Accountancy in Transition

Edited by Richard P. Brief, NEW YORK UNIVERSITY

A GARLAND SERIES

Accounting Method

C. Rufus Rorem

Garland Publishing, Inc.
New York & London 1982

This facsimile has been made from a copy in the
Yale University Library.
Reprinted by permission of the McGraw-Hill Book Company.

Library of Congress Cataloging in Publication Data

Rorem, C. Rufus (Clarence Rufus), 1894–
Accounting method.

(Accountancy in transition)
Reprint. Originally published: Chicago : University of Chicago Press, 1928. (Materials for the study of business)
Bibliography: p.
Includes index.
1. Accounting. I. Title. II. Series. III. Series: Materials for the study of business.
HF5635.R75 1982 657 82-48382
ISBN 0-8240-5327-3

The volumes in this series are printed on acid-free, 250-year-life paper.

Printed in the United States of America

MATERIALS FOR THE STUDY OF BUSINESS

ACCOUNTING METHOD

THE UNIVERSITY OF CHICAGO PRESS
CHICAGO, ILLINOIS

THE BAKER & TAYLOR COMPANY
NEW YORK

THE MACMILLAN COMPANY OF CANADA, LIMITED
TORONTO

THE CAMBRIDGE UNIVERSITY PRESS
LONDON

THE MARUZEN-KABUSHIKI-KAISHA
TOKYO, OSAKA, KYOTO, FUKUOKA, SENDAI

THE COMMERCIAL PRESS, LIMITED
SHANGHAI

ACCOUNTING METHOD

BY

C. RUFUS ROREM

CERTIFIED PUBLIC ACCOUNTANT

ASSISTANT PROFESSOR OF ACCOUNTING
THE UNIVERSITY OF CHICAGO

THE UNIVERSITY OF CHICAGO PRESS
CHICAGO · ILLINOIS

Published August 1928

Composed and Printed By
The University of Chicago Press
Chicago, Illinois, U.S.A.

TO

G. M. R.

PREFACE

This book introduces accounting as *a method of measuring and interpreting the business transactions of a given economic enterprise.* The problem of measurement is what the accountant usually refers to as the problem of "valuation." "Interpretation" involves the classification, summarization, and comparison of accounting data. The "double-entry" system, when viewed in its proper perspective, must be regarded as a technical device which facilitates interpretation—a procedure for classifying and summarizing data in records and reports. An introduction to accounting must, therefore, include more than the principles of double-entry accounting; it must also deal with the theory underlying accounting valuation and the various aspects of interpretation. The first two parts of the text introduce double-entry accounting as the procedure which differentiates accounting from other types of scientific method, particularly statistics. Parts III and IV explain and illustrate the general principles underlying accounting valuation and accounting interpretation, respectively. Throughout the text, accounting method is emphasized as a means to an end—as a tool for administrative control.

This text is intended for college students, preferably of sophomore or senior-college rank; the different sections make it possible for schools to place emphasis on portions which are most suited to their needs. The entire book would serve as the basis for a year's work totaling about six semester-hours of credit; more might be granted if students were given additional reading and problem assignments (including the practice set, pp. 561–65). Ordinarily the first twenty chapters would comprise the first half-year's work (three hours of credit); the last twenty chapters, including the practice set, would normally be suitable for the second half-year's work (three hours of credit). The elimination of certain parts or certain chapters makes it possible to treat subjects which are of most value to the school using the book as the basis of instruction. A three-hour course might cover chapters i–xiii, xxi–xxiv, xxxiii–xxxvi; a four-hour course would include chapters i–xvi, xxi–xxiv, xxxiii–xxxvi, including the practice set.

Accounting Method has been used at the University of Chicago for two years as the basis for the introductory course in accounting. Among the colleagues who have read and criticized portions of the manuscript are the following: L. C. Marshall, Director of Economics and Business; W. J. Graham, C.P.A., and H. C. Daines, C.P.A., of the Department of Accounting; T. O. Yntema, C.P.A., Assistant Professor of Statistics; J. L. Palmer, C.P.A., Assistant Professor of Marketing; W. N. Mitchell, C.P.A., Assistant Professor of Production Control. Leroy D. Stinebower and Sidney Perlstadt aided in the correction of manuscript and proof.

H. A. Fountain, Treasurer, The Ohio Public Service Company, Cleveland, Ohio, read the manuscript from the point of view of an engineer and business man who uses accounting for control. F. B. Andrews, C.P.A., of F. B. Andrews and Company, Chicago, made numerous helpful suggestions which grew out of his experience as a professional accountant.

C. Rufus Rorem

University of Chicago
July 1, 1928

TABLE OF CONTENTS

PART I. THE ROLE OF ACCOUNTING IN MODERN ECONOMIC LIFE

PART II. DOUBLE-ENTRY ACCOUNTING

A. THEORY OF DOUBLE-ENTRY ACCOUNTING

PART I

THE RÔLE OF ACCOUNTING IN MODERN ECONOMIC LIFE

CHAPTER I

ACCOUNTING AS A TOOL FOR ECONOMIC CONTROL

Accounting is a tool for use in the control of economic activity. It is a device for measuring and interpreting certain quantitatively expressed facts of an enterprise, meaning by "enterprise" any type of organization which deals with the manipulation of those social resources commonly called "economic goods." Accounting is a special method for dealing with the economic facts of a given enterprise.

Many types of enterprise use accounting information.—The need for the services of accounting is by no means confined to the business enterprise. Accounting may be used by a privately owned business operated for profit, a non-profit institution, a government, an association of enterprises, or the individual in his rôle of consumer of economic goods.

All sorts of business enterprises which are operated for profit depend more or less upon accounting for the control of their operations. This is true alike of farm, mine, factory, fishery, bank, railroad, insurance company, and wholesale or retail store. It makes no difference whether a business enterprise is organized as a partnership, a corporation, a business trust, an individual proprietorship, or some other form of the business unit. It makes no difference whether the persons desiring information are the managers and employees of the enterprise, the stockholders or partners, the financial institutions from which funds are borrowed, the vendors from whom merchandise is purchased, or the government officials who are collecting taxes from the concern. Whatever the form of organization, and whatever the purpose for which precise quantitative information is desired accounting is the device which supplies information as to the various activities of an enterprise: marketing, production, purchasing, personnel, and finance. The information is expressed in such terms as "income from sales," "manufacturing costs," "wages," "interest," "taxes" and "profit."

When individual business men or business enterprises wish to co-operate with one another in carrying out some policy, they depend to a great degree upon information provided by accounting. For example, if a group of wholesale dry-goods merchants wish to determine the average costs of selling a certain group of commodities, they turn to the accounting records of the various firms for the information on which to base their calculations. Or when a group of educational institutions form an association for the co-operative purchase of building-supplies, the prices quoted to them may depend upon the previous purchases of the member-institutions, information which it is the peculiar function of accounting to provide.

Non-profit institutions, such as churches, lodges, museums, schools, educational foundations, and hospitals, also use accounting data in controlling their activity. Information concerning dues, fees, subscriptions, membership, sources of income, and causes of outgo—all such data are provided by accounting and are important for control of the economic activities of these organizations. The financial success or failure of a metropolitan art museum or a civic opera company is not, of course, the criterion of its social usefulness. Nor is it the purpose of accounting to attempt to measure the social usefulness of institutions. Accounting is not used by non-profit institutions to justify or condemn their existence, but rather to insure the wise administration of the economic goods under their control.

Governmental organizations—nations, states, counties, townships, cities—all use accounting information for control of their activities. Accounting data are continually used by public officers to aid in the intelligent solution of such problems as legislative appropriations, tariff schedules, tax rates, executive salaries, etc. Governments also use accounting for the control of private business enterprise, as in the regulation of railroad rates, the control of banking operations, or the supervision of activities of trade associations.

The individual citizen as a consumer of economic goods also relies upon accounting to supply him with information concerning his own affairs. Even the simple problem of administering a household budget may well require some method of accounting, so that the household income may be effectively apportioned among the necessities and luxuries of life—food, rent, clothing, education, and entertainment.

Accounting especially vital to business enterprise.—Accounting deals with economic facts which may be expressed quantitatively; and as the term is commonly used, it is limited to economic facts expressed in terms of money. The facts with which accounting deal may be broadly subdivided as being of two main types: facts which describe the economic status of an enterprise at a particular moment of time; and facts which summarize the economic operations during a given period of time. It is the task of the accounting method so to treat the economic facts that the exact status of an enterprise can be determined at any time, with appropriate explanations as to the causes of changes in status from time to time. The extensive use of accounting information depends upon an adequate system of permanent records from which accounting information may be drawn. Accordingly one function of accounting is that of providing competent records of all the facts with which it deals. Without written records, the manager of an enterprise would be forced to rely upon personal observation and direct contact with his associates to secure important facts. This would be ineffective, in fact impossible, in the present stage of economic development.

Certain aspects of modern business make accounting of vital importance in the control of a specific enterprise. In the first place, modern business is complex; the operations of a single factory comprise such varied and technical activities as the mixing of chemicals, transportation of materials, assembling of parts, generation of power, testing of finished products, and supervision of workmen. It will often lie beyond the power of the most intelligent business manager to supervise and direct personally the varied processes being carried on under his control. His task is rather to co-ordinate the work of certain technical specialists who are responsible for the varied activities. In the second place, business enterprise is frequently operated on such large scale that its very size would prevent one man from directing it personally.

Many enterprises employ thousands of men to carry on their activities. And even if the tasks of all these men were simple enough to be understood by a business manager, it would be impossible for him to maintain direct control over the activities of each employee. In the third place, the geographical areas of enterprise are often so great that peculiar problems of control arise. Many large companies employ salesmen and establish branches which operate in all parts of the world. Even a simple enterprise doing a moderate amount of business must maintain accounting records when the employees are continuously absent from the center of business activity. Other characteristics of modern business could be cited to emphasize the need for some device to supplement direct personal observation and contact in the control of a given enterprise. Enough have been mentioned to demonstrate that the powers of the individual manager must be multiplied if he is to maintain control over important areas of economic activity. This multiplication of powers may be accomplished through recorded data, properly classified, summarized, and interpreted.

The private business enterprises have been keenly aware of the importance of accounting in the control of their affairs and have made great progress in developing accounting technique applicable to their individual needs and purposes. This is because private business is inspired by the profit motive, and accounting makes possible the efficient control of resources to the end that profit may be increased. Accounting is, of course, applicable equally to the problems of the non-profit organizations. The failure, in individual cases, of other types of enterprise to follow the lead of private business in the adaptation of accounting to their needs has sometimes resulted in their being poorly administered.

QUESTIONS ON CHAPTER I[1]

1. Accounting in the generic sense means "explaining" or "giving an account of." What does accounting attempt to explain or account for in connection with an economic enterprise?

[1] The questions are intended to serve as the basis for independent thinking and discussion, rather than as mere "quiz" questions on the contents of the chapters. Many of them are not answered in the text, itself; they require application of the ideas in the book to special and general situations.

2. Does a modern city need a more complex method of measuring and recording its operations than did the medieval town? Specify reasons for your answer. Will the needs for accounting increase in the future?
3. Does the United States Steel Corporation need a more detailed system of measuring, recording, and reporting than the corner drug store operated by the proprietor? Indicate in detail the reasons for your answer.
4. Would the corner drug store need a more detailed accounting system if it were run by a hired manager as one of a chain system? Why or why not?
5. Many small businesses today have very simple and undeveloped accounting systems; their records are not worked out in great detail. How do the managers obtain the information necessary to formulate their policies intelligently?
6. Explain the ways in which a large university makes use of accounting. A church. A lodge. A museum. What types of receipts and expenditures would each type of enterprise need to account for?
7. Why have business enterprises outstripped other agencies in the elaboration and development of their accounting systems? What concrete advantages does accounting offer for the management of private enterprise?
8. Would accounting be more or less necessary in a socialistic or communistic society than it is in the present economic order?

CHAPTER II

ACCOUNTING AS A TYPE OF QUANTITATIVE METHOD

Accounting has been defined as a tool for the control of economic activity, a special method for measuring and interpreting the economic facts of a given enterprise which can be quantitatively expressed. The method of accounting is an application of the quantitative method of scientific analysis, a method which confines itself to those aspects of phenomena which can be measured. Quantitative method is particularly applicable to the measurement of economic transactions, although it has been most fully developed in the natural sciences, where laboratory technique makes it possible to segregate phenomena for continued and accurate observation.

Quantitative method involves measurement of phenomena and the interpretation of data.—Quantitative method may be subdivided into two basic steps or processes. The first process is *measurement* of the phenomena to be studied. The phenomena may be the heat-producing qualities of certain foods, the tensile strength of metals, the mental capacities of factory employees, or the expenditures of a local government; the phenomena to be measured will vary with the field in which the quantitative method is being applied. The second process is *interpretation* of the data. This process usually involves classification and summarization, followed by the measurement of important relationships between classes and groups of data. The relationships are usually those which can be expressed in such terms as ratios and averages.

Recording is not included as a basic process in the quantitative method. Records are, of course, necessary to the application of quantitative method; in fact, records must be maintained during each phase of its application. Recording, then, is not a single process in quantitative method; it is rather a requirement which must accompany each of the processes, if the data are at all numerous.

Accounting and statistics as special applications of quantitative method.—There are two main types of quantitative method which may be applied to the analysis of economic phenomena—statistics and accounting. "Statistics" is the broader term, and sometimes the expression "statistical method" is used as synonymous with "quantitative method." Both statistics and accounting, however, may be regarded as applications of the same general method of analysis. Accounting usually limits its measurement of economic phenomena to the facts which can be expressed in terms of money; statistics deals with economic phenomena in any of their aspects, selecting any unit of measure (including money) which may be of use for the purpose at hand. Accounting classifies and summarizes the data from the point of view of a specific enterprise; statistics, on the other hand, is subject to no such limitation. It may deal with data from the point of view of one portion of an enterprise or from the point of view of the entire economic order of which the enterprise is a part. Statistical data are often very important in the administration of a specific enterprise, and should be used by the managers whenever they can be secured.

Some attempt has been made to differentiate statistics and accounting by the fact that workers in statistics have developed the technique of measurement and interpretation farther than have the accountants. This distinction is purely historical, and cannot be regarded as basic. The special technique of statisticians is the common property of all workers in quantitative method. The failure of accountants to use more refined methods in measuring phenomena and interpreting data is not evidence of a difference in accounting and statistical method. It merely indicates that such technique has not been considered necessary by accountants—mistakenly enough, in some cases—for dealing with the financial data of an economic enterprise. One purpose of this text is to emphasize the need for the best possible technique in the accounting application of the quantitative method.

Measurement involves selection and application of a unit of measure.—The phenomena with which accounting deals are the economic transactions of an enterprise—the events which change the status of an enterprise, such as investment of funds in an enterprise, purchase of materials, payment of wages, sale of merchandise, or use of supplies in manufacturing operations. The task of measuring economic transactions is twofold. It involves selecting a unit of measure, and applying the unit to the phenomena, the economic transactions.

Selecting the unit of measure.—To measure the length of an article of furniture one must select some appropriate unit of measure. It may be the width of a hand, the length of a pencil, or the depth of an ink-well; usually one selects some well-known unit of linear measure, such as the inch or centimeter. The measurement of the amount of food a person has consumed may be carried on in terms of volume, weight, or temperature. The measurement of a man's labor may be made in terms of hours of employment or pounds of material handled. Each of the types of phenomena mentioned above—furniture, food, labor—may be measured in terms of different units of measure. No single unit, however, would serve to compare the different important characteristics of furniture, food, and labor. The relative dimensions of furniture and food are obviously of no significance for most purposes; moreover, labor cannot be expressed in terms of linear measure. Similarly, the other units of measuring physical characteristics (such as volume, temperature, or duration of time) are not concurrently applicable to widely different phenomena.

Accounting, in its treatment of economic phenomena, typically selects the unit of exchange value as the basis of its measurements. Exchange value is a characteristic common to all types of economic phenomena; and it serves to reduce furniture, food, and labor to a common denominator. In the United States, the dollar is the unit for measuring exchange value. By the selection of the dollar as a unit of measure, accounting limits itself to only those aspects of economic transactions which can be expressed in terms of money. Money as a unit of measure is, of course, subject to certain limitations. It will not measure the loyalty of an employee, the power factor of an electric motor, or the heat of a blast furnace; yet these items often are very important in deciding whether an enterprise will be a financial success or failure. Money value is widely applicable to a large number of different economic phenomena, but it does not deal with all the important aspects of these phenomena.[1]

Applying the unit of measure.—After a satisfactory unit of measure has been selected, it must be applied correctly to the phenomena, a task which is often exceedingly difficult. In the first place, the measurement may be affected by *bias* on the part of the persons securing the data. For example, a business man may overstate the amount of his profit when preparing an income-tax return. The direction of personal bias is affected by the uses to which data are to be placed, sometimes tending to overstatement of measurement, sometimes to understatement.

In the second place, the accuracy of measurement may be affected by the *adequacy of the technique* used for securing the data. For example, a person measuring the height of a mountain above sea-level will ordinarily apply the principles of trigonometry to his task, thus securing more accurate data than if he expressed his opinion without such aid. A person cannot correctly estimate the population of a city by walking about the streets and getting an "idea" of the size of the town. Census enumeration requires an elaborate technique of interviewing individuals properly to account for non-residents, transients, recent arrivals, etc. Personal observation may be satisfactory for counting the number of sacks of sugar on the shelf of a grocery store; it would be inadequate for calculating the number of pounds of sugar sold in a given city during a certain period of time. A person unfamiliar with the principles of trigonometry might say that it would be impossible to measure the height of a mountain; likewise a person unskilled in dealing with large numbers might assert that the population of a city or the amount of sugar sold therein could not be determined. Complex and numerous phenomena require special techniques for their measurement. Failure to select, or inability to apply, proper technique may result in measurements being no more accurate than the crudest type of personal conjecture.

[1] The financial unit may itself change in value, either because of fluctuations in international exchange rates or because of changes in the general price level. The accountant typically assumes that the dollar is of constant value, although there are some cases where changes in the value of the monetary unit have been recognized in accounting measurement.

In the third place, the measurement of economic phenomena is conditioned by the *purpose* for which the value is being determined. A motor truck may be worth \$2,000 for the purpose of transporting goods; it may be worth only \$1,000 for the purpose of immediate sale in the second-hand automobile market. Yet each amount may properly be said to indicate the value of the motor truck; in other words an economic phenomenon may have several values, each of which is correct for the purpose for which it is computed.

Interpretation involves classification and summarization; also the measurement of relationships between classes and groups of data.—The interpretation of quantitative data—of which accounting data are a type—is the second basic process in accounting method. The process of interpretation begins with the attempt to segregate data into fundamentally similar classes and to summarize these classes into larger, more significant groups. It is carried forward by the search for measurable relationships among the classes and groups of data, particularly those relationships which are important for purposes of administrative control.

Classification and summarization are conditioned by purpose and effective technique.—The basis for classifying quantitative data will vary with the purpose of the measurement and the technique available for the classification. For example, one hundred persons may be classified according to their heights, measured in feet and inches. The persons may also be classified according to such characteristics as their weight, age, experience, education, or race; the purpose of the classification will determine which basis or combination of bases is most useful.

So, also, in the accounting field, the classification of economic data is conditioned by the purpose of the analysis. Accounting data are assembled to express in financial terms the economic status and operations of a specific enterprise; consequently the accounting data of an enterprise are first of all classified as to those which express *status* (set forth in the balance sheet) and those which reflect *operations* (set forth in the statement of income and expense). A subclassification of the balance-sheet data provides such headings as "Cash," "Merchandise," "Accounts receivable," "Buildings," "Accounts payable," and "Capital stock." The income and expense data appear in such subclasses as "Interest," "Salaries," "Sales," "Purchases," "Taxes," "Profits," "Depreciation," "Rent," and "Income from royalties."

The technique of recording the accounting data usually employs the device called tabulation, which consists of arranging the data in rows and columns, segregated and grouped in accord with the avowed purpose of the accountant. Increases and decreases in each type of accounting data are offset against each other in two parallel contiguous columns, each pair appearing under a title which designates the type of data recorded therein. The method by which the accounting data are properly recorded in these tabular records is known as the double-entry system of accounting.[1]

The recorded data may be grouped to summarize the financial aspects of economic status or operations. The type of summary that will be prepared varies with the use it is to serve. For example, a report may be made showing the various items of merchandise owned by an enterprise at a given time, or the various types of expenses incurred during a period of time. In some cases, the reports may, of course, consist of complete financial summaries of status or operations. The technique of presenting the summarized data also varies with the purposes for which reports are prepared. Graphic presentations are very common; they include straight lines, curves, pictures, maps, etc. The graphic form of presentation is easily comprehended and is very useful in the expression of general facts; it is not well adapted to reports which must show a great amount of detail. Another method of presenting accounting facts is the tabular method, which consists of assembling the numerical data into rows and columns, with groups

[1] There is a vast amount of economic data in the auxiliary records of a business enterprise which cannot conveniently be reduced to the double-entry system of classification, that is to say, are not ordinarily expressed in terms of monetary units. Such items may be described as "non-value data"; illustrations would be tons of coal, yards of cloth, barrels of oil, pounds of metal, hours of labor, hours of idleness. Non-value data are often very important in the administration of an economic enterprise, and the methods of classifying and summarizing such data may well engage the attention of a manager. This text will mention from time to time the rôle which non-value data play in accounting control.

and subgroups. This method of presentation is well adapted to accounting data and is capable of expressing a great amount of important detail, but it is not as easily comprehended as graphic presentation. Both graphic and tabular methods of presenting data are useful in accounting, although accountants have in the past confined themselves almost entirely to the preparation of tabular reports.

The importance of relationships in the accounting data varies with the purpose or end sought.—The interpretation of data extends beyond the classification and summarization of data. Interpretation also includes the discovery and measurement of important *relationships* between the data in reports. For example, a banker may be interested in the ability of an enterprise to repay a sixty-day loan. He would thus wish to know the *ratio* between the resources which could be realized upon promptly, on the one hand, and the existing obligations which must be met in the near future, on the other. Significant accounting relationships may also be expressed as *averages* and variations from averages. A sales manager of an enterprise may be interested to know that the average monthly sales for a year were $15,000. He may also be interested to know that the sales for individual months varied from an amount as low as $5,000 to an amount as high as $25,000. Knowledge of this average and of the variations therefrom might serve as the basis for action designed to secure more regular income from the sale of merchandise. The computation of averages and variations is an important part of the task of interpreting accounting data. Important relationships may also be revealed by the discovery of *trends* in the economic conditions of an enterprise, separate and apart from any geographical variations or temporary fluctuations. Interpretation may reveal, for example, that the average sales per month of an enterprise are increasing from year to year. The technique of discovering trends in economic activity requires the use of some of the most elaborate devices of interpretation. Throughout all interpretation of summarized data, the particular ratios, averages, variations, and trends to be sought for will vary with the purpose for which the data are to be used.

This book organized around the basic processes of quantitative method.—The basic processes in the quantitative method have been shown to be: (1) measurement of phenomena; and (2) interpretation of data. The accountant, like all other workers in quantitative method, makes use of these processes; but he has come to apply to them a specialized terminology. The measurement of business transactions is usually referred to by the accountant as "valuation." The "interpretation" of accounting data comprises the theory of accounting classification and summarization, as well as the discovery and measurement of important relationships between the data. The steps in measurement and interpretation merge into and influence each other to a degree that makes the dividing lines between them at times almost indistinguishable. This text begins with a discussion of *double-entry accounting* as the basic technique for maintaining records which classify and summarize the accounting data of an enterprise. The book then takes up the underlying theory and problems of *valuation* and *interpretation*. The parts of the text are as follows:

Part II. Double-Entry Accounting
Part III. Accounting Valuation
Part IV. Interpretation of Accounting Data

This order is selected because the double-entry accounting system is the one feature of accounting which distinguishes it from other applications of quantitative method. Moreover, the principles of double-entry accounting can be explained and illustrated without regard to theories of valuation or interpretation. It seems best, therefore, to begin with the double-entry system of classifying and summarizing accounting data, and to follow with a treatment of the broader problems of measurement and interpretation. The entire text will emphasize the unity of the accounting method and the extent to which each step is affected by the purpose for which the method is applied.

QUESTIONS ON CHAPTER II

1. Mention and explain the basic processes in accounting method.
2. Why is the money-value unit of such great importance in controlling economic operations today? Does this unit of measurement have any

serious limitations or imperfections? Is it conceivable that a highly specialized society could function successfully without the use of some value unit of measurement?

3. Name several non-value units of measurement which would be useful in measuring economic operations. What are the peculiar advantages and limitations of non-value measurement?
4. What bias is apt to affect the income-tax returns rendered the U.S. government? The evaluation of the property owned by a public utility? The net profit of operations of a company in a period of prosperity? The statement of the same company in a period of depression? The statement of a company whose general manager is paid a bonus out of profits?
5. The accounting data are frequently summarized into reports. What forms do accounting and statistical reports most frequently take? Indicate some reports which may prove serviceable to a manager.

PART II

DOUBLE-ENTRY ACCOUNTING

A. THEORY OF DOUBLE-ENTRY ACCOUNTING

CHAPTER III

THE BALANCE-SHEET EQUATION

The scope of double-entry accounting.—Double-entry accounting, as it will be explained in the following chapters, is a device for classifying and summarizing in financial terms the economic data of an enterprise. Although the principles of double-entry accounting are applicable to any form of enterprise, most of the transactions which will be selected to illustrate the principles will be taken from business.[1] The justification for beginning with transactions of the business enterprise in the illustration of the double-entry accounting principles is threefold: business is the most common type of economic enterprise; most students of accounting plan to engage in business; many students are familiar with the common terms of business, whereas few are acquainted with the transactions of hospitals, governments, social clubs, etc.

Double-entry accounting is limited to those business transactions which may be measured in terms of a common unit. That unit is *money* value. One very important assumption will be made in the present study of double-entry accounting: that the accounting data have been correctly determined by accurate measurement. The question will not be raised in this part of the text as to whether the business transactions have been properly evaluated; this problem will be dealt with in Part III.

The accounting data are of two main types: those which express *status*, and those which reflect *operations*. The whole process of classification and summarization leads forward to the preparation of two main financial reports: the balance sheet, which is a financial summary of status; and the statement of income and expense, which is a financial summary of business operations.

[1] The term "business" may, strictly speaking, be applied to any type of economic enterprise, even though it is government-owned or a non-profit enterprise; in practice, however, the term is usually restricted to a privately owned enterprise operated for profit. The principles of double-entry accounting are, of course, the same for all types of enterprise.

The balance sheet is the financial summary of status and is the basic accounting equation.—What is a balance sheet? The study of this question will be introduced by consideration of certain data which represent the balance sheet of the enterprise designated as the Gibson-Spence Grocery Store.

GIBSON-SPENCE GROCERY STORE

BALANCE SHEET—JANUARY 1, 19—

Cash	$ 1,100.00	Merchandise creditor	$ 2,000.00
Merchandise	5,900.00	Holder of building mortgage	7,000.00
Building	10,000.00	Holder of promissory note	6,000.00
Furniture	4,200.00	T. E. Gibson, proprietor	5,000.00
Motor truck	2,800.00	L. M. Spence, proprietor	4,000.00
Total	$24,000.00	Total	$24,000.00

The foregoing balance sheet consists of two columns, each totaling $24,000. The two sides contain apparently different types of data. Why are two columns necessary to a complete financial summary of status, and what do these two equal sides of the balance sheet represent? They will be discussed separately.

The various items of wealth invested in a business enterprise are known as the "assets" of that business. Illustrations of assets in a mercantile business are: money, merchandise, claims against customers, buildings, machinery, tools, furniture, land, franchise privileges, patent rights, insurance protection, etc. Assets are of many types and forms. They may consist of tangible or intangible wealth; in fact, an asset may be anything which has an exchange value and can be measured in terms of money. Moreover, there may be numerous subclasses of each of these types of assets, which vary with each individual business enterprise. The assets of the Gibson-Spence Grocery Store appear in the left column of the balance sheet and, as here listed, are five in number: cash, merchandise, building, furniture, and motor truck. Each of these assets possesses some economic value, the amount of which is set opposite the name. The total equals $24,000.

A statement of the assets of an enterprise is not a complete statement of financial condition, for it merely indicates the nature, types, and amounts of wealth invested therein. It says nothing about the sources from which the wealth has come; it gives no indication as to what persons or types of persons have contributed the assets for the use of the enterprise and who now may be regarded as having proprietary claims against the assets. A complete summary of economic status would include a statement of the property rights (claims of ownership) in the assets, such as are found in the right-hand column of the balance sheet of the Gibson-Spence Grocery Store. This column indicates the sources from which the assets have come, as well as the nature and extent of the property rights in those assets. Five different persons are listed in the right-hand column: merchandise creditor; holder of building mortgage; holder of promissory note; T. E. Gibson, proprietor; and L. M. Spence, proprietor. The extent of the property rights of each of these five persons is set forth separately; the total is $24,000.

The central fact concerning the economic status of the Gibson-Spence Grocery Store is that property with a total value of $24,000 has been invested in the enterprise. The word "property" implies two things: that there exist specific items of wealth (assets) which possess given economic values; and that there is a specific person or group of persons in whom the property rights in the assets reside. There can be no assets without owners; nor can there be owners without assets. The balance sheet may, therefore, be looked upon as an expression of two aspects of the total property invested in the enterprise. The left column expresses the total as types and amounts of assets; the right column expresses the total as types and amounts of property rights. The value of the assets of the Gibson-Spence Grocery Store equals the value of the property rights existing in them. Each is $24,000. This equality is not accidental; it is fundamental. The two columns of the balance sheets are merely two different aspects of the same thing—the total economic value inherent in, or comprising, the enterprise. Of course, the equality of the assets and of the property rights in an enterprise is an equality of totals only. The two columns of a balance sheet may set forth the total economic value in entirely different numerical subdivisions. Such is the case in the Gibson-Spence Grocery Store balance sheet, in which no asset corresponds in value to any of the various property rights. The persons listed in the right column do not ordinarily have rights in specific assets; they have claims upon the total only.

Liabilities and proprietorship represent two main classes of property rights in assets.—In the illustrations thus far given, there has been no indication that the various property rights in the assets represent different types and degrees of control; as a matter of fact, the property rights of the different persons may vary greatly according to the terms under which each one advances assets for use in the enterprise. Two main classes of persons may be distinguished according to the nature of their property rights in the total assets. These classes are commonly treated separately in business practice, and are generally referred to as proprietors and creditors, and their rights as *proprietorship* and *liabilities*.

Proprietorship is the type of ownership enjoyed by persons who invest their property more or less permanently in an enterprise. They assume the primary responsibility for the success of the business operations; in this capacity they reap the benefits of any financial gains, as well as bear the burdens of financial losses. They are usually referred to as proprietors or "owners" of the business, in popular language; all other holders of claims against the assets are usually designated by some other title.

A second type of property right is vested in persons who merely loan assets for use in the business. Such property rights are known as *liabilities*, and reside in a group of persons referred to as "creditors." Creditors are primarily interested in the return of values equal to the property they lend to a business. If a creditor lends cash to a business, he expects to have equivalent cash ultimately returned to him, meanwhile to receive additional amounts periodically as interest. If a creditor sells merchandise to a business on credit terms, he normally expects to receive in return only the value of the goods, that is, an amount equal to their selling price.

Liabilities and proprietorship are very similar in their basic characteristics: they both represent property rights. Creditors and proprietors may, broadly speaking, be regarded as joint participants in an enterprise. To be sure, the creditors invest their assets under different conditions than do the proprietors; nevertheless they contribute to the total assets of the enterprise, and, until they withdraw their portions, they have certain definite rights over the assets of the enterprise. These rights are often very limited, yet they exist; and in certain emergencies the creditors may legally exercise control that sweeps the rights of the proprietors temporarily aside.

It is the basic similarity between the property rights of creditors and proprietors that justifies listing the liabilities and proprietorship in the same column of the balance sheet. It is the practical difference that justifies segregating them in different parts of the column. The right column of the balance sheet of the Gibson-Spence Grocery Store appeared as follows:

Merchandise creditor	$ 2,000.00
Holder of building mortgage	7,000.00
Holder of promissory note	6,000.00
T. E. Gibson, proprietor	5,000.00
L. M. Spence, proprietor	4,000.00
Total	$24,000.00

Of the persons designated above, the first three would be regarded as creditors of the Gibson-Spence Grocery Store; Gibson and Spence would be considered the proprietors. The liabilities and proprietorship of the creditors and proprietors comprise a total of $24,000. The complete balance sheet, with the property rights of creditors and proprietors separated, would appear as follows:

GIBSON-SPENCE GROCERY STORE

BALANCE SHEET—JANUARY 1, 19—

ASSETS		LIABILITIES AND PROPRIETORSHIP		
Cash	$ 1,100.00	*Liabilities:*		
Merchandise	5,900.00	Accounts payable	$2,000.00	
Building	10,000.00	Mortgages payable	7,000.00	
Furniture	4,200.00	Notes payable	6,000.00	$15,000.00
Motor truck	2,800.00			
		Proprietorship:		
		T. E. Gibson, capital	5,000.00	
		L. M. Spence, capital	4,000.00	9,000.00
Total	$24,000.00	Total		$24,000.00

The two sides of the balance sheet are still equal. The student should observe that the subdivisions of the right-hand column are here expressed as types of liabilities and proprietorship rather than as individual creditors and proprietors. The advantage of such procedure is that it provides descriptive headings under which to group various persons who enjoy the same type of property rights. In the case of liabilities, for example, the term "Accounts payable"[1] is broad enough to include the property rights of numerous creditors. Similarly, under the heading of proprietorship general titles can be used to indicate the rights of all the proprietors of an enterprise. Corporations which have large numbers of shareholders set forth the contributions of corporate proprietors under the general caption "Capital stock." If the Gibson-Spence Grocery Store were organized as a corporation, the balance sheet might appear somewhat as follows:

GIBSON-SPENCE GROCERY STORE

BALANCE SHEET—JANUARY 1, 19—

ASSETS		LIABILITIES AND PROPRIETORSHIP		
Cash	$ 1,100.00	*Liabilities:*		
Merchandise	5,900.00	Accounts payable	$2,000.00	
Building	10,000.00	Mortgages payable	7,000.00	
Furniture	4,200.00	Notes payable	6,000.00	$15,000.00
Motor truck	2,800.00			
		Proprietorship		
		Capital stock		9,000.00
Total	$24,000.00	Total		$24,000.00

The balance sheet maintains a continuous equilibrium.—The equality of the assets and property rights of an enterprise has been introduced as the basic fact of the balance sheet. This condition of equality is sometimes referred to as the "accounting equation,"

[1] The question immediately arises: How is the balance sheet to set forth the amounts owing to individual creditors? The answer is that the balance sheet usually does not carry a list of individual creditors, debtors, or proprietors; such information is ordinarily available only in specialized records devised for the purpose of maintaining detailed data of this kind. For the present, the discussion of double-entry method will assume that summary information will serve the purpose of the manager of an enterprise.

or the "balance-sheet equation"; it is the basis of the double-entry scheme of classifying and summarizing accounting data. The equation may be expressed as follows: value of assets equals value of property rights in them, or simply:

Assets = property rights.

The property rights may be subdivided into two main classes—liabilities and proprietorship; hence the sum of the liabilities and proprietorship equals the total assets. The equation then becomes:

Assets = liabilities plus proprietorship.

Using the first letter of each word as a symbol, the equation may be expressed as follows:

$$A = L + P.$$

This form of the accounting equation serves as the starting point for analyzing the effects of all the transactions of an enterprise. The transactions of an economic enterprise may cause changes in the individual items in the balance sheet and in the totals, but none of these changes can affect the equilibrium of the accounting equation. At every stage in the operations of a business enterprise, the total value of the assets will equal the total value of the liabilities and proprietorship. The truth of this statement will be demonstrated by analysis of the various types of business transactions, showing how they may be dealt with in terms of their effect on the accounting equation.

The basic types of business transactions.—Business transactions may be differentiated in two broad classes, as far as their effects on the left and right sides of the equation are concerned. They may cause:

1. Changes affecting the balance-sheet totals. This type of transaction causes an increase or a decrease in the total assets, as well as in the total of liabilities plus proprietorship. It affects *both* sides of the accounting equation.
2. Interchanges of the balance-sheet items. This type of transaction does not affect the totals of the balance sheet. It merely shifts value from one item to another on the same side of the equation. It may affect *either* side of the balance sheet, but *not both*.

The two types may be subclassified as follows:

I. Changes affecting the balance-sheet totals:

A. Increases:

1. Increase of assets and proprietorship
2. Increase of assets and liabilities

B. Decreases:

3. Decrease of proprietorship and assets
4. Decrease of liabilities and assets

II. Interchanges of the balance-sheet items:

A. Interchanges of assets:

5. Increase of one asset; decrease of another

B. Interchanges in liabilities and proprietorship:

6. Decrease of one liability; increase of another
7. Decrease of one proprietorship item; increase of another
8. Decrease of liability; increase of proprietorship
9. Decrease of proprietorship; increase of liability

Type I—Changes affecting the balance-sheet totals.—The first group of changes includes those which affect the total values in the balance-sheet columns. They may increase the assets, also the liabilities and proprietorship; or they may decrease them.

Increased totals.—Balance-sheet totals may be increased by business transactions which introduce new assets into the enterprise. The assets may be provided by either proprietors or creditors.

First example (increase of assets and proprietorship): Mr. X invests $10,000 cash in a business. The asset "Cash" is increased $10,000; and the proprietorship item "X, capital" is increased $10,000. The balance sheet of the company appears as follows:

ASSETS		PROPRIETORSHIP	
Cash................	$10,000.00	X, capital...........	$10,000.00

Second example (increase of assets and liabilities): Merchandise is purchased on credit terms for $4,000. The asset "Merchandise . . . . $4,000" appears; the liability "Accounts payable. . . . . $4,000" also finds a place in the balance sheet. The assets and the liabilities are each now increased by $4,000. The balance sheet becomes:

ASSETS		LIABILITIES AND PROPRIETORSHIP	
Cash	$10,000.00	*Liabilities:*	
Merchandise	4,000.00	Accounts payable	$ 4,000.00
		Proprietorship:	
		X, capital	10,000.00
Total	$14,000.00	Total	$14,000.00

The equilibrium of the equation is undisturbed.

Decreased totals.—Balance-sheet totals may also be reduced by the transactions of an enterprise. Each decrease causes a reduction of the total assets, accompanied by a corresponding reduction of the liabilities or proprietorship.

Third example (decrease of proprietorship and assets): Two hundred dollars in cash is withdrawn by the proprietor. The asset "Cash" is decreased $200; the proprietorship item "X, capital" is decreased $200. The balance sheet becomes:

ASSETS		LIABILITIES AND PROPRIETORSHIP	
Cash	$ 9,800.00	*Liabilities:*	
Merchandise	4,000.00	Accounts payable	$ 4,000.00
		Proprietorship:	
		X, capital	9,800.00
Total	$13,800.00	Total	$13,800.00

The assets have been reduced and proprietorship has also been reduced. Liabilities remain the same. There has been an equal reduction on both sides of the equation.

Fourth example (decrease of liabilities and assets): Seven hundred and fifty dollars in cash is paid to a short-time creditor. The asset "Cash" is decreased $750, and the liability "Accounts payable" is decreased $750. The balance sheet would now be:

ASSETS		LIABILITIES AND PROPRIETORSHIP	
Cash	$ 9,050.00	*Liabilities:*	
Merchandise	4,000.00	Accounts payable	$ 3,250.00
		Proprietorship:	
		S, capital	9,800.00
Total	$13,050.00	Total	$13,050.00

The total of each side has been decreased by the same amount.

Type II—Interchanges of the balance-sheet items.—The second main group of transactions comprises those which do not affect the total values in the balance-sheet columns. They consist merely of interchanges of values among assets, liabilities, or proprietorship; and each transaction affects items on only one side of the balance sheet.

Interchanges of assets.—Some transactions consist merely of changes in the various types of assets. They have the effect of shifting certain parts of the total value from one asset or group of assets to another. Such transactions do not affect the total assets; nor do they change the types or amounts of liabilities and proprietorship.

Fifth example (increase of one asset; decrease of another): Purchase of merchandise for $160 cash. The asset "Merchandise" is increased $160, and the asset "Cash" is decreased the same amount. There has been no change in the liabilities or proprietorship. The balance sheet would now be:

ASSETS		LIABILITIES AND PROPRIETORSHIP	
Cash.................	$ 8,890.00	*Liabilities:*	
Merchandise..........	4,160.00	Accounts payable...	$ 3,250.00
		Proprietorship:	
		X, capital.........	9,800.00
Total............	$13,050.00	Total.........	$13,050.00

Interchanges of liabilities and proprietorship.—Changes may occur which affect only the right-hand column of the balance sheet, without increasing or decreasing any of the assets. Such transactions may consist either of interchanges of liabilities and proprietorship or of substitutions of one type of liability or proprietorship for another.

Sixth example (decrease of one liability; increase of another): A payment of $1,750 is made to a creditor by giving him a promissory note. The liability "Accounts payable" is decreased $1,750; the liability "Notes payable" is increased $1,750. There is no change in the total amount of liabilities; nor is there any change in proprietorship or assets. The balance sheet is now:

ASSETS		LIABILITIES AND PROPRIETORSHIP	
Cash	$ 8,890.00	*Liabilities:*	
Merchandise	4,160.00	Accounts payable	$ 1,500.00
		Notes payable	1,750.00
		Proprietorship:	
		X, capital	9,800.00
Total	$13,050.00	Total	$13,050.00

Seventh example (change of proprietorship): Proprietor X sells $1,500 of his interest in the business to Z. The proprietorship item "X, capital" is decreased $1,500; the proprietorship item "Z, capital" is increased $1,500. The balance sheet is now:

ASSETS		LIABILITIES AND PROPRIETORSHIP		
Cash	$ 8,890.00	*Liabilities:*		
Merchandise	4,160.00	Accounts payable	$1,500.00	
		Notes payable	1,750.00	$ 3,250.00
		Proprietorship:		
		X, capital	8,300.00	
		Z, capital	1,500.00	9,800.00
Total	$13,050.00	Total		$13,050.00

Eighth example (decrease of liability; increase of proprietorship): Mr. Y, to whom the note for $1,750 was given, becomes a proprietor and cancels the note. In terms of the balance sheet, the liability "Notes payable" is decreased $1,750, and the proprietorship item "Y, capital" is increased $1,750. The change is shown as follows:

ASSETS		LIABILITIES AND PROPRIETORSHIP		
Cash	$ 8,890.00	*Liabilities:*		
Merchandise	4,160.00	Accounts payable		$ 1,500.00
		Proprietorship:		
		X, capital	$8,300.00	
		Y, capital	1,750.00	
		Z, capital	1,500.00	11,550.00
Total	$13,050.00	Total		$13,050.00

Ninth example (decrease of proprietorship; increase of liability): Proprietor Z withdraws from the firm. He accepts a promissory note signed by X and Y in exchange for his proprietorship. The proprietorship item "Z, capital" disappears and the liability "Notes payable" $1,500 appears on the balance sheet as follows:

ASSETS		LIABILITIES AND PROPRIETORSHIP		
Cash..........	$ 8,890.00	*Liabilities:*		
Merchandise...	4,160.00	Accounts payable...	$1,500.00	
		Notes payable.....	1,500.00	$ 3,000.00
		Proprietorship:		
		X, capital.........	$8,300.00	
		Y, capital.........	1,750.00	10,050.00
Total.....	$13,050.00	Total..................		$13,050.00

In the nine examples just given it has been shown that no transaction properly recorded can disturb the equilibrium of the accounting equation. The first type adds *or* subtracts equal amounts on *each side* of the equation. The second type adds *and* subtracts equal amounts on the *same side* of the equation. All transactions may be reduced to terms of one or both of the foregoing types.

QUESTIONS ON CHAPTER III

1. What is a balance sheet? What is a statement of income and expense?
2. Why are there two columns in a balance sheet? Why must the two columns always be equal?
3. Define "assets." Illustrate five typical assets of each of the following types of enterprise: gold mine; drygoods store; textile mill; wheat farm; grocery store.
4. The right side of the balance sheet indicates the persons or types of persons who have claims upon the assets. Would it also be true to say that it indicates the persons to whom the property rights in new assets will be assigned?
5. Do the creditors and proprietors of an enterprise each have definite claims on specific assets of an enterprise? Why or why not?
6. How would you classify the following in terms of assets, liabilities, and proprietorship: cash; delivery truck; amount invested by a partner in an enterprise; amount receivable from the taxpayers of a government; amount payable to a bank; ten acres of land; mortgage on land payable to an insurance company.
7. If total assets always equal the total of liabilities plus proprietorship, a change in one total must of necessity affect the other. Explain.

8. Some transactions merely change the form of assets or the type of the ownership. Explain.
9. Give two illustrations of each of the following types of transactions:
   (1) Increase in assets and increase in proprietorship
   (2) Increase in assets and increase in liabilities
   (3) Decrease in assets and decrease in proprietorship
   (4) Decrease in assets and decrease in liabilities
   (5) Increase in one asset and decrease in another asset
   (6) Increase in one liability and decrease in another liability
   (7) Increase in one part and decrease in another part of proprietorship
   (8) Decrease in liabilities and increase in proprietorship
   (9) Increase in liabilities and decrease in proprietorship
10. Analyze each of the following transactions in terms of its increase or decrease of assets, liabilities, or proprietorship. Be sure that each transaction can be reduced to one of the nine types illustrated in the foregoing question.

    S. H. Hopkins invests $13,000 to establish a retail drug store, of which he becomes the sole proprietor. The sum of $6,000 is borrowed from T. Arandson, a one-year note bearing interest at 7 per cent per annum. The following assets are purchased for cash: land and building, $4,000; fixtures, $1,000; office equipment, $300; miscellaneous supplies, $300; drugs, $2,000. Additional drugs to the amount of $3,000 are secured from the Gayson Laboratories on a 60-day open account. The partnership borrows $2,000 from the Z State Bank and uses $1,000 of it to make a payment on the amount due the Gayson Laboratories.
11. State the effect of each of the following upon the balance sheet: investment by proprietor; borrowing of funds; cash purchase of land; cash purchase of postage stamps; credit purchase of stock in trade; embezzlement by cashier; collection of cash from customers; payment of amount due a creditor; payment of freight and handling charge on materials; donation of land to corporation; loss by fire; payment of half the loss by an insurance company; loss on a customer's account which proves uncollectible.

CHAPTER IV

THE ACCOUNT—DEBIT AND CREDIT

The equilibrium of the accounting equation has been demonstrated at length in chapter iii. But no explanation has been given of the method of classifying and recording the effects of transactions upon assets, liabilities, and proprietorship. The balance sheet served in previous illustrations as the place for recording the effects of every transaction; but the task of preparing a balance sheet after each business transaction would be impossible and undesirable for any enterprise operating under normal conditions. The transactions of an enterprise occur in rapid sequence, and revision of the balance sheet after each transaction would require a great amount of work; moreover, much of the work would be unnecessary, because most transactions would affect only certain aspects of the balance sheet. Some devices must be found to provide more adequate treatment of the accounting data, devices which will permit the effects of transactions to be accumulated in the records before the data are reduced to the form of the balance sheet.

The account; a device for recording changes in the accounting data.—The account is a device for accumulating records of the increases and decreases in assets, liabilities, and proprietorship. One account is maintained for each type of balance-sheet item, and the captions or titles of the accounts correspond to the subdivisions of the data which appear in the balance sheet itself, such as "Cash," "Merchandise," "Buildings," "Notes Payable," and "Capital."[1] The extent to which accounting data will be subdivided in the balance sheet and in the accounts will, of course,

[1] The custom will be followed in this text of capitalizing the first letter of all words or expressions which represent the titles of "accounts," but not those which merely designate a group or class of certain accounting data. The following sentence will illustrate this principle, applied to the word *cash*. "All receipts and disbursements of cash will be entered in the Cash account." In some cases the titles of accounts will be used without the word *account* following them. For example "Two accounts were affected: 'Cash' and 'Notes Payable.' "

depend upon the need for detailed information. The records in the accounts are limited to such information as can be expressed in terms of exchange value, which means that certain important aspects of the economic phenomena are omitted from the records. For example, the cash of an enterprise may consist of paper money, gold, and silver of various denominations and of various dates of issue. The Cash account, however, would (normally) show records only of the increases and decreases in the total amount of cash, no record being made therein of the color, denomination, or metallic composition of the coins or other currency. The restriction of the account to data expressed in terms of exchange value simplifies the task of maintaining accounting records; for exchange values are affected by only one type of variation, change in *amount*. Exchange value may increase or decrease, and it is the purpose of each account merely to set forth the increases and decreases of the balance-sheet item with which it deals.

The form of the account is as simple as its purpose; it is arranged to contain the records of increases and decreases of a specific balance-sheet item, such as "Cash" or "Merchandise." For example, the Cash account would appear as follows:

CASH

The Cash account has two sides; data may be recorded either to the left or right of the vertical line which divides the space beneath the account title. The form of the Cash account illustrates the general form of all accounts, a form which varies in detail with the purposes for which used. But in every case the account includes a title, under which specific balance-sheet data may be arranged, and two vertical parallel columns,[1] in which the in-

[1] The account might of course take other forms; for example, the parallel columns might be horizontal, or all data might be recorded in one vertical column. The

creases and decreases may be accumulated and offset against each other, as follows:

ACCOUNT TITLE

Record of changes in amount	Record of changes in amount

The two columns may be designated as the "left" and "right" columns of the account, or as the "left side" and "right side" of the account respectively. The question arises: How shall the two sides of the account be used? They are, of course, established to record increases and decreases in balance-sheet data, with opposite sides to be used for offsetting tendencies. But which side shall be used for increases, which for decreases? Theoretically it would make no difference: one might arbitrarily decide, for example, that all increases in account totals should be recorded on the left sides of all accounts, and all decreases on the right sides. There are practical reasons, however, why some other method serves the accountant's purpose better.

Records in accounts consistent with arrangement of balance sheet.—The final balance sheet of the enterprise used in chapter iii to illustrate the effects of certain business transactions is set forth below:

ASSETS		LIABILITIES AND PROPRIETORSHIP		
Cash..........	$ 8,890.00	*Liabilities:*		
Merchandise...	4,160.00	Accounts payable...	$1,500.00	
		Notes payable......	1,500.00	$ 3,000.00
		Proprietorship:		
		X, capital.........	$8,300.00	
		Y, capital.........	1,750.00	10,050.00
Total.....	$13,050.00	Total..................		$13,050.00

single-column account would be very serviceable (and is often used) where the data are continuously increased (with no offsetting decreases) during the time the account is in use. More than two columns are sometimes used, the extra columns to express subtotals of either side or the amounts by which the data on one side exceed those on the other.

In this balance sheet, as was true in all previous balance sheets, the assets are listed on the left side, the liabilities and proprietorship on the right. This method of arranging information on the balance sheet suggests a basis for arranging the detailed information within each account; in fact, each individual account provides data from which some aspect of financial status can be determined, and the various accounts together contain exactly the same information as appears in the balance sheet. Custom has placed assets on the left side, and liabilities and proprietorship on

Cash (asset)	
$8,890.00	

Merchandise (asset)	
$4,160.00	

Accounts Payable (liability)	
	$1,500.00

Notes Payable (liability)	
	$1,500.00

X, Capital (proprietorship)	
	$8,300.00

Y, Capital (proprietorship)	
	$1,750.00

the right side, of the balance sheet.[1] The accounts which contain detailed information concerning financial status may be grouped into exactly the same general classes as the balance-sheet data. There are asset accounts, liability accounts, and proprietorship accounts. Each account has its two sides, which are used in a manner consistent with the conventional arrangement of the balance sheet; that is to say, assets appear on the left sides of

[1] Enterprises organized in Great Britain use the reverse order in the balance sheet, in conformity with the British Companies Act of 1862 which suggested this form of balance sheet for limited companies (corporations). The practice of the limited companies has set the standard for individual proprietorships and partnerships. British enterprises, however, use the accounts in the manner to be described in this text.

the asset accounts, liabilities and proprietorship on the right sides of their respective accounts. This consistency of arrangement of balance-sheet data and account data serves many practical purposes in accounting, and is the method used in most countries where double-entry accounting has been adopted. The accounts which contain the data of the foregoing balance sheet are shown on page 35.

Recording increases in the accounts.—The foregoing accounts show the values of the assets in the left columns of the asset accounts; they also show the values of the liabilities and proprietorship in the right columns of their accounts. If any one of these items is increased as the result of a transaction, an additional amount is recorded below that already in the account. To demonstrate the use of the account, let us record the effects of the following simple transaction: the investment of $1,000 additional cash by X, one of the proprietors. The result of the transaction would be an increase of the asset "cash" and an increase of the proprietorship item "X, capital." The increase of the asset would be recorded on the left side of the Cash account. The increase of proprietorship would be recorded on the right side of the X, Capital account. The accounts affected would then appear as follows:

Cash	
$8,890.00	
1,000.00	

X, Capital	
	$8,300.00
	1,000.00

The transaction has illustrated increases of account totals—additions to totals already appearing in the accounts. Increases in the assets are recorded in the left columns of the asset accounts. Increases in the liabilities or proprietorship items are recorded in the right columns of their accounts.

Recording decreases in the accounts.—But how shall *decreases* be recorded? The Cash and the X, Capital accounts just illustrated reveal the fact that only one side of each account has been affected by the increases in the accounts. This suggests the possibility of using the "other" side of each of these accounts for the record of decreases. If this method is adopted, the decrease column for cash is the *right* side of the Cash account, whereas the decrease column for X's proprietorship is the *left* side of the X, Capital account. To illustrate, assume that X withdraws $140 cash from the enterprise. The effects of the transaction will be a decrease of the asset "Cash" and a decrease of the proprietorship item "X, capital." If the *other* side is used in each case to record the decrease of the data, the asset account will be reduced by a record on the right side, the proprietorship account by a record on the left side. The two accounts, after the records are made, would appear as follows:

Cash	
$8,890.00 1,000.00	$140.00

X, Capital	
$140.00	$8,300.00 1,000.00

Asset decreases are recorded in the right columns; liability and proprietorship decreases are recorded in the left columns. The uses of the left and right sides may be shown more clearly by the following diagrams:

Assets	
Increases	Decreases

Liabilities	
Decreases	Increases

Proprietorship	
Decreases	Increases

Substituting signs and symbols for the terms used above, the facts may be set forth as follows:

A	
+	−

L	
−	+

P	
−	+

Debit and credit refer to data in left and right columns of accounts.—Accounting data appearing in the left columns of accounts are known as *debits*. Accounting data appearing in the right columns of accounts are known as *credits*. The words "debit" and "credit" are also frequently used as verbs, referring to the act of making records in the accounts: to debit an account means to record information on the left side; to credit an account means to record information on the right side.

The terms "debit" and "credit" need carry no meaning, when considered in terms of accounting records, other than left and right, respectively. The use of these terms is sometimes confusing, however, to persons unfamiliar with accounting; for they discover that asset accounts are increased by "debits," whereas they are used to considering assets as something to their "credit"; they also find that liability accounts are increased by "credits," whereas they are accustomed to thinking of liabilities as synonymous with "debts" (debits). The confusion arises from failure to keep in mind the viewpoint of the double-entry system, which is the viewpoint of the enterprise as a separate entity.[1]

The explanation of the account may now be summarized in terms of debit and credit. It has been shown that increases in the asset accounts are recorded on the left side, decreases on the right side; increases in the liability and proprietorship accounts are recorded on the right side, decreases on the left side. Regrouping these statements, it is clear that:

Left-hand records (debits) consist of

a) Original (or increases in) assets
b) Decreases in liabilities
c) Decreases in proprietorship

Right-hand records (credits) consist of

a) Decreases in assets
b) Original (or increases in) liabilities
c) Original (or increases in) proprietorship

[1] The use of the terms "debit" and "credit" arose from the custom of Italian merchants who maintained lists of their customers and vendors with whom deferred payment agreements had been drawn up. A customer was a person who owed the enterprise or the enterpriser (*debet*=he owes), and the customers were listed as debtors of the firm. A vendor was a person who intrusted assets to the enterprise (*credit*=he trusts), and the vendors were shown as the creditors of the firm.

The terms "debit" and "credit," so useful for the expression of these personal relationships between the enterprise and outsiders, were later extended to other accounts and resulted in the personification of all the aspects of financial status and operations. Each account was dignified as a separate financial entity, having debtor-creditor relations with the other accounts. This text will deal with debit and credit strictly in terms of increases and decreases of balance-sheet data, without regard to the meaning of the words in the early stages of double-entry technique.

Reduced to the symbols, *A*, *L*, *P*, and expressed in terms of plus and minus signs, the debit and credit grouping may be shown as follows:

Debits	Credits
$+A$	$-A$
$-L$	$+L$
$-P$	$+P$

Business transactions cause equal debits and credits in the accounts.—The effects of every business transaction may be expressed as debits and credits; for debits and credits are merely symbols for expressing certain aspects of the balance-sheet data. The main types of transactions will be analyzed in terms of this assertion:

I. Changes affecting the balance-sheet totals:
  A. Increases:
    1. Increased asset ($+A$; debit); increased proprietorship ($+P$; credit)
    2. Increased asset ($+A$; debit); increased liability ($+L$; credit)
  B. Decreases:
    3. Decreased proprietorship ($-P$; debit); decreased asset ($-A$; credit)
    4. Decreased liability ($-L$; debit); decreased asset ($-A$; credit)

II. Interchanges of the balance-sheet items:
  A. Interchanges in assets:
    5. Increase of one asset ($+A$; debit); decrease of another ($-A$; credit)
  B. Interchanges in liabilities and proprietorship:
    6. Decrease of one liability ($-L$; debit); increase of another ($+L$; credit)
    7. Decrease of one proprietorship item ($-P$; debit); increase of another ($+P$; credit)
    8. Decrease of liability ($-L$; debit); increase of proprietorship ($+P$; credit)
    9. Decrease of proprietorship ($-P$; debit); increase of liability ($+L$; credit)

Every business transaction illustrated above results in both a debit and a credit to the accounts. In view of the fact that no transactions disturb the equilibrium of the balance sheet (which is the summation of the data in the accounts), it is necessary that the debits and credits of each transaction be equal in amount. Each transaction must result in equal debits and credits, which can be classified in terms of whether they increase or decrease the assets, liabilities, or proprietorship. The task of analyzing each transaction for purposes of double-entry classification is the task of determining just what kinds and amounts of debits and credits have resulted therefrom. The types of debits and credits may, of course, be expressed in terms of signs and symbols; and these devices often aid in the analysis of transactions.[1]

Some transactions cause several debit or credit entries, or both.—Not all transactions are as simple as those which have been illustrated in the text thus far. Some are complex in their effects upon the accounts; consequently they require careful analysis by the person dealing with them. A few illustrations of complex transactions will be given. Assume that a machine used in a factory and recorded in the accounts at a value of $1,000 is delivered to a creditor to satisfy an $800 liability. The creditor chooses to allow only $900 for the machine (and this is agreed to). This amount, however, is $100 more than the debt owed to the creditor, who, upon receipt of the machine, accordingly sends his check for $100. Before the effects of the transaction are recorded, the accounts containing the record of the machine and the obligation would appear as follows (many other accounts, of course, would typically exist as records of the enterprise):

[1] The general application of the rule may also be demonstrated by stating the accounting equation in algebraic form. The accounting equation has been shown to be: Assets equal liabilities plus proprietorship, or:

$$A = L + P$$

Subtract equal amounts from each side of the equation. Since $A = L + P$, we may subtract the quantity $(L+P)$ from the left side, and the quantity A from the right side, without destroying the equality. We then have:

$$A - (L+P) = L + P - A,$$

which is:

$$A - L - P = L + P - A.$$

This final equation provides a formula for all of the foregoing types of debits and credits. Debits are at the left side of the equation; credits at the right.

Machinery	
$1,000.00	

Accounts Payable	
	$800.00

The debits and credits to classify the effects of the delivery of the machine to the creditor at an agreed value of $900 would affect the accounts as follows:

		Debit	Credit
Debits:	Increased asset—Cash	$100.00	
	Decreased liability—Accounts payable	800.00	
	Decreased proprietorship—Capital	100.00	
Credit:	Decreased asset—Machinery		$1,000.00

This transaction has resulted in debits to three accounts, representing each type of debit. Only one account has been credited in this particular case. The debit to the Capital account represents a reduction of proprietorship as a result of this transaction, for the $1,000 asset "Machinery" is given in payment of an $800 liability and for $100 in cash, total debits of only $900. The loss resulting from the transaction causes a debit to the proprietorship account, Capital. The effects of the transaction are shown below:

Cash		Machinery		Accounts Payable		Capital	
$100.00		$1,000.00	$1,000.00	$800.00	$800.00	$100.00	

A second illustration will serve to demonstrate complex transactions further. A machine valued at $2,000 is received from a creditor to whom the business is already indebted to the extent of $300. The following agreement is made and carried out. The creditor is to cancel his claim against the business, and in return is to receive $1,000 cash, an old machine recorded in the accounts at $400, and a promissory note for $800. The following debits and credits will be made:

		Debit	Credit
Debits:	Increased asset—Machinery	$2,000.00	
	Decreased liability—Accounts payable	300.00	
Credits:	Decreased asset—Cash		$1,000.00
	Decreased asset—Machinery		400.00
	Increased liability—Notes payable		800.00
	Increased proprietorship—Capital		100.00

The total debits and credits are equal. Among the debits, the asset "Machinery" is increased, and the liability "Accounts payable" decreased. Total debits are $2,300. The following credits appear: The assets "Cash" and "Machinery" are decreased, and the liability "Notes payable" is increased. The total of these credits is $2,200, which indicates that a new property right must be recorded. The balance is accordingly credited to "Capital," the account with the proprietors. The $100 represents extra proprietorship resulting from this interchange of assets and liabilities. The effects of all business transactions may ultimately be reduced to balance-sheet elements (assets, liabilities, proprietorship). The resulting debits and credits may always be expressed in terms of the changes just described. At times, however, a transaction results in two or more debits or credits at the same time. A transaction may give rise both to increased assets and to decreased liabilities or proprietorship—several types of debits. The equivalent credit, on the other hand, might comprise both reduced assets and increased liabilities or proprietorship—several types of credits.

The complexity of the foregoing transactions indicates that it is not always easy to classify the effects of transactions in terms of the balance-sheet equation. The task becomes particularly burdensome and difficult if these complex transactions recur frequently. Such a condition creates a need for supplementary or intermediate accounts to classify certain recurring transactions until they can be reduced to the balance-sheet elements. These supplementary accounts are known as "Income accounts" and "Expense accounts," and will be introduced in chapter v.

QUESTIONS ON CHAPTER IV

1. What is an "account?"
2. What is the form of the account? Why does it have two sides? Would there be any advantage if an account had three or four columns in which data could be recorded?
3. Mention some of the reasons why the balance sheet would be inadequate as a basis for elaborate accounting records.
4. What is the relation of the account to the balance sheet? Are the left and right columns of the accounts for exactly the same purpose as the left and right columns of the balance sheet?

5. How are increases of balance-sheet items recorded in the accounts? Decreases? Answer in terms of assets, liabilities, and proprietorship.
6. What is the meaning of the term "debit"? Of "credit"? Frame the answer in terms of the balance-sheet elements.
7. Analyze the transactions in questions 4 and 5 at the close of chapter iii in terms of debits and credits.
8. Indicate the accounts to be debited and credited as result of the following transactions:
   a) Purchase of a truck for $1,000, one-half paid in cash, one-half on credit terms.
   b) The truck is exchanged for the following: $200 cash; a note receivable for $700; and a motorcycle valued at $300.
9. A machine is purchased at a cost price of $8,000. One thousand dollars is paid in cash, a note is given for $3,000, and the balance remains unpaid on "open account." Analyze the complete transaction in terms of debits and credits.
10. A parcel of land recorded in the accounts at a value of $12,000 is disposed of for $14,000, received as follows: $5,000 cash, a promissory note for $4,000, a mortgage on the land for the balance of the total selling price. Indicate the resulting debits and credits.

CHAPTER V

INCOME AND EXPENSE ACCOUNTS

All business transactions may be analyzed in terms of their effects on assets, liabilities, and proprietorship. But it is not always expedient to attempt such an analysis of each transaction at the time it occurs. Moreover, immediate classification in terms of balance-sheet data would provide no accounting record of the operations by which financial status is changed. Consequently, intermediate or supplementary accounts are often introduced to accumulate data concerning business operations, data which are later reclassified in terms of their effect upon financial status.

Income and expense accounts reflect business operations.— The primary objective of private enterprise is the making of profit —the manipulation of economic goods in such manner as to increase the property rights of the proprietors. This objective is striven for by engaging in business transactions; profit results when the assets received possess greater value to the proprietors than the assets surrendered or liabilities incurred.

The computation of the profit from individual transactions gives rise to two difficulties: some business operations are so complex in their nature that the task of computing the values received and expended at the time of each transaction would be almost impossible; some business operations recur so frequently and in such rapid sequence that they could not be analyzed and classified as they take place. But these difficulties can be surmounted by accounting methods. Usually it is not important to determine the exact profit resulting from each individual transaction. The real problem of the business manager is to conduct his affairs so that his operations as a whole during a period of time cause an increase of proprietorship. Income and expense accounts describe and measure in financial terms the different business operations carried on in the effort to realize a profit. The data of such accounts are summarized periodically to reveal their net effect on proprietorship, also to provide information for purposes of administrative control.

Income accounts illustrated.—The A and B Law Firm prepares a balance sheet to express its financial status on January first of a certain year, which appears as follows:

A AND B LAW FIRM

BALANCE SHEET—JANUARY 1, 19—

ASSETS		PROPRIETORSHIP	
Cash	$3,600.00	A, capital	$1,800.00
		B, capital	1,800.00
Total	$3,600.00	Total	$3,600.00

During the course of two months the firm renders services to clients, for which it receives cash in numerous small amounts. The total cash received is $4,000. If any one of these receipts of cash—say for seven dollars—were analyzed in terms of the accounting equation, it might be treated as follows:

Debit: Cash	$7.00	
Credit: A, capital		$3.50
B, capital		3.50

But such a detailed analysis of the effects of each cash receipt upon the Capital accounts would entail considerable labor, much of which would serve no useful purpose. The task may be reduced by accumulating the credits in a single account which would offset the cash received for the legal services rendered. Such an account would also provide a record of the total earnings of the firm during the period. An account of this type is known as an "income account." The proper title for an income account is the title which most accurately describes the source of the income. For example, a satisfactory title for the case just described would be "Legal Services" or "Income from Fees."

The recording and later treatment of income data may also be illustrated by data of the A and B Law Firm. Before the period of operations, the accounts of the firm would have been:

CASH		A, CAPITAL		B, CAPITAL	
$3,600.00			$1,800.00		$1,800.00

At the end of two months, the Cash account would have been affected by debits amounting to $4,000. An income account entitled "Legal Services" would also have accumulated a total credit of $4,000. The accounts at the close of operations would contain the following amounts:

Cash	
$3,600.00	
4,000.00	

A, Capital	
	$1,800.00

Legal Services	
	$4,000.00

B, Capital	
	$1,800.00

Now, if the proprietorship of the firm is to be correctly shown, the Legal Services account containing a credit of $4,000 must be apportioned to the Capital accounts of A and B. The apportionment may be accomplished by the following transfer:

Debit: Legal services	$4,000.00	
Credit: A, capital		$2,000.00
B, capital		2,000.00

After this change is made, the accounts would be:

Cash	
$3,600.00	
4,000.00	

A, Capital	
	$1,800.00
	2,000.00

Legal Services	
$4,000.00	$4,000.00

B, Capital	
	$1,800.00
	2,000.00

The Legal Services account now merely reflects the business operations of the period. The data accumulated in the account have been reclassified in terms of the balance sheet to show their effect on proprietorship. The assets and proprietorship of the A and B Law Firm have been increased by $4,000. The balance sheet would now be:

A AND B LAW FIRM

BALANCE SHEET—MARCH 1, 19—

ASSETS		PROPRIETORSHIP	
Cash	$7,600.00	A, capital	$3,800.00
		B, capital	3,800.00
Total	$7,600.00	Total	$7,600.00

The foregoing treatment of the Legal Services account illustrates a principle applicable to any other type of income transaction. There are numerous sources of business income; illustrations are brokerage services, royalties, rentals, interest, dividends, profit on sale of buildings or land, and profit on sale of merchandise, to mention only a few.

Expense accounts illustrated.—Mention may now be made of the assets expended (or liabilities incurred) in the operations entered into for profit. For example, assume that the A and B Law Firm has expended total cash of $1,072 during the two months' period of operations for the following: rent, $400; light, $22; telephone, $50; office salaries, $600. For purposes of this illustration we may also assume that these cash expenditures were paid after the rental privileges, light, telephone service, and office help, respectively, had been enjoyed. What accounts are to be used to reflect the various causes of the total cash expenditures? Of course, the debits to offset the cash expenditures could be entered in the Capital accounts; but, as in the case of income apportionment, the task of dividing the various debits between the two Capital accounts would require much labor, and would merge the records of different types of business operations. Consequently temporary accounts—*expense accounts*—may be used to accumulate the debits later to be offset against the Capital accounts, also to describe the various business operations involving the cash expenditures. Expense accounts may be used also to reflect the expenditure of assets other than cash, as well as transactions which result merely in the incurrence of liabilities. The appropriate titles for expense accounts are those which most adequately describe the causes or circumstances of the expenditures of assets or incurrence of liabilities.

Income and expense accounts summarized to determine net effect on financial status.—The accounts of the A and B Law Firm at the close of two months' operations, giving effect to the income and expense transactions, would be:[1]

Cash	
$3,600.00	$400.00
4,000.00	22.00
	50.00
	600.00

A, Capital	
	$1,800.00

B, Capital	
	$1,800.00

Legal Services	
	$4,000.00

Rent	
$400.00	

Light	
$22.00	

Telephone	
$50.00	

Office Salaries	
$600.00	

Three of the foregoing accounts are balance-sheet accounts representing financial status—Cash, A Capital, and B Capital. The other accounts reflect business operations (income and expense) which must be summarized to show their effects on financial status. The reclassification of the data in the Legal Services account—an income account—was accomplished in the previous illustration by merely dividing the credit in the Legal Services account between the Capital accounts of A and B. The reclassification of the data in the various expense accounts might, of course, be accomplished in the same manner, with one-half of each of the expense-account debits finding its way to each Capital account. Such treatment of income and expense data would be impracticable, however, unless the number of such accounts were small; for the mere task of apportioning the totals of a large num-

[1] The amount in each account represents what in practice would consist of numerous smaller amounts involved in separate transactions. The four accounts, Rent, Light, Telephone, and Office Salaries, are *expense accounts* which offset the credits in the Cash account.

ber of accounts would be unduly great. Such procedure would offer no practical advantages; in fact it would have the disadvantage of obscuring the total effects of the income and expense transactions during a fiscal period.[1] In practice, a different method is followed in calculating the effect of income and expense transactions upon proprietorship. The method consists of offsetting the various income and expense data in one account to determine the net excess of income or expense. The net excess then represents the net change of proprietorship, and may be apportioned to the Capital accounts in the proper amounts. The account to be selected for the purpose of assembling the income and expense data will vary with the needs of the case. It may be one of the income accounts, one of the expense accounts, or a special account introduced solely for this purpose of summarizing the income and expense data. The following illustration will use a special account entitled "Income and Expense" as the place of summarization to determine net change in proprietorship. After transferring the income and expense data to the Income and Expense account, the accounts of the A and B Law Firm would be:

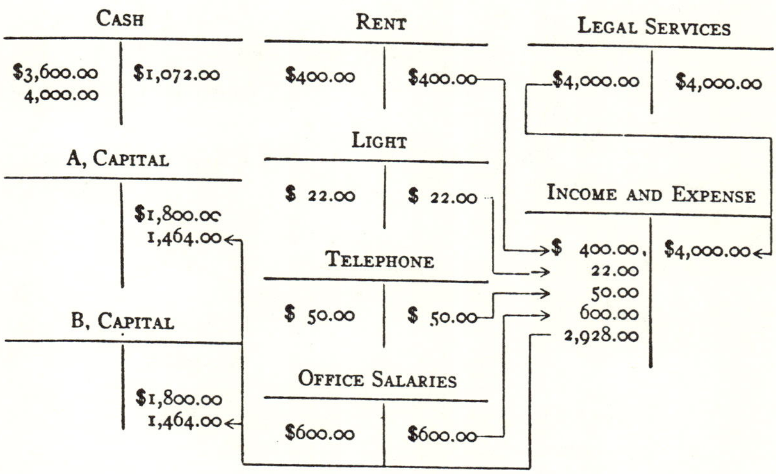

[1] A period of business operations selected as the basis of summarization of income and expense data is known variously as a "fiscal period," an "accounting period," or an "operating period." Such periods may be of any length; usually they are expressed in terms of calendar periods of time, such as the month or year.

The Income and Expense account receives credits of $4,000 and debits of $1,072 by the transfer of the income and expense data thereto. The excess credit of $2,928 is apportioned to the Capital accounts of A and B, as net increases of their proprietorship resulting from the profit of the operations during the period. The balance-sheet accounts (Cash; A, Capital; and B, Capital) now express the financial status of the enterprise at the close of two months' operations. The data in the various income and expense accounts have been reclassified in terms of the balance sheet, and the amounts in them merely reflect the business operations of the two months' period. The balance sheet would now be:

A AND B LAW FIRM

BALANCE SHEET—FEBRUARY 28, 19—

ASSETS		PROPRIETORSHIP	
Cash	$6,528.00	A, capital	$3,264.00
		B, capital	3,264.00
Total	$6,528.00	Total	$6,528.00

Income and expense data as basis for summary report of business operations.—The income and expense accounts provide the data for the calculation of financial profit or loss from the business operations during a period of time. They may be summarized in the Income and Expense account specially intended for the purpose, and may be regarded as the basis for a report of business operations which sets forth the causes of the net change in pro-

A AND B LAW FIRM

STATEMENT OF INCOME AND EXPENSE—FOR THE TWO MONTHS ENDING FEBRUARY 28, 19—

Income:		
Legal services		$4,000.00
Expense:		
Rent	$400.00	
Light	22.00	
Telephone	50.00	
Office salaries	600.00	1,072.00
Profit (increase of capital)		$2,928.00

prietorship during a period of time. A report of this type has been referred to at various times as a statement of income and expense; it may be prepared directly from the data of the Income and Expense account. Such a report for the A and B Law Firm is shown on page 50.

The sale transaction presents special difficulties of classification.—Many business enterprises reap their main profits from the sale of tangible merchandise. An account to reflect the income from sales would contain a total equal to all the assets received from the sale of merchandise. If, for example, merchandise were sold for $40 cash, the entry would be:

Debit: Cash..................	$40.00	
Credit: Sales...................		$40.00

But sales of merchandise differ from other income transactions in that they involve the surrender of ownership in certain merchandise at the time new assets are received in exchange for it. The credit in the Sales account, therefore, must be regarded as representing both the reduction of the asset "Merchandise" and the profit ultimately to be apportioned to the Capital accounts. Assume the cost value of the goods sold to be $35. This means that the manager has engaged in a transaction which results in a profit to him of five dollars, and reduces the merchandise on hand by $35. But where sale transactions occur frequently during a period of financial operations, such analysis of each sale would be very difficult and probably of little value to the proprietor. Consequently the custom is usually followed of crediting a Sales account to record the total receipts from the sale of merchandise, and reclassifying the total later in terms of sold merchandise and profits on its sale.

Illustration of the sales account.—A business enterprise has on hand $3,000 worth of merchandise, and the proprietor owns the stock in its entirety. Assume that he does not replenish his stock (sixty oriental rugs, for example); also that he sells them in typical oriental fashion on the street, so that no other assets are invested in the business. The balance sheet of the enterprise would be:

Z RUG BUSINESS

BALANCE SHEET—APRIL 1, 19—

ASSETS		PROPRIETORSHIP	
Merchandise..........	$3,000.00	Z, capital............	$3,000.00
Total............	$3,000.00	Total............	$3,000.00

The accounts showing the facts of this balance sheet would be:

MERCHANDISE	
$3,000.00	

CAPITAL	
	$3,000.00

During a month Z sells rugs for which he receives $2,500 in cash. He makes records equivalent to the following in their totals:

Debits to cash......... $2,500.00
Credits to sales.............. $2,500.00

At the end of the month the accounts would contain the following totals:

MERCHANDISE	
$3,000.00	

CASH	
$2,500.00	

Z, CAPITAL	
	$3,000.00

SALES	
	$2,500.00

When the time arrives to prepare a summary of financial status, it will be necessary to reclassify the credit total in the Sales account in terms of its effect on both assets and proprietorship. Assume the original cost of the sold merchandise to be $2,000. This amount must properly be credited to the Merchandise account and debited to the Sales account. The transfer would be effected as follows:

Debit: Sales.................. $2,000.00
Credit: Merchandise................ $2,000.00

The remaining credit in the Sales account is, strictly speaking, increased proprietorship. This amount may now be removed from the Sales account and properly classified as an increase of Capital:

Debit: Sales.................... $500.00
  Credit: Z, capital.................... $500.00

After the foregoing transfers have been effected, the accounts would be:

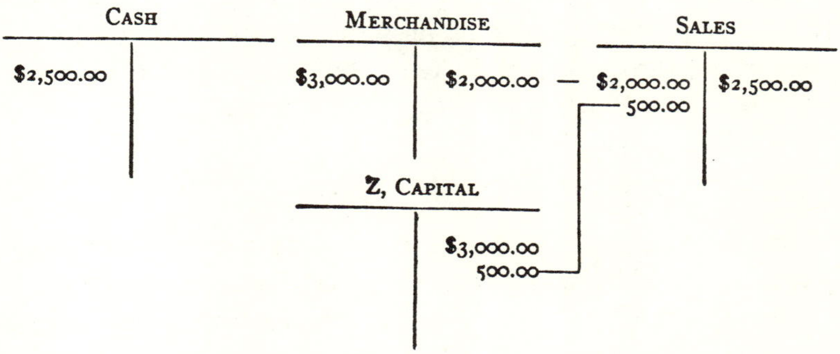

The balance sheet at the close of these operations would appear as follows:

Z RUG BUSINESS

BALANCE SHEET—MAY 1, 19—

ASSETS		PROPRIETORSHIP	
Cash................	$2,500.00	Z, capital............	$3,500.00
Merchandise..........	1,000.00		
Total............	$3,500.00	Total............	$3,500.00

The gain from the merchandise transactions is reflected in proprietorship by the $500 increase of Z's capital.

Business operations not limited to cash transactions.—The foregoing illustrations of income and expense transactions have been limited to operations affecting the cash of an enterprise. But income and expense accounts may, of course, reflect operations which involve any of the assets, as well as the liabilities. The account with Legal Services illustrated above would have reflected income transactions equally well if the assets received had been merely the clients' promises to pay the amounts at a later time. The record for such transactions would then have been:

Debit: Accounts receivable.... $4,000.00
Credit: Legal services.............. $4,000.00

Later, when the clients paid their obligations to the law firm the asset "Accounts receivable" would have been converted into the asset "Cash."

The account with Rent likewise would have reflected expense transactions, even though promissory notes were given to the landlord for the amount of the rent payable. The accounts affected would, under such conditions, be as follows:

Debit: Rent..................... $400.00
Credit: Notes payable................ $400.00

When the notes were paid at a future date, the liability "Notes payable" would be reduced and the asset "Cash" correspondingly decreased. In each of these illustrations, the cash receipt or cash payment is not concurrent with the income or expense transaction which leads up to it. Income and expense operations are not mere receipts and disbursements of cash but include many other transactions which increase and decrease assets and liabilities in the effort to realize an ultimate profit.

Accounts at times contain data which represent both status and operations.—Previous discussion has drawn a rather sharp line between the accounts which represent financial status (assets, liabilities, and proprietorship) and those which reflect various types of business operations (income and expense). But in practice, the line is not always so easily drawn; the character of the data in many accounts changes from time to time, so, that unless the data be continuously revised, some accounts may prove to contain both balance-sheet data and income or expense data at the same time. Accounts of this type—which contain data representing both status and operations—are known as "mixed" accounts.

Merchandise as a mixed account.—The merchandise sold to customers during a period of operations is delivered to them in relatively small amounts during this time. The gradual decrease in the asset merchandise, however, is typically recorded by a credit in the Merchandise account only at the end of the period, at which time the total in the Sales account is correspondingly reduced by an offsetting debit. The expiration of merchandise value is a business operation in the same sense as the payment of cash or the incurrence of a liability; in fact, complete accounting for the expenditure of the asset "Merchandise" requires the use of an expense account to reflect the cost of goods surrendered in the business operations. Such an account might well be given the title "Merchandise Sold," "Cost of Goods Sold," or some similar designation. The periodic adjustment of the Merchandise account would be accomplished as follows, using the data of the Z Rug business illustrated above:

Debit: Cost of goods sold..... (an expense account)	$2,000.00	
Credit: Merchandise................		$2,000.00

The accounts affected would appear:

Merchandise		Cost of Goods Sold	
$3,000.00	$2,000.00	$2,000.00	

Previous to the adjustment just illustrated, the debit in the Merchandise account contains data of dissimilar nature. A part, $1,000, represents merchandise on hand at the close of the period; the remainder, $2,000, represents goods no longer on hand. Consequently the Merchandise account must be credited with $2,000. A corresponding debit must be made in the Sales account or in an expense account which reflects the operations which have caused the reduction of the asset merchandise. Such an expense account has been given the title "Cost of Goods Sold" in the foregoing illustrations; it would be set forth in a statement of income and expense for a given period of business operations.

Rent as a mixed account.—Take another illustration which appears to present a more difficult problem. Suppose, for example, a merchant had rented a store for $100 per month and that he had paid $100 cash to insure a month's occupancy. The transaction would be recorded as follows:

Debit: Rent.....................	$100.00	
Credit: Cash.........................		$100.00

The transaction does not, strictly speaking, decrease the net assets of the enterprise at the time of the cash payment; for the merchant regards the one-month rental privilege to be equal in value to the cash he has paid. The Rent account may, for the time being at least, be regarded as an asset account. As the weeks pass, however, the value of the rental privilege grows smaller, until at the end of the month, the merchant must vacate the store or pay $100 for another month's occupancy. The asset "Rent" is itself now completely *expended.* By the end of the month, the Rent account is no longer an asset account; by that time it serves merely to show that one month's occupancy of the building has been enjoyed. The Rent account, as here discussed, is a *mixed* account. At any given moment during the month, the $100 debit in the Rent account would contain two types of data; part would represent the unexpired occupancy privilege (an asset), part would represent the expired privilege (an expense).

Expense accounts as mixed accounts.—The possibility that accounts may contain mixed data—for example, both expired and unexpired values—makes it now desirable to restate the nature of the expense accounts. Expense accounts are, of course, accounts which describe certain business operations. But they are also accounts which indicate (at a given moment in time) that certain assets have been expended or liabilities have been incurred. The entries in the expense accounts may be made at the same time, before, or after these assets are actually expended or liabilities are actually incurred. In the case of the Rent account previously illustrated, the entry was made *before* the rental privilege had expired; in the case of the merchandise sold in the business operations the expense transaction was recorded *after* the asset "Merchandise" had been disposed of. Many asset accounts are gradually reduced in value during a period of business operations. At the time the accounts are summarized, the expended values in these accounts must be treated as expense items. As expenses, these amounts must be transferred to expense accounts specially provided for them, or must be offset directly against the accumulated credits in the proper income accounts.

The theory of double-entry accounting reviewed.—The various steps in the classification and summarization of business transactions by means of double-entry accounting have now been traced. Let us briefly review the essential points of the foregoing chapters.

The *balance sheet* is a summary of the financial status of a business enterprise; it is a statement which sets forth the *assets* on the one side, *liabilities* and *proprietorship* on the other. Assets are always equal to liabilities plus proprietorship. This equality may be regarded as the basic accounting equation (balance-sheet equation) and expressed algebraically as follows: $A = L + P$.

Business transactions of all kinds may be reduced to terms of their effect on the accounting equation. Every transaction may be analyzed as causing:

1. Increases *or* decreases in *both* sides of the equation.
2. Increases *and* decreases in *either* side of the equation.

The *account* is a device with two sides, used for keeping separate record of the increases and decreases of each type of asset, liability, or proprietorship. The increase and decrease side of a particular account is determined by its position in the balance-sheet equation. *Debits* are records on the left side of the accounts; *credits* are records on the right. In terms of the accounting equation, and using symbols for increases and decreases, we have the following: debits are $+A$, $-L$, $-P$; credits are $-A$, $+L$, $+P$.

Some transactions either are so complex or occur so frequently that it is desirable to record them in temporary accounts not classified as assets, liabilities, or proprietorship. The accounts used to reflect business operations of these types are called *income* accounts and *expense* accounts. Whenever a balance sheet is to be prepared, the income accounts and expense accounts are summarized to show the net effect of the business operations upon financial status. This is accomplished by transferring income and expense account totals to a summary account, and the difference thence to proprietorship. The data in the summary account provide the basis for a financial summary of business operations which explains the change in the proprietorship. This summary is known as the *statement of income and expense.*

QUESTIONS ON CHAPTER V

1. Some transactions *cannot be easily reduced* to the balance-sheet elements at the time they occur; consequently either their debit or credit elements are first classified in terms not included in the original balance-sheet equation. They are later finally reclassified into their balance-sheet elements. Illustrate.
2. Some transactions *occur so frequently* that their debit or credit elements are recorded in temporary accounts. This is done to provide important historical data for the management. The data in these temporary accounts are then reduced to their balance-sheet elements whenever a summary of the transactions and their effect on the balance sheet is required. Explain.
3. The title given to the income account represents the source from which certain effects on the balance sheet arise. It is a description of a transaction. Illustrate.
4. The title given to an expense account is intended to describe a transaction which has an effect on the balance sheet. It contains debit items only, but may be offset by reductions in assets or increases in liabilities. Illustrate.
5. What is the real nature of the credit in the *Sales* account?
6. What is the purpose of the Income and Expense (summary) account? In practice the account used for this purpose is often referred to as the "Profit and Loss" account. Discuss the adequacy of these titles as descriptions of the data included in such an account.
7. What is a mixed account? What elements are mixed in the Merchandise account? In the Sales account?
8. Analyze the following transactions into debits and credits in terms of the balance sheet and income and expense accounts. Sale for cash; sale on open account; purchase for cash; purchase on credit; payment of account to creditor; receipt of payment from customer; receipt of interest on note of customer; payment of interest to bank; payment of taxes; purchase of supplies on credit; payment of sales salary; payment of income tax; sale of building for $500 more than value shown in the accounts; return of goods by customer and cancellation of his account; return of goods bought from vendors and receipt of cash; allowance to customer for defective goods.

B. GENERAL CLASSIFYING DEVICES AND SUMMARIES

CHAPTER VI

THE JOURNAL AND LEDGER

Preceding chapters have outlined the theory of double-entry accounting as a method of classifying and summarizing the accounting data of a specific enterprise. They have introduced the account as the basic device for accomplishing the classification, thus making possible reports showing the financial summaries of status and operations—the balance sheet and statement of income and expense. The theory of double-entry accounting has been explained; attention is now turned to a discussion of the technique by which its objectives are accomplished.

Business papers necessary to double-entry classification.—Business transactions are recorded at the time of their occurrence, or as soon thereafter as it is expedient to recognize their effects on the condition of the enterprise. The form of the original record of a business transaction will vary with the type and size of the enterprise, also the nature of the transaction. No one document can be satisfactorily used by all businesses, even for identical types of transactions. On the other hand, no enterprise could satisfactorily use the same type of record for each of its own varied transactions, such as cash sales, receipts of cash from customers, sales on credit terms, borrowing of funds by giving promissory notes, payment of expenses, or purchases of equipment, fixtures, and buildings.

The original records of business transactions are sometimes referred to as business papers, documents, or vouchers. The terms are used interchangeably in business practice, and will be so used in this text, except in such cases as a special, limited application is indicated. The business papers provide the first record of the data which find their way into the accounts; they may be prepared by any persons connected with the various transactions, regardless of whether these persons are responsible for the later records and classification of the facts they write down. For example, when a sales person in a retail establishment sells an article on credit terms, he would typically record certain information on a slip, indicating the amount and other essential facts concerning the transaction.[1] The preparation of business documents is not an integral part of what is known as double-entry accounting. It does, however, provide the data which are to be recorded and summarized in terms of the double-entry system; a complete set of business papers is a prerequisite to any adequate system of accounting records.

The ledger, the book of accounts.—As has been indicated in preceding chapters, the accounting data of an enterprise are segregated in accounts under titles selected to describe particular aspects of financial status or operations. The total group of accounts for a business enterprise is known as the "ledger." The form of the ledger is not standardized; it may be a bound volume in which the accounts follow each other on separate pages or in which several accounts appear on the same page. The ledger may consist of a series of loose leaves or cards, each carrying the information of one account. The device which will be used in practice depends in part on the needs to be served by the ledger after the records are made and in part on the frequency of transactions to be recorded. For example, removable cards would make it possible for several interested persons to examine different parts of the ledger data at the same time or to record data therein. Whatever the form of the ledger, it is to be regarded as the permanent record of the accounting data—the book in which the significant financial facts of an enterprise are segregated in terms of accounts.

Form of the ledger page.—Inasmuch as the account is the basis of the ledger, a study of the form of the ledger page is essentially a study of the form of the account. We already know that the account is divided into two portions, one side for recording in-

[1] Enterprises may keep merely an informal chronological record of the business transactions, recording them all on a sheet or in a book. Such a type of original record is known as a "daybook"; its use is rapidly disappearing in modern business practice, for reasons which will become apparent as accounting technique is discussed. It is the present custom to record each business transaction on a separate document.

creases, the other for recording decreases. In the standard form of account each side of the account is subdivided to show four aspects of each *entry:* (1) date; (2) explanation; (3) folio (cross-reference to the journal); and (4) money values. The term "entry" is usually applied to any portion of the accounting data appearing in the formal records—the journal and ledger described in the following paragraphs. The journal is sometimes called a book of *original* entry, the ledger a book of *final* entry. An illustration of the form of the ledger account is shown below:

Account Title

Year						Year					
Month	Day	Explanation	Folio	Debits $	¢	Month	Day	Explanation	Folio	Credits $	¢

The "date" and "money" columns are self-explanatory. The use of the "folio" columns will be made clear when the journal—a preliminary classifying device—is explained. An "explanation" column may be used in various ways; it may contain the title of some other account which is debited or credited concurrently as a result of the same transaction, or it may merely indicate some minor detail of information. The explanation column of the account is not always used.

Advantages of journal for preliminary classification.—The data of the original records must find their way to the accounts for classification in terms of the accounting equation; each transaction must be reduced to terms of assets, liabilities, proprietorship, income and (or) expense. But what is to be the technique of expressing the effects of each transaction, and of recording the data in the proper accounts? The process consists of two separate steps: the determination of the accounts and amounts which are to be debited and credited; the actual work of recording the debits and credits. This means that some person must examine each business paper, analyze each transaction, and then proceed to record the data in the proper accounts. After the data are recorded in the accounts, the business paper may be marked or filed away to indicate that its important facts have been recorded in the ledger; the ledger accounts may in turn be marked to indicate the source of the data.

This method of transferring accounting data to the ledger has two limitations. First, it is practicable only when the analysis and recording of each transaction are carried on by the same person; for no person but the analyst would know the proper entries to be made. Second, it necessitates immediate transfer of the data to the accounts after the classification has been decided upon; otherwise the task of analysis would have to be repeated when the entries were later recorded. To remove these limitations it is customary to use an intermediate record called the "journal" in which to classify and store the data previous to their being recorded in the ledger. The data in the journal may be transferred to the ledger accounts at some later time. This procedure permits a division of the accounting labor with two resulting advantages: the work of analyzing business transactions may be done by an accountant who is trained in such work; the task of transferring accounting data from the journal to the accounts may be carried on by anyone sufficiently accurate and intelligent to follow the instructions.[1]

Form of the journal.—The form of the journal is not standardized; however, certain aspects of business transactions are of such general importance that most journals provide a record of them. These aspects are: (1) date; (2) titles of accounts affected; (3) explanation (i.e., description of transaction); (4) folio (cross-reference to ledger data); and (5) money values. The illustration on page 65 represents the form sometimes referred to as the "standard" journal page.

Journalizing.—Journalizing (or the journalizing process) involves the decision as to the proper debits and credits resulting

[1] The limitations referred to would, of course, also be removed if one person were to analyze the transactions represented by the business papers and were to write on the original documents adequate instructions for others to follow in recording the data in the accounts. As a matter of fact, modern practice has the effect of just such procedure. (Cf. Chap. xvii.)

from a transaction and the recording of this decision in the journal. The division of the transaction into its debits and credits is the more important and difficult part of the process. If, for example, an amount which should properly be debited to an asset account were recorded as an expense, a balance sheet prepared at the time would be inaccurate. Likewise, if an amount which should be credited to "Accounts payable" were credited to "Notes payable," the balance sheet would be inaccurate. The classes and titles under which accounting data are recorded affect the reports greatly, and they must be selected with intelligence and care.

Account titles should be selected to describe accurately the types of information they contain. They should be complete, yet

JOURNAL

Year							
Month	Day	Titles of accounts affected. Description of transaction.	Folio	Debits $	¢	Credits $	¢

not too cumbersome for use in the records and reports. If an account were maintained for the traveling expenses of salesmen in a certain territory, it is conceivable that a title like the following might be selected: "Traveling Expenses of Salesmen in the Chicago, Illinois, Branch Territory." A briefer title might be merely, "Travel Expenses." The first title seems too long for convenient use in financial summaries. The second appears indefinite, although it might prove sufficient for some purposes. The account title selected will vary with, and should meet the needs of, the business using the term. Whatever the account title in the ledger may be, this title should be used in the journal entries. The journal is the "instruction sheet" for entries in the ledger; it should be prepared in terms of the ledger accounts.

It is not always necessary for descriptions to be written out completely. In some cases the description may merely be a reference to some original document which served as the first evidence of the transaction. But when descriptions are included in the journal, they should be carefully expressed. Adequate description involves a thorough understanding of the nature of each transaction and its effect on the accounts in the ledger. For example, assume that a retail dealer in motorcycles has sold two machines of a certain make and model for $700 cash. The entry for such a transaction would be recorded as follows in a standard journal:

JOURNAL (Page 1)

19—							
March	1	Cash..	1	$700	00		
		Sales..	12	.....	..	$700	00
		To record the sale of 2 Banderson motorcycles, model 4B					

The recording of accounting information in a formal journal presents no particular difficulties. The date of each transaction is first recorded in the proper column. The debit elements are recorded on the same line of the page, the account titles appearing in the "explanation" column and the values in the left-hand money column. On the next horizontal line (or lines) are written the credit elements resulting from the transaction—the account titles being placed in the explanation column, and the values in the right-hand money column. The account titles in the journal entries must always agree exactly with the account titles under which the data are to appear in the ledger. The left and right money columns of the standard journal page are used to designate the accounts to be debited and credited, respectively. Where a standard journal page is not used, the credit items (both titles and values) would be recorded below and slightly to the right of the debit items. Such arrangement enables the reader to recognize at a glance the accounts to be debited and credited, also to identify certain entries with specific transactions.

Posting.—The process of transferring information from the journal to the ledger is known as "posting." It consists merely of following carefully the instructions of the journal entries. All debits and credits must be correctly transferred to the proper accounts, and in the proper amounts as indicated in the journal. It is important that cross-reference to the ledger be correctly indicated in the folio column, so that the ledger entries may be traced from the journal data. In the journal record of the cash sale of $700 previously illustrated, there are two numbers in the folio column. The numeral 1 on the first line indicates that the record of the debit to the Cash account will be found on page 1 of the ledger. Similarly, the numeral 12 on the following line shows that the credit to Sales has been entered on page 12 of the ledger.

The ledger accounts to reflect the transfer of the data from the journal are shown below:

LEDGER

CASH (Page 1)

19—											
March	1	Sales.......	1	700	00						

SALES (Page 12)

						19—					
						March	1	Cash.......	1	700	00

The Cash account contains a debit entry; the Sales account, a credit entry. In each account the date column is used; the explanation column shows the "other" account affected; the folio column refers to the page of the journal from which the entry has come; the money column shows the financial value involved.

Suggestions concerning posting procedure.—Accounting information may be transferred immediately from the journal to the ledger. Promptness is especially desirable in connection with customers' accounts, since it is important to know the amounts due from individual debtors at all times. Under some conditions, however, it is preferable to permit journal entries to accumulate and then to transfer a large number of data during one working period; this makes it possible for an office worker who does not give all his time to bookkeeping to devote a half-day or day to posting. Concentration on a particular duty tends to promote speed and accuracy. There is no general rule as to the routine procedure of posting. There is some advantage, however, in transferring either all the debits or all the credits of a given journal page to the ledger accounts in direct sequence. This practice reduces the tendency to enter amounts on the wrong side of the accounts. In addition it sometimes saves labor, for the accounts to be debited are often separated in the ledger from those to be credited.

"Paging" is a very important part of the posting process. This consists of entering the proper cross-reference page numbers in the folio columns of the journal and ledger. The folio columns should never be filled until the money values have actually been transferred to the ledger accounts. If the folio column of the journal were filled before the data were entered in the ledger, the posting of certain entries might never be completed in case the bookkeeper were interrupted in his work.

Illustrative problem showing use of journal and ledger.—In the following illustration of a retail store operated by D. L. Wander there is listed a series of twenty-three business transactions intended to represent one month's operations. In the books of such a store the number of transactions recorded would actually be much larger; each type of transaction would, of course, appear more frequently and would typically involve smaller amounts. In the journal the transactions are recorded in chronological order. There are forty-six entries to be recorded in ten ledger accounts; consequently several of the accounts will have entries made in them several times during the period. The reader should observe carefully the method of recording the data, tracing the transactions from journal to ledger and verifying the folio references.

TRANSACTIONS OF D. L. WANDER

1. Investment of $8,000 cash in a business by D. L. Wander
2. Payment of store rent, $200
3. Purchase of merchandise for $1,900 cash
4. Purchase of merchandise for $2,100 cash

5. Cash sales of merchandise, $1,020
6. Receipt of $1,800 cash from bank in exchange for 30-day note payable
7. Merchandise purchase, on account, $470
8. Cash sale of merchandise, $493
9. Sale of merchandise on account, $1,326
10. Cash purchase of merchandise, $497
11. Cash purchase of store fixtures, $350
12. Payment of $25 for stationery and office supplies
    Receipt of bill for advertising, $35
    Purchase of merchandise on account, $230
13. Merchandise sales on account, $589
    Payment of $200 to merchandise creditors
15. Sale of merchandise on account, $350
    Receipt of incoming freight bill, $24
16. Receipt of cash from customer to apply on account, $481
17. Sale of merchandise on account, $492
18. Purchase of merchandise on account, $278
19. Reduction of investment by withdrawal of $1,000 cash
    Payment for heating of office, in cash, $131

Account titles.—The following accounts will be used for classifying the transactions in the ledger; all journal entries must be made in these terms: "Cash," "Accounts receivable," "Merchandise," "Furniture and fixtures," "Accounts payable," "Notes payable," "D. L. Wander, capital," "Sales," "Sales Expense," "Office Expense "

D. L. WANDER

JOURNAL (Page 1)

19—							
July	1	Cash	1	$8,000	00		
		D. L. Wander, capital	7			$8,000	00
		Investment in retail business located at 5464 Woodlawn Ave.					
	2	Office expense	10	200	00		
		Cash	1			200	00
		Payment of July store rent					
	3	Merchandise	3	1,900	00		
		Cash	1			1,900	00
		Cash purchase of merchandise*					
	4	Merchandise	3	2,100	00		
		Cash	1			2,100	00
	5	Cash	1	1,020	00		
		Sales	8			1,020	00
	6	Cash	1	1,800	00		
		Notes payable	6			1,800	00

* Explanations will not be written to describe each of the other entries. They would consist of descriptions of the transactions, or references to the original sources of the data recorded.

(Page 2)

19—					
July	7	Merchandise	3	$ 470 00	
		Accounts payable	5		$ 470 00
	8	Cash	1	493 00	
		Sales	8		493 00
	9	Accounts receivable	2	1,326 00	
		Sales	8		1,326 00
	10	Merchandise	3	497 00	
		Cash	1		497 00
	11	Furniture and fixtures	4	350 00	
		Cash	1		350 00
	12	Office expense	10	25 00	
		Cash	1		25 00
		Sales expense	9	35 00	
		Accounts payable	5		35 00
		Merchandise	3	230 00	
		Accounts payable	5		230 00
	13	Accounts receivable	2	589 00	
		Sales	8		589 00
		Accounts payable	5	200 00	
		Cash	1		200 00
	15	Accounts receivable	2	350 00	
		Sales	8		350 00
		Merchandise	3	24 00	
		Accounts payable	5		24 00
	16	Cash	1	481 00	
		Accounts receivable	2		481 00
	17	Accounts receivable	2	492 00	
		Sales	8		492 00
	18	Merchandise	3	278 00	
		Accounts payable	5		278 00
	19	D. L. Wander, capital	7	1,000 00	
		Cash	1		1,000 00
		Office expense	10	131 00	
		Cash	1		131 00

LEDGER OF D. L. WANDER

Cash

(Page 1)

19—					19—				
July	1		1	$8,000 00	July	2		1	$ 200 00
	5		1	1,020 00		3		1	1,900 00
	6		1	1,800 00		4		1	2,100 00
	8		2	493 00		10		2	497 00
	16		2	481 00		11		2	350 00
						12		2	25 00
						13		2	200 00
						19		2	1,000 00
								2	131 00

Accounts Receivable

(Page 2)

19—						19—					
July	9		2	$1,326	00	July	16		2	$ 481	00
	13		2	589	00						
	15		2	350	00						
	17		2	492	00						

Merchandise

(Page 3)

19—											
July	3		1	$1,900	00						
	4		1	2,100	00						
	7		2	470	00						
	10		2	497	00						
	12		2	230	00						
	15		2	24	00						
	18		2	278	00						

Furniture and Fixtures

(Page 4)

19—											
July	11		2	$ 350	00						

Accounts Payable

(Page 5)

19—						19—					
July	13		2	$ 200	00	July	7		2	$ 470	00
							12		2	35	00
									2	230	00
							15		2	24	00
							18		2	278	00

Notes Payable

(Page 6)

						19——					
						July	6		1	$1,800	00

D. L. Wander, Capital

(Page 7)

19——						19——					
July	19		2	$1,000	00	July	1		1	$8,000	00

Sales

(Page 8)

						19——					
						July	5		1	$1,020	00
							8		2	493	00
							9		2	1,326	00
							13		2	589	00
							15		2	350	00
							17		2	492	00

Sales Expenses

(Page 9)

19——											
July	12		2	$ 35	00						

Office Expense

(Page 10)

19——											
July	2		1	$ 200	00						
	12		2	25	00						
	19		2	131	00						

QUESTIONS ON CHAPTER VI

1. Describe the function of the journal and the ledger in the accounting process. What is meant by the term "entry" when applied to accounting technique?
2. The journal is called a book of original entry. Why? Name several forms or records on which the first notations of transactions are made.
3. Describe in detail the standard form of account. Explain the purpose and exact nature of the entries to be made in each column of the account.
4. Describe in detail the form of the standard journal. Explain fully the entries to be made in each column.
5. Of what significance is the journal explanation? How detailed should the explanation be? Can it be dispensed with or abbreviated under any circumstances?
6. Why should the journal have two money columns? Could one column be used? More than two columns?
7. Could a set of accounts be kept satisfactorily without maintaining a journal? In such a system what difficulties might be encountered in tracing down an error of entry; in obtaining information concerning a particular transaction; in auditing or verifying the accuracy of the records.
8. Would the entries in the accounts be made differently if no journal were kept? If so, describe and explain these differences.
9. Suggest some characteristics of a good account title. Are the following satisfactory? Real estate; Receivables; Reserves?
10. In planning an accounting system for a business, in what order should the following be worked out? Data needed in reports? Journals? Ledgers?
11. Explain the process of posting. What use is made of the folio columns of the journal and the ledger?

CHAPTER VII

TYPES OF ACCOUNTING ENTRIES

The data in specific accounts may be said to pass through certain phases in the course of the accounting process. The application of the principles underlying the dealings with accounting data must be clearly understood if the technical procedure is to be thoroughly mastered.

Accounts opened when the first entries are recorded therein.—An account is said to be "opened" when the first entry is made in it; the record may be a debit or a credit. For example, when D. L. Wander invested his $8,000 cash in the grocery business the transaction affected two accounts in his ledger: Cash, and D. L. Wander, Capital. As a result of the transaction, the Cash account was opened with a debit entry of $8,000 and the D. L. Wander, Capital account with a credit entry of $8,000. The term "opening entry" is used to describe the record in each of these accounts; from the viewpoint of the individual accounts this debit and this credit "open" the two accounts—Cash and D. L. Wander, Capital. The accounts would have appeared as follows after the first entries were made:

CASH (Page 1)

19—											
July	1		1	$8,000	00						

D. L. WANDER, CAPITAL (Page 7)

						19—					
						July	1		1	$8,000	00

The term "opening entry" is also used in a different sense to refer to the first entry in a journal—an entry which serves to authorize the opening of the various ledger accounts of an enterprise. The transaction just discussed would serve to illustrate this second meaning of "opening entry" also, for the journal entry to record the investment of cash would be the opening entry in the journal of D. L. Wander.

Current entries accumulate data in the accounts.—Subsequent entries illustrated in chapter vi served to increase the debits in the Cash account of D. L. Wander, as well as partially to offset these debits by a series of credits. Entries made during a period of operations are sometimes referred to as "current entries," to distinguish them from records which open or close the accounts. At the end of the month's operations illustrated above, the Cash account of D. L. Wander appeared as follows:

Cash

19—						19—					
July	1		1	$8,000	00	July	2		1	$ 200	00
	5		1	1,020	00		3		1	1,900	00
	6		1	1,800	00		4		1	2,100	00
	8		2	493	00		10		2	497	00
	16		2	481	00		11		2	350	00
							12		2	25	00
							13		2	200	00
							19		2	1,000	00
									2	131	00

The total debits in the Cash account have accumulated to $11,794; the total credits, to $6,403. Other accounts likewise have been affected by current entries; for example, the Accounts Receivable, Merchandise, Accounts Payable, and Sales accounts all contain five or more entries which have been made to reflect the operations during July.

Accounts balanced to determine net effect of data they contain.—The financial status of an enterprise is expressed by the data in the accounts. The important fact concerning an account at any particular time is the net effect of the total data accumulated therein. The Cash account shown above contains debits of $11,794, credits of $6,403. The essential fact of these data is the excess of debits over credits, an amount which represents the cash presumably on hand for the use of the enterprise. The data in the account reflect the amounts of cash which have been received and paid by the enterprise during the month of July. The difference between them is the amount on hand July 19; it may be computed from the account data as being the excess of debits over credits, which is $5,391. The excess of either debits or credits in an account is known as the account "balance." The process of computing this amount and setting it forth in an account is called "balancing" the account. The process is illustrated below, using the data of D. L. Wander's Cash account.

Cash (Page 1)

19—						19—					
July	1		1	$ 8,000	00	July	2		1	$ 200	00
	5		1	1,020	00		3		1	1,900	00
	6		1	1,800	00		4		1	2,100	00
	8		2	493	00		10		2	497	00
	16			481	00		11		2	350	00
							12		2	25	00
							13		2	200	00
							19		2	1,000	00
									2	131	00
								Balance	✓	*5,391*	*00*
				$11,794	00					$11,794	00
July	19	*Balance*	✓	$ 5,391	00						

The amount by which the debit total in the Cash account exceeds the credit total is added to the entries on the credit side of the account. This process equalizes the amounts in the debit and credit columns, and each one is accordingly totaled and "ruled off" with double horizontal lines. The amount added is the *balance*. The balance is carried forward on the side of the account which originally contained the larger total. The process of totaling the entries on the two sides of an account is sometimes referred to as "footing" the columns. Balances indicate the condition of the individual accounts and may be used in the preparation of financial summaries. The method illustrated in balancing the Cash account is applicable to the balancing of any account, either an account with financial status or one with business operations. Where the number of either debit or credit entries greatly exceeds those of the opposite type, it is customary to draw a diagonal line through the unused portion of one side of the account, as was done in the foregoing illustration. This practice prevents tampering with the account after it has once been balanced; consequently it aids in detecting unauthorized entries.

Account balances may be determined whenever such information is desired—ordinarily at the end of an operating period when financial summaries are to be prepared. However, it is often necessary or desirable to determine the balances at various times during an operating period. This is especially true of the Cash account and the accounts with individual customers or creditors. The balances of such accounts may, therefore, be computed more frequently and in a less formal manner. In such cases, the accumulation of debits and credits may be "footed" as penciled subtotals inserted at various points in the debit and credit columns respectively. If desired, the explanation column of the account may then be used to show the balance.

Trial balance verifies equality of total debits and credits or debit and credit balances.—It has been emphasized continuously in the text that the debits and credits resulting from each transaction are equal; consequently the ledger data resulting from a group of transactions must comprise equal total debits and total credits. Unless some mistake has been made in the posting process, the total of left-hand entries will equal the total of right-hand entries. The equality of debits and credits in the ledger may be tested by the preparation of a *trial balance*, which is a list of the account titles, with parallel columns indicating the total debits and total credits in the various accounts. If the totals of the two columns are equal, the ledger is "in balance." The following trial balance, prepared from the accounts of D. L. Wander, shows that the debit and credit entries are equal.

D. L. WANDER

TRIAL BALANCE—JULY 19, 19—

	Debits	Credits
Cash	$11,794.00	$ 6,403.00
Accounts receivable	2,757.00	481.00
Merchandise	5,499.00	....
Furniture and fixtures	350.00	....
Accounts payable	200.00	1,037.00
Notes payable	....	1,800.00
D. L. Wander, capital	1,000.00	8,000.00
Sales	....	4,270.00
Sales expense	35.00	....
Office expense	356.00	....
Total	$21,991.00	$21,991.00

The foregoing trial balance has been prepared by listing the total debits and total credits from each account. In some accounts there are both debit and credit entries; consequently the same proof of the equilibrium of the ledger could be obtained by merely adding the excess debits or credits in each account, that is, by listing the account "balances." The trial balance of D. L. Wander, consisting of a list of account balances, appears as follows:

D. L. WANDER

TRIAL BALANCE—JULY 19, 19—

	Debits	Credits
Cash	$ 5,391.00	....
Accounts receivable	2,276.00	....
Merchandise	5,499.00	....
Furniture and fixtures	350.00	....
Accounts payable	....	$ 837.00
Notes payable	....	1,800.00
D. L. Wander, capital	....	7,000.00
Sales	....	4,270.00
Sales expense	35.00	....
Office expense	356.00	....
Total	$13,907.00	$13,907.00

Limitations of the trial balance.—A trial balance will reveal errors which cause unequal totals of debits and credits. But many errors occur which do not disturb the equilibrium of the ledger.

For example, an entry which is properly a debit to "Accounts receivable" might be posted by mistake as a debit in the Cash account. The trial balance of the ledger would not reveal such an error. The error could be discovered only by inspection of the actual cash in the possession of the firm, and by a careful check upon the correctness of the Accounts Receivable. Errors of this kind are often more serious than those causing inequalities in the trial balance. They might cause misstatements which affect the reports of financial status or operations.

Trial-balance errors.—The following may be stated as the causes of unequal trial-balance totals: (1) duplicate posting of a debit or credit; (2) failure to post a debit or credit; (3) posting of an incorrect amount; (4) posting on the wrong side of an account. The first two are the result of careless bookkeeping and must be discussed as problems of psychology and office management rather than accounting. The third and fourth types of error, however, may be mentioned briefly. The entry of one or more incorrect amounts among the debits and credits may result from inability to read the figures, with the resultant recording of the wrong digits. On the other hand, the error may result from a transposition of digits to be recorded, as when 67 is written as 76, or 45,678 is written as 46,578. When a transposition is the only cause of the inequality, the error is always divisible by 9. If the totals of two trial balances are unequal in an amount divisible by 9, the difference is probably caused by one or more transpositions in the records. This simple trick of discovering transpositions by dividing the amount of error by nine arises from the arithmetic rule that shifting of digits causes changes in numbers which are multiples of nine. Assuming the original digits remain the same, any rearrangement of the digits will cause a change divisible by nine.

If a ledger entry has been made in the wrong side of an account (that is, an entry properly to be recorded as a debit has been posted as a credit item, or vice-versa) the trial-balance totals will show a difference twice as great as the amount incorrectly entered. If, for example, a debit to Accounts Receivable of $225.75 has been incorrectly entered as a credit, there would result an understatement of Accounts Receivable by $451.50. When the accountant is attempting to discover the cause of an error, he frequently divides the error by two and searches through the journal to see if any transaction has occurred involving such an amount. If the error has been caused by posting on the wrong side of an account, this method will often prove useful—especially if only one error has been made.

Data may be reclassified in whole or in part by transfer to other accounts.—Accounting data are prepared for certain purposes. When they have served the purposes for which they were secured and classified, they should be summarized or otherwise disposed of. Consequently one encounters the term "closing" in connection with accounts; to "close" an account is to transfer its balance to some other part of the ledger under a different account title. A "closing entry" is one by which certain ledger data are reclassified under a new account title. Usually the term is restricted to the transfer of income or expense data to a summary account, by which the business operations are summarized to show their net effect on proprietorship. Broadly speaking, however, a closing entry is any entry which removes a previously existing debit or credit balance from an account, regardless of what other account or accounts are affected.

An account may be said to be "closed" if it contains debits and credits of equal amounts; if it is in balance. Likewise any account may be said to be "open" if it contains unequal debits and credits, indicating that it is not closed. The terms "open" and "closed," therefore, may refer to balance-sheet accounts as well as to income or expense accounts. In the case of balance-sheet accounts, however, the elimination of an account balance is usually the result of current entries rather than of periodic reclassification. The method of closing an account by transfer of the "balance" is similar to the balancing process. The difference between the totals of the debits and credits in the account to be closed is added to the entries in the column containing the smaller total. This difference—the balance—reappears in the new account to which the data are to be transferred. Closing entries in the ledger may be authorized by journal entries, in which case complete folio references would appear in both journal and ledger. Entries to close the data in the Sales, Sales Expense, and Office Expenses accounts to the Income and Expense account of D. L. Wander would be journalized as follows:

(Page 3)

19——							
July	19	Sales	8	$4,270	00		
		Income and expense	11	....	..	$4,270	00
		Income and expense	11	35	00		
		Sales expense	9	....	..	35	00
		Income and expense	11	356	00		
		Office expense	10	....	..	356	00

At times it is necessary to transfer only a part of the balance in an account. This requirement was encountered earlier in the text (chap. v), where it was found necessary to reclassify part of the total debit in the Merchandise account, transferring this portion to an expense account entitled "Cost of Goods Sold" or directly to the Income and Expense summary account. If it were determined that goods valued at a cost price of $3,200 had been sold by D. L. Wander, the entry to reclassify this portion of the Merchandise account data would be:

July	19	Income and expense	11	$3,200	00		
		Merchandise	3	....	..	$3,200	00

This entry adjusts the merchandise account to its proper value by reclassifying a portion of the data as expense. The data in the Income and Expense account express the net effect of business operations on proprietorship. In the foregoing illustration, the credits to income and expense exceed the debits by $679. The journal entry to transfer the resulting credit balance to the proprietorship account, D. L. Wander, Capital, would be as follows:

July	19	Income and expense	11	$679	00		
		D. L. Wander, capital	7	....	..	$679	00

Accounting data are sometimes transferred to other positions in a ledger, where they reappear under identical account titles. Such transfers may be accomplished by first balancing the account in the usual manner, and then carrying the balance forward on a different ledger page. The principles of dealing with the various accounting entries—opening entries, current entries, closing entries—may be illustrated briefly by setting forth the D. L. Wander ledger, with the accounts properly balanced and with the income and expense data summarized to show their net effect on proprietorship. The accounts would appear as follows:

D. L. WANDER

LEDGER

CASH (Page 1)

19—						19—					
July	1		1	$8,000	00	July	2		1	$ 200	00
	5		1	1,020	00		3		1	1,900	00
	6		1	1,800	00		4		1	2,100	00
	8		2	493	00		10		2	497	00
	16		2	481	00		11		2	350	00
							12		2	25	00
							13		2	200	00
							19		2	1,000	00
									2	131	00
								Balance.....	✓	*5,391*	*00*
				$11,794	00					$11,794	00
		Balance.....	✓	$ 5,391	00						

ACCOUNTS RECEIVABLE (Page 2)

19—						19—					
July	9		2	$ 1,326	00	July	16		2	$ 481	00
	13		2	589	00						
				1,915	*00*						
	15		2	350	00						
	17		2	492	00						
				2,757	*00*						

MERCHANDISE (Page 3)

19—						19—					
July	3		1	$1,900	00	July	19	Income and expense...	3	$3,200	00
	4		1	2,100	00			*Balance*.....	√	*2,299*	*00*
	7		2	470	00						
	10		2	497	00						
	12		2	230	00						
	15		2	24	00						
	18		2	278	00						
				$5,499	00					$5,499	00
July	19	*Balance*.....	√	$2,299	00						

FURNITURE AND FIXTURES (Page 4)

19—											
July	11		2	$350	00						

ACCOUNTS PAYABLE (Page 5)

19—						19—					
July	13		2	$200	00	July	7		2	$470	00
							12		2	230	00
									2	35	00
							15		2	24	00
							18		2	278	00
										1,037	*00*

NOTES PAYABLE (Page 6)

						19—					
						July	6		1	$1,800	00

D. L. Wander, Capital (Page 7)

19—						19—					
July	19	*Balance.....*	2 ✓	$1,000 7,679	00 00	July	1 19	Income and expense...	1 3	$8,000 679	00 00
				$8,679	00					$8,679	00
						July	19	*Balance.....*	✓	$7,679	00

Sales (Page 8)

19—						19—					
July	19	Income and expense	3	4,270	00	July	5 8 9 13 15 17		1 2 2 2 2 2	$1,020 493 1,326 589 350 492	00 00 00 00 00 00
				$4,270	00					$4,270	00

Sales Expense (Page 9)

19—						19—					
July	12		2	$35	00			Income and expense...	3	$35	00

Office Expense (Page 10)

19—						19—					
July	2 12 19		1 2 2	$200 25 131	00 00 00	July	19	Income and expense...	3	$356	00
				$356	00					$356	00

INCOME AND EXPENSE (Page 11)

19—						19—					
July	19	Merchandise.	3	$3,200	00	July	19	Sales........	3	$4,270	00
		Sales expense	3	35	00						
		Office expense.....	3	356	00						
		D. L. Wander, capital	3	679	00						
				$4,270	00					$4,270	00

One account has been added to those shown in chapter vi, the Income and Expense account. It contains data transferred (closed) to it from the Sales, Merchandise, Sales Expense, and Office Expense accounts. The balance resulting from these entries is a credit amount of $679, which has been "closed" to the D. L. Wander, Capital account and represents an increase of proprietorship.

All of the individual income accounts and expense accounts in the ledger of D. L. Wander are *closed;* the balance-sheet accounts are *open*. The Cash, Merchandise, and D. L. Wander accounts are balanced in the formal manner illustrated earlier in the chapter. The Accounts Receivable and Accounts Payable accounts are marked with "penciled" totals (as shown by the small italics inserted between the regular entries) to indicate the total debits and credits, respectively, which have been accumulated. The Furniture and Fixtures and Notes Payable accounts have not been balanced, because they contain only one entry each. It is possible now to present the asset, liability, and proprietorship balances in the form of a balance sheet; also to present the income and expense data in the form of a statement of income and expense. The balance sheet would be:

D. L. WANDER

BALANCE SHEET—JULY 19, 19—

ASSETS		LIABILITIES AND PROPRIETORSHIP	
Cash...............	$ 5,391.00	*Liabilities:*	
Accounts receivable..	2,276.00	Accounts payable......	$ 837.00
Merchandise........	2,299.00	Notes payable........	1,800.00
Furniture and fixtures	350.00	*Proprietorship:*	
		D. L. Wander, capital..	7,679.00
Total..........	$10,316.00	Total............	$10,316.00

The statement of income and expense would be:

D. L. WANDER

STATEMENT OF INCOME AND EXPENSE—JULY 1–19, 19——

Income:		
Sales		$4,270.00
Expense:		
Merchandise	$3,200.00	
Sales expense	35.00	
Office expenses	356.00	3,591.00
Net profit (increased capital)		$ 679.00

The reader may be puzzled by the fact that, although the enterprise has earned a profit from operations to the extent of $679, the final proprietorship on July 19 is less than D. L. Wander's original investment of $8,000 on July 1. The explanation is to be found, of course, in the fact that previous to the summarization of the accounts on July 19, D. L. Wander had withdrawn $1,000 cash from the enterprise.

Arrangement of the ledger accounts.—How shall the accounts themselves be grouped within the ledger? This question may be answered in terms of two requirements: placing data *in* the ledger; obtaining data *from* the ledger. The first requirement implies that the best arrangement of accounts is one that minimizes the labor of posting the data from the journal. One arrangement sometimes encountered is a sequence of accounts in alphabetical order: Advertising, Buildings, Cartage, etc. This enables bookkeepers to find accounts quickly after they are familiar with the various titles. Another arrangement groups similar accounts in the same portions of the ledger: Asset, Liability, Proprietorship, Income, and Expense accounts, respectively, are grouped within the ledger. Within these groups, further subdivision is often desirable. The arrangement of ledger accounts should be decided upon in terms of the ultimate uses of the data, as well as types of summaries which will probably be required by the management. At this stage in our discussion we may say that the following sequence of accounts will prove most useful, from both the standpoint of bookkeeping convenience and the preparation of accounting reports: Assets, Liabilities, Proprietorship, Income,

Expense. This places the balance-sheet items first, followed by the data to be summarized in the statement of income and expense.

Summary of double-entry technique.—After business transactions have been recorded, they are classified in terms of their effect on the financial status of the enterprise. The effects of each transaction are first classified in the *journal*, which indicates the debits and credits resulting from each transaction. The process of determining the proper debits and credits, and of recording them in the journal is called *journalizing*. The data of the journal are then transferred to the *ledger*, where they are recorded in the respective accounts. The process of transferring the data from the journal to the ledger is called *posting*. Accounting data, after being classified in the ledger, may then be *balanced* and summarized to reflect their net effect on financial status. The account balances provide the information from which to prepare the financial summaries of status and operations—the balance sheet and the statement of income and expense. These reports are the goals toward which the accounting data move, wending their way through the classifying media of the journal and ledger. They are the justification of the accounting process itself. Classified data are well-nigh useless, unless they are ultimately summarized into intelligible reports to reveal the data which the management needs for administrative control. The technique of double-entry accounting procedure is illustrated by the diagram on page 88. This diagram traces the course of the accounting data from the original business papers to the journal in which they are given a preliminary double-entry classification. The data are then transferred to the ledger, from which the information for the balance sheet and statement of income and expense is obtained. The record of every business transaction must pass through these phases of the double-entry procedure.

BUSINESS PAPERS, DOCUMENTS, VOUCHERS

ORIGINAL RECORDS OF BUSINESS TRANSACTIONS

Cash slips, check books, inventory cards, deposit tickets, labor tickets, sales slips, sales invoices, return slips, purchase invoices, etc.

↓

JOURNALIZING

Separating data into debits and credits and entering them in Journal

↓

THE JOURNAL

BOOK OF TRANSACTIONS

Accounts to be debited
Accounts to be credited

Complete explanation, if entry is not self-explanatory.

↓

POSTING

Transferring data to Ledger

↓

THE LEDGER

BOOK OF ACCOUNTS

Asset accounts	Liability accounts
Expense accounts	Income accounts

Proprietorship accounts

Summarization accounts

↓

REPORTING

Preparing data in various reports needed for management

↓

BALANCE SHEET

SUMMARY OF FINANCIAL STATUS

THE STATEMENT OF INCOME AND EXPENSE

SUMMARY OF BUSINESS OPERATIONS

QUESTIONS ON CHAPTER VII

1. What is meant by the term "opening entry"? Is it possible that a transaction may cause only one account to be opened?
2. What is an account *balance?* Of what advantage are account *balances* in the preparation of accounting reports?
3. Describe in detail the process of *balancing* an account. How often should an account be balanced?
4. What is the advantage of penciled subtotals in the accounts which are not balanced?
5. Define and describe the *trial balance.* Why is it given this name? Suggest other more descriptive titles.
6. Distinguish between a trial balance consisting of debit and credit totals and one composed of debit and credit balances.
7. What are the advantages of a trial balance? Does the equality of debits and credits prove that all transactions have been correctly posted? Does it prove they have been correctly journalized?
8. What type of errors may appear in the accounts? How may each one be detected by an accountant who is attempting to discover and correct all errors?
9. To what uses may the trial balance be put in the preparation of financial reports?
10. Describe the methods of transferring accounting data from one page to another.
11. What does it mean to close an account?
12. Income and expense data are closed into the Income and Expense account. Why to this account?
13. Why might the credit balance resulting from data in an Income and Expense account differ from the net increase in proprietorship during the period to which the income and expense transactions relate?
14. What methods may be used for arranging accounts within the ledger? Discuss the advantages of each method.

CHAPTER VIII

TYPICAL BALANCE-SHEET ACCOUNTS

The technique of accounting classification and summarization must be applied to all aspects of the financial status and operations of an enterprise. This chapter will discuss typical subdivisions of the data which appear in the balance sheet—the accounts which represent assets, liabilities, and proprietorship. The basis for subdividing the various aspects of financial status will vary with the purpose for which the data are to be used; consequently any account or group of accounts here discussed must be regarded merely as typical of those necessary in practice rather than as indicating titles universally applicable. The groups of accounts will be discussed below in terms of their significance to an enterprise rather than in terms of the specific types of wealth or property rights which they might describe. The groups selected are as follows:

Assets: Cash, Accounts Receivable, Notes Receivable, Merchandise, Supplies, Deferred Charges (Prepaid Expenses), Furniture and Fixtures, Machinery, Delivery Equipment, Buildings, Land, Investments. *Liabilities:* Accounts Payable, Notes Payable, Long-Term Liabilities. *Proprietorship:* Proprietor, Capital; Proprietor, Personal; Corporate Proprietorship.

Asset accounts segregate the data concerning the types of wealth invested in an enterprise.—There are many types of assets; any type of commodity or article of wealth may conceivably be listed in the balance sheet of an enterprise. Assets in the technical accounting sense, must, however, be sharply differentiated from economic wealth from the point of view of society as a whole. Assets must be considered solely in terms of one specific economic enterprise. For example, an amount of $100 receivable by enterprise A from a customer, enterprise B, would appear as an asset—an Account Receivable—in the ledger of enterprise A, which had sold the goods. But in the ledger of the customer, enterprise B, which had purchased these goods, the $100 would also appear as an asset—Merchandise—in the form of goods on hand. The tangible goods involved in the sale would thus serve as the basis for $100 of assets appearing in the ledgers of each of these two enterprises; $100 in the ledger of A as an account receivable from enterprise B; $100 as tangible merchandise in the ledger of B.[1]

Cash.—What is cash? What items should be recorded as increasing or decreasing the Cash account? Cash is a term used synonymously with "money"; it includes such items as metallic currency, paper currency, checks, drafts, money orders, etc. The cash in any business usually comprises a very small portion of the total assets in its control, for the profits of an enterprise are usually derived from dealings in other types of economic goods. The Cash account may be affected by a wide variety of transactions: it may be received from customers to whom goods have been sold, from creditors who are loaning money to the business, or from proprietors who are investing additional funds in the enterprise. It may be paid out to vendors from whom goods or services have been purchased, to debtors to whom money is being loaned, to employees who have rendered valuable services, or to proprietors who withdraw all or a portion of their original contributions. Transactions affecting the Cash accounts occur frequently and form a large part of the business activities of some enterprises. A business may, of course, maintain several Cash accounts —an account for each of several portions of the total cash of the business. Typical account titles might be: "Cash—First National Bank"; "Cash—In Petty Cash Drawer"; "Cash—At Branches."

Accounts Receivable.—"Accounts Receivable" is a general term customarily used to include the various amounts due from

[1] The transaction which gave rise to the Account Receivable on the books of the vendor, enterprise A, also gave rise to an Account Payable on the books of B, the purchasing enterprise. From the viewpoint of society as a whole, the debts due from one enterprise to another do not affect total economic wealth; from the viewpoint of each enterprise concerned, these contractual obligations may bulk large in an expression of financial status, as assets and as liabilities. The analysis of transactions by double entry must never forsake the viewpoint of a specific enterprise, even though the "assets" of a group of enterprises thereby combine to make a larger total than the economic wealth invested in them.

the customers of a business enterprise. It sometimes also includes amounts which are receivable from other debtors. Examples of other accounts receivable are amounts borrowed by employees or proprietors, rent receivable from tenants (where leasing of real estate is not the main income-producing activity of an enterprise), and interest receivable from debtors on promissory notes given to a business. A proper classification of accounts would separate these items from the Accounts Receivable from customers who have purchased merchandise from or enjoyed the regular services of the enterprise. Other amounts receivable might well be designated as "Advances to Employees," "Rent Receivable," "Interest Receivable," etc. All types of amounts receivable from debtors of an enterprise may be supported by subsidiary data which will inform the management just how much is due from each debtor. The securing of such data does not involve any digression from the principles applicable to keeping the record of total amounts. It does, however, involve the use of certain specialized classifying devices.[1]

Notes Receivable.—"Notes Receivable" is a term to represent amounts receivable from debtors who have given formal and written promises to pay their obligations. They may arise from any of the transactions discussed under the head "Accounts Receivable," although in most businesses the total number of notes receivable is not as large as the number of accounts receivable. Notes Receivable, as an accounting term, usually includes trade acceptances and drafts receivable.

Merchandise.—Merchandise transactions constitute a large part of the operations of many enterprises; previous discussion has illustrated and discussed such transactions in much the same manner as dealings in the other assets. The importance of merchandise transactions, however, has given rise to special treatment of them; the merchandise data are not usually grouped in one account at the time the transactions occur, but are segregated

[1] Any asset or liability group may be accounted for in such a way that only one account is used to express the total value of a large number of individual items. The detailed data would be recorded as subsidiary information to support the central facts of the ledger account. Compare chapters xiv and xv, which deal with special columns in the journal and controlling accounts in the ledger.

in special accounts which reflect the various operations. The data representing merchandise operations are periodically summarized to determine their net effect on the status of the merchandise. The method of maintaining and summarizing the accounts with merchandise operations will be discussed further in chapters ix and x.

Supplies.—In every business there are certain materials which are purchased for use in the income-producing operations. They are not to be sold to customers, but are to be gradually consumed in the regular course of the business operations. Examples of supplies are: stationery, pens, ink, and accounting records in an office; stencils, boxes, paint, crates, twine, and wrapping materials in a shipping room; oil, waste, polish, and fuel in a factory. The number of accounts that a particular business will maintain for the various items of "supplies" will vary with the needs of the classification. In some enterprises one account—Supplies—might suffice. In others, separate accounts might be provided, such as Office Supplies, Shipping Supplies, and Factory Supplies. In still other cases separate accounts might be maintained with each type of supplies used by the enterprise. It is customary to record the individual receipts of supplies at the time they enter the business, but not to attempt to record their diminishing value from daily consumption. The value of supplies which have been used during a given operating period is accordingly estimated from an inspection of the goods, which shows the value of the unused supplies on hand at various times. The technique of adjusting the Supplies accounts to make their balances conform to the actual condition of the business will be discussed at length in chapter x.

Deferred Charges (*prepaid expenses*).—There are certain expenses incurred, the benefits of which will be enjoyed during future periods. The expenses incurred are carried as assets on the balance sheet, and are charged off as current expenses according to a planned schedule. Some of the items included by various enterprises as *deferred charges* are the expenses of organizing an enterprise, of advertising a new product, of insuring physical property for a long period of time. Certain of the deferred charges are sometimes designated on a balance sheet as *prepaid expenses*, with such subcaptions as "Prepaid Rent," "Prepaid Interest," "Prepaid Insurance." The term "prepaid expenses" is often expanded to include unused supplies.

In practice the term "charge" is frequently used synonymously with "debit." To charge an account is to debit it; a deferred charge to an expense account is a deferred debit to that account. The term "deferred charges" is a shorter term for *deferred charges to expense*, which implies that certain items normally chargeable as expenses have been temporarily classified as assets. They will later be charged to expense. The term "deferred expenses," when encountered in accounting reports is synonymous with deferred charges. Some attempts have been made to establish a logical distinction between prepaid expenses and deferred charges. Such attempts must fail, however; for the terms are merely different methods of expressing the same concept—that of an asset being procured, the benefits of which will be enjoyed during future periods. The limited life of such assets, as well as the impossibility (usually) of recovering their benefits except by continued operations, leads the accountant to designate them as "prepaid" expenses, items which will be charged as expenses during future periods. The recognition of these items as current expenses is for the time being *deferred.*[1]

Furniture and Fixtures.—This is a heading often used to designate the equipment of offices and salesrooms, such as desks, chairs, show cases, removable shelves. As a rule, furniture and fixtures are not disposed of through the process of sale; they are used by the business until worn out or replaced for some other reason. Consequently the accountant uses the Furniture and Fixtures account primarily for the accumulation of values of new articles of equipment which enter the business. The gradual re-

[1] Where the captions "Prepaid Expenses" and "Deferred Charges" designate separate groupings of assets on the same balance sheet, the classification must be recognized as adopted for purely practical purposes. Usually the distinction is drawn between expenses which are recurrent and non-recurrent in normal business operations. The recurrent items are sometimes called "Prepaid Expenses" and include such expenses as insurance, rent, interest, royalties, advertising, supplies, etc. The non-recurrent items are sometimes called "Deferred Charges" and cover such expenses as costs of selling securities, special losses from accidents or storms, costs of organizing a "going" enterprise, etc.

duction in value caused by wear and tear is deducted periodically and charged as expenses of the operations of the business. The costs of installing furniture and fixtures are generally looked upon as increasing their value, and such costs are debited to the Furniture and Fixtures account or accounts.

Machinery.—Machinery includes the wide variety of permanent assets necessary in the manufacture of goods for sale. Illustrations are lathes, planers, molds, benches, vats. The Machinery account or accounts are increased from time to time as new items are purchased for use by the enterprise. They are decreased when machinery is sold or when values of the various items have been decreased through use. All costs of installing machines and of making them available for use increase their value to the business; hence these costs are properly to be debited to the Machinery accounts.

Delivery Equipment.—Most enterprises own some equipment for the purpose of delivering merchandise to customers or of bringing purchased goods to the place of business. Examples are trucks, automobiles, motorcycles, bicycles, wagons, harnesses, horses. The classification of the items of delivery equipment in the accounts will vary with the amount of the equipment and the advantages to be gained from detailed information. The Delivery Equipment accounts are increased when amounts are paid for new items. They are decreased when the values have been reduced by the wear and tear of business operations or when equipment is sold.

Buildings.—Buildings are usually separately recorded in the accounts. The building accounts are not often increased by current business transactions (purchase or sale); however, buildings continually decrease in value from wear and tear or from the passage of time. These reductions in values require periodic recognition in the accounts.

Land.—Land on which a concern's buildings are situated should be accounted for separately. In many instances the value of land is independent of the value of the buildings thereon; moreover, land as a building site is not subject to exhaustion or depreciation from wear and tear. The value of land may fluctuate, of course, but its intrinsic value as a site for building construction does not necessarily decrease with its use. As a matter of fact, land values usually increase; and the proper method for recording this increase gives rise to many important questions of business policy.

Investments.—This is a general term to designate assets not used in the regular operations of the business. Investments may consist of bonds or stock of other companies, real estate not used by the enterprise, short-term notes receivable purchased with funds temporarily not needed by the enterprise, or government bonds. Investments made for short periods of time are sometimes designated as "temporary"; investments which will not be disposed of within a relatively short period of time are sometimes referred to as "permanent." Investments may, of course, include assets of widely different physical aspects or legal characteristics. The term "Investments" is not usually selected as an account title; the importance of each investment usually entitles it to a separate place in the ledger accounts. Thus, one sometimes sees on the balance sheet a series of investment items listed under a general heading, such as:

Investments:		
Bonds of Jackson Co.	$ 2,600.00	
Stock of Bender Co.	10,000.00	
Unimproved Real Estate	4,500.00	
Sixty-day notes, Johnson & Decker	9,400.00	
Total		$26,500.00

Liability accounts classify and measure the property rights of creditors.—Every asset is owned by someone; the property right of every owner must be included in the balance sheet of an enterprise. The property rights of creditors are known as liabilities, and they may comprise numerous types and amounts of claims applicable to the assets of any specific enterprise.

Accounts Payable.—This account contains the amounts due to creditors of the business enterprise who have not asked for written evidence of their claims. It is usually limited in its application to amounts due to the trade creditors of the enterprise. There are other items not technically regarded as accounts payable, because no invoice or other demand has yet been received to evidence the transaction. Examples would be Interest Payable, Rent Payable, Wages Payable, or Taxes Payable. A separate record of some kind should be kept for each of these payable items, although they may be listed in a balance sheet under the general heading of Accounts Payable.

Notes Payable.—Notes Payable include promissory notes of all kinds. The term is often expanded to cover accepted drafts, trade acceptances payable, etc. Notes Payable may include notes given for any purpose, such as for cash borrowed from banks or to liquidate a liability to merchandise creditors. The term may include amounts which are due in the near or distant future. In most cases the title is limited to notes which are due and payable within one or two years.

Long-term liabilities.—When funds have been borrowed by a business enterprise for use over a long period of time before repayment, the terms of the agreement usually provide that some assets be pledged to insure the ultimate payment of the debt. Consequently the designation of such a liability in the accounts often indicates the condition under which the obligation was assumed. Mortgages Payable is a common title for long-term promissory notes, payment of which is "secured" by the pledging of permanent assets, such as buildings or lands. Bonds Payable represent a particular type of written obligation in accordance with which payments are due to a large group of holders. Bonds are payable at definite dates; they bear interest, and are often secured by property which has been pledged to guarantee the payment of the debt; they are issued under special or general permission by governmental units, and are otherwise to be distinguished from ordinary notes payable.

Proprietorship accounts classify and measure the claims of proprietors on the assets of an enterprise.—The proprietors usually enjoy only the residual or secondary claims in the assets of an enterprise. As a rule, the contractual agreements by which creditors loan assets to an enterprise give the creditors special preferences and protection in case of liquidation. Nevertheless the proprietors' claims on the assets are more valuable in other ways than those of the creditors. One of the most striking advantages enjoyed by the proprietors is the possibility of their ownership being increased by successful business operations. The proprietors' claims may, of course, be decreased by unsuccessful operations.

Proprietor, Capital.—Accounts may be maintained with the various proprietors of a business enterprise. Each such account would indicate separately the total ownership enjoyed by an individual proprietor of a business. It is usually desirable that records be maintained which segregate the data concerning original contributions and the later fluctuations of the proprietors' interests. The term "Capital" is generally used to indicate the portions of the proprietors' ownership which are the result of their original or other more or less permanent contributions to a business. Such accounts are usually headed with the various proprietors' names followed by the word "Capital," as: E. W. Dredge, Capital; R. L. Lorton, Capital; etc. The Capital accounts carry credit balances (usually), and are credited to offset new assets contributed to the business or to reflect the income arising from successful operations.

Proprietor, Personal.—When the business operations result in profits or losses to be assigned to the various proprietors, it is often desirable to make the first records of these changes of proprietorship in intermediate or temporary accounts. The first record is accordingly entered in a "Personal" account, so named to indicate the temporary nature of the increase or decrease in proprietorship. The amounts appearing as debits or credits in the proprietors' Personal accounts may be periodically transferred to the Capital accounts. The proprietors' personal transactions with the business during current operations may also be recorded in Personal accounts. Illustrations of such transactions are: temporary borrowings, temporary loans, withdrawals of merchandise or other assets for personal use, or withdrawals of cash in advance to apply on agreed salary payments. Several "Personal" accounts may be opened with each proprietor, in case the number of the proprietors is large enough and the recurrence of the transactions frequent enough to justify such treatment.

Corporate proprietorship.—In the previous illustrations of proprietorship accounts attention has been centered on businesses controlled by one or more individual proprietors or owners. In the form of business organization known as the corporation, the proprietors are designated as "stockholders." The number of stockholders is usually so large that the data in the separate accounts with each of the proprietors could not conveniently be placed on a balance sheet. Consequently corporate proprietorship is commonly set forth as a composite item on the balance sheet under the heading "Capital Stock" or some similar title. The total proprietorship is divided into shares of stock; the owners of these shares are the stockholders. As the proprietorship of the stockholders increases and decreases from time to time, the increases and decreases are recorded in an account known as "Surplus." The Surplus account represents the undivided proprietorship of the entire group of stockholders, and corresponds in part to the Personal accounts of the individual proprietors or the partners. Portions of the surplus are sometimes segregated under separate accounts entitled "Reserves." Such accounts are used when parts of the surplus need to be designated as applicable to specific purposes, and as not available for realization by the stockholders through the withdrawal of assets. The term "Undivided Profits" is an account title sometimes encountered to designate surplus not definitely assigned to the proprietors. In the case of financial institutions, this portion of the proprietorship is often affected by definite legal requirements established by statutory regulation. The term "Undivided profits" may be encountered in the balance sheet of either a corporation or a partnership. When the stockholders of a corporation have decided to distribute assets among themselves, they segregate a part of the surplus in an account entitled "Dividends Payable." Such an account has the legal status of a liability.

QUESTIONS ON CHAPTER VIII

1. Analyze the following, indicating the nature and titles of the accounts to be debited and credited: (*a*) cash received from customers in payment of accounts, \$389; (*b*) cash received in payment of note receivable, \$200; (*c*) cash received from sale of building, \$5,000; (*d*) cash borrowed on

note payable, $1,000; (*e*) cash obtained by issuing bonds, $10,000; (*f*) cash invested by sole proprietor, $8,000. Name the most frequent cash receipt transactions.

2. Analyze the following: (*a*) cash paid for delivery truck, $375; (*b*) cash paid to close account payable, $95; (*c*) cash paid to bank to retire note payable, $500 for face of note, $5 for interest; (*d*) cash paid for site for factory, $5,000. Name the most frequent types of cash disbursements.
3. Analyze the following transactions: (*a*) supplies are purchased on account, $75; (*b*) $5,000 cash is invested in Liberty bonds; (*c*) show cases are purchased for $175, for which a note is given; (*d*) a new factory machine is purchased for $270; (*e*) an old factory machine valued at $150 is sold for that price.
4. A building is purchased for $40,000, subject to a $24,000 mortgage, the $16,000 balance payable in cash. Record this transaction on the books of the purchasing company.
5. The Z Company sells for $3,500 cash, a piece of land which originally cost $3,000 and which appears on the books at cost. Record the transaction on the books of the Z Company.
6. Money is borrowed by the issuance of $60,000 bonds payable. The bonds are later paid in cash. Make the entries to record the issuance and payment of the bonds.
7. *a*) L. C. Ramsdell, a partner, invests additional cash in an enterprise to the extent of $800. (*b*) D. L. Bye, a partner, withdraws $600 permanently. Journalize the transactions.
8. Journalize: M. D. Watkins loans $300 cash to an enterprise in which he is a partner. H. I. Temm, a partner, borrows $600 cash from an enterprise.
9. Journalize: Shares of stock valued at $7,500 are issued by a corporation in exchange for a building.
10. Eight hundred dollars of the surplus of a corporation is declared payable as dividends to the stockholders. This amount represents a liability of the corporation. Use any account titles you may wish to indicate the effects of this transaction.

CHAPTER IX

TYPICAL INCOME AND EXPENSE ACCOUNTS

The time element in business operations makes it very important that a clear understanding of the nature of income and expense data be had. Income data are accumulated on the credit side of certain accounts which describe the sources of the income or the business operations creating it. Expense data are accumulated on the debit side of certain accounts which describe the business operations causing the expenditure or the types of assets involved.

Income accounts measure and classify business operations expressed in the accounts by credit data.—The ultimate effect of any business operation upon financial status can usually be determined by analysis. But it is often important to accumulate the total effects of a group or series of operations before they are reduced to terms of the balance sheet. This is particularly true of business operations which are not mere exchanges of assets and liabilities but which tend to increase proprietorship. The account titles selected to reflect the amounts and classes of the various income operations must vary with the nature of the operations and the purposes for which the data are secured. One enterprise may carry on income operations vastly different from those of another. The main income operations of a few types of business enterprises may be differentiated by the various account titles shown in the diagram on page 102. Each of these enterprises would probably receive other income from various minor sources. For example, a mercantile establishment may receive interest payments due on the interest-bearing notes of customers, or rental payments from the leasing of portions of storage space. Moreover, some enterprises may be of such nature that they carry on two or more main types of income operations, as in the case of a real estate company which both sells and leases land and buildings. The income titles to be selected will vary with the sources of the income and the characteristics of the transactions.

Type of Enterprise	Major Type of Income Operations	Typical Income-Account Titles
Mercantile establishment	Sales of merchandise	Sales
Professional firm	Professional services	Fees, Professional Services, Retainers, etc.
Financial institution	Loaning of funds	Interest, Discount, Commissions
Insurance company	Insurance protection	Premiums, Interest
Real estate firm	Sale and leasing of real estate	Commissions, Rent

Expense accounts classify and measure business operations expressed in the accounts as accumulated debits.—The payment of $100 for one month's occupancy of a building would ordinarily be journalized as follows:

Rent....................	$100.00	
Cash.........................		$100.00

The debit to the Rent account represents an asset valued at $100. This debit one month later, however, serves merely to indicate the expired value of the rental privilege. The $100 becomes an expense item, just as if the entry had been made in the Rent account at the close of the period. Assets purchased during a period of business operations may be gradually expended; the data in the asset accounts thus change from data which express certain aspects of financial status to data which reflect certain types of business operation. It is this phenomenon of gradual change that makes so important the careful distinction between asset accounts and expense accounts. For very often the difference between asset and expense data is dependent entirely upon the moment at which the data are considered.

From the standpoint of accounting technique, the expense transactions may be given immediate or deferred recognition in the ledger. In the first instance, the business operations are recorded as expenses immediately when certain assets are expended or liabilities incurred. Examples are: the payment of current advertising bills, salaries, insurance, repairs, maintenance expenses, etc. At the time cash is paid (or the liability recognized) the transaction is immediately recorded as an expense. In the second instance, the business operations are recorded as expenses only at the time when a summary of financial status is prepared. This is accomplished by adjusting the values of certain assets, such as merchandise, receivables, buildings, supplies, or prepaid expenses; or by bringing new liabilities into the ledger, such as salaries payable or interest payable. The periodic adjustments to reflect expense operations at the time of summarization will be discussed in the following chapter.

Capital vs. revenue expenditures.—Some expenditures result in bringing to an enterprise assets which continue in existence up to the time of preparing a balance sheet. The purchase of new machinery or fixtures is an expenditure of this type, which is usually referred to under the general designation of "capital expenditures." Expenditures which are chargeable as expenses of the fiscal period in which they occur are known as "revenue expenditures." An example would be the cost of repairing or attending a machine. "Revenue expenditure" is, of course, merely another designation for an expense transaction, a term used to differentiate such a transaction from one increasing the assets of an enterprise. It is not always easy to distinguish capital and revenue expenditures, especially in cases where short-lived assets are purchased for use in current operations. This problem will be discussed at length in chapter xxiv as one of the difficulties involved in the valuation of fixed assets.

Merchandise transactions often recorded in separate accounts at time of occurrence.—The importance of merchandise operations often makes it desirable for a manager to maintain very definite control over the receipts and outgo of merchandise, as well as over the amount on hand at any given time. Accordingly modern practice usually provides accounts to reflect the various aspects of the merchandise operations in separate accounts; these accounts are summarized periodically to determine the amount on hand at any particular time (the merchandise inventory), also the amount disposed of during a period of time (the cost of goods sold). Some of the accounts used in the summarization of the merchandise transactions to determine the goods on hand and goods sold are Merchandise Inventory, Merchandise Purchases, Purchases Returns, Purchases Allowances, Cost of Goods Sold. The last-mentioned account is, in its ultimate effect, an expense account; but it also serves as a place for a periodic summarization of the other data. The Sales account, with its offsets in the forms of returns and allowances, may also be regarded as expressing merchandise operations; in fact the sales data are at times offset in the accounts directly against the cost of goods sold.[1]

Merchandise Inventory.—This account is used to record the amount of merchandise on hand whenever a balance sheet is prepared. The amount is changed periodically whenever the inventory on hand is evaluated by actual inspection and count. The adjustment may be accomplished either by addition to or subtraction from the previously entered value. Or it may be effected by transferring the old amount to the Cost of Goods Sold account and replacing it with the new inventory—the cost of goods *not* sold. Some enterprises maintain a continuous record of outgoing merchandise; the Merchandise Inventory account of such firms always expresses the value of merchandise on hand at any given time.

Merchandise Purchases.—The value of the commodities purchased during a given period is very important information for administrative control. The account containing this amount is entitled "Merchandise Purchases" (or "Purchases"); it is an account which accumulates the value of goods purchased during a given period. When the goods enter the business, debits are recorded in this account; and corresponding credits are posted to Cash or Accounts Payable, as illustrated below:

Purchases......................	$9,500.00	
Cash (or Accounts payable)............		$9,500.00

Merchandise is usually recorded in the Purchases account at cost price, that is, at the amount paid or payable to the vendor of the

[1] In chapter xx the Trading account is discussed as a specialized type of summarizing device used to assemble all data concerned with the receipt and outgo of merchandise.

goods. In some instances the amount paid or payable for incoming transportation is also regarded as if it increased the value of the purchased merchandise; hence it is added to the invoice value of the commodities.

Purchases Returns.—Purchases Returns is an account to reflect the return of merchandise to vendors; it is credited when goods in serviceable condition are returned to creditors to apply against Accounts Payable. If the creditor has been previously paid in full, the firm returning the goods may be reimbursed in cash. The entry to be made when goods are returned to the vendor (assuming an amount of $84 to be involved) is:

Accounts payable (or Cash)..........	$84.00	
Purchases returns.......................		$84.00

Purchases Allowances.—Purchases Allowances is an account in which are recorded reductions allowed by a creditor for goods damaged or otherwise not desirable. In such cases, the goods are not returned to the creditor. When it is known by the firm claiming an allowance that an allowance will be made by the creditor, the transaction should be recorded as follows (assuming an amount of $92 to be involved):

Accounts payable..................	$92.00	
Purchases allowances....................		$92.00

The journal entry does not imply that a vendor would allow full credit for undesirable goods and also would permit the purchaser to keep them. The $92 refers only to the portion of the invoice cost which is being reduced by the purchase allowance.

Cost of Goods Sold.—The value of the goods sold is an important expense item of an enterprise; this value must be determined if the status of the asset "Merchandise" is to be known at the time of preparing a balance sheet. But often this very important item must be calculated after the value of merchandise on hand is known, rather than before. With the aid of Merchandise Inventory values determined through actual count of goods on hand, the cost value of goods sold may be determined by summarizing the data in the various accounts with merchandise operations. The method consists of first transferring the balances of the various merchandise accounts to the Cost of Goods Sold account, and then removing therefrom the value of the merchandise on hand at the end of the period (the "ending" inventory). The balance represents the cost value of the goods sold during the period, and represents an "expense" item which should be summarized in the Income and Expense (Profit and Loss) account.

Cash discounts.—When merchandise has been sold on credit terms, it often happens that the vendor indicates specifically that privileges are to be granted the buyer when he pays his account. One of the privileges typically granted is the allowance of a deduction from the amount payable, if the account is paid on or before a certain date. For example, a 2 per cent discount may be allowed if an account is paid within ten days following the date on which an invoice is rendered to the purchaser to notify him of the amount payable. When such terms are extended, the symbol "2/10" is sometimes placed on the invoice; the 2 refers to the amount of discount to be allowed; the 10, to the number of days during which the discount privilege may be availed of. Additional facts concerning terms of sale may also be specified. An account may be payable at face value (net) thirty days following the date of the invoice. The symbol "2/10/n/30" means that a 2 per cent discount will be allowed if paid within ten days, the total amount being due not later than thirty days following the date of the invoice. Different terms of sale are offered by different firms. A discount may be granted if an account is paid on or before a certain date in the succeeding month. The expression "2 per cent 10th prox" (or "proximo") means that a 2 per cent discount will be allowed for payment on or before the tenth day of the month following the one during which the goods are sold. If goods are sold on such terms during the month of March, a discount of 2 per cent would be allowed on March invoices paid by April 10.

The discounts on amounts which are paid on or before certain dates are referred to in business practice as "cash discounts." When they are granted on accounts payable to vendors, they are called "purchases discounts"; when they are granted on accounts receivable from customers they are called "sales discounts." The allowance of a cash discount obviously causes entries in the books of both creditor and debtor. To the buyer the allowance is a discount on goods purchased—purchases discount; to the seller the allowance is a discount on goods sold—sales discount. To illustrate a cash discount allowed on purchases, assume that goods have been bought at a price of $2,000 on 2/10/n/30 terms. At the time of the purchase, the following entry will be made:

Purchases	$2,000.00	
Accounts payable		$2,000.00

If the goods are paid for within the discount period, the following entry will be made on the books of the purchasing company:

Accounts payable	$2,000.00	
Cash		$1,960.00
Purchases discount		40.00

On the books of the selling company the foregoing transactions will be recorded in an exactly opposite manner; by this company the transaction must be accounted for as a sale on which a sales discount is allowed at time of payment. The following entry will be recorded at the time of the sale.

Accounts receivable	$2,000.00	
Sales		$2,000.00

Ten days later, when the customer takes advantage of his cash-discount privilege, the following entry will be made:

Cash	$1,960.00	
Sales discount	40.00	
Accounts receivable		$2,000.00

Sales.—The Sales account has been discussed in chapter v as an account representing a source of income. It is credited when goods are sold; appropriate offsetting accounts (usually Cash or Accounts Receivable) are debited. The Sales account need not be discussed in more detail at this time.

Sales Returns.—When a customer is permitted to return goods which are in serviceable or salable condition the transaction causes either a reduction in the customer's account receivable or a refund of cash to the customer. The account to be debited in such a case may be entitled Sales Returns. When goods are returned they affect the accounts at sales price. The record of a transaction in which $81 credit is granted for merchandise returned by a customer would be as follows:

Sales returns	$81.00	
Accounts receivable (or Cash)		$81.00

Sales Allowances.—This is an account to record the effects of allowances made to customers on merchandise which has been sold. An allowance may cause either a reduction in the amount receivable from a customer or a payment of cash to him. A sales allowance may be made for any of various reasons, such as damage to the merchandise, or shipment of the wrong size, style, or amount of the merchandise. The journal entry to analyze the effects of a Sales Allowance of $30 would be:

Sales allowances....................	$30.00	
Accounts receivable (or cash)............		$30.00

The student should observe that merchandise returns and allowances may affect either goods sold or purchased; the purchases and sales returns and allowances differ from each other only in the viewpoint from which they are analyzed. When goods are returned from one enterprise to another, the transaction is, of course, recorded on the books of both companies. On the books of the company returning them to the original vendor, the transaction is a return of goods previously purchased—a purchases return. On the books of the company receiving the goods returned from the original customer, the transaction is a return of goods previously sold—a sales return. This difference in viewpoint on purchases and sales returns is applicable also to purchases allowances and sales allowances.

Summary accounts for business operations.—Mention has been made of the necessity for summarizing the accounts expressing business operations to determine their net effect upon financial status. The summarization of data may apply to any or all of the various income accounts and expense accounts, such as those dealing with merchandise sales and purchases, with manufacturing operations, or with any other types of business operations. Two summary accounts have already been illustrated in previous discussion: Cost of Goods Sold, and Income and Expense. The former account may, of course, be dispensed with at the time of summarization by transferring the merchandise data which represent cost of goods sold directly from the Merchandise account to the Income and Expense account. The Income and Expense account is very frequently referred to in business practice as the "Profit and Loss account." Whenever the latter title is referred to in later parts of this text, it will be used synonymously with Income and Expense.

QUESTIONS ON CHAPTER IX

1. Analyze the following transactions of the X Company for entry in the accounts:
   a) Miscellaneous cash sales of merchandise for day, $45.
   b) Sale to James Folan, 2/10/n/30, $80.
   c) Sales to K. H. Madden, $225; took his 6 per cent 60-day note for the amount.
   d) Sale to Henry Gamble, $600. He paid cash $100, gave a 6½ per cent 90-day note for $300, and left the balance on open account, 1/20/n/60.
2. Analyze the following transactions: (*a*) commissions earned (payment not yet received, $27; (*b*) interest earned and received, $36; (*c*) rent income received, $70; (*d*) dividends received, $500.
3. Analyze the following: (*a*) purchase of supplies on credit, $30; (*b*) payment of wages, $350; (*c*) payment of interest, $10; (*d*) depreciation of building for past year, $300; (*e*) payment of rent, $50; (*f*) payment of sales salaries, $200.
4. A customer who owes the X business $150 on 2/10/n/30 terms pays the account less the discount. Record the transaction on the books of the X business.
5. Why should a sales discount be offered by a vendor? What is the nature of the debit to the sales discount account?
6. The X business pays a trade creditor a $500 account less a discount of 1 per cent. Record the payment on the books of the X business.
7. Why should a business take purchase discounts? What rate of interest would a business pay for the use of the money if it failed to take a discount when the terms were 2/10/n/30? What is the nature of the credit entry in the purchase-discount account?
8. Analyze these transactions: (*a*) sales allowance, $14 (customer's account not paid up); (*b*) sales allowance and return of cash, $20; (*c*) sales return, $10 (customer's account not paid up); (*d*) sales return and return of cash to customer, $31.
9. Analyze the following : (*a*) purchase for cash, $240; (*b*) purchase on account, 1/10/n/30, $175; (*c*) purchase, $400, for which a 6 per cent 90-day note is given; (*d*) purchase of $700: $200 cash, $200 on account, 2/10/n/60, and balance covered by non-interest-bearing note running 90 days; (e) purchase return of goods not yet paid for, $75; (*f*) purchase return of goods paid for, $50; (*g*) purchase allowance on goods paid for, $25; (*h*) payment of freight-in, $10.

CHAPTER X

PERIODIC ADJUSTMENT AND SUMMARIZATION

A balance sheet which expresses financial status correctly must reflect the net effects of all business operations which have occurred. This requirement makes necessary periodic adjustment of the ledger data to express certain operations which have not been given previous recognition in the accounts. The business operations to be expressed by this periodic adjustment may comprise both expense and income transactions; the recording of these transactions may be accomplished by adjusting either the assets or the liabilities. The entries to record such business operations introduce no new principles of double-entry accounting; they merely apply the basic principles of debit and credit to transactions, the effects of which have been gradually accruing. The adjustments affect the balance sheet and statement of income and expense in exactly the same way as other transactions do. In some cases the adjustments are recorded in accounts which have been maintained currently during the period of operations; in other cases additional accounts are required to classify the data. The types of adjustments which may be necessary at the time of summarizing the ledger data may be classified as follows:

I. To record *expense* not previously accounted for:
   - A. By decreasing certain assets, for example:
     1. Merchandise
     2. Supplies
     3. Prepaid expenses
     4. Receivables
     5. Permanent assets
   - B. By increasing certain liabilities, for example:
     1. Wages payable, interest payable, rent payable.

II. To record *income* not previously accounted for:
   - A. By increasing certain assets, for example:
     1. Interest receivable, rent receivable.

B. By decreasing certain liabilities, for example:

1. Advance rentals, deferred interest income, etc.

Adjustments necessary to record expense not previously accounted for.—Certain expense operations must be recognized in the accounts at the time of summarizing the data of an enterprise. The adjustment of the accounts to record such expense transactions may be accomplished: (1) by writing down the values of certain assets which have been gradually disappearing; and (2) by increasing certain liabilities which have been incurred but not recorded.

Expenses may be recognized by decreasing certain assets.—The first type of expense adjustment to be illustrated is that which is effected by the reduction of specific assets. Any of the assets may conceivably require adjustment to give effect to expense operations. The principle will be illustrated in the cases of merchandise, supplies, prepaid expenses, accounts receivable, permanent assets. The account title selected in each case to reflect the expense operations will vary with the nature of the transaction which has affected the asset.

Adjustment of the merchandise accounts.—The merchandise data, whether assembled in one account or in several, must be adjusted to indicate the value of the goods sold during the period for which the expenses are being summarized. This is accomplished (where only one merchandise account is used) by transferring the cost value of goods sold from the Merchandise account to an expense account, Cost of Goods Sold, or directly to the Profit and Loss account. The task of calculating the value of goods sold is accomplished by evaluating at cost price the goods known to be on hand at the end of the period; the remainder are then regarded as having been sold.

To illustrate, assume that an account with merchandise has accumulated total debit entries of $15,711 during the six months' period ending June 30. Of this total, $1,946 represents the amount of goods which were on hand on the preceding January 1; $13,765 represents goods which have been purchased during the intervening period. The account would appear as follows before any adjustment is made:

Merchandise

Jan. 1	Balance..........	$1,946.00	
16	Cash.............	4,500.00	
Mar. 18	Accounts payable..	2,600.00	
May 15	Accounts payable..	4,240.00	
June 15	Cash.............	2,425.00	

It is apparent that this account does not represent the actual status of the asset merchandise, for it contains only debit entries; no credit entries have been made in the Merchandise account to record the outgoing or sold merchandise. If the total goods on hand June 30 were determined to have cost $3,142, the value of the goods sold would, by subtraction, be established at $12,569.

Total merchandise debits January 1 to June 30..	$15,711.00
Actual merchandise on hand June 30.......	3,142.00
Cost of goods sold January 1 to June 30.......	$12,569.00

The amount $12,569 may be removed from the Merchandise account and debited to the expense account Cost of Goods Sold.

Cost of goods sold............	$12,569.00	
Merchandise........................		$12,569.00

The Merchandise account now contains a debit balance of $3,142 which may be carried forward in the account in the usual manner. The accounts affected would appear as follows after the journal entry and the balancing of the Merchandise account.

Merchandise

Jan. 1	Balance.........	$ 1,946.00	June 30	Cost of goods sold..........	$12,569.00
16	Cash............	4,500.00		*Balance.........*	*3,142.00*
Mar. 18	Accounts payable	2,600.00			
May 15	Accounts payable	4,240.00			
June 15	Cash............	2,425.00			
		$15,711.00			$15,711.00
June 30	*Balance........*	$ 3,142.00			

The debit balance of $3,142 in the Merchandise account above represents an asset which should appear on a balance sheet of June 30. The debit of $12,569 in the Cost of Goods Sold account is an expense item which should appear in the summary statement of income and expense.

If the merchandise data had been separated in the accounts, the Cost of Goods Sold account might have been used as a summary account in which to compute the value of goods sold. The summarization of the merchandise data (if previously recorded in Merchandise Inventory and Merchandise Purchases accounts) would have been recorded as follows:

MERCHANDISE INVENTORY

Jan. 1	Balance.........	$1,946.00		

MERCHANDISE PURCHASES

Jan. 16	Cash............	$4,500.00		
Mar. 18	Accounts payable.	2,600.00		
May 15	Accounts payable.	4,240.00		
June 15	Cash............	2,425.00		

The transfer of these two balances to the Cost of Goods Sold account would be accomplished by the following entries:

Cost of goods sold............	$1,946.00	
Merchandise inventory...............		$1,946.00
Cost of goods sold............	$13,765.00	
Merchandise purchases...............		$13,765.00

The Cost of Goods Sold account would now contain a debit total of $15,711.[1] This amount contains both the amount sold and the amount on hand June 30. The latter amount must be removed to the Merchandise Inventory account, as follows:

Merchandise inventory........	$3,142.00	
Cost of goods sold...................		$3,142.00

[1] The adjustment is sometimes accomplished by transferring the inventory to Merchandise Purchases. When the final inventory is removed therefrom, the Merchandise Purchases account contains a balance equal to the cost value of the goods sold; this balance may be transferred directly to the Profit and Loss account. No Cost of Goods Sold account would be used.

The Cost of Goods Sold account balance would be closed to the Profit and Loss account in the same manner as the data in any other expense account. The closing entry would be:

Profit and Loss	$12,569.00	
Cost of goods sold		$12,569.00

After the foregoing adjusting and closing entries were posted, the accounts would appear as follows:

MERCHANDISE INVENTORY

Date	Item	Amount	Date	Item	Amount
Jan. 1	Balance	$ 1,946.00	*June 30*	Cost of goods sold	$ 1,946.00
June 30	Balance	$ 3,142.00			

MERCHANDISE PURCHASES

Date	Item	Amount	Date	Item	Amount
Jan. 16		$ 4,500.00	June 30	Cost of goods sold	$13,765.00
Mar. 18		2,600.00			
May 15		4,240.00			
June 15		2,425.00			
		$13,765.00			$13,765.00

COST OF GOODS SOLD

Date	Item	Amount	Date	Item	Amount
June 30	Inventory, Jan. 1	$ 1,946.00	June 30	Inventory, June 30	$ 3,142.00
	Purchases	13,765.00		Profit and Loss	12,569.00
		$15,711.00			$15,711.00

PROFIT AND LOSS

Date	Item	Amount	Date	Item	Amount
June 30	Cost of goods sold	$12,569.00			

Adjustment of the supplies accounts.—Many supplies are purchased for use in the current business operations. All incoming supplies are recorded as debits in the various supplies accounts. As in the case of the merchandise accounts, credits are not usually made to the supplies accounts at the time supplies are consumed. The reductions in values are recorded only when it is necessary to summarize the operations of a period. Consequently the total debits in the supplies accounts, before analysis, represent two types of items: supplies on hand (assets) and supplies consumed (expenses). The adjustment is made by crediting the various supplies accounts and debiting appropriate expense accounts for the values of the consumed supplies. To illustrate, assume that total debits of $985 have been entered in an account entitled "Factory Supplies."

FACTORY SUPPLIES

Dec. 31	Balance	$214.00			
Mar. 2	Cash	190.00			
Apr. 17	Accounts payable	321.00			
June 10	Cash	260.00			

Assume also that an evaluation of the factory supplies on hand at the time of analyzing the accounts shows them to be worth only $320. This means that during the foregoing period $665 worth of factory supplies have been consumed. The adjustment of the account may be accomplished by crediting the Factory Supplies account $665 and debiting Factory Supplies Expense $665. The journal entry would be:

Factory supplies expense	$665.00	
Factory supplies		$665.00

The accounts, after the adjustment, would appear as follows:

FACTORY SUPPLIES

Dec. 31	Balance	$214.00	June 30	Factory supplies expense	$665.00
Mar. 2	Cash	190.00			
Apr. 17	Accounts payable	321.00			
June 10	Cash	260.00			

FACTORY SUPPLIES EXPENSE

June 30	Factory supplies	$665.00			

The debit entry in the Factory Supplies Expense account will be summarized with the other expense items of the period. The remaining balance in the Factory Supplies account will appear as an asset on the balance sheet. The account may be balanced, if it is so desired, to show the amount of unused supplies on hand June 30.

FACTORY SUPPLIES

Dec. 31	Balance	$214.00	June 30	Factory supplies expense	$665.00
Mar. 2	Cash	190.00			
Apr. 17	Accounts payable	321.00			
June 10	Cash	260.00		*Balance*	*320.00*
		$985.00			$985.00
June 30	*Balance*	$320.00			

The same principles that have been illustrated here in the adjustment of Factory Supplies would apply to other accounts with supplies and materials. Examples are Office Stationery, Fuel, Oil, Waste, etc.

Prepaid expenses.—Rent, insurance, interest, etc., are sometimes paid in advance for several periods of business operations. At the time each payment is made, the appropriate asset account is debited and the Cash account or some liability account is credited. The benefits from these transactions will be enjoyed during several ensuing operating periods. Consequently the original amounts must be reduced periodically, with only the remaining balances appearing as assets on the balance sheet. Assume that an insurance premium of $1,200 has been paid in advance for three years from January 1. The account to represent the prepaid insurance would appear as follows on January 1 at the time of the payment.

INSURANCE

Jan. 1	Cash	$1,200.00	

The debit in the Insurance account represents a valuable asset, which will be of service to the enterprise for three years. Its value constantly decreases, however; and at the end of one year, one-third of the value of the insurance will have expired. If a balance sheet is prepared on December 31, the account with Insurance will be adjusted to record the expired value of the insurance protection. This may be accomplished by transferring one-third of the debit in the Insurance account to an appropriate expense account by the following entry:

Insurance expense..................	$400.00	
Insurance..............................		$400.00

This journal entry will be given effect in the accounts as follows:

INSURANCE

Jan. 1 Cash............. $1,200.00	Dec. 31 Insurance expense.... $400.00

INSURANCE EXPENSE

Dec. 31 Insurance.......... $400.00	

The Insurance account illustrated above is represented as an asset account, which is periodically written down when expenses are to be summarized. The expired portions of the prepaid insurance must be transferred periodically to an Insurance Expense account, or summarized directly in the Profit and Loss account.

The illustration of Insurance as a prepaid expense, whose original debit balance represents an asset, is applicable to other types of services or privileges which are purchased. Typical account titles representing assets of this nature are "Rent," "Interest," "Royalties," etc. In some cases the original debits from payments for these items are made in accounts entitled "Prepaid Insurance," "Prepaid Rent," "Prepaid Interest."[1]

[1] The foregoing method of adjusting supplies and prepaid-expense data is analogous to the first method illustrated for adjusting the Merchandise account when all merchandise data are kept in one account. But it would also be possible to keep separate accounts for the "inventories" of supplies and prepaid expenses on the one hand, and for the transactions (the "purchases") which increase these items on the other. When such accounts are maintained, the adjustment of the supplies and prepaid-expense data would involve essentially the same procedure as adjustment of the merchandise data under these conditions. The old "inventories" would be merged with the current data; the new "inventories" would be credited to the current expense accounts and established in the inventory (asset) accounts to appear on the balance sheet.

Adjustment of the receivables.—At the end of a period of business operations there will usually be a substantial debit balance in the Accounts Receivable account. This balance represents the amount to be later collected in the form of cash. Business experience has demonstrated, however, that some of these receivable items will not be collected in full. Some of the debtors, because of poor financial condition or dishonesty, will fail to pay their obligations in full to the enterprise. A firm knows that such losses will occur, and it considers them a part of the expenses of an enterprise which sells merchandise on credit terms. The total of Accounts Receivable should accordingly be reduced to approximately the amount that will be collected. In some businesses the percentage of reduction will be large; in others it will be small. At any rate, the total Accounts Receivable must be divided into: good debts (collectible), and bad debts (uncollectible). The journal entry to provide such an adjustment would be as follows, assuming total Accounts Receivable of $59,876 on March 1 and an allowance or reduction of 5 per cent to provide for bad debts:

	Debit	Credit
Bad debts	$2,493.80	
Accounts receivable		$2,493.80

The account before adjustment might appear as follows:

ACCOUNTS RECEIVABLE

Jan. 1	Balance	$47,900.00	Feb. 1	Cash	$36,800.00
Feb. 1	Sales	52,600.00	Mar. 1	Cash	45,200.00
Mar. 1	Sales	41,376.00			*82,000.00*
		141,876.00			

After the entry is posted, the accounts affected would be:

ACCOUNTS RECEIVABLE

Jan. 1	Balance	$47,900.00	Feb. 1	Cash	$36,800.00
Feb. 1	Sales	52,600.00	Mar. 1	Cash	45,200.00
Mar. 1	Sales	41,376.00			*82,000.00*
		141,876.00	Mar. 1	Bad debts	2,493.80

Bad Debts

Mar. 1 Accounts receivable $2,493.80	

The debit in the newly established Bad Debts account is an expense item. The remaining debit in the Accounts Receivable account represents the estimated good debts, the net amount which should appear on the balance sheet as an asset. The percentage by which the Accounts Receivable total has been adjusted is relatively small, as compared with the adjustment of the other asset accounts illustrated in the previous paragraphs. The nature of this adjustment, however, is fundamentally the same as those which have been discussed; it involves writing down an asset, "Accounts receivable" to reflect an expense, the loss on bad debts.

Allowance for Bad Debts account.—There is a fundamental objection to accounting for the losses on bad debts in the manner just illustrated. The credit to Accounts Receivable is, of course, a subtraction representing the estimated uncollectible items. But how is the accountant to know exactly which customers should be given credit for the subtraction? Obviously he cannot deduct 5 per cent from the amount due from each customer; for some receivable items will be collected in full, and others will be entirely uncollectible. A method of dealing with this situation is the establishment of a temporary credit account, in which to accumulate the deductions for bad debts, thus postponing the entry in the Accounts Receivable account. Such an account may be designated as "Allowance for Bad Debts," "Reserve for Bad Debts," or "Deduction for Uncollectible Items." The journal entry to reflect the adjustment would be:

Bad debts	$2,493.80	
Allowance for bad debts		$2,493.80

The Allowance for Bad Debts account would appear as follows:

Allowance for Bad Debts

	Mar. 1 Bad debts......... $2,493.80

The journal entry shown above does not provide for an immediate credit to the Accounts Receivable account. The credit to the Allowance for Bad Debts account may be regarded as a postponed deduction from the Accounts Receivable; it appears in a balance sheet as follows:

Accounts receivable...........	$59,876.00	
Less: Allowance for bad debts..	2,493.80	
		$57,382.20

When accounts receivable from specific customers are discovered to be uncollectible, the known losses may be transferred from the Allowance for Bad Debts account and recorded as direct deductions from the Accounts Receivable.[1] Assume that soon after the Allowance for Bad Debts account was established on March 1 it is discovered that a customer has become bankrupt. One-half of his total account of $970 is declared uncollectible. The journal entry to deduct $485 from Accounts Receivable will be :

Allowance for bad debts.............	$485.00	
Accounts receivable.....................		$485.00

The Allowance for Bad Debts account would become:

Allowance for Bad Debts

Mar. 5 Accounts receivable... $485.00	Mar. 1 Bad debts........ $2,493.80

[1] The method of keeping detailed records of the amounts due from each customer will be discussed in chapter xv.

Inasmuch as the estimated allowance for bad debts is expected to cover the actual losses which will be incurred, the Allowance for Bad Debts account would normally have a very small credit balance, if any, at the close of each operating period before the accounts were adjusted; in fact it may contain a debit balance.

Adjustment of permanent asset accounts.—Most assets which are referred to as "permanent" assets gradually wear out in the course of business operations or lose their value by the mere passage of time. This gradual reduction of value is not recorded in the books from day to day; the accounts are adjusted periodically to reflect the changes. The fact of reducing value is generally described as "depreciation."[1] Accordingly, one or more expense accounts are opened periodically to record the depreciation of the various permanent assets. Adjustments to reflect the reducing values must consist of credits to the asset accounts and debits to the expense accounts representing depreciation. To illustrate, assume that a building with an original cost value of $50,000 is estimated to have depreciated 4 per cent during a period of business operations. The journal entry to record the depreciation for the period might be:

Depreciation on building........	$2,000.00	
Building............................		$2,000.00

The debit to the Depreciation on Building account is an expense item which should be summarized with the other expenses.

It is not always desirable to record the expiration of the asset values directly in the asset accounts, because of the highly tentative character of the depreciation estimate and because of the advantages of maintaining a permanent record of the original costs of the assets. The difficulty can be avoided by entering the credit in a temporary account with a title such as "Allowance for Depreciation," "Reserve for Depreciation," or "Provision for Depreciation." A balance sheet prepared from the accounts may thus show the original costs of the permanent assets as well as the deductions which have been made to estimate the accrued

[1] Methods of determining the amount of depreciation to be charged to a given period of business operations are treated fully in chapter xxv.

depreciation. The journal entry to record the depreciation on the building referred to above would be:

Depreciation on building........	$2,000.00	
Allowance for depreciation on building..		$2,000.00

The accounts affected would appear as follows:

DEPRECIATION ON BUILDING

Dec. 31	$2,000.00		

ALLOWANCE FOR DEPRECIATION ON BUILDING

		Dec. 31	$2,000.00

The credit in the Allowance for Depreciation on Building account is, in its ultimate effect, a credit to the Building account, and grows larger during the service life of the asset. If depreciation is charged at a rate which apportions the cost of the asset over the length of time it is used, the total in the allowance for depreciation account will accumulate until it exactly equals the cost value in the asset account. Allowance for depreciation accounts may be maintained with all permanent assets. On a balance sheet the accumulated allowances for depreciation might appear as follows at the end of seven years:

Building....................	$50,000.00	
Less: Allowance for depreciation	14,000.00	
		$36,000.00

The Allowance for Depreciation account would be:

ALLOWANCE FOR DEPRECIATION ON BUILDING

		Dec. 31, 1922	$2,000.00
		Dec. 31, 1923	2,000.00
		Dec. 31, 1924	2,000.00
		Dec. 31, 1925	2,000.00
		Dec. 31, 1926	2,000.00
		Dec. 31, 1927	2,000.00
		Dec. 31, 1928	2,000.00

Expense operations recognized by increasing certain liabilities.— Assume that a group of employees are usually paid on a bi-weekly basis on Saturdays, and that the closing date of a given fiscal period is the Saturday between pay days. The business at this date has enjoyed one week's services of these employees; moreover, it has incurred a liability for the payment of the wages to these employees, even though the cash need not be delivered until the following Saturday. The expense which has been incurred should be reflected in the accounts by debiting an expense account and crediting the liability which has become payable. If the bi-weekly pay-roll of this company were $680, the journal entry to record one week's labor expense and the wages payable therefor would be:

Labor	$340.00	
Wages payable		$340.00

The "Labor" debit is an expense item, which must be added to other debits previously recorded in the Labor account. The "Wages payable" credit is a liability. After these data are posted, the accounts might appear as follows:

LABOR

Jan.	13	Cash	$680.00	
	27	Cash	680.00	
Feb.	10	Cash	680.00	
	24	Cash	680.00	
Mar.	10	Cash	680.00	
	24	Cash	680.00	
	31	Wages payable	340.00	

WAGES PAYABLE

	Mar. 31 Labor $340.00

The total debit in the Labor account becomes $4,420, an amount which will appear on a statement of income and expense for the three months' period ending March 31. The credit in the Wages Payable account is a liability as of March 31. The liability "Wages payable" illustrates a type of special liability which must be given recognition in periodic balance sheets. The adjustments illustrated in the case of labor would apply equally well to any other type of expenses, such as taxes, interest, rent, royalties.

Adjustments necessary to record income not previously recognized in the accounts.—Some income operations affect the financial status of an enterprise gradually; they tend to increase proprietorship continuously during a period of business operations, either by adding to certain assets or reducing certain liabilities. Both of these types of income operations must be recorded in the ledger accounts if a balance sheet is to express accurately the financial status of an enterprise.

Income operations recognized by increasing certain assets.—Assume that an enterprise is the legal owner of a note for $20,000 which bears interest at the rate of 5 per cent per annum, payable annually on December 31 of each year during its life. On June 30, the enterprise wishes to prepare a balance sheet and to include among its assets the amount of interest which has accrued during the first six months of the year. The entry to recognize the earnings on the note as income of the six months' period and as an amount receivable on June 30 would be as follows:

	Debit	Credit
Interest receivable................	$500.00	
Interest income........................		$500.00

The credit item will be added to other credit entries which have previously accumulated in the Interest Income account up to June 30. The accounts affected by the foregoing entry might appear as follows:

INTEREST RECEIVABLE

Debit		Credit	
June 30 Interest income.....	$500.00		

INTEREST INCOME

Debit		Credit	
		Mar. 31 Cash...............	$310.00
		May 31 Cash...............	265.00
		June 30 Interest receivable...	500.00

The "Interest receivable" debit represents an asset item, and should appear on a balance sheet of June 30. The total credit of $1,075 in the Interest Income account would appear in the statement of income and expense for the six months' period ending June 30. "Interest receivable" is one of a group of similar assets which appear on periodic balance sheets. Receivables of this type are sometimes segregated on the balance sheet under the general heading "Accrued income" or "Accrued income receivable." The principles illustrated in the interest transaction would be applicable to income from other sources, such as rent, commissions, royalties, etc.

Income operations recognized by decreasing certain liabilities.— Certain liability accounts must be adjusted when financial summaries are prepared; illustrations are the liabilities established when assets are received in advance of certain income-producing operations. The problem presents itself continuously in the treatment of cash received in advance for rental privileges or other services. Assume that a firm which makes a business of leasing property on five-year terms collects a five-year rental price of $6,000 in advance. The journal entry at the time of the receipt of cash might be made as follows:

Cash..........................	$6,000.00	
Advance rentals..................		$6,000.00

The account with Advance Rentals would be:

ADVANCE RENTALS

	Jan. 1	$6,000.00

The credit in the Advance Rentals account measures the rent income to be earned during the ensuing five years. At the time of entry the $6,000 represents a liability to grant the tenants five years' free occupancy. The liability continues until the rental privileges have been availed of; it is gradually liquidated as the period of the lease expires. The credit in the Advance Rentals account should accordingly be periodically reduced by transfer to an income account as the lease draws to a close. At the end of the first year, one-fifth of the total liability represented by Advance Rentals will have been discharged; one-fifth of the total $6,000 received as cash may, therefore, be recognized as earned during the foregoing year. The journal entry to transfer the proper amount from Advance Rentals to an account to represent current rent income might be:

Advance rentals................	$1,200.00	
Rent income......................		$1,200.00

The accounts affected would appear as follows:

ADVANCE RENTALS

Dec. 31 Rent income...... $1,200.00	Jan. 1 Cash.............. $6,000.00

RENT INCOME

	Dec. 31 Advance rentals... $1,200.00

The remaining credit balance of $4,800 in the Advance Rentals account is still a liability item and would appear on a balance sheet of December 31. The credit balance in the Rent Income account is an income item and would appear on a statement of income and expense for the year ending December 31. Liabilities of the type just illustrated by Advance Rentals are, in the last analysis, merely deferred credits to various income accounts, and they commonly are designated on the balance sheet under some general caption indicating their nature, such as "Deferred Income," "Deferred Credits to Income," etc. Typical accounts of this nature, other than Advance Rentals, are: Deposits on Sales, Insurance Premiums Received, Deferred Interest Income.[1]

Closing the income and expense accounts.—The foregoing extensive discussion of the periodic adjustment of the accounts has shown how certain business operations are given eventual recognition in the books of an enterprise. The adjustments record these operations in the accounts and have the effect of segregating the balance-sheet data and the income and expense data in the ledger. The next step in the summarization of the accounting data is that of offsetting the income and expense operations against each other; the income and expense accounts are therefore "closed" into the summary account referred to above as the "Income and Expense account," and typically designated in practice as the "Profit and Loss account." The balance of the Profit and Loss account, then, represents an increase or decrease in proprietorship, and is accordingly transferred to a proprietorship account, either to the proprietor's Personal accounts or to corporate Surplus. After the accounts have been adjusted and the income and expense balances closed, the ledger accounts contain open records with balance-sheet items only. From these data, an accurate balance sheet may be prepared. The data for a statement of income and expense may be secured from the entries in the Profit and Loss account. The technique of adjusting and closing the ledger accounts will be illustrated in detail in chapter xi.

QUESTIONS ON CHAPTER X

1. Certain transactions occur during an accounting period, the effects of which are recorded only periodically. Into what main classes of entries may the adjustments necessary to record these transactions be divided? Explain fully.

[1] The reader should be warned at this point that in practice many bookkeepers do not clearly segregate the "deferred" income from the income applicable to current periods of operations. Not infrequently all credits which will ultimately be recognized as income are entered in the current income accounts; the credit accumulations are later analyzed into those portions applicable as income to current periods and those to be deferred and treated as income of ensuing periods. For example, in the illustration above, one single account, such as Rent Income (or Rent), would suffice to accumulate the advance rentals. The account would be adjusted periodically by transferring part of the credit to the Income and Expense summary account. The remainder would be deferred to later periods and would appear on the balance sheet as a liability.

2. The ending inventory adjustment serves to split the total cost of goods to be accounted for (beginning inventory plus purchases) into two parts —the cost of the goods *sold* and the cost of the goods *on hand* at the end of the period. In which statements do the cost of goods sold and the ending inventories appear?
3. Explain in detail the steps in the process of recording the inventory adjustment and summarizing the various elements necessary to obtain the cost of goods sold when separate purchases, inventory, and other auxiliary accounts are maintained.
4. Why is the allowance for bad debts recorded in an account separate from the receivables and not deducted directly from them? Why is the allowance for depreciation recorded in an account separate from that carrying the original asset value?
5. An expense may be recognized in the accounts by decreasing certain assets; that is, by transferring the expired value to appropriate expense accounts. Show how this statement is applicable to the adjustment of the following assets: (*a*) supplies; (*b*) accounts receivable; (*c*) buildings; (*d*) prepaid expenses.
6. Journalize the necessary entries for recognizing the following conditions in the books of account:

   Beginning inventory: $21,250 (ending inventory $14,765). Current purchases were $184,293. Compute the cost of goods sold, and show the status of the various accounts affected after the posting.
7. Unused supplies are $248. A total of $1,864 has been debited to a "Supplies" account. Journalize the adjustment.
8. A payment of interest amounting to $295 was made on July 1. It represented a semi-annual payment of 5 per cent annual interest on a note payable for $10,800. It is now October 1. The debit was made to "Interest." Journalize the necessary adjustment.
9. Insurance premiums were paid a year ago amounting to $1,500. The premiums covered insurance for a period extending over five years. The original debit was to "Insurance." Journalize.
10. Distinguish carefully between Bad Debts and Allowance for Bad Debts; Depreciation and Allowance for Depreciation.
11. A building which has been constructed at a cost of $46,000 is now ten years old. Depreciation for the past year is estimated at 3 per cent of the original cost. It has not yet been recorded in the accounts. Record it.
12. Three months ago $900 cash was received as interest on a note receivable. It covered the interest of the present year at 5 per cent on an $18,000 loan. Assume (*a*) that the original credit was to Interest Income; (*b*) that the original credit was to Deferred Interest Income. Journalize.
13. A tenant has been permitted to use a warehouse for a year with the understanding that at the end of the time he will pay a rental of $1,800. Six months of this period of occupancy have gone by, and no entries have

yet been made in the books. (*a*) Make appropriate entries. (*b*) Handle the situation also on the assumption that the following entries had been made in the books at the first of the year: debit: "Rent receivable, $1,800"; "Advance rentals, $1,800." (*c*) On the assumption that the following entry had been made: debit: "Rent receivable, $1,800;" credit, "Rent income, $1,800."

14. A wage bill will be payable in two weeks amounting to $500. The last payment was made and the last entries for wages were posted two weeks ago. Make the necessary adjustment.

15. Adjustments affect *both* the *balance sheet* and the *statement of income and expense.* What would be the effect on *each* of these reports if the following adjustments were omitted: (*a*) accrued income, such as accrued interest income; (*b*) accrued liabilities (or expense) such as accrued wages; (*c*) deferred charges to expense such as supplies on hand; (*d*) deferred credits t income such as unearned rent; (*e*) allowance for bad debts; (*f*) depreciation?

CHAPTER XI

CLOSING THE LEDGER—THE WORK-SHEET

This chapter will be devoted to the technique of adjusting and closing the accounts preliminary to the preparation of a balance sheet and statement of income and expense. It will introduce no new matters of theory, but will illustrate the points discussed in chapter x.

Illustration of adjusting entries.—As the basis for a series of adjusting entries, let us use the following trial balance taken from the ledger of D. L. Keller. The debit and credit balances here recorded represent the amounts appearing in the different accounts before they are adjusted.

D. L. KELLER

TRIAL BALANCE—DECEMBER 31, 19——

Account Title	*Debit*	*Credit*
Cash	$ 1,400.00	
Notes receivable	5,000.00	
Accounts receivable	17,500.00	
Allowance for bad debts	....	$ 450.00
Merchandise inventory, Jan. 1, 19——	9,500.00	
Furniture and fixtures	2,250.00	
Allowance for depreciation on furn. and fix.	....	225.00
Delivery equipment	2,800.00	
Allowance for depreciation on equipment	....	1,120.00
Buildings	21,000.00	
Allowance for depreciation on buildings	....	6,000.00
Land	4,500.00	
Accounts payable	....	3,025.00
Notes payable	....	4,920.00
Mortgage payable	....	18,000.00
D. L. Keller, capital	....	19,000.00
D. L. Keller, personal	....	....
Sales	....	50,950.00
Purchases	32,000.00	
Office supplies	1,000.00	
Interest expense	400.00	
Interest	....	350.00
Insurance	840.00	
Advance rentals	....	1,900.00
Taxes	550.00	
Sales salaries	5,800.00	
Advertising	1,400.00	
Total	$105,940.00	$105,940.00

The following data are to be given recognition in the accounting records by the journalizing and posting of appropriate adjusting entries:

1. Merchandise inventory 12/31/19, $8,900.
2. Estimated loss on bad debts, 2 per cent of sales (not including the allowance already shown in the trial balance).
3. Depreciation on furniture and fixtures, 10 per cent; delivery equipment, 20 per cent; buildings, 4 per cent.
4. Office supplies on hand, $350.
5. Interest accrued on notes payable, $270.
6. Interest accrued on notes receivable, $84.
7. Insurance paid was for a three-year period, which began one year previous to the present date.
8. Cash was received six months ago for a full year's rent income. The entire amount, $1,900, was credited to Advance rentals.
9. Sales salaries payable have accrued, but are not due, $400.

The journal entries necessary to record the adjustments would be those shown on page 132. Explanations are omitted, the adjusting entries being listed in the same order as the data to which they apply. The method of "adjusting" the accounts to recognize certain expense and income transactions varies with the needs of the enterprise. In the following pages the method of adjustment illustrated is the same as that described in chapter x. Special accounts have been established to contain certain expense and income items previous to their transfer to the Profit and Loss account; similarly certain temporary assets and liabilities have been established to reflect the "accrued" items which are "receivable" or "payable." Other methods of effecting the adjustments are mentioned at the close of this chapter, also in the footnote on page 117.

A series of closing entries is shown on page 133. Each of these entries transfers the data of one income or expense account to the Profit and Loss account. The total income data or expense data could, of course, be transferred by a compound entry which would close all the income or expense accounts with one debit to Profit and Loss.

ADJUSTING ENTRIES

Date		Account	L.F.	Debit	Credit
19—					
Dec.	31	Cost of goods sold	20	$ 9,500.00	
		Merchandise inventory	5		$ 9,500.00
		Cost of goods sold	20	32,000.00	
		Purchases	19		32,000.00
		Merchandise inventory	5	8,900.00	
		Cost of goods sold	20		8,900.00
		Bad debts	29	1,019.00	
		Allowance for bad debts	4		1,019.00
		Depreciation	30	225.00	
		Allowance for depreciation on furniture and fixtures	7		225.00
		Depreciation	30	560.00	
		Allowance for depreciation on delivery equipment	9		560.00
		Depreciation	30	840.00	
		Allowance for depreciation on building	11		840.00
		Office-supplies expense	32	650.00	
		Office supplies	20		650.00
		Interest expense	22	270.00	
		Interest payable	33		270.00
		Interest receivable	34	84.00	
		Interest income	23		84.00
		Insurance expense	35	280.00	
		Insurance	24		280.00
		Advance rentals	25	950.00	
		Rent income	36		950.00
		Sales salaries	27	400.00	
		Salaries payable	37		400.00

The foregoing journal entries are to be posted to the general ledger accounts shown in the trial balance and to other general ledger accounts established to record the accrued assets and liabilities.

Illustration of closing entries.—We shall now illustrate the entries necessary to transfer the balances in the expense and income accounts to the Profit and Loss account, and thence to a proprietorship account, D. L. Keller, Personal. The ledger of D. L. Keller is shown on succeeding pages. It should be examined carefully in order that the reader may observe how adjusting and closing entries affect the accounts.

Closing Entries

Dec.	31	Sales	18	$50,950	00		
		Profit and loss	31	....	..	$50,950	00
		Interest income	22	434	00		
		Profit and loss	31	....	..	434	00
		Rent income	35	950	00		
		Profit and loss	31	....	..	950	00
		These entries close the income account balances to Profit and Loss at the end of one year's operations.					
		Profit and loss	31	32,600	00		
		Cost of goods sold	20	....	..	32,600	00
		Profit and loss	31	650	00		
		Office supplies expense	32	....	..	650	00
		Profit and loss	31	670	00		
		Interest expense	22	....	..	670	00
		Profit and loss	31	280	00		
		Insurance expense	35	....	..	280	00
		Profit and loss	31	550	00		
		Taxes	26	....	..	550	00
		Profit and loss	31	6,200	00		
		Sales salaries	27	....	..	6,200	00
		Profit and loss	31	1,400	00		
		Advertising	28	....	..	1,400	00
		Profit and loss	31	1,019	00		
		Loss on bad debts	29	....	..	1,019	00
		Profit and loss	31	1,625	00		
		Depreciation	30	....	..	1,625	00
		All the foregoing entries are made to close expense accounts to Profit and Loss.					
		Profit and loss	31	7,340	00		
		D. L. Keller, Personal	17	....	..	7,340	00
		To close the Profit and Loss account balance to D. L. Keller's personal account.					

Ledger accounts after being adjusted and closed.—The following accounts represent the condition of the ledger after the adjusting and closing entries have been properly entered in them. The income and expense accounts are all closed; their balances have been transferred to the Profit and Loss account. The Profit and Loss balance has been transferred to the D. L. Keller, Personal account. The amounts in the ledger accounts represent the balances as they would appear on December 31 before adjustment. The total data of each of the various accounts would typically consist of series of debits, or credits, or both. The ledger accounts are set forth in "skeleton" form, without special rulings for the debit and credit money columns, and without folio columns for cross-indexing the ledger entries with the journal entries. Each account is given a page or number, the numbers following in sequence; in practice one account might be given several pages in a ledger, or several accounts might appear on the same ledger page.

LEDGER OF D. L. KELLER

CASH (Page 1)

Dec. 31	$1,400.00			

NOTES RECEIVABLE (Page 2)

Dec. 31	$5,000.00			

ACCOUNTS RECEIVABLE (Page 3)

Dec. 31	$17,500.00			

ALLOWANCE FOR BAD DEBTS (Page 4)

		Dec. 31		$ 450.00
			Bad debts	1,019.00

MERCHANDISE INVENTORY (Page 5)

Jan. 1	$9,500.00	Dec. 31	Cost of goods sold	$9,500.00
Dec. 31	$8,900.00			

FURNITURE AND FIXTURES (Page 6)

Dec. 31	$2,250.00			

Allowance for Depreciation on Furniture and Fixtures (Page 7)

		Dec. 31	$ 225.00
		Dec. 31 Depreciation	225.00

Delivery Equipment (Page 8)

Dec. 31	$2,800.00		

Allowance for Depreciation on Delivery Equipment (Page 9)

		Dec. 31	$1,120.00
		Dec. 31 Depreciation	560.00

Buildings (Page 10)

Dec. 31	$21,000.00		

Allowance for Depreciation on Buildings (Page 11)

		Dec. 31	$6,000.00
		Dec. 31 Depreciation	840.00

Land (Page 12)

Dec. 31	$4,500.00		

Accounts Payable (Page 13)

		Dec. 31	$3,025.00

Notes Payable (Page 14)

		Dec. 31	$4,920.00

Mortgages Payable (Page 15)

		Dec. 31	$18,000.00

D. L. Keller, Capital (Page 16)

			Dec. 31	....	$19,000.00

D. L. Keller, Personal (Page 17)

			Dec. 31	Profit and loss.....	$7,340.00

Sales (Page 18)

Dec. 31	Profit and loss...	$50,950.00	Dec. 31	....	$50,950.00

Merchandise Purchases (Page 19)

Dec. 31	....	$32,000.00	Dec. 31	Cost of goods sold.	$32,000.00

Cost of Goods Sold (Page 20)

Dec. 31	Inventory.......	$ 9,500.00	Dec. 31	Inventory........	$ 8,900.00
	Purchases.......	32,000.00		Profit and loss....	32,600.00
		$41,500.00			$41,500.00

Office Supplies (Page 21)

Dec. 31	....	$1,000.00	Dec. 31	Profit and loss.....	$ 650.00
				Balance.........	350.00
		$1,000.00			$1,000.00
Dec. 31	*Balance*..........	$ 350.00			

Interest Expense (Page 22)

Dec. 31	....	$400.00	Dec. 31	Profit and loss.......	$670.00
Dec. 31	Interest payable.....	270.00			
		$670.00			$670.00

Interest Income

(Page 23)

Dec. 31	Profit and loss...	$434.00	Dec. 31	....	$350.00
			Dec. 31	Interest received....	84.00
		$434.00			$434.00

Insurance

(Page 24)

Dec. 31	....	$ 840.00	Dec. 31	Insurance expense..	$ 280.00
				Balance...........	560.00
		$ 840.00			$ 840.00
Dec. 31	*Balance*..........	$ 560.00			

Advance Rentals

(Page 25)

Dec. 31	Rent income......	$ 950.00	July 1	....	$1,900.00
	Balance..........	950.00			
		$1,900.00			$1,900.00
			Dec. 31	*Balance*...........	$ 950.00

Taxes

(Page 26)

Dec. 31	....	$ 550.00	Dec. 31	Profit and loss.....	$ 550.00

Sales Salaries

(Page 27)

Dec. 31	....	$5,800.00	Dec. 31	Profit and loss.....	$6,200.00
31	Salaries payable...	400.00			
		$6,200.00			$6,200.00

Advertising

(Page 28)

Dec. 31	....	$1,400.00	Dec. 31	Profit and loss.....	$1,400.00

Loss on Bad Debts (Page 29)

Date	Item	Amount	Date	Item	Amount
Dec. 31	Allowance for bad debts..........	$1,019.00	Dec. 31	Profit and loss.....	$1,019.00

Depreciation (Page 30)

Date	Item	Amount	Date	Item	Amount
Dec. 31	Allow. for Depr. on:		Dec. 31	Profit and loss.....	$1,625.00
	Fix. and furn....	$ 225.00			
	Del. equip......	560.00			
	Buildings.......	840.00			
		$1,625.00			$1,625.00

Profit and Loss (Page 31)

Date	Item	Amount	Date	Item	Amount
Dec. 31	Cost of goods sold.	$32,600.00	Dec. 31	Sales...........	$50,950.00
	Office supplies....	650.00		Interest income....	434.00
	Interest expense..	670.00		Rent income......	950.00
	Insurance........	280.00			
	Taxes...........	550.00			
	Sales salary......	6,200.00			
	Advertising......	1,400.00			
	Loss on bad debts	1,019.00			
	Depreciation.....	1,625.00			
	D. L. Keller, personal.........	7,340.00			
		$52,334.00			$52,334.00

Office Supplies Expense (Page 32)

Date	Item	Amount	Date	Item	Amount
Dec. 31	Office supplies.......	$650.00	Dec. 31	Profit and loss.......	$650.00

Interest Payable (Page 33)

Date	Item	Amount	Date	Item	Amount
			Dec. 31	Interest expense.....	$270.00

Interest Receivable (Page 34)

Date	Item	Amount	Date	Item	Amount
Dec. 31	Interest income......	$84.00			

INSURANCE EXPENSE (Page 35)

Dec. 31 Insurance	$280.00	Dec. 31 Profit and loss	$280.00

RENT INCOME (Page 36)

Dec. 31 Profit and loss	$950.00	Dec. 31 Advance rentals	$950.00

SALARIES PAYABLE (Page 37)

		Dec. 31 Salaries	$400.00

The balance-sheet accounts.—An examination of the ledger accounts of D. L. Keller shows that only the balance-sheet accounts are "open"; the income and expense accounts are "closed." An accountant wishing to prepare a balance sheet could do so by merely transcribing the balances in the asset, liability, and proprietorship accounts to a report on which the balance-sheet items were to be portrayed. Such a balance sheet would appear as follows:

D. L. KELLER

BALANCE SHEET—DECEMBER 31, 19—

ASSETS			LIABILITIES AND PROPRIETORSHIP	
Cash		$ 1,400.00	Accounts payable....	$ 3,025.00
Notes receivable		5,000.00	Notes payable	4,920.00
Accounts receivable ...	$17,500.00		Mortgage payable ...	18,000.00
Allow. for bad debts..	1,469.00	16,031.00	D. L. Keller, capital..	19,000.00
Merchandise inventory		8,900.00	D. L. Keller, pers	7,340.00
Furniture and fixtures.	2,250.00		Advance rentals.....	950.00
Allow. for deprec.....	450.00	1,800.00	Interest payable.....	270.00
Delivery equipment ...	2,800.00		Salaries payable.....	400.00
Allow. for deprec....	1,680.00	1,120.00		
Buildings	21,000.00			
Allow. for deprec....	6,840.00	14,160.00		
Land		4,500.00		
Office supplies		350.00		
Insurance (unexpired)		560.00		
Interest receivable		84.00		
		$53,905.00		$53,905.00

The account titles are listed on page 139 in the order in which they appear in the ledger; they might, of course, be listed in other sequences.

Income and expense accounts.—The facts necessary for a summarized statement of income and expense may be found in the Profit and Loss account. Here the income items are listed on the right side of the accounts; the expense items, on the left. Inasmuch as the Profit and Loss account is closed, the difference between the income and expense totals is listed on the debit side to indicate its transfer to the D. L. Keller, Personal account. This amount represents the net increase of proprietorship resulting from the period's income and expense transactions. The data of the Profit and Loss account, when summarized into a report, might appear somewhat as follows:

D. L. KELLER

STATEMENT OF PROFIT AND LOSS—JANUARY 1 TO DECEMBER 31, 19—

Income:		
Sales	$50,950.00	
Interest	434.00	
Rent	950.00	
Total		$52,334.00
Expenses:		
Cost of goods sold	$32,600.00	
Interest	670.00	
Taxes	550.00	
Sales salaries	6,200.00	
Advertising	1,400.00	
Bad debts	1,019.00	
Depreciation	1,625.00	
Office supplies	650.00	
Insurance	280.00	
Total		$44,994.00
Net increase of proprietorship		$ 7,340.00

The work-sheet.—In the discussion of the adjusting and closing entries there have been indicated appropriate journal entries to be posted to the ledger accounts. The adjustment and summarization have been illustrated as integral parts of the regular accounting procedure, which were necessary to the preparation of reports of financial condition and operations.

But it is conceivable that the accountant or business manager might wish to prepare a balance sheet and statement of income and expense without first making a formal adjustment and summary of the ledger accounts. Or it may be necessary to prepare the statements so quickly that it would be impossible first to journalize and post the adjusting and closing entries. To meet such situations there has been devised a *work-sheet*, on which the accountant can make an informal analysis and summary of the ledger data. From the data of the work-sheet he can later enter the adjusting and closing entries in the journal and the ledger. The work-sheet enables him to prepare a complete balance sheet and statement of income and expense without making formal adjustments in the ledger accounts.

The work-sheet usually contains eight parallel columns with headings as illustrated below:

Account Titles	Trial Balance		Adjustments		Profit and Loss		Balance Sheet	
	Debit	Credit	Debit	Credit	Debit	Credit	Debit	Credit

The first two debit and credit columns contain the figures of the unadjusted trial balance as the account balances would appear before analysis and summarization. The next two columns are for entering the effects of the adjusting entries. The adjustment columns in their vertical aspects may be regarded as the parallel columns of a journal in which the adjustments would be recorded. The horizontal lines on which the figures are entered may be regarded as the columns of ledger accounts in which the debits or credits would be posted. All figures on the same horizontal line affect the same account, the title of which is shown at the left side of the work-sheet.

D. L. KELLER

WORK SHEET—DECEMBER 31, 19—

Account Titles	Trial Balance		Adjustments		Profit and Loss		Balance Sheet	
	Debit	Credit	Debit	Credit	Debit	Credit	Debit	Credit
1. Cash	$ 1,400 00						$ 1,400 00	
2. Notes receivable	5,000 00						5,000 00	
3. Accounts receivable	17,500 00						17,500 00	
4. Allowance for bad debts		$ 450 00		$ 1,019 00				$ 1,469 00
5. Merchandise inventory	9,500 00		$ 8,900 00	9,500 00			8,900 00	
6. Furniture and fixtures	2,250 00						2,250 00	
7. Allowance for depreciation		225 00		225 00				450 00
8. Delivery equipment	2,800 00						2,800 00	
9. Allowance for depreciation		1,120 00		560 00				1,680 00
10. Buildings	21,000 00						21,000 00	
11. Allowance for depreciation		6,000 00		840 00				6,840 00
12. Land	4,500 00						4,500 00	
13. Accounts payable		3,025 00						3,025 00
14. Notes payable		4,920 00						4,920 00
15. Mortgage payable		18,000 00						18,000 00
16. D. L. Keller, capital		19,000 00						19,000 00
18. Sales		50,950 00				$50,950 00		
19. Merchandise purchases	32,000 00			32,000 00				
20. Cost of goods sold			{ 9,500 00 32,000 00	8,900 00	$32,600 00			
21. Office supplies	1,000 00			650 00			350 00	
22. Interest expenses	400 00		270 00		670 00			
23. Interest income		350 00		84 00		434 00		
24. Insurance	840 00			280 00			560 00	
25. Advance rentals		1,900 00	950 00					950 00
26. Taxes	550 00				550 00			
27. Sales salaries	5,800 00		400 00		6,200 00			

28. Advertising	1,400 00				1,400 00			
29. Bad debts			1,019 00		1,019 00			
			225 00		225 00			
30. Depreciation			560 00		560 00			
			840 00		840 00			
32. Office supplies expense			650 00		650 00			
33. Interest payable				270 00				270 00
34. Interest receivable			84 00				84 00	
35. Insurance expense			280 00		280 00			
36. Rent income				950 00		950 00		
37. Salaries payable				400 00				400 00
Total	$105,940 00	$105,940 00	$55,678 00	$55,678 00				
31. Profit and loss					7,340 00			
17. D. L. Keller, personal								7,340 00
					$52,334 00	$52,334 00	$64,344 00	$64,344 00

NOTE.—Observe that the first four columns (reading from left to right) serve to "accumulate" certain net totals in the accounts, the data of each account being distributed in the four columns to the right. The net amount which appears on a given horizontal line of the first four columns is the same as appears in the last four columns. The "adjustment" columns indicate the effects of the adjusting entries shown on page 132. The Profit and Loss columns set forth the effects of the closing entries on page 133, by which certain income and expense data are transferred to the Profit and Loss account. The Balance-Sheet columns represent the "open" balances of the accounts with assets, liabilities and proprietorship.

The term "work-sheet" need not be limited to a work-sheet for representing the adjusting and closing procedure. It may also be employed to describe any sheet on which an accountant makes a temporary classification and summarization of accounting data.

The four columns at the right of the work-sheet are classification columns for assembling the facts to appear in a balance sheet and statement of income and expense. The "Profit and Loss" columns may be looked upon as the two sides of the Profit and Loss account, after the income and expense accounts have been transferred thereto. The "Balance Sheet" columns contain the asset, liability, and proprietorship balances existing after all adjusting and closing entries have been recognized. The work-sheet for preparing the statements of D. L. Keller illustrates how this device is used.

In D. L. Keller's work-sheet, the credit items in the Profit and Loss columns exceed the debit items by $7,340. This is the amount that appeared as the credit balance in the Profit and Loss account in the ledger. Moreover, the total debits in the Balance Sheet columns exceed the credits by $7,340. In the ledger the credit balance in the Profit and Loss account is actually transferred to the proprietor's personal account. To simulate this transfer on the work-sheet it is customary to "balance" the Profit and Loss columns by adding the excess of debits or credits to the column containing the lesser total. The same procedure may be applied to the Balance Sheet columns of the work-sheet. The data in the Profit and Loss columns now are sufficient for preparing a formal statement of income and expense. The data in the Balance Sheet columns contain information for preparing a balance sheet. The form and arrangement of balance sheets and statements of income and expense will be discussed in detail in chapters xii and xiii.

Post-closing trial balance.—A trial balance prepared after all adjusting and closing entries have been posted is known as a "post-closing" trial balance. It consists of the asset, liability, and proprietorship account balances which have not been closed; these accounts contain totals identical with those appearing in the Balance Sheet columns of the work-sheet (after the Profit and Loss credit has been closed to the Personal account).

Alternative method of adjusting the ledger data.—In the foregoing illustrations the adjustments of the books have necessitated the introduction of some additional expense and income accounts which were not used during the period of business operations. These new accounts were opened at the time the ledger balances were adjusted, and were closed immediately to the Profit and Loss account.

It is possible to adjust assets and liabilities without introducing any new accounts, and such a method is often employed by accountants. Let us illustrate with the case of insurance. In the ledger account of D. L. Keller, the original debits for insurance were made to an Insurance account to the extent of $840. One-third of this total was later transferred to an Insurance Expense account and from there closed to the Profit and Loss account. The alternative method would be to handle the adjustment of the Insurance account and closing of the Insurance Expense account with one journal entry. This would be accomplished by regarding the Insurance account as containing expense data, a part of which should be periodically transferred to the Profit and Loss account. The amount transferred would be summarized in the statement of income and expense. The remaining debit balance would represent an asset in the form of unexpired insurance protection; it would appear on a balance sheet prepared at the time. The journal entry to adjust the Insurance account by removing the expired value would be:

Profit and loss.....................	$280.00	
Insurance..............................		$280.00

This journal entry serves both as an adjusting and closing entry. It removes the expense element from the Insurance account and transfers it directly to the Profit and Loss account. The Insurance account after this entry would appear as follows:

INSURANCE

Jan. 1	....	$840.00	Dec. 31	Profit and loss.......	$280.00
				Balance.............	560.00
		$840.00			$840.00
Dec. 31	*Balance*............	$560.00			

The same method illustrated here may be applied to all prepaid items, such as supplies, interest, rent, etc. It is also applicable to the deferred credits to income. For example, in the case of advance rentals, the income credits could have been accumulated in an account entitled "Rent Income" (or merely "Rent"). The balance of Advance Rentals in the ledger of D. L. Keller was $1,900. If the credits had been accumulated in an account entitled "Rent Income," an entry to remove the earned income from this account on December 31 would be:

Rent income	$950.00	
Profit and loss		$950.00

The Rent Income account after the entry would be:

RENT INCOME

Dec. 31	Profit and loss	$ 950.00	July 1		$1,900.00
	Balance	950.00			
		$1,900.00			$1,900.00
			Dec. 31	*Balance*	$ 950.00

The balance in the Rent Income account is a liability item and would appear on a balance sheet of December 31.[1]

Payment and receipt of accrued items.—In the accounts of D. L. Keller the adjustment of the Salaries account necessitates the opening of a special liability account, Accrued Salaries Payable. After the summarization, this account carries a credit balance of $400. When the total salaries of $800 are paid one week later the following entry will be made:

Salaries	$400.00	
Salaries payable	400.00	
Cash		$800.00

[1] The practitioner does not always keep the various accrued and deferred items segregated in the accounts. Very often a single account will be used to record current operations, as well as items which must be "deferred." In some cases a single account such as Interest Expense may contain data which represent current interest expenses and prepaid interest, and at times be used to "accrue" the interest expenses payable.

Of the total cash expended, one-half liquidates the accrued liability for salaries of the preceding period; the other half is debited as a current expense to Salaries. Similar treatment may be given to the accrued receivable items. For example, when cash is received by D. L. Keller to apply on interest income, part of the amount will be credited against the $84 Interest Receivable. The journal entry to record the receipt of $250 cash for interest would be:

Cash	$250.00	
Interest receivable		$ 84.00
Interest income		166.00

QUESTIONS ON CHAPTER XI

1. State in detail the proper sequence of operations in adjusting and closing a set of books.
2. What is the relation of the statement of income and expense to the Profit and Loss account? Does it carry the same information? Is the information classified in the same way?
3. What are closing entries? Is it conceivable that some methods of handling the accounts might merge the adjusting and closing of the accounts into the same entries? If so, what would be examples?
4. Trace the sequence of the net profit credit as it appears in the Profit and Loss account until it reaches its final resting-place in the ledger of a single proprietorship; a partnership; a corporation.
5. What is the work-sheet? What is its relation to the ledger accounts? to the journal?
6. Describe the eight-column work-sheet. At what stage of the closing process should it be prepared? Of what service is it?
7. Describe the entry of the adjustment for the merchandise inventories in the work-sheet.
8. Why is it advisable to prepare the financial statements directly from the work-sheet before journalizing the adjusting and closing entries?
9. How would you proceed to obtain a balance sheet and a statement of profit and loss from the accounts after all adjustments and closing entries have been made?

CHAPTER XII

THE BALANCE SHEET

(A SUMMARY OF FINANCIAL STATUS)

The study of accounting began with the balance-sheet equation as the basis for the entire system of debit and credit. All business transactions were interpreted in terms of their effects on the balance-sheet elements—assets, liabilities, and proprietorship. Moreover, the whole system of journals and ledgers was explained as being primarily a set of classifying devices for accumulating the data of a balance sheet. We now come to an analysis of the construction of the balance sheet—the basic accounting report summarizing financial status. Other titles under which the balance-sheet data sometimes appear are "Statement of Resources and Liabilities," "Financial Statement," "Statement of Financial Condition," "Statement of Assets and Liabilities."

The work-sheet of D. L. Keller, illustrated in chapter xi, lists a series of balance-sheet items; these amounts comprise the post-closing trial balance, and represent the "open" balances in the asset, liability, and proprietorship accounts. Such balances are the data for the balance sheet and will serve in this chapter as the basis for illustrating the arrangement of balance-sheet data. The balance sheet of D. L. Keller is shown on page 149.

The balance-sheet elements may be grouped in terms of characteristics which affect financial status. Some of the bases on which accounting data may be segregated and summarized have been discussed at various points in previous chapters. The present discussion of the bases for summarizing data will therefore involve some repetition.

Assets grouped according to intended use by the enterprise.—Classification of accounting data is affected by the uses for which the data are secured. This general fact was discussed at some length in chapter ii, and has been illustrated from time to time in the explanation of double-entry theory and technique. This suggests also that grouping of the assets might well be in terms of the intended uses to which they are to be placed. Such a basis for grouping assets leads to an underlying distinction between current and fixed assets.

D. L. KELLER

BALANCE SHEET—DECEMBER 31, 19__

ASSETS		
Current assets:		
Cash		$ 1,400.00
Notes receivable		5,000.00
Accounts receivable	$17,500.00	
Allowance for bad debts	1,469.00	16,031.00
Merchandise inventory		8,900.00
Insurance (unexpired)		560.00
Interest receivable		84.00
Office supplies		350.00
		$32,325.00
Fixed assets:		
Furniture and fixtures	$ 2,250.00	
Allowance for depr.	450.00	$ 1,800.00
Delivery equipment	$ 2,800.00	
Allowance for depr.	1,680.00	1,120.00
Buildings	$21,000.00	
Allowance for depr.	6,840.00	14,160.00
Land		4,500.00
		$21,580.00
Total		$53,905.00

LIABILITIES AND PROPRIETORSHIP	
Current liabilities:	
Accounts payable	$ 3,025.00
Notes payable	4,920.00
Interest payable	270.00
Salaries payable	400.00
Advance rentals	950.00
	$ 9,565.00
Fixed liabilities:	
Mortgage payable	$18,000.00
Total liabilities	$27,565.00
Proprietorship:	
D. L. Keller, capital	$19,000.00
D. L. Keller, personal	7,340.00
Total proprietorship	$26,340.00
Total	$53,905.00

Current assets.—Current assets are those assets which are intended to be consumed or converted into other assets in the normal course of business operations within a relatively short period of time. This definition requires some amplification. First, it must be said that current assets include cash, an asset continuously disposed of and replenished in normal business operations. Second, current assets are "consumed or converted"; this qualification brings into this class the supplies to be consumed in business operations and the merchandise to be sold to customers for cash or receivables. Broadly interpreted, the phrase "consumed or converted" will apply also to other types of receivables and the prepaid expenses: the receivable items will be converted into cash; the prepaid expenses will be consumed by the enjoyment of valuable services rather than tangible goods. Third, the assets must be consumed or converted "within a relatively short period of time." Just what constitutes a relatively short period of time cannot be stated arbitrarily. For most purposes, however, current assets are those which continue for only one year, or at most two years. Assets which meet the general requirements referred to above, but which are of longer duration, should be carefully analyzed before being given a final classification as "current." Fourth, the asset is affected by the "normal course of business operations." For example, it may be that a store building is to be sold for cash within the ensuing twelve months. Such intended disposal is not within the scope of the normal operations of a mercantile concern and cannot operate to classify a store building as a current asset of such an enterprise. Finally, the whole problem of classification is affected by the "intention" of the management. Many assets may from time to time be readily salable; but if there is no intention of disposing of them, they cannot be regarded as current assets. This aspect of intent is especially important in the classification of land, securities, etc. Intention implies an ability to realize the intended use. For example, it assumes that accounts receivable are collectible. If they are not collectible, the difficulty must be solved, not by reclassifying the accounts receivable, but by eliminating them from the balance sheet.

It is apparent that the essence of the current-asset classification is not to be found in any physical characteristics of the assets; current assets comprise such varied tangible items as cash, supplies, and merchandise,[1] as well as the intangible rights growing out of contractual agreements, such as accounts and notes receiv-

[1] Merchandise may, of course, consist of land, buildings, machinery, bonds, or receivables, as well as the conventional forms of personal property.

able, prepaid rent, interest, or insurance, bonds, and shares of stock. The current-asset classification is, in the last analysis, affected by the viewpoint of a specific enterprise. A building which is sold as the stock-in-trade of a real estate company cannot be regarded as the stock-in-trade of a mercantile concern which purchases the building as a place of business. Any asset may be classified as a current asset of a specific enterprise if the enterprise intends that it shall be consumed or converted into other assets in the normal course of business operations within a relatively short period of time.

The balance sheet should be prepared so as to segregate the current assets of an enterprise. The prepaid expenses (frequently referred to as "deferred charges"), the accrued receivables, and the short-term investments are often given separate classification under the headings just mentioned. Similarly the cash, receivables, and merchandise are sometimes designated "quick" assets, as being particularly susceptible to realization in the form of cash. In the balance sheet of D. L. Keller, the following assets may be said to meet the requirements of the current-asset classification just discussed: "Cash," "Accounts receivable," "Notes receivable," "Merchandise inventory," "Interest receivable," "Office supplies," "Insurance (unexpired)."

Fixed assets.—Fixed assets likewise are to be differentiated in terms of the purpose for which they are held by an enterprise. They are assets which it is intended shall *not* be consumed or otherwise disposed of within a relatively short period of time. Ordinarily the class includes such tangible property as land, buildings, machinery, fixtures; also certain long-term intangible assets which increase the earning capacity of a given enterprise, such as patents, copyrights, franchises, good-will, etc. It may also include securities held as long-term investments by an enterprise. The fixed-asset classification is sometimes set forth as comprising only the tangible fixed assets used in the main business operations, with intangibles and long-term investments finding their place in the balance sheet under separate headings.

Some attempt has been made to differentiate fixed assets from current assets on the basis of certain physical characteristics, and in many cases the plan has proved useful. For example, fixed assets have been said to be those which serve the enterprise in their original form without physical depletion by use in the enterprise. This criterion serves to distinguish a machine from the supplies used in maintaining it, but will not hold when applied to certain other fixed assets such as timber lands, stone quarries, or clay pits, which are subject to depletion. Fixed assets are sometimes said to be those which remain in an enterprise a long period of time. This designation serves to classify many fixed assets, but it would not be applicable to a parcel of land which is to be sold in accord with a proposed change in plant location. Ease of convertibility into cash is sometimes suggested as the basis for distinguishing current and fixed assets. This characteristic will not serve generally as the sole criterion for recognizing current and fixed assets; for office supplies to be consumed may have practically no cash value, whereas a building may be desired by several buyers who stand willing to purchase it for cash at any time. The ultimate criterion of a fixed asset is its intended use by the enterprise over a relatively long period of time. The assets of D. L. Keller which appear to meet this qualification are: "Furniture and fixtures," "Delivery equipment," "Buildings," "Land."

Liabilities grouped according to length of life.—Liabilities may be grouped in terms of various characteristics, such as "amount involved," "security pledged," or "length of life." The last of these three bases is of most importance to management, for it determines the amounts of cash to be needed from time to time for payment of the liabilities; this basis also makes possible additional subdivision in terms of security pledged, if such subdivision is useful in expressing financial status.

Current liabilities.—Current liabilities are those which in the normal course of business operations will be liquidated within a relatively short period of time; they may be secured or unsecured. They include accounts payable to merchandise vendors; short-term notes payable to banks; and miscellaneous amounts payable in the near future for such expenses as wages, interest, taxes. The amounts payable for the current expenses are sometimes given a separate grouping on the balance sheet under the heading

"Accrued expenses" or "Accrued expenses payable." A special type of current liability is that sometimes grouped under the heading "Deferred credits" or "Deferred credits to income." It includes those credits made when assets are received in advance of certain income operations, such as cash received by real estate operators from tenants for rent, or by brokerage houses from customers to serve as margins or commissions. The balances remaining in such accounts represent liabilities, and appear under such titles as "Advance rentals," "Commissions prepaid," "Advance interest received," etc. The accounts in the balance sheet of D. L. Keller which may be listed as current liabilities are Accounts Payable, Notes Payable, Advance Rent Income, Interest Payable, and Salaries Payable.

Fixed liabilities.—Fixed liabilities comprise the long-term obligations of an enterprise, whether secured or unsecured by the pledging of specific assets. They include mortgages payable, bonds payable, long-term notes, debentures, or other debts which do not mature until after a relatively long period of time; the periods may vary in length from approximately one or two years to much longer periods such as twenty, or even fifty, years. The only liability of D. L. Keller which would be classed as a fixed liability is the "Mortgage payable."

Proprietorship subdivided as permanent and temporary contributions of capital.—The term "proprietorship" includes the various aspects of the proprietors' rights in an enterprise. Other expressions used to designate proprietorship are "net worth," "net capital," "net assets." Proprietorship includes two basic sub-divisions: (1) the original or permanent capital contributions; and (2) the fluctuating accumulations of profits from various periods of operations. In the single proprietorship or partnership form of enterprise, the permanent or original contributions are designated as "capital"; the fluctuations in proprietorship are recorded in "Personal" accounts. The original corporate proprietorship arises from the sale of capital stock; it is not disturbed by increases or decreases resulting from operations. The profits or losses are posted to an account entitled "Surplus," which appears on the balance sheet as a proprietorship item. The surplus proprietorship sometimes appears on the balance sheet in subdivisions, under such titles as "Reserves," "Reserve for plant extension," "Reserve for contingencies," etc..

Illustrations of proprietorship section of the balance sheet.—The assets and liabilities on the balance sheet of D. L. Keller would serve equally well to illustrate typical assets and liabilities of a partnership or corporation. The proprietorship section, however, would need to be revised to indicate the proper division of proprietorship for these other forms of business organization. The proprietorship section for D. L. Keller appears as follows:

Proprietorship:	
D. L. Keller, capital	$19,000.00
D. L. Keller, personal	7,340.00
Total	$26,340.00

The total proprietorship, which is here shown as $26,340, might also appear on a balance sheet as the investment of two or more partners:

Proprietorship:	
D. L. Keller, capital	$10,000.00
J. D. Persons, capital	9,000.00
D. L. Keller, personal	5,340.00
J. D. Persons, personal	2,000.00
Total	$26,340.00

Likewise, this same total proprietorship could be expressed as the ownership of a group of stockholders in a corporation:

Proprietorship:	
Capital stock	$19,000.00
Surplus	7,340.00
Total	$26,340.00

The "Surplus" may, of course, be subdivided to include various "reserve" items. The balance sheet of D. L. Keller, revised to represent the balance sheet of a corporation with equal proprietorship might appear as follows:

KELLER MERCANTILE COMPANY

Balance Sheet—December 31, 19—

ASSETS

Current assets:		
Cash		$ 1,400.00
Notes receivable		5,000.00
Accounts receivable	$17,500.00	
Reserve for bad debts	1,469.00	16,031.00
Merchandise inventory		8,900.00
Interest receivable		84.00
Prepaid insurance		560.00
Office supplies		350.00
		$32,325.00
Fixed assets:		
Furniture and fixtures	$ 2,250.00	
Reserve for depr.	450.00	$ 1,800.00
Delivery equipment	$ 2,800.00	
Reserve for depr.	1,680.00	1,120.00
Buildings	$21,000.00	
Reserve for depr.	6,840.00	$14,160.00
Land		4,500.00
		$21,580.00
Total		$53,905.00

LIABILITIES AND PROPRIETORSHIP

Current liabilities:	
Accounts payable	$ 3,025.00
Notes payable	4,920.00
Interest payable	270.00
Salaries payable	400.00
Advance rent income	950.00
	$ 9,565.00
Fixed liabilities:	
Mortgage payable	$18,000.00
Total liabilities	$27,565.00
Proprietorship:	
Capital stock	$19,000.00
Surplus	2,000.00
Reserve for contingencies	5,340.00
Total proprietorship	$26,340.00
Total	$53,905.00

Working capital and fixed capital.—"Working capital" is a term frequently encountered in business practice and used by banks as synonymous with "current assets." The use of the term "capital" to refer to the assets of an enterprise, rather than to the proprietors' equities in the assets, runs counter to the terminology introduced in previous chapters of this text. The practice illustrates one of the confusions of terms with which the accountant must deal intelligently if he is to serve business men and financial institutions in the preparation of accounting statements. "Net working capital" is the amount by which the current assets exceed the current liabilities in a particular balance sheet. In the balance sheet of D. L. Keller, the current assets (including the deferred and accrued items) total $32,325; the current liabilities (including deferred and accrued items) amount to $9,565; the resulting net working capital is $22,760. The term "fixed capital" is used synonymously with fixed assets. "Net fixed capital" is the difference in value between the fixed assets and the fixed liabilities. The total of the fixed assets on the balance sheet of D. L. Keller is $21,580; the total of the fixed liabilities is $18,000; the resulting net fixed capital amounts to $3,580. The sum of the net working capital and the net fixed capital is, of course, equal to the total net worth of an enterprise. In the balance sheet of D. L. Keller, the total of the net working capital $22,760, plus the net fixed capital $3,580, equals $26,340, the total net worth or proprietorship shown on the balance sheet.

Sequence of balance-sheet items.—In the foregoing illustrations of the balance sheets, the current assets and the current liabilities have been placed in the first positions of the left and right columns, respectively. This arrangement assumes that the assets most readily reducible to cash are those of greatest importance and that the liabilities which must be paid first are those of greatest significance. Some individuals may, of course, be primarily interested in the extent and nature of the fixed assets and liabilities; an example would be a prospective creditor who contemplates advancing funds for a long term of years, payment for which is to be secured by special claims on the fixed assets. Some balance sheets display the fixed assets and fixed liabilities as the first items on the balance sheet, with the current items following them. In either method of listing the assets and liabilities, however, the proprietorship should appear on the lower right-hand side.

Another aspect of the arrangement of balance-sheet data is the sequential relation of the assets, liabilities, and proprietorship. All previous discussion of the balance sheet has assumed that data should be arranged with assets in one parallel column and liabilities and proprietorship in another. This arrangement is an expansion of the balance-sheet equation from its general form: $A = L + P$. But the equation may also be expressed as: $A - L = P$; and this statement of the equation gives the cue for arranging all data in one column, setting forth the assets first, with the liabilities subtracted immediately below to reveal the total proprietorship. The first or usual form of the balance sheet is referred to as the "account form"; the second is designated as the "report form." Both are encountered in business practice. The account form lends itself more readily to the presentation of large amounts of elaborate data on one sheet; the report form is sometimes easier for the business man to understand, because it sets forth proprietorship as a residual amount after the subtraction of liabilities from total assets.

Balance sheets may contain a vast amount of detailed data, covering several pages of facts closely printed. Others may be prepared in condensed form, with the explanatory or subsidiary data appearing in attached schedules containing the detailed information. A condensed balance sheet containing the facts appearing in D. L. Keller's balance sheet might appear as follows:

D. L. KELLER

CONDENSED BALANCE SHEET—DECEMBER 31, 19—

Current assets	$32,325.00	Current liabilities	$ 9,565.00
Fixed assets	21,580.00	Fixed liabilities	18,000.00
		Proprietorship	26,340.00
Total	$53,905.00	Total	$53,905.00

Some attempt has been made by business men and accountants to arrive at satisfactory sequences and terminology for balance-sheet data which could be recommended to all business men for use in their reports. Uniform reports would be useful in the analysis of financial condition; they would make possible the comparison of similar items on successive balance sheets of one company or on concurrent balance sheets of similar enterprises.

General rules of balance-sheet construction.—The balance sheet is a report to be used for control by the management of a business enterprise. Accordingly the preparation of the data to appear on the balance sheet is very important. The following suggestions for balance-sheet construction should be studied carefully; all of them cannot be followed in the preparation of every balance sheet, but they should be kept constantly in mind during the preparation of a statement of financial condition.[1]

a) *All assets and liabilities should be stated gross*, with reserves or special deductions indicated on the face of the balance sheet. This is particularly applicable to allowances for bad debts, depreciation, stock discount, etc.

b) *The balance sheet should distinguish current and fixed items.* —This rule applies to both assets and liabilities, and facilitates the computation of net working capital and net fixed capital by examination of the balance sheet.

c) *Group headings and totals should stand out clearly.*—This may be accomplished by larger or heavier lettering, underlining, or indentation of detailed items under the general headings. Subtotals should, if convenient, be extended into a separate column to the right of the detailed items.

d) *Groups should be logically arranged.*—This involves logical order of asset, liability, and proprietorship items. The sequence of current and fixed assets and liabilities should be consistent, within the limits of the same report. The proprietorship items should follow each other in the same portion of the balance sheet; they should not be separated.

All of the general rules laid down in the foregoing statement may, with slight change, be made applicable to the preparation of statements of income and expense, or various subsidiary schedules and reports. The reader should have them in mind when studying the following chapter on the construction of statements of income and expense.

Limitations of the balance sheet for management.—The balance sheet contains important data which may be used by the business manager in the control of his enterprise. It tells him the financial condition at a particular moment, and successive balance sheets provide a "moving" picture of the various stages of financial condition. The comparison of balance sheets, especially when they are prepared uniformly, is very important; it reveals much significant information about the trend of business. But at best

[1] These rules are suggested by a pamphlet published by the Illinois Manufacturers' Cost Association, entitled *The Preparation and Use of Financial Statements.*

the balance sheets can only reveal a succession of conditions. They cannot describe the various business activities which have resulted in the changes. They do not contain a statement of the income and expense transactions during a period of business activity. Such data are, of course, available in the accounts, but they are periodically summarized and their net effect is merged with the proprietorship data. Consequently it is necessary that the balance sheet be supplemented by the income and expense data, which will serve as an explanation of the changes which have occurred in the balance sheets. The net profit or loss, computed by offsetting income and expense items, serves to measure and explain the periodic changes in the proprietorship section of the balance sheet. At times the income and expense data are very important; for some purposes they may be more significant than the data of the balance sheet. The following chapter is devoted to the construction and preparation of the statement of income and expense as a report for the use of the management.

QUESTIONS ON CHAPTER XII

1. Define the term "balance sheet." Name several other titles for the balance sheet.
2. Define or explain the following group titles to be found in the balance sheet: current assets; quick assets; deferred charges to expense; investments; fixed assets; intangible assets; current liabilities; deferred credits to income; net worth or proprietorship.
3. Discuss the differences in the net-worth section of a balance sheet for (*a*) a sole proprietorship, (*b*) a partnership, and (*c*) a corporation.
4. Describe the various common sequences of groups in the balance sheet. Compare their merits and shortcomings, and select the arrangement which seems to you to be most desirable.
5. Contrast the account form and report form of balance sheet. What are the merits of each?
6. Distinguish between the detailed and condensed balance sheets.
7. Would every business have the same items and groups of items in its balance sheet? If not, why not?
8. Discuss the advantages and limitations of a standard form of balance sheet.
9. Discuss the possibilities and the limitations of the balance sheet as a managerial report.

CHAPTER XIII

THE STATEMENT OF INCOME AND EXPENSE

(A SUMMARY OF BUSINESS OPERATIONS)

The statement of income and expense is a summary of the business operations of an enterprise during a period of time; the data are classified in terms of income and expense. The excess of the income or expense gives the net effect of the operations on the financial condition of the enterprise; it explains the net profit or loss during a period of time.

Statement of income and expense summarizes business operations of fiscal period.—The data for a statement of income and expense are obtained directly from the ledger of a business enterprise. Inasmuch as the various income and expense accounts are usually summarized in the Profit and Loss account, the statement of income and expense may be regarded as a transcript of the data appearing therein. The credit or debit balance appearing in the Profit and Loss account thus corresponds to the net profit or loss computed by offsetting the income and expense items in the statement of income and expense.

The statement of income and expense is given various titles in practice, some of which are: "statement of profit and loss," "income statement," "income account," "income sheet," "statement of income," "statement of earnings and expenses," "statement of revenue and expenses," "statement of operations." "Statement of profit and loss" is a title frequently encountered. The heading of the statement of income and expense should include the complete name of the enterprise and the period for which the operations are summarized. Typical headings might be:

D. L. KELLER

STATEMENT OF INCOME AND EXPENSE—JANUARY 1 TO DECEMBER 31, 19__

KELLER WHOLESALE COMPANY

STATEMENT OF INCOME AND EXPENSE—FOR THE YEAR ENDING DECEMBER 31, 19__

Illustration of statement of income and expense.—The Profit and Loss account of D. L. Keller, after the income and expense accounts were summarized therein, carried total credits of $52,334 and total debits of $44,994. These entries gave a resulting credit balance of $7,340, the net profit during the period of business operations from January 1 to December 31, 19—. In the accounts of D. L. Keller this balance was transferred to the D. L. Keller, Personal account, where it was classified as a part of the proprietorship of the enterprise. The statement of income and expense for D. L. Keller sets forth as an administrative report the same information as appears in the Profit and Loss account in the ledger.

Data of the statement of income and expense may be arranged in various ways. The most simple arrangement merely offsets the income and expense items in parallel columns, after much the same manner as they appear in the accounts. The excess can thus be computed and shown clearly at the foot of the statement, where the total income is offset against the total expense. Such a form for the statement of income and expense corresponds to the parallel columns of balance-sheet data, and is sometimes referred to as the "account form." An alternative method of displaying the data is to list all income items first and to subtract the total expense items directly beneath, with the net profit for the period as the remainder. This form is known as the "report form." The statement of income and expense for D. L. Keller might, therefore, appear in either of the arrangements.

Grouping similar income and expense data facilitates interpretation of reports.—Each of the illustrations of the statement of income and expense on page 162 present a simple comparison of income and expense totals, the difference between them being the measure of net profit. But there are other methods of arranging the data from which the net profit is computed, methods that make it possible to reveal special aspects of the income and expense data. Various balances, subtotals, and remainders appear in most statements of income and expense, and are often of great importance for administrative control. The task of preparing a statement of income and expense usually consists of two

D. L. KELLER

STATEMENT OF INCOME AND EXPENSE—JANUARY 1 TO DECEMBER 31, 19—

(Account Form)

EXPENSE		INCOME	
Cost of goods sold	$32,600.00	Sales	$50,950.00
Interest	670.00	Interest	434.00
Taxes	550.00	Rent	950.00
Sales salaries	6,200.00		
Advertising	1,400.00		
Bad debts	1,019.00		
Depreciation	1,625.00		
Office supplies	650.00		
Insurance	280.00		
Total expense	$44,994.00		
Net profit	7,340.00		
Total	$52,334.00	Total	$52,334.00

D. L. KELLER

STATEMENT OF INCOME AND EXPENSE—JANUARY 1 TO DECEMBER 31, 19—

(Report Form)

Income:		
Sales	$50,950.00	
Interest	434.00	
Rent	950.00	
		$52,334.00
Expense:		
Cost of goods sold	$32,600.00	
Interest	670.00	
Taxes	550.00	
Sales salaries	6,200.00	
Advertising	1,400.00	
Bad debts	1,019.00	
Depreciation	1,625.00	
Office supplies	650.00	
Insurance	280.00	
		44,994.00
Net profit		$ 7,340.00

parts: the subclassification of income and expense data, and the offsetting of particular items of income against particular expense items to arrive at significant balances.

Classification of income.—Most enterprises receive the major portion of their income from only a few sources. For a mercantile business, the main source of income would be sales; for a brokerage firm, it would be commissions; for a bank, it would be interest earned; for a real-estate firm, it would be rentals or commissions. The classification of the main sources of income usually takes the form of a classification according to types of customers, products, terms of sale, etc. Very often the subdivision of the income data is recognized only in subsidiary records and reports, which are not made a part of the double-entry accounts. Enterprises usually receive some income from miscellaneous operations incidental to the main purpose of the business. This fact has led many accountants to classify income in terms of its major and minor sources. The major or main business activity is often spoken of as providing the *operating* income, the minor or incidental activities as being the sources of *non-operating* income. Income which is to be grouped in the non-operating classification will vary with the particular industry and enterprise. Interest earned might be an incidental source of income for a retail store; it would be the main source of income for a banking institution.

Classification of expense.—The expense items on the financial reports may also be given their first classification in terms of operating and non-operating items. *Operating* expenses are those connected with or incurred to further the main income-producing operations. *Non-operating* expenses are those not related to or connected with the major operations of the business enterprise. As in the case of income, transactions which would be looked upon as the operating expenses for one firm might be the non-operating expenses for another. The classification of particular expense items into non-operating and operating expenses must differ with each particular industry and enterprise. The non-operating expense items are usually not large in number or amount, and may be listed in the statement of income and expense under the general caption "non-operating expense."[1]

Grouping the data of the statement of income and expense.—It was mentioned earlier in this chapter that advantages might be gained from a series of computations appearing on the face of the statement of income and expense. Some attention will now be devoted to the grouping of the income and expense items. The following arrangement is very frequently encountered:

Gross sales (or other major source of income)		....
Deductions (subtract)		....
Net sales		....
Cost of goods sold (subtract)		....
Gross profit on sales		....
Operating expenses (major items, classified according to system adopted by the enterprise) (subtract)		....
Operating profit		....
Non-operating income (incidental to main activity)	....	
Non-operating expense (incidental to main activity)	....	
		....
Net profit		....

The captions and groupings shown above are not to be regarded as the ideally correct ones, or those which are most commonly encountered in practice. These classes and phases of income and expense data are, however, of such general importance that they should be clearly understood, even though not always explicitly recognized in a statement of income and expense. Accountants are not in complete agreement as to the captions to be given to the various classes of data, although they usually agree on the subdivisions into which the data may be segregated.

[1] The terms "operating" and "non-operating" (although widely used in modern business) must be regarded as unsatisfactory in any treatment of accounting which states that expense and income accounts reflect business "operations." For obviously, if expense and income represent operations, there can be no "non-operating operations." However, the terms "operating" and "non-operating" have received wide approval in modern business practice and will be used in this text as a point of departure for further discussion of the classification problem.

Before discussing the various groups in a statement of income and expense and the data which they include, let us prepare the simple report of D. L. Keller on the basis of the foregoing outline. It would appear as follows:

D. L. KELLER

STATEMENT OF INCOME AND EXPENSE—JANUARY 1 TO DECEMBER 31, 19__

Gross sales		$50,950.00
Cost of goods sold		32,600.00
Gross profit on sales		$18,350.00
Operating expenses:		
Interest	$ 670.00	
Taxes	550.00	
Sales salaries	6,200.00	
Advertising	1,400.00	
Bad debts	1,019.00	
Depreciation	1,625.00	
Office supplies	650.00	
Insurance	280.00	$12,394.00
Operating profit		$ 5,956.00
Non-operating income:		
Interest	434.00	
Rent	950.00	$ 1,384.00
Net profit		$ 7,340.00

Gross sales (gross income).—The gross income classification includes the main sources of income and is generally used as synonymous with operating income. The main source of income to a mercantile enterprise is the sale transaction; accordingly the gross income account generally is entitled "Sales" or "Gross Sales." This account is credited with the total sale price of the merchandise sold to customers; the total includes all items appearing on the invoices and received or receivable from the customers.[1]

Deductions from gross sales—net sales.—Some charges against the gross income are of such nature that they should not be considered as expenses of operation, but rather as cancellations of the

[1] The term "gross income" is given a special meaning in modern income-tax legislation. The federal revenue acts have used the term to include "gains, profits, or income from any source whatsoever." It is, therefore, the sum of all income, including what has been classified above as both operating and non-operating.

original transactions; illustrations are sales returns and allowances. In the case of a sales return, the goods come back to the firm which sold them and are available for resale to other customers. In the case of a sales allowance, the goods are not returned by the customer, but the amount collectible from him is reduced. The amount shown as income from sales is accordingly reduced. For this reason "Sales returns" and "Sales allowances" may be treated in the statement of income and expense as direct deductions from "Gross sales." The resulting balance is entitled "Net sales," and would be set forth as follows:

Gross sales	$86,795.00
Less: Returns and allowances	1,800.00
Net sales	$84,995.00

Cost of goods sold—gross profit on sales.—"Cost of goods sold" is usually not listed with the other expenses, but separately classified in a statement of income and expense. This method of treatment may be justified on the grounds that the relation between the cost price and sale price of goods sold is a very important feature in administrative control. Consequently an arrangement of data which contrasts these items on the face of the statement serves a useful purpose. When "Cost of goods sold" is deducted directly from "Net sales," the resulting balance is entitled "Gross profit on sales." The item "Cost of goods sold" is usually supported by a schedule showing the method of arriving at the amount; in fact, the computation very often appears on the face of the statement of income and expense. The computation of the "Cost of goods sold" and the subtraction from "Net sales" might be set forth as follows:

Gross sales		$86,795.00
Less: Sales returns and allowances		1,800.00
Net sales		$84,995.00
Cost of goods sold		
Merchandise inventory Jan. 1	$20,800.00	
Merchandise purchases	52,000.00	
Total	$72,800.00	
Merchandise inventory Dec. 31	17,500.00	$55,300.00
Gross profit on sales		$29,695.00

In the illustration above, the final inventory is set forth as being $3,300 less than the beginning inventory. This means that the cost value of goods sold is $3,300 greater than the cost value of the goods purchased. Consequently the computation could have been made by simply adding $3,300, the decrease in inventory, to the goods purchased:

Purchases	$52,000.00	
Add: Decrease in inventory	3,300.00	
Cost of goods sold		$55,300.00

This method may be used generally to compute the value of any items which have been disposed of, such as office supplies, factory material, etc. If the ending inventory is smaller than the beginning inventory, the decrease should be added to the total purchases to determine the cost value of goods consumed or sold. If the remaining balance is larger, this excess should be deducted from the total purchases.

The "cost of goods sold" may be affected by several very important transactions, such as purchase allowances and purchase returns. Such data should be subtracted from the total purchases at the end of a fiscal period to determine the net purchases to be accounted for. The "cost-of-goods-sold" section of a statement of income and expense affected by such transactions might appear as follows:

Cost of goods sold:			
Merchandise inventory, Jan. 1, 19—			$15,780.00
Merchandise purchases		$65,640.00	
Less: Purchases returns	$240.00		
Purchases allowances	774.00	1,014.00	
Net purchases			64,626.00
			$80,406.00
Merchandise inventory, December 31, 19—			17,940.00
			$62,466.00

Other expenses subtracted to determine net profit.—The other expenses of operation, exclusive of cost of goods sold, are deducted from the gross profit on sales. The various *operating* expenses usually compose the largest portion of the statement, and a completely classified list of the operating expenses often comprises a very large number of items. The resulting balance, after the operating expenses are subtracted from the gross profit on sales, may be designated as *operating profit.* This term is used to distinguish it from the ultimate net profit computed from all income and expense data. The *non-operating* income and expense may be offset against each other, and the difference added to or subtracted from the operating profit. The sum or remainder is then shown as *net profit*, and corresponds to the balance remaining in the Profit and Loss account after the income and expense items have been closed thereto. Net profit may be regarded as the ultimate objective of the business operations of a private enterprise; the proper determination of this item depends greatly upon adequate definition of income and expense transactions.

Detailed classification of operating expenses.—Most expenses of a business enterprise are incurred for the direct furtherance of the major operations of the firm. The expenses should, if possible, be classified in such a way as to indicate responsibility. The statement of income and expense should contain information which may serve as a measure of the efficiency of the different parts of the enterprise. Such account titles as "Wages," "Interest," "Fuel," and "Supplies," give no indication of the purposes for which wages or interest was paid, fuel or supplies were consumed, or under whose jurisdiction such expenses were incurred. The various bases for grouping expense data will vary with the enterprises maintaining the accounts. Items separately classified by one company may properly be merged in the accounts of another; no classification of expenses will be adequate for all firms or lines of business. One objective, however, may well be kept in view when any data are summarized for the statement of income and expense: the expenses should be classified in terms of the portions of the organization responsible for their occurrence. For one enterprise, this may result in a broad grouping of expenses according to the different territories served; for another, the classification may be begun in terms of types of product or administrative functions. The following list of expense groups is intended to suggest the importance of the problem of expense classification. It should not be regarded as a suitable classification for all purposes and for all firms. It illustrates, however, a classification based on what may be regarded as the functional activities of a business enterprise:

1. Production expenses
2. Marketing expenses
3. Financial expenses
4. Personnel expenses
5. Controller's expenses
6. General administration expenses

The individual expenditures such as taxes, labor, interest, depreciation, etc., should, strictly speaking, all be very carefully apportioned to the various classes of operating expenses; and, in fact, such apportionment actually is achieved by enterprises which attach great importance to the control of expense. There are many cases, however, where a rough-and-ready apportionment is necessary, or where the assignment of certain expenses in their entirety to a particular class may be advisable, even though not strictly scientific. Expense classification is a device established by management for its own use; it should not be allowed to defeat its own practical purposes. The expenses of D. L. Keller, arranged on a functional basis, might be grouped somewhat as follows:

Marketing expenses:			
Sales salaries	$6,200.00		
Advertising	1,400.00	$7,600.00	
Financial expenses:			
Interest	$ 670.00		
Bad debts	1,019.00	1,689.00	
General administration:			
Office supplies	$ 650.00		
Depreciation	1,625.00		
Insurance	280.00		
Taxes	550.00	3,105.00	
Total operating expense			$12,394.00

The classification of the eight expense accounts of D. L. Keller illustrates the difficulties encountered when an adequate grouping of the data is attempted. Some persons might argue, for example, that "Bad debts" should be charged as a marketing expense necessarily incurred in the distribution of merchandise. Likewise, the "Depreciation" might be separated in terms of depreciation on the delivery equipment, the furniture and fixtures, and the building; such subdivision would, for example, make possible the grouping of delivery-equipment depreciation under marketing expenses. The problem of apportioning various expenses to different aspects of the business activity is one of the most important to be solved by the accountant; it is also one about which the least can be said by way of establishing categorical rules for all purposes. Each business man must select the grouping which will be most useful for his own purposes; and the accountant must consider the classification of any group of expenses in terms of the needs of each enterprise.[1]

Other summaries of business operations.—The statement of income and expense is not a summary of all business transactions during a period, for it lists only those transactions entered into directly for the realization of profit. In fact, the Profit and Loss account may be regarded as containing detailed data which would otherwise have found their way directly to some proprietorship account of the balance sheet. There are other balance-sheet accounts which also may be analyzed, the data of which may be set forth in financial reports. Such treatment is very often accorded to the data of the Cash account, which are summarized as the "Statement of Cash Receipts and Disbursements." Although the amount of cash on hand at one time is relatively small, the amount of cash which passes through the deposit accounts of a business is typically very large. The total amount of income earned in a given operating period corresponds in some degree to the amount of cash received. But the cash receipts will not equal the income —or the cash disbursements, the expense—unless the income and expense accounts are all maintained on a "cash basis"; even then,

[1] Compare chapter xxxiii, "Theory of Accounting Classification."

a discrepancy will often result from cash transactions involving the purchase and sale of fixed assets.

Attempts have been made by groups of business men to standardize the financial summaries of business operations used in their trade or industry. The reports suggested by them are based upon uniform classifications of accounts. Certain governmental bodies also have been instrumental in standardizing accounting reports; for example, the Federal Reserve Board has prescribed a form which must be used by all firms applying to member-banks for loans under this system. Various other governmental agencies have suggested uniform methods of presenting statements of earnings. The Interstate Commerce Commission and the public utility commissions of the different states have prescribed the forms on which reports must be rendered to them. The Internal Revenue Bureau has, of course, standardized the forms on which taxable income must be set forth. Taxable income is not synonymous with the net profit as ordinarily computed by business men; the revenue act specifically exempts certain types of income from taxation, as well as disallows the deduction of some of the usual items of expense.[1]

The statement of income and expense is a useful device in the control of business policies and administration. When expense and income items are properly classified, the report is the basis for placing responsibility and rewarding efficiency within an organization. It serves to inform interested outside parties of the progress of the enterprise. In many instances the statement of income and expense is more important than the balance sheet.

Summary.—This chapter concludes the discussion of the general technique of accounting classification and summarization. But there are many specialized devices of double-entry accounting which have been developed both to reduce the labor of bookkeeping and to increase the value of the results which may be obtained by the accounting process. Some of them will be discussed at length in the following chapters. Those readers who do not wish

[1] The form and arrangement of the summaries of business operations are discussed at length in chapter xxxv, entitled "Summaries of Business Operations."

to pursue the study of accounting technique beyond the generalizations already established may well turn immediately to the sections on Accounting Valuation and on Interpretation of Accounting Data.

QUESTIONS ON CHAPTER XIII

1. What is a statement of income and expense? Name several other possible titles for this statement and comment on their acceptability. Explain fully the relation of the statement of income and expense to the balance sheet.
2. Statements of income and expense show much greater variations in form and content than balance sheets. Explain.
3. Distinguish clearly between a statement of income and expense and a statement of cash receipts and disbursements.
4. Define: "gross income," "deductions from gross income," "cost of goods sold," "gross profit on sales," "operating expenses," "operating profit," "non-operating income," "non-operating expenses," "net profit."
5. What is gained by grouping separately the operating and non-operating elements of a statement of income and expense?
6. Distinguish "deductions from gross income" from "expenses." Give illustrations of deductions from gross income.
7. Discuss the advantages and limitations of a standard statement of income and expense. The government uses a standard form for income-tax-return purposes. Might such a statement well be adapted to managerial needs?
8. From a managerial point of view, would you say the statement of income and expense was more or less useful than the balance sheet?

C. SPECIALIZED CLASSIFYING DEVICES

CHAPTER XIV

SPECIAL COLUMNS IN THE JOURNAL

The complete double-entry accounting process has been explained and illustrated in the foregoing chapters. Business transactions are first recorded on documents or vouchers, such as invoices for sales on account, invoices for purchases on account, cash-sales tickets, cash-disbursements memoranda, labor tickets, supplies requisitions, sales-return memoranda, credit memoranda for purchase returns, cash-deposit tickets, etc. The data are then recorded in a preliminary classifying device known as the journal, after which they are transferred to and reclassified in the accounts of the ledger. The ledger data are periodically summarized into a balance sheet and a statement of income and expense. The process of summarization is usually preceded by a series of adjustments of certain accounts. The accounting data of every business transaction appear in two parts of the double-entry records —in the journal and in the ledger.

Standard journal and ledger subject to certain limitations.— A journal arranged according to the standard form carries a record of each transaction as a unit; such a record provides a chronological statement of the business activities. Any person who inspects the journal and reads all explanatory matter carefully will be able, it is intended, to gain a clear idea of each transaction which has occurred. He will not, however, be able to determine with accuracy the trend of the condition of the business; for the data affecting particular ledger accounts are not grouped within the journal. The reader of the journal will be compelled to trace similar transactions to the ledger in order to determine the facts concerning any asset, liability, proprietorship, income, or expense item. If a business manager wished, for example, to know the total sales during a given period, he would be required to seek this information in the Sales account.

A journal in which all the transactions of an enterprise are entered is often referred to as a "general journal," to differentiate it from a "specialized journal" in which only certain kinds of transactions appear. A general journal need not, however, always assume the standard form that has been illustrated in previous chapters. Use of the two-column, or "standard," journal necessitates separate posting of each debit and each credit, even to those accounts which are affected frequently by the transactions of a business. It is desirable that some method be devised to reduce the amount of labor involved in maintaining the accounts, especially if this can be accomplished without diminishing the usefulness of the data. This chapter illustrates some ways in which *special columns* make the journal a more useful device for administrative control.

The purposes of the journal and ledger are to classify and summarize data for use in administrative control. The journal and ledger contain the same facts, differently arranged. In the standard journal only one column is provided for debits; only one for credits. The effects of all transactions must be classified as debits or credits in these two columns. In the ledger the data are arranged in debit and credit columns also, but the data are no longer segregated according to transactions; the accounts are the units for assembling the data in the ledger. The transfer of data from the journal to the ledger, then, is primarily a method of regrouping the debits and credits in terms of accounts rather than transactions. The regrouping necessitates, of course, rewriting in the accounts all the money values previously recorded in the journal.

Special columns in journal provide preliminary classification of data and reduce the task of posting.—The standard form of journal is subject to two very important limitations: it provides no preliminary classification of similar accounting data, and it entails a vast amount of posting labor in the transfer of data to the ledger. By the introduction of *special columns* in the journal, both of these limitations can be removed. Special columns are additional columns placed parallel to the regular debit and credit columns of the standard two-column journal. Each of the special columns is used to accumulate debits or credits to some specific ledger account, the title of which appears at the head of the column. The amounts to be posted to these accounts are entered in the respective special columns, which provide a preliminary classification of similar data before transfer to the ledger, and also make possible the posting of these data in totals rather than in numerous small amounts. All other debits and credits are listed in general columns, which are used in exactly the same manner as the columns of the standard journal; each general column may be headed "Sundry," to indicate the fact that it contains debits or credits to several accounts.

The following illustration shows the arrangement of a general journal—a special-column general journal—which contains

SPECIAL-COLUMN GENERAL JOURNAL

(Two Special Columns)

Date	Account Titles	Sundry Dr.	A/c Rec. Dr.	Sundry Cr.	Sales Cr.

special columns to accumulate debits to the Accounts Receivable account and credits to the Sales account.

Journals may contain a large number of special columns, depending upon the frequency with which certain debits or credits result from the transactions. The selection of special columns is affected by the desirability of a preliminary classification of certain data before they are posted; also the number of times certain similar data are recorded. Some of the types of data usually given special columns in the general journal are the following: debits to cash; credits to cash; debits to accounts receivable; credits to accounts receivable; debits to accounts payable; credits to accounts payable; debits to purchases; credits to sales. Under given conditions any type of entry may be accorded a special column, depending upon the importance of the data and the frequency of the transactions. Illustrations of special-column headings less frequently encountered are sales discounts, purchases discounts, sales returns, sales allowances; special columns may also be used for specific frequently recurring expenses.

Special-column journal illustrated.—The advantages of special columns in the journal may be illustrated by journalizing and posting the following transactions:

Jan. 1. Investment by O. S. Wildman of $6,000 cash in a business enterprise. Payment of January rent in cash, $200.
2. Purchase on account from F. R. Ormes, $4,000 worth of merchandise.
3. Sale on account to J. L. Palmer, $1,000.
4. Cash sales to sundry customers, $1,200.
5. Sale on account to C. R. Heeter, $800.
6. Cash purchase of merchandise, $1,600.
8. Payment of one-half of account due to F. R. Ormes. Sale on account to B. Clows, $1,400.
9. Purchase on account from J. C. Dunn, $1,000.
10. Receipt of advertising bill from L. K. Watson, $180.
12. Receipt of cash from J. L. Palmer in full payment of his accounts. Sale to J. Hawkins, $1,500, $700 being paid in cash with balance remaining on open account.
15. Cash disbursement for weekly pay-roll: Sales salaries, $180; office salaries, $120.
Sale to H. Bent, $1,600 on account.

The transactions shown above are entered in a journal on page 179 which contains special columns for debits to Accounts Receivable and for credits to Sales. The use of special columns in the journal for Accounts Receivable debits and Sales credits makes it possible to post these items in total after they have been summarized at the foot of the journal page. The debits to Accounts Receivable and the credits to Sales need not be posted individually. To indicate that the posting of these items has not been overlooked, however, the folio column should contain some symbol; often a check mark (√) is used. All other debits and credits should be posted in the usual way. Ledger page numbers for the amounts posted individually should, of course, be entered in the folio column of the journal as a cross-index to the record of

O. S. WILDMAN

Special-Column Journal (Page 1)

19—				Sundry Dr.	A/c Rec. Dr.	Sundry Cr.	Sales Cr.
Jan.	1	Cash	1	$ 6,000 00			
		O. S. Wildman, capital	4			$ 6,000 00	
		Original investment					
		Rent	9	200 00			
		Cash	1			200 00	
		Payment of January rent					
	2	Purchases	6	4,000 00			
		Accounts payable	3			4,000 00	
		Purchase from F. R. Ormes					
	3	Accounts receivable	√		$1,000 00		
		Sales	√				$1,000 00
		Sale to J. L. Palmer					
	4	Cash	1	1,200 00			
		Sales	√				1,200 00
		Misc. cash sales					
	5	Accounts receivable	√		800 00		
		Sales	√				800 00
		Sale to C. R. Heeter					
	6	Purchases	6	1,600 00			
		Cash	1			1,600 00	
		Misc. cash purchases					
	8	Accounts payable	3	2,000 00			
		Cash	1			2,000 00	
		Paid on acct. to F. R. Ormes					
		Accounts receivable	√		1,400 00		
		Sales	√				1,400 00
		Sale to B. Clows					
	9	Purchases	6	1,000 00			
		Accounts payable	3			1,000 00	
		Purchase from J. C. Dunn					
	10	Advertising	10	180 00			
		Accounts payable	3			180 00	
		Bill rendered by L. K. Watson					
	12	Cash	1	1,000 00			
		Accounts receivable	2			1,000 00	
		Received from J. L. Palmer					
		Cash	1	700 00			
		Accounts receivable	√		800 00		
		Sales	√				1,500 00
		Sale to J. Hawkins					
	15	Sales salaries	7	180 00			
		Office salaries	8	120 00			
		Cash	1			300 00	
		Weekly pay-roll					
		Accounts receivable	√		1,600 00		
		Sales	√				1,600 00
		Sale to H. Bent					
		Sundry debits	√	$18,180 00			
		Accounts receivable debits	2		$5,600 00		
		Total debits	√	$23,780 00			
		Sundry credits	√			$16,280 00	
		Sales credits	5				$7,500 00
		Total credits	√			$23,780 00	

these transactions in the accounts. Posting to the accounts which are given special columns in the journal may take place whenever the recorded data fill the columns of a journal page, or at other times suitable to the conditions under which the accounting records are maintained. The totals in the special columns may either be carried forward from page to page as subtotals or be added only at the times the totals are posted. The amounts in the special columns are first totaled; their sums are then posted to the accounts bearing the titles of the special-column headings. These summary posting entries take the place of the series of postings of individual amounts that would have been made from time to time if no special columns had been introduced into the standard journal. At the foot of the special-column journal previously illustrated, there is shown a debit of $5,600 to be posted to Accounts Receivable, also a credit of $7,500 to be posted to Sales. These totals replace the larger number of entries which would have been posted separately from a journal of the standard form. The data in the special-column journal were proved by adding the totals of each of the columns, and comparing debits with credits.

The total of the debit columns must, of course, equal the total of the credit columns. The accumulated entries in the special columns may be cross-indexed in the same manner as the individual items, with the ledger page numbers being written in the folio columns. This practice was followed in the foregoing journal, but it sometimes requires the use of numerous horizontal lines, especially if the number of special columns is large. In such cases bookkeepers frequently enter the special-column folio numbers on one horizontal line, each ledger-page number appearing directly beneath the total of the special column to which it refers.

The Accounts Receivable account and the Sales account contain one debit and one credit, respectively, after the data of the special columns are posted thereto on January 15. The Accounts Receivable account also contains one credit entry, posted on January 12 from the sundry credit column of the general journal. The Accounts Receivable and Sales accounts would appear as follows on January 15:

ACCOUNTS RECEIVABLE

19—			19—		(Page 2)
Jan. 15	1	$5,600.00	Jan. 12	1	$1,000.00

SALES

19—			19—		(Page 5)
			Jan. 15	1	$7,500.00

Other forms of the special-column journal.—In the journal previously described, only two types of entries have been selected to illustrate the use of the special column. Special columns may, however, be introduced to provide for summarizing any types of similar data before they are transferred to the ledger. The number of special columns may conceivably be increased to cover all the accounts in the entire ledger of a business enterprise. The form of the special-column journal also may be varied to suit the needs of a particular business. The account titles may be placed between the debit and credit columns of the journal, as illustrated on pages 182–83. This journal is divided so as to show all debits on the left side of the sheet and all credits on the right. This arrangement tends to reduce errors of posting to the ledger accounts, for attention of the bookkeeper can be directed to the debit data as a series of postings, to be followed later by transfers of the credit totals. It should be observed also that this journal introduces six special columns for accumulating the data of O. S. Wildman's transactions; consequently the number of entries recorded in the sundry columns is greatly reduced. Of the entire group of entries, only seven require the use of the sundry columns. All the other entries of the transactions shown on this journal find their places in the various special columns, whence they are ultimately posted to the ledger accounts as parts of accumulated totals.

O. S. WILDMAN, SPECIAL-COLUMN JOURNAL

(Page 1)

A/c Rec. Dr.	Purchases Dr.	Cash Dr.	Sundry Dr.	Date 19—		L F	Account Titles and Explanation	Sundry Cr.	Cash Cr.	Sales Cr.	A/c Pay. Cr.
		$6,000 00		Jan.	1	√	Cash				
						4	O. S. Wildman	$6,000 00			
							Original investment				
			$200 00			9	Rent				
						√	Cash		$200 00		
							Payment of January rent				
	$4,000 00				2	√	Purchases				
						√	A/c payable				$4,000 00
							Purchase from F. R. Ormes				
$1,000 00					3	√	A/c receivable				
						√	Sales			$1,000 00	
							Sale to J. L. Palmer				
		1,200 00			4	√	Cash				
						√	Sales			1,200 00	
							Misc. cash sales				
800 00					5	√	Accounts receivable				
						√	Sales			800 00	
							Sale to C. R. Heeter				
	1,600 00				6	√	Purchases				
						√	Cash		1,600 00		
							Misc. cash purchases				
			2,000 00		8	3	Accounts payable				
						√	Cash		2,000 00		
							Paid to F. R. Ormes				
1,400 00						√	Accounts receivable				
						√	Sales			1,400 00	
							Sold to B. Clows				
	1,000 00				9	√	Purchases				
						√	Accounts payable				1,000 00
							Purchase from J. C. Dunn				
3,200 00	*6,600 00*	*7,200 00*	*2,200 00*				*Total forward*	*6,000 00*	*3,800 00*	*4,400 00*	*5,000 00*

(Page 2)

A/c Rec. Dr.	Purchases Dr.	Cash Dr.	Sundry Dr.	Date 19—		L F	Account Titles and Explanation	Sundry Cr.	Cash Cr.	Sales Cr.	A/c Pay. Cr.
$3,200 00	$6,600 00	$7,200 00	$2,200 00	Jan.	9		*Balance forward*	$6,000 00	$3,800 00	$4,400 00	$5,000 00
			180 00		10	10	Advertising				
						√	Accounts payable				180 00
							Bill rendered by L. K. Watson				
		1,000 00			12	√	Cash				
						2	Accounts receivable	1,000 00			
							Received from J. L. Palmer				
		700 00				√	Cash				
800 00						√	Accounts receivable				
						√	Sales			1,500 00	
							Sale to J. Hawkins				
			180 00		15	7	Sales salaries				
			120 00			8	Office salaries				
						√	Cash		300 00		
							Weekly pay-roll				
1,600 00						√	Accounts receivable				
						√	Sales			1,600 00	
							Sale to H. Bent				
$5,600 00	$6,600 00	$8,900 00	$2,680 00				*Totals*	$7,000 00	$4,100 00	$7,500 00	$5,180 00
②	⑥	①	√		15		*Folios*	√	①	⑤	③

The reader should observe the method by which the subtotals accumulated up to January 9 are carried forward on page 2 of the special-column journal. Postings are made of the special-column data on January 15. The posting folios are indicated as ledger page numbers at the foot of each of the special columns; the ledger folios are encircled to distinguish them clearly from other numerals entered in the various columns.

The explanation of each transaction need not always be written out in full. Some enterprises have adopted the practice of numbering serially all business papers which give rise to transactions entered in the general journal. The serial numbers, therefore, may be used to indicate the sources of the journal data and thus make unnecessary the writing of a description of each transaction. Persons interested in verifying the sources of the journal entries can do so by referring to the files of business papers.

Advantages and limitations of special columns in the general journal.—Considerable emphasis has been laid on the advantage of the special column in effecting a reduction in the labor of transferring accounting data from the journal to the ledger. But it also serves another important function—that of providing a preliminary classification of certain information before it reaches the accounts. The special sales column, for example, contains information regarding sales which could not be obtained unless one examined either the Sales account in the ledger or the business papers—sales invoices—on which the data were originally recorded. The special columns may be regarded as accumulating detailed ledger information, which will be transferred in summary to the ledger accounts before they are given a final classification in the ledger.

Useful as the special columns in a journal may be in the preliminary classification and in the posting of data, a special-column general journal is still subject to several very definite limitations. In the first place, it does not permit division of labor, either in journalizing or posting; for only one clerk can use the accounting records, either for journalizing or posting, at one time. Another disadvantage arises from the fact that many transactions do not require the use of special columns. If such transactions comprise a large portion of the business activities, they should be recorded in a separate standard journal; for otherwise they rapidly fill the elaborate special-column journal pages. If the bookkeeper is following the practice of carrying totals forward or of posting them from the foot of each journal page, numerous entries in the sundry debit and credit columns increase the frequency with which the special-column data must be adjusted. The summarization and posting of the special-column data involve considerable work and should be done as infrequently as the form of the journal will permit. A third limitation of the special-column journal is that, of itself, it does not reduce the work of journalizing transactions; in fact it may increase the task of journalizing, because it requires extreme care in entering the data in the proper special columns. Each transaction must be journalized completely. The debit and credit account titles and amounts must all be written in full, even though the explanations be eliminated by the substitution of serial numbers referring to the business papers. The use of serial numbers of business papers (or business vouchers) is not a practice limited to transactions recorded in a special-column journal; in fact, it could be equally well adapted (and often is) for entries in the standard journal.

After all, the special column must be regarded as the expression of a principle in bookkeeping practice rather than as an absolute end in itself. It is a device by which the journal may accumulate data preliminary to summary posting in the ledger, thereby providing significant current information. The principles and advantages of special columns may be enjoyed along with other devices, to be illustrated in chapters xvi and xvii, which reduce the task of journalizing business transactions. One more very important application of the special column as an aid in posting data remains to be discussed, namely, the way in which it facilitates the posting of summary and detailed data concurrently during a period of business operations. This subject is introduced in chapter xv.

QUESTIONS ON CHAPTER XIV

1. It is the function of the books of original entry to provide: (*a*) a chronological record of events; (*b*) the analysis of transactions in double-entry terms; (*c*) a preliminary classification of entries. How satisfactorily does the simple journal meet these requirements?
2. Why is it desirable to provide a preliminary classification of entries when they are first recorded? Answer specifically.
3. What factors govern the selection of columns for a special-column journal? Name the accounts which in most businesses would be given special columns.
4. Under what conditions is the use of the special-column journal to be recommended? Is it a satisfactory record if the volume of transactions is too large for one individual to handle? If the number of accounts having frequent entries is very large?
5. Why do the account titles and explanation appear in the center of the page in some special-column journals? What is the advantage of recording the explanation to the right of the account title rather than beneath it? Why are explanations sometimes omitted and reference made to the original document merely by file number? Suggest other devices for conserving space.
6. Does the adoption of a special-column journal necessitate the discard of the simple journal, or may the two be used together?
7. Describe the process of "proving" the special-column journal. Of what importance is this procedure?
8. Does the use of special columns in the general journal reduce the labor of journalizing transactions?
9. Of what advantages are the special columns for managerial control?

CHAPTER XV

CONTROLLING ACCOUNTS

There may be different grades of accounting data in the records of a business enterprise. This fact has been suggested at various times in previous chapters; it will be discussed and explained at this point as a specialized classifying device which may be used in administrative control.

The principle of controlling and subsidiary data.—All aspects of accounting data are not equally important for administrative control; some information may with advantage be placed before the management in groups or classes rather than as detailed recitals of specific facts. For this reason accounting technique should provide for classification of data in groups defined as broadly as practical purposes will permit. Illustrations of such groups of data appear in accounts such as Buildings, Merchandise, Accounts Receivable, Accounts Payable, and Bonds Payable. Such accounts contain data which show in summary certain aspects of financial status. But there are conditions under which the general information of such accounts is not adequate for the purposes at hand. For example, a plan for replacing or repairing buildings must be based on specific data concerning each factory, warehouse, store building, or garage owned by an enterprise. Likewise the procedure of collecting amounts due from individual customers is dependent upon specific information as to the amounts charged to and received from each debtor.

It is desirable that the accounting records provide a means of displaying concurrently the summary and detailed information concerning any aspect of financial status or operations. And modern practice makes possible the keeping of such data through the principle of summary and subsidiary accounts. The summary accounts are known as *controlling accounts;* they contain in total the subsidiary information appearing in detailed records. The term "controlling" is particularly applicable to this relationship, for the total data in a summary account may be based on computations which are independent of the summation of the detailed records. The controlling accounts thus prove the accuracy of the detailed data which support them.

Records for the controlling and subsidiary data.—The concept of subsidiary data implies a method for maintaining the record of them, as well as a place to marshal such data for use from time to time. In a sense the subsidiary data may be regarded as "duplicate" data, for they do not add to or detract from any of the general information appearing in the controlling accounts. It would be incorrect to add the subsidiary data to amounts contained in the conventional ledger; for the introduction of the data would destroy the equilibrium. The subsidiary data, therefore, must be maintained in separate records which do not affect the equality of total debits and credits. They must be regarded as explanatory, rather than as additional, information concerning financial status or operations.

The subsidiary records may take the form of the conventional ledger accounts, and they usually do take this form in cases where the account which "controls" them (their controlling account) is one affected by both debits and credits during a period of operations. Illustrations of this type are the subsidiary accounts with various assets and liabilities, particularly the accounts receivable from specific customers or payable to individual creditors. Where, however, the controlling account merely accumulates debits or credits, as is usually the case with income and expense accounts, the subsidiary data may be recorded in single columns under appropriate headings. Illustrations of the second type would be the tabular records of sales by departments, prepared from an analysis of the outgoing invoices.

The subsidiary data which support a given controlling account are often spoken of as comprising a *subsidiary ledger;* in contrast to this term, the central or main ledger of an enterprise, in which the controlling accounts appear, is referred to as the *general ledger*. Not all accounts in the general ledger are controlling accounts; many general-ledger accounts are not supported by subsidiary data. The type of ledger illustrated in the preceding chapters has been a "general" ledger; it has been used for all accounts. The subsidiary ledgers are frequently given special names to indicate the nature of the detailed data they contain: illustrations of such titles are "customers' ledger," "creditors' ledger," "bondholders' ledger," "stockholders' ledger," "plant and equipment ledger," etc. The customers' ledger and creditors' ledger are sometimes referred to as the "sales ledger" and "purchases ledger," respectively. These titles were probably selected originally to describe amounts receivable arising from sales and purchases, on the assumption that most merchandise transactions were carried on under credit terms.

Other data are often set forth on the subsidiary ledger pages along with the account titles. Accounts with persons often include: (1) the address of the customer or creditor; (2) the credit limit of the customer; (3) the terms of sale or purchase; (4) the type of business of the customer; (5) the rating which the customer is given by the commercial companies; (6) the prices quoted, etc. An illustration of a subsidiary account for a customer is given below:

Rating	Dun—D-2	Name	Jamestown Automobile Co., Inc.
Business	Auto. Garage & Agency	Address	1425 Cedar Street
			Jamestown, Colorado
Price	40% from list	Terms	2% 10th proximo

Special columns in journal facilitate concurrent posting to controlling and subsidiary accounts.—The posting of accounting information both to controlling accounts and to subsidiary records requires more labor than the maintenance of the summary accounts alone. If the task were to be attempted by using the standard two-column journal for the preliminary classification, there would be need of two ledger-folio numbers in the journal, one to refer to the controlling account and one to the subsidiary account involved. For example, if O. S. Wildman were to decide to maintain subsidiary accounts receivable, he might journalize his first sale on account as follows:

Jan.	3	Accounts Receivable....................... (J. L. Palmer-subsidiary)................ Sales................................... *Sale to J. L. Palmer*	2 5 5	$1,000	00	 $1,000	 00

The first folio numeral, 2, indicates that the debit entry of $1,000 will appear on page 2 of the general ledger. The second numeral, 5, refers to page 5 in the subsidiary ledger of Accounts Receivable—the sales ledger—in which the entry will also be made. The third numeral, which also is 5, is the ledger page for the Sales account in the general ledger of O. S. Wildman, which will be credited $1,000. The task of posting the debit in both the general ledger and subsidiary ledger accounts entails a dual entry for each amount affecting the Accounts Receivable. This duplication of work seems hardly justified unless the controlling account is to be of real use to the management. In fact, one might prefer to dispense with the controlling account entirely, removing the summary data from the general ledger and substituting therefor the data of the subsidiary accounts. If later it should become important to know the total accounts receivable from customers or payable to creditors, these amounts could then be determined by totaling the balances in the subsidiary accounts.

The posting to the controlling accounts is made easier by the use of special columns in the journal. The special columns can be used to accumulate debits and credits to the controlling accounts, the totals of which may be posted from time to time. The subsidiary accounts (which, in the case of accounts receivable in some concerns, may number several thousand) may be posted continuously, thus enabling the management to know at any time the amount receivable from each customer. On the other hand, the general ledger would contain only one account with these customers as a group. The special-column journal on pages 192–93 indicates the method of posting to controlling and subsidiary accounts. The transactions of O. S. Wildman illustrated are the same as those which have appeared in other special-column journals in chapter xiv. This journal differs from the one on pages 182–83 only in the number of special columns and in their arrangement on the page of the journal. Special columns are provided for both debits and credits to Accounts Receivable and Accounts Payable, these being controlling accounts supported by subsidiary data.

No cross-index numerals appear in the vertical folio column, except for amounts recorded in the sundry columns and for data which are to be posted to subsidiary accounts. All entries to Accounts Receivable and Accounts Payable are cross-indexed with the subsidiary ledger by the use of folio numbers written in the vertical folio column. The account title in each case indicates specifically just which customer or creditor is affected by each transaction; the special columns in which the amounts are recorded inform the bookkeeper as to whether the subsidiary entry is intended for the customers' or creditors' ledger. For example, the first transaction affecting a subsidiary account is the purchase of $4,000 worth of goods from F. R. Ormes. The transaction is journalized by writing the account titles "Purchases" and "F. R. Ormes," and by writing the amount "$4,000" in the special columns headed "Purchases" and "Accounts Payable," respectively. No entry is made to either of these latter accounts immediately, but the amount payable to F. R. Ormes is posted at once to the subsidiary account under his name on page 2 of the creditors' (accounts payable) ledger. The totals of the special columns are posted from the second page, where the pages of the general-ledger accounts are indicated by the numerals below the amounts accumulated in each column. This method of entering the ledger folios reduces the amount of vertical space on the journal page required for this purpose.

The reader may have observed that certain cross-index numerals appear to affect different accounts; for example, the numeral 2 is used for postings of three distinct types in the special-column journal illustrated on pages 192–93. The numeral 2 is set opposite the name of F. R. Ormes, as well as B. Clows, in the

SPECIAL-COLUMN JOURNAL

(Illustrating Method of Posting to Controlling and Subsidiary Accounts) (Page 1)

Date		Account Titles	L F	Sundry Dr.	Sundry Cr.	Accounts Receivable Dr.	Accounts Receivable Cr.	Accounts Payable Dr.	Accounts Payable Cr.	Cash Dr.	Cash Cr.	Purchases Dr.	Sales Cr.
Jan.	1	Cash	√							$6,000 00			
		O. S. Wildman, capital	4		$6,000 00								
		Original investment											
		Rent	9	$ 200 00									
		Cash	√								$ 200 00		
		Payment of January rent											
	2	Purchases	√									$4,000 00	
		F. R. Ormes	2						$4,000 00				
		Purchase from F. R. Ormes											
	3	J. L. Palmer	5			$1,000 00							
		Sales	√										$1,000 00
		Sale to J. L. Palmer											
	4	Cash	√							1,200 00			
		Sales	√										1,200 00
		Misc. cash sales											
	5	C. R. Heeter	4			800 00							
		Sales	√										800 00
		Sale to C. R. Heeter											
	6	Purchases	√									1,600 00	
		Cash	√								1,600 00		
		Misc. cash purchases											
	8	F. R. Ormes	2					$2,000 00					
		Cash	√								2,000 00		
		Paid to F. R. Ormes											
		B. Clows	2			1,400 00							
		Sales	√										1,400 00
		Sale to B. Clows											
	9	Purchases	√									1,000 00	
		J. C. Dunn	1						1,000 00				
		Purch. from J. C. Dunn											
		Total forward		*200 00*	*6,000 00*	*3,200 00*		*2,000 00*	*5,000 00*	*7,200 00*	*3,800 00*	*6,600 00*	*4,400 00*

Date		Account Titles	L F	Sundry Dr.	Sundry Cr.	Accounts Receivable Dr.	Accounts Receivable Cr.	Accounts Payable Dr.	Accounts Payable Cr.	Cash Dr.	Cash Cr.	Purchases Dr.	Sales Cr.
Jan.	9	*Balance forward*	√	$ 200 00	$6,000 00	$3,200 00		$2,000 00	$5,000 00	$7,200 00	$3,800 00	$6,600 00	$4,400 00
	10	Advertising	10	180 00									
		L. K. Watson	3						180 00				
		Bill rendered by L. K. Watson											
	12	Cash	√							1,000 00			
		J. L. Palmer	5				$1,000 00						
		Received from J. L. Palmer											
		J. Hawkins	3			800 00							
		Cash	√							700 00			
		Sales	√										1,500 00
		Sale to J. Hawkins											
	15	Sales salaries	7	180 00									
		Office salaries	8	120 00									
		Cash	√								300 00		
		Weekly pay-roll											
		H. Bent	1			1,600 00							
		Sales	√										1,600 00
		Sale to H. Bent											
		Totals		$ 680 00	$6,000 00	$5,600 00	$1,000 00	$2,000 00	$5,180 00	$8,900 00	$4,100 00	$6,600 00	$7,500 00
	15	*Folios*		√	√	②	②	③	③	①	①	⑥	⑤

vertical folio column; it also appears at the foot of the special columns entitled "Accounts Receivable, Dr." and "Accounts Receivable, Cr." The explanation of this fact is as follows: the folio number 2, when set opposite the name of F. R. Ormes, refers to page 2 in the subsidiary accounts-payable ledger—the purchases ledger; the folio number 2, when set opposite the name of B. Clows, refers to page 2 in the subsidiary accounts-receivable ledger—the sales ledger; the numeral 2, when placed at the foot of one of the special columns with Accounts Receivable, refers to page 2 of the general ledger. It is only by circumstance that the number 2 refers to the pages of these particular subsidiary and controlling accounts. (Several other digits are also used as cross-references to more than one part of the accounting records.) Wherever there are several ledgers in a set of accounting records, the pages on each ledger will ordinarily be numbered in sequence, beginning with page 1. Consequently the bookkeeper who is cross-indexing the postings must bear in mind that the folio numbers may refer to any of several ledgers, depending on the folio column in which they appear, as well as the special columns in which the amounts are recorded.[1]

The general-ledger entries which are accumulated in special columns in the journal are Accounts Receivable, Dr. and Cr.; Accounts Payable, Dr. and Cr.; Cash, Dr. and Cr.; Purchases, Dr.; Sales, Cr. The accounts are shown on page 195, as they would appear after the data were posted from the special-column journal. Two of these accounts are controlling accounts: Accounts Receivable and Accounts Payable. The data of the subsidiary ledgers are a part of the general-ledger records. They appear in subsidiary records, to which data are posted directly from the special-column journal, as evidenced by the ledger-folio numbers in the vertical folio column. The subsidiary accounts, as they

[1] The pages in the separate ledgers may, of course, be given special groups of members: for example general-ledger pages may be numbered from 1 to 199; sales-ledger pages from 200 to 399; purchase-ledger pages from 400 to 599; plant-and-equipment-ledger pages from 600 to 699, etc. Or the page numbers in the ledgers may be differentiated in the folio columns by the use of letters or other symbols, such as S1 for page 1 in the sales ledger, P6 for page 6 in the purchases ledger, etc.

ACCOUNTS IN GENERAL LEDGER

19—— CASH (Page 1)

Jan.	15		2	$ 8,900	00	Jan.	15		2	$ 4,100	00

19—— ACCOUNTS RECEIVABLE (Page 2)

Jan.	15		2	$ 5,600	00	Jan.	15		2	$ 1,000	00

19—— ACCOUNTS PAYABLE (Page 3)

Jan.	15		2	$ 2,000	00	Jan.	15		2	$ 5,180	00

SALES 19—— (Page 5)

						Jan.	15		2	$ 7,500	00

19—— PURCHASES (Page 6)

Jan.	15		2	$ 6,600	00						

would appear in the accounts-receivable ledger and accounts-payable ledger are shown below:

ACCOUNTS-RECEIVABLE LEDGER

(Sales Ledger)

(Individual customers' accounts supporting the controlling account *Accounts Receivable* in the general ledger)

H. Bent (Page 1)

Jan.	15		2	$ 1,600	00						

B. Clows (Page 2)

Jan.	8		1	$ 1,400	00						

J. Hawkins (Page 3)

Jan.	12		2	$ 800	00						

C. R. Heeter (Page 4)

Jan.	5		1	$ 800	00						

J. L. Palmer (Page 5)

Jan.	3		1	$ 1,000	00	Jan.	12		2	$ 1,000	00

ACCOUNTS-PAYABLE LEDGER

(PURCHASES LEDGER)

(Individual creditors' accounts supporting controlling account *Accounts Payable* in the general ledger)

J. C. DUNN (Page 1)

Jan.	13					Jan.	9		1	$ 1,000	00

F. R. ORMES (Page 2)

Jan.	8		1	$ 2,000	00	Jan.	2		1	$ 4,000	00

L. K. WATSON (Page 3)

						Jan.	10		2	$ 180	00

The equality of the controlling and subsidiary data may be tested by preparing schedules of the account balances and comparing them with the balances of the controlling accounts. Schedules of both Accounts Receivable and Accounts Payable are shown below:

ACCOUNTS RECEIVABLE
JANUARY 15, 19__

H. Bent	$1,600.00
B. Clows	1,400.00
J. Hawkins	800.00
C. R. Heeter	800.00
TOTAL	$4,600.00

ACCOUNTS PAYABLE
JANUARY 15, 19__

J. C. Dunn	$1,000.00
F. R. Ormes	2,000.00
L. K. Watson	180.00
TOTAL	$3,180.00

The total of $4,600 in the subsidiary schedule of accounts receivable exactly equals the net balance in the Accounts Receivable controlling account; the subsidiary accounts payable total of $3,180 also is equal to the net balance in the Accounts Payable controlling account. The continuous posting of subsidiary data to the accounts with customers and creditors is a necessary procedure in the administration of cash receipts and disbursements. For, unless the data affecting specific individuals are up-to-date, many undesirable mistakes may be made, such as attempts to collect amounts which customers have already paid, failures to prepare correct statements of amounts receivable, or failures to take advantage of purchases discounts available.

There is no general rule which can be laid down covering the question of when and how often one should post data to controlling accounts. Some bookkeepers prefer to post to the general-ledger accounts from the foot of each page. This practice entails considerable labor, but it has the advantage of keeping the general ledger up-to-date. Other workers with accounts adopt the policy of accumulating special-column data over comparatively long periods, such as one or two months. This practice frees the general ledger from much detail and thus facilitates the testing of ledger equilibrium when a trial balance is prepared. It has the disadvantage of postponing the discovery of errors which might be brought to light by a more frequent comparison of controlling accounts with their subsidiary records.

Controlling and subsidiary accounts are the devices generally used for keeping concurrent records of summarized and detailed data. The duplicate entries to controlling and subsidiary accounts do not disturb the equality of general-ledger debits and credits, for the subsidiary data are not recorded in the general ledger. Controlling and subsidiary accounts are not limited in their usefulness to the accounts with the debtors and creditors of an enterprise; they may also be used with data representing other assets. Corporations use subsidiary records of the proprietorship of individual stockholders in their capacities as subscribers to, as well as holders of, shares of stock. The principle of controlling and subsidiary data may be applied to the records covering any aspect of economic status or operations.

QUESTIONS ON CHAPTER XV

1. What is a controlling account? a subsidiary ledger? Give illustrations of each. When is it desirable to adopt a controlling account?
2. Is a controlling account a general-ledger account? Do the subsidiary accounts appear in the general ledger?
3. Would it be desirable to operate many controlling accounts if all transactions were recorded in a two-column standard journal? Is the usefulness of the controlling account promoted by the adoption of special-column journals? Answer specifically in each case.
4. Assuming the existence of accounts-receivable and accounts-payable subsidiary ledgers and the two corresponding controlling accounts, describe in detail the process of posting from the special-column journal to the general ledger and to the subsidiary ledgers. Discuss the relative merits of posting the totals of each page and of carrying forward the totals and of posting the accumulated total at the end of each accounting period.
5. What entries should be made in the ledger-folio column of the special-column journal?
6. The entries affecting the customers' and creditors' accounts should be posted daily (or oftener), whereas the posting to the general ledger may be done when the page is completed or at the end of the accounting period. Why the daily posting to the customers' and creditors' accounts?
7. An entry in a standard two-column journal which affects an account in a subsidiary ledger must be posted both to the subsidiary account and to the controlling account. Why? Do these two postings of a single debit or credit throw the books out of balance or maintain the balance?
8. Are subsidiary ledgers specialized ledgers? Do they facilitate specialization of duties in the accounting organization and specialization of accounting methods?

CHAPTER XVI

SPECIALIZED JOURNALS

Special columns serve to accumulate similar debits or credits in a journal, which may be posted in total to the proper ledger accounts. By this process the task of posting the accounting data is materially reduced, and the general ledger accounts are thus freed of much detail. The special column lightens the otherwise burdensome task of maintaining the subsidiary records. But the use of special columns does not reduce the task of journalizing accounting transactions; for in the special-column general journal every account title must be written out in full, even though the data are posted in summary from the special columns.

Specialized journals reduce labor of journalizing transactions.—Special columns in a journal, then, are a very useful device for preliminary classification and summary posting of similar debits or credits. But the special-column principle may be carried one step farther by actual segregation of the special columns from the columns containing sundry debits and credits. Each special column thus becomes the basis for a separate *specialized journal.* For example, all transactions causing debits to Cash may be recorded on a separate page of a journal or in a separate journal.

The segregation of the special columns into specialized journals does not lessen any of the inherent advantages of special columns for preliminary classification and summary posting. It increases their usefulness in two ways. First, this segregation of the special-column data avoids the necessity of re-writing the title of the account each time a transaction recorded in the special column is journalized. Second, the separation of the journal data makes it possible for several persons to journalize transactions at the same time. This advantage tends to promote efficiency by simplifying the process of classifying the transactions; it also makes it possible for certain bookkeepers to specialize in dealing with the records of certain operations. For example, one clerk may record transactions in a journal which accumulates credits to Sales, another may work with only debits to Cash. Likewise the bookkeepers who post to the ledgers may be assigned the tasks of entering data from certain types of journals only. Several bookkeepers may thus concurrently post to the subsidiary ledgers, or even to the general ledger, if the ledger pages are of the loose-leaf type.

There may be specialized journals maintained to accumulate entries of any type; the specialized journals adopted by a specific enterprise will depend upon the frequency with which certain types of entries recur and upon the extent to which division of labor in journalizing is advantageous. Most enterprises maintain specialized journals for cash and merchandise transactions because of the frequency with which such transactions occur and the necessity of maintaining close control over them. Thus there may be specialized journals in which are accumulated, and from which are posted, the data of all transactions resulting in debits to Cash (cash receipts), credits to Cash (cash disbursements), credits to Sales, debits to Purchases, debits to Notes Receivable, credits to Vouchers Payable,[1] debits to Sales Returns, etc.

Specialized journals illustrated.—The specialized journals vary in form and complexity according to the needs of the enterprise using them. In some instances a single-column journal serves the purposes for which the journal is needed; in other cases the specialized journal may be very complex, with special columns introduced within the specialized journal.

Single-column specialized journal.—A single money column in a specialized journal will prove satisfactory if all the items in the column are to be posted individually to the accounts involved, with the total posted to the opposite side of some other account. The Cash Receipts journal illustrated below is one of this type. The title of this journal indicates that all entries recorded therein refer only to cash receipts. Certain accounts are credited as each

[1] No mention has been made previously of an account entitled "Vouchers Payable." Such an account is sometimes used to accumulate all current liabilities which are to be paid in cash. It comprises accrued expenses payable to employees and dividends or other claims payable to stockholders, as well as the conventional Accounts Payable due to vendors of merchandise or service.

item of cash is received; the titles of these accounts are listed in the column headed "Accounts to Be Credited," and the ledger folios appear in the folio column. Only one debit is made to the Cash account. This comprises the total of all cash receipts, computed by adding the items in the money column. This journal possesses the advantage of summary posting to the Cash account, and provides a preliminary classification of the Cash debits. But it should also be observed that the amount of money involved in each of the nine transactions is recorded only once in the foregoing journal. Moreover, the account title "Cash" is not re-written

CASH RECEIPTS JOURNAL
(Single Column) (Page 1)

19—		Accounts to Be Credited	Explanation	Folio		
June	1	A. C. Miller, capital	Investment	4	$10,000	00
	4	Sales	Cash sales	5	1,200	00
	6	Sales	Cash sales	5	700	00
	8	Sales	Cash sales	5	600	00
	12	Accounts receivable	R. J. James, on account	2	396	00
		Accounts receivable	W. N. Mitchell, on account	2	990	00
		Accounts receivable	L. Cox, on account	2	1,386	00
	15	Accounts receivable	E. L. Parkhurst, on account	2	500	00
		Sales	Cash sales	5	1,200	00
		Cash	Dr.	1	$16,972	00

each time a cash receipt is journalized. These advantages reduce the labor of journalizing to approximately one-half that necessary for the record of these transactions in a general journal. In the specialized journal only ten account titles are written out—those to be credited as a result of the nine transactions, and the Cash account which is to be debited once. Likewise, the writing of the money values is reduced; for the amounts involved are written only once for each transaction, and are then totaled for one summary posting to the Cash account.

A specialized journal with a single money column is restricted in its usefulness to much the same extent as the standard form of general journal. It serves very well for transactions to be posted in total to one account and in detail to others. It also serves where the transactions are identical as to both debits and credits, so that the same total may be posted to two general-ledger accounts. But it has limitations when both controlling and subsidiary accounts are to be posted concurrently. It will serve such requirements only when the transactions are similar, and when only one of the general-ledger accounts affected is a controlling account; in such cases the vertical folio column can be used for cross-reference to the subsidiary records. The total may then be posted to each of the general-ledger accounts from the foot of the column. The Sales Returns journal shown below illustrates this principle:

SALES RETURNS JOURNAL

(Single Column) (Page 1)

19——		Credits to Sales Ledger	Explanation	L F		
Dec.	2	R. U. Straight	Sales Return Memo. #24	24	$ 175	00
	5	I. M. Nott	Sales Return Memo. #25	20	260	00
	7	P. D. Quick	Sales Return Memo. #26	22	384	00
	19	X. L. Ling	Sales Return Memo. #27	19	75	00
	26	F. I. Dodge	Sales Return Memo. #28	9	114	00
			Accounts receivable Cr.	7	$1,008	00
			Sales returns, Dr.	17	$1,008	00

The explanation column of the foregoing Sales Returns journal contains a list of the sales returns "memoranda," that is to say, the business papers containing a detailed record of each transaction. These memoranda are given individual serial numbers, by which they may be identified in case of future reference; the serial numbers may be regarded as a "cross-index" to the original business papers, similar in many ways to the ledger folios which serve as a cross-index to the ledger data.

Special columns in the specialized journals.—The special columns in the general journal provide a preliminary classification of data and help to reduce posting labor; they also facilitate the keeping of controlling and subsidiary records. Special columns may also bring these same advantages to the specialized journals. The advantages are demonstrated by the illustration of the Cash Disbursements journal of J. C. Beals shown on page 204. In the

CASH DISBURSEMENTS JOURNAL
(With Special Columns)

(Page 1)

19—		Account Titles	Explanation	L F	Purchases Dr.	Accounts Payable Dr.	Sundry Dr.
July	1	H. L. Morris	On account	5		$ 82.00	
		Purchases	Miscellaneous	√	$ 140.00		
		A. D. Hole	On account	3		92.00	
		H. A. Brinton	On account	1		16.00	
		J. C. Beals, personal	Drawings	15			$ 28.00
		M. S. Markle	On account	4		73.50	
		J. C. Beals, personal	Drawings	15			12.00
		D. M. Edwards	On account	2		90.00	
	2	Purchases	Miscellaneous	√	160.00		
		A. D. Hole	On account	3		24.00	
	3	Purchases	Miscellaneous	√	210.00		
		H. A. Brinton	On account	1		36.00	
		H. L. Morris	On account	5		19.00	
	4	Purchases	Miscellaneous	√	170.00		
		Office salaries	Weekly pay-roll	19			120.00
		Office equipment	New typewriter	9			81.00
		A. D. Hole	On account	3		25.00	
	5	Purchases	Miscellaneous	√	90.00		
		D. M. Edwards	On account	2		32.00	
		J. C. Beals, personal	Drawings	15			19.00
		H. A. Brinton	On account	1		64.00	
		Purchases, Dr.		10	$ 770.00		
		Accounts payable, Dr.		9		$553.50	
		Sundry, Dr.		√			$260.00
		Cash, Cr.		1	$1,583.50		

Cash Disbursements journal of J. C. Beals, the three columns segregate the types of debits resulting from the transactions. The cash purchases are recorded in the first column and posted in total from the foot of the journal page. The Accounts Payable column makes possible the debiting of individual creditors' accounts, with summary posting of the total. The Sundry column accumulates all debits which do not come under the classes of purchases or accounts payable.

Transactions may involve more than one specialized journal.—Specialized journals are based upon the principle of segregating similar debits or credits which are common to a series of transactions. They may be constructed to deal with any type of debits or credits, such as cash debits, sales credits, purchases debits. Whenever the frequency or importance of similar debits or credits justifies such action, a specialized journal may be introduced to accumulate them for preliminary classification and summary posting to the ledger. There are, of course, some transactions which may be classified in either of two types of specialized journals. Cash sales, for example, cause both debits to Cash and credits to Sales; they are, accordingly, eligible for entry in either a Cash Receipts journal or a Sales journal. What shall be done with such transactions? Shall they be entered in both journals? If so, what technique is to be adopted to avoid duplication in posting the data to the Cash and Sales accounts, respectively?

An advantage will be gained if cash sales are recorded in both the Cash Receipts journal and the Sales journal; for such procedure permits each journal to accumulate all of the entries for which it was established. That is, the Cash Receipts journal will thereby contain all the debits to Cash; the Sales journal will contain all the credits to Sales. The data in the journals thus will indicate the trend of cash receipts and of sales during a period of operations, without an examination of the ledger accounts. Duplicate posting may be avoided by posting from each journal only those aspects of the cash-sale transactions for which the specialized journal was created, that is, by posting the debits to Cash from the Cash Receipts journal and the credits to Sales from the Sales journal. The method of posting from the specialized journals under such conditions is illustrated by the two journals of A. C. Miller which are shown on page 207, and in which cash-sale transactions to the extent of $3,700 are recorded in both a Cash Receipts journal and a Sales journal.

The Sales journal sets forth the amounts of cash sales in a special column; the entries therein total $3,700. The amount of $3,700 is included to compose the total credit to Sales from the Sales journal. However, this amount is not debited to the Cash account from the Sales journal; it is included as part of the total debit to Cash from the Cash Receipts journal.

The Cash Receipts journal contains a special column for the cash-sale transactions; the column contains the same amounts as were listed in the Cash column of the Sales journal, which total $3,700. This amount is included in the total debit to Cash from the Cash Receipts journal. However, it is not posted as a credit to Sales from the Cash Receipts journal; for such entry would be made from the Sales journal, in which the $3,700 would be included in a summary credit to the Sales account.[1]

The accounts with Cash and Sales after the postings from the specialized journals of A. C. Miller are shown on page 208. The folio columns in the Cash and Sales accounts contain symbols indicating the specialized journal from which the data have been posted. CR refers to the Cash Receipts journal, S to the Sales journal. The practice of using symbols to indicate specialized journals facilitates reference to the books of original entry and is often followed.

Discount columns in the cash journals.—Previous illustrations of the Cash Receipts journal have indicated only the net amounts of cash received from customers. Assume that the terms of sale offered by A. C. Miller provide that customers who pay within 10 days are entitled to 1 per cent discount on the amounts

[1] Each of the journals of A. C. Miller contains a special column from which neither subsidiary nor controlling data are posted. Consequently the question arises as to whether such columns serve any useful purpose. In the foregoing illustrations the special columns for cash and sales, respectively, served to point out to the reader the exact duplication of journal entries. As a practical matter, the cash-sale amounts could have been merged with the data in the sundry columns of the Sales journal and the Cash Receipts journal.

receivable from them. The receipts of actual cash from customers on June 12 do not, therefore, represent the total amounts by

SALES JOURNAL

(Cash Items Not Posted to Cash Account) (Page 1)

19—		Account Titles	Explanation	L F	Cash Dr.	Accts. Rec. Dr.
June	4	W. N. Mitchell	Invoice #1	5		$1,000 00
		E. L. Parkhurst	Invoice #2	6		800 00
		Cash	Cash slips, 101–25	√	$ 1,200 00	
	5	R. J. James	Invoice #3	4		800 00
	6	L. Cox	Invoice #4	2		1,400 00
		Cash	Cash slips, 126–47	√	700 00	
	8	D. L. Hanson	Invoice #5	3		800 00
		Cash	Cash slips, 148–72	√	600 00	
	12	G. Brewer	Invoice #6	1		1,600 00
	15	Cash	Cash slips, 173–200	√	1,200 00	
		Cash	Dr.	√	$ 3,700 00	
		Acco	unts receivable Dr.	2		$6,400 00
		Sale	s Cr.	5	$10,100 00	

CASH RECEIPTS JOURNAL

(Sales Items Not Posted to Sales Account) (Page 1)

19—		Account Titles	Explanation	L F	Sales	Accts. Rec.	Sundry
June	1	A. C. Miller, capital	Investment	4			$10,000 00
	4	Sales	Cash slips, 101–25	√	$ 1,200 00		
	6	Sales	Cash slips, 126–47	√	700 00		
	8	Sales	Cash slips, 148–72	√	600 00		
	12	R. J. James	Received on acct.	4		$ 396 00	
		W. N. Mitchell	Received on acct.	5		990 00	
		L. Cox	Received on acct.	2		1,386 00	
	15	E. L. Parkhurst	Received on acct.	6		500 00	
		Sales	Cash slips, 173–200	√	1,200 00		
		Sales	, Cr.	√	$ 3,700 00		
		Accou	nts receivable, Cr.	2		$3,272 00	
		Sundr	y, Cr.	√			$10,000 00
		Cash,	Dr.	1	$16,972 00		

which the Accounts Receivable account must be reduced. The complete entries for these three transactions would show total credits to Accounts Receivable as follows: R. J. James, $400; W. N. Mitchell, $1,000; E. L. Parkhurst, $1,400. The differences between these amounts and the amounts debited to Cash represent the sales discounts for prompt payment.

CASH (Page 1)

June	15		CR–1	$16,972	00						

SALES (Page 5)

						June	15		S-1	$10,100	00

The journal entries to record the effects of the sales discounts allowed could be made in a special-column general journal, with a special column for recording the offsetting credits to the subsidiary accounts receivable and for summarizing the total as a credit to the Accounts Receivable controlling account in the general ledger. The practice just mentioned, however, possesses a disadvantage in that it separates the effects of a single transaction, namely, the receipt of cash from a customer. For example, when R. J. James pays an account receivable for $400, he does so by sending cash to the extent of $396. The journal entry to record this transaction would be recorded as follows:

Cash........................	$396.00	
Sales discount.................	4.00	
Accounts receivable................		$400.00

The foregoing entry could not be recorded in the specialized journals previously illustrated. The effects of the transaction would be journalized in two places. The receipt of cash would be recorded in a Cash Receipts journal; the allowances of the sales discount in a Sales Discounts journal or a "general" journal. There is a close relationship between the receipt or payment of cash from customers or to creditors and the allowance of sales and purchases discounts for prompt payment of the accounts receivable or payable. This relationship makes it desirable, if possible, to record all the data arising from the receipt or payment of cash "on account" in the same journal. Consequently, the strict logic of the cash journals is often violated to the extent of providing extra columns therein for entries to the Sales Discount and Purchases Discount accounts. This makes it possible to enter in one journal all the data which arise from cash receipts from customers or payments to creditors. The Cash Receipts journal of A. C. Miller will be chosen to illustrate the use of the discount column in the cash journals. It appears on page 210.

This journal provides special columns for both debits and credits. The total of the first two, which are credit columns, equals the total of the last two, which are debit columns. The previous cash journals which were shown did not contain a separate column for totaling the debit to Cash; a special column was unnecessary. Even in the present case, the debit to Cash could be computed by subtracting the sales-discount debit from the total of the credit columns. The special column for debits to Cash is convenient, however, in proving the mathematical correctness of the column totals. It also has another advantage: that of providing a record of actual cash receipts. Sometimes the "cash" column is headed with the name of a bank in which cash is deposited and on which checks are drawn.

It should be observed that in the Cash Receipts journal illustrated on page 210 the cash-sale items are listed in the Sundry column. No credits are made to the Sales account for these items; they would ordinarily be posted from a Sales journal.

The cash book—A combined cash journal and cash account.— There is no reason, in strict theory, why the Cash Receipts journal and Cash Disbursements journal should be adjacent in the accounting records of an enterprise. But there is, in modern practice, an important practical reason for such an arrangement: by this method the Cash Receipts and Cash Disbursements journals are made to comprise a complete record of the transac-

CASH RECEIPTS JOURNAL

(With Discount Column)

(Page 1)

19—		Account Titles	Explanation	L F	Sundry Cr.	Accounts Rec. Cr.	Sales Discount, Dr.	Cash, Dr.
June	1	A. C. Miller, capital	Investment	4	$10,000.00			$10,000.00
	4	Sales	Cash slips, 101–25	√	1,200.00			1,200.00
	6	Sales	Cash slips, 126–47	√	700.00			700.00
	8	Sales	Cash slips, 147–72	√	600.00			600.00
	12	R. J. James	Received on account	4		$ 400.00	$ 4.00	396.00
		W. N. Mitchell	Received on account	5		1,000.00	10.00	990.00
		L. Cox	Received on account	2		1,400.00	14.00	1,386.00
	15	E. L. Parkhurst	Received on account	6		500.00		500.00
		Sales	Cash slips, 173–200	√	1,200.00			1,200.00
		Totals		√	$13,700.00	$3,300.00	$28.00	$16,972.00
		Folios		√	√	(2)	(6)	(1)

tions affecting incoming and outgoing cash. Moreover, if some provision could be made for offsetting the ultimate credits to cash before they were posted, the Cash account in the ledger might be dispensed with. This result is often accomplished by placing the journal records of cash receipts and of cash disbursements on opposite pages of a journal entitled the "cash book." At the foot of each page, or at convenient times, the offsetting credits and debits caused by the cash transactions may be posted to the proper accounts. The debits and credits involving cash need not, however, be posted to the Cash account. The cash book itself may be treated as a Cash "account" with "Cash" columns on opposite pages of the cash book serving as debit and credit columns of the account. The "Cash" columns may be balanced periodically, with the "balance" carried forward in the debit column as the cash on hand.

The cash book in this way serves two purposes. It is a journal for recording cash transactions by listing the account titles and amounts to be debited and credited as a result of these transactions. It is also a detailed Cash account which may be balanced from time to time to show the cash on hand. Where the cash book is substituted for the Cash account in the general ledger, the balance in the cash book must be included in each trial balance.

Limits of journal specialization.—The principle of specialization as applied to journals may be extended to any limit. Special columns may be used in the specialized journals to reduce posting; and whenever the number of transactions recorded in a special column justifies such action, a new journal may be created. Transactions which do not give rise to entries accumulated in the specialized journals may be recorded in a general journal, either of the standard two-column type or one containing special columns. In most enterprises, a general journal is included as part of the original-entry records, if for no other purpose than to contain the adjusting and closing entries at the end of a fiscal period. It is conceivable that a specialized journal may be used for every type of business transaction, limiting all entries in each journal to those transactions which have both debits and credits alike. The maintenance of specialized journals is often combined with the use of business papers or vouchers as direct media for posting to the subsidiary ledger accounts.

QUESTIONS ON CHAPTER XVI

1. Is the general journal with a number of special columns adequate (*a*) when the volume of transactions is too large for one individual to handle, and (*b*) when a large number of accounts are very active?
2. Why are the Sales, the Purchases and the Cash journals the most common of the specialized journals? Would it be desirable under some circumstances to adopt a Labor journal; an Expense journal; a Purchase Returns and Allowances journal; a journal to record the receipt of notes; a journal to record the purchase of fixed assets?
3. Describe the single-money-column form of specialized journal. What advantages does this introduce as compared with two-column general journal? Describe the posting from this journal to the ledger.
4. If a controlling account and a subsidiary accounts receivable ledger are in use, how must sales be recorded in the single-money-column type of Sales journal? How should cash sales and note sales be treated?
5. A single-money-column special journal may be used (*a*) if all the items in the column are to be posted individually to the accounts involved and the total is to be posted to the contra side of some account; or (*b*) if only the total is to be posted to the debit and to the credit of the two accounts involved; or (*c*) if the terms are to be posted individually to the accounts in a subsidiary ledger and the total is to be posted to the two accounts in the general ledger, one of which is of course the controlling account. Illustrate. If a single-column journal is to be used in connection with a controlling account (case *c*), what may be said as to the necessity for the homogeneity of the transactions recorded in it? Why?
6. Describe the process of posting from a Sales journal with the following money columns: Sundry, Dr.; Notes Receivable, Dr.; Accounts Receivable, Dr.; Sales, Cr. Assume a controlling Accounts Receivable account and a subsidiary accounts-receivable ledger.

APPENDIX TO CHAPTER XVI

The following transactions are introduced to illustrate the concurrent use of several specialized journals. Some of the transactions are recorded in one journal; some in two journals; however, no entries are posted from more than one journal. Some of the explanations in the various journals appear as references to the business papers which originally evidenced the transactions. Others consist of descriptions of the transactions or of certain conditions which distinguish them. The Cash Receipts and Cash Disbursements journals are maintained in such manner that they set forth the cash balance, and serve as a Cash account.

It is suggested that the reader test his knowledge of the principles of specialized journals by verifying the trial balance which follows the journals of Henry Osgood. This may be done by posting the data in appropriate general ledger and subsidiary accounts, and comparing the balances thus obtained with those of the trial balance.

TRANSACTIONS OF HENRY OSGOOD, SOLE PROPRIETOR, JANUARY 1–6, 19___

January 1. Invested the following assets in a business: $5,000 cash; delivery truck, $1,000. Rented a store building, paying $200 for rent for January. Bought furniture and fixtures for $3,000, paying $2,000 cash and giving a note for $1,000. Purchased merchandise on account from the Bryson Company, $8,000.

January 2. Sold merchandise for cash, $500. Sold merchandise on account as follows: R. U. Green, $350; I. M. Gray, $250. Paid repair expense on delivery truck, $25. Purchased merchandise on account, as follows: I. R. White, $750; the Bryson Company, $400.

January 3. Cash sales, $600. Sales on account: E. B. Black, $150; R. U. Green, $50. Purchased merchandise from the Bryson Company, $1,000: paying $500 cash, giving a note for $300, and leaving the balance on open account.

January 4. Mr. Osgood withdrew merchandise for own use, $100. Sold merchandise on account to E. B. Black, $50. Returned merchandise to the Bryson Company, $250. Received on account from R. U. Green, $200, less 2 per cent cash discount. Paid on account to I. R. White, $500, less 5 per cent cash discount.

January 5. Purchased merchandise on account from I. R. White, $30. Paid on account to the Bryson Company, $2,000, less 1 per cent cash discount. Gave a note on account to the Bryson Company for $4,000. Received a note on account from I. M. Gray, $150. Received merchandise from R. U. Green, $35. Purchased merchandise on account from the Bryson Company, $2,000.

January 6. Paid expenses as follows: clerk's salary, $25; garage bill, $20; supplies, $15. Withdrew cash for personal use, $100. Cash sales, $800. Sold merchandise on account to I. M. Gray, $200.

CASH BOOK (LEFT-HAND PAGE)

CASH RECEIPTS

(Page 1)

19—		Account Titles	Explanation	L F	Sundry Cr.	Accounts Receivable Cr.	Sales Discount Dr.	Cash Dr.
Jan.	1	Henry Osgood, capital	Investment	√	$5,000.00			$5,000.00
	2	Sales	Sales slips, 1–15	√	500.00			500.00
	3	Sales	Sales slips, 16–23	√	600.00			600.00
	4	R. U. Green	On account	3		$200.00	$4.00	196.00
	6	Sales	Sales slips, 24–30	√	800.00			800.00
		Totals		√	$6,900.00	$200.00	$4.00	$7,096.00
		Folios			√	(3)	(18)	√
	6	Balance		√	$1,756.00			$1,756.00

CASH BOOK (RIGHT-HAND PAGE)

CASH DISBURSEMENTS

(Page 2)

19—		Account Titles	Explanation	L F	Sundry Dr.	Accounts Payable Dr.	Purchases Discount Cr.	Cash Cr
Jan.	1	Rent	Check No. 1	14	$ 200.00			$ 200.00
		Furniture and fixtures	Check No. 2	√	2,000.00			2,000.00
	2	Delivery expense	Check No. 3	15	25.00			25.00
	3	Purchases	Check No. 4	√	500.00			500.00
	4	I. R. White	Check No. 5	2		$ 500.00	$25.00	475.00
	5	The Bryson Co.	Check No. 6	1		2,000.00	20.00	1,980.00
	6	Salaries	Check No. 7	16	25.00			25.00
		Supplies	Check No. 8	17	15.00			15.00
		Delivery expense	Check No. 9	15	20.00			20.00
		H. Osgood, personal	Check No. 10	9	100.00			100.00
		Balance		√	*$1,756.00*			*$1,756.00*
		Totals		√	$4,641.00	$2,500.00	$45.00	$7,096.00
	6	Folios			√	(7)	(19)	√

SALES (Page 1)

19—		Account Titles	Explanation	L F	Sundry Dr.	Accounts Receivable Dr.	Notes Rec. Dr.	Sales Cr
Jan.	2	Cash	Sales slips, 1–15	√	$ 500.00			$ 500.00
		R. U. Green	Sales invoice, #001	3		$ 350.00		350.00
		I. M. Gray	Sales invoice, #002	2		250.00		250.00
	3	Cash	Sales slips, 16–23	√	600.00			600.00
		E. B. Black	Sales invoice, #003	1		150.00		150.00
		R. U. Green	Sales invoice, #004	3		50.00		50.00
	4	H. Osgood, personal	Withdrawal	9	100.00			100.00
		E. B. Black	Sales invoice, #005	1		50.00		50.00
	6	Cash	Sales slips, 24–30	√	800.00			800.00
		I. M. Gray	Sales invoice, #006	2		200.00		200.00
		Totals		√	$2,000.00	$1,050.00		$3,050.00
	6	Folios			√	③		⑫

PURCHASES (Page 1)

19—		Account Titles	Explanation	L F	Sundry Cr.	Accounts Payable Cr.	Notes Payable Cr.	Purchases Dr.
Jan.	1	The Bryson Co.	Purchase invoice #1	1		$ 8,000 00		$ 8,000 00
	2	I. R. White	Purchase invoice #2	2		750 00		750 00
		The Bryson Co.	Purchase invoice #3	1		400 00		400 00
	3	The Bryson Co.	Purchase invoice #4	1		200 00	$300 00	500 00
		Cash	Purchase invoice #4	√	$500 00			500 00
	5	I. R. White	Purchase invoice #5	2		30 00		30 00
		The Bryson Co.	Purchase invoice #6	1		2,000 00		2,000 00
		Totals		√	$500 00	$11,380 00	$300 00	$12,180 00
	6	Folios			√	⑦	⑥	⑩

NOTE: Purchase invoice No. 4 is listed above in two portions, the amount paid in cash being segregated. The $500 cash purchase is also recorded in the cash disbursements journal.

GENERAL JOURNAL

(Page 1)

Sales Returns Dr.	Notes Receivable Dr.	Accounts Payable Dr.	Sundry Dr.	19—		Account Titles	L F	Sundry Cr.	Accounts Receivable Cr.	Notes Payable Cr.	Purchases Returns Cr.
			$5,000 00	Jan.	1	Cash	√				
			1,000 00			Delivery equipment	5				
						Henry Osgood, capital	8	$6,000 00			
						Original investment of miscellaneous assets by Henry Osgood					
			3,000 00			Furniture and fixtures	4				
						Cash	√	2,000 00			
						Notes payable	√			$1,000 00	
						Purchase of certain furniture and fixtures for store					
		$ 250 00			4	The Bryson Co.	1				
						Purchases returns	√				$250 00
						Bryson credit memorandum #1					
		4,000 00			5	The Bryson Co.	1				
						Notes payable	√			4,000 00	
						To apply on account					
	$150 00					Notes receivable	√				
						I. M. Gray	2		$150 00		
						To apply on account					
$35 00						Sales returns	√				
						R. U. Green	3		35 00		
						Sales credit memorandum #1					
$35 00	$150 00	$4,250 00	$9,000 00			*Totals*		$8,000 00	$185 00	$5,000 00	$250 00
⑬	②	⑦	√		6	*Folios*		√	③	⑥	⑪

H. OSGOOD—TRIAL BALANCE

JANUARY 6, 19——

1. Cash	$ 1,756.00	
2. Notes receivable	150.00	
3. Accounts receivable	665.00	
4. Furniture and fixtures	3,000.00	
5. Delivery truck	1,000.00	
6. Notes payable		$ 5,300.00
7. Accounts payable		4,630.00
8. H. Osgood, capital		6,000.00
9. H. Osgood, personal	200.00	
10. Purchases	12,180.00	
11. Purchases returns		250.00
12. Sales		3,050.00
13. Sales returns	35.00	
14. Rent	200.00	
15. Delivery expense	45.00	
16. Salaries	25.00	
17. Supplies	15.00	
18. Sales discount	4.00	
19. Purchase discount		45.00
Total	$19,275.00	$19,275.00

The foregoing journals indicate that subsidiary accounts are to be opened with customers and creditors. The amounts in the trial balance represent the balances in the controlling accounts only. It is possible to maintain the specialized journals in such manner that no transactions are journalized in more than one part of the records. Cash sales, for example, would then appear in the Cash Receipts journal or in the Sales journal, but not in both. This procedure does not, of course, enable the specialized journals to serve as complete records of all the transactions causing certain types of entries. Whether or not this limitation is significant depends upon the purposes for which the journals are maintained.

CHAPTER XVII

MODERN DEVELOPMENTS IN ACCOUNTING TECHNIQUE

Anyone who has journalized large groups of business transactions, recording them either in a general journal or with the aid of specialized journals, must realize that the task is enormous. When one considers, also, that journalizing is merely a preliminary step to the final ledger classification, he is forced to regard this process as at best a necessary evil. But is it necessary? Is it not possible for the business papers themselves to serve some or all of the important functions for which journals are ordinarily maintained?

These functions are: (1) to provide chronological records of transactions; (2) to provide preliminary classifications of similar data; (3) to provide media for transferring data from the business papers to the ledger (posting media). This chapter will illustrate some modern technical methods of exercising these functions.

Business papers as chronological records of transactions.—It is not fundamentally necessary to re-write the description of each transaction in a journal, provided the detailed data have been recorded on the business paper which authorizes the entries. The practice of doing so arose out of conditions where an original document was not made for each transaction, and the chronological record in a bound volume constituted the first written evidence that the transaction in question had occurred. The task of journalizing in modern days may well be lightened (and in practice *is* lightened) by the elimination of the descriptions of transactions from the formal journal records. In place of descriptions, the bookkeeper may merely employ a symbol which indicates the source of the journal data. The references may take the form of serial numbers assigned to the original documents, with all documents numbered and filed in one series, or in separate concurrent series.[1] The substitution of references for descriptions may take place either in the general or in specialized journals. The practice not only greatly reduces the task of journalizing transactions; it also reduces the space necessary for recording them in the journal. The principle of substituting symbols for explanations is widely applied in modern accounting technique. It may be used concurrently with the advantages of special columns in the general journals or with the specialized journals, whether of the single-column or special-column type. Several commonly used types of specialized journals will be discussed at this point to illustrate the principle.

Journals for receipt and issuance of notes and drafts.—The receipt or issuance of notes or drafts is an important and frequently recurring type of transaction in the activities of some enterprises. In such cases, specialized journals may be maintained to authorize the summary posting to the Notes Receivable or Notes Payable account. Such journals may be single-column journals, as in the cases where notes receivable arise only from sales on account, or where notes payable are issued only for purchases on account. But more often the journals for recording such note transactions contain several special columns permitting the classification and accumulation of various aspects of the accounting data. They serve as indexes of the notes received or issued, and thus often take the place of subsidiary accounts with the signers or holders. The general ledger accounts, Notes Receivable or Notes Payable, are debited or credited for the total of the entries in the note journals. The offsetting accounts to be debited or credited may be posted either individually in the general ledger or as totals accumulated in the special columns of the note journals. The Notes Payable journal of the Peterson Engineering Company serves as a medium for posting credit entries to the Notes Payable account and debits to certain other accounts at

[1] The files of various types of business papers may be accompanied by indexes which contain descriptions of them. These lists of documents are sometimes called "registers" and often serve only to facilitate reference to the original business papers. This type of register which serves as an index of original papers must be sharply distinguished from specialized journals, which are sometimes referred to as registers, but which also serve to authorize ledger postings.

NOTES PAYABLE JOURNAL—PETERSON ENGINEERING COMPANY (Page 1)

Date of Entry 1926	Date of Note or Draft 1926	Time to Run	Interest Rate	File No.	Payee	L F	Accounts Payable Dr.	Cash Dr.	Interest Dr.	Sundry Dr.	Account Title	Notes Payable Credit	Due Date	Date Paid
June 1	June 1	60 days	5	1	A. L. Marcus	32	$ 500 00					$ 500 00	8/1/26	
9	7	90 days	5	2	T. P. Jones	21	400 00					400 00	9/7/26	
11	10	1 yr.	6	3	First Nat'l Bank	√		$4,000 00				4,000 00	6/10/27	
15	15	60 days	6	4	R. L. Conklin	√		594 00	$ 6 00			600 00	8/15/26	
		30 days	5	5	L. D. Pinker	57	175 00					175 00	7/15/26	
29	25	6 mo.	6	6	Acme Mfg. Co.	17				$1,200.00	Machinery	1,200 00	12/25/26	
30	30	2 yr.	5	7	John Doan	9			30 00	600.00	Mortgage payable	630 00	6/30/28	
					Total		$1,075 00	$4,594 00	$36 00	$1,800.00		$7,505 00		
June 30					*Folios*	√	(11)	√	(19)	√		(12)		

NOTE.—This is a journal for recording the effects of issuing notes payable to creditors. The data recorded therein are posted to the accounts of the ledger. No formal explanation is written out in this journal; the explanation is substituted for by additional data at the left of the page and the file numbers of duplicate notes payable.

the same time. The debits to Cash are not posted from this journal; the "Cash, Dr." column is checked to indicate that the amount is being posted from some other journal.

Journal for issuance of vouchers payable.—Some enterprises maintain a system of bookkeeping records under which separate documents are prepared for all current liabilities and for other obligations which involve the ultimate disbursements of cash. These documents are known as "disbursement vouchers" or "accounts-payable vouchers," and are credited to an account known as Vouchers Payable. No subsidiary records need be kept of these vouchers in terms of the persons to whom they are payable; the vouchers are numbered serially and paid by check at the times of maturity. The issuance of the disbursement vouchers is journalized in a specialized journal usually referred to as the *voucher register* (sometimes Vouchers-Payable journal), with special columns to accumulate the debits offsetting the credit to Vouchers Payable.[1] The method of using the voucher register will be illustrated by recording the issuance of vouchers for the following transactions in the register appearing on page 224.

June 1. Rent for month of June becomes payable to H. B. Ackerson, $300.
2. Merchandise is purchased on account from Hendrickson and Company, $4,000, 2/10/n/30.
3. An advertising bill is received from the Crane Advertising Service, Inc., $180.
5. Merchandise is purchased from C. N. Cole, $1,450.
6. Purchase of merchandise from L. W. Raymond, $600.
Purchase of merchandise from N. W. Bryan, $1,300.
7. Purchase of new office equipment from Library Bureau, Inc., $2,000.
8. Purchase motor truck from Nash Sales Company, $950.
15. Certain office salaries become payable, $240; interest accrues on note payable to First National Bank, $120.

The voucher system.—The system under which vouchers are issued to authorize all cash disbursements is often referred to in practice as the "voucher system." Strictly applied, it extends to

[1] The voucher register (the Vouchers-Payable journal) is a type of specialized journal which removes the need for certain other journals and ledgers. The purchases ordinarily recorded in a Purchases journal may be listed in a special column in the voucher register. The accounts-payable ledger is no longer an absolute necessity; for each voucher is paid separately to an individual vendor for a particular invoice.

VOUCHER REGISTER (Page 1)

Date 19—		Payee	Voucher No.	Vouchers Payable Cr.	Purchases Dr.	Rent Dr.	Sales Salaries Dr.	Sundry Dr.	L F	Account Titles	How Paid
June	1	H. B. Ackerson	001	$ 300 00		$300 00			√		Ck. 101
	2	Hendrickson & Co.	002	4,000 00	$4,000 00				√		Ck. 104
	3	Crane Adv. Co.	003	180 00				$ 180 00	12	Advertising	Ck. 106
	5	C. N. Cole	004	1,450 00	1,450 00				√		
	6	L. W. Raymond	005	600 00	600 00				√		Ck. 102
		N. W. Bryan	006	1,300 00	1,300 00				√		Ck. 103
	7	Library Bureau	007	2,000 00				2,000 00	7	Furn. and Fix.	Ck. 108
	8	Nash Sales Co	008	950 00				950 00	8	Del. Equip.	
	15	Sales pay-roll	009	240 00			$240 00		√		Ck. 105
		First National Bank	010	120 00				120 00	14	Interest Exp.	Ck. 107
		Total		$11,140 00	$7,350 00	$300 00	$240 00	$3,250 00	√		
		Folios		(4)	(8)	(11)	(13)	(√)	(√)		

payment not only of the conventional types of current liabilities for merchandise purchases but also of the accrued liabilities for such items as salaries, taxes, interest, insurance, dividends, personal withdrawals, etc. The central feature of the voucher system, from an administrative viewpoint, is that it compels formal recognition and approval of all cash disbursements. But *the voucher register is not a cash-disbursements journal;* it is merely the journal for accumulating and posting the effects of the vouchers which must be prepared to authorize each cash disbursement. In some cases the voucher is prepared just before payment, as in the case of a pay-roll; in other cases the voucher may be prepared at the time of the transaction which gives rise to a liability, such as the purchase of merchandise on sixty-day terms. Ordinarily the issuance of a note payable or a group of bonds payable would not give rise to the immediate issuance of a "voucher payable." But a voucher would have to be issued before the note or bonds were paid in cash. Vouchers payable, then, are not the only type of liabilities which are recognized under the voucher system; they do, however, comprise a class through which all other liabilities must pass before they are liquidated.

There is no standard form which the disbursement voucher must assume. The only requirement is that it adequately describe the nature of the liability which is to be paid, so that it can be classified in the voucher register and so that the check may be prepared at the correct time payable to the proper person or persons. Very often the face of the voucher contains a place for indicating the accounts to be affected and the number of the check by which it is ultimately paid.[1]

[1] It is common practice for firms to deposit all cash receipts in a bank and to make all payments by check. Most firms, however, object to preparing checks for small amounts; consequently they set a minimum below which they refuse to issue them. For the purpose of paying small amounts—such as expenditures for postage, stationery, and express charges—a "petty cash fund" is often provided. From this fund, payments are made in currency. A widely used plan of operating the petty cash fund is known as the "imprest system." Under this plan a clerk called the "petty cashier" is placed in charge of the fund. A voucher is made payable and a check is issued to the clerk to establish a fund, and checks issued later to replenish it are drawn in his favor; he cashes these checks and makes payments of small amounts in currency. When the fund runs low, he presents an itemized statement or voucher to the general cashier, supported by receipts and other memoranda in his possession. Another check is issued for the amount expended. The currency fund is restored to the original amount when the petty cashier cashes the check.

The check register.—The Cash Disbursements journal used under a voucher system is usually very simple, for each check is issued in direct payment of a specific "vouchered" liability. The journal, therefore, often consists solely of a *check register* to authorize credits to the Cash account and debits to the Vouchers

CHECK REGISTER

(For Use with Voucher Register) (Page 1)

19—		Check No.	Voucher No.	Voucher Payable Dr.		Purchase Discount Cr.		Cash Cr.	
June	1	101	001	$ 300	00			$ 300	00
	6	102	005	600	00			600	00
	6	103	006	1,300	00			1,300	00
	12	104	002	4,000	00	$80	00	3,920	00
	15	105	009	240	00			240	00
		106	003	180	00			180	00
		107	010	120	00			120	00
		108	007	2,000	00			2,000	00
		Total		$8,740	00	$80	00	$8,660	00
		Folios		(4)		(9)		(1)	

VOUCHERS PAYABLE ACCOUNT

(After Posting from the Voucher Register and Check Register)

19— 19— (Page 4)

June	15	Check register....	1	$ 8,740	00	June	15	Voucher register....	1	$11,140	00
		Balance.....		2,400	00						
				$11,140	00					$11,140	00
						June	15	Balance.....		$ 2,400	00

Payable account. A check register is shown above, indicating that eight of the ten vouchers have been paid. The Vouchers Payable account sets forth the balance of unpaid vouchers; this information can also be determined from the face of the voucher register, which contains a column at the extreme right of the page for indicating which vouchers have been paid. Vouchers are sometimes prepared in such manner that they also serve as receipts from the creditors. This is accomplished by including on each one a statement which authorizes withdrawal from the bank account of the firm issuing the voucher. The voucher is thus a combined device for authorizing payment and acknowledging receipt of cash, and is sometimes referred to as a "voucher check."

The voucher system has certain limitations which should be mentioned in this survey of its operations. First, it provides no method for keeping track of the amounts purchased from individual creditors during a given period of time. The vouchers are typically not classified according to payees. Such information is often important for managerial control, and must be provided by some other device not an integral part of the voucher system, such as cards on which records are kept of the purchases made from various vendors. A second limitation of the voucher system is the rigor with which it must be carried out; it permits few exceptions to its routine. The handling of unusual transactions, such as partial payments, returns, forfeited purchases discounts, etc., cause very great difficulty in the record-keeping. Where the conditions of the business make these transactions of frequent occurrence, the voucher system is not a convenient method of controlling cash disbursements.

Business papers as preliminary classifying devices.—The business papers, it has been shown, may be used in such a manner as to eliminate much of the task of writing the explanations of transactions. Such use was illustrated in the cases of the note journal and voucher register. But business papers may also serve to reduce the task of journalizing by making unnecessary the writing out of numerous account titles and amounts. For example, the amounts involved in similar transactions may be summarized into one total and journalized as one transaction. The file of business papers from which the total is computed may thus be substituted for the entries in the specialized journals or the special columns in those journals. For example, a group of papers representing individual cash sales may be journalized as one transaction with one debit to Cash and one credit to Sales; the task of journalizing the whole group would therefore be no greater than the entry for any one of the cash sales. Similar treatment could be given to cash purchases, sales on account, sales returns, purchases returns, etc. The entries to the general-ledger accounts could be recorded in a standard form of general journal, unless, of course, provision had to be made for posting to subsidiary accounts, in which case the special-column form would be needed. But this leads to a discussion of a third advantage of business papers for journalization—their use as media for posting to the subsidiary (and also general-ledger) accounts.

Business papers as posting media.—The business papers serve admirably as explanations of transactions and as preliminary classifying devices. But they are also very well adapted to serve as the basis for "direct posting" to the ledger accounts, without the use of a formal journal of either the standard or the specialized type. The following figure, which represents a credit-sale ticket, contains information which may well serve as the basis for posting to the ledger.

SAMPLE STORE — No. 1751
CHICAGO — May 17, 1927

CREDIT SALE

E. S. Carroll
5529 University Ave.

5 pr. Men's Hose @ 75c.................... $3.75

Debit: Accounts Receivable Folio: *3*	Credit: Sales Folio: *27*

This memorandum serves as evidence of the sale of goods to a credit customer. It could be (and in practice *would be*) used as the medium for a debit to Accounts Receivable and a credit to the Sales account. If one were in doubt as to how to classify the effects of the foregoing sale, he need only consult the data at the foot of the memorandum, where full instructions as to posting are indicated, with only the ledger page numbers remaining to be entered in the folio spaces. These spaces serve the purpose of the folio column of the conventional journal. The ledger accounts to which the data were posted would carry a cross-reference to the serial number of the sales memorandum rather than to the page of a journal.

The direct method of posting data eliminates the task of journalizing the individual transactions. But it does not, of itself, reduce the task of posting data to the general ledger, or provide a classification of similar data preliminary to their entry in the ledger. The direct method is, however, very useful for posting to the subsidiary accounts; moreover, such posting does not interfere with summary posting through the medium of a conventional journal. This practice is commonly adopted for posting to individual customers' and creditors' accounts. Under ordinary conditions, individual credit-sale tickets would be used as the basis for posting only to the customers' accounts in the sales ledger. The total of a number of sales tickets would then be posted to the general-ledger accounts, namely, Accounts Receivable and Sales.

It has been stated at different times that the data of a group of similar business papers may be accumulated before being journalized for transfer to the general-ledger accounts. The files of original documents can thus be said to serve as "subsidiary journals," the totals of which are periodically transferred to a columnar controlling journal. The controlling journal may be of the standard two-column form, on which are periodically entered the effects of large numbers of similar transactions, or it may contain "special columns."

Business papers for posting to the general ledger.—Previous discussion dealt with business papers as media for posting to the subsidiary ledgers, implying that general-ledger accounts would be posted from a general or specialized journal of the columnar type. But it is possible, and often desirable, to post the general-ledger data also directly from the business papers, whether the documents represent individual transactions or the summation of numerous similar transactions. Business papers which authorize direct entries to the general-ledger accounts are sometimes referred to as "general-journal vouchers," or as "journal vouchers." They replace the general journal of an enterprise; and when used, they make unnecessary the conventional system of columnar journals, which were at one time so indispensable to adequate accounting procedure. In some enterprises one finds no journals of the columnar type for the authorization of entries to either the general or subsidiary ledgers, although in many cases indexes or registers of the business papers are maintained for purposes of historical reference. The real journals—the preliminary classifying devices and posting media—are the files of business documents or vouchers. The form of voucher used to authorize general-ledger posting is usually similar for all types of general-ledger entries. In some cases journal vouchers serve to summarize totals of subsidiary vouchers; in other cases they are prepared for infrequent transactions which must be posted individually to the general ledger. Illustrations of such transactions are purchases of fixed assets, periodic adjustments of inventory, allowances for bad debts or depreciation, declaration of dividends, etc.

The following illustration indicates in general the form and content of a journal voucher.

MERRIMAN MANUFACTURING COMPANY
Merriman, Indiana

Journal Voucher

Semi-annual dividend 6% preferred stock, par value			
$100—1,000 shares	$3,000	00	

Debit:	*Folio*	*Credit:*	*Folio*
Surplus $3,000.00	141	Dividends Payable $3,000.00	215

A journal voucher usually authorizes the entry of only one transaction or group of transactions; however, there may be several different accounts debited and/or credited from each document.

Grades and types of subsidiary records.—There may be more than two grades of journals and ledgers in an enterprise. Subsidiary journals may, for example, be used to accumulate data at different places. The totals of the various parts may then be forwarded to a central point where similar totals are accumulated. The grand total may then be computed and recorded on a journal voucher from which it is posted to the respective controlling accounts affected. During the process of accumulating the total amounts, the individual documents may be posted to subsidiary accounts. For example, assume that an enterprise maintains sales branches at various points in its territories and that each of the sales branches carries a detailed ledger showing the amounts receivable from the customers in the territory it serves. When sales are made to customers, sales invoices are prepared which serve as the basis for charging the individual customers' accounts. The total shown by the sales invoices, when computed, is the basis for debiting the branch controlling account, Accounts Receivable, and also for crediting the Sales account in the branch general ledger. A journal voucher might be prepared at the branch to authorize the debit to Accounts Receivable and the credit to Sales; also to serve as evidence of the transactions for entry at the home office.

The accounts at the home office of the enterprise would not be affected until a copy of the journal voucher was received. From the viewpoint of the central records at the home office, however, this journal voucher would itself be regarded as a document for posting to a subsidiary account, that is, the amount receivable at one of several branches. The data of the voucher may be debited to the subsidiary account for the amounts receivable from customers at this branch. The document would then be totaled with other similar documents from other branches, and the final posting would be authorized by a journal voucher prepared at the home office. This voucher would authorize a total debit to Accounts Receivable, and a credit to Sales, in the general ledger of the enterprise. The principle just discussed is illustrated by the diagram on page 232.

The illustration of the accumulation of the sales-invoice totals, coupled with the periodic posting of the detailed information in subsidiary accounts, is typical of the practice encountered in modern business enterprises. In some cases the document which serves as the posting medium to the general ledger will be a journal voucher which records totals only. In such cases, all subsidiary accounts must be posted direct from the original documents. In other cases, the posting medium will be a register of the original documents, sometimes containing special columns to aid in summary posting. In cases where subsidiary accounts are not to be provided for, the subsidiary journal may be a mere column

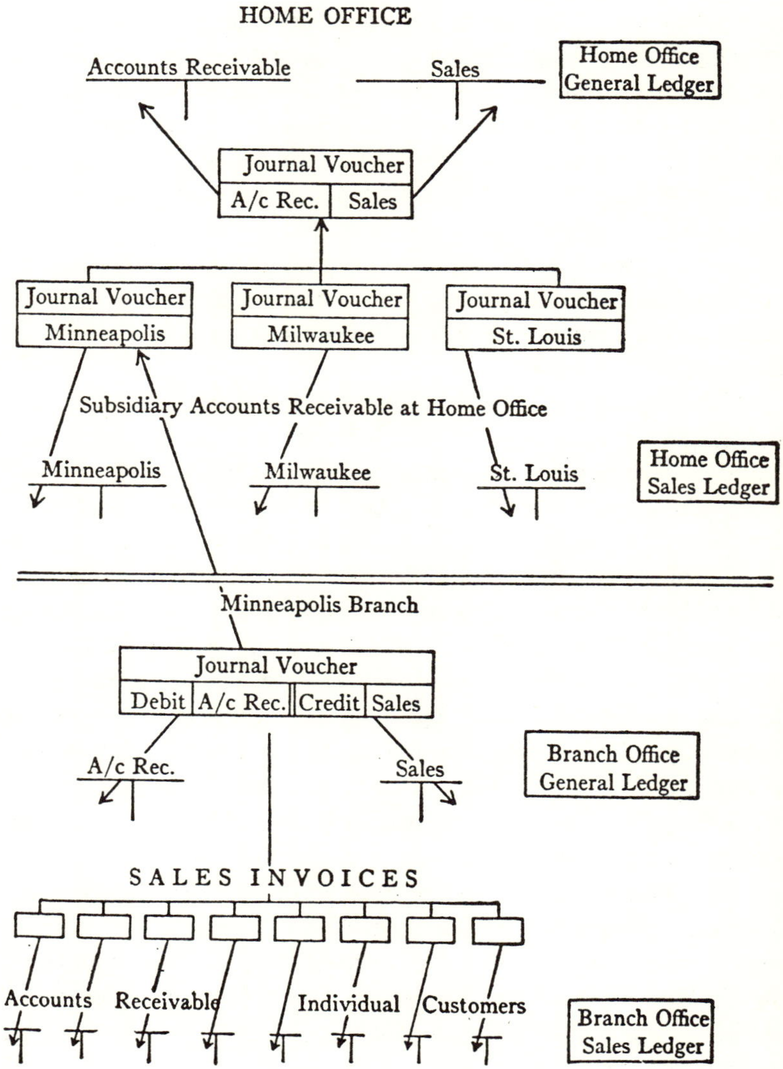

of figures on a sheet appropriately headed to indicate the accounts affected. For example, when cash-sales tickets are received from the various departments of a store, the amounts might be continuously transferred to a sheet entitled "Cash Sales." The total would later be posted to the Cash account and to the Sales account..

Mechanical equipment now widely used to reduce bookkeeping labor and to provide important detail.—The tremendous growth in business activity has increased the demand for business records to the point where all possible labor-saving devices must be introduced. The efficiency of business control has waited upon the introduction of classifying and recording methods which would provide adequate information for use in management. Certain specialized classifying devices have been described in the foregoing chapters; but the features pointed out have been those for avoiding repetition of the classifying and summarizing processes. These devices still leave a vast amount of work to be done in the actual recording, classification, and summarization of business facts. It is apparent that if some of the mechanistic phases of this work could be turned over to machines, two great advantages would result: (1) the accuracy and speed of machine methods would increase the amount of exact information made available for control; and (2) a great amount of human energy would be released for intellectual effort in the management of the business. In response to this need, mechanical devices have been invented and manufactured to meet the requirements of business in all phases of the classification and summarization of economic data.

Classes of mechanical equipment.—The machines used to reduce the labor and increase the accuracy of bookkeeping procedure may be grouped under four general headings. The first group includes machines used in the *preparation of the original vouchers*. Billing machines may be used for writing sales invoices, purchase orders, shipping orders, bills of lading, or numerous other forms used in the bookkeeping procedure. Other machines for preparing data for entry in the accounts are autographic registers used for the preparation of sales slips, cash registers to contain cash and maintain a record of its receipt and disbursement, and time-recording devices for showing the amounts and types of labor expended by individuals and groups of workers.

The second group of business machines are *those which record data directly in the accounts*, and which are commonly referred to in business as "bookkeeping machines";[1] they may be used for posting, balancing, and transferring accounting data in the ledger. Some of the bookkeeping machines contain adding or other calculating devices which make it possible to post entries in an account, total them, compute the resulting balance, and prove the accuracy of the computations without removing the ledger card or page from the machine. The third group may be designated the *measuring aids in accounting method.* They are used in the basic mathematical processes of addition, multiplication, subtraction, and division; some of the various machines used for these purposes are adding machines and calculating machines. Adding machines usually imprint a record of the amounts which are totaled; whereas the calculating machines typically do not provide a printed record of the amounts involved in the various calculations. Other measuring aids are cash registers, coin-changing devices, coin-counting and coin-wrapping machines, slide-rules, tabulating machines, correlation machines, etc. The fourth group is the *miscellaneous group of office appliances* which may be adapted in one way or another to prepare accounting records or reports. It includes typewriters for use in preparing financial statements, signature devices for authorizing receipts or disbursements, and duplicating machines for making possible the distribution of accounting data. Many other devices which are less directly connected with accounting procedure could be mentioned, such as addressing machines, special communication devices, filing sys-

[1] The discussion in this paragraph is intended merely to introduce the advantages and extent of mechanical equipment in accounting method. Many of the mechanical devices here mentioned may be grouped within several of the classes. It goes without saying that mechanical equipment serves accounting method best where the records, both vouchers and ledgers, are maintained in loose-leaf or card form. The specialized bookkeeping processes require great flexibility in the accounting records. Moreover, the mechanical equipment serves best when it is necessary to use several copies of the original document. Multi-copy records imply loose-leaf records, for the duplicate copies are useful only when distributed to different persons or departments. A full discussion of the advantages of mechanical equipment may be found in the *Office Appliance Manual*, published for the National Association of Office Appliance Manufacturers, 1926.

tems, etc. Mechanical equipment which requires manipulation may be operated by hand or electric power. The method used will vary with the rate at which the machines must be operated, the length of time they are used, the skill required in their manipulation, and the differences in their complexity and cost.

Accounting records vary with the types and complexity of business operations.—The types of accounting records encountered in business practice will, of course, differ from those used for illustrations and explanations in a treatise on accounting technique. *All accounting systems are different* from each other in that they all are, or should be, devised to suit the needs of particular enterprises; nevertheless *all accounting systems are similar* fundamentally, in that they involve the analysis and recording of business transactions in accord with a common principle. Every set of accounting records illustrates and applies in some way the basic theory of double-entry classification and summarization.[1]

It is impossible either to describe or to illustrate all possible types of accounting records. The following list of forms and records used by business firms will, however, give some idea of the extent to which accounting data may be subdivided in practice. Readers who are particularly interested in the technique of accounting procedure would do well to make a special study of the accounting system of some business enterprise with which they are familiar.

[1] The term "single entry" is sometimes used to designate any method of keeping accounts which does not record equal debits and credits for all transactions. Some transactions are completely journalized and posted; others are merely recorded informally for managerial use from time to time. The completeness of the records varies with the supposed needs of the business; consequently there are no two single-entry methods exactly alike. In reality single-entry accounting is another name for incomplete accounting, the incompleteness varying with the needs for which data are gathered or with the whims of the bookkeepers.

Business papers (some of which may be media for posting to general or subsidiary ledgers).—

Accounts-payable vouchers
Bank-deposit tickets
Bank drafts and checks
Bills of lading
Bond coupons
Cash-receipt memoranda
Freight and express bills
General-journal vouchers
Materials requisitions
Materials-issued memoranda
Merchandise requisitions
Pay-roll checks
Pay-roll summaries
Petty-cash vouchers
Production orders
Promissory notes
Purchase invoices
Purchase orders
Received-goods reports
Returned-goods reports
Sales invoices
Sales orders
Sales tickets
Stock certificates
Time cards
Warehouse receipts

Specialized journals (some of which may accumulate data for posting from other journals).—

Cash book
Check register
Collections record
Claims register
Invoice register (miscellaneous items)
Journal-voucher register
Notes-payable journal
Notes-receivable journal
Pay-roll sheet
Petty-cash book
Production-order register
Purchases journal
Returns-and-allowances journals
Sales journal
Stock-transfer register
Supplies journal
Subscription book
Vouchers-payable register

Subsidiary ledgers (some of which may contain several grades of subsidiary accounting data).—

Bond ledger
Claims ledger
Consignment ledger
Cost ledger (goods-in-process)
Creditors' ledger
Customers' ledger
Equipment ledger
Factory ledger
Instalment-sales ledger
Insurance ledger
Investment ledger
Merchandise ledger
Materials ledger
Plant ledger
Supplies ledger
Stockholders' ledger
Subscribers' ledger

QUESTIONS ON CHAPTER XVII

1. What is meant by a "business paper"? Were business papers originally intended as official evidence of transactions or as preliminary classifying devices?
2. What advantages may be derived from maintaining a register of certain types of business papers? Does not such procedure involve extra work? If so, what are the advantages?
3. Is the Cash Disbursements journal more simple or more complex when the voucher system is used? What are the limitations of the voucher system?
4. Is it necessary to maintain an accounts-payable ledger where the voucher system of authorizing cash disbursements is used? Is it advisable to maintain a record of transactions with individual vendors? Why? How may this be done?
5. What differences are there between the note records which are used as posting media, and those which are used merely as an informal record of notes received or given?
6. Do you gain the impression that the voucher register is a Cash Disbursements journal? Is it a Vouchers Payable journal?
7. What is a petty cash fund?
8. Would the direct posting of the data on each business voucher reduce the bookkeeping labor? What part of the bookkeeping routine would be eliminated?
9. What is meant by the statement that business papers may be regarded as subsidiary journals? Illustrate cases in which the data may be posted direct to subsidiary accounts from the business papers.
10. What are journal vouchers? Under what conditions are they used? May journal vouchers be used to journalize summarized data as well as individual transactions?
11. What advantages may be derived from the use of mechanical equipment for the carrying on of bookkeeping procedure?
12. Is it necessary for an employee to understand the principles of accounting to successfully operate mechanical bookkeeping equipment? Be specific in your reply.

CHAPTER XVIII

SPECIAL ACCOUNTS FOR PARTNERS' PROPRIETORSHIP

The proprietors of a business enterprise have been referred to at various times as partners in its ownership and management. The relations among partners give rise to certain aspects of financial status and operations which require special recognition in the double-entry accounts.

Partners' proprietorship affected by legal considerations.—The legal relationships between partners do not affect the principles of double-entry accounting; however, these relationships often affect the extent of each partner's proprietorship. A partnership agreement is a contract of two or more competent persons who place their money, effects, labor and skill, or some or all of them, in a lawful commerce or business and divide the profits and bear the losses in certain proportions. The partnership relation can be established by the investment of labor or skill, as well as other assets, provided the members of the partnership decide to share the loss or profit in agreed proportions.

The essentials of the partnership relation from the standpoint of financial status and operations are mutual agency and profit-and-loss sharing. The partnership relation may not exist where one man only is the agent of the other. Each partner must be liable for the acts of the other in so far as these acts are within the scope of the partnership agreement, expressed or implied. Common ownership of property does not in itself create a partnership; the aspects of mutual agency as well as agreement to share in profits or losses must be present. Courts have held an agreement on both of these points to be prima facie evidence of an intention to form a partnership.

The partnership relation is essentially a personal relation. Parties to a partnership agreement may not substitute persons in their places without the consent of all the other members of the partnership. The substitution of a partner through sale of one's investment really dissolves the original partnership and gives rise to a new one; however, these legal formalities are not always recognized in the accounting records. In the absence of an agreement to the contrary, profits and losses are assumed to be shared equally by the partners. Partners are not entitled to interest earnings on either Capital of Personal accounts unless they have so agreed; nor are they entitled to salaries, commissions, or compensation for special service. Any legal agreement covering these matters will, of course, be binding and effective between the partners.

Types of partnership.—Partnerships may be classified according to the nature of the liability of the partners or the scope or continuity of the partnership activities. On the basis of liability, *general* partnerships refer to those in which all the partners are unlimitedly liable for all the activities of the other partners. A *limited* partnership refers to one in which some of the partners (not all) have limited their liability to definitely agreed amounts, also the extent of their control over business policies. These amounts are known to outsiders who carry on the business transactions with the enterprise. There must be at least one partner with unlimited liability in every partnership.

The terms "general" and "limited" are also applicable to the scope or continuity of the business. For example, a general partnership in the grocery business would be one formed for the purpose of carrying on any transactions related to operating a grocery, such as purchasing, storage, borrowing money, selling, transportation, payment of wages, etc. It is also assumed that a general partnership of this type is continuous. A partnership may be limited as to the nature of certain business operations. An individual may be a partner with one man who leases apartment houses; he may be a partner with another man who leases hotels. This man is a party to two partnership agreements. Neither of his partners may hold him responsible or act as his agent in the activities outside the field for which each partnership relation is established.

A partnership may also be limited as to a period of time, or may end with the completion of a particular project. Partners may, for example, join in the construction of a particular building; their partnership relation does not remain in effect for the construction of other buildings. Partnerships formed for the purpose of carrying on specific projects are often referred to as "joint ventures."

Types of partners.—There may be various types of partners. A *general* partner is one who assumes unlimited liability and has authority to represent other members of the firm in all its activities. He holds himself out to the public as a partner of the enterprise and as one who is willing to assume responsibility for its activities. All partners are assumed to be general partners unless there is some definite notice or agreement to the contrary. Other terms are frequently used to designate partners who bear peculiar relations to the activities of the business. A *nominal* partner is a person who is a partner in name but not in fact. His name appears in the title of the firm, but he is not typically regarded by creditors as having liability for the payment of debts. The buying public alone considers this man as a member of the firm. A *silent* partner is a partner in fact, but not in name; he is liable for obligations of the partnership. His proprietorship in the firm is known to mercantile creditors and business houses which advance money or merchandise to the enterprise. The customers of the enterprise, however, typically do not know of this man's connection with the firm.

Partners' proprietorship classified in capital and personal accounts.—The problem of adequately expressing the partners' proprietorship in an enterprise may be divided into two parts: (1) expressing the original proprietorship at the time the business is organized or the partnership relation is established; (2) expressing the fluctuations in the proprietorship of the individual partners from time to time. Consequently two main types of partners' proprietorship accounts are used: Capital accounts to reflect original contributions and permanent additions and subtractions; Personal accounts to reflect periodic or temporary fluctuations.

Partners' capital accounts.—At the time a business enterprise is organized under the partnership form of control, a Capital account is opened for each of the partners. The total amount of proprietorship assigned to each partner is (usually) the value at which the investment of each partner is entered among the assets of the enterprise. Assume that A. B. Jones and J. D. Kunz decide to form a partnership and operate a mercantile enterprise; also that Mr. Jones contributes $10,000 in cash and $5,000 in merchandise, whereas Mr. Kunz contributes $2,000 in cash and a building to be valued in the accounts at $12,000. The entry to record the effects of this transaction and to open the books of the newly formed partnership would be as follows:

Debit: Cash	$12,000.00	
Merchandise	5,000.00	
Building	12,000.00	
Credit: A. B. Jones, capital		$15,000.00
J. D. Kunz, capital		14,000.00

The Capital accounts to reflect the total contributions of each partner would be:

A. B. Jones, Capital

	Jan. 1	$15,000.00

J. D. Kunz, Capital

	Jan. 1	$14,000.00

Partners' Personal accounts.—Periodic fluctuations in the proprietorship of the various partners may arise from any of several different sources. The effects of such fluctuations are not usually entered directly in the accounts which represent the permanent proprietorship of the partners. More often they are accumulated in temporary or intermediate accounts, pending their ultimate assignment to the Capital accounts. The intermediate accounts are referred to as Personal accounts, and are designated by titles consisting of the partners' names followed by the word, "personal." The data in the Personal accounts may be transferred to the Capital accounts whenever the partners wish to have it done.

Personal account for profits and losses.—A typical source of fluctuations in the partners' proprietorship is the net income or net loss from current business activities. The effects of the business operations are summarized in the Profit and Loss account; the balance in this account, after the income and expense items have been transferred thereto, represents the net loss or net profit of the period. This amount may be regarded as a deferred debit or credit to the proprietorship accounts. It is first transferred to the intermediate proprietorship accounts—the Personal accounts. Later it finds its way to the Capital accounts. Assume that on June 30 the Profit and Loss account of Jones and Kunz carries a credit balance of $6,000 after income and expense items have been summarized at the close of six months' operations. The journal entry to transfer the $6,000 credit from the Profit and Loss account to the Personal accounts of Jones and Kunz would be as follows:[1]

Debit: Profit and loss...............	$6,000.00	
Credit: A. B. Jones, personal..............		$3,000.00
J. D. Kunz, personal...............		3,000.00

If a balance sheet were prepared at this time, it would set forth total proprietorship which included $6,000 under the captions "A. B. Jones, personal" and "J. D. Kunz, personal." The proprietorship section would be:

Proprietorship:

A. B. Jones, capital.............	$15,000
A. B. Jones, personal............	3,000
J. D. Kunz, capital.............	14,000
J. D. Kunz, personal............	3,000

Suppose that Jones now decides to treat his newly acquired proprietorship as permanent Capital, whereas Kunz decides to withdraw cash equal to the amount shown in his Personal account.

[1] In the absence of specific agreement, partners share profits and losses equally regardless of relative capital investments. The journal entry above assumes that no agreement as to profits has been made or that the agreement states that profits will be shared equally.

The following entry would be made to close the Personal accounts of the partners:

A. B. Jones, personal	$3,000	
J. D. Kunz, personal	3,000	
A. B. Jones, capital		$3,000
Cash		3,000

The Capital and Personal accounts of the two partners, after posting, would appear as follows:

A. B. JONES, CAPITAL

		Jan. 1		$15,000.00
		June 30	A. B. Jones, personal	3,000.00

A. B. JONES, PERSONAL

June 30	A. B. Jones, capital	$3,000.00	June 30	Profit and loss	$3,000.00

J. D. KUNZ, CAPITAL

	Jan. 1	$14,000.00

J. D. KUNZ, PERSONAL

June 30	Cash	$3,000.00	June 30	Profit and loss	$ 3,000.00

A balance sheet prepared after the adjustment would include a proprietorship section as follows:

Proprietorship:

A. B. Jones, capital	$18,000.00	
J. D. Kunz, capital	14,000.00	
		$32,000.00

The capital of Jones has been increased $3,000; the capital of Kunz has not been changed. The Personal accounts have been closed in the ledger; hence do not appear on the balance sheet.

Personal accounts for other partners' relationships.—There are types of transactions other than income and expense which affect directly the proprietorship of the individual partners. Examples are loans, borrowings, interest allowances on invested capital, regular or occasional withdrawals of funds, and salary allowances. The effects of all of these transactions should be entered in the Personal accounts before they are finally recorded in the Capital accounts. But it is not necessary to record all such transactions in one Personal account. It may prove advantageous to maintain several Personal accounts with each partner, and, as a matter of fact, such procedure is very often followed. One encounters in the books of a partnership enterprise such account titles as the following: "A. B. Jones, Interest"; "A. B. Jones, Salary"; "A. B. Jones, Loan"; etc. Accounts may be opened to designate any type of business relationship which the partners assume toward the enterprise. Separate accounts are often opened to show that salaries are still payable to partners, that interest items are payable to or receivable from them, or that commissions have affected their proprietorship.[1]

Valuation of partners' proprietorship depends upon agreement.—Assume that a partner contributes a building as his share of the investment in an enterprise. Should this building be recorded in the accounts at original cost price, at market price, or at some other value? Fortunately the answer is not as difficult as it first appears. The valuation of an asset for the partnership accounts is essentially a private matter between the partners. Creditors may agree with or deny the valuation set upon these

[1] In the last analysis, all Personal accounts of the partners in the business enterprise may be considered Capital accounts. They are Capital accounts of special nature, which, on account of business policy, have not yet been merged with the accounts showing original or permanent investment. In case of liquidation, Personal accounts are treated as increases or decreases of the original capital investment. A partnership agreement may provide for various types of preferences in the claims on the assets and in the liability for losses. From the standpoint of outsiders, however, such agreements may be entirely ignored, except where they are known and specifically approved by such outsiders.

assets by the partners; but for the partners' own purposes, any reasonable values may be placed upon them. There is no limit to what may be considered as reasonable, except the limit of fraud or deception on the part of the partners in their relations with outsiders. Similarly the resulting partnership capital may be assigned to the partners in any proportions agreed upon by them. The assets contributed by a specific partner may, for example, be carried on the books of the partnership at a value of $10,000. The proprietorship assigned to the contributing partner may be more or less than $10,000, depending on the partnership agreement. Or it may be that one partner contributes $10,000 in tangible assets, whereas the other brings only his skill or good-will to the enterprise. The amounts credited to the Capital accounts upon the investment of the $10,000 may be divided equally, or in any other ratio, between the partners.

Admission of new partners.—Accounting for partnership formation introduces the problem of assigning correct amounts of capital to the original partners. The same problem also appears whenever a new partner is admitted to an existing partnership; here again the amount of capital assigned to an incoming partner is dependent upon the partnership agreement.[1] The introduction of a new partner may take place in two ways: (1) the incoming partner may bring additional funds to the business; (2) he may take over all or part of the proprietorship previously assigned to some other partner.

Assume that C. L. Downs purchases an interest in the partnership of Jones and Kunz for $10,000 and places the money in the business. The entry on the books of the partnership would be:

Cash....................	$10,000.00	
C. L. Downs, capital.............		$10,000.00

The total assets of the partnership are increased $10,000 by this transaction. The proprietorship is increased accordingly by the addition of the C. L. Downs, Capital account. By agreement the

[1] In the strict sense, it is impossible for a partner to be admitted to an existing partnership. The very admission of a new partner constitutes the establishment of an entirely new partnership. The previous partnership is dissolved; a new one is formed.

amount of proprietorship assigned to C. L. Downs might have been more or less than $10,000. The difference would be adjusted by additions to or subtractions from the Capital accounts of the original partners.

A partner may wish to withdraw from a partnership completely or partially. In such a case, he may either withdraw cash from the assets of the business or sell a portion of his proprietary rights to a new partner. If he chooses the latter course, an entry must be made to reassign the proprietorship in the first partner's Capital account. If A. B. Jones were to decide to withdraw partially from the partnership by selling $4,000 of his proprietary rights to H. C. Clem, the entry to record the transfer would be:

A. B. Jones, capital.........	$4,000.00	
H. C. Clem, capital...............		$4,000.00

This transaction does not give rise to an increase in total assets or in total proprietorship. The only accounts affected are the Capital accounts: the A. B. Jones, Capital account is decreased; the H. C. Clem, Capital account is given a place in the ledger. The price at which the proprietorship changed hands is of no consequence from the viewpoint of the double-entry records. It might have been more or less than the $4,000 involved in the shifting of capital proprietorship.

Partnership assets and liabilities may be assumed by an individual or by a corporation.—Partners may, if they so desire, dispose of the assets which they control in common, using part of them to repay the creditors and dividing the remainder among themselves. Frequently a partnership is dissolved for the express purpose of permitting new proprietors to carry forward the operations. Under such conditions, the new proprietors assume the assets and liabilities of the old partnership, and "pay off" the original owners in cash or other assets. From the standpoint of the double-entry records, this shifting of total proprietorship should be accounted for by completely closing the ledger of the partnership which is going out of business. This involves transferring all assets and liabilities to an account with the incoming proprietor, recording the receipt of the cash or other assets from the new proprietor, and finally reflecting the distribution of the cash or other assets to the original partners.[1]

In some instances a partnership is dissolved to permit the continuance of business operations by a corporation organized to assume the assets and liabilities of the partnership. The steps in closing the partnership books may be illustrated by using the data of the following balance sheet:

JONES AND KUNZ

BALANCE SHEET—JUNE 30, 19____

Assets:		*Liabilities:*	
Merchandise........	$13,250.00	Accounts payable....	$ 4,000.00
Accounts receivable..	6,750.00	Notes payable......	3,000.00
Buildings...........	11,000.00		
Delivery equipment..	8,000.00		$ 7,000.00
		Proprietorship:	
		A. B. Jones, capital..	$18,000.00
		J. D. Kunz, capital...	14,000.00
			$32,000.00
Total..........	$39,000.00	Total............	$39,000.00

The assets and liabilities of the partnership are to be transferred to the Newcomb Corporation. At the time the corporation assumes responsibility for the assets and liabilities, the following entry might be made on the books of the partnership:

Receivable from Newcomb Corporation..	$32,000.00	
Accounts payable....................	4,000.00	
Notes payable.......................	3,000.00	
Merchandise............................		$13,250.00
Accounts receivable......................		6,750.00
Buildings................................		11,000.00
Delivery equipment.......................		8,000.00

[1] In practice, however, the change of ownership is more often accomplished by an entry which transfers the proprietorship from one group of proprietors to another. When the new proprietors are a group of stockholders, the transfer may be effected by closing the individual Capital accounts with the partners, and substituting therefore a controlling account to represent the stockholders interests. Such an account may be entitled "Capital Stock."

When the Newcomb Corporation issues stock to the partnership in exchange for the assets and liabilities, the entry would be:

Newcomb Corporation capital stock....	$32,000.00	
Receivable from Newcomb Corporation.........		$32,000.00

The only asset of the partnership at this stage in the negotiations is the capital stock of the Newcomb Corporation. When the stock is distributed to the partners, the Capital accounts must be debited. The books of the partnership are then closed and may be discontinued. The entry would be:

A. B. Jones, capital..................	$18,000.00	
J. D. Kunz, capital..................	14,000.00	
Newcomb Corporation capital stock............		$32,000.00

None of the foregoing entries would affect the accounts of the corporation. The accounting records of the corporation would have no connection with those of the dissolved partnership. The partnership accounts are closed after the recording of the entries illustrated above. The opening of the books of the corporation is a separate task and a separate problem.

If the accounting records of the corporation were to be maintained in the same ledgers as were the records of the partnership, the last entry of the illustration would have sufficed to transfer the capital from the partners to the stockholders. It would have appeared essentially as follows:

A. B. Jones, capital..................	$18,000.00	
J. D. Kunz, capital..................	14,000.00	
Capital stock............................		$32,000.00

The Capital Stock account of the foregoing entry is the proprietorship account of the newly formed corporation. The asset and liability accounts are unchanged when the partners sell out to the stockholders; the stockholders may, in fact, be the same individuals as the partners. The only change in the accounting records when such a change of ownership is effected is the recognition of a new firm name and the introduction of one or more new Capital accounts.

QUESTIONS ON CHAPTER XVIII

1. Distinguish clearly between the partners' Capital accounts and their Personal accounts. Is the distinction a practical one for purposes of determining the financial condition of an enterprise? Explain.
2. A partner withdraws cash from an enterprise. Does he become a debtor of the business, or is he merely reducing his proprietorship? What difference would it make to a creditor of the enterprise as to which way the transaction is interpreted?
3. Journalize the following transactions, using only one Personal account. Post those which affect the Personal account, and indicate the debit or credit balance which would appear therein. (*a*) Under a previous agreement, partner T. R. Ingram is allowed 5 per cent interest on a capital investment of $10,000. (*b*) Ingram borrows $1,200 from the business, with the intention of paying it back soon. (*c*) He repays the loan of $1,200, and at the request of the other partners lends $600 to the enterprise. (*d*) At the end of a month, Mr. Ingram is credited with his agreed monthly salary of $325; he does not withdraw the amount immediately. (*e*) The enterprise repays Ingram $300 of the money he had advanced, also the salary with which he had been credited. (*f*) Mr. Ingram takes home for his personal use, merchandise valued at a cost price of $75. It has been agreed among the partners that such amounts should be regarded as sales of the enterprise, even though they are to be credited at cost price.
4. Journalize the transactions of Question 3, using as many Personal accounts for Mr. T. R. Ingram as you think it would be advisable to use.
5. Is the partnership a legal person? Can a partnership be sued? If not, how does a creditor proceed to collect a bad debt contracted by a partnership enterprise? What is a "silent" partner? A "nominal" partner?
6. In what ways may a partnership be limited? Illustrate or explain in detail.
7. Carl D. Longworth and V. C. Montgomery are partners in an enterprise with the following capital investments: Longworth, $6,400; Montgomery, $3,600. A. E. Borough purchases the interest of Montgomery. Journalize the transaction. Longworth and Borough admit M. L. Rourke as a third partner upon the payment of $5,200 in cash. Journalize the transaction.

CHAPTER XIX

SPECIAL ACCOUNTS FOR CORPORATE PROPRIETORSHIP

The principles of double-entry accounting are not affected by the type of enterprise for which the accounting records are maintained. Consequently an explanation of corporation accounts introduces no new phases of accounting theory. The problems of corporation accounting arise from the peculiarities of the proprietorship in a corporation, not from the types of transactions it carries on. A study of corporation accounts, then, must be introduced by a preliminary study of the general nature of corporations.

Corporate proprietorship affected by legal considerations.—The corporation in modern industrial society is an association of individuals, in some ways similar to the association of individuals in the partnership relation. But, unlike the partnership, the corporation itself is a legal person; it exists separate and apart from the individuals who are associated in the enterprise. Moreover, the individuals organizing a corporation are not the mutual agents of each other, nor are they ordinarily liable for the acts of each other or for those of the corporation. The corporation comes into existence through an act of the governing body under which it operates. It is a product of the government and is organized with the consent of the government for definite, stated purposes. The corporate form of organization is not limited to profit-seeking enterprises; cities and towns are incorporated, as are many hospitals, clubs, lodges, etc.

The corporation a device for accumulating funds.—The features of corporate organization with which we have to do here are those connected with raising of its funds, and the apportionment on the books of the corporation of the capital accruing to each contributor to those funds. The features of the corporation which make it an effective device for raising funds are:

1. *Limited liability of stockholders.*—Individuals who advance funds to a corporation are given certificates stating the amount of their ownership in the corporation. The holder of a certificate is not liable for loss beyond the amount of his original contribution (usually). He may lose the amount he invests in an enterprise; but, except in a few cases prescribed by the statutes, he cannot be called upon further to pay the obligations of the corporation.

2. *Transferability of corporate securities.*—Unlike the case of a partnership, the holder of a share of stock may sell his right in a corporation without destroying the corporate entity. He may also purchase securities without obtaining permission from other security holders.

3. *Division of capital into small units.*—The units of ownership are rarely exceedingly large; often the units range from $100 down to $1, or even less. Consequently people of moderate means may join with those of greater wealth in providing funds for the corporation. This feature makes it possible for ownership to be widely distributed, but with control to be centralized in a small group of stockholders.

4. *Various classes of corporate securities.*—Corporate proprietorship is often divided into common and preferred capital stock with various provisions distinguishing the holders' claims.[1] This situation makes it possible for the corporation to appeal to investors of different temperaments. The large aggregates of capital thus accumulated are in themselves suggestive of strength and stability; consequently they attract additional investors.

Administrative features of the corporation.—Large numbers of individuals are often associated in the corporate organization; hence the problem of administration becomes one of great importance. In the partnership the problem of administrative responsibility is settled by contract between the partners. Where the number of partners is large, the contract often must be very detailed and complex. Likewise, in the corporation the administrative control must be carried on in terms of a definite contract to which the investors subscribe at the time they purchase securities. This contract is expressed in the conditions governing the issue of the stock and in the by-laws of the corporation. Administrative responsibility for a corporate enterprise is usually delegated to a committee of stockholders known as the *board of directors.* The directors act as the official representatives of the corporation,

[1] The legal relations of the stockholders to the corporation vary with each class of stock; but the method of accounting for the issuance, transfer, and cancelation of shares is identical for all types of Capital stock. The transactions selected to illustrate corporate accounts will deal simply with capital stock, without regard to its classification.

and usually elect a chairman, who is chief administrative head of the enterprise. Directors are required by the laws of most states to be stockholders of the corporation. They, in turn, usually select from their number certain members who act as the executive officers of the corporation, such as president, vice-president, treasurer, and secretary. The administrative organization for the management of the incorporated business varies with the business activities of the corporation.

Relations between Corporation Ownership and Management

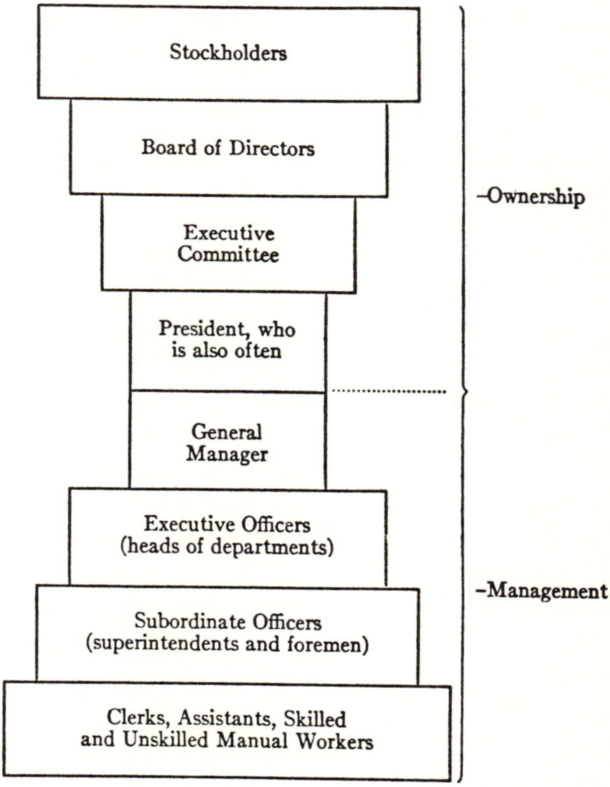

Limitations on corporate management.—All the acts of the directors must be performed in terms of a body of rules known as the *by-laws*,[1] which are prepared for and usually approved by the

[1] The by-laws are also known by other names, varying with the statutory requirements, such as "code of regulations."

entire group of stockholders. The by-laws of a corporation cover, among other things, the details concerning such points as the election and removal of officers, the borrowing of funds, and the distribution of income. The by-laws themselves are drawn in terms of and are limited by the *charter* of the corporation, which has been granted by the state or governing body. The charter (sometimes referred to as the "articles of incorporation") states the conditions under which the corporation has been organized and may operate. It covers such points as the total amount and number of shares of stock which may be issued and the type of activity in which the corporation may engage. The articles of incorporation are drawn up in terms of the constitution or statutes of the state government creating the corporation. Each state is, of course, limited in its powers by Acts of Congress and by the Federal Constitution.

Corporate proprietorship divided into proportionate shares of capital stock.—The stockholders of a corporation are joint owners in, and the ultimate managers of, the enterprise. The ownership is divided into *shares* of stock, which represent the portions of the total proprietorship to which each stockholder is entitled. If the articles of incorporation authorize the issuance of 1,000 shares of stock, each share represents $\frac{1}{1000}$ of the proprietorship, when all the shares are issued. If only one-half of the shares are issued, each share represents $\frac{1}{500}$ of the total proprietorship. Each stockholder holds one or more *stock certificates* which evidence the amount and nature of his interest in and control over the corporate property and activities. A stock certificate is, in effect, merely an evidence of a contract with the corporation. The corporation secures money or other assets from the stockholder; the certificate serves both as a receipt for funds and as evidence of an agreement. The corporation agrees to use the assets in certain definite ways, and to return equivalent assets, if possible, when the corporation ceases to exist. The corporation may also agree that certain stockholders shall have preference as to earnings or voting power. The details of stock agreements vary with the particular type of contract evidenced by the certificate.

Value of corporate shares.—Each share of stock is usually given a nominal or *par* value. This value serves as the basis for stating proprietorship in a corporate balance sheet. If, for example, 250 shares of stock have been issued by a corporation, and each share has been declared to have a par value of $50, the total proprietorship will be 250×$50, or $12,500. If it develops later that the actual proprietorship, as shown by the accounting records, should be more or less than $12,500, the adjustment is accomplished by entries in the Surplus account. Under such circumstances, the real value of stock must be regarded as some value other than par; accordingly shares of stock are often spoken of as having a *book* value. Book value is the proportionate value of each share in the total proprietorship as evidenced by the books (the accounts). If the accounts show the total proprietorship represented by 250 shares to be $14,000, the book value of each share is then $56, as compared to its par value of $50. Book value may be higher or lower than par value. *Market* value is the price at which shares of stock are exchanged in the open market, without regard to their par value or their book value. In view of the fact that the market values of shares are determined by proportionate interests in the total proprietorship, rather than by the nominal value known as par, many corporations have adopted the policy of issuing shares of stock for which a par value is not specified. Such shares are known as *no-par-value* shares, and are now legally authorized by the statutes of many states.

Capital Stock accounts.—Special accounts are necessary to record the holdings of the stockholders of a corporation—the total amount of stock which has been issued and is still "outstanding" at a given time. A controlling account should be maintained for the proprietorship represented by each class of stock. The total amount of all types of shares appears on the balance sheet under the heading "Capital stock." Information showing the number of shares of stock held by individual stockholders may be carried in a subsidiary *stockholders' ledger*. Such a ledger contains a record of the first issue of shares, as well as of transfers from one stockholder to another after shares have been issued. Changes in the ownership of shares do not affect the totals in the controlling accounts; in fact, independent subsidiary journals may be kept for authorizing the changes of the individual holdings. The first double-entry accounting records necessary for a corporation are those to record the acquisition of assets. Assets are usually first advanced to the corporation by people who are to become stockholders; their action is accompanied by the issuance of capital stock equal in par value to the agreed value of the assets. A journal entry must record the assets received and the stock issued. It would be made as follows:

Cash	$50,000.00	
Capital stock		$50,000.00
(To record the issuance for cash of 500 shares of $100 par value stock to miscellaneous stockholders.)		

The balance sheet of the corporation after such a transaction would be:

ASSETS		PROPRIETORSHIP	
Cash	$50,000.00	Capital stock	$50,000.00

Subsequent receipts of assets in exchange for capital stock would be recorded in the same way, until the total amount authorized had been issued.

Surplus.—In partnership records, the Capital accounts are adjusted only periodically; such procedure preserves the integrity of the original and permanent contributions of the partners. Similarly, in the corporation it is desirable—at times compulsory—to keep the records of capital stock separate from the records of periodic increases or decreases in proprietorship. Consequently a "*Surplus*" account is usually introduced to record the increase in the value of stockholders' interests from time to time. Profits or losses from business operations are transferred from the Profit and Loss account to the Surplus account at the close of each fiscal period. The balance in the Surplus account at any given time is added to the balance in the Capital Stock account to make up the total proprietorship on the corporation's balance sheet.

Capital stock	$40,000.00	
Surplus	10,000.00	
Total proprietorship		$50,000.00

When the business operations of a fiscal period result in a net loss to the corporation, this loss appears first as a debit in the Profit and Loss account. It is then transferred to the debit side of the Surplus account. When the Surplus account carries a debit balance, this amount is subtracted from the capital stock of the corporation to determine the total proprietorship. The debit balance in the Surplus account is usually referred to as a *deficit.* The outstanding capital stock, less the deficit existing at a given time, shows the net proprietorship.

Capital stock	$40,000.00	
Deficit	5,000.00	
Net proprietorship		$35,000.00

Classes of capital stock involve special privileges and responsibilities.—The privileges of all stockholders in corporations are not of equal rank. Some stockholders enjoy various preferences over others.

Common stock.—Common stock comprises the shares which entitle their holders to no assured privileges in the way of financial return. If the earnings of the corporation are large, the common stockholders receive the benefits. If the earnings of the corporation are small, or are negative, the common stockholders receive no return. Some of the general privileges ordinarily enjoyed by holders of common stock are: proportionate voting power; proportionate shares of current earnings; proportionate shares of assets remaining when the corporation is dissolved. These privileges are usually described on the face of the stock certificate; invariably they are set forth in the by-laws or the charter of the corporation.

Preferred stock.—Preferred stock is stock which enjoys a preference over the common stock, as well as all the privileges of common stock, unless expressly withheld according to the stock contract. The terms under which preferred stock shares are issued are carefully specified in the contract which the preferred stockholders make with the corporation when they purchase or subscribe for shares.[1] Some of the special ways in which preferred stock may be privileged are:

a) Voting power.—Preferred shareholders frequently have contingent voting power which enables them to protect their interests when these become endangered. This authority may be exercised when the financial status of the corporation is not in accord with the original agreement with the preferred stockholders.

b) Earnings.—The earnings of the company are apportioned to the preferred stock before being apportioned to the common stock. If the total income of the corporation is not sufficient to pay dividends to all stockholders, the preferred stockholders are given first consideration. These earnings are usually payable regularly in designated amounts, as, for example, annual dividends of 7 per cent on the par value of the stock. Preferred stock earnings may be *cumulative.* This means that if the income of the corporation is not great enough to pay dividends at the regular time, these dividends must ultimately be paid before common stockholders may share in the earnings of the corporation at later periods. The preferred stock, after receiving its income, may *participate* in additional earnings along with and on the same basis as the common shares; in practice most preferred stock is non-participating.

c) Protection.—Stock may also be preferred in the matter of protection of the original investment. In case of liquidation, preferred stockholders are usually given their share of the assets represented by their stock before the common stockholders are provided for.

Treasury stock.—After stock has once been issued, it may be transferred from one owner to another or may be turned back to the treasury of the corporation. In the latter case the corporation typically would pay cash or some other consideration to the stockholder; the share or shares in the hands of the corporation would then be available for reissue or for ultimate retirement. "Treasury stock" is a term used to describe stock which has been once issued but has been returned to the treasury of the corporation either by purchase, donation, or forfeiture. It is not to be confused with "unissued stock," which is stock that has never been issued. When stock is acquired by the company which issued the

[1] Guaranteed stock is stock the dividends of which are guaranteed by some corporation other than the issuing company. Watered stock is a popular phrase used to indicate stock that has been issued in exchange for assets known or assumed to be worth less than the par value of the shares. It has no technical meaning for accounting purposes.

shares, the accounting for the return of the stock is often very simple. The asset surrendered is credited, and a debit is made to an account entitled "Treasury Stock," as follows:

Treasury stock...........	$10,000.00	
Cash..........................		$10,000.00
(To record the purchase of 100 shares of stock at par value.)		

The treasury-stock total, together with unissued stock, should be deducted from authorized stock to determine the amount "outstanding," which appears on the balance sheet of a corporation:

Capital stock authorized................		$100,000
Less: Unissued stock.......	$50,000	
Treasury stock.......	10,000	60,000
Outstanding....................		$ 40,000

Stock premium and discount.—Stock may be sold at prices higher or lower than the par value of the shares issued. The question arises: How shall this excess above par value, usually referred to as *premium*, or the amount below par value—the *discount*—be treated? Obviously the premium on the capital stock issued must be considered additional proprietorship of the corporation. But how should it appear in the accounts and on the balance sheet? It could, of course, be merged with the surplus; on the other hand there are good arguments for maintaining its separate identity in the records. One argument is that the premium may thus be offset by the discount on other shares of stock which are sold at other times at prices below par.[1]

The following journal entries show the method of recording sales of stock at a premium or discount:

Cash.......................	$51,000.00	
Capital stock, preferred..............		$50,000.00
Preferred stock premium.............		1,000.00
(To record the sale of 500 shares of $100 par value preferred stock at a price of $102 per share.)		

[1] Most states do not permit the sale of stock at a discount. All shares must be paid for in full, before they can be issued to the stockholders. But even in states which permit the issuance of shares as fully paid, when they have been sold below par, the contract is good only between the stockholders and the corporation. Creditors of the corporation may insist, in case of a deficit, that the difference between the amount paid by the stockholder and the par or other value at the time of sale be paid by the stockholders who have purchased such shares at a discount.

Cash	$49,000.00	
Preferred stock discount	1,000.00	
Capital stock, preferred		$50,000.00

(To record the sale of 500 shares of $100 par value preferred stock at a price of $98 per share.)

Special accounts necessary to record subscriptions for shares of stock previous to their issuance.—In the foregoing illustrations it has been assumed that each share of capital stock issued was completely paid for at the time of issue. It often happens, however, that purchasers of stock do not wish to pay for the shares immediately. They "subscribe for" (that is, agree to purchase) certain shares of stock which they intend to pay for later, either at one time or in a series of instalments. This practice requires the introduction of accounts which will show the amounts receivable and received from these subscribers. There must also be accounts to show the total amount of stock which has been subscribed for but which at a particular moment of time still remains unissued. To illustrate, assume that 500 shares of capital stock have been subscribed for by a group of prospective stockholders. The journal entry would be:

Subscriptions receivable	$50,000.00	
Capital stock subscribed		$50,000.00

(To record the subscription for 500 shares $100 par value capital stock.)

The account entitled "Subscriptions Receivable" is, in effect, an account receivable; it shows the total amount receivable from the individuals who have agreed to purchase shares of stock. The debit balance in the Subscriptions Receivable account is reduced by receipts of cash or other assets from individual subscribers. The Subscriptions Receivable account is usually a controlling account supported by subsidiary records with each subscriber. The subsidiary information is contained in the *subscribers' ledger*. The accounts with the subscribers may be similar in form to the accounts with other debtors of the corporation. The journal entry to record a partial payment of the subscription would be as follows:

Cash	$25,000.00	
Subscriptions receivable		$25,000.00

(To record the payment of $50 per share on 500 shares $100 par value capital stock.)

To continue the illustration, assume that the final payments were made in merchandise and real estate, in equal amounts. The journal entry would be:

Merchandise	$12,500.00	
Land and buildings	12,500.00	
Subscriptions receivable		$25,000.00

After the foregoing entries were posted, the account Subscriptions Receivable would be in balance and would appear as follows:

SUBSCRIPTIONS RECEIVABLE

Capital stock subscribed	$50,000.00	Cash	$25,000.00
		Merchandise	12,500.00
		Land and buildings	12,500.00
	$50,000.00		$50,000.00

Turn now to the Capital Stock Subscribed account. It shows the total amount of stock which has been subscribed for but which is not yet issued. It is opened with a credit balance, which is reduced when the shares are issued to the subscribers. In the case illustrated above, no shares would be issued until the final payment had been made for them. The issuance of the shares of stock is recorded by transferring the credit balance in the Capital Stock Subscribed account to the Capital Stock account, which contains a record of the capital stock issued and outstanding. The following journal entry is required:

Capital stock subscribed	$50,000.00	
Capital stock		$50,000.00

(To record the issuance to subscribers of 500 shares $100 par value capital stock.)

The account with Capital Stock Subscribed is in balance, after posting, and appears as follows:

CAPITAL STOCK SUBSCRIBED

Capital stock	$50,000.00	Subscriptions receivable	$50,000.00

The receipt of the cash or other assets from the subscribers is journalized independently of the issuance of the stock to them. The transactions are separate; the assets must be received and subscriptions must be paid in full before stock is issued to subscribers.

Records of authorized and unissued stock need not be (but may be) of double-entry type.—The Capital Stock account which has been illustrated contains a record of the par value of the total issued and outstanding shares of a certain class of stock. It is a controlling account supported by a stockholders' ledger, which contains detailed information concerning the holdings of each stockholder. The Capital Stock account gives no indication, of itself, as to the amount of stock authorized and unissued; such information, however, may well be set forth on the balance sheet, even if not made a part of the formal double-entry records. A special memorandum account may be opened entitled "Capital Stock Authorized," or "Authorized Capital Stock." It would not be listed in a trial balance of the ledger accounts or adjusted when capital stock is subscribed for or issued. It would serve merely for information at the time of preparing a balance sheet. Assume that the shares subscribed for and issued in the foregoing illustration were part of an original issue of 1,000 shares. The ledger would contain a memorandum entry of the authorization to issue 1,000 shares. At the time a balance sheet was prepared, the accountant could compare this information with the credit balance in the Capital Stock account. From these two sources he would observe that 500 shares were still unissued; and he would prepare his balance sheet accordingly, somewhat as follows:

Capital stock:		
Authorized	$100,000.00	
Unissued	50,000.00	
Outstanding		$50,000.00

It is possible, however, to bring the data concerning authorized and unissued stock into the ledger by opening accounts with each item. For example, the authorization of 1,000 shares of $100 par value capital stock might be recorded as follows:

Unissued capital stock	$100,000.00	
Authorized capital stock		$100,000.00

These two accounts offset each other; the difference between them represents the capital stock outstanding, which, of course, at the time of authorization is none. When shares of stock are issued, they would be credited to the Unissued Capital Stock account, thereby reducing the amount of stock recorded as unissued. The less "unissued," the more "issued." The entry for the issuance of 500 shares of stock at par would be:

Cash........................	$50,000.00	
Unissued capital stock...............		$50,000.00

In case the shares had been subscribed for previous to their issue, the entry to record their issue would have been:

Subscribed capital stock.......	$50,000.00	
Unissued capital stock...............		$50,000.00

When the Unissued Capital Stock account is used, the credit entries (not credit "balance"—this account has a debit balance, if any) therein are the controlling general-ledger records for the stockholders' ledger. The general ledger contains no separate account for the capital stock outstanding; this amount can be determined only by comparing the credit balance in the Authorized Capital Stock account with the debit balance in the Unissued Capital Stock account. The balance sheet would set forth the data in the same manner as illustrated above.

Corporate proprietorship may be reduced by dividends.—A corporation may increase its net assets through financial operations or additional contributions and thus build up its Surplus account. Frequently it is desirable, however, definitely to apportion part of the increased surplus among the stockholders. By such action, assets may be prevented from accumulating beyond the immediate or expected requirements of the enterprise. The term "dividends payable" is used to indicate the liability of a corporation which has declared a dividend from its surplus, an amount payable to the stockholders.[1]

[1] The corporation's contract with holders of preferred stock usually states that these stockholders shall receive regular payments of cash amounting to a certain percentage of the par value of the shares (when, as, and if the net earnings of the corporation are equal to this amount, and when the dividend is declared payable by the directors). The ownership of the different corporate shares is evidenced by

The declaration of dividends.—Dividend transactions comprise two distinct steps—their declaration and their payments. The first takes place in the meeting of the board of directors, after the board has decided that the financial status of the corporation warrants the distribution of a part of the assets among the stockholders. The second is the routine procedure of paying the proper amounts to the holders of shares on which dividends have been declared. The entry to record the creation of a liability for the payment of dividends would be:

Surplus	$3,500.00	
Dividends payable		$3,500.00

(To record the declaration of annual dividends payable of 7 per cent on 500 shares of $100 par value preferred stock.)

The amount $3,500 appears in the ledger and on the balance sheet of the corporation as a liability.

Payment of dividends.—The liability for the payment of dividends is ultimately liquidated in the same way that other corporate liabilities are reduced. Dividends paid or payable in cash are known as *cash dividends*. An entry to liquidate the 7 per cent dividend illustrated above would be made as follows:

Dividends payable	$3,500.00	
Cash		$3,500.00

(To record the payment in cash of 7 per cent dividends declared payable on 500 shares of $100 par value preferred stock.)

The assets of a corporation may be of such types that it is inconvenient to pay declared dividends with cash. In these cases a corporation may distribute written evidences of the liability. These written certificates are known as "scrip"; they indicate when and under what conditions the holders may turn them back

stock certificates, record of which is maintained by the corporation itself or an independent "registrar." Transfers are recorded by the corporation; and the stockholders' ledger, of course, indicates the number of shares held by each stockholder. Dividends are usually declared payable to the stockholders whose names appear in the records as of a certain date. This date may be before or after the date of the declaration of the dividend. The date of payment of the dividend may be any time after its declaration.

to the corporation in exchange for cash. Dividends payable or paid by the issuance of scrip certificates are known as *scrip dividends.*

There may be times when it is unnecessary or unwise to distribute assets among the stockholders; it may suffice definitely to assign the surplus proprietorship to the individual stockholders by issuing more shares of stock to them. Stockholders who wish cash may then dispose of their new shares at the prevailing market prices. The process of converting the surplus into capital stock is known as the declaration and payment of *stock dividends.* The dividends are declared payable in the usual way. They are then paid by the issuance of stock certificates instead of by the payment of cash. Entries to reflect the declaration of a dividend and its payment in shares of stock are illustrated below:

Surplus........................	$5,000.00	
Common dividends payable............		$5,000.00

(To record the declaration of a 20 per cent dividend on 250 shares of $100 par value common stock.)

Common dividends payable......	$5,000.00	
Capital stock, common................		$5,000.00

(To record the payment in capital stock of a 20 per cent dividend on 250 shares of $100 par value common stock.)

The declaration of a dividend, and its payment in capital stock, does not increase the book value of stockholders' ownership in the corporation. The transaction merely changes the form of the proprietorship from surplus to capital stock.

Bonds an important source of corporate funds.—One very important source of corporate funds has not been discussed. This is *bonds.* The issuance of bonds is not a privilege legally restricted to the corporate form of organization; individuals or partnerships may issue bonds if they wish. As a practical matter, however, the issuance of bonds for sale on the open market is a procedure followed almost exclusively by corporations. Consequently the accounting entries necessary to record the issuance and repayment of bonds will be illustrated at this point. If a corporation were to issue its bonds in the total amount of $100,000 in order to secure funds, the following entry would be made:

Cash...................... $100,000.00
Bonds payable.................... $100,000.00
(To record the issuance at par of $100,000 5 per cent, 20-year bonds.)

Bonds bear a specified rate of interest, which is usually payable annually or semiannually. The payment of the interest on bonds payable is usually recorded as an expense transaction. Each semi-annual interest payment on the bonds described above would be recorded as follows:

Interest expense................ $2,500.00
Cash............................. $2,500.00
(To record the payment of the semi-annual interest on $100,000, 5 per cent, bonds payable.)

Bonds are not, of course, representations of corporate proprietorship. They are in the legal sense of the term the liabilities of the corporation; they are the property rights of creditors rather than of proprietors. It is true that creditors may at times exercise extensive control over corporate policy and management. Nevertheless, the distinction should be sharply drawn between bondholders as creditors and stockholders as proprietors.

A corporation may assume the assets and liabilities of another enterprise.—A corporation may purchase the assets and assume the liabilities of another enterprise, an individual proprietorship, a partnership, or a corporation. Payment therefor may be made in cash, other assets, or in shares of stock in the purchasing corporation. The following conditions illustrate typical entries on the books of a corporation when stock is issued in exchange for the resources and obligations of another enterprise. Assume that the American Corporation decides to take over the assets and liabilities of Allison & Doliver, partners, whose balance sheet includes the following data:

ASSETS		LIABILITIES AND PROPRIETORSHIP	
Accounts receivable...	$ 21,000.00	Accounts payable.....	$ 18,000.00
Merchandise.........	48,000.00	J. B. Allison, capital...	60,000.00
Building............	60,000.00	O. B. Dolliver, capital.	67,000.00
Land...............	16,000.00		
Total...........	$145,000.00	Total.............	$145,000.00

Journal entries may be recorded which will bring the assets and liabilities of the partnership into the accounts as assets and liabilities of the corporation. The difference between them will represent an amount due to the partners from the corporation. This may be paid in cash or by the issuance of capital stock. The journal entries follow:

Accounts receivable	$21,000.00	
Merchandise	48,000.00	
Building	60,000.00	
Land	16,000.00	
Accounts payable		$ 18,000.00
J. B. Allison and O. B. Dolliver, vendors		127,000.00

(To record receipt of certain assets and assumption of certain liabilities of the partnership, Allison & Dolliver.)

J. B. Allison and O. B. Dolliver, vendors	$127,000.00	
Capital stock, common		$127,000.00

(To record the issuance of 1,270 shares $100 par value common stock to J. B. Allison and O. B. Dolliver, vendors of certain assets and liabilities of the partnership formerly carried on under the name of Allison & Dolliver.)

The controlling accounts only are shown here. The stock certificate book and transfer book would carry the data for opening accounts in the stockholders' ledger with Allison & Dolliver. Complete accounting for the proprietorship of a large corporation requires the maintenance of specialized journals for posting to the controlling and subsidiary accounts with subscribers and stockholders. For discussion and illustration of this specialized technique the reader is referred to the classified group of works on accounting which appears in the rear of this book.

QUESTIONS ON CHAPTER XIX

1. Why is it true that the accounting problems which are distinctly those of the corporation center around the correct expression of proprietorship? Why is the problem of expressing proprietorship more complex for the corporation than for other forms of business organization?
2. What characteristics of the corporation make it an effective device for accumulating funds? Does the corporation possess any administrative advantages which are not common to other forms of large-scale enterprise?

3. What is a share of stock? Is it an asset on the balance sheet of the issuing corporation? Is it an asset on the balance sheet of the stockholder?
4. What is the meaning of the term "par value"? "book value"? "market value"? "no-par value"?
5. Explain the nature of the following phases of proprietorship accounts: Capital Stock; Surplus; Treasury Stock; Reserves; Undivided Profits; Subscriptions Receivable; Capital Stock Unissued; Capital Stock Authorized; Capital Stock Subscribed; Stock Discount; Stock Premium.
6. What is meant by preferred stock? common stock?
7. What are dividends? Are they assets, liabilities, or proprietorship? In what way may dividends be "paid off"? What are the essential accounting steps in recording dividend transactions?
8. What journal entries are necessary when a corporation purchases the assets and assumes the liabilities of a partnership? Assume that the partners are paid in cash. Assume that partners are paid in capital stock. Is the problem for purchasing the business of the partnership essentially different from the issuing of stock in exchange for other assets?
9. What are bonds? Are they proprietorship items in the technical or legal sense? Do bondholders have control over the assets of the business? Do they have voting power? Do they have special protection?
10. Journalize the transactions to record the following:
    a) Issue of $20,000, 5 per cent, 20-year bonds at face value.
    b) Payment of annual interest instalment.
    c) Payment of the bonds at maturity.
11. Journalize the following, and post to appropriate accounts:
    a) Authorization of $100,000 preferred stock; $100,000 common stock.
    b) Receipt of subscriptions for $14,000 common stock, $36,000 preferred stock.
    c) Receipt of cash payment of 50 per cent from all common-stock subscribers.
    d) Receipt of payments in full from one-half of the preferred-stock subscribers; issuance of the shares which are fully paid.
    e) Sale for cash and issue of $40,000 preferred stock.
    f) Half the common-stock subscribers pay up in full and receive their stock certificates.
    g) $50,000 of common stock is issued in exchange for miscellaneous assets.
12. Indicate how the facts in the accounts of Question 11 would appear on the balance sheet.

CHAPTER XX

MANUFACTURING AND OTHER SUMMARY ACCOUNTS

The double-entry system provides a technique for general classification of data in terms of accounts which express financial status and reflect business operations. The classifying devices may be specialized to serve the specific needs of individual enterprises or to deal with certain types of activity. Similarly the process of summarizing the data may be specialized—the effects of business operations may be grouped to reveal the net results of certain activities. It is the purpose of this chapter to indicate some of the activities with which certain income and expense data may be identified, and to show how these operations may be summarized in the accounts.

The trading account summarizes merchandise operations.— The statement of income and expense frequently is arranged to segregate all operations which involve merchandise, such as purchases, sales, returns, allowances, and discounts. The net result of such computations is to arrive at a figure known as "gross profit on sales," from which may be subtracted the various expenses of other business operations. The merchandise data may be summarized in a "*Trading*" account. All previous inventory balances are transferred to the Trading account, and the ending inventories are removed therefrom at the time of summarization. The net credit or debit balance in the Trading account then represents the gross profit (or loss) on merchandise operations. This amount may be transferred to the Profit and Loss account to be offset against or added to the various other expenses of operation which appear on the conventional statement of income and expense. The Trading account on page 269 illustrates the types of data which may be summarized therein.

The Cost of Goods Sold account may itself be used as a clearing account, from which the "Cost of goods sold" is transferred to the Trading account. Similarly the net sales may be determined by offsetting the sales returns and allowances in the Sales account, the resulting balance being transferred to the Trading account.

TRADING

Mdse. Inv., Jan. 1	$1,600.00	Sales, Jan. 1–June 30	$7,600.00
Purchases, Jan. 1–June 30	6,500.00	Purchase returns, Jan. 1–June 30	110.00
Sales returns	200.00	Mdse. Inv., June 30	2,100.00
Balance to profit and loss	1,510.00		
Total	$9,810.00	Total	$9,810.00

Manufacturing accounts summarize factory operations.—In the previous chapters it has been a simple problem to compute the cost of goods sold. The total goods on hand at the opening of an operating period were added to those purchased during the period. The amount still on hand was determined by inspection and appraisal of the goods. The remainder was considered to have been sold during the period of operations. But manufacturing enterprises face a more complex problem in the computation of the cost of goods sold. The task is complicated by the fact that the product sold by the enterprise is different from the materials purchased. The materials purchased are subjected to various treatments within the plant, so that the same units of measure will not suffice to estimate the quantities both of goods purchased and of goods sold. Materials are changed by the labor of workmen who apply tools to them or by the operations of certain machinery and equipment. The value of the human labor and the other processes must be regarded as adding to the value of the materials consumed in factory operations. Consequently accounts must be established to assemble the costs of various products or services, in order that the total cost of the goods sold can be computed.

The materials of a manufacturing concern, it has been suggested, pass through an intermediate stage between their purchase and sale, the stage of manufacturing operations. They are transformed from raw materials by the various processes of manufacture. They later emerge as finished product. Accordingly, the inventory accounts should separate the total materials in terms of the stage before, during, and after which they are affected by the manufacturing processes. To accomplish this segregation, the accounting records of a factory must contain three separate types of merchandise inventories; these are known as *raw materials* (before operations), *goods in process* (during operations), and *finished goods* (after operations). As the raw materials pass to the finished-goods stage, they accumulate other values, including direct factory labor and the various indirect expenses of operations (factory burden). The materials and labor which can be easily identified with a specific product or service are often referred to as the "direct costs" of that product or service. Those which cannot be so traced are called the "indirect costs."[1] Complete accounting for factory operations comprises a record of all direct and indirect costs incurred, and summarizes them in the ledger of the enterprise.

The following diagram compares the steps in the calculation of cost of goods sold for a mercantile and a manufacturing concern.

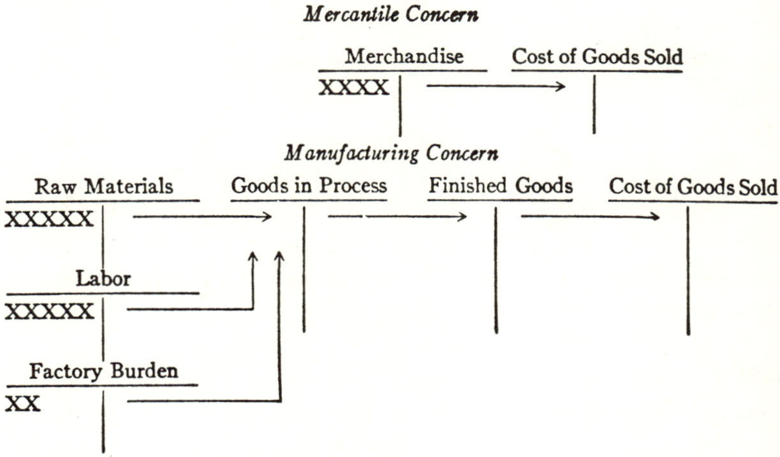

[1] Chapter xxxix, "Administrative Uses of Cost Data," discusses the characteristics of direct and indirect costs, in so far as they affect business policies and control. Factory burden is synonymous with "indirect costs," or "overhead costs," as far as the items composing them are concerned. The term "factory burden" is sometimes used to refer to a summary or clearing account through which the various indirect costs pass.

The Goods in Process account is debited with the value of materials consumed and of labor expended upon them; it is credited with the value of products completed which pass over into the finished-goods classification. The Goods in Process account would normally carry a debit balance, if the entries were made currently to represent the factory operations. This debit balance would represent the inventory of goods in process at any given time. But the Goods in Process account is sometimes used only for periodic summarization, at which times the values of the inventories of total raw materials and finished goods are determined.

To illustrate the method of summarizing costs of manufacture in the Goods in Process account, assume that the following amounts represent debit balances in certain accounts of the general ledger of a manufacturing concern.

Raw materials	$25,867.00
Direct labor costs	32,654.00
Depreciation	3,250.00
Superintendence	2,400.00
Power, heat, light	450.00
Taxes and insurance	325.00
Indirect labor costs	1,390.00
Miscellaneous	624.00
Goods in process (inventory)	4,310.00
Finished goods (inventory)	5,416.00

Two of the accounts contain inventory balances as of a previous date: they are Goods in Process and Finished Goods. These accounts should be adjusted to show the amounts on hand at the present time. But they cannot be adjusted properly until all entries have been made in them which should be charged to the accounts. Assume that the remaining inventories are valued as follows: raw materials, $1,450; goods in process, $3,516; finished goods, $6,312. These inventories make it possible to compute the costs of two important types of operations: cost of goods manufactured; cost of goods sold. The assembling of the manufacturing costs and of the cost of goods sold is not difficult. The amounts of materials consumed, the labor costs, and the indirect costs are transferred to the Goods in Process account, where they are added to the beginning inventory of goods in process.[1] The value of the goods completed is transferred to the Finished Goods account. The necessary adjustments to reflect the manufacturing and mercantile operations are shown below:

Debit: Goods in process	$24,417.00	
Credit: Raw Materials		$24,417.00
Debit: Goods in process	32,654.00	
Credit: Direct labor costs		32,654.00
Debit: Factory burden[2]	8,439.00	
Credit: Depreciation		3,250.00
Superintendence		2,400.00
Power, heat, light		450.00
Taxes and insurance		325.00
Indirect labor costs		1,390.00
Miscellaneous		624.00
Debit: Goods in process	8,439.00	
Credit: Factory burden		8,439.00
Debit: Finished goods	66,304.00	
Credit: Goods in process		66,304.00
Debit: Cost of goods sold	65,408.00	
Credit: Finished goods		65,408.00

The accounts, graphically portrayed to represent the summary of the cost data, are shown on page 273.

The Raw Materials, Goods in Process, and Finished Goods accounts each carry debit balances, following the closing entries just illustrated. These balances represent inventories of goods in

[1] The present illustration does not separate the raw materials on hand at the beginning of the fiscal period from those purchased during the period. In practice, all goods may be charged to the Raw Materials account at the time of purchase, from which they are charged individually to the costs of manufacture at the time they are used. The detailed records of raw materials would thus represent a "perpetual inventory" of the raw materials on hand at any one time. The controlling account with Raw Materials would not typically be adjusted whenever goods were consumed in factory operations, but only when it became necessary to compute the total costs of goods manufactured and sold. It will be assumed (for the sake of illustration) that the total debit in the Raw Materials account comprises an inventory of $1,320, established as a balance when the account was last adjusted.

[2] The expenses charged into the Factory Burden account are the "indirect" costs of operation, which must be allocated to the different products manufactured. They are first summarized in the Factory Burden account, in order that the total may be assigned in whole or in part to the cost of the "goods in process."

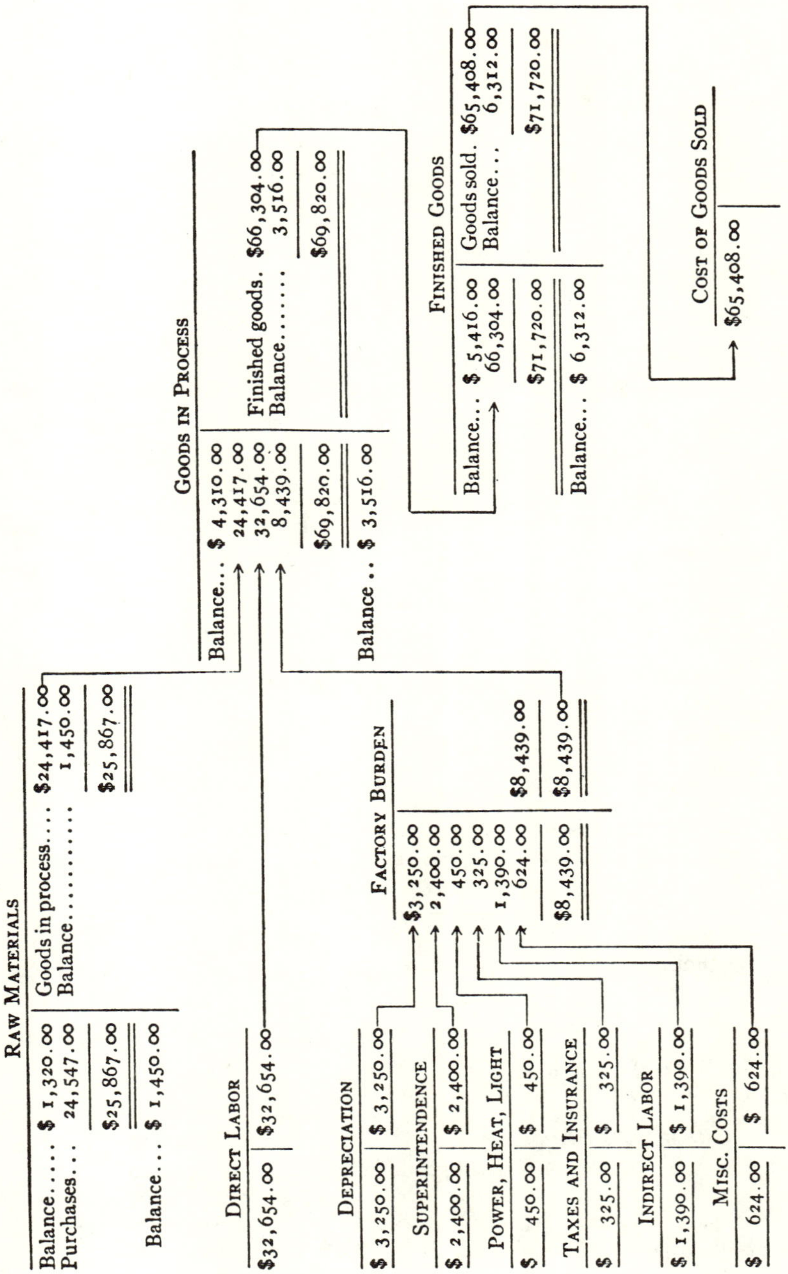
Raw Materials
Balance..... $ 1,320.00
Purchases... 24,547.00
$25,867.00
Balance... $ 1,450.00
Goods in process.... $24,417.00
Balance............ 1,450.00
$25,867.00
Direct Labor
$32,654.00
$32,654.00
Depreciation
$ 3,250.00
$ 3,250.00
Superintendence
$ 2,400.00
$ 2,400.00
Power, Heat, Light
$ 450.00
$ 450.00
Taxes and Insurance
$ 325.00
$ 325.00
Indirect Labor
$ 1,390.00
$ 1,390.00
Misc. Costs
$ 624.00
$ 624.00
Factory Burden
$3,250.00
2,400.00
450.00
325.00
1,390.00
624.00
$8,439.00
$8,439.00
$8,439.00
Goods in Process
Balance... $ 4,310.00
24,417.00
32,654.00
8,439.00
$69,820.00
Balance.. $ 3,516.00
Finished goods. $66,304.00
Balance....... 3,516.00
$69,820.00
Finished Goods
Balance... $ 5,416.00
66,304.00
$71,720.00
Balance... $ 6,312.00
Goods sold. $65,408.00
Balance... 6,312.00
$71,720.00
Cost of Goods Sold
$65,408.00

the three stages of manufacture; the inventories would appear on a balance sheet as follows:

Merchandise inventory:		
Raw materials..........	$1,450.00	
Goods in process........	3,516.00	
Finished goods..........	6,312.00	
Total........................		$11,278.00

Manufacturing-cost schedule.—The cost-of-goods-sold section of a statement of income and expense is more complex for a manufacturing concern than for a mere trading enterprise. The change in form of the materials and the assembly of manufacturing costs must be completely expressed. If we use the data of the foregoing illustration, the costs of goods manufactured and sold would be set forth as follows:

Raw materials:				
Beginning inventory...	$ 1,320.00			
Purchases...........	24,547.00			
	$25,867.00			
Ending inventory.....	1,450.00	$24,417.00		
Direct labor costs.................		32,654.00		
Factory burden:				
Depreciation.........	$ 3,250.00			
Superintendence......	2,400.00			
Power, heat, light....	450.00			
Taxes and insurance..	325.00			
Indirect labor costs...	1,390.00			
Miscellaneous........	624.00	8,439.00		
Total manufacturing costs..........		$65,510.00		
Beginning inventory goods in process (add)....................		4,310.00		
		$69,820.00		
Ending inventory goods in process (subtract)..................		3,516.00		
Cost of goods manufactured................			$66,304.00	
Beginning inventory finished goods (add)......			5,416.00	
			$71,720.00	
Ending inventory finished goods (subtract)....			6,312.00	
Cost of goods sold..............................				$65,408.00

The same data can be expressed in condensed form as follows:

Raw materials purchased	$24,547.00
Less: Increased raw-material inventory	130.00
Raw materials consumed	$24,417.00
Add: Direct labor	32,654.00
Factory burden	8,439.00
Decreased work-in-process inventory	794.00
Cost of goods manufactured	$66,304.00
Less: Increased finished-goods inventory	896.00
Cost of goods sold	$65,408.00

Subsidiary records identify certain costs with specific units of product or service.—No mention has been made of the subsidiary accounts which might be adopted to support the main inventory accounts of a manufacturing concern. Each of the controlling accounts would typically be supported by elaborate subsidiary data, which show in detail the main facts shown elsewhere in summary. The data include complete records of the materials consumed and the labor expended during a period of operations; also the detailed items of indirect costs. These records support the Raw Materials, Direct Labor, and Factory Burden accounts, respectively. The most complex records, however, are those which are subsidiary to the Goods in Process account. The various phases of the goods in process must be accounted for in terms of cost units selected for the purpose at hand. An appropriate unit for accumulating subsidiary manufacturing cost data is a very important aid to production control. The manufacturing costs may be assembled merely in terms of the types of product or types of manufacturing processes. But often the sub-classification of the cost is very detailed and identifies certain costs with designated portions of the output or the manufacturing processes. For example, a hat-manufacturing company may wish to compute the total cost of manufacturing ten hats of a certain size, style, and quality, or a chemical company may wish to determine the total cost of dissolving twenty pounds of certain chemical solids.

Cost accounting.—The manipulation of the subsidiary journals and ledgers for assembling cost data in terms of products or services known as "cost units" is the particular function of *cost ac-*

counting. Cost accounting is, of course, applicable to selling costs as well as to manufacturing costs. It has been most generally and most fully developed in the latter field, where the selection of adequate units for assembling the subsidiary cost data has been carefully studied. The identification of certain costs of manufacture with units of product is not an easy task. One may ask: What is the total cost of manufacturing ten hats of a certain style, size, and quality? The direct costs are ordinarily easily computed. It can be determined, for example, that five square yards of felt valued at $5 per square yard were used in the processes; also that three laborers expended a total of ten hours of time valued at $1 per hour. This makes a total cost of materials and labor to be $35, computed as follows:

Five yards of material @ $5.00........	$25.00
Ten hours of labor @ $1.00...........	10.00
	$35.00

But does $35 represent the total cost of manufacturing the ten hats? No. For many other indirect manufacturing costs must also be added, such as rent, light, foreman's salaries, etc. All of these other expenses (sometimes referred to as the "overhead" or "overhead costs") are as much a part of the cost of making the hats as the materials consumed and the labor expended. But how much of the individual or total indirect expenses should be charged against the cost of these ten hats? This question is not easily answered. It must be dealt with in terms of an agreed schedule for apportioning factory burden to the cost units. The methods of estimating total indirect costs and of apportioning them equitably to specific processes or units of product comprise the technique of cost accounting. It is not the function of the present chapter, or of this text, to explain the technique of assembling costs. Such technique must be mastered by study of books devoted to the subject of cost accounting and by contact with the problems of factory administration. But the reader should have gained from the foregoing comments the realization that accounting for manufacturing operations is not different in principle from accounting for mercantile operations. Manufacturing data are classified and summarized according to the general principles of double-entry accounting. Their treatment is differentiated from other accounting methods only by the peculiar conditions encountered and by the devices necessary for dealing with them.

Conclusion.—The principle underlying a "summary" account should be sharply distinguished from that underlying "controlling" and "subsidiary" accounting data. A summary account groups or offsets accounting data of the same order, such as when the general-ledger accounts with incomes and expenses are closed to the Profit and Loss account. A controlling account, on the other hand, is merely one which contains in total the data appearing in detailed subsidiary records, such as Accounts Receivable supported by the data in the customers' ledger. The data in the controlling and subsidiary records are often maintained concurrently. Summary accounts, as well as the accounts which are summarized therein, may at the same time be "controlling" accounts supported by subsidiary data.

QUESTIONS ON CHAPTER XX

1. The Trading account summarizes the results of the transactions affecting merchandise? What are these transactions? What is the net figure resulting from the data in the Trading account?
2. What costs should be regarded as costs of manufacturing goods? In what way is the classification of manufacturing costs into direct costs and indirect costs a useful division? What are indirect costs?
3. What advantage is gained by summarizing the various indirect costs into the Factory Burden account before transferring the total to the cost of goods in process?
4. Why is it necessary to maintain subsidiary records of the following: raw materials; labor; indirect expenses; goods in process; finished goods? What practical advantages may be gained from knowing at all times just what various units of output have cost the enterprise?
5. Do you think it would be advisable to attempt to summarize various aspects of the selling costs as well as of the cost of manufacture? Which of the following would you suggest as satisfactory cost units for accumulating selling expenses during a given period: products, territories, departments, sales persons?
6. Do you think it would be easier or more difficult to maintain subsidiary records of the selling costs than it is to maintain subsidiary records of production costs? Explain your position.
7. Distinguish "summary" accounts and controlling accounts.

PART III

ACCOUNTING VALUATION

CHAPTER XXI

THE ACCOUNTING-VALUATION PROBLEM

Accounting method begins with the valuation (measurement) of the transactions of an enterprise. In sequence, the process of valuation precedes the double-entry classification and summarization by which the interpretation of the accounting data is facilitated; in this text, however, the double-entry system has been explained first, as the aspect of accounting which distinguishes it from other applications of quantitative method. Many accounting transactions are easily evaluated. For example, any accountant will brand as absurd a procedure by which an account receivable is recorded as showing an amount greater than a customer has agreed to pay. The absurdity is apparent, for such practice is in direct contradiction to evidence that a smaller amount will be received. But there are many problems of valuation which are not so easily analyzed and solved; this section of the text will discuss some of them.

Accounting valuation is measurement of the transactions of an enterprise.—The accountant's valuation problem—the problem of measuring transactions—at first appears very simple. One might say, for instance, that an incoming asset should be recorded at its "value." But what is the value of an asset? This question is more easily asked than answered; nevertheless, the accountant must answer it in some way before he proceeds to the task of recording transactions in the double-entry accounts. The accountant's search for value is not an attempt to discover some vague attribute dependent upon a particular philosophical or psychological interpretation. The accountant wants merely to discover economic value which can ultimately be reduced to money terms. Accounting valuation is, therefore, the measurement of certain transactions in terms of financial units. The very word "transaction" implies the "exchange" of values, and it is the potential exchange value of assets which an accountant must discover in his measurement of financial status and operations.

Exchange value is a dynamic thing; it implies exchange transactions. Valuation looks toward the immediate future or the distant future, depending upon the transactions to be measured. The value of an asset to an enterprise must be regarded as an estimate of its present exchange power, to be realized either through the process of sale or through gradual use in business operations. The correctness with which the values of certain assets are estimated very often determines whether an enterprise is successful or not. Financial status as expressed by the balance sheet must be regarded as the present value of the exchange capacity of the various items. The balance sheet is definitely pointed toward the future, and the validity of its data is affected by the reasonableness of the prediction as to what events will follow.

The problem of valuation is primarily concerned with assets. But an approach to the problem necessarily involves all other types of accounting phenomena, such as liabilities, proprietorship, income, and expense. The accountant must have a clear understanding of when and to what extent liabilities have been incurred, as well as of what transactions are to be regarded as income or expense operations. Cash borrowed from a bank becomes an asset of the enterprise for the same amount, and at the same time, that the note payable to the bank becomes a liability. Likewise an account receivable from a customer becomes an asset for the same amount, and at the same time, that the sale of merchandise occurs. Very often the decision as to whether a certain asset is to be included in a balance sheet depends upon whether a certain liability has been incurred or whether an income or expense transaction has taken place. Any study of valuation, therefore, must give attention to the criteria by which certain types of business transactions may be recognized.

Valuation of assets affected by their intended use.—The value of an asset is measured by its power to command other goods in exchange. There are many different ways, however, by which an asset may be exchanged or disposed of, and the expected use of an asset affects the amount of value which may properly be assigned to it. Some of the uses will be discussed in the paragraphs immediately following.

Sale or conversion in normal course of business.—Some assets are held for sale to customers in the regular course of business operations. Such assets have been referred to in previous chapters as "merchandise," and are, at least in theory, most correctly evaluated at the prices they will command in the sale market. Assume that an enterprise owns twenty tons of coal which it is estimated can be sold for $8.00 per ton. This fact would seem to establish the value of the coal at a total amount of $160. But how may one be sure, unless the coal is actually sold, that the enterprise will receive $160 in money if it chooses to sell? The answer may be that an offer has been made to purchase it, and that, since such an offer is open to acceptance at any time, it suffices as objective evidence of the value of the coal as an item of salable merchandise. The offer is a fact which may reasonably serve as the basis for estimating the value of the coal. As a matter of common practice, selling prices are very seldom used in commercial balance sheets, even for the valuation of merchandise; this is because of the possibility of losses from fluctuation in market values. Merchandise is more often evaluated at the original purchase price or the cost of replacement, whichever of the two is lower. The limitations and advantages of this practice will be discussed in chapter xxiii.

Productive use in business operations.—The selling price of twenty tons of coal was referred to in the previous paragraph as being estimated at $160. But suppose that the manager of the enterprise did not intend to sell the coal; in fact, had made definite plans to burn it under the boilers of the factory power plant. The selling price is a value of slight importance to the enterprise under such conditions. The owner might even refuse to part with the coal at double the selling price, unless immediate replacement were assured. The manager may argue that the value of the coal is $320, even more, because the power generated from burning the fuel is worth a certain amount in the manufacturing processes. The question of whether the value of the coal as fuel, or of any other asset in productive use, can be accurately estimated is one to which no categorical answer can be given. But one very important fact may be observed, namely, that a value which is satisfactory for one purpose may be entirely unacceptable for another. The coal may be assigned one value when regarded as salable merchandise, another when looked upon as an irreplaceable source of factory power.

Some assets serve an enterprise through periods of time without being depleted or changed in physical form; for example, buildings and machinery retain essentially their original shape and dimensions during their entire useful life. Nevertheless, such assets are used in business operations for limited periods of time, and they may be evaluated at their worth for purposes of productive use. It is not easy to measure the total value of a fixed asset in productive use, for it involves the apportionment of the value to various segments of the output and to various periods of time. A fixed asset may, of course, possess a certain value in the sale market as well as a value in productive use. The sale value may even be higher than the estimated value in productive use, but the increased market value must be ignored unless the fixed asset is available for sale at the market price.

Immediate sale.—If an asset is to be sold quickly, regardless of existing market conditions, the price it will bring may be quite different from its value in the normal sale market or when held for productive use in business operations. For example, the receiver for a bankrupt enterprise may be instructed by the court to dispose of all assets immediately at the best price obtainable under the circumstances. The prices obtained under these conditions are sometimes called "forced sale" prices and are usually lower than the values of assets for other purposes; they may, of course, be higher.

Scrap.—After assets have served their full period of productive use, it is possible that much physical capacity may remain in the worn-out materials. A machine which is considered useless for productive purposes may be sold as old metal at scrap value. The time at which a specific asset will be discarded as worthless, except for scrap, will vary with the circumstances. An asset may be in good physical condition, only slightly affected by wear and tear, yet be obsolete and essentially valueless to the firm owning it. Assets considered obsolete for one purpose may, of course, actually be adequate for productive use in another.

Different values for different purposes.—Any of the foregoing uses of assets may, under certain conditions, be used as the basis for establishing their values. This means that an asset may have two or more values at the same time, each of which is correct. A machine, for example, may exchange for $2,000 if offered for sale in the normal market, may render services valued at $4,000 in productive use, may bring $1,000 if disposed of at forced sale, and may be worth only $200 as scrap metal. It is the task of the accountant first to determine which type of value should be selected under given conditions, and then to estimate the value correctly in terms of the circumstances. The technique of valuation is a tool which the accountant must learn to use. The skill with which he applies it will determine his success as a constructive interpreter of financial values; as an intelligent and reliable business adviser.

The viewpoint of the person using the data is a very importent consideration in arriving at correct value. A frequently recurring manifestation of this fact is the attitude of banking institutions which make short-term loans on the basis of the current assets from which the debts may be paid. The recognized values of the fixed assets in productive use are not of primary interest to a banker who is considering a short-term loan. The most important assets for short-term security are the assets, now on hand or to be procured, which may be easily converted into cash. Other assets are often given slight consideration in the granting of short-term loans.

Accuracy of valuation depends upon adequacy of methods employed.—It is not always easy to measure value, even though the purposes of the valuation have been agreed upon. Certain limitations at once appear, either in the attitude and skill of the observer or in the technique employed by him. First, the element of *bias* may greatly affect the values assigned to given assets. A business man might, for example, be unduly optimistic over the possibility of collecting certain accounts receivable, and thus might make an inadequate allowance for bad debts in his balance sheet. Similarly he may be influenced by the smooth-working efficiency of a factory machine and thus overlook the fact that modern inventions have lowered its value in productive use. On the other hand, an interested person may be too pessimistic in regard to asset values, not to mention the possibility of deliberate understatement with intent to avoid liability for taxes or to induce investors to sell their interests at low prices. The accountant should approach the problem of valuation in the rôle of a scientific observer, reporting the facts as he sees them, without regard to the prejudices of interested persons.

Some problems of valuation are difficult, and require *special technique* for their solution. For example, the valuation of interest-bearing securities, leaseholds, or instalment contracts involves the application of algebraic formulas and the more elaborate devices of "actuarial science." The valuation of manufactured merchandise demands a mastery of the technique of cost-accounting methods, a technique which often taxes the powers of the most ingenious accountant.

There is an ideally correct value for each asset.—Some assets are acquired for purposes of sale, others for gradual consumption or continuous use in business operations. But in every case the value an asset has to a business is its ultimate exchange capacity; this capacity may be exercised at one time through sale or gradually through the service it renders to the enterprise. Every asset contains a certain amount of potential exchange value, which it will ultimately yield to the enterprise in some manner.

The actual value of an asset, therefore, is the total value of the services it will render, if used in the manner intended.[1] Where the value of an asset is to be realized through a transfer of ownership,

[1] The influence of "intended use" is continually felt in accounting-valuation procedure. The accountant is faced, on the one hand, with the necessity of preparing a balance sheet dependent for its validity upon future events and, on the other hand, with the possibility of unpredictable events occurring which will make his balance-sheet values incorrect. This possibility illustrates the tentative nature of accounting valuation and the need for an awareness of its practical limitations. The accountant is charged with the exercise of reasonable judgment in the prediction of future events (especially losses); but he rightfully insists that he be freed from responsibility for predicting the numerous fortuities (such as floods, land booms, inventions) which may invalidate his estimates.

the task of estimating the value is relatively easy; for the total value can be calculated by considering only one transaction—the ultimate sale of the asset. But if an asset is to be consumed gradually or used continuously during a period of time, the valuation problem is more difficult to solve. It involves an estimate, not only of the total value of the services of the asset, but also of the periods during which the services will be enjoyed. Some services will be enjoyed in the present (speaking in relative terms), some in the future. Those in the future must be "discounted" to the value which they have at the present, the time of determining financial status. The real value of any asset at any given time, therefore, may be said to be the *present value of its future services.*[1] The future value of these future services must be discounted to the value they would have if they were all to be realized upon immediately.

Standards for recognizing future services.—If assets are to be valued in terms of future services, some standards must be established by which these "future services" may be recognized and given a place in the accounting records. The establishment of such standards is often very difficult, so difficult, in fact, that most accountants hesitate to use the ideally correct method of valuation for any assets except those whose values can be computed by mathematical formulas and whose validity can be established in terms of legally enforceable rights against responsible persons. Illustrations of such assets are bonds, contracts, and leaseholds.

What is to be done about it?—The task of evaluating assets is not easy; in fact, the problem as here expressed seems to be well-nigh impossible. Nevertheless, the process of valuation must go on. The following chapter will indicate some of the ways in which the accountant has dealt with the problem in his daily practice.

[1] The concept of capitalized value is a familiar one to economists and to engineers. It has been employed only recently by practical accountants and business men. One of the most prominent advocates of correct valuation, R. H. Montgomery, in his revised edition of *Auditing Theory and Practice* emphasizes the fact that there are different values for different purposes, such as liquidation, sale, rate regulation, taxation. He concludes one paragraph with the statement: "Perhaps the most trustworthy value is that which is established by capitalizing the use of the property to be valued. It is almost the sole criterion of those who buy and sell properties" (p. 207).

QUESTIONS ON CHAPTER XXI

1. "Exchange value is dynamic; it looks toward the future." Explain and discuss.
2. Does an asset have only one correct value at a given time? If so, how is the value ascertained? If not, cite different values which may properly be assigned to a commodity.
3. The basis of accounting valuation should depend upon the purpose for which the valuation is made. Illustrate this point by using the following assets:
   a) Ten automobile tires were originally purchased for use on certain delivery trucks. The trucks have been disposed of, and the tires are of the wrong size for the trucks now in use.
   b) A machine for the manufacture of a specialized product. Assume any conditions necessary in order to give an opinion as to its value.
4. What elements of bias might be encountered in the valuation of inventory by a business man when he is computing his taxable income?
5. The present value of its future services is the correct value for each and every asset. Is it conceivable that these services of an asset might be realized simultaneously? Give illustrations.
6. Some assets are utilized so soon in the future that the problem of discounting their services can be ignored. Illustrate and discuss.
7. Why do you suppose mathematical formulas have been applied to the valuation of bonds in greater degree than to the valuation of merchandise? State your answer in terms of the differences in the characteristics of the two types of assets, and the purposes for which the values are established.

CHAPTER XXII

THE COMMON RULES OF ACCOUNTING VALUATION

Accounting value is dependent upon the purpose for which the value is established and upon the adequacy of the technique employed in its computation. The accountant realizes the advantages to be gained from definiteness in his data, but he is also confronted by the need for promptness in his measurement of business operations. The large number of business transactions during an accounting period must be evaluated according to some well-ordered routine if accounting is to keep pace with modern business.

Accountants make certain assumptions as to purposes and technique of valuation.—The accountant must, if possible, avoid the vagueness arising from differences in purpose, and also must reduce the enormous task of separately evaluating numerous complex transactions. He accomplishes these results by handling most of his transactions according to an agreed pattern, from which he traces the values with sufficient accuracy for ordinary purposes. The pattern is based upon various assumptions as to the purpose and technique of valuation, assumptions which are applicable to most situations and which permit the establishment of useful working rules.[1]

The "going-concern" assumption.—The accountant typically makes one very sweeping assumption as to the *purpose* underlying his valuation of assets: he assumes that an enterprise will function normally and will continue its operations over a reasonable period of time. This implies that the assets of an enterprise will all be used in the manner intended; for example, that merchandise

[1] W. A. Paton, in *Accounting Theory* (chap. xx), has set forth some of the "Postulates of Accounting" which have influenced both theory and practice. The first three of the assumptions mentioned in the present chapter were suggested directly by Mr. Paton's "postulates." The importance of recognizing the assumptions implicit in any given line of argument need hardly be defended to practical men or to workers in scientific method.

will be sold within the usual period of time, that supplies will be consumed in normal operations, and that plant and equipment will be depreciated gradually through continuous service. The assumption is often referred to in practice as the "*going-concern*" *assumption*, meaning that a concern expects to continue its normal operations rather than to discontinue them and to dispose of its property. The going-concern assumption is consistent with the facts of modern economic life, for most enterprises do continue their normal operations for a reasonable period of time and most assets are used in the manner intended by the management. To be sure, fixed assets are sometimes sold and merchandise is sometimes held for long periods of time; nevertheless, such procedures must be regarded as unusual and not typical of the practices of business. When unusual conditions appear, such as when an enterprise faces the discontinuing of operations, the going-concern assumption must be brushed aside to make room for the existing facts.

Assumption that cost gives value.—The accountant also makes several assumptions as to the *technique* of estimating value. The first of these is that *the cost of an asset determines its value, for purposes of initial statement.* In his search for a measure of value at the time an asset is acquired, the accountant ignores all considerations of selling price, scrap value, use value, etc. Regardless of the special purpose for which the asset has been procured, he considers it worth the price paid. Even if the price paid appears extravagant in terms of one purpose, the accountant assumes that the price must have been justified for some other purpose in the mind of the buyer. No accountant insists, of course, that an asset remain on the books forever at cost price. This value is established only for purposes of initial statement. It may be changed very soon; it may never be changed.[1]

Assumption as to value of money.—A second assumption affecting valuation technique is that the measuring unit, the dollar,

[1] "Cost is only an incident. The value of an asset to a business is measured solely by the value of the *use*. It may be that the cost was justified, or that a bargain purchase was made. When the cost was not justified, or when an extravagant purchase was made and the profitable *use* of the asset stops or diminishes, 'cost' should not be confused with 'value' " (R. H. Montgomery, *Auditing-Theory and Practice*, p. 207).

is of constant value. The accountant typically ignores the fluctuations in the value of the dollar which arise out of economic conditions. This assumption at times causes misstatement in the values of assets, especially those which serve a particular enterprise over a long period of time. Accountants have made some attempt to offset the influence of the changing value of the dollar by using index numbers in comparing the values of fixed assets. The efficacy of index numbers in practical business affairs will be tested by the extent to which values based upon them are accepted. There is some evidence that long-term creditors recognize the inadequacy of measurements made on the assumption of a dollar of constant value; it may be that in the future all accountants will supplement their formal reports by additional data compensating for the errors which have arisen from changes in the general price level.

Conservatism in accounting valuation.—Another aspect of the accountant's estimating technique is the influence of conservatism. By "conservatism" is meant an attitude which strives to avoid the overstatement of the proprietorship of an enterprise. It leads to a relatively low valuation of assets, with a relatively high valuation of liabilities. The effect of conservatism as a factor in accounting valuation has been very great. The notion that *conservatism* is a desirable feature of accounting valuation *is more than a mere assumption* on the part of the accountant; *it is a conviction.* This conviction is probably shared by most business men; for they feel that an understatement of their proprietorship is of less danger than an overstatement which might lead to unwise expansion of operations or to distribution of assets. As a working rule, conservatism is very useful in business administration, particularly where assets may be evaluated in terms of different purposes. In such cases, a conservative policy compels the recognition of the lower of two possible values. Where conservatism is applied to prevent unwarranted increases in the statement of proprietorship, it is a useful device for administrative control. Where it serves to obscure actual values from the view of interested persons or to prevent progress in economic efficiency, it cannot be commended.

Assumptions give rise to certain working rules of accounting valuation.—Accountants have developed several working rules for accounting valuation, rules which have been applied successfully under normal conditions. All of the rules have been affected by the practical assumptions of the accountant; they will be stated and discussed briefly in the paragraphs immediately following.

Current assets should be valued at cost or market, whichever is the lower.—This rule means that, when the original cost value and the present replacement value are both known, and are different in amount, the lower of the two values should be adopted. It presents two problems which must be solved if the rule is to be applied: the definition and measurement of "cost" value; the definition and measurement of "market" value. These problems are not always easily solved. Typically the "cost-or-market" rule is applied to all current assets, particularly merchandise, supplies, and temporary investments. When extended to receivables, it results in their being shown at face value, minus adequate allowances for bad-debt losses.

Fixed-asset value should be cost price less depreciation.—This rule establishes original cost price as the correct basis for the original accounting valuation. Depreciation is subtracted from this amount to give the value for the balance sheet. Assets not subject to depreciation are, of course, listed continuously at cost price. According to this rule, such assets would not increase or decrease in value during the time held. The rule assumes that each fixed asset will be used in the manner originally intended, that no unpredictable events will occur to change the value of the service, and that no variations in the value of money will influence the exchange value of its future services. The influence of conservatism is present in the refusal to recognize upward tendencies in replacement cost, although the effects of conservatism are partially offset by the adherence to cost value after replacement values have declined. The application of the cost-less-depreciation rule presents two very important requirements: accurate definition and measurement of fixed-asset cost; accurate definition and measurement of fixed-asset depreciation. This rule is usually applied to any type of long-term assets, including fixed tangible assets, intangible assets, and permanent investments.

Include all liabilities at their maximum value.—The valuation of liabilities is usually not a matter involving judgment on the part of the proprietor of an enterprise; it is his main task to include all liabilities in his balance sheet and to make sure that the amounts are at least as large as those ultimately expected by the creditors. But it is not always possible to determine the exact amount of a liability, or even to tell whether a liability has been incurred or not. Moreover, in the case of a liability which is due in the future, the time element may affect the value which should properly appear on the balance sheet.

Assets minus liabilities equal proprietorship.—The task of estimating proprietorship is an easy one if the assets and liabilities have been correctly evaluated; proprietorship is merely the residual ownership of the stockholders or partners in an enterprise, after the creditors' interests have been deducted from total assets. Some problems appear, however, in the apportionment of total proprietorship among the individual proprietors or the various classes of proprietors. Likewise some differences of opinion appear concerning the dividing line between the rights of creditors and proprietors.

Anticipate no unrealized income, and provide for all possible expenses.—This rule covers the typical treatment of income and expense transactions, which is closely linked with the measurement of financial status. The influence of conservatism is apparent in this rule, which recommends provision for all "possible" losses, even though not yet actually incurred, whereas the profits to be recorded by the accountant must not include those which are "unrealized." A rule of this type implies that certain standards have been established for determining the realization of profits and the possibility of losses; otherwise an accountant would have no means of applying the rule to actual situations. A discussion of the standards for measuring income and expense is, therefore, properly a part of a study of the problem of valuation.

The purposes for which assets are held by an enterprise

greatly influence their valuation; likewise the technical difficulties of estimating their value affect the accuracy with which values can be determined. For these reasons the discussion of valuation in the following chapters is divided in terms of the characteristics of the accounting situations and the technique necessary for dealing with them. The problems of valuation will be discussed under the following headings: Current Assets, Fixed Assets, Investments, Intangible Assets, Liabilities, Proprietorship, Income, and Expense. Many of the problems of valuation are common to several of these classes, but the subdivision is practicable for the purposes of this discussion.

QUESTIONS ON CHAPTER XXII

1. What are the advantages of the assumptions which the accountant makes in approaching the subject of valuation? Do they make his results more accurate? Do they make his task lighter?
2. Consider the going-concern assumption in the problem of valuation. Does this assumption definitely throw out any of the following bases of valuation: purchase market; present sale market; future sale market; original cost; reproduction cost; forced sale value; scrap value? Does the going concern point to any one value as the correct value for all assets and for all purposes?
3. Is the accountant justified in assuming that cost gives value for purposes of initial statement? Is the assumption always valid?
4. The accountant for the most part assumes that the dollar is a constant unit of measurement. Is this generally a permissible assumption? Is it always reasonable?
5. The clear indication in the balance sheet of the basis of valuation selected is frequently of no less importance than the particular basis adopted. Do you agree? If not, is there a significant kernel of truth in this statement?
6. The basic rule of conservatism underlying the common rules of accounting valuation is that no profits should be anticipated and all losses should be provided for. Illustrate the application of this rule in the valuation of current assets, fixed assets, and liabilities.
7. Valuations placed upon assets are to some degree estimates or matters of opinion. Do you agree? What would probably be the last significant figure in the total of assets valued at $24,597,831.27?
8. The rule of "cost or market whichever is lower" has been widely quoted as a practicable rule of accounting valuation. If it is a good rule for a valuation of current assets, why might it not be applied with equal reasonableness to fixed assets?

9. Would you say that "cost less depreciation" was in all cases a conservative rule for the valuation of fixed assets?
10. Why is the valuation of liabilities usually omitted from the discussions of balance-sheet valuation? Is the overstatement of liabilities consistent with the basic assumptions of the accountant?
11. Why should income and expense be included in a discussion of accounting valuation? Give illustrations of the effects of income and expense measurement upon the values at which assets and liabilities appear in the balance sheet.

CHAPTER XXIII

VALUATION OF CURRENT ASSETS

The valuation of assets is affected by the purposes for which they are held. Consequently, those assets of an enterprise which it is intended to use in a similar manner may be discussed as a group. The present chapter will present some of the problems of valuation which arise in connection with current assets.

The nature of current assets affects their valuation.—Current assets were defined in chapter xii as those assets which are intended to be consumed or to be converted into other assets in the normal course of business operations within a relatively short period of time. Usually the period of time is twelve months or less. The group of assets includes cash, receivables, merchandise, short-term investments, and prepaid expenses. When an asset normally regarded as a current asset fails to qualify as such under the foregoing definition, its place in the balance sheet must be examined carefully, with a view to its reclassification or revaluation. The purposes for which these assets are held affect the values to be placed on them.

Assume that a sixty-day note receivable for $400 is uncollectible at the present but is owed by a debtor whose financial condition indicates that he will pay the amount in full in about four years. The classification of this note must be changed; the note is no longer a current asset of the company holding it. A note receivable which will not be paid in less than four years, and possibly not then, is either a fixed asset or no asset at all (a bad debt.) For purposes of immediate conversion into cash, such a note may have very little value; on the other hand, the note may conceivably be listed at face value as a fixed asset, given the assurance that the money will be forthcoming at some later date.

As a second illustration, assume that merchandise inventory suddenly becomes obsolete, even though in perfect physical condition. Shall unsalable merchandise (for example, ladies' shoes of an obsolete style, purchased at a price of $10) be regarded as a current asset? The solution of this problem is not as difficult as it first appears. It is to be found, not in a change of the classification, but in a change of the valuation. The shoes may be salable at $6; at $4; at $2. They must be valued at their worth as merchandise inventory. If they cannot be sold at any price, they must be taken from the balance sheet entirely.

Assets which are intended to be held for long periods of time may be salable at a moment's notice. Nevertheless, these items are not to be regarded as current assets of a business which does not intend to dispose of them. It is apparent, then, that any given asset may be admitted to or excluded from the current asset classification on the basis of the purpose for which it is owned. A building might be a current asset (part of the inventory) for a real estate concern; a building would not be a current asset for a retail merchant who used it as a store. An auto truck is a current asset for a motor-car agency, but not for a factory using it to transport materials.

The method of realizing on the values of current assets simplifies the problem of their valuation, for such items as cash, receivables, and merchandise are usually disposed of in definitely measurable units. The expected sale of an article of merchandise or the probable collection of an account receivable is a single transaction which presumably will occur in the near future. The nearness of the single event thus makes possible relative certainty as to the correct value; it also reduces the allowance which must be made through the process of "discounting" one or more future services. To be sure, the time element cannot be ignored in the valuation of current assets; nevertheless, it is of less importance than in the valuation of assets which serve the enterprise through longer periods of time.

The "cost-or-market" rule and conservatism.—Accountants have been greatly influenced by two considerations in their valuation of current assets: the desire to state profits and net worth conservatively, and the difficulties of ascertaining current values. They have been led, on the one hand, to consistent understatement of values, whenever there might be possible doubt as to a correct amount; and, on the other hand, to a persistent use of the known data of the past rather than the more significant, but often less definite, data of the present. Many accountants have, accordingly, adhered strictly to the working rule for the valuation of current assets: *cost or market, whichever is lower*. By "cost" is meant the purchase price, that is to say, the market price at the time of acquisition; by "market" is usually meant the replacement price at the time of the valuation.[1]

The "cost-or-market" rule recognizes all decreases but no increases in the values of current assets. The inconsistency is declared to be justified on the grounds of conservatism. The argument is often advanced that no harm can come from an understatement of values, whereas an overstatement may lead to great injustice. If the accountant were forced to choose between understatement or overstatement, the weight of business judgment would fall on the side of understatement. But the accountant is presumably interested in accurate statement of business values. If a significant value can be accurately determined, it should not be overlooked by interested parties.[2]

Assume that two partners are dissolving their business relations and that the merchandise inventory carries a known replacement-cost value of $15,000 but has cost only $12,000. Must

[1] The difference between "cost" and "market" in practice can be recognized and explained only when there has been agreement as to the definition of "cost" and "market." In the first place, the amount which an item "has cost" (original cost) is merely the "past-market" price which existed at the time of the purchase. In the second place the amount which an article "would cost" (replacement cost) is merely the "present-market" price. The rule of "cost or market, whichever is lower" could, therefore, be expressed in either of the following ways: "original or replacement cost, whichever is lower" or "past or present market, whichever is lower."

[2] In discussing some "Criteria of Balance Sheet Valuation," T. O. Yntema makes the following suggestions: "The basis of valuation: (1) should be *simple*—easy to understand and to calculate; (2) should be such that sufficient evidence is available to allow objective verification of the value by independent observers. That is, the value of the asset should be definitely *ascertainable* within reasonable limits of error. (3) Should be *conservative*—but only within the range of doubt or uncertainty. (4) Should give a figure which is *as near value, i.e., market price, as is reasonably possible* in the light of the necessity for simplicity and for sufficient evidence to allow objective verification" (*Publications of the American Association of University Instructors in Accounting*, December, 1925).

the withdrawing partner accept an amount of $6,000 as his share in the inventory, thus leaving the other partner to reap the entire benefits of the rise in price? No partner would have the courage to insist on or be willing to agree to any such division. In this instance, cost value, a very significant fact in the records of a business, tends to work a great injustice to the partner who wishes to realize on his equity in an enterprise. If the market value had been lower, let us say $10,000, both partners would no doubt have agreed to a division on such a basis. From the viewpoint of all interested parties, the prevailing market values are of great significance. In most cases an attempt to approximate prevailing values will result in less injustice than will any other policy. Where such values are not known, and cannot be estimated with any reasonable degree of accuracy, they should not replace the known fact of cost. This means, of course, that values can be written neither up nor down, unless prevailing market value is known.

Valuation of cash requires careful definition.—In chapter viii cash was defined as money, or any asset which in its present form may be used currently as money in economic transactions. This definition automatically excludes any item the value of which depends upon the opinion of the person receiving it in exchange. An illustration would be a government bond of known market value but which a creditor chooses to accept at some other amount. Unless sellers or creditors currently accept government obligations in exchange transactions, such securities cannot be logically considered as cash. Items which normally should be excluded from the cash classification are stamps, I O U's of employees, dishonored checks, and notes of officers. Items which normally may be included are checks from customers, metallic and paper currency, bank deposits subject to withdrawal, and funds in the hands of agents or branches. Negotiable notes or accepted drafts, even though they can be discounted and converted into cash at known prices, should not be considered cash, for they are not currently accepted by creditors under all circumstances. Cash items are typically accepted at face value, in terms of the money of the realm. This value is uniform, is recognized by all citizens.

and does not usually change appreciably during the time cash is in one's possession. An exception is foreign currency, the value of which may fluctuate with international policies and economic conditions. In such cases, it may be necessary to make adjustments to allow for variations in the exchange ratios.

Valuation of receivables involves an estimate of the amounts collectible.—The amounts receivable from debtors of an enterprise must be carefully appraised for admission to the balance sheet. Some of them may be uncollectible because of the dishonesty or financial insolvency of the debtors; others may prove to be invalid as claims upon the alleged debtors of the enterprise. Two groups of receivable items are usually recognized in a balance sheet: accounts receivable and notes receivable. They will be discussed separately.

Accounts receivable.—The term "accounts receivable" is usually restricted to the amounts due from the customers of a business enterprise, customers who have incurred debts to the business for merchandise sold or services rendered. Amounts receivable from other classes of debtors are usually given special descriptive titles, to separate amounts due from employees, officers' borrowings, rent receivable, interest receivable, and commissions receivable. The problems of evaluating all these types of receivables are essentially the same; consequently they may be discussed as a group. In general practice accounts receivable are accepted at their face value less a suitable allowance for bad debts. The adequacy of the allowance will depend upon the nature of the obligations, the length of time for which the accounts have been outstanding, and the success with which the collections are carried on.

Allowance for bad debts.—Various methods are used for estimating a proper allowance for bad debts. One method very commonly employed is the computation of a percentage of the gross sales during a fiscal period. Assume that the total sales during a year were $1,350,000, that the goods were sold on sixty-day terms, and that at the close of the fiscal period the total accounts receivable were $250,000. An allowance for bad debts equal to 1 per cent of the total sales for the period would be $13,500.[1]

Another method of estimating a proper allowance for bad debts is the calculation of a percentage of the accounts outstanding at a particular period of time. In the illustration above, for example, a deduction of 5 per cent may be made from the $250,000, giving a total allowance for bad debts of $12,500. Whether or not this or any other allowance for bad debts is adequate must be determined later from the actual losses sustained. A modification of the second method is the detailed analysis of the conditions of the various classes of accounts. They may, for example, be classed according to due date, those not yet due, those thirty days past due, those sixty days past due. The estimated percentage of loss on each class would vary. The resulting total would be the amount to be credited to the Allowance for Bad Debts account.

Deductions for sales discount and other items.—Other amounts which might be deducted from the accounts receivable to determine their exact value are sales discounts, estimated collection expense, possible sales returns, and interest on investment in accounts receivable. Usually these items are ignored in the valuation of the accounts receivable and are charged as expenses or income deductions only after the transactions occur. The argument for deducting the probable sales discounts from the face value of the accounts receivable is the very reasonable contention that all the accounts will not be collected in full as cash; that some allowances will be made for cash discounts to customers who pay

[1]Where this basis is used, the addition to the Allowance for Bad Debts at the end of a fiscal period would be just large enough to make the total Bad Debts charged as expenses a certain percentage of sales. For example, if in the foregoing illustration, $6,000 of accounts receivable had already been charged off as uncollectible, the additional adjustment would create a credit in the Allowance for Bad Debts account of $7,500, and a corresponding debit to Bad Debts, the expense account.

The method may also be applied by debiting all actual bad debt losses to the Allowance for Bad Debts account, even though this procedure results in building up a debit balance in the account during a fiscal period. At the time of adjustment, the Allowance for Bad Debts account may be credited for the full 1 per cent of sales, and the Bad Debts account may be debited for the same amount.

within the ensuing discount periods. At any given time the expected sales-discount allowances may be a substantial percentage of the total accounts receivable. This is particularly true of cases where the normal sales discounts are large, such as 5 or 10 per cent of the sales-invoice price. The United States Treasury Department permits the deduction of allowable sales discounts as business expenses in the calculation of taxable income,[1] provided they are deducted currently at the times sales are made.

Notes receivable.—Notes receivable are typically listed at face value in balance sheets, although they should, strictly speaking, be evaluated with full regard to the probability of bad debts and of expenses in collection. In cases where notes are receivable at definite dates in the future, the question also arises as to the desirability of discounting the notes to their "present values," using some agreed rate of interest earnings on the obligations during their lives.

The discounts on notes receivable for the ordinary mercantile concern are not large items. Consequently the discounts are often regarded in their entirety as immediate earnings and are credited to Interest Income. The discount items may be, at times, large enough to affect seriously the validity of a balance sheet; this would be particularly true in the case of a firm which received its main income from the purchase and discount of short-term securities.

Valuation of merchandise requires careful definition and accurate technique.—The valuation of merchandise is one of the most important tasks before the accountant when he is preparing a balance sheet. The rapid changes in the merchandise items themselves, as well as the frequent changes in their market values, make it very necessary for the accountant to bring to his task the greatest degree of care and business judgment.

Elements of merchandise value.—Merchandise inventory includes all goods which are secured and held for sale by a mercantile enterprise, even though they are in the hands of agents or branches. It excludes all items which are not the property of the enterprise, even though they are in the possession of the firm. In

[1] *Cumulative Bulletin I-1*, page 51; *Income Tax Unit Decision*, 1348.

some cases, the first consideration in inventory valuation is the determination of the owner, the location of legal title. Only after ownership is established may the other problems of definition and estimated value be raised.

What are the elements of merchandise value? In the wholesale and retail enterprises, the purchase-invoice price is generally regarded as the main element in total merchandise value. Other items usually added are the expenses connected with bringing the goods to a marketable condition or location; some of them are incoming freight, temporary storage and insurance charges, and expenses of unpacking and repacking. The items which may be included in total cost are usually limited to those necessary to bring the goods to the condition in which, or to the place where, they will be sold. Other costs are usually regarded as distribution expenses. Merchandise which has not been purchased, but has been manufactured, by an enterprise must include as cost more than the mere expenses of procuring the materials; it must also include the direct and indirect expenses of the manufacturing processes, for the expenses of manufacturing are assumed to be imbedded in the materials used in the processes. The technique for assigning the labor and other manufacturing expenses to particular units of product is a part of that branch of accounting known as "cost accounting."[1]

Types of merchandise inventory.—The merchandise of a manufacturing enterprise passes through three stages: raw materials; goods in process; finished goods. *Raw materials* for a particular business are the materials in the forms in which purchased from vendors. *Goods in process* are materials which have gone through a part of the manufacturing process, and to which have been added some of the labor and other manufacturing expenses applicable to these materials. *Finished goods* are those which have passed through all stages of the manufacturing process. The terms "raw material" and "finished goods" are relative terms, and no commodities can be regarded as always in one class or the other; iron ore would be finished goods of a mine but raw material for a

[1] Compare chapters xx and xxxix of this text, where other aspects of cost accounting are discussed.

smelting plant; pig iron would be finished goods of a blast furnace but raw material for a foundry; iron castings would be the finished goods of a foundry but raw materials for a machine shop. Goods in process are the unfinished materials between any stages of production indicated by the iron ore, pig iron, castings, or tools. The problem of evaluating the merchandise inventory must deal with all phases of the inventory of an enterprise. Typically, however, the materials and finished goods are those which permit of the greatest choice in selection of values. Goods in process are usually evaluated on the basis of raw materials consumed plus the expenses of "processing" the materials to a certain percentage of completion. The change in the market value of a large stock of raw materials or finished goods greatly affects the financial condition of a business. To meet this problem, and also to deal with situations where it is impossible to assign accurate costs to merchandise, various methods have been adopted for evaluating inventory. All of the methods are attempts to recognize the actual economic importance of the merchandise at the moment of the valuation.[1]

Cost value of merchandise.—Cost price is a term sometimes difficult to define; moreover, it is often very hard to compute. What is the "cost" of goods remaining at the close of a period during which several different purchase prices have prevailed? The price at the opening of the period? at the end of the period? an average of the prices during the period? The accountant must decide what cost price shall be recognized in the balance sheet. When an *average* price is adopted as being most significant, it may be computed by adding the different prices and dividing by their number. Such a procedure provides a simple-average cost, which may give disproportionate weight to an unusually high or low price which was in effect only a short time.

In some cases, the averages are computed to give proper weight to the prices at which the largest amounts are purchased; the result in such instances is a *weighted-average* cost. In other

[1] Even the most conservative accountants at times admit the reasonableness of recognizing present market values (replacement-costs) in balance sheets. The discussion in the following pages illustrates some of the devices by which current practice has been affected by tendencies to recognize existing values.

cases, an average is computed from most recent purchase prices; those are weighted to apply to the goods on hand. This method proceeds on the assumption that goods purchased first are those sold first, and is sometimes called the *first in—first out* method. It is often applied to the estimation of the values at which raw materials are charged to the goods-in-process accounts.

A method sometimes called the *most-recent-invoice* method is that of evaluating all goods on the balance sheet at the price appearing on the most recent invoice of goods purchased during the period. In effect, this method is an attempt to approximate present-market price, that is, the current *replacement cost.*

The following data illustrate some typical cost values which may be selected for evaluating merchandise on hand. Assume that 250 articles of a certain kind are in stock and that the prevailing replacement cost is $3.00 per article on June 30.

PURCHASES

January 10	300 articles	@	$3.70 =	$1,110.00
March 1	400 articles	@	3.60 =	1,440.00
May 15	75 articles	@	4.00 =	300.00
June 20	125 articles	@	2.80 =	350.00
June 25	100 articles	@	2.90 =	290.00
	1000		$17.00	$3,490.00

INVENTORY VALUES

Simple average	=250×$3.40 ($17.00÷5)	=$850.00
Weighted average	=250×$3.49 ($3,490÷1,000)	=$872.50
First in—first out	=100× 2.90=$290.00	
	125× 2.80= 350.00	
	25× 4.00= 100.00	$740.00
Most recent invoice	=250× 2.90=	725.00
Replacement cost	=250× 3.00=	750.00

Market value an important element in the valuation of merchandise.—The accountant is often faced with the problem of selecting a proper value for merchandise inventory when an otherwise acceptable cost value is greater or less than prevailing replacement price. "Replacement cost" (present market) not infrequently differs widely from original cost computed by any of the other methods just described. In case of such difference between original and replacement cost, which value shall appear in the balance sheet? How shall the accounts be adjusted if present market value is selected as the value to appear in the balance sheet? The answers to these questions will vary with the accountant's convictions concerning the purpose of his valuation. If his balance sheet is to reflect current conditions, the market values must appear on it. On the other hand, if the accountant is to be true to his conservative training, he must take care not to recognize temporary fluctuations which are of no practical significance. He sees the desirability of displaying market value on the balance sheet; he also recognizes the advisability of indicating original cost. He desires a method which will indicate the relation between cost and market values and will permit interested parties to attach such importance to the variations as they wish. In harmony with the very useful principle of conservatism, he could always include the lower value in the asset-column total.

Various methods have been suggested for accomplishing the objective of indicating which is the lower price, cost or market. One very useful device is to supplement the account title representing merchandise on the balance sheet with a parenthetical statement indicating which value appears thereon. Such a statement might be "At cost, which is lower than market" or "At market, which is lower than cost."[1] Other methods provide for the maintenance of "reserve" accounts in which the variations between market values and cost values may be clearly shown on the balance sheet.[2] Regardless of the technique used to display it, market value, as the prevailing replacement cost, is a very important figure and should find its place on the balance sheet. When market is lower than the original cost price, the value may be included in the summation of total assets. When market price is greater than cost, it need not (and probably should not) be

[1] This device was suggested by E. L. Kohler in an article in the *Accounting Review* entitled "Tendencies in Balance Sheet Construction," June, 1927.

[2] An extended discussion of the use of "reserves" to reflect inventory fluctuations appears in the *Accounting Review*, Vol. I, No. 1. The discussion was led by DR Scott, of the University of Missouri, and was participated in by several eminent accounting teachers and practitioners.

included in the column of net-asset values. Nevertheless, it should appear on the face of the balance sheet. The market value may be dealt with in several ways: by representing market price as a gross inventory value from which a special valuation "reserve" is deducted; by including the market value as a parenthetical notation but not including it in the summation of total assets; by indicating the market value in a footnote to the balance sheet on which the original "cost" values appear.

Selling price less estimated selling costs.—Some firms adopt the practice of evaluating certain parts of their merchandise on the basis of selling price, but of making allowances for probable costs to be incurred in marketing the goods. This method is most frequently used in the evaluation of obsolete merchandise or of goods for which no cost price can be easily determined, as, for example, by-products of the regular processes of manufacture. To illustrate, assume that a meat-packing enterprise owns some beef hides which are quoted on the market at $7.00 per hundred pounds and which it is estimated can be sold by incurring selling expenses of 50 cents per hundred pounds. The price at which these hides would appear in the balance sheet would be $6.50 per hundred pounds.

Retail method.—Another method of evaluating inventory is known as the "retail method." It is used widely in department stores, where it is necessary to enlist the aid of a force of sales people to inspect and count large numbers of items. The method consists of preparing a list of all items of merchandise at their selling prices. These values, either singly or in groups, are then adjusted to an estimated cost value by applying a percentage of reduction equal to the expected gross profit. In the last analysis, this method is an attempt to establish replacement cost by an indirect method, a method which does not require the revealing of cost prices to all employees engaged in verifying the stock on hand.

Base stock or cushion method.—This is a method which establishes a fixed price for the permanent value of a certain minimum amount of inventory—a minimum which must always be kept on hand to insure a supply of materials for sale or manufacture. This method is sometimes applied to metals such as lead or copper. The price for the basic minimum of stock is maintained continuously at a given price, regardless of fluctuations in market values. The inventory on hand in excess of the base stock is evaluated according to the policy adopted by the enterprise as most useful for its purpose. Where the base stock is a large proportion of the average inventory on hand, this method tends to equalize current profits—at least to the extent of offsetting variations which would result from recognizing all inventory fluctuations in the records.

Conclusion.—In general it may be said that the ideal value to be ascribed to current assets is the present market value, or as near to such a value as it is practicable to estimate. The accountant must frequently choose between very accurate, but delayed, data on the one hand, and less accurate, but more promptly available, data on the other. Frequently cost and market are so near in value that either will serve adequately for the balance sheet. The basis selected will depend upon the purposes of the valuation as they are seen by the interested parties. Most frequently, of course, current assets have been valued at "cost or market whichever is lower," without regard to the effects of such a policy.

QUESTIONS ON CHAPTER XXIII

1. What are current assets?
2. Classify the following items into current or fixed assets on the basis of intended use: (*a*) cash; (*b*) old-style dresses in a ladies' ready-to-wear store; (*c*) old-style dresses in a costumer's establishment; (*d*) land for a factory site; (*e*) land for sale by a real estate company; (*f*) accounts receivable, good and collectible within thirty days; (*g*) notes receivable, collectible, but not due for four years.
3. The balance sheet of the Alleson Mercantile Company shows the item "Cash." An examination shows that "Cash" includes the following:
   a) Customers' checks returned dishonored
   b) I O U's of employees
   c) Stamps in cash drawer
   d) Notes of customers, due but not presented for payment
   e) Currency in cash drawer
   f) Branch working funds
   g) Cash in bank for which checks have been issued but not yet presented
   How should each of the foregoing items be shown on the balance sheet?

4. Should all notes receivable be stated at their face value in the balance sheet? On what other basis might they be evaluated? Should the balance-sheet value be different for interest-bearing and non-interest-bearing notes?
5. Which of the following items are usually deducted from the accounts receivable in estimating their value for a balance sheet: (*a*) bad debts; (*b*) collection costs; (*c*) sales discounts; (*d*) sales allowance; (*e*) losses on sales returns; (*f*) interest on investment until time the debts are paid?
6. What is properly to be regarded as merchandise inventory? Should the following items be included?
   a) Merchandise on hand for which invoices have not yet been received
   b) Merchandise received on consignment from other companies
   c) Merchandise consigned to other companies
   d) Orders received from customers for future deliveries but not yet filled
   e) Merchandise for which the company has been billed, but which has not yet been received by it
   f) Merchandise sold and paid for but held for later delivery at request of customer
7. Which of the following items are to be included in determining the *cost* of merchandise inventory: purchase invoice price; freight, express and cartage in; expense of unpacking; expense of arranging on shelves; expense of repacking for sale in smaller parcels; freight, express, and cartage out?
8. What objections may be raised to the rule of "cost or market, whichever is the lower" in the valuation of inventories? What may be said in defense of the rule?
9. Is not cost price just another name for the market price which prevailed at the time the inventory was purchased? If so, might the rule be stated "past or present market, whichever is the lower"?
10. Explain the meaning of each of the following methods of valuing inventory: (*a*) selling price less cost of selling; (*b*) base stock, or cushion method; (*c*) retail method.

CHAPTER XXIV

VALUATION OF FIXED ASSETS

Fixed assets are those which are held for continuous use in a business enterprise and which are not to be converted into cash or otherwise quickly expended in business operations. They remain with the enterprise for several fiscal periods. The assets usually regarded as meeting the requirements given above are land, buildings, machinery, delivery equipment, furniture and fixtures, permanent investments, intangibles, and some types of deferred charges.

The nature of fixed assets affects their valuation.—Most fixed assets are subject to gradual reduction in value during their life, that is to say, the periods of their usefulness. Each asset has a definitely limited life, which varies in length with certain factors, such as the uses to which it is placed, the continuity and severity of service, the methods of maintenance and repair, and the probabilities of its becoming superseded by some other type of asset. The criterion of a fixed asset is the purpose for which it is held by a specific enterprise, not its physical characteristics. Land and buildings, for example, may be the merchandise inventory (current assets) of a real estate company; fixtures, machinery, or delivery equipment likewise may be the salable product of some factory or mercantile organization; similarly, securities may be regarded as the stock-in-trade of an investment-bank concern. In the previous paragraph, intangible assets and securities held for long periods of time were listed as types of fixed assets. The valuation of intangible fixed assets and long-term investments presents special problems; consequently their valuation will be separately discussed in chapters xxvi and xxvii. The present chapter will limit itself to the valuation of tangible fixed assets held for productive use in the main business operations.

The time element.—Fixed assets are acquired for use during a succession of accounting periods. The problem of fixed-asset valuation, therefore, is a continuing one; it involves not only the establishment of initial values at the times of acquisition but also the periodic revaluation for purposes of calculating costs of operation and of expressing financial status. Attention will first be given to the problem of determining the initial value of fixed assets, then to the measurement of decreases and increases of their values in the course of business operations. The present chapter and the one following will present the problem of fixed-asset valuation under the following general topics:

1. Initial valuation
    a) Ideal value (present value of future services)
    b) Cost (an approximation to ideal value)
2. Revaluation
    a) Decreases in value
        (1) Depreciation
        (2) Depletion
    b) Increases in value
        (1) Betterments
        (2) Appreciation

Ideal value is present value of future services.—A business man typically intends to use a fixed asset over a period of several years; he plans to enjoy its value in the form of the continuous services which it will render in his various business activities. Buildings are erected for the protection of life and property; automobiles or trucks are manufactured for the transportation of people or materials. Whatever value a building or motor vehicle may possess arises out of the protection or transportation service it can render. No other value of a fixed asset (such as value for purposes of sale) is of importance to an owner who intends to keep it.

The problem of measuring fixed-asset value, then, is the problem of measuring the value of the services which fixed assets will render during their lives. If an accountant is computing the value of a truck which will run 60,000 miles, he must estimate the value to the enterprise of 60,000 miles of transportation. His estimate will, of course, be made before the truck is worn out; for it is necessary that the value of the truck be listed periodically among the assets of a firm's balance sheet. The value of the truck at any given time will be the value of the services which it may be expected to render in the future in the form of transportation.

The value of a fixed asset is the total value of the services it will render if used in the manner intended. The services typically will be rendered during a succession of operating periods; hence the value of a fixed asset may be defined as the value (at the present time) of its future services. The *present value of the future services* is often referred to as the capitalized value of these services. It is the total present value of the future services which will be later enjoyed in the course of business operations. For example, if a factory machine is estimated to be useful for ten years, and to render services valued at $500 per year, the total value of these services will be $5,000. All of these services will not, of course, be realizable immediately; consequently the total value of the future services must be discounted to give recognition to the fact that some services will be deferred. This adjusted value (the discounted value) of the future services represents the real value of the asset at a given moment of time. This value may be higher than cost or market; it may be lower. The principle of "discounting" future values when estimating their importance at the present is encountered in all aspects of valuation. The amount by which the value of a future asset will be discounted will, of course, vary with the length of time the realization of the value is postponed and the "rate" at which the future values are discounted. The process of discounting future values or services finds its most specific application in the valuation of long-term investments, especially bonds. Dealers in bonds actually compute the values of bonds for sale in the open market by discounting their future services with the aid of compound-interest formulas.

The values of tangible fixed assets are not usually established by computing the present value of their future services; for the difficulty of imputing values to specific assets often makes this method very impracticable. For example, in a factory which employs one hundred machines of ten different types, how shall an accountant determine the values of the services which each one renders in producing the output of the plant? It is difficult enough to estimate the total value of the services of the entire plant; the task of assigning different parts of the total to specific fixed assets is often impossible.

Cost an approximation to ideal value.—How, then, is the accountant to estimate the value which may be imputed to the future services of each fixed asset? What is to be the starting-point for the evaluation? When one considers the large number of variables in such a computation—changes in demand for the product, varying productive processes, changes in selling prices—the problem of evaluating a specific fixed asset on the basis of future services seems almost unsolvable. But the accountant analyzes the problem from a practicable, reasonable point of view. He assumes that the values which will be yielded by a fixed asset will be equivalent to those which a business originally yielded in order to secure it. In other words, the accountant assumes that, for purposes of initial valuation, *assets are worth what they have cost.* To be sure, it may be difficult at times to determine the cost; nevertheless, the accountant turns his attention first of all to the measurement of cost as the expression of the value of the future services. His second consideration is the proper apportionment of this cost to the periods or units of business activity. If it can be established that a machine has cost $10,000, the machine is assumed to have been worth $10,000 at the time of purchase. The ultimate value of the future services may prove to be more than this figure; it may be less. The problem of subsequent revaluation is separate from the original valuation at the time of acquisition.

Elements of fixed-asset cost.—Assume that a machine has been purchased from a manufacturer at an invoice price of $10,000. Is this the total cost of the machine? No; for other costs are yet to be incurred before the machine may be considered one of the useful assets of the enterprise. Some of the other costs are to cover incoming transportation, installation, testing, adjustment, special licenses. If the asset has been manufactured by the present owner, he may wish also to include the interest on his investment during the process of construction. In some cases, the invoice price may be a relatively small portion of the total cost of a fixed asset. An illustration of such a case would be a device for carrying materials which must be suspended from an overhead track; the expense of installing the track and adjusting the carrying devices is typically greater than the invoice cost of the equipment.

It may be said, in general, that the total cost of a fixed asset should include all costs which are expended in making it available for its intended use. In some cases, the costs of installation and testing will bulk large in the total costs; in others, the invoice price of the physical asset will be the main component. The real problem is to make sure that all elements of cost are included in the initial valuation. The problem is of special importance when a fixed asset, such as a building, is constructed by the enterprise which owns it. Cost of construction must, in such cases, include all items of materials, labor, and overhead expense, including interest on borrowed money during the period of construction.

Revaluation of fixed assets involves measurement of periodic depreciation.—Depreciation is the gradual reduction in the value of a fixed asset. It may be due to many causes, such as wear and tear in business operations; physical deterioration from action of the elements, or obsolescence caused by changes in business conditions, arts, or procedures. The accountant is not primarily concerned with the physical causes of depreciation; such problems are the particular province of the engineer. However, the matter of depreciation in value interests the accountant greatly; for as a person who estimates and classifies changes in value, he must frequently turn his attention to the measurement of the periodic reductions in fixed-asset values.

One of the typical rules of accounting valuation is that fixed assets should appear in the balance sheet at *cost less depreciation.* But it is apparent to any practical business man that such an amount is not always easily established. In the first place, cost cannot be accurately determined in every instance; the estimating of cost requires the application of definite rules concerning the admission and exclusion of items at the time of acquisition. It is not always easy to come to an agreement on what an asset has cost an enterprise. In the second place, the measurement and apportionment of accrued depreciation requires a knowledge of the rates and causes of depreciation in value—knowledge which is very often limited because of inadequate data. Cost less depreciation, which may be accepted as a very useful approximation to value, is not, however, an amount which is always easily determined.

Estimating the periodic depreciation.—The task of estimating the depreciation in the value of a fixed asset during a given period of time is threefold; that is to say, the actual estimate of depreciation depends upon, and is, the result of two other estimates which must first be made. The steps in the process of estimating periodic depreciation are as follows:

1. Estimate of depreciable value, which equals
   a) Initial value when secured, less
   b) Final value when discarded
2. Estimate of the life of the asset
3. Apportionment of depreciable value to periods of the life of the asset

Assume that a motor truck has been purchased at an initial cost of $5,000, an amount which is accepted as the initial value; also that the final value of the truck when discarded will be $200, its scrap value. The total *depreciable value* of the truck is the first amount less the second, or $4,800. The next task is to estimate the *life of the truck.* But what is meant by the life of a truck? In what units shall it be measured? A business man may select years of service, miles traveled, tons hauled, or some such factor as the basis for calculating the future services he will receive from a truck. Some unit must be found before any satisfactory basis of apportioning depreciation can be adopted. The units which may be used for estimating the life of a fixed asset are numerous and varied, but they may all be reduced to a basic classification under one of the following headings: (1) time; (2) service. The meaning of this statement will become clearer in the specific illustrations given in later paragraphs.

The final task is the *apportionment of the depreciable value* to periods of the life of the asset. In the case of the truck described above, the apportionment will be in terms of time or service, depending on which is selected as the basis. The amount of depreciation assignable to any given period may be determined by merely dividing the total depreciable value by the number of periods in the life of the truck, whether measured in units of time or service. In such a case the depreciable value would be apportioned uniformly over the life of the truck. But it is also possible to apportion the depreciable value to the periods of useful life in decreasing or increasing amounts. The method which will be used by a particular enterprise will vary with the purposes for which the depreciation is being computed and the available technique for estimating the decrease in value. The problem of accounting for the depreciation of fixed assets is of such general importance that it will be developed more fully in chapter xxv, which explains the various methods of computing the amounts applicable to individual accounting periods, as well as some of the economic and legal problems involved in recognizing depreciation as an expense of operations.

Depletion of fixed assets a problem in their valuation.—Some assets of a more or less permanent nature, such as mines, timber, quarries, and other natural resources, serve the business by being physically consumed. Accounting for the decreasing value of these assets—often referred to as *wasting-assets*—requires the measurement of their physical depletion. Broadly speaking, the problem is essentially the same for the apportionment of depletion to accounting periods as for the apportionment of depreciation, for in each case the accountant attempts to measure and record the total value to be yielded up by the asset, and to assign this amount to successive periods of business operations.

Assume that a mine which has cost $250,000 is estimated to contain 500,000 tons of iron ore of a quality suitable for extraction; also that the contents of the mine will in all probability be removed during the ensuing four years. The purchase price of the ore is 50 cents per ton, and the total value of the property is subject to depletion in the course of the mining operations. This value, like the value of depreciable assets, may be apportioned to operating periods in terms of calendar years or in terms of its service, that is to say, output measured in tons of ore. Usually depletion is calculated on the basis of some unit of weight or dimension and is apportioned to accounting periods in direct proportion to the cost of the original property. If, for example, 120,000 tons of ore were extracted from the mine referred to, the allowance for depletion would be $60,000, calculated on the basis of 50 cents per ton. An asset account, such as "Mining Properties," would be credited for this amount; and an expense account, such as "Depletion," would be debited. The journal entry might appear somewhat as follows:

Depletion........................	$60,000	
Mining properties......................		$60,000

(To record an allowance for the depletion of leasehold, No. 26; 120,000 tons of iron ore at 50 cents per ton.)

The task of properly estimating the contents of a mine is very difficult; nevertheless, it must be attempted if adequate accounting is to be achieved. The technique of estimating the contents and value of a wasting-asset is beyond the scope of this text. The rule "cost less depletion" is the rule most frequently adopted for computing the remaining value for purposes of balance-sheet presentation. Some value other than cost may be selected for purpose of the initial value; in fact many wasting-assets, such as mines, timber lands, or quarries, are often evaluated by scientific appraisals which attempt to determine the volume or weight of the ore, timber, stone, or clay which can be obtained from them. Where such estimates are used as the basis for entering periodic depletion in the accounting records, they are subject to the same need for revision as the values of depreciable assets.

Fixed assets may increase in value through additions or betterments.—The remainder of the present chapter deals with accounting for increases in fixed-asset values. Although the processes of depreciation and depletion speed the fixed assets on their inevitable journey to the scrap pile, certain other influences tend to postpone the trip. Two main types of transactions may be differentiated as increasing the values of fixed assets: additions and betterments. Both of these transactions come under the general classification of *capital expenditures* (see chap. ix); they are to be sharply distinguished from *revenue expenditures*, such as maintenance and repairs, which are incurred solely for the purpose of making possible the continuance of current business operations.

Additions.—Additions to fixed assets are the features added to property already in service at the beginning of operations, which do not take the place of similar assets previously in service. An illustration would be the construction of a new wing or story on a building. *"Additions" may be regarded as "quantitative" changes in the nature of an asset, by which the total dimensions are increased. They are not to be confused with "replacements,"* which merely substitute one asset for another substantially similar in nature. The purchase of a new machine to replace one which has been worn out cannot be regarded as increasing the value of the asset being discarded. The expenditure for the new asset is, to be sure, a capital expenditure; but it is to be accounted for by bringing the new asset into the books as an independent entity, not by writing up the value of the one previously owned.

Betterments.—Betterments are changes in assets intended to make them of greater capacity or to prolong their usefulness for a greater period of time than would otherwise have been the case. An illustration is the remodeling of a machine to make possible the manufacture of a new product, or the substitution of a tile roof on a building for one of shingle. *Betterments are not to be confused with "maintenance" and "repairs"* of the existing fixed assets or with improvements and expenditures necessary to keep them in serviceable condition. For example, the cost of cleaning the carbon out of the cylinders of a motor would not be regarded as a betterment of an automobile, but rather an expenditure necessary in its "maintenance." Likewise, the replacement of glass in the broken windows of a building would be regarded as a repair of the building, a charge against current operations. A betterment need not consist of an actual physical change in the shape or construction of assets; it may be the mere rearrangement of them to improve or prolong their usefulness. The transfer of machines from one room to another and their reinstallation as equipment of a different department involve expenditures which may under certain conditions properly be capitalized as a betterment. *"Betterments" may be regarded as "qualitative" improvements in fixed assets, which increase the amount or quality of service although they do not change the physical dimensions or essential characteristics of assets.*

Accounting for additions and betterments proceeds independently of periodic allowances for depreciation. These transactions affect the depreciation schedules, of course, by increasing the estimated depreciable value or the estimated service life, or both.

It should be mentioned at this point that both additions and betterments may result from expenditures which consist, in part, of either current maintenance or repairs. Only those parts of the expenditures which actually increase the value of the asset above that existing at the beginning of the period's operations should be capitalized; the remainder should be charged as current expenses.

Difficulties in separating capital and revenue expenditures.— Difficult problems of classification sometimes appear when portions of fixed assets are replaced. The question arises as to whether the accountant should regard some particular expenditure as resulting in a current expense or as an increase in the value of an asset. The answer is usually to be found in the method used for classification of the fixed assets. Assume that a new door is constructed to replace one which has been destroyed. Is this transaction a "replacement" of the fixed asset "Door," or is it a "repair" of the fixed asset "Building"? The accounts will suggest the proper method of dealing with such a transaction. If a separate record is kept of each door, the entry must undoubtedly provide for the disposal of the old door and the construction of the new one. If, on the other hand, the accounts do not carry a separate record of each physical component of the buildings, the erection of the new door must be regarded as merely an expense of operations, a current repair necessary for the continued use of a particular building.

The difference between capital and revenue expenditures is easily drawn in theory—but the practical apportionment of expenditures to capital and expense is not always simple. Many accountants and business men are of the opinion that consistency is more important than strict accuracy as the basis for classification at the time of the expenditure. They hold to this opinion because of the fact that over a series of operating periods all fixed assets are ultimately charged off as expenses. It does not always matter, they argue, whether specific items are charged as expenses immediately or gradually through the depreciation account. To meet the needs for consistency in the classification of expenditures, manuals are often prepared for the guidance of bookkeepers. These manuals give specific instructions regarding all items which are to be "capitalized" in the accounts; the rules generally are framed in terms of objects of expenditure and are applied without regard to the purposes of the expenditures. Other companies adopt the policy of classifying expenditure on the basis of amount, regardless of the object of expenditures: all items over a specified amount are capitalized; all under this amount are regarded as current expenses.

Changes in market conditions may increase the value of fixed assets.—Fixed assets may increase in value as the result of changes in general price levels, independently of financial expenditures for additions or betterments.

Appreciation.—The increase in market value may result in the cost of replacement of fixed assets being greater in amount than the original cost of construction or purchase. Land used as a building site for business operations often "appreciates" in value, as do various natural resources, such as timber, mines, and farm land; moreover, machinery, furniture, or fixtures may increase in financial value because of changes in the conditions of an industry or in the general price level. Where such appreciation is recognized in the accounts, it should be recorded separately, and not be merged with the depreciation data. When the value of the asset is increased in the accounts, the offsetting credit may be entered in one of two ways: as an earning of the current period, to be immediately credited to "Surplus"; or as a deferred credit to the income of future periods, to be entered in a special reserve account. Illustrations of each method follow:[1]

[1] On the consolidated balance sheet of the Goodyear Tire and Rubber and Subsidiary Companies, June 30, 1927, the following appears as a parenthetical comment, explaining the item "Surplus": "Including $15,314,274.68 arising from appreciation of properties prior to 1921 and from the valuation placed on goodwill and patents at March 1, 1921."

Land	$3,400.00	
Surplus		$3,400.00

(To adjust the Land and Surplus accounts to give effect to revaluation by the National Appraisal Company, July 30, 1927.)

or,

Land	$3,400.00	
Reserve for land appreciation		$3,400.00

The Reserve for Land Appreciation is an account which would appear on the balance sheet as a deduction from the fixed-asset totals, together with the allowances for depreciation. The credit to this account offsets the increase in the asset account; the net effect on the proprietorship account is to leave it undisturbed by the adjustment. The only advantage of the Reserve for Land Appreciation account under such a method of accounting would be administrative in nature; the account would serve to direct attention to the fact that the value of the fixed assets was higher than cost. The Reserve for Land Appreciation account might, of course, be listed among the proprietorship accounts, with the asset "Land" appearing in the accounts at the total appraised value. A person examining the balance sheet could thus tell how much of the proprietorship represented accumulated earnings and how much had resulted from revaluation of the land.

Reproduction cost.—Assume that an accountant is convinced that cost less depreciation does not represent the real value of a specific asset—for example, a special type of building, such as an electric power plant. He therefore wishes to establish a new value in terms of its replacement cost under prevailing conditions. How is he to discover the present value of the power plant? This question cannot be easily answered, for probably no two power plants are exactly alike; and even if they were, they would not be located on exactly similar land sites or depreciated to the same degree of physical efficiency. The estimate of the present value of such a specialized asset must be established by more elaborate technique than mere reference to current quotations in the market.

The discovery of a suitable value may be accomplished by obtaining bids from companies which would be willing to purchase the plant, or by securing estimates from construction companies as to the present approximate cost of building a similar power plant or one of the same efficiency and expected life as the original plant.[1] From the figure thus obtained, the accountant could deduct an amount to represent the depreciation which should be regarded as already accrued. Such a value is often used by appraisers for regulatory commissions who are attempting to establish current values on which service charges will be based; it is referred to as "*reproduction cost.*" Reproduction cost is often considered in the valuation of public-service corporation property by the representatives of regulatory commissions. Public-service corporations are permitted to charge rates for utility service calculated to produce income equal to an amount arrived at by applying a certain percentage on an approved valuation. This percentage is what the commission allows as the rate for "fair or reasonable return" on the investment found to be dedicated to public service. Sometimes the valuation is determined from the records of the corporation; at other times, by appraisal. The commissions prescribe the accounting procedure to be followed in regard to classification of accounts and in the treatment of capital and revenue expenditures.

QUESTIONS ON CHAPTER XXIV

1. Define the term "fixed assets." Give some typical illustrations of items usually regarded as fixed assets. May some of these be regarded as current assets under certain conditions? If so, under what conditions?
2. Cost less depreciation is often said to be the proper measure of the value of a fixed asset. Indicate why it may be difficult to determine cost and to estimate depreciation.

[1] Ordinarily a power plant or specialized factory building or machine would not be duplicated, even though it might be replaced. For even though the capitalized value of the remaining future services might be greater than depreciated cost price, the plant would be obsolete, when judged in the light of current knowledge and inventions. For this reason the market value cannot be determined by mere summation of the replacement costs (less depreciation) of the component parts of the fixed asset.

A distinction should be made between the cost of reproducing a physical plant of *identical size and proportions* and the cost of reproducing a plant which will *render identical or equivalent service*. The two costs might be different, depending upon the progress in the industry and special inventions which would render the original equipment obsolete.

3. What is meant by "the present value of the future services"? Is this value an estimate or is it an absolute fact? Is this the figure which cost attempts to approximate at the time of purchase?
4. Would a practical business man ever pay more than goods were worth to him at the time he purchased them? If not, would you say that the cost value of a fixed asset could either understate or overstate the present value of its future services?
5. The accountant is interested in value changes only, not in the physical changes of assets. Explain. Is the depreciation which the accountant records a deduction in value, in physical condition, in functional efficiency?
6. What is depletion? Is depletion a form of depreciation in the ordinary sense? May it be so regarded?
7. Define, illustrate, or explain: addition; replacement; betterment; maintenance; repairs.
8. Is it possible to evaluate the individual assets of a plant on the basis of capitalized earnings? What difficulties are present in the imputation of total income to specific assets?
9. What is appreciation? Is it always the result of general changes in price levels? What other factor might give rise to appreciation? How should it be recorded in the accounts?
10. What is meant by reproduction cost when applied to the valuation of fixed assets? How would it be determined in the case of fixed assets which are still in use but are of a type which is no longer being constructed—assets which will ultimately be replaced by a different type of assets?

CHAPTER XXV

SOME ASPECTS OF DEPRECIATION

The present chapter deals with the problem of calculating depreciation on fixed assets. Depreciation will be discussed both as a current expense chargeable to various fiscal periods and as a deduction from initial cost to establish the value of fixed assets.

Depreciation an expense chargeable to current fiscal periods. —Fixed assets are consumed in business operations in much the same manner as are current assets. To be sure, a building or a machine is not gradually dismembered during its service life in the same way that a stock of merchandise or of consumable supplies is depleted. Nevertheless, the values of depreciable assets steadily decrease during the assets' service lives, even though capital expenditure and appreciation postpone the dates of their abandonment. Depreciation of a fixed asset, therefore, is as much an expense chargeable to current operations as wages, interest, or taxes. Depreciation is allowable as a deduction for the computation of taxable income under the Federal Revenue Act.[1] It must be accounted for by all public utilities and other enterprises operating under the supervision of regulatory commissions. Accountants, economists, and the courts agree that depreciation is an expense chargeable against the fiscal periods during which assets are owned. The loss of value through depreciation must be recognized before any profits can be regarded as earned and available for distribution. It is not within the discretion of the management of a corporation to include or to exclude depreciation as expense when calculating profits available for distribution to stockholders. Moreover, the courts have held that depreciation must be accounted for periodically according to a schedule which apportions the depreciable value equitably over the various accounting

[1] Sec. 214, 2 (8), describes depreciation as "a reasonable allowance for wear and tear of property used in business, including a reasonable allowance for obsolescence."

periods.[1] The corporation is not at liberty to vary the periodic charges for depreciation to suit the conditions of prosperous and unprofitable years. Depreciation, then, is to be regarded as an expense chargeable to the periods during which an asset is owned. Depreciation continues whether business operations are carried on or not;[2] it is not an item to be used for equalizing the net profits of successive periods of business activity.

Depreciation may be apportioned to accounting periods in uniform, increasing, decreasing, or fluctuating amounts.—One important purpose underlying the measurement of depreciation is the discovery of costs of business operations. Consequently it is very important that depreciation estimates, no matter how they are calculated, be accounted for in terms of fiscal periods of financial activity. For this reason the element of *time* must be regarded as a very important factor in the apportionment of depreciable value; in practice it is not uncommon to apportion the value of most fixed assets to accounting periods without regard to their physical deterioration or amount of service. Nevertheless, there are circumstances where the *service* of an asset is the deciding factor in estimating periodic depreciation.

From the point of view of the various accounting periods, the total depreciable value may be apportioned in uniform, increasing, decreasing, or fluctuating amounts. The apportionment of depreciation in uniform amounts (whether in terms of time or service) is usually referred to as the "straight-line" method, and is the method most commonly used in business practice. The practice of apportioning depreciation in varying amounts is less frequently followed, because of the difficulty of computing the

[1] The Interstate Commerce Commission requires the companies under its regulation to compute the depreciation on the basis of rules "derived from a consideration of the company's history and experience. Companies should be prepared to furnish the Commission, upon demand, the rules and sworn statements of the facts, expert opinions, and estimates upon which they are based."—*Uniform System of Accounts for Telephone Companies*, first issue, p .67.

[2] This statement should be qualified, especially where the useful life is measured in terms of product or services, rather than years. In some cases the amount that an asset depreciates may bear a very direct ratio to the amount of service that is rendered—hence, to the total business operations. This condition would apply to heating apparatus that is affected by continued use; also to transportation equipment on which depreciation bears a close relation to tonnage hauled or mileage traveled.

periodic depreciation and verifying its correctness. Where these methods are used, the amount of depreciation is usually increased or decreased by a constant percentage of that apportioned to the previous year, although the change may be a constant amount or a varying amount. Where the amount of periodic depreciation is increased, the rate of increase often bears some relation to an actual or hypothetical interest accumulation; the method of apportioning increasing amounts which will be illustrated is the one known as the "sinking-fund" method. The method selected to illustrate decreasing amounts of depreciation is called the "fixed-percentage-of-diminishing-balance" method.[1]

Straight-line method.—The most commonly used method of estimating accrued depreciation is the one which apportions the expiring value in direct proportion to the passage of time.[2] To illustrate, let us use the previously mentioned $5,000 truck, with its scrap value of $200 and its estimated life of six years. This means that the total depreciable value, $4,800, must be apportioned to the six years during which the truck will be in service; it means also that one-sixth of this amount must be regarded as the expense of each of the years during which the truck is used. The annual allowance for depreciation would, therefore, be $800. A schedule showing the periodically depreciated value of the truck during the six years would be as follows:

Time, End of:	Annual Depreciation Expense	Allowance for Depreciation	Remaining Value of the $5,000.00
First year	$800.00	$ 800.00	$4,200.00
Second year	800.00	1,600.00	3,400.00
Third year	800.00	2,400.00	2,600.00
Fourth year	800.00	3,200.00	1,800.00
Fifth year	800.00	4,000.00	1,000.00
Sixth year	800.00	4,800.00	200.00

[1] A detailed classification of methods of apportioning depreciation may be found in R. B. Kester's *Accounting Theory and Practice*, Vol. II; also in E. A. Saliers' *Principles of Depreciation*.

[2] The term "straight line" is an outgrowth of an attempt by the engineering profession to portray graphically the amount of decrease in the value of a fixed asset. A graph is prepared which portrays money values marked off on the vertical axis and years of service on the horizontal. Depreciable value is apportioned equally to each year (or fiscal period) and is represented by dots on the graph. A line drawn through the dots is a "straight line." Lines to represent apportionment in increasing, decreasing, or fluctuating amounts would be "curved" or "broken."

The straight-line method of apportioning depreciation in direct ratio to passage of time during the expected service life has the advantage of simplicity. A fixed percentage is applied to the original cost at the close of each fiscal period. Its disadvantage lies in the fact that uniform depreciation charges are made during normal periods, periods of depression, and periods of unusual activity. Where costs are used as the basis for estimating the selling prices of products or services, there would be unequal loading of depreciation on the costs of the product. It is true that the depreciation allowance should not be a mere equalizer of net profits; nevertheless, business practice and the accountant's interest in clearly reflecting income require that depreciation be established in the light of the individual circumstances rather than by arithmetical calculations.

Sinking-fund method.—A second method of apportioning depreciation during the estimated life of a fixed asset is one by which the amount of periodic depreciation increases during the life of the asset. The depreciation may increase in constant amounts or in constant percentages. When a constant rate of increase is applied, the rate selected for the increase usually approximates the current rate of interest. The annual allowance for depreciation increases at a compound-interest rate for successive periods until the end of the estimated service life of the asset. The amounts of the annual credits to the Allowance for Depreciation account are such that the total credit will equal the depreciable value at the end of the service life. Let us again refer to the truck used in the illustration made above. The first problem is to select an original amount which may be charged as depreciation the first year but which will increase at a certain rate each year. This is done by the aid of compound-interest formulas. If we assume a rate of increase of 5 per cent, the amounts of depreciation for each year necessary to write off the total depreciable value of $4,800.00 would be as follows:[1]

[1] The Depreciation Expense charge increases each year by 5 per cent over that of the previous period. The credit to Allowance for Depreciation increases at the same rate as would a sinking fund in which annual deposits of $705.68 were made, each deposit earning interest at 5 per cent. See Appendix at close of this chapter.

Time, End of:	Annual Depreciation Expense	Allowance for Depreciation	Remaining Value of the $5,000.00
First year	$705.68	$ 705.68	$4,294.32
Second year	740.96	1,446.64	3,553.56
Third year	778.01	2,224.65	2,775.35
Fourth year	816.91	3,041.56	1,958.44
Fifth year	857.76	3,899.32	1,100.68
Sixth year	900.68	4,800.00	200.00

The depreciation charge increases each year, from $705.68 in the first year to $900.68 in the sixth year—a total difference of $195.00. The justification usually advanced for such a depreciation schedule is that the accounts thus show more exactly the actual depreciation of the asset; that is to say, depreciation of an asset is assumed to progress slowly at first, increasing in rate toward the end of its service life.[1] Another argument sometimes put forth is the claim that the reserve for depreciation should keep pace with a replacement fund which may be established by periodic contributions each year. Periodic contributions of $705.68, accumulating interest at 5 per cent per year, would amount to $4,800.00 in six years.

Fixed-percentage-of-diminishing-balance method.—A third method of apportioning depreciation on the basis of time apportions the depreciable value in decreasing amounts to operating periods; the amount allowed annually for depreciation grows smaller in the later years of the life of the asset. This procedure, when adopted, is claimed to be justifiable on the assumption that the total annual charges for repairs and depreciation combined should be ap-

[1] This argument may be correct, theoretically, as far as functioning efficiency is concerned. From the standpoint of realizable value, however, it would typically be incorrect. For the realizable value of an asset often falls rapidly during the first period of use. As an example one may point to the low prices of second-hand automobiles or specialized machinery.

[2] This argument, however, does not square with the purposes for which depreciation charges are computed. There is no inevitable relation between the amount of depreciation of an asset used for business purposes and the amount of a sinking-fund which would replace it. Moreover, the mere allowance for depreciation provides no funds with which an asset can be replaced. If a "sinking-fund reserve" is to be established, it must grow independently of any charges for depreciation expense.

proximately equal. Inasmuch as the repair charges are smaller in the early years of the life of the asset, the charge for depreciation should be relatively large during this period. During the later years when the repair charges increase, the depreciation charges should be reduced.[1] The amount by which annual depreciation decreases from year to year may be a constant value; or the amount of decrease itself may grow smaller, as in the case where the annual depreciation is a fixed percentage of the diminishing value of the asset. The fixed-percentage method permits the accountant to deduct each year a certain percentage of the value on the books at the beginning of the year. The method applied to the $5,000 truck would require an approximate annual charge of about 40 per cent on the diminishing balance in the asset account. The rate of 40 per cent does not bring the remaining value to exactly $200 at the end of six years, but this rate will illustrate the principle of the fixed-percentage method. The schedule would be as follows:

Time, End of:	Annual Depreciation Expense	Allowance for Depreciation	Remaining Value of the $5,000.00
First year	$2,000.00	$2,000.00	$3,000.00
Second year	1,200.00	3,200.00	1,800.00
Third year	720.00	3,920.00	1,080.00
Fourth year	432.00	4,352.00	648.00
Fifth year	259.20	4,611.20	388.80
Sixth year	155.52	4,766.72	233.28

Depreciation on a service basis.—Broadly speaking, the only difference between the time basis and the service or output basis is the unit in which the serviceable life is measured. In one case, it is measured in terms of time—calendar months or years. In the other, the unit of life is a unit of service or of output. The service life of a machine, for example, could be estimated in terms of working-hours instead of mere passage of time. By "working-hours" is meant the actual periods of time during which an asset

[1] There is merit to the argument that costs of depreciation and repairs should be accounted for as mere parts of the whole costs of using a fixed asset during its service life. A depreciation policy, therefore, which tends to distribute the composite cost of depreciation and repairs on some reasonable basis must be commended as being logical, even if not practicable in all cases.

is in use or motion, as opposed to the mere length of time it is in the possession of an enterprise. The service of a fixed asset may also be measured in terms of the physical output of product which is affected by the asset during its life. For example, depreciation on a rock-crushing machine may be computed in proportion to carloads of crushed stone; or the depreciation on a power loom in a textile mill may be computed in proportion to square yards of cloth woven on the loom.

When depreciation is computed on the basis of units of service rather than of time, the value is usually written down in direct proportion to the amount of service on a straight-line basis, when considered in terms of the service life of the asset. When depreciation calculated on a straight-line service basis is apportioned to calendar periods, the amounts charged against the various fiscal periods are not equal. The charges vary with the amount of service rather than with the mere passage of time. In so far as the use of an asset is dependent upon the amount of income earned, this method of calculating depreciation tends to equalize current net profits by charging a relatively small amount of depreciation against a period of relative inactivity.

Assume that the depreciation on the truck previously referred to is to be apportioned to fiscal periods on the basis of mileage, which is estimated in advance to be 60,000 miles. Inasmuch as there is a total of $4,800 to be charged off as depreciation, this would mean that 8 cents should be charged for each mile traveled. If the truck traveled 10,000 miles the first year, the depreciation would be estimated at $800. If it traveled 14,000 miles the second year, the depreciation would be $1,120. The annual depreciation charge would vary with the mileage traveled. The total depreciation at the end of the service life will be $4800, assuming that the truck renders 60,000 miles of service, no more or less.

Time, End of:	Annual Mileage	Annual Depreciation Expense	Allowance for Depreciation	Remaining Value of the $5,000.00
First year..........	10,000	$ 800.00	$ 800.00	$4,200.00
Second year........	14,000	1,120.00	1,920.00	3,080.00
Third year.........	4,000	320.00	2,240.00	2,760.00
Fourth year........	16,000	1,280.00	3,520.00	1,480.00
Fifth year.........	8,000	640.00	4,160.00	840.00
Sixth year.........	8,000	640.00	4,800.00	200.00

Effects of using different methods.—In the foregoing illustrations, the annual depreciation charges varied with the methods of computing them. The following schedule and chart are presented to compare the reducing net values of the assets when the following methods are used: straight line,[1] sinking-fund, fixed percentage of diminishing balance, service (miles of travel).

COMPARISON OF VALUE OF TRUCK, DETERMINED ANNUALLY ON BASIS OF STRAIGHT-LINE AND OTHER METHODS OF ESTIMATING DEPRECIATION

Time, End of:	Straight Line	Sinking-Fund	Fixed Percentage	Service
Original	$5,000.00	$5,000.00	$5,000.00	$5,000.00
First year	4,200.00	4,294.32	3,000.00	4,200.00
Second year	3,400.00	3,553.56	1,800.00	3,080.00
Third year	2,600.00	2,775.35	1,080.00	2,760.00
Fourth year	1,800.00	1,958.44	648.00	1,480.00
Fifth year	1,000.00	1,100.68	388.80	840.00
Sixth year	200.00	200.00	233.28	200.00

COMPARISON OF ANNUAL DEPRECIATION OF A TRUCK WHEN COMPUTED ON STRAIGHT-LINE AND OTHER BASES

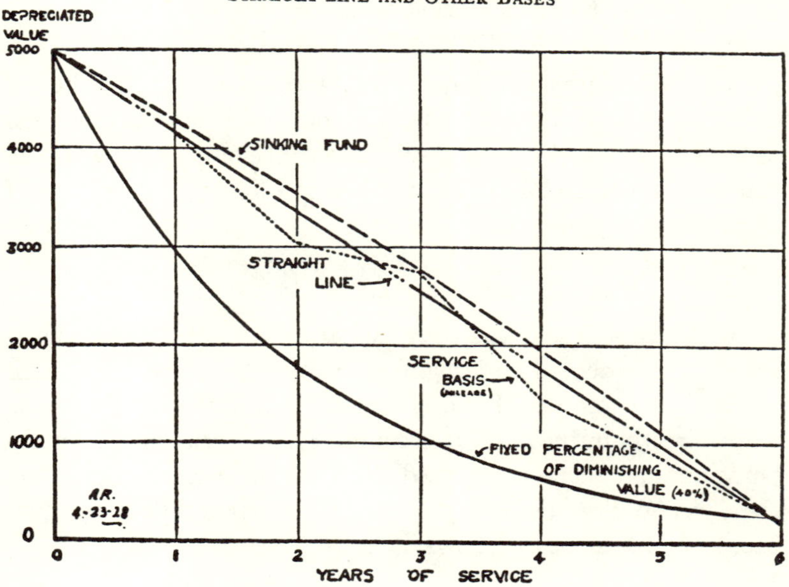

[1] The straight-line time-basis method of calculating periodic depreciation is probably used more than all other methods combined. For most practical purposes, the inaccuracies arising from its use are offset by the convenience of its application.

All of the different methods of computing depreciation bring the net value of the asset to approximately $200 at the end of six years. The book values at the end of the various years of service, however, are noticeably different. The facts of the table are set forth in Chart on page 331.

Disposal of partly depreciated assets.—Fixed assets are sometimes discarded or replaced before their depreciation has been entirely accounted for. The Allowance for Depreciation account for such an asset should be closed, however, even though it is not sufficient entirely to offset the original book value at which the asset was recorded. To illustrate, assume that a machine which was purchased at a price of $600, and on which depreciation of $60 per year has been charged for six years, is to be discarded. The depreciation allowance would have accumulated by the end of the sixth year to a total of $360. This deferred credit to the asset account should now be deducted from the face value to indicate clearly the book value of the depreciated asset. The entry would be accomplished as follows:

Allowance for depreciation on machinery..	$360.00	
Machinery and equipment (lathe No. 46)......		$360.00

The Machinery and Equipment account would now be reduced by $360, and the subsidiary account carrying a record with lathe No. 46 would show a resulting balance of only $240. If the machine is disposed of at book value, the following entry would be made:

Cash..............................	$240.00	
Machinery and equipment...............		$240.00

If the asset is sold at a price higher or lower than book value, the difference should be recognized as an income or expense item affecting the surplus of the enterprise. An adjustment may be made directly in the Surplus account or in a special income or expense account temporarily used to record the gain or loss. If the lathe were disposed of at a price of $220, there would be a loss of $20, to be recorded as follows:

Cash..............................	$220.00	
Loss on sale of fixed assets...........	20.00	
Machinery and equipment...............		$240.00

If, on the other hand, the lathe were sold for $260, the net result of the transaction would be a profit of $20. It would be shown as follows:

Cash	$260.00	
Profit on sale of fixed assets		$ 20.00
Machinery and equipment		240.00

Effects of excessive depreciation charges.—It happens not infrequently that fixed assets enjoy a longer serviceable life than was anticipated at the time they were purchased. Strict adherence to the depreciation schedule would cause the book value to be written down more rapidly than the actual service life of the asset draws to its close. In such cases, the owner may find himself in possession of valuable assets of recognized serviceability, after they have been recorded on the books of the enterprise as entirely depreciated. What should be done? It is impossible to continue charging depreciation after the original values have been written off.[1] Moreover, it would be impracticable to attempt to restate at such late date the expenses for depreciation which have been charged against previous periods; such adjustments, even if they could be made, would be of very slight significance for the administrative control of current operations.

The accountant has two choices. In the first place, he may ignore the existence of the asset, in so far as depreciation charges are concerned, but may carry it on the balance sheet at a nominal figure, such as $1.00, for purposes of information only. Instances of this type are not uncommon in the cases of financial institutions, whose conservative policies sometimes result in the writing off of building or fixtures value long before the assets themselves are discarded.[2] In the second place, he may revalue the asset, increas-

[1] The manager of a lumber company, however, did continue to write down the value of his saw mills, even after the original book value had been fully depreciated. He thereby accumulated a credit which he designated as an "Insurance Reserve," presumably to absorb any losses which might arise from fires, against which the insurance companies would not insure him. The Insurance Reserve account, in fact, represented accumulated surplus. There can be no loss (for accounting purposes) when unrecorded financial values are destroyed.

[2] The published statement of condition of the Illinois Merchants Trust Company, Chicago, at the close of business, December 31, 1926, lists the asset "Illinois Merchants Bank Building" at a value of $1.00, with the following parenthetical comment inserted in the body of the statement: "Actual Cost of Building, Furni-

ing its book value to an amount equal to its estimated present worth, and then record depreciation on the new value during succeeding periods on the basis of a revised depreciation schedule. Either method ultimately affects the financial summaries in the same way. The first method, by omitting the depreciation charge from operating expenses, makes possible the showing of larger earnings and a consequent accumulation of surplus; the second method creates additional proprietorship at the time the asset is revalued, but loads future operating periods with greater charges for depreciation.

QUESTIONS ON CHAPTER XXV

1. Depreciation is both a measure of the expense of operations during a period and of the reduction in the original value of a fixed asset. As such it affects both the statement of income and expense and the balance sheet. Explain.
2. Do you think the practice of accounting for depreciation would be continued by business men even though they were taxed on the original costs of assets, without regard to the net income derived from them? Explain your position.
3. The preceding chapter stated that the steps in establishing a depreciation rate consisted of (*a*) estimating the depreciable value; (*b*) estimating the life of the asset; (*c*) apportioning the depreciable value to periods in the life of the asset. Select an illustration, and make the arithmetical calculations to explain this procedure.
4. When depreciable value is apportioned to fiscal periods in uniform amounts, the method is referred to in practice as the "straight-line" method. Why this name? May the term "straight line" be applicable to cases where life of the assets is measured in terms of service or output? Explain.
5. "Decreasing" amounts may vary from each other in constant amounts, in constant percentages, or the amount of decrease in periodic depreciation may be arbitrary. Illustrate by using the case where depreciation during the first accounting period is estimated to be $400.
6. "Increasing amounts" of periodic depreciation may increase by constant amounts, by constant percentages, or by arbitrary amounts. Illustrate.

---

ture, Fixtures, and Safety Deposit Vaults—$15,815,498.00." The building is an exceedingly valuable income-producing asset, rising more than twenty stories above street level and housing the activities of nearly 2,000 bank employees as well as several thousand workers in the offices of firms which rent space in the building.

7. What are the usual arguments in favor of increasing and decreasing amounts of depreciation during a succession of accounting periods? Would the schedule to be adopted be influenced by the type of asset involved and the conditions under which it was used and owned? Illustrate by selecting assets from the following: a patented process of manufacture; a building on leased land; an automobile truck.
8. What arguments can be advanced for charging off depreciation in proportion to such items as the following: gross income; net profit; units of output?
9. What alternatives does an accountant face when he finds that the depreciable values of an asset have been written off in the accounts, but the asset still continues in use?

APPENDIX TO CHAPTER XXV

The determination of all amounts involving compound-interest calculations is based upon the mathematical principle that an amount (P) which increases at compound interest at a given rate (i) for a given number of compounding periods (n) will grow to a sum (S) which may be expressed as $P\ (1+i)^n$. The value P, which is the "present worth" of the sum S, may likewise be expressed as $S \div (1+i)^n$. For example, let i equal 0.06, n equal 10, and S equal \$10,000. The present value (P) of the amount (S) is $P \div (1+i)^n$, or \$10,000 ÷ $(1.06)^{10}$, which is \$10,000 ÷ 1.79085, or \$5,583.95. This amount is used in an illustration of the text on page 340.

These simple expressions form the basis for calculating the present and future values of series of amounts (annuities), as well as of individual amounts. The formulas are developed in practice to solve problems in which any of the foregoing symbols are the unknowns, namely, P, S, i, or n. In the case of the sinking-fund method of estimating periodic depreciation, the unknown quantity is an amount which, when increased by a constant percentage and charged against succeeding fiscal periods, will cause the total Allowance for Depreciation to equal the agreed "depreciable value." In the case of the truck mentioned in chapters xxiv and xxv, this amount proved to be \$705.68, where the ultimate sum (S) was \$4,800, the rate of interest of increase (i) was 0.05, and the number of compounding or fiscal periods (n) was six.

CHAPTER XXVI

VALUATION OF INVESTMENTS

The present chapter deals with certain types of property known as investments, a group which may be separated for purposes of discussion because of special, indirect relations which such property bears to the business operations.

Investments are special assets not employed directly in the major income-producing activities.—Investments may be defined as those assets of a business which are not used in the main income-producing operations. They are obtained for various purposes, varying with the financial conditions and policies of each specific enterprise. One purpose of investments is to obtain earnings from excess funds not required for the major business activities. An example of an investment for this purpose is the purchase of interest-bearing securities which may be disposed of on short notice. A second and very important purpose is to extend control over new areas of business operations. An investment for business control is the acquisition of securities of a factory or mine from which raw materials are to be produced, or the establishment of a retail store through which a manufactured product is to be sold. A third purpose is to reap a profit by resale of the asset purchased. This is not regarded by business men as a desirable basis for investing surplus assets, or one that is consistent with sound business practice. This objective is, however, frequently justified; in fact, it is sometimes regarded as auxiliary to the main income-producing operations of buying and selling merchandise. An illustration would be purchases of an unusually large supply of materials in anticipation of a probable advance in price.

Scope of investment classification.—The investment classification cuts across the boundaries of all other classes of assets; it is not limited to any particular type of objects. Investments may take the form of current assets, fixed assets, or intangibles. The test of whether a particular asset is to be classified as an investment in the balance sheet is the purpose for which it is held. If it is not to be used directly in the income-producing operations, it must be regarded for the time being as an investment. Illustrations are savings-bank deposits, government bonds, short-term notes, raw-material inventories, industrial bonds, capital stock, land, buildings, machinery, patents, copyrights. Each of these assets may be owned under such circumstances that it should be regarded as an investment in a balance sheet. The problem of evaluating an investment is similar to that of estimating the worth of any other current or fixed asset; the value of an investment to an enterprise must be estimated in terms of the particular purpose for which it is owned. Assets which are purchased to be held for a short time are sometimes referred to as *temporary* investments. They are usually procured to insure moderate earnings on temporary excess funds or an immediate trade advantage because of fluctuations in business conditions. Assets to be held for long periods of time are usually purchased to insure control over a source of raw material or an outlet for finished product. They are referred to as *permanent* investments. Temporary and permanent investments will be discussed separately in this chapter, special attention being given to the latter.

Market value important in valuation of temporary investments.—The first consideration in the valuation of temporary investments is their probable market value; such investments are usually made with a view to being liquidated on short notice. This consideration applies to any type of temporary investment, including excess stocks of merchandise as well as the corporate securities of other enterprises. At times market price must give way to other approximations of value for purposes of balance-sheet presentation. The alternative to market price is usually cost price, an amount which is very often easily determined and generally known and which is frequently the only value which can be assigned to investments.

The rule "cost or market, whichever is lower" may be applied to temporary investments as well as to other current assets. Where both cost value and market value are known, they may both be shown on the balance sheet by the use of a valuation account to record the effects of periodic fluctuations. Chapter xxiii indicated that fluctuations in inventory value might be reflected in an account which recorded such changes. A similar account may also be used for recording variations in the value of investments.

Many types of assets are held as permanent investments.— Permanent investments are those held for long periods of time with a view to securing indirect gains to the enterprise. They may be fixed assets of any nature, such as buildings, land, bonds, stock, etc. The rule generally applied to the valuation of permanent investments is the same as for other fixed assets—"cost less depreciation." The rule implies, of course, that the accountant is able to determine cost, and also depreciation. Depletion, capital expenditures, and appreciation also present problems in the valuation of permanent investments. In the case of tangible physical property, such problems may be solved in essentially the same way as for other fixed assets.

But the ownership of corporate securities presents certain valuation problems which are peculiar to them; they often change gradually in value, without, of course, being subject to depreciation. Some changes occur as a result of the mere passage of time; this condition is particularly true of bonds as they approach maturity. Other changes follow trends in general business conditions or fluctuations in the earning power of the issuing corporations; this situation applies especially to shares of stock. The accounting problems of bonds and stocks as permanent investments will be discussed separately in the paragraphs immediately following.

Bond investments evaluated on present-worth principle.— Bonds of other companies or of governments are frequently purchased to be held as long-term investments; they may be obtained directly from the issuing corporations or purchased in the open market.

Characteristics of bond investments.—The valuation of bonds held as permanent investments is affected by three specific conditions not present in the problem of evaluating other fixed assets: a recognized face value, a definite maturity date, a series of definitely contracted interest payments. All of these factors must be taken into consideration in the initial valuation of permanent investments and in their revaluation during the time they are held. The face value of the bonds represents the value which the bonds will have at maturity; it is the amount which the issuing company has pledged itself to pay and which the company holding them expects to receive at the time of redemption. Face value is a very important factor in bond valuation and may well be regarded as the central consideration in evaluating long-term bond investments; consequently, the face value of bond investments should appear on the balance sheet, even though this amount differs from the purchase price. Cost values and periodic market values are often important factors in arriving at the proper values for bond investments. They also should find their way into the accounts, although it is not always necessary for such values to be given separate records in the ledger. Differences between face values and other values of bond investments may be reflected by the use of discount or premium accounts, depending upon which values are the higher.

Present worth in bond values.—It has been asserted in previous discussions that the real value of an asset is the present value of its future services or earnings. This principle is applied literally in the valuation of bonds by many financial institutions; they compute the present value of all the future receipts from a bond, including both the periodic interest earnings and the face value at maturity. The total future receipts from a bond are "discounted" to their "present value" at the rate of interest which the investor is to receive on his money. The resulting "present value" of the future receipts thus represents the price which he will pay for a bond at a given time. To illustrate, assume the case of $10,000 worth of 5 per cent, ten-year bonds, interest payable annually. The purchaser who obtains these bonds is receiving the right to two distinct types of assets: a payment of $10,000 ten years hence; and ten $500 annual interest payments, beginning one year later. If the investor wishes to receive 6 per cent on the money which he actually invests, he will "discount" these future assets to their "present value" at a rate of 6 per cent. He will pay a sum at the present time equal to the discounted value of the future receipts, including both the principal of the bond and the annual interest coupons. For example:

$10,000, ten years hence, 6 per cent basis	=$5,583.95 now
Ten $500 interest payments, 6 per cent basis	= 3,680.05 now
	$9,264.00

The "present value" of the bonds to an investor who wishes to receive 6 per cent earnings on his money is $9,264.[1] This is the amount an investor would pay and the value which should appear on a balance sheet. The bonds would, therefore, be discounted in the amount of $736 by an investor who wished to receive 6 per cent on his money. On a balance sheet the bond investment might appear as follows:

Morton Company bonds..................	$10,000.00
Bond discount......................	736.00
	$ 9,264.00

The "Bond discount" should be periodically amortized[2] by transfer to Surplus or to the Interest Income account. The amortization may proceed on a straight-line or compound-interest basis. A comparison of the two rates of amortization follows:

AMOUNT OF BOND DISCOUNT AMORTIZED ON TEN-YEAR BONDS PURCHASED AT DISCOUNT OF $726.00

Time, End of:	Straight-Line Amortization	Compound-Interest (6%) Amortization
First year............	$ 73.60	$ 55.84
Second year...........	147.20	115.03
Fourth year...........	294.40	244.30
Sixth year............	441.60	389.48
Eighth year...........	588.80	552.70
Tenth year............	736.00	736.02

[1] Good treatments of the general subject of compound-interest calculations may be found in such books as Finney, *Actuarial Science*, and Vinal, *Mathematics for the Accountant*.

[2] Amortization is the process of writing down an accounting value. It is a term applied to bond discount and premium, as well as to debts and capital values generally. Literally, to amortize means to extinguish; hence, amortization is any process of extinguishing a value by payment or consumption. In practice the term "amortization" is also applied to the writing down of capital assets because of obsolescence or inadequacy; it was used by the Bureau of Internal Revenue to refer to the amortization of manufacturing facilities used in the production of materials for the prosecution of the war.

Assume that an investor buys the X Company 5 per cent bonds on a 4 per cent basis. He will, of course, discount the par value and the interest earnings on a 4 per cent basis, paying the following amounts:

$10,000, ten years hence, 4 per cent basis	=	$ 6,755.64 now
Ten $500 annual interest payments, 4 per cent basis	=	4,055.45 now
		$10,811.09

An investor purchasing the X Company bonds on a 4 per cent basis will, therefore, pay a premium of $811.09 for them. The premium should appear on the balance sheet as an addition to par value and be amortized periodically as a deduction from interest income at the time the interest earnings are received. The bond premium may be amortized on a straight-line or compound-interest basis, in exactly the same way as has been illustrated for the bond discount.

Accounting for bond discount.—The variation between the cost and face value of a bond investment should be clearly shown in the accounts at the time of acquisition. For example, if certain bonds of the Morton Company, carrying a face value of $10,000, were purchased at 90,[1] the entry would be:

Morton Company bonds........	$10,000.00	
Cash................................		$9,000.00
Bond discount......................		1,000.00

(To record the purchase at 90 of $10,000 worth of first mortgage, 5 per cent bonds of the Morton Company, due in ten years.)

As the maturity date of the bonds approaches, portions of the bond discount should be transferred to the Surplus account, or to some income account pending transfer to the Profit and Loss account. The Bond Discount account may be regarded as an interest account, carrying deferred credits to Interest Income earned on the bonds. As such, the credit in the Bond Discount account may be gradually transferred to an Interest Income account and added to the amount of interest earned as computed on

[1] The term "at 90" means at a price of 90 cents per dollar of face value; it does not refer to the actual amount paid for each bond. The face value of the individual bonds may have been any amount, such as $100, $500, or $1,000.

the basis of the "nominal" interest. "Nominal interest" is a term used to refer to the ratio of the annual interest paid on a debt to the face value of the bond or other evidence of the debt. This ratio is permanent during the life of the bond. The "nominal" rate of interest is often contrasted with the "effective" rate. The former is the ratio of the annual interest to the face value of the bonds; the latter is the ratio of the annual interest to the amount which a purchaser has paid. The actual rate of interest earnings of securities bought at a discount will, of course, be higher than the nominal rate quoted in the bond agreement. The value of the bonds will increase as the maturity date approaches, for the bonds will be redeemed at par by the issuing company.

The amortization of the Bond Discount credit may be carried on in uniform or increasing amounts during the time before maturity of the bonds. Where the amortization progresses at an increasing rate based upon compound-interest accumulations, the transfer is said to be effected according to the "scientific" method. The entry shown below illustrates amortization computed on the straight-line basis; such an entry would be made at the time cash was received for annual interest, and one-tenth of the discount transferred to the Interest Income account:

Bond discount	$100.00	
Cash	500.00	
Interest income		$100.00
Interest income		500.00

(To record the receipt of annual interest and to recognize as interest income one-tenth of the bond discount on $10,000 worth of Morton Company bonds.)

The entry may also be condensed to the following form:

Bond discount	$100.00	
Cash	500.00	
Interest income		$600.00

Accounting for bond premium.—When bonds are purchased at a price above face value, both the face value and the premium should be entered in the accounts. The entry for the purchase of

$10,000 worth of Morton Company 5 per cent ten-year bonds at 110 would be made as follows:

Morton Company 5 per cent bonds	$10,000.00	
Bond premium	1,000.00	
Cash		$11,000.00

The debit in the Bond Premium account is a deferred charge to Interest Expense, which must be charged off during the life of the bonds. The premium represents prepaid interest and may accordingly be gradually reduced by transfer to an Interest Expense account during each succeeding period. The premium may be regarded as a payment to the vendor of the bonds to insure cash receipts as interest earnings which are larger than those which could have been obtained from other types of investment. For that reason accountants do not usually transfer the premium on bond investments to an Interest Expense account. More often they treat the reduction of bond premium as an offset to the interest income from the bonds. An entry to record the receipt of an interest payment and to adjust the Bond Premium account would be:

Interest income	$100.00	
Cash	500.00	
Interest income		$500.00
Bond premium		100.00

(To record the receipt of annual interest and to write off as a deduction from Interest Income one-tenth of the bond premium on $1,000 worth of Morton Company bonds.)

The two entries to the Interest Income account may, of course, be offset against each other with the following result:

Cash	$500.00	
Bond premium		$100.00
Interest income		400.00

Permanent stock investments affected by element of cost.—Shares of stock held for investment cannot be evaluated with the same mathematical exactness as bonds which bear definite maturity dates and are conditioned by contractual interest payments. The accountant cannot look forward with any definiteness to the time when shares of stock will be converted into cash by the issuing company; moreover, he cannot even be sure that regular dividend payments will be received. For these reasons the accountant typically attaches great importance to original cost price in the valuation of shares of stock as long-term investments; he adjusts the value of capital-stock investments on his books with the same hesitancy that he would adjust the valuation of tangible fixed assets such as machinery, buildings, or land. He is not concerned with the problem of periodic depreciation, which is so important in the evaluation of tangible property, for, although shares of stock may change in value, the change is not usually continuous or always in the same direction. Cost, then, is the value most frequently adopted for the initial valuation of shares of stock purchased as a long-term investment. Cost may, of course, be identical with the prevailing market price at the time of purchase. If one hundred shares of X Company $100 par value common stock were purchased at $74 per share, the entry to record them at cost price would be:

X Company common stock	$7,400.00	
Cash		$7,400.00

(To record the purchase of one hundred shares of X Company $100 par value common stock at 74.)

The investment in stock would appear on the balance sheet at cost price, with appropriate explanation:

X Company common stock	$7,400.00

(One hundred shares at cost.)

If, when later balance sheets were prepared, the prevailing market value for such shares were higher, the variation could be pointed out by means of a footnote, somewhat as follows: "Market value of X Company common stock on May 1, 1927, was $85.00 per share."

Fluctuations in value.—Should temporary fluctuations in the market value of permanent stock investments be given recognition in the accounts of the company holding the securities? Probably not, because of the fact that during a period of time upward and downward fluctuations might offset each other. Moreover, the fluctuations in "book" value (which underlie the changes in market value) cannot be realized upon by an investing company, unless such an enterprise owns enough shares to control the financial policy of the corporation which has issued them. Where a continued upward or downward trend, however, appears to express a permanent increase or decrease in the value of shares, the investment accounts should be adjusted to reflect the new conditions. The problem of adjusting permanent stock investments in accord with fluctuations in the book value of the shares is not easily solved in practice. It is affected by the conditions under which the shares are owned, particularly with regard to whether they represent controlling or minority interests in the company which has issued them.

Controlling interest.—When a stock investment represents a controlling interest in the issuing company, there is often a good argument for evaluating the shares at a price proportionate to the total book value of the issuing company's proprietorship. To illustrate, assume that the Walter Hagen Sporting Goods Company purchases 1,500 shares of the stock of the Chick Evans Amusement Park, incorporated. The par value of the shares is $100 each, and there is a total of 2,000 shares outstanding. The purchase price is $105 per share. The journal entry to record the purchase of this stock, as entered on the books of the Hagen Company, would be:

Chick Evans Amusement Park stock..	$157,500.00	
Cash..................................		$157,500.00

Assume also that the price of $105 per share represents the proportionate interest of each share in the total net assets of the Evans Company. This means that the proprietorship section of the Evans Company would have appeared somewhat as follows:

Proprietorship:		
Capital stock............	$200,000.00	
Surplus..................	10,000.00	
		$210,000.00

The $210,000 represents the book value of the 2,000 shares of stock outstanding: of this total, three-fourths represents the book value (also the purchase price) of the 1,500 shares now held by the Hagen Company. But let us assume that the surplus of the Evans Company increases from \$10,000 to \$50,000 as the result of earnings, making a total net worth of \$250,000. The book value of each share of stock consequently increases to \$125; the total book value of the Hagen Company stock investment increases to \$187,500. If the rise in book value were to be recognized, the adjustment would be made as follows:

Chick Evans Amusement Park stock....	\$30,000.00	
Surplus....................................		\$30,000.00

Adjustments of this type are justified in cases where one company holds a large enough portion of stock to control the policy of another corporation.

Minority interests.—Stock investments which represent minor portions of the outstanding stock of the issuing corporation are called "minority interests." Where they appear as assets on the balance sheet of a company owning the shares, they may well appear at cost, without regard to temporary fluctuations in book value.

Funds a special type of investment.—Certain assets of an enterprise may be designated as available for specific, limited purposes; such items are usually separately accounted for under the general heading "funds." A fund account may be a controlling account containing the totals of various subsidiary accounts. The subsidiary accounts may be numerous; moreover, they may be of a specialized nature, each containing records of subsidiary debits or credits only. The subsidiary data, when combined, reveal a net amount equal to the value of the available assets comprising a particular fund.

Sinking-fund accumulations.—The most simple and frequently encountered type of fund account is one in which a record is made of assets set aside periodically to make possible a future payment. Such funds are known as "sinking-funds," and the assets which comprise them are usually invested in such manner that they earn some fixed rate of interest. The interest earnings are accordingly added to the fund, along with certain regular contributions agreed upon when the fund is established. The fund is therefore increased by two factors: (1) periodic contributions, and (2) interest earnings on the contributions. In view of the fact that the interest earnings are themselves reinvested immediately upon their receipt, it can be said that each periodic contribution increases at a uniform compound-interest rate during the existence of the fund. The term "sinking-fund" has, therefore, come to refer to any amount which is increased by a series of payments and which grows at a constant rate.

The term "sinking-fund" should be distinguished from "retirement fund." A sinking-fund is one which grows continuously (whether or not at increasing rate) until it is finally used for its intended purpose. A retirement fund, on the other hand, may be depleted from time to time by periodic withdrawals which are used to reduce (retire) the obligations gradually. Sinking-funds, according to the foregoing definition, grow in constantly increasing amounts. The amounts charged periodically to a fund which increases in this manner become larger as the fund grows, for, although the periodic payments remain the same, the interest earnings are larger each period. The funds should be shown separately among the assets on a balance sheet. An illustration of the investment section of a balance sheet, in which funds are shown, appears below:

Investments:		
Handley Company stock	$16,000.00	
Jensen Company bonds	15,000.00	
Funds:		
Sinking fund for 5 per cent, twenty-year, first mortgage bonds	5,536.60	
Retirement fund for 6 per cent preferred stock	3,480.00	
		$40,016.60

QUESTIONS ON CHAPTER XXVI

1. What classes of items may appear in the investment section of the balance sheet? Describe other ways of classifying these items.
2. What are the characteristics distinguishing temporary from permanent investments?

3. Temporary investments are customarily valued at cost or market, whichever is lower. Is there any reason, other than conservatism, to recommend this rule?
4. Suggest a method of showing temporary investments at market in the balance sheet by means of reserves adjusting cost to the market figure.
5. For what purposes are permanent investments acquired or held? Is cost, with recognition of depreciation in value, if large, a satisfactory basis for the statement of these assets? Give reasons.
6. Why is it necessary to distinguish between permanent stock and permanent bond investments for purposes of valuation?
7. Why are bonds purchased at a premium or a discount?
8. A $10,000 block of 6 per cent, ten-year bonds was purchased at 95. (*a*) Journalize the purchase; the receipt of an annual interest payment; the liquidation of the investment at maturity. (*b*) Journalize the transactions as they would appear if the purchase had been made at 105.
9. Controlling stock investments are stated at cost, plus, or minus pro rata shares of profits or losses, with deductions for dividends received. Non-controlling stock investments are carried at cost, with allowance for decline in value if great. Are these consistent rules? Do you agree with them? Why were they adopted?
10. Distinguish between a "sinking-fund" and a "retirement fund" as types of investments owned by an enterprise.

CHAPTER XXVII

VALUATION OF INTANGIBLES

Intangible assets may, broadly speaking, be regarded as comprising a subdivision of fixed assets; they possess certain peculiarities, however, which justify their being treated separately in a discussion of valuation.

Typical intangible assets explained.—Previous chapters have given only passing mention to the nature and scope of the intangible assets. A discussion of the problems of their valuation, therefore, may well be preceded by an explanation of the characteristics of various assets listed under this classification.[1]

Good-will.—Good-will is a characteristic of a business organization which gives it an earning capacity in terms of its total assets which is greater than that earned by the representative firm in the same industry. Good-will may result from an advantageous location, a desirable reputation, a well-known firm name, or personal skill. None of these advantages, however, are of any significance for estimating good-will from an accounting standpoint, unless they give rise to potential earning capacity or actual increased earnings.

Patents.—Patents are rights granted by the federal government, permitting persons to engage in the manufacture and sale of certain described articles to the exclusion of all other persons. In the United States a patent usually remains in effect for seventeen years. In most instances, the rights existing under them are transferable. Patent rights may not be renewed: this restriction is of little significance, however, inasmuch as most patents become obsolete or inadequate before they expire.

Copyrights.—Copyrights are privileges granted by the government to persons, involving the exclusive right to publish

[1] In legal parlance, the term "intangibles" is often used to apply to stocks, bonds, and notes, especially when they are being classified for purposes of taxation. But this terminology seldom, if ever, finds a place in commercial balance sheets.

certain written material. The right is granted to the person originally composing the material, or to his agents, and may not be infringed upon.

Trade-marks.—Trade-marks are the rights to use specific marks of identification on merchandise manufactured by or for a particular enterprise. The rights may not be infringed upon by competitors, even though the trade-marks have not been registered with a government agency.

Formulas and trade secrets.—Some businesses, particularly those engaged in chemical or other scientific processes as a part of manufacturing, possess certain secret formulas to which they attach very great value. Illustrations of such companies are the manufacturers of beverages or patent medicines. The formulas and trade secrets of manufacturing processes are sometimes listed at high values among the assets of these enterprises.

Franchises.—Franchises are special privileges granted to private persons, either individuals or corporations, to use natural resources or public property for their own profit. The holder of the franchise rights typically is restricted by the government granting them in the method of using public property or in the "rates" the franchise owner may charge for services rendered to customers. Illustrations of franchises are the rights to use a street, to harness a waterfall, or to exploit a mine on government land. Franchises are sometimes classified as to time as follows: (1) perpetual; (2) indeterminate—revocable by the government at any time; (3) determinate—with limited life, at the end of which the privileges expire.

Licenses or concessions.—Private enterprises may be granted temporary licenses or concessions to ply their trades in particular locations where this grant is exclusive and not open to all persons. The exclusive right to occupy a location may be very valuable. News-stand corners, for example, actually exchange at prices of from $500 to $10,000.

Organization expenses.—Organization expenses are those costs of a business which are incurred before the regular activities are begun. Illustrations are costs of selling stock and advertising expenses before the date of opening. These costs may be deferred and charged against future operating periods. They are often carried on the balance sheets of the enterprise as deferred charges to expense. Such costs are sometimes listed among intangible assets; they are, in fact, classified as intangibles in the *Uniform Classification of Accounts for Telephone Companies* prescribed by the Interstate Commerce Commission.[1]

Going-value.—Going-value is very much like organization expenses, except that it may also include some costs (or even net losses) of operation during the early life of the enterprise before it is able to earn a reasonable rate of profit. It represents the difference between the exchange value of the total assets of the enterprise as inanimate objects and their earning value as property of a living enterprise. Going value may be brought into the books of a company by capitalizing some of the expenses of operation during the early periods of the business growth. The purpose of such capitalization is to avoid showing losses as such; the practice is asserted to be justifiable because of future earnings which will result after the enterprise is firmly established. Going-value is frequently considered in the valuation of the assets of public utilities; the asset represents value upon which the regulatory bodies sometimes permit these utilities to earn a "fair" rate of return.[2]

The ideal valuation for intangible assets.—Some intangible assets are not purchased at definite cost prices. The questions arise immediately: Should such assets be included in the balance sheet of an enterprise; and, if so, at what values should they be entered? On the assumption that an intangible asset has not been purchased or developed at a definitely known money cost, the accountant is faced with the following alternatives: of

[1] Page 36 describes "Organization" (a subaccount of Intangible Capital) as follows: "This includes the cost of preparing and distributing prospectuses, the cost of soliciting subscriptions for stock (but not for loans nor for the purchase of bonds or other evidence of indebtedness), cash fees paid to promoters, and the actual cash value at the time of organization of securities paid to promoters for their services in organizing the enterprise; counsel fees; cost of preparing and issuing certificates of stock; and cost of procuring certificates of necessity from state authorities, and other like costs."

[2] For a discussion of the economic and legal aspects of "going-value," see W. G. Glaeser, *Outlines of Public Utility Economics*, pp. 487–501.

excluding the assets from the balance sheet because of the difficulty or actual impossibility of estimating their value; or of bringing them on to the balance sheet at definite though estimated prices based upon his opinion of the present values to the business of their future services. The calculation of the present value of the future services of an intangible asset is not different in theory from the valuation of any other type of asset. The task is made difficult, however, by two conditions: first, the services of an intangible asset are necessarily merged with the total services of the property of a going concern; second, the continuity of the services of an intangible asset is not predictable, but may be destroyed by conditions over which an enterprise has no control.

Computation of good-will value.—The calculation of the value of an intangible asset may be illustrated by the case of good-will. The recognition of good-will assumes the existence of earning power or future income in amounts greater than would be expected from the tangible assets of a typical going concern. The earning power which is not directly attributable to specific tangible or intangible assets is said to be the result of good-will, an asset which has made the unusual earnings possible. Accordingly, the future services might be discounted to their present value and capitalized for purposes of inclusion in the balance sheet. The idea of good-will as capitalized excess earnings implies, of course, that there exists a "normal" or reasonable rate of earnings, in relation to which the excess earnings can be computed.

Assume that a particular business enterprise, the A Company, earns net profits of $25,000 on a net investment of $200,000. This is an average net earning of 12½ per cent on the investment. Assume also that the average firm in this line of business enjoys only a 6 per cent average profit on its investment; other firms, with a capitalization of $200,000 would then normally receive annual net profits of only $12,000. The earnings of the A Company are $13,000 per year higher than the normal rate. The proper value for the good-will may be estimated on the basis of the time for which the excess profits are expected to continue. If they are estimated to continue five years, the total ultimate value of the excess earnings would be $65,000. The present value of these five years of excess earnings computed on a 6 per cent basis would be approximately $55,000.

Cost an approximation to intangible asset value.—Cost is usually accepted as the most practicable valuation for an intangible asset; in fact, some accountants insist that cost is the only basis which should be accepted for valuing intangibles on the balance sheet. Cost is, of course, a very significant figure where assets are purchased; yet, as in the case of other types of assets, the cost of an intangible asset may be much higher or lower than its real value. The cost of developing a patent, for example, may be very high because of long periods of experimentation and the use of expensive materials; in some instances the results accruing from a patent are negligible; in others they are very considerable. Copyrights or franchises may be granted for absurdly small sums —at times the mere costs of applying for the privileges. In such cases the costs of special privileges would not be a clear indication of their ultimate worth, either for exchange in the market or for productive use. Intangible assets may, of course, lose their value quickly and without advance notice of their worth as so reduced. A patent may become obsolete long before its legal privileges expire.

Modern practice in good-will valuation.—The ideal value for an intangible asset is the present value of its future services. Cost value is sometimes regarded as the market equivalent of the ideal value, but it can be used only when the good-will has been purchased by the company claiming it as an asset. The difficulty of computing the ideal value of good-will has led business men and accountants to establish its value by simpler formulas based upon total gross earnings or total net profits; the amount of good-will computed on such bases varies with the size of the enterprise, the amount of net profit and its ratio to sales, and the length of time during which the profits may be expected to continue. In some cases enterprises make careful analyses of conditions before they insert good-will in the balance sheet; in others the value may be arrived at by common agreement of the interested parties, an agreement followed later by arguments and formulas which justify the procedure.

Intangible asset values subject to change.—It is impossible to forecast the value of an intangible asset with unfailing accuracy. Nevertheless, the valuation must be attempted for purposes of initial statement. Intangible asset values may, of course, be changed because of unexpected increase in earning power or because of the gradual expiration of the earning capacity.

Depreciation.—The mere passing of time makes necessary the writing down of intangible values which have a definite length of life, such as patents. In some cases patents are valuable until final expiration, after which time they should be removed from the balance sheet because the privileges originally enjoyed are no longer the special property of the company. An illustration of this fact is the case of a safety razor company which enjoyed immense profits during the entire life of a patented safety-razor device. At the expiration of the seventeen-year period, a razor which had previously been sold at a price of $5.00 was reduced to $1.00 and within a few years was being offered on the market by shaving-soap companies as a bonus with purchases of toilet articles.

Obsolescence.—Intangible assets may, of course, decline very rapidly in value, thus becoming worthless long before the end of their legal life. For example, a patent or special privilege may become obsolete because of changes in styles or customs. Privileges at county fairs, once very valuable assets to the individuals holding them, are much less valuable than they were twenty years ago, because of the reduced attendance at local fairs. The stage-coach privileges granted to carriers are still in existence but are not availed of by their holders. A trade-mark for a particular confection becomes of less value after competition has brought similar products on the market under other names. Likewise, special formulas for soft drinks fluctuate in value with changes in fads and tastes.

Improved methods in manufacturing may render obsolete certain patents and processes which were once very important. Mining processes, even though they are the exclusive right of a particular company, are of slight value if other more efficient methods of mining have been developed. Changes in physical conditions also affect the value of franchises. For example, the privilege of harnessing the power from a waterfall may be very valuable at the time it is granted but would be ignored, of course, if the stream were to diminish greatly in volume during the period of the franchise.

Depreciation rates.—The rate at which intangible assets should be depreciated varies with the specific assets, the particular conditions under which they are enjoyed, and the prospects for their continued life. One general rule may be laid down: most intangible assets should be subjected to proportionately greater depreciation charges during the early years of their life. This is due to the fact that intangible assets are often superseded before the end of their expected period of usefulness. High depreciation rates thus make probable the writing down of most of the original valuation before the end of the actual service life.

The good-will dilemma.—A paradoxical situation appears in the writing down or elimination of good-will. In years when satisfactory profits are earned and the good-will is most clearly a genuine asset, the company can, and often does, remove it from the books. On the other hand, in years when profits are low and the good-will is rapidly decreasing (if it has not already disappeared), it cannot be removed from the assets without greatly affecting the statement of the financial condition of the company. The situation is a paradoxical one, for when good-will is most needed to show a satisfactory financial condition, it is not properly admissible to the balance sheet; when it is least needed because of profitable operations, it is rightly accorded a place among the assets.[1]

Intangibles on the balance sheet.—Intangibles should be

[1] A business man who read the foregoing paragraph in typescript has commented on it by saying: "Profits fall off for other reasons than diminishing good-will. Good-will is an asset attaching to a business because of the friendly regard of customers; this friendly regard may be retained even though the purchasing power of the customers disappear. Good-will is not related to temporary purchasing power, but rather to continuing purchasing desire, together with long-run purchasing power. Good-will at the time of its admission to the balance sheet reflects value placed on continuing purchasing desire or long-run purchasing power. In good years the business may well write it down; in lean years I see no necessity for writing it down further; in fact, it may be that if good-will did not exist, the lean year would be leaner."—H. A. Fountain, treasurer, Ohio Public Service Company.

clearly shown on the balance sheet, under a special section which lists as subdivisions the various items to which the intangible values are presumed to attach. This practice makes it possible for interested parties to determine which intangible values are transferable, which would disappear upon reorganization of the enterprise, also for what period of time such assets will probably serve the enterprise. Methods of dealing with intangible asset values in financial reports are illustrated in the balance sheets of the companies discussed in chapter xxxiv. In the broad sense, of course, any economic force which increases earning power might be regarded as an intangible asset, such as: loyalty and morale of employees; business judgment and capacity of executives; potential increase in the density of population. Such items, however, do not find their way into the double-entry accounts, although they often influence practical accounting valuation.

QUESTIONS ON CHAPTER XXVII

1. What items are typically listed among the intangible assets? Are they the only assets which are intangible in the physical sense?
2. Define, illustrate, or explain: good-will; patent; copyright; trade-mark; organization expense; going-value; franchise.
3. Cost less depreciation is sometimes presented as the ideal basis for evaluating intangible assets. What objections can be offered to this rule from a practical viewpoint? from a theoretical viewpoint? What points may be advanced in its favor?
4. Should all intangible assets be depreciated? If so, what basis would you recommend? straight-line? increasing rate (sinking-fund basis)? decreasing rate? Support your arguments.
5. An intangible value may be included in the balance sheet in any of the following ways: (*a*) as an asset, included in the asset total; (*b*) as an asset, not included in the asset total; (*c*) as a footnote; (*d*) as a deduction from net worth. What arguments may be advanced in favor of each?
6. Should intangible values which have not been purchased be included in a balance sheet? If so, at what values?
7. Explain the meaning of "present value of excess future earnings." Can it always be easily computed?
8. Assuming a normal rate of return in an industry to be 7 per cent, what amount of good-will should be recognized in an enterprise which earned 11 per cent on a capital of $300,000? Assume that this earning would continue for six years. Ignore compound interest.
9. What items would you include in estimating the cost of the following intangible assets: patents; copyrights; organization expense; franchises?

CHAPTER XXVIII

VALUATION OF LIABILITIES

The problem of evaluating liabilities has been described by some writers as presenting few practical difficulties, and this assertion is essentially true if applied to total liabilities. There are, however, many problems of preference among liabilities; there are also cases where interested parties are in disagreement as to the proper valuation of specific liabilities—as to whether or not they really exist—and as to their distinction from proprietorship.

Valuation of fixed liabilities affected by time element.—The valuation of long-term liabilities presents a very important problem arising out of the time between the preparation of a balance sheet and the maturity of the obligations. In the interests of correct accounting, care should be taken to recognize the influence of time and market conditions on liabilities payable in the future. This caution is especially applicable to long-term bonds; it is important to a lesser degree in computing the amounts of current liabilities.

Bonds payable.—Bonds are specific types of long-term liabilities which are payable at definite times, according to specific agreement. The amounts payable at the dates they mature are accordingly very important figures, and should appear on the balance sheet. Where the face values are different from the prices at which they have been issued, the differences may be shown as additions to or discounts from the face values of the bonds at the time of issue. The resulting values are the amounts which would (theoretically) have to be paid if the debts were to be liquidated; sometimes they are higher than face value, sometimes lower. Bonds issued below par may rise to market values considerably above face value, or vice versa. If the present values of the liabilities are to be set forth, fluctuations in market value may well be recognized on the balance sheet from time to time.

Scientific valuation of bonds payable.—The valuation of bonds payable presents the same problem as the valuation of bonds held as permanent investments. The debtor assumes a dual type of obligation; he must not only pay the face value of the debt at maturity; he must also pay a series of interest obligations as long as the debt exists. The amount of the debt at any one time, then, is made up of two parts: (1) the discounted value of the main obligation to be paid; (2) the discounted value of the interest payments. If the debt and interest payments are discounted at the rate of interest which the bond bears, the sum will exactly equal the face value of the bond. For example, let us take the case of $10,000 worth of 5 per cent, ten-year bonds. The present values, discounted on a 5 per cent basis are computed as follows:

$10,000, ten years hence	= $6,139.13	now
Ten $500 annual interest payments =	3,860.87	now
	$10,000.00	

The present values five years closer to maturity would still total $10,000 if discounted on a 5 per cent basis. For example:

$10,000, five years hence =	$7,835.26	now
Five $500 annual payments =	2,164.74	now
	$10,000.00	

There are times, however, when the nominal interest rate (the percentage which the payments bear to face value) is not equal to the market rate. It may be higher or lower than the rates at which creditors could loan their money for other purposes. The rate at which the creditors discount the future payment of the debt and the annual interest payments will determine the amount which they will advance to the company issuing the bonds.

Bond premium is the amount by which the cash received exceeds the future value of the bond obligation. It may be regarded as a deferred credit to the interest accounts of the issuing company, a credit which offsets the extra cash paid by the buyer of the bonds. In this sense it is a special liability incurred at the time of the bond issue, a liability which is gradually written down at the interest-payment periods.

Bonds which bear a relatively low rate of interest are often issued for amounts below their face value, the reduction from face value being a concession granted to the buyer of the bonds.

Bond discount may be regarded as a prepaid interest item to offset a low nominal rate of interest and hence may be listed as a deferred charge to expense. In another sense, however, it may be regarded as a valuation deduction from the face of the bonds—a deduction which shows the actual "present" liability at the time of issue. Bonds issued at a discount may under some conditions be redeemed at a discount before the time of maturity.

Accounting for bond premium.—The following entries would be made to record the issuance of $100,000 worth of 8 per cent, twenty-year bonds at 110.

Cash	$110,000.00	
Bonds payable		$100,000.00
Bond premium		10,000.00

The credit in the Bond Premium account is, in effect, a deferred credit to interest expense and as such may be offset against current interest expense at the close of each interest period. The credit in the Bond Premium account is transferred gradually to the credit of the Interest Expense account at the time cash payments are made to the bondholders. The entries to record the writing off of one-twentieth of the bond premium, and the payment of 8 per cent annual interest, would be:

Bond premium	$ 500.00	
Interest expense		$ 500.00
Interest expense	$8,000.00	
Cash		$8,000.00

These two entries may be combined into one, as follows:

Interest expense	$7,500.00	
Bond premium	500.00	
Cash		$8,000.00

The reduction of bond premium replaces a debit which would otherwise be made to Interest Expense, and thereby reduces the total recorded interest expense. The $8,000 annual interest payment consists, in part, of a return of the cash premium contributed by the purchasers of the bonds at the time they were issued.[1]

[1] The reader will observe that the treatment of bond premium and discount in this chapter is different from that in chapter xxvi. The difference arises from the fact that in chapter xxvi premium and discount were discussed as items affecting the values of assets—bond investments—whereas in this chapter they affect the amount of liabilities—bonds payable.

Accounting for bond discount.—Bond discount affects the balance sheet and the income and expense accounts differently than does bond premium. A journal entry to record the issuance of $100,000 worth of 5 per cent, twenty-year bonds at 90 would be:

Cash	$90,000.00	
Bond discount	10,000.00	
Bonds payable		$100,000.00

The annual bond interest payments would be recorded as follows:

Interest expense	$5,500.00	
Cash		$5,000.00
Bond discount		500.00

Each year the bond discount total is reduced by a transfer of a portion of the interest expense account along with the current interest expense items. The gradual amortization of the bond discount has the effect of increasing the annual interest expense incurred by the issuance of the bonds.

Unissued bonds.—Bonds which have been authorized for issue but which have not actually been placed in the hands of creditors are not liabilities of a business enterprise. They are merely the legal rights to incur liabilities, and need not appear on a balance sheet. When it is desirable, however, to show the total bonds authorized, this amount should be reduced by the amount still unissued at any one time to give the amount outstanding.

Current liabilities give rise to certain problems of valuation.—The valuation of current liabilities does not involve to great degree the difficulties of "present value" or periodic fluctuations; it is concerned more directly with the problem of securing evidence which establishes the existence and the gross amounts of the obligations.

Notes and accounts payable.—Notes and accounts payable within one or two fiscal periods are usually entered at face value in the accounts. However, the effect of interest earnings cannot properly be ignored in measuring short-term liabilities. For example, a six months' note payable for $1,000 which bears no interest is not the equivalent of a liability for $1,000 at the time it is given. The creditor who accepts such a payment does so, realizing full well that his note will not accumulate to a value of

$1,000 until its maturity. If a note of this type were discounted to its present value at a rate of 6 per cent, it would be reduced by approximately $30; strictly speaking, it could appear on a balance sheet at a figure of $970. It is not necessary for a business man to follow this method of measuring liabilities in the accounts in order to recognize the time element in their computation; it is important, however, for him to bear such facts in mind. Probably in many cases the inaccuracy resulting from stating future liabilities at face value is less serious in its nature than the possibility of overstating proprietorship.

Accrued liabilities.—From time to time accrued liabilities must appear on the balance sheets. The problem arises, therefore, of how to evaluate these items, particularly in view of the fact that very often the amounts are estimated from incomplete data. Such liabilities as bond interest payable may, of course, be very definitely computed on the basis of time; consequently they may be placed on the balance sheet at amounts which represent actual liabilities. But often it is necessary to bring estimated accrued expenses on to the balance sheet; for example, to include the liability for income taxes or property taxes which have not yet been assessed. The fact that these liabilities must be estimated does not mean that they are unreal. It merely means that the accountant must use extra care in estimating their amount. They should be definitely listed and classified in the liability section of a balance sheet.[1]

Deferred credits to income.—When assets are received in payment for, but in advance of, the completion of an income transaction, the offsetting credits are made to accounts classified under the general heading "Deferred Credits to Income." Cash might be received from a customer in advance of a shipment of goods to him or before the passage of title; similarly, money might be received from a tenant to cover rental services which will extend

[1] It has been held, however, that accrued income taxes estimated at mid-year upon the basis of probable taxable income for the entire year were not an actual liability for purposes of determining the net capital invested in the enterprise at the time. (See *B. T. A.* [1925], I, 1135, "L. S. Ayres & Co."). This type of accrual must, of course, be estimated before any taxable income has been assured; losses during the second half of the fiscal year might offset the first six months' earnings.

over several operating periods. The credit made whenever cash has been received in advance to insure a delivery of merchandise should be treated as a liability. It is a deferred credit to income, a liability which can be liquidated only by the shipment of merchandise to the customer or by the return of his cash. A typical illustration is the receipt of cash in advance for meals at a hotel or restaurant. The meal tickets are liabilities of the issuing enterprise; often they are transferable. The only way in which the obligation can be discharged is by dispensing meals to the holders or by refunding their cash.

Deferred credits to income on the balance sheet may be evaluated on the basis of time, as in the case of the rent received from a tenant; on the basis of stage of completion, as in the case of the building under construction; or on the basis of any other standard, such as the shipment of goods or passage of legal title. The valuation of deferred credits to income is a problem of deciding when liability elements change to the income classification. It is thus very closely connected with the problem of the measurement and the timing of income, a matter which will be discussed in chapter xxxi.

Special payable items.—Special payable items, such as loans from partners or dividends payable to stockholders, should be recognized on the balance sheet at their ultimate face value, although, of course, they may be written down to present worth if the amounts are large enough to justify a more accurate analysis of financial condition. Dividends payable are actual liabilities of a corporation, after having been declared by the directors. If the dividends have been declared under conditions which comply with statutes and court rulings under which the corporation operates, the declared dividends are on a basis of preference equal to that of ordinary unsecured creditors. Directors who have declared dividends are personally liable for losses to creditors directly resulting from the payment of dividends under conditions prohibited by the charter or other legal restrictions. Dividends may be paid in any of several ways: with cash or other assets, with scrip, or with stock. The manner in which they are paid has no effect upon the ultimate amount of the liability.

Special types of liabilities are incurred by brokers who buy and sell stock or bonds. In one instance a broker sold stock, and borrowed certain shares from another broker in order to make delivery to his customer. He did not purchase shares in his own name immediately, and the price of the shares rose so rapidly that he was unable to pay the market price for the shares he had borrowed. The original owner of the shares sued for the market value of the stock and forced the broker into bankruptcy on the basis of the liability. The court which adjudged the broker a bankrupt at first refused to permit the loss on the transaction as a deduction in the computation of taxable income for the period, the basis for the refusal being the contention that the loss had not yet been "realized." It was pointed out by counsel that the liability for the value of the stock was real enough as a basis for adjudging the broker bankrupt and hence the transaction should be regarded as real enough to be given recognition in the computation of taxable income.

Contingent liabilities require careful definition and treatment.—The question arises as to the proper treatment of liabilities which have not come into existence, and may never do so, but which are contingent upon the happening of some event. Should they be included in the periodic balance sheets? If so, how should they be shown and at what values?

Endorsement liability.—When the payment of liabilities of another enterprise has been guaranteed by endorsement, the liability for the payment of the debts may develop into a direct obligation of the endorsing firm. This liability need not appear in the accounts, however, unless the approximate amount can be estimated with reasonable accuracy. The most satisfactory method of showing such liabilities is by the use of footnotes attached to the balance sheet. Special treatment is sometimes accorded, however, to indorsements made in order to dispose of notes receivable. The contingent liability in such cases is often brought on to the balance sheet through entry in a special account such as Notes Receivable Discounted, which would be subtracted on the balance sheet from the original total of accounts receivable. The liability for refunding the cash which might result from the customer's failure to pay his note would thus be constantly before the eyes of the accountant. When the discounted notes receivable were paid by the signer, the credit in the Notes Receivable Discounted account would be transferred to the Notes Receivable account.

Guarantees and reserves for losses.—Many companies guarantee their products against unsatisfactory service resulting from defects in workmanship or material used. Liability for losses on such guarantees should invariably be given recognition in the balance sheet, the only problem facing the accountant being the measurement of its amount. The amount to be allowed will be computed on the basis of the probable losses, estimated in terms of the experience and opinions of those acquainted with the industry. The entry at the close of each fiscal period might appear somewhat as follows:

Estimated loss on guarantees........	$350.00	
Reserves for guarantees................		$350.00

The Estimated Loss on Guarantees account is an expense account and should appear on the statement of income and expense. The Reserve for Guarantees is a liability which should appear on the balance sheet. The credit will be used to absorb future losses from goods which are defective in workmanship or material. If an allowance were made to a customer the entry would be:

Reserve for guarantees................	$25.00	
Cash (or Accounts receivable).............		$25.00

Provisions of this type which are established to absorb losses of unknown extent, but which will in all probability occur, are real liabilities of an enterprise. Such reserves should appear on the balance sheet among the liability items and should not be regarded as a part of the proprietorship. Other examples are reserves for pension liabilities and for workmen's compensation insurance. Border-line cases arise, however, when the reserves accumulate beyond the actual needs of an enterprise. Moreover, estimates for pensions and compensation insurance have been held not deductible for purposes of compulsory taxable income. The actual amounts paid out for such items are, of course, deductible as business expenses.

QUESTIONS ON CHAPTER XXVIII

1. The principal problem in the valuation of liabilities is to insure the inclusion and full statement of all items. Why may there be a bias operating to exclude or minimize the liabilities?
2. State the basis of distinction between current and fixed liabilities. In which group would you place bonds maturing within the next three months (*a*) if the bonds are to be retired by payment out of current assets; (*b*) if the bonds are to be refinanced; (*c*) if there exists a sinking-fund sufficient to retire the bonds?
3. Should trade discounts or cash discounts be deducted from the face values of accounts payable for statement in the balance sheet? Should non-interest bearing payables be discounted to a present-worth basis?
4. Explain and give three illustrations of deferred credits to income.
5. Contingent liabilities fall into two groups: (*a*) those which arise as secondary obligations out of the guarantee of performance of another party and which carry the right to recover from the party primarily liable; (*b*) those which become full primary obligations of the business without any such right of recovery. Give two illustrations of each class.
6. Are the reserves for contingent losses, arising out of pending lawsuits and the guarantees of product, liabilities or proprietorship items? How would you regard reserves for taxes?
7. How may cumulative preferred stock dividends unpaid for two years be shown in the balance sheet?
8. "Bond discount is a deferred charge to expense." "Bond discount is a deduction from the face amount of the bond liability in order to ascertain its present worth." With which of these do you agree? What is the nature of bond premium?
9. Explain the straight-line and "scientific" methods of amortizing bond discount or premium. Describe the entries to record the payment of bond interest including the amortization of discount or premium.
10. How should unissued bonds be stated in the balance sheet?
11. Journalize the following transactions: (*a*) Issuance of sixty $1000 bonds at 90, bearing interest at 4 per cent and payable in 40 years; (*b*) payment of annual interest for any given year; (*c*) final payment of annual interest and redemption of bonds at face value.
12. Journalize the following transactions: (*a*) issuance of eight hundred $500 bonds at 105, bearing interest at 6% and payable in 15 years; (*b*) payment of semi-annual interest for any given year; (*c*) final payment of interest and redemption of bonds at face value.

CHAPTER XXIX

VALUATION OF PARTNERS' PROPRIETORSHIP

The valuation of proprietorship may be approached indirectly either through the valuation of assets and liabilities or through the measurement of income and expense. The first approach may be referred to as the single-entry method; proprietorship is merely the difference between the assets and liabilities existing at a certain time. The second approach may be called the double-entry method: the amount by which income exceeds expense represents the increase in proprietorship for the period. This amount added to the original proprietorship gives the new correct valuation of proprietorship, after allowances for withdrawals and original contributions. The foregoing chapters have implied that valuation of proprietorship was a normal by-product of the correct valuation of assets and liabilities; and this implication is justified for most purposes of dealing with total proprietorship. Nevertheless, there are problems of apportionment of proprietorship to individuals and to groups of proprietors. Some of them will be discussed in the present chapter and in the one following. The task of calculating changes in proprietorship through the measurement of income and expense will be discussed in chapters xxxi and xxxii.

Partners' original capital affected by agreement.—The proprietorship accounts of partners represent the total amounts of their ownership in the enterprise at any given time. It was stated in chapter xviii[1] that partners' proprietorship typically is divided into two main classes, represented by data in the Capital accounts and the Personal accounts.

Capital accounts.—The Capital accounts of the partners indicate their invested proprietorship, as represented by original contributions plus that portion of additional contributions and earnings which are to be regarded as permanently invested in the

[1] The present chapter should be read in connection with chapter xviii, which deals with the conditions which require the use of special accounts for partners' proprietorship.

enterprise. Personal accounts represent temporary phases of the partners' proprietorship and may carry debit or credit balances. Entries in the Personal accounts may result from any of a wide variety of transactions; some of them will be mentioned after the problems of the Capital accounts have been discussed.

Capital accounts are usually credited with the book values of the assets contributed by the partners at the time of forming the partnership. In such cases, the problem of accounting for the original capital is easily solved. When an incoming partner merely buys out the capital of another, the price at which the proprietorship is transferred is not a matter for entry in the books of account. If, for example, partner E. B. Andrews buys one-half of the capital of H. L. Underhill, the total of which was valued at $12,000, it would be immaterial for purposes of the accounting records whether the price were above or below $6,000. The accounting records in such a transaction would be affected similarly whether the capital changed hands at $4,000 or at $8,000.

When an incoming partner makes an investment to secure an interest, the value of the contributed assets affects the resulting amount of the capital that is to be assigned to him. The value of the assets received must equal the total new capital created, even though the capital assigned to the incoming partner be more or less than the book value of the assets contributed. The problems of reconciling the asset contributions and the new capital of an incoming partner are of two types: investments credited at less than the book value of the previous assets, and investments credited at more than book value. The reconciliation may be effected either by a change in the book values of the assets or by special treatment of the previously existing capital accounts.

Incoming partners' capital below book value of contributed assets.—The following balance sheet represents the financial condition of the partnership of Jones & Kunz:

ASSETS		PROPRIETORSHIP	
Cash	$ 5,000.00	A. B. Jones, capital	$18,000.00
Merchandise	15,000.00	J. D. Kunz, capital	14,000.00
Building	12,000.00		
	$32,000.00		$32,000.00

Assume that C. L. Downs has expressed a willingness to become a one-third owner of the enterprise by contributing $13,000 to the business. The problem now arises of properly recording the receipt of the cash and the assignment of one-third of the resulting proprietorship. What will be the resulting proprietorship? Several methods of answering this question may be given:

a) The total proprietorship may be regarded as $50,000, the original total plus C. L. Downs's contribution. Downs's one-third share in the new total will be $16,666.67, even though he has actually paid $18,000 into the business. The journal entry to record the admission of Downs would be:

Cash...........................	$18,000.00	
C. L. Downs, capital.....................		$16,666.67
A. B. Jones, capital......................		666.67
J. D. Kunz, capital......................		666.66

C. L. Downs has increased the total assets and the total capital of the partnership to the extent of $18,000. Not all of the increased capital is assigned to Downs, however, for it has been agreed that he is to be given only one-third interest in the enterprise. One-third of the new total proprietorship is $16,666.67; the remainder of Downs's contribution, $1,333.33, is assigned to the other partners. Jones and Kunz regard this as a gain to themselves and share it in the agreed profit ratio.

b) It might be assumed that the total value of the assets after Downs's $18,000 cash contribution is increased to $54,000. Such an assumption is said to be justified on the grounds that since Mr. Downs is willing to pay $18,000 for a one-third interest, the total value of the net assets must be three times the amount of Mr. Downs's contribution. Such treatment implies that the original assets of the corporation must have been undervalued; therefore they should now be increased in value so that the total assets, including Downs's contribution, will be $54,000. This procedure requires an entry which shall increase the assets and proprietorship by $4,000.

The question arises: What accounts shall be debited to represent the change in total asset value? It is possible either to debit specific assets for the total amount or to apportion the increase proportionately over all assets (except the cash and the receivable items). A third choice is to establish a new account to carry the value being written into the records; such an account may be entitled "Good-will." A journal entry to record the good-will on the books and to assign the increased proprietorship equally to the original partners would be:

Good-will..................	$4,000.00	
A. B. Jones, capital...............		$2,000.00
J. D. Kunz, capital...............		2,000.00

The journal entry then to record the cash contribution would be:

Cash.....................	$18,000.00	
C. L. Downs, capital.............		$18,000.00

The balance sheet resulting after the adjustment illustrated would be:

ASSETS		PROPRIETORSHIP	
Cash...............	$23,000.00	A. J. Jones, capital....	$20,000.00
Merchandise........	15,000.00	J. D. Kunz, capital....	16,000.00
Building............	12,000.00	C. L. Downs, capital...	18,000.00
Good-will..........	4,000.00		
	$54,000.00		$54,000.00

Incoming partners' capital above book value of contributed assets.—There also are cases in which a partner receives capital in greater proportion to total capital than his contribution bears to the book value of the total net assets. Suppose, for example, that in the partnership illustrated above, Mr. Downs is to be given a one-third interest if he contributes $12,000 in cash. The original total of the assets and capital is $32,000. Mr. Downs increases the assets to $44,000. He contributes $\frac{12}{44}$ of the total assets, which is $12,000; but he is to be assigned one-third of the total capital, which is $14,666.67. How shall this difference of $2,666.67 be reconciled in the accounts?

a) It may, in the first place, be reconciled by debiting the existing Capital accounts of Jones and Kunz for a total of $2,666.-67 and adding this amount to the $12,000 which would under ordinary conditions be ascribed to Downs's Capital account. This would be accomplished by the following entry:

Cash	$12,000.00	
A. J. Jones, capital	1,333.34	
J. D. Kunz, capital	1,333.33	
C. L. Downs, capital		$14,666.67

The foregoing debits to the Capital accounts must be regarded as losses sustained by Jones and Kunz upon the admission of Downs into the partnership. The amount of $2,666.67 represents a bonus granted to Downs to induce him to join the partnership.

b) Another method of handling the problem would be to assume that since Downs is to purchase a one-third interest for $12,000, the previous assets must have had a real value of only $24,000 before the admission of Downs. Consequently a revaluation should be made to reduce the total original asset values and proprietorship to $24,000. The result is accomplished by debiting the capital accounts $8,000, charging this amount against Jones and Kunz as a loss. But where shall the credit entry be posted? Shall all the assets be written down? or only a few of them? or shall a suspended reduction be made which shall apply against the total assets? Where the last-mentioned practice is adopted, the credit is sometimes entered to an account entitled "Reserve for Overvaluation." It is a valuation deduction from the asset totals but is usually listed on the right-hand side of the balance sheet just above the proprietorship items. If the total asset values actually increase in later periods, this credit account may be reduced, and the credit balance may then be transferred to the Capital accounts.

The entry for such an adjustment of the assets would be:

A. B. Jones, capital	$4,000.00	
J. D. Kunz, capital	4,000.00	
Reserve for Overvaluation		$8,000.00

The journal entry for the admission of Downs as a partner would be:

Cash	$12,000.00	
C. L. Downs, capital		$12,000.00

Additions and withdrawals of capital require special accounting procedure.—The capital accounts of partners are affected by various transactions, such as earnings and losses from operations, and also by temporary or permanent additions and withdrawals of funds.

Partners' personal accounts.—The Personal accounts of Proprietors represent special aspects of their total proprietorship. But it should be emphasized strongly that the distinction between partners' Capital and Personal accounts does not correspond in the legal sense to the distinction between a corporation's Capital Stock and its Surplus accounts. The partnership is not a legal entity; consequently any segregation of the proprietorship accounts must be regarded as solely for the convenience and information of the partners. Partners' loans and borrowings are debited and credited to special Personal accounts. These accounts are not, strictly speaking, asset or liability accounts. The debit in an account entitled "Partners' Withdrawals" is not an amount receivable from the partner. It is rather a postponed debit to his Capital account. Likewise the credit in a Partner's Loan account does not represent a liability of the partnership of the same nature as an obligation to outside creditors. Such an amount represents increased proprietorship of the partner who has loaned funds temporarily to the enterprise. Loans are ordinarily preferred claims against the total assets, but the preference exists only as between the partners.

Partnership profits and losses.—The distribution of the current income of a partnership is usually carried on in terms of a contract which deals with all matters pertaining to the apportionment of regular and irregular profits. Where no agreement is made, the common law and statutes prescribe the proper method of treatment. In the absence of agreement to the contrary, interest is not allowed on funds loaned to the business by an individual partner; nor is it charged on assets withdrawn from the business by a member of the partnership. By agreement, interest rates may be provided for. Salaries also are not considered to be payable to partners, unless the agreement specifically states the amounts and conditions under which they are to be paid. Profits and losses of a partnership are assumed to be shared equally by the partners. This equal ratio applies regardless of the comparative capital contributions.

But the partners may agree to use other ratios as the basis for the distribution of profits and losses. They may, in fact, agree upon a percentage equal to the ratio between the proprietorship accounts of the partners. A problem arises when an agreement has been made to distribute profits and losses on the basis of proprietorship. What is the correct proprietorship for purposes of such calculations, when the totals are continuously shifting in the accounts of the partners? It might be the original contributions, the proprietorship at the beginning of a fiscal period, or at the time of the distribution. The profit-and-loss ratio may be based upon average proprietorship, recognizing the additions and withdrawals during the operating period. The answer must be found in the intention of the partners themselves, and in practice the calculation of the partners' proprietorship which is to serve as the basis for profits distribution is a major consideration in partners' settlements. Such an important problem should be treated specifically in a partnership agreement.

Partnership dissolution.—Important partnership problems center around the distribution of the net assets at the time a partnership is dissolved. Assets are returned to the partners in proportion to the Capital account balances after all adjustments have been made for profits and losses. In the distribution of partnership assets, the following order of preference is recognized: preferred creditors (liabilities for taxes, wages, etc.); secured creditors; partners' loans, salaries, etc., where agreed to by other partners; partners' undrawn profits; partners' capital contributions.

A partner's personal relations with the business are given preference over his capital or proprietary relations; loans and undrawn salaries, for example, are paid in full before distributions are made to the partners as return of capital. Profits and losses arising from liquidation are shared in the same proportion as current earnings and losses. An amount due to a partner may be withheld to offset a deficiency in his Capital account. An amount receivable from a partner who has borrowed funds may be deducted from the amount otherwise distributable to him. This principle that partners' Personal accounts may affect the amount distributable to the various partners upon liquidation is known in practice as the principle of "offset." It is frequently encountered in partnership-dissolution problems.

QUESTIONS ON CHAPTER XXIX

1. "Capital accounts are *usually* credited with the book values of the assets contributed by the partners at the time of forming the partnership." Why *usually?* Why not *always?*
2. Distinguish between the procedure by which a partner sells out to a new partner and the procedure by which a new partner contributes additional assets to a partnership.
3. When a new partner joins an enterprise, must the new capital be exactly equal to the book values at which the new assets are entered in the accounts? Is the new capital necessarily apportioned solely to the new partner? Why or why not?
4. What are Personal accounts? Are they proprietorship accounts?
5. What is the general rule in the sharing of partnership profits and losses? In the allowance of interest on investment? Salaries for personal services?
6. E. Scrooge and J. Marley are partners with Capital accounts showing credit balances of $15,000 and $25,000 respectively. Journalize the entries to admit R. Cratchit as a partner with a one-third interest under the following conditions:
   a) Cratchit pays into the business $20,000 cash
   b) Cratchit pays into the business $23,000 cash
      (1) Assets not to be adjusted
      (2) Assets to be adjusted
   c) Cratchit pays into the business $17,000 cash
      (1) Assets not to be adjusted
      (2) Assets to be adjusted

   Assume that Scrooge and Marley have been sharing all losses and profits equally.
7. Three partners have the following Capital accounts: A, $3,000; B, $4,000; C, $5,000. Profits are to be distributed after a 6 per cent allowance on investment to each partner. (*a*) Distribute the current profits of $3,500 (before allowing for interest) (1) on an equal basis; (2) on the following basis: A, 50 per cent; B, 30 per cent; C, 20 per cent. (*b*) Make the entries to effect a distribution of $1,000 current profit (1) on an equal basis; (2) on the 50 per cent, 30 per cent, 20 per cent basis.

CHAPTER XXX

VALUATION OF CORPORATE PROPRIETORSHIP

A corporation is a legal entity, separate and apart from the individuals who organize it and direct its affairs; it may own assets, and it is responsible for its own obligations.

The theory of corporate organization affects the method of accounting for corporate capital.—The large number of proprietors in the typical corporation makes it necessary for the legislatures and courts to provide some device by which creditors may be protected against the possibility of loss from the withdrawal of assets by proprietors. This has been done by declaring that all property intrusted to a corporation in exchange for capital stock is in reality a "trust fund" for protection of creditors against losses. It is not permissible to distribute assets to the holders of shares of stock to the extent of reducing their proprietorship below the face value (or stated capital) of the outstanding shares. Accordingly a sharp line is drawn between "capital stock" and "surplus." Capital stock represents the permanent or stated capital on which creditors rely for protection of their interests; it measures the value of net assets which may be withdrawn by the stockholders only under special conditions specified by the statutes, by the corporate charter, by the by-laws, or by agreement with creditors. Surplus is the excess proprietorship available for apportionment among the stockholders in such manner as they wish, subject to restrictions provided in the articles of incorporation or in the by-laws. It is necessary, in accounting for corporate proprietorship, to observe the distinction between capital stock and surplus. These two aspects of proprietorship bear different relationships to the rights of creditors. Typically, surplus arises from current business operations or from dealings in fixed assets; it may also be the result of dealings in shares of the capital stock itself. Surplus accounts may be either positive or negative; they may contain debit as well as credit balances. Negative surplus is usually referred to as a "deficit."

The first part of the present chapter deals with the definition and valuation of capital stock, the stated capital of a corporation; the second part, with the definition and valuation of surplus.

Capital-stock values affected by conditions under which shares are issued.—The values of shares of stock may be expressed in terms of at least three distinct types of value; (1) par value, (2) book value, and (3) market value. These values were defined briefly in chapter xix.[1] The par value of stock is merely the amount which is assigned as the nominal value of a share. Book value of a share of stock is the par value plus or minus a proportionate share of the surplus or deficit properly assignable to this particular share. Market value is the value at which a share of stock is bought and sold in the open market. Market value may be higher or lower than either par value or book value; it is a representation of the value it has for a particular purchaser at the time of acquisition.

Stock premium.—Shares of stock are not always issued at their nominal or par value. They are sometimes issued at prices above or below par; the difference is referred to as "stock premium" or as "stock discount," respectively. The journal entry for the issue of 100 shares of stock having $50 par value for a cash consideration of $55 per share would be:

Debit: Cash	$5,500.00	
Credit: Capital Stock		$5,000.00
Stock Premium		500.00

What does the credit in the Stock Premium account represent? Is the premium an amount payable as a liability to the subscribers for stock? Is it a deferred credit to the income account which should be recognized only gradually as earnings of this enterprise? Or is it a proprietorship item which increases the book value of the capital stock immediately? This last interpretation of stock

[1] Many of the general statements made here in regard to corporate proprietorship have been previously made in chapter xix. They are repeated here for the convenience of those readers who have not wished to study the details of the specialized classifying devices.

premium appears to come nearest to a statement of its actual nature; it represents additional proprietorship in excess of the face value of the shares. Capital stock premium must be credited to proprietorship at the time the shares are issued, if the premium is to be considered proprietorship at all. There are no regular interest payments with which the amortization of stock premium can be correlated. It must be classified immediately as part of either the liabilities or the proprietorship. Stock premium may, at the discretion of the directors, be classified as surplus available for the declaration of dividends; however, certain corporations are organized under charters and by-laws which forbid such action.[1] Surplus proprietorship resulting from the sale of stock at a premium is sometimes designated "premium surplus" or "capital surplus" to distinguish it from surplus arising from current income and expense operations.

Stock discount.—What is the nature of the stock-discount debit resulting from the sale of stock below par? Is it an amount receivable from the stockholders, which may be called upon in case of emergency? Is it a deferred charge to expense which should be written off periodically during future periods? Is it a deduction from capital-stock value which should be subtracted from par value on the balance sheet? Strictly speaking, stock discount should be considered as an offset to proprietorship. It arises out of the fact that stock has been issued for assets which are not equal in value to the par value of the shares. The real value of the issued shares is the value of the assets received in exchange. Because of the conventional practice of recording stock at par value in the accounts, the discount account is introduced to maintain the equality of the debits and credits.

Not infrequently stock discount is listed among the assets of an enterprise, being so classified on the assumption that the stock discount is an expense of carrying out a financial program, which may be deferred to future periods. It is alleged to be an asset akin

[1] Under the laws of most states, banks are required to accumulate a certain amount of surplus which must appear in their balance sheets. This may result either from issuing shares of stock at a premium or from the accumulation of earnings. Very frequently a certain amount of surplus must be accumulated before the bank can begin operations.

to organization expense; and, as a matter of common practice, the discount is sometimes merged with organization expense or other intangible assets. Such practice, however, cannot be regarded as clearly reflecting financial status, even though one were to agree that stock discount represents an asset at the time of sale of the shares. If stock discount is to be capitalized and charged against future periods, the accounts should indicate clearly the procedure followed. Stock discount can, however, be regarded as an asset from another point of view; it represents potential values receivable from stockholders in case the tangible assets are insufficient to protect the interests of creditors. The legal theory of corporate organization requires that assets equal to the par value of shares—the stated capital—be ultimately paid to the corporation by stockholders.

Can stock discount be written "out" of the accounts, by being charged against current profits or accumulated surplus? From a practicable viewpoint, such procedure is certainly reasonable, regardless of the theory adopted as to its inherent nature. If stock discount is to be capitalized as an organization expense, it should be apportioned to future periods. If it is an offset to capital stock, it may well be reduced as future earnings increase the proprietorship. If it is an amount receivable from the stockholders, the discount may be reduced when tangible assets are retained in the business which would otherwise be paid out as dividends. Whether or not creditors of a corporation must abide by the bookkeeping entries which apply current earnings or surplus to the amortization of stock discount would depend upon the view adopted by the courts. It is conceivable that creditors might insist that all payments on capital stock should be actually paid into the corporation's treasury in the form of cash, and not be written down by charges against profits which have been more than offset by later losses.

Subscribed stock.—Subscribed stock partakes of the nature of both liabilities and proprietorship. Capital Stock Subscribed is a temporary account in which the subscriber's equity is carried pending complete payment for and issue of the actual shares. The account may, in one sense, be regarded as a liability; the corporation is obliged to issue stock certificates to the subscribers when they comply with the terms of the subscription agreement. This obligation can be removed only by return of the cash paid in or by the issue of stock. In a more correct sense, the Capital Stock Subscribed account may be said to represent proprietorship, for the offsetting subscriptions receivable are in fact realizable assets based upon valid agreements to pay cash or other assets to the corporation. The Capital Stock Subscribed account evidences a first claim on the unissued stock of the corporation. One might say that for practical purposes capital stock subscribed is equivalent to capital stock outstanding, varying in name and legal status only because of formal requirements of the statutes of incorporation. The subscriber to capital stock must be regarded as acting a dual rôle from the viewpoint of financial status. He is a debtor in the sense that he has incurred the obligation of paying certain assets to the corporation; he is a creditor or proprietor in the sense that the corporation is obliged to issue shares of stock to him when certain contractual requirements have been met.

Capital stock may be reduced by cancellation or purchase.—It is possible for a corporation to reduce the amount of its stated capital by the cancellation of some of its outstanding shares of stock. Such procedure can be followed only, however, when specifically authorized by the stockholders, in compliance with the terms of the articles of incorporation and the by-laws, and with the permission of creditors who have relied upon certain stated capital in previous dealings with the corporation.

Shares of stock may be returned to the treasury of a corporation as the result of gifts by stockholders or through purchase with available funds of the enterprise. Such transactions do not result in cancellation of the shares; they do, however, affect the corporate proprietorship at the time they occur. When capital stock is returned to the treasury of a corporation, it must be recorded as reducing the amount of outstanding stock. This result may be accomplished by debiting the Capital Stock account; more commonly it will be achieved by debiting a special Treasury Stock account. Assume that a corporation purchases, for cash, twenty of its own shares of stock at par value, which is $100. The entry would be:

Treasury stock	$2,000.00	
Cash		$2,000.00

Treasury stock is not an asset; it must be considered as an offset to outstanding capital stock. On the balance sheet of a corporation, treasury stock should most properly be shown as a deduction from the authorized capital stock, somewhat as follows:[1]

Capital stock authorized		$50,000
Less: Unissued	$20,000	
Treasury stock	2,000	22,000
Outstanding		$28,000

If the authorized capital stock is not to be shown on the balance sheet, the transaction may be handled somewhat as follows:

Capital stock outstanding	$30,000.00
In treasury	2,000.00
	$28,000.00

A corporation may repurchase its own shares at prices higher or lower than their par value. The difference between the book values of the assets paid out and the par value of the shares received must be adjusted by revision of the Surplus account. The adjustment may be made directly in the Surplus account or indirectly through the use of a temporary account such as Treasury Stock Surplus. When it carries a credit balance, it is added to the surplus total. When it carries a debit balance, it is offset against the surplus total. When capital stock is returned to a corporation as a gift or donation, the entire par value of the shares may be credited to Surplus, although the amount may very properly be given a special title such as "donated surplus," to distinguish it from the "general surplus."

No-par-value stock requires special treatment in the accounts.—The par value of a share of stock very often differs ma-

[1] Treasury stock is, of course, often listed among the assets, presumably on the theory that it can be sold for cash without materially altering financial status. The resale of treasury stock increases the amount of capital stock outstanding in exactly the same way as the original issue. Likewise, the purchase of treasury stock reduces the total par value of outstanding stock.

terially from its sale price in the investment market; this nominal value may be more or less than the proportionate interest which the shareholder enjoys in the total corporate proprietorship. Par value is little more than a label to designate the alleged values for which shares were originally issued. After several periods of business operations have gone by, par value may be of slight significance in the formation of financial policies. Within the past decade, corporations have been authorized by the state legislatures to issue shares referred to as "no-par-value stock." These shares represent definite proportionate interests in the proprietorship of the issuing corporation, but they may be offered to the public at any price (usually with minimum and maximum limits).

Issuance of no-par-value stock.—The shares are issued as fully paid at certain agreed prices. The amount to be credited to the Capital Stock account would (typically) be the book value of the assets received in exchange for them. For example, if 300 shares of no-par-value stock were issued at $18 per share, the entry would be:

Cash............................	$5,400.00	
Capital stock, no-par-value................		$5,400.00

The introduction of no-par-value shares appears at first to simplify the task of accounting for capital stock. But the absence of the par-value designation makes more difficult the important problem of the segregation of the capital stock and the surplus in the accounts and in the balance sheets. As a general rule, dividends cannot legally be declared payable if their declaration impairs the capital stock of the corporation. In the case of par-value shares, this rule means that no dividends may be declared which reduce the proprietorship below the par value of the outstanding shares of stock. Dividends, therefore, must be declared only out of surplus; they must not create a deficit to be deducted from the par value of capital stock issued.[1]

The foregoing rule—that dividends may not be declared out

[1] There are cases where dividends paid by a liquidating corporation are permitted, even though they "impair" capital stock. They are looked upon as a return of corporate capital to the stockholders. There are other cases where a minimum amount of surplus must appear in the accounts continuously.

of capital—implies that a definite line can be drawn between capital and surplus. The line tends to be obscured in transactions with no-par-value stock, particularly where the shares are issued at different prices. What portion of the consideration received for no-par-value stock should be credited to Capital Stock; and what portion, if any, should be credited to Surplus? The legislatures of the various states have attempted to answer the question in the following manner: (1) by establishing both minimum and maximum values per share which may be credited to Capital Stock; and (2) by permitting corporations to decide within these limits just how much of the consideration received for each authorized issue (or each group of shares) is to be credited as capital stock.

In general the capital stock (the stated capital) is assumed to be the value of the assets contributed in exchange for the shares of no-par-value stock. Where the corporation and the purchasers of shares of stock so agree, however, the total proprietorship may be apportioned between capital stock and surplus in any reasonable proportions. In some states a minimum stated value per share is prescribed; Illinois uses $5.00 as the stated value, an amount which for many practical accounting purposes is the equivalent of a par value. The amounts by which the assets received exceed the stated minimum value may be treated in whole, or in part, as stated capital, and accordingly may be added to the amount shown as capital stock.[1]

Dividends on no-par-value stock.—Dividends may be declared and paid on no-par-value stock in much the same manner as on par-value shares. Dividends are, of course, declared in terms of dollars per share rather than as percentages of the par value of each share. Declared dividends may be paid in cash, in scrip, or in stock. The declaration and payment of stock dividends on no-par-value stock presents a special problem in that these results may be accomplished by mere transfer of a portion of surplus to the credit of capital stock without the issuance of additional cer-

[1] The problems of apportioning proprietorship in terms of stated capital and surplus have been summarized in a monograph by Carl Robbins, *No-Par-Value Stock.*

tificates. Such a transfer affects merely the total capital stock and serves as notice to creditors of the increase in stated capital. When capital stock has been increased by a stock dividend accounted for in the foregoing manner, the new amount of capital stock may be reduced only as prescribed by law. Increases of capital stock arising from stock dividends have the same legal status as the capital stock arising from the issue of the first shares. Stock-dividend transactions may also be accompanied by the issuance of new certificates; transfer of proprietorship from the surplus to the capital-stock classification would be similar to the procedure previously described.[1]

Corporate surplus expresses variations in proprietorship.—The creditors of a corporation are protected by law against the withdrawal of funds which reduce the net assets below the stated capital. But they do not ordinarily share in or have jurisdiction over the surplus proprietorship above the stated capital; the surplus represents unrestricted proprietorship of the stockholders.

The Surplus account.—The title "surplus" is often restricted solely to that portion of the total proprietorship above stated capital which is characterized by two features: (1) that it is the result of the major business activities; (2) that it is available for apportionment and distribution as dividends among the individual stockholders without legal restrictions.[2]

The Surplus account is not always subdivided in corporation accounts; one account may be used to reflect all the periodic fluc-

[1] The stockholders' ledger supporting the controlling account with no-par-value stock outstanding would typically be maintained only in terms of shares rather than of financial values. The ledger accounts with each stockholder would indicate the relative amounts of proprietorship which each stockholder enjoyed.

[2] R. H. Montgomery in his *Auditing Theory and Practice* divides surplus into three general groups: (1) capital surplus; (2) earned surplus; (3) appropriated surplus. By *capital surplus* he means surplus arising from such transactions as reappraisals of assets, gifts, premiums on capital stock, dealings in capital assets. By *earned surplus* is meant the surplus arising from current operations, particularly those comprising the main income-producing operations of the enterprise. It is the account against which operating losses and dividend declarations are charged. It is sometimes referred to as "available surplus" or "undivided profits," although this latter term has a definite legal connotation in banking statutes. *Appropriated surplus* is that portion of the surplus which has been specially designated as not available for distribution as dividends. Ordinarily this part of proprietorship appears under the heading of *reserves*, which are segregated in accord with compulsory legal agreements or voluntarily because of financial considerations.

tuations in corporate proprietorship. This account, typically designated by the general title "surplus" (or "general surplus"), will be affected directly or indirectly by any of the various transactions which increase or decrease corporate proprietorship. The surplus of a corporation, whether it be expressed in one or in several accounts, is the focusing point for all income and expense transactions. Some income and expense transactions affect the surplus indirectly by being classed and summarized with other current operations; others are recorded directly as immediate adjustments of the Surplus account. The line for distinguishing the transactions which affect operating profit from those which are direct surplus adjustments cannot always be clearly drawn in practice.

The most important characteristic of that portion of the proprietorship known as the surplus is that the directors may legally apportion it as dividends payable to the stockholders. One should not conclude from this statement, however, that the declaration of dividends to the full extent of existing surplus is either permitted by law or consistent with sound financial administration. There are many circumstances under which all surplus proprietorship should not be distributed as dividends. For example, plans might have been laid for an expansion of plant and equipment; or it might be desirable to maintain a minimum surplus which will insure regular dividend declarations in future periods. Dividends payable are, of course, liabilities rather than proprietorship. They are given preference over the general claims of stockholders in case of liquidation.

Reserves.—There are occasions when it is advisable, or even legally compulsory, to designate portions of the accumulated surplus as not available for distribution as dividends. This may be accomplished by transferring portions of the surplus credit to other accounts entitled "reserves." Such accounts represent proprietorship of the stockholders but indicate that no dividends will be declared from these amounts unless a change in policy is effected. Reserve accounts may be established for a variety of purposes; the titles vary with the administrative plans of the corporation whose accounts are being maintained.

Reserve accounts are, of course, proprietorship accounts; they represent special portions of the surplus which are designated as not available for declaration as dividends. They are sometimes spoken of as "appropriated surplus," or *proprietorship reserves;* they are to be sharply distinguished from other credit balances sometimes listed under the headings of reserves, such as reserves for bad debts or for depreciation. The latter items are allowances or deductions from the book values of assets and are merely deferred credits or offsets to specific asset values; they are often referred to as *valuation reserves.* A third type of credit for which the term "reserve" is sometimes used includes certain estimated accrued obligations, such as "reserves" for taxes or accrued interest. Such reserves are in reality *liabilities* of a corporation, and they should be listed as such on the balance sheet. The mere fact that their amounts are not definitely known does not change their reality as obligations. Estimates are continually resorted to in the valuation of assets; they may also be applied to liabilities.[1] A credit balance in a reserve account does not signify that specific assets have been set aside for a particular purpose. A reserve account merely labels a certain portion of the proprietorship in such a way that interested parties can interpret the plans and policies of the corporation. Stockholders might, for example, request a distribution of profits if they were to observe a large surplus item on the balance sheet, whereas the term "reserve" would show that business policy would not permit the declaration and payment of dividends.

QUESTIONS ON CHAPTER XXX

1. What is meant by the "book value" of stock? "par value" of stock? "market value" of stock?
2. May the "capital" of an enterprise be distributed among its owners? What is the capital of an enterprise? Is there a legal distinction between "capital" and "surplus"?

[1] The three types of accounts mentioned above may be said to be credits applicable to the three parts of the balance sheet: assets, liabilities, and proprietorship. The valuation (asset) reserves are offsets against original asset values and may well be given some title such as "allowance" or "deduction." The liability reserves are, in fact, liabilities and should be listed among the accrued items payable as current liabilities. The proprietorship reserves are a part of proprietorship.

3. Discuss the following conceptions of stock discount: an account receivable from the stockholders; a deduction from capital-stock value; a prepaid expense.
4. Discuss the various conceptions of stock premium: an amount payable to stockholders; an addition to capital-stock value; a deferred credit to income (a liability).
5. Is unissued stock an asset or a deduction from proprietorship?
6. What is the nature of the Subscriptions Receivable account? of the Capital Stock Subscribed account?
7. What is no-par-value stock? How is the book value of such stock determined?
8. Illustrate the journal entries for the purchase by a corporation of twenty shares of its own preferred stock (par value, $100) at $90 per share.
9. Journalize the cancellation of fifty shares of $100 par-value common stock: (*a*) if equal cash value is withdrawn; (*b*) if the shares are converted into bonds at par; (*c*) if the shares are converted into 500 shares of no-par-value common stock.
10. Are "reserves" typically a part of proprietorship? What is the nature of a Reserve for Dividends account? Is it a liability?
11. To whom is the surplus assigned in case of liquidation? Do all stockholders share alike? Do unpaid dividends receive preference?
12. "Donations may consist of the contribution of additional assets or the surrender of claims over the existing assets." Does a donation of stock increase the assets of a corporation? Does it increase the proprietorship? Does it change the form of the proprietorship?

CHAPTER XXXI

THE MEASUREMENT OF INCOME

The problem of valuation extends beyond the appraisal of the assets, liabilities, and proprietorship existing at a given time. For a balance sheet is affected by all income and expense transactions which have occurred prior to its preparation; in fact, the increase or decrease in proprietorship corresponds in considerable degree to the difference between the income and expense of the preceding period.

Measurement of income requires establishment of standards. —In chapter xxii it was stated that the accountant frequently adopts the following conservative rule in his treatment of income and expense: *Anticipate no unrealized income, and provide for all possible expenses.* Certainly the first part of the rule must be approved. It means in effect: Do not record income until it "comes in." Accountants agree that income should not be recorded before it is earned—that income transactions should not be recognized in the account before they occur. When accountants disagree on such matters, it is solely in regard to what evidence is to be accepted to prove that given income transactions have occurred. They subscribe unanimously to the rule, "Anticipate no unrealized income." They disagree violently as to what constitutes the realization of income.

It is easy to say that "no unrealized income" should be recognized and that "all possible expenses" should be provided for. But it is a more difficult matter to state what is meant by the realization of income and what constitutes a possible expense. Since the problem of valuation depends upon the correct measurement of income and expense, it is important that satisfactory standards be established for recognizing and measuring the effects of income and expense transactions. This chapter will concern itself with the standards by which individual income transactions are to be measured.

The time element affects the measurement of income.—The proper measurement of income and expense is affected by a *time* element. The accountant must not only determine what is to be the ultimate effect of an income or expense transaction; he must also determine what portion, if any, of an income or expense transaction has actually transpired up to a given moment in time.

Very often the question of whether an asset or liability is to be admitted to the balance sheet is a question of whether or not a certain income or expense transaction has occurred. When, for example, should the fee earned by a lawyer be listed as an amount receivable from his client? at the time of the first consultation? at various times during the period of engagement? at the time of the final settlement? The answer is, of course, that the accrued amount receivable from the client should be entered at the time the fee is "earned." But when is a fee earned? When is any type of income earned? The answers to these questions force us to establish certain standards which may be applied for the measurement of income.

This measurement is essentially a matter of "timing" the income transactions—of deciding what portions are earned before or after certain moments in time, such as the dates for the preparation of balance sheets. The measurement of the total income very seldom causes difficulty; the greater task is the satisfactory apportionment of the total to periods of time. This problem is particularly important for an income transaction such as the construction of a building which continues over several years. Does the contractor earn his money gradually during the period of construction, or at one time—either at the beginning or at the end of the operations? This question, like the problem of the lawyer's fee, requires the establishment of standards for timing the income.

Standards for measuring income are standards for timing its occurrence.—The valuation of income must recognize the time element; the accountant must mark off periods of time during which certain income can be regarded as earned. Some standard must indicate the progress of each income transaction—its beginning and its end. Various events or criteria for the recognition of income are used by different enterprises and lines of industry or trade. Although the various criteria of income may appear to be widely different, they are all selected with one purpose in mind—to designate clearly the time when an incoming value actually becomes an asset of an enterprise. The stage in the income operations at which the incoming value may be listed as an asset will often vary with the purpose for which the valuation is being made. Some of the standards for recognizing income as "realized" will be discussed in the following paragraphs.[1]

Cash receipts.—The receipts of cash are sometimes selected to measure the earnings over a period of time. The income from a sale on credit, for example, may be entered in the accounts as income only when the cash is received. On the other hand, if cash is received in advance, the income is recognized immediately, even though the sale is not completed. The cash-receipts method may be applied, of course, to sales which give rise to a series of instalment receipts of cash, and also to transactions extending over long periods of time, for which payments are received at intervals or only at completion.

Credit transactions.—When a mercantile transaction has been completed and goods have been sold to a customer on credit terms, the credit sale may be the signal for recording sales income in the books. The credit sale is the most commonly recognized standard for the measurement of income. In most mercantile transactions the shipment of the goods is made at the time of the sale; in cases where the shipment of the goods and their sale do not occur at the same time, firms must use special accounts to show the condition of affairs.

Percentage of completion.—The income from a transaction extending over several operating periods may be measured in terms of the progress of the activity—the "percentage of completion" of the income transaction. The basis selected as most satisfactory for recognizing different stages of completion will vary with the purposes of the valuation. It may be any of the following:

[1] Compare Paton, *Accounting Theory*, chap. xix, on the "Criteria of Income." Mr. Paton discusses the criteria at considerable length; the discussion in the present chapter is influenced greatly by the terminology and argument presented in Mr. Paton's book.

1. Percentage of physical completion: A ten-story building is being constructed and sold at a price of $3,300,000. The gross income might be recognized as the construction progressed; for example, $300,000 of income might be recorded upon the completion of the foundation and of each floor. If, at the end of the first year, the foundation were laid and the framework of four of the stories were erected, the total gross income from the building contract would thus be evaluated at $1,500,000.

2. Percentage of total financial expenses: Assume that the building previously mentioned was to be erected at an estimated total cost of $2,400,000 to the contractor. At the time $1,200,000 had been expended, the contractor might regard the construction project as half-completed and the income as half-earned. The amounts of gross income recognized by the contractor could be accrued in the books in the proportion to expected gross income that expenses incurred bear to the estimated total costs. If, at the end of the first year, $1,200,000 had been expended, the gross income to be recognized would thus be one-half of the total $3,300,000, or $1,650,000.

3. Percentage of time: The mere passage of time also might be the standard of income earnings on a long-term transaction. If, for example, the construction of the building were estimated to continue for two years, one-fourth could be recorded as earned during each six months' period.[1]

Price fluctuation.—Income may also be recognized at times when the market prices of assets change. The market-price fluctuations may be very significant for some purposes, particularly for resale of marketable securities or of fixed assets held for speculation or for temporary investment. Prices may, of course, decrease as well as increase; consequently, price fluctuations are a possible measure for losses or expense, as well as for income.

Some practical problems in income determination.—The task of timing income is often a difficult one, and under many circumstances the events selected to indicate the realization of income must be chosen in terms of the specific purposes at hand. A few such cases will be discussed in the following paragraphs.

Long-term contracts.—It has been suggested that "percentage

[1] Mr. Paton mentions "physical completion" as a criterion of income. Under the foregoing classification this criterion would be merely 100 per cent physical completion. There is a difference, however, in the concept of total completion and of percentage of completion, for in the former case no income would ever be recognized on unfinished transactions or contracts. In some cases physical completion as a criterion obviously has decided merit, particularly where the task is one which could not be completed by a person substituted in the business contract. An illustration would be a contract to construct an elaborate hand-made calculating machine, the design and principle of which were understood only by the inventor, who was also the manufacturer.

of completion" may be used as the index of the realization of income earned over several periods of business operations. Assume that a contractor has agreed to construct a hotel for a hotel-operator at a price of $400,000. Assume, also, that the transaction is to continue over three years and that the gross income is to be apportioned on the basis of time. At the beginning of construction the following entry could be made in the contractor's accounts:

Oswego Hotel Company, owner...... $400,000.00
  Unearned contract sales.................... $400,000.00
  (To record the amount receivable from the owner and the deferred income from the hotel contract.)

The credit in the Unearned Contract Sales account is a deferred credit to the income from the contract sale. It may be transferred to a current-income account at the close of each fiscal period in amounts proportionate to the time during which the contract will continue in effect. At the end of the first year the following entry would be made:

Unearned contract sales............. $133,333.33
  Contract sales............................ $133,333.33
  (To record as income one-third of the gross earnings from the hotel contract.)

The credit to Contract Sales represents current income which may be closed to the Profit and Loss account. The entry is independent of the expected cash instalment which may be later received, either when the building reaches a certain stage of completion or at some agreed date. When the first instalment is received from the Oswego Hotel Company, it will be handled in the same manner as any other account receivable. The entry to record the receipt of one half the total amount due from the owner would be:

Cash........................... $200,000.00
  Oswego Hotel Company, owner.............. $200,000.00
  (To record the receipt of first instalment on hotel contract.)

The foregoing entries have not, of course, shown the procedure for recording the expenses of the construction company. They have dealt only with gross income entries, which would be offset by the expenses incurred during the period of construction. The net income to be credited to each fiscal period would depend, of course, on the method of accounting for the total expenses of carrying out the terms of the contract.

Instalment sales.—When merchandise or fixed assets are sold on instalment terms, the accounting problem is essentially the same as that arising in connection with long-term service contracts. The amounts receivable are shown as assets, but instalment sales are credited to income only when actual amounts of cash are received from the customers. In the case of merchandise, the high percentage of defaulted payments often makes it unwise to recognize income in advance of actual receipts of cash. The Federal Revenue Act classifies as instalment sales those sales on which the original payment is 25 per cent or less of the total sale price. Net profit on such sales may be reported as income immediately; it may be computed in direct ratio to the payments of instalments; or it may be deferred until the total receipts equal the cost, after which all receipts are to be regarded as net income.

Sales on approval.—Many retail establishments and mail-order houses sell goods on approval, with privilege of return after inspection. In such cases the customer often returns all the merchandise placed in his hands by the seller. In other cases he retains only a part of the total shipment. To deal with such situations it is generally desirable to separate the records of the sales on approval from the sales made on regular terms. To illustrate, assume that three dresses valued at $30 each are shipped on approval to a customer, who decides to keep two. The other one is returned. The entries would be:

Approval accounts receivable	$90.00	
Approval sales		$90.00
(To record the shipment of three dresses on approval.)		

At the time the one dress is returned and the other two accepted by the customer:

Approval sales	$60.00	
Sales		$60.00
(To record the sale of two dresses formerly on approval.)		
Accounts receivable	$60.00	
Approval sales	30.00	
Approval accounts receivable		$90.00
(To record the return of one dress formerly on approval and to charge the customer for the two sold.)		

C.O.D. sales.—C.O.D. sales may be handled by a method similar to that previously illustrated, that is, by entering the amounts receivable from C.O.D. customers in a temporary account until the money orders arrive in payment. In view of the fact that most C.O.D. shipments are accepted, it is usually unnecessary to establish a temporary account for the record of the sale. An illustration would be:

C.O.D. receivables	$85.00	
Sales		$85.00
(To record C.O.D. shipment No. 4,589.)		

When the payment for the shipment is received, the entry would be:

Cash	$85.00	
C.O.D. receivables		$85.00
(To record the receipt of cash from C.O.D. shipment No. 4, 589.)		

The student should bear in mind that all business enterprises will devise suitable accounting forms for the records of these transactions. The entries may be made informally in a columnar record, may be posted on separate cards, or may be entered individually to formal ledger accounts. The purpose of the entries given above is merely to indicate the ultimate effect of such transactions on the financial condition of a business enterprise.

Purchases discounts.—What is the nature of the credit entered in the Purchases Discount account when advantage is taken of the cash discount privileges allowed by vendors? It may be regarded either as a source of income or as an offset to the cost value of the total goods purchased during the period. Strictly speaking, the latter view must be regarded as the correct interpretation of purchases discount, for the purchases discount allowance is, in fact, merely a transaction by which the purchaser secures title to the goods for a less sum than would have otherwise been the case.[1]

[1] Obviously, either interpretation of purchases discounts results in the same net profit to the enterprise. Any discussion of the merits and demerits of a given accounting procedure must, therefore, center around the advantages which it offers for administrative control. The foregoing attitudes toward the real nature of purchases discount, with several modifications of each one, are discussed at length in W. S. Krebs's *Outlines of Accounting*, II, 444–90.

Sales on consignment require special treatment.—Merchandise is sometimes sold through agents known as factors or commission merchants; goods are shipped to these agents, who sell them for the owners. The disposal of goods in this manner is referred to in mercantile and legal practice as a *sale on consignment.* The agent is the custodian of the goods and has a right to dispose of the possession and title to the goods; however, the title to the goods often passes directly from the shipper to the ultimate buyer. The owner of the goods is known as the *consignor;* the agent, as the *consignee.*

The question arises: When should the income from a sale on consignment be recognized, and what accounts should be maintained to record the movement of the merchandise and the liability of the agent at different steps in the proceedings? Current practice avoids the recognition of the income until a sale of the merchandise has actually been consummated by the agent. In some instances this also means that income is not to be recorded in the accounts until a formal report, an "account sales," has been received from the agent. The accounts which may be maintained in the interim between shipment to the consignee and receipt of the account sales will vary with the purposes of the records. The records of consignment transactions may, of course, be merged with the other income and expense transactions. Very often they are given separate recognition in the accounts and recorded in a manner that reveals the net income from each sale on consignment.

The following transactions will serve as the basis for illustrating two methods of handling consignments on the books of the consignor: June 1, the James Wholesale Company consigns to Glenn Drake ten motorcycles, the inventory value of which is $175 each. The James Company prepays $45 freight. June 3, Glenn Drake pays $35 storage and insurance charges, which the James Company agrees to bear. August 1, Glenn Drake sells the machines for $300 each, on which he is allowed a commission of 5 per cent; he sends an account sales to the James Company. This is accompanied by a check for the amount due to the James Company, after the deduction of commission, storage, and insurance.

Consignment account as an "inventory" account.—The James Wholesale Company, the consignor, does not surrender its title to the goods at the time of the shipment. The consignee, Glenn Drake, is not the purchaser; he merely intends to find a purchaser and to act as custodian of the goods during the period of his agency. For this reason the only entry required at the time of shipment is an entry which will inform the owner of the location of his property. Accordingly a temporary merchandise account is opened under the name "Consignment—Glenn Drake." The inventory value of the consignment is recorded in this account, being transferred thereto from the Merchandise Purchases account.[1]

Consignment—Glenn Drake	$1,750.00	
Merchandise purchases		$1,750.00

If the goods are no longer in the hands of Glenn Drake at the close of a fiscal period, the Consignment—Glenn Drake account may be closed. It has served its purpose as an inventory account; consequently the balance may be returned to the Purchases account from which it was originally removed.

Merchandise purchases	$1,750.00	
Consignment—Glenn Drake		$1,750.00

(To return to the Purchases account the record of the goods formerly on consignment to Glenn Drake.)

In the meantime the records of the expenses and sales connected with the consigned goods may be made in the regular income and expense accounts. The journal entries on the books of the James Wholesale Company would be:

June 1, 1927

Freight expense	$ 45.00	
Cash		$ 45.00

(Payment of freight bill on consignment to Glenn Drake.)

[1] The credit entry may be and sometimes is, made to a temporary account established for the purpose, such as "Consignments Out," a general account to offset the total cost values of the goods on consignment. The Consignments Out account and the individual Consignment accounts are later closed concurrently when the consignment transactions for which they were opened have been completed. For illustrations of different methods of accounting for consignments, see Finney, *Principles of Accounting*, Vol. I.

August 1, 1927

Cash	$2,815.00	
Commissions	150.00	
Storage and insurance	35.00	
Sales		$3,000.00

(Receipt of account sales from Glenn Drake for shipment of ten motorcycles.)

Consignment account as a "summary of operations."—The account entitled "Consignment—Glenn Drake" was used above as a temporary inventory account, established solely for the purpose of indicating the location of a part of the firm's merchandise. It is sometimes given a broader interpretation and used for accumulation of all the income and expense transactions affecting a particular consignment. The original debit to the account is regarded as the cost of goods to be sold; expense entries are likewise entered in the account on the debit side. The credits arising from the sale of the goods are entered on the right side of the account. The resulting balance is the net income or loss resulting from the consignment, and may be closed to the general Profit and Loss account as an income item. The first entry would be identical with the one given above:

June 1, 1927

Consignment—Glenn Drake	$1,750.00	
Merchandise purchases		$1,750.00

(To open an account for the consignment of ten motorcycles to Glenn Drake, June 1.)

The $45 freight expense would be added to the debit in the Consignment—Glenn Drake account, thus increasing the cost of the goods to be sold. The journal entry would be:

June 1, 1927

Consignment—Glenn Drake	$45.00	
Cash		$45.00

(Payment of freight on shipment of ten motorcycles to Glenn Drake.)

If it were learned that Glenn Drake had paid the $35 storage and insurance, the Consignment account would typically be charged at once therefor. On the other hand, such an expense might be recognized only when the cash is received from the consignee. When Glenn Drake sells the machines, collects the cash from the purchasers, and sends in the proper amount, the following entry would be recorded, which makes proper allowance for his commission deductions and for the payments for storage and insurance.

AUGUST 1, 1927

Cash	$2,815.00	
Consignment—Glenn Drake		$2,815.00

(To record cash receipt as shown by account sales of Glenn Drake.)

The Consignment account would now appear as follows:

CONSIGNMENT—GLENN DRAKE

June 1	Purchases	$1,750.00	Aug. 1	Cash	$2,815.00
	Freight	45.00			
Aug. 1	To profit and loss	1,020.00			
		$2,815.00			$2,815.00

The credit balance in the Consignment account after the transactions are completed represents the profit from the consignment to Glenn Drake. It is accordingly transferred to the Profit and Loss account with other income items at the close of an operating period.

The account sales rendered by Glenn Drake August 1 would appear somewhat as follows:

ACCOUNT SALES TO JAMES WHOLESALE COMPANY

AUGUST 1, 1927

Cash sales, Aug. 1, 1927, ten motorcycles @ $300.00		$3,000.00
Deductions: Commission	$150.00	
Storage and insurance	35.00	$ 185.00
Check inclosed		$2,815.00

Records of consignee.—The methods of maintaining the consignment records of a consignor will vary with the needs of the particular enterprise and trade. Similarly, the records of the consignee may be prepared in any manner which will suit his purposes; in fact, the consignee's records may be much simpler, inasmuch as he is not concerned with the computation of income or net profit on the different consignments. He is interested primarily in setting up records which will represent his liability to, or claim against, the consignor.

When the goods are received, no entry need be made on the books of Glenn Drake,[1] except a memorandum to the effect that certain motorcycles are in his warehouse and are the property of the James Wholesale Company. Such an entry need not be in terms of financial values, nor need it be considered a part of the double-entry accounting records. When Glenn Drake pays the insurance and storage charges, he will debit an account with James Wholesale Company, the consignor, indicating that he is to be reimbursed for this amount, as follows:

Consignment No. 10—James Wholesale Company........	\$35.00	
Cash..		\$35.00

At the time the machines are sold and the cash is collected, the entry will be:

Cash..	\$3,000.00	
Consignment No. 10—James Wholesale Company.........		\$3,000.00

This entry records the amount for which Glenn Drake is responsible to the consignor on the consignment from the James Wholesale Company. It changes the small "account receivable" from the James Wholesale Company, (\$35) to an "account payable" to the James Wholesale Company (\$2,965). The account payable later is liquidated by deducting \$150 commissions and making a cash payment of \$2,815. The entry would be:

Consignment No. 10—James Wholesale Company...	\$2,965.00	
Cash..		\$2,815.00
Commissions earned..................................		150.00

The account with the consignor after these transactions are recorded would appear as follows:

[1] Sometimes the same practice is followed by consignors. No records are made of the shipments of merchandise to consignees until financial transactions occur which change ownership of the consigned goods.

Consignment No. 10—James Wholesale Company

June 1	Cash	$ 35.00	Aug. 1	Cash	$3,000.00
Aug. 1	Commission	150.00			
	Cash	2,815.00			
		$3,000.00			$3,000.00

QUESTIONS ON CHAPTER XXXI

1. Can the problem of valuation—so often looked upon as a matter of appraisal—be considered as essentially a problem of measuring "incoming" values and "expended" values? If we start with an accepted value, add the new values, and subtract the expired values, do we not automatically obtain the remaining values?
2. If valuation is dependent upon a proper measurement of income and expense, this means that we should have satisfactory criteria for recognizing income and expense. What are some of the possible criteria of income?
3. What transaction should be the signal for recognizing income in the case of the following: (*a*) consignments, (*b*) approval sales, (*c*) instalment sales?
4. Is it possible that companies might find it preferable to recognize the income from consignment transactions before the consignee actually buys or disposes of the goods? Under what conditions might such procedure be justified? How might the accounts be handled in such instances?
5. Suggest a method of accounting for approval sales. To illustrate your point, assume that four dresses are shipped to a customer on approval. They each have a selling price of $35. You do not expect the customer to keep more than two—possibly only one; possibly none. Journalize the entry at the time the goods are shipped; at the time one is accepted.
6. When should the income on a C.O.D. sale be recognized? When the goods are shipped? When the cash is received? Give the journal entries necessary in the case of each assumption stated above.
7. When should the income be recognized on instalment sales? If it is to be considered as earned gradually during the period of the instalment payments, how would the transactions appear in the account?

CHAPTER XXXII

THE MEASUREMENT OF EXPENSE—NET PROFIT

The essence of economic activity is the balancing of income against expense. The interest of private business, moreover, is in making income exceed expense. A comparison of income and expense necessitates the application of standards in their measurement, and proceeds upon the assumption that devices have been made available for identifying income and expense with periods of time.

The measurement of expense involves apportionment to periods of time.—Expense accounts reflect business operations which have occurred during an accounting period. The measurement of total expense or of individual expenses must be preceded, therefore, by identifying them with certain periods of time. For example, two men may agree that a cash payment of $100 was made on December 1 for advertising services. But they may not agree as to whether the entire $100 should be charged as an expense of the present calendar year or be charged in part to the ensuing year. This simple question of whether a certain advertising cost is an expense of one period or another is typical of those encountered continuously by business men. The ways in which these questions are answered affect greatly all aspects of financial status.

The widely accepted rule for dealing with expense is: "Provide for all possible losses." In practice, this rule has become: "Recognize all expenses which have been incurred up to the time at which financial status is being determined." The recognition of expenses implies the existence of certain earmarks of expense, which will identify them with particular periods of time. Accountants will agree generally that all expense transactions should be recognized, but not all accountants will recognize the same business transactions as expenses. The difference of opinion among accountants arises from the fact that they use different criteria for the recognition of expense operations. They do not often disagree as to the amounts involved in certain transactions, but they very often disagree as to what portions of the totals are to be apportioned to or identified with certain periods of time. It is easy to ask: When is an expense incurred? What is the signal for recognizing the occurrence of an expense transaction? But no one answer to either of these questions will serve for all types of expenses or for all purposes. Some of the typical standards for identifying expense with certain periods of time are cash expenditures, the incurring of liabilities, depletion or depreciation, price fluctuations.

Cash expenditures.—A cash expenditure may be regarded as the index of an expense transaction. The total cash payments would thus be the measure of the expense incurred during a given period. The cash expenditure standard may, of course, be applied to all types of expenses, including such dissimilar transactions as payments for labor or transportation, the liquidation of liabilities, or the cash purchase of merchandise. The limitations of the cash expenditure as a standard for expense determination are apparent from the widely different natures of the transactions just mentioned. In some of the cases the cash payments are made to purchase new assets; in others the cash is used to pay debts long since incurred. Most practical men refuse to regard the purchase of assets or the payment of debts as expense operations, for such transactions do not immediately affect the net proprietorship of an enterprise.

Cash expenditures may under some circumstances serve very satisfactorily as a measure of total expense incurred, for example, where the fiscal period under consideration is considerably longer than the length of time the individual assets are retained in the business or the individual liabilities remain unpaid. Cash payments might, for example, suffice for practical purposes as an estimate of total expense transactions of an enterprise during a period of 40 years; for in that period most of the original buildings would have depreciated and the original long-term bonds would have been paid off. A different illustration would be a grocery store the stock of which is sold and replenished monthly. The small stock on hand at any one time and the unpaid liabilities would not, for practical purposes, be important variables in calculating an entire year's expenses. These two types of circumstances are, of course, similar, in that the total expenditures during the fiscal period in each case bear a high ratio to the assets on hand at any one time.

As a practical matter, a statement of cash receipts and expenditures is often regarded as equivalent to a statement of business operations, particularly in cases where no private interests are to be compared and subdivided. Illustrations are the transactions of governments, clubs, professional societies, and churches. The adequacy of such statements for purposes of administrative control will depend upon the circumstances in each case. Taking the cash payment as a criterion for the recognition of expense transactions has certain advantages. It is an overt transaction, easily recognized, with the resultant advantage of definiteness in its application. This criterion has been universally applied by enterprises of widely different natures; in fact, until the passage of revenue acts which made it desirable to develop more refined methods of expense determination, cash receipts and disbursements were commonly used as the basis for estimating business profit. At the present time, business enterprises have, for the most part, discontinued the use of the cash expenditure as the measure of expense. The following paragraphs will indicate some of the other bases for measuring expense transactions.

Incurrence of liabilities.—It is possible to regard the incurrence of a liability as the criterion of expense. For example, the amount involved in the purchase of coal may be considered as expended at the time the coal is purchased, without regard to when it is paid for, received, sold, or consumed. In some cases, of course, the liability may be incurred and the cash expended at the same time (or essentially so, as in the case of the payment of daily wages at the close of each day). Typically, the practice of regarding the incurrence of a liability as a criterion of expense leads to just as great inaccuracies as does the practice of taking cash expenditures as a criterion. This is especially true in cases where the total investment in a business bears a high ratio to the total financial transactions carried on during a period, or where transactions continue over considerable periods of time.

Depletion or depreciation.—In the case of continuing transactions, it is necessary to find some criterion which will measure the gradual expenditure of value; it is not enough to designate certain events which are presumed to mark the sudden disappearance of assets. The treatment of continuing-transactions requires a measure for portions of the expense transaction, a measure which will serve to designate the stage of its progress. "Percentage of completion" was introduced for the measurement of income, with three standards set up for measuring the stages of progress. They were physical completion, financial expenses, and the passage of time. The first and the last of these bases suggest standards which may be used for expense measurement; the second, of course, is the very phenomenon we are trying to measure.

The expenditure of an asset may be measured in terms of the percentage of its physical depletion during a given period of time. An obvious illustration of this principle would be the measure of coal expenditure in terms of the tons consumed from a given supply. Another would be the calculation of the proportionate value of metallic ore taken from a mine, measured in terms of cubic yards or tons extracted. The principle of depletion may, of course, be applied to any type of goods which are gradually consumed in business operations. Strictly speaking, the principle of percentage of depletion is applied to salable merchandise, particularly in cases where a perpetual inventory of goods is maintained. Even the periodic appraisal of goods on hand has the effect of estimating the periodic depletion of the total amount of goods comprising those on hand at the beginning of, and received during, a period.

A more difficult problem of expense measurement appears in those cases where the decrease in value of an asset cannot be measured by physical units of gradual decrease but must nevertheless be apportioned to periods of time. Illustrations which come to mind immediately are, of course, machinery and buildings used in carrying on business operations without changing their form. Machines are not depleted (usually) by a process of gradual dismemberment; they lose their value through the process described as "depreciation." The depreciation may be caused by wear and tear, obsolescence, inadequacy, or by any or all of these; usually it is measured in terms of some unit which will serve for practical purposes to apportion the value adequately to periods of time.

Price fluctuations.—Downward changes in prices may, in some circumstances, be regarded as causing reductions of values which should be recorded in the accounts. Accountants apply this rule very frequently to the recognition of decreases in the market value of salable merchandise. When the cost of replacing merchandise at the time of preparing a balance sheet is less than the original financial outlay of securing the merchandise, the variation is usually regarded as important enough for record in the accounts. The actual accounting entries do not, of course, reveal such adjustments of merchandise value unless a perpetual inventory is maintained. Nevertheless the fluctuation in the inventory value has its effect on total expense by reducing the value of the inventory below its original cost and accordingly increasing the cost of goods sold. Downward fluctuations in the values of permanent assets are not usually recognized in the current records as business expenses. Persistent downward trends in market price may, of course, be reflected in the accounts by increases in the amount of depreciation charged against the fiscal periods during which fixed assets will be used.

Practical uses of expense standards.—All of the various standards of timing expense which have been discussed above may, under some circumstances, be useful for the purpose of a manager in the measurement of specific expenses or groups of expenses. In practice it is not uncommon for a business man to use them concurrently for specific conditions where they appear to be applicable. For example, the "cash expenditure" might be used to deal with small items paid from a petty-cash fund; the "incurrence of a liability" would suffice when an invoice for transportation service was received from a carrier of outgoing merchandise; "physical depletion" would serve to estimate the supplies consumed during a period; "depreciation" would be the basis for calculating the reduced values of fixed assets; "price fluctuations" in merchandise inventory on hand would be charged against the period which had just come to a close.[1] The business man must recognize the advantages and limitations of each criterion of expense. He must recognize also that the adequacy of a given standard very often depends upon the purpose for which the calculations are being made.

Net profit affected by standards of income and expense.—The total income of an enterprise during a period may be offset against the total expense during the same period. The difference represents a net addition to or subtraction from proprietorship—the net profit or the net loss. In practice, three types of questions must be answered when dealing with income and expense transactions: What transactions reflect income or expense operations and hence affect proprietorship? What transactions affect proprietorship directly, without being income or expense operations? What transactions are neither income nor expense nor affect proprietorship directly? The answers to these questions must be given in terms of the purposes for which net profit is being computed; or, to put it differently, in terms of the definition or conception of net profit which has been adopted.

Profits as net increase in proprietorship.—Net profits are sometimes regarded as being merely the net increase in proprietorship between two periods of time. According to this concept, income and expense would include all transactions which affect the actual or potential exchange value of resources and liabilities. Income would include appreciation in the value of both current and fixed assets, although there would need to be reasonable assurance that the increased fixed asset values could be realized through higher prices of products. The valuation of each asset or liability at the end of an operating period would be based on the expected use to which it would be placed. This concept of profit as the net increase of proprietorship is never held to in practice; it is necessarily modified to allow for permanent withdrawals of capital, either by payment of dividends or cancellation of stock; also for the investment of additional capital through the admission of new partners or through the sale of capital stock.

[1] Such fluctuations would (if recognized in the accounts) probably be charged directly against accumulated surplus rather than against current operations.

Most business men would exclude also the gains or losses from dealings in capital stock sold above par or redeemed below par. There is a strong feeling that no income ought to be realized or expense sustained by an enterprise through dealings in the distributive shares of its own proprietorship. As a matter of fact, the federal revenue acts of the United States have consistently refused to recognize dealings in a corporation's own capital stock as affecting taxable net income.[1]

Profits as gains from operations.—This concept varies from the first in two distinct respects. In the first place, it ignores fluctuations in price, as elements of income or expense, however much they may affect proprietorship. In the second place, this concept requires the elimination from the net profit calculations of all incidental transactions not directly related to the major business operations. The idea of profits as gain from operations is the concept of income adopted by the typical business man, and it is supported generally by the courts. Business men vary this general rule in one important respect. They consistently give recognition to fluctuations in merchandise value, as long as the fluctuations do not carry the value above the original purchase price. A consistent application of the concept of net profit as gain from operations would, of course, exclude fluctuations in merchandise value from the income and expense classification. Strictly speaking, the differences between cost and market values of merchandise should be accounted for as direct adjustments of proprietorship.

Net profits and dividends.—It is a commonplace of corporate law that the capital stock of a corporation may not be impaired by the declaration of dividends. This means that dividends payable must be charged against the surplus of a corporation, or against current net profits which would otherwise have been credited to the Surplus account. For purposes of computing net profits, the courts have assumed that profits include all the net changes in proprietorship. Although the courts have been slow to approve appreciation as a source of income, they have held that surplus arising from an appraisal of fixed assets is subject to distribution as dividends. The courts have made some attempt to

[1] Sec. 230, Act of 1926; Reg. 69, Art. 2.

differentiate between gains from operations and non-operating gains, but they have not regarded the distinction as important for purposes of dividend declaration. Some of the "border-line" types of transactions which are generally regarded as creating surplus distributable as dividends are gifts, appraisals, sale of stock above par, and redemption of stock below par.

In computing the net gain from operations, the courts have approved the business man's attitude toward the problem of income and expense. They have included as expenses all ordinary financial costs, such as materials, labor, rent, taxes, and interest on borrowed capital. They have also included the other actual diminutions of assets, such as depreciation and depletion, and have regarded interest on investment as an expense for some purposes, notably for the establishment of normal rates of profit allowed to public-service corporations.

Net profits and taxable income.—For purposes of taxing income, the various governments have made certain arbitrary definitions as to what receipts and what expenditures shall be used in the computations. The United States has avowedly set out to include as gross income all "gains, profits, incomes, from every source whatsoever,"[1] The list of receipts classified as gross income is very inclusive; but certain receipts are regarded as non-taxable, either on the ground of public policy or because the recipient cannot be said to have realized actual income. Among the excluded items are income (salaries or interest) from governments, gifts; dividends from domestic corporations (exempt from normal tax, which the corporation pays), stock dividends, and premiums on sale of stock. As far as expenses are concerned, the law permits deductions which correspond closely to the business man's idea of business expense. Personal expenses are not deductible, being excluded on the theory that they are chargeable against net profits and hence correspond to a dividend; capital expenditures

[1] Section 213 (*b*), Act of 1926, Reg. 69, Art. 31. It is significant that the income-tax laws of Great Britain have laid great stress upon the concept of periodicity or regularity in their taxation of income. They have ordinarily not taxed "casual" gains under the class of income. In line with this rule, they have been slow to recognize depreciation as an allowable expense and have not yet permitted the depletion of wasting-assets to be deducted in all cases.

are omitted on the ground that they do not affect expense of the period in which they occur. Among the special inclusions of deductions to be noted are taxes and interest on a personal dwelling-house (rent for a residence is not deductible) and contributions to charitable institutions.

Net profits and surplus.—Accountants frequently assume that as many expenses should be charged against the income of a period as can be so treated. They adjust Surplus with considerable reluctance, feeling that most transactions can be regarded as part of the main operations of an enterprise. Consequently the term "expenses" is sometimes extended to include the dividends on preferred stock, losses from various contingencies and accidents, and provision for the increase of the assets of an enterprise. The treatment of these items is usually handled by the gradual building of a "reserve" which covers all such expenses, and against which the expenditures can be charged when they actually occur.

The dividing line between expenses, on the one hand, and charges against net profit or surplus, on the other, is not an easy one to draw. The concept of net profit is one of the most elusive concepts in accounting theory, and about which no dogmatic rules can be laid down that will cover all cases. The answer to the problem of determining net profit is to be found in the criteria of income and expense that are adopted and in the bases selected for identifying them with periods of time.

QUESTIONS ON CHAPTER XXXII

1. What are the advantages of the "cash-expenditure" as a criterion of expense transactions? Is it consistent with the principle of conservatism? Under what conditions is it useful for the measurement of expense?
2. Do credit transactions—the incurrence of liabilities—correctly measure the expense transactions? Why or why not?
3. What disadvantages would be encountered in accounting for fixed assets as "expenses" at the times they were discarded rather than through periodic depreciation charges?
4. Under what conditions might it be practicable to charge buildings off as expenses when *discarded?* Under the same conditions might it be equally practicable to charge them as expenses when *erected?*
5. Do you consider the depletion of natural resources a proper charge against current operations? What factors enter to make the problem

of apportioning depletion more difficult than the apportionment of depreciation?

6. Expenses include all the outlays for materials and services during a period of operations. They may be said to represent the *distribution* of the total income under such groupings as *interest* paid to financial creditors, *wages* paid to laborers, and *rent* to property owners, *commodities* purchased from mercantile creditors. *Net profit* is what is left for the proprietors. Under the foregoing definition would you regard dividends paid on stock as expenses? Would it make any difference whether the dividends were on preferred or common stock? If dividend payments are not expenses, what are they?
7. Net profit is the difference between the income and expense during an accounting period. What are some of the variations in the concepts of net profit which are held for the following purposes: (*a*) expressing changes in financial conditions; (*b*) measuring gains from major business operations; (*c*) determining an amount on which to base a tax on incomes; (*d*) deciding on the availability of surplus for dividends?
8. Accountants attempt to differentiate between transactions which affect *net-profit* and those which affect *surplus*. What is the advantage of such a distinction for practical purposes? Which theories of net profit underlie the attempt to make such distinctions?
9. Do you see any connection between the accountant's tendency to make a large number of transactions come within the classification of income or expense (especially expense) and his conviction that conservatism is a good thing? How is such a policy conservative?
10. What should be the accountant's stand on the matter of recognizing appreciation in land values or other fixed assets in a balance sheet? Is the income from appreciation taxable before it is realized through actual sale of the assets? Has the income been realized in the sense that a banker might increase the amount of money which he would loan with the asset as security?

PART IV

INTERPRETATION OF ACCOUNTING DATA

CHAPTER XXXIII

THEORY OF ACCOUNTING CLASSIFICATION

The text up to this point has dealt with some of the problems which must be solved in *accounting valuation* (chaps. xxi–xxxii); it has also explained the theory and technique of *double entry*, a special method for classifying and summarizing accounting data (chaps. iii–xx). The closing chapters will be concerned with the *interpretation* of accounting data for control; also the application of accounting data to some problems of administrative and social control.

Interpretation affects each step in the accounting method.—Interpretation is the critical analysis and appraisal of the accounting data secured by the processes of measurement; it involves classification, summarization, and the discovery of important relationships between different facts set forth in the accounting reports. Interpretation is more than a mere process in accounting method; it is also an attitude which influences every move in accounting procedure. In turn, interpretation is affected greatly by the uses to which accounting data are to be placed.

The process of interpretation may be said to begin when the observer attempts to differentiate business objects or transactions and to group them in terms of basic similarities. Consequently the present discussion of interpretation opens with this chapter on the "Theory of Accounting Classification"; this is followed by two chapters entitled "Balance Sheets and Other Summaries of Financial Status" and "Summaries of Business Operations," respectively. The process of interpretation, of course, goes farther than the search for similarities and differences in the accounting data. It also involves comparison—the discovery of quantitative relationships between classes of data, as revealed by ratios, averages, variations, and trends. Accordingly the study of interpretation continues with the following chapters: "Ratios in Accounting Data"; "Averages and Trends in Accounting Data"; and

"Analysis of Comparative Balance Sheets." The text closes with two chapters illustrating the uses of accounting data in modern economic enterprise. They are: "Administrative Uses of Cost Data" and "Social Control through Accounts."

Classification of accounting data conditioned by purposes or ends sought.—The classification of accounting data raises two questions: *To what degree* are the data to be subdivided before they are summarized in the accounting reports? *On what bases* are groups of data to be summarized in the accounting reports? The answers to both questions must be made in terms of the purposes of the classification in view. For some purposes the assets of an enterprise may be subdivided into three accounts; for other purposes three hundred might be needed. The data of an entire balance sheet may be grouped into three accounts—Assets, Liabilities, and Proprietorship—if the purpose is merely to set forth the net worth of an enterprise. A classification to this degree would not, of course, serve for forming a judgment on a given policy for collecting accounts receivable or for establishing a practical standard for controlling inventories. Purposes of these latter types require detailed information as to causes and extent of bad debts, or as to the items of merchandise on hand.

The selection of bases for the classification of accounts, as well as the degree of sub-classification, must be made with regard to the purposes which the accounts are to serve. No one basis will serve for all conceivable purposes; nor will any one basis serve a given purpose under all conditions. The balance-sheet equation implies that certain broad classes of data must be recognized before the accounts of an enterprise may be further subdivided: namely, the accounts which express financial status (Assets, Liabilities, Proprietorship) and the accounts which summarize business operations (Income, Expense). Some accounts, of course, may be *mixed* in character from time to time; nevertheless their elements are always separable in terms of the main divisions. The real problem of accounting classification may be said to begin, therefore, after the recognition of such classes of accounting data as assets, liabilities, proprietorship, income, and expense. The bases of classification which may be applied to subdivisions of these broad classes of accounting data will be discussed under four headings:

1. *Intended uses or purposes* of the objects or transactions. (Special characteristics independent of the qualities or properties of objects or transactions, and arising entirely out of their relations to uses and purposes in a business.)
2. *Inherent qualities or properties* of the objects or transactions. (General characteristics attaching to the objects or transactions themselves.)
3. *Administrative responsibility* for the objects or transactions. (Classification by units of administrative organization; this grouping is in essence a special application of the first basis.)
4. *Financial appropriations or ventures* (*funds*). (This basis separates the objects or transactions in terms of special projects, grouping the balance-sheet and income and expense accounts under the general headings of financial appropriations or ventures.)

Each of these bases is limited in its applicability, yet each has found a place in the practice of modern business. Very often several of the bases are used concurrently in the accounting records of the same enterprise.

An illustrative classification of accounts.—Various bases of classification might be applied to the ledger data of a large enterprise. Two bases of classification are apparent in the general grouping shown below: *Intended uses or purposes* are reflected by such captions as "Current assets," "Fixed assets," "Deferred charges." *Administrative responsibility* is the basis for the expense classification under such general headings as "Production expenses," "Marketing expenses," "Financial expenses."

1. *Assets*
   11. Current assets
   12. Deferred charges
   13. Fixed assets
   14. Permanent investments
   15. Intangibles
2. *Liabilities*
   21. Current liabilities
   22. Deferred credits
   23. Fixed liabilities
3. *Proprietorship*
   31. Capital stock
   32. Capital stock premium
   33. Capital stock subscribed
   34. Reserves
   35. Undivided profits
   36. Surplus
4. *Clearing accounts*
5. *Income*
   51. Gross income
   52. Non-operating income
   52A. Non-operating expense (debits)
6. *Expenses*
   61. Production expenses
   62. Marketing expenses
   63. Financial expenses
   64. Personnel expenses
   65. Controllers' office expenses
   66. Executive supervision

Each of the groups of accounts listed above might be subdivided into a detailed classification. The Current Assets, for example, might be subdivided according to the *inherent qualities or properties* of the items of wealth. Subgroups of this type would be Cash, Merchandise, Receivables. A detailed classification of account titles appears at the close of this chapter.

Classification by intended uses or purposes applicable to main divisions of accounting data.—Accounting data may be classified in terms of the intended use or purposes of the objects or transactions underlying them. This basis of classification can be applied to the data in any of the broad groups of accounting phenomena, either balance-sheet data or income and expense accounts.

Balance-sheet data.—Assets which are characterized in terms of their intended use by an enterprise fall into two major classes: *current* and *fixed.*[1] These groups are themselves subdivided in the typical balance sheet so as to present detailed information concerning the financial status. The uses of the terms "current" and "fixed" are not standardized; they may have very broad or very limited meanings. Modern practice tends to give them rather arbitrary limited meanings and to admit a large number of other groups as main divisions of assets. The classification of assets as current or fixed arises out of the particular relationships which they bear to the organization and transactions of a given enterprise. The terminology selected for the basic groups is not always the same.[2]

[1] Compare chapter xii, where the meaning of the terms "current" and "fixed" in relation to assets and liabilities were discussed at length.

[2] A government regulating body of one state has prescribed the following major groups for the classification of the assets of certain public utilities: I, Fixed Capital (tangible fixed assets, land, buildings, etc.); II, Investment (securities and property of other companies, advances to other companies); III, Re-acquired Securities (treasury stock or bonds); IV, Funds (special assets accumulated to pay liabilities, replace assets, or absorb losses); V, Special Deposits (money available for special legal requirements, such as interest or dividends); VI, Current Assets (cash, receivables, materials, supplies); VII, Accrued Assets (rents and interest receivable); VIII, Deferred Charges (organization and investigation costs, casualties, abandoned property). (Taken from *A Uniform Classification of Accounts for Natural Gas Utilities* prescribed by the Public Utilities Commission of the State of Ohio. Effective January 1, 1921.)

Liabilities are, of course, also divisible into groups classified as "current" and "fixed." The current group is sometimes differentiated from the groups of "accrued" expenses and "deferred" credits to income. Likewise certain "contingent" liabilities may be set forth separately in the balance sheet.

The "current-fixed" grouping of assets also finds its counterpart in the subdivisions of Proprietorship usually encountered in a balance sheet. The Capital or Capital Stock accounts represent, in a sense, "fixed" proprietorship. The Personal or Surplus accounts likewise may be regarded as "current" or temporary proprietorship. This distinction is emphasized particularly in the accounts of a corporation, because specific legal and economic considerations underlie the separation of capital stock and surplus. The Capital Stock account represents a permanent investment in the enterprise which can be withdrawn only in accord with special legal provisions. Surplus is the undivided proprietorship of the stockholders, and may be distributed among them in the form of new shares, may be reduced by the payment of cash, or may be given a special designation to reflect business policies, such as "Reserves." Capital stock itself may be classified on the balance sheet according to the different types of stock which are outstanding, such as preferred and common.

Income and expense.—Many enterprises attempt to differentiate income and expense transactions according to their relation to the major business activities. Consequently one encounters such terms as "operating" and "non-operating" in the published statements of income and expense. The items which are to be regarded as operating or non-operating will vary from one enterprise to another.[1] It is very important to classify business operations, both income and expense, in terms of their relations to the main activities of an enterprise; for such separation enables a manager to trace the sources of his profits or losses. Not infre-

[1] In governmental accounting, one finds such headings as "revenue" and "non-revenue." For example, under the heading of "revenue receipts" appear items received as the result of regular governmental services: from the collection of taxes, licenses, special assessments, fees, fines, forfeits, subventions, grants-in-aid. Under "non-revenue receipts" are the earnings of publicly owned utilities, and cash from issuance of bonds or from sale of property.

quently the incidental (non-operating) activities of an enterprise grow to such proportions that they must be reclassified as major activities or must be segregated and carried on as separate enterprises.[1]

The grouping of expenses by intended uses or purposes also makes possible such groupings as "direct vs. indirect," or "current vs. fixed." These groupings are often important in administrative control, although they very seldom find their way into the published statements. Both of these classifications of expense data will be discussed fully in chapter xxxix, "Administrative Uses of Cost Data."

Classification by inherent qualities or properties generally applicable to minor subdivisions of accounting data.—Differentiation of accounting data in terms of the inherent qualities or properties of the objects or transactions is applicable generally to all types of data. It is both the easiest and the most difficult method of classification to apply in practice. In its simplest aspects, it may be applied by mere casual observation; in its more complex manifestations, it requires very accurate definition of the data to be classified.

Balance-sheet data.—Classification of assets and liabilities according to their inherent qualities or properties has its greatest advantage in the extent to which it permits subdivision of the items. The asset "Merchandise inventory," for example, might be listed as a single item in a balance sheet. But this general heading may itself be subdivided into numerous groups. The account grouping shown below indicates how a Merchandise Inventory account could be subdivided to show the different classes of merchandise held in stock by a manufacturer of rubber goods.

[1] The International Harvester Company established a small steel mill to furnish a portion of the steel for use in manufacturing farm implements. The steel mill was able to prepare more than enough material for the manufacture of implements; hence it began to sell some of its output to other firms. Ultimately the steel enterprise grew until it became a large concern; it was separately incorporated and is now managed as a subsidiary corporation, serving the industrial world generally. Sales to the parent company absorb only a minor portion of its total output. (Compare chapter xiii of this text on the use of the terms "operating" and "non-operating.")

115. *Merchandise inventory*
  1151. Belting
  1152. Packing and hose
  1153. Drug sundries
  1154. Tires
  1155. Tubes
  1156. Aeronautic supplies
  1157. Soles and heels

The subdivisions illustrated above merely indicate the method of breaking the Merchandise Inventory account into sub-classifications. In practice, each of the groups would be divided into styles, types, and sizes. An adequate system of numbers or symbols is a very important part of a classification plan; it simplifies the task of referring to the accounts, either for the purpose of posting data therein or for verification of the facts recorded.

The classification of assets in terms of inherent qualities or properties is the ultimate or final subdivision to which they may be subjected; hence it is most useful when made a part of a broader grouping, such as current or fixed assets. The classification must be preceded by accurate definition of items and carried out by persistent conformity to a uniform procedure. To meet these requirements, many enterprises prepare elaborate accounting manuals in which are carefully described the objects or transactions which are to be listed under each general heading. Such manuals are also issued by government regulatory bodies to insure uniformity in the accounts of enterprises under their supervision.[1]

[1] As an example of the detail with which accounts may be classified and described, the following facts are cited from the explanatory text in the *Uniform System of Accounts for Telephone Companies* as prescribed by the Interstate Commerce Commission, 1913. The asset accounts are first divided under the following headings: "Permanent and long-term investments," "Working assets," "Accrued income," "Deferred debits." "Permanent and long-term investments" include, as one subdivision, the item "Fixed capital." Under "Fixed capital," one of the subheadings is "Station equipment." Under "Station equipment," the subheading "Station apparatus" appears. "Station apparatus" is defined as follows: "231. *Station Apparatus.*—This account should include the cost of station apparatus, such as telephone sets, intercommunicating sets, bells, backboards, desk stands, coin boxes, protectors, battery boxes, initial batteries and cords, special station-switching devices not otherwise classified, and telephone and telegraph instruments or parts thereof when owned by the company and installed for service."

Income and expense data.—A classification of expenses in terms of the inherent qualities or properties of the objects or transactions provides such account titles as "Heat," "Light," "Supplies," "Interest," "Taxes," "Wages," "Insurance," and "Depreciation." Such account titles are widely used in the records of business enterprises. They are most practicable when applied to small numbers of accounts solely for the purpose of determining net profit, or when made a subdivision of some broader class.

The Bureau of Internal Revenue recommends classification of expenses in terms of the inherent qualities of the objects or transactions for use by individuals and corporations when setting forth taxable income. The Federal Revenue Act does not insist that the reports of taxable income be used by the enterprises in their management; the purpose of the returns is merely to explain how net taxable income is computed. The expenses shown on the face of the income-tax return are listed as "deductions." On the corporation return (form 1120) are included such items as officers' compensation, rent, repairs, interest, taxes, losses, bad debts, depreciation, depletion, salaries, and wages.

When income transactions are classified according to the inherent properties of the objects or transactions, the data are usually described in terms of the sources from which income has been derived. The sources may be income-earning assets or business transactions. The Federal Reserve Act of 1926 classifies the sources of income (for an individual with a net income of more than $5,000) under the following headings:[1]

1. Salaries, wages, commissions
2. Business or profession
3. Bank deposits, notes, bonds, etc.
4. Partnerships, fiduciaries, etc.
5. Rents and royalties
6. Dealings in fixed assets or other property
7. Capital stock of corporations
8. Other sources

Classification according to administrative responsibility, desirable for control.—Accounting classification is pointed toward

[1] These items appear on the face of the income tax return (Form 1040) for individuals with net incomes of more than $5,000, or with net incomes, regardless of amount, if derived from a profession or business, including farming.

the ultimate use of data in the control of an enterprise. A classification of accounts which is to be used for administrative control may well reflect the form of the organization of the enterprise. Such a basis for subdivision would make possible the placement of responsibility upon the proper members of the administrative organization.

Types of administrative organization.—The importance of the type of organization upon account classification may be made clearer by a discussion of the various units in terms of which an enterprise may be organized. For example, an enterprise may be organized in terms of administrative functions, territories, or commodities.

A functional organization is one which apportions administrative authority and responsibility according to what may be termed "functions," that is to say, groups of related or similar activities, such as those connected with marketing, finance, production, personnel, or accounting and statistics. A chart indicating in general the lines of administrative responsibility is shown below:

FUNCTIONAL TYPE OF ORGANIZATION*

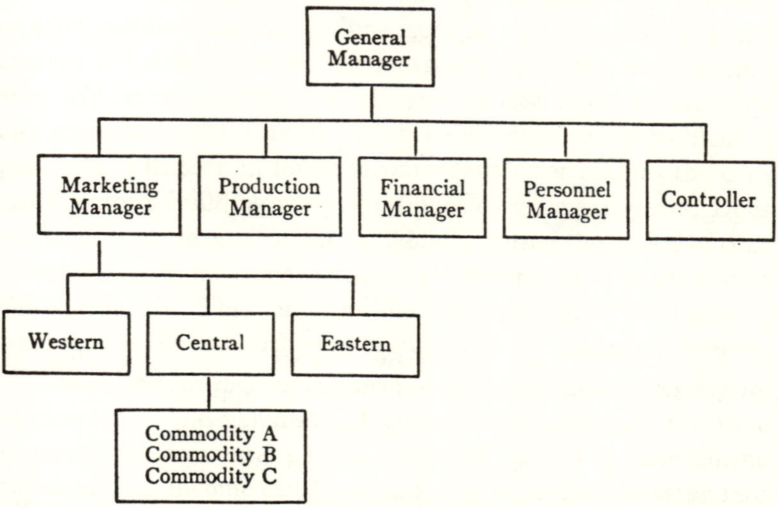

* This chart is meant to illustrate an organization in which functions are the basis for the first main division of administrative responsibility. Subdivisions would consist of departments classified according to "territories" (geographical areas) and "commodities." This chart is not complete, that is to say, all the subdivisions of an enterprise are not shown thereon. It is intended merely to indicate the ways in which the various bases of administrative organization can be adopted and used concurrently by an enterprise.

A classification of operating expenses to reflect an organization with the main divisions established according to administrative functions would be:

2. *Operating expenses*
    21. Marketing
        211. Western district
        212. Central district
            2121. Commodity A
            2122. Commodity B
            2123. Commodity C
        213. Eastern district
    22. Production
    23. Personnel
    24. Finance
    25. Controllership

A *territorial organization* is one in which responsibility is apportioned in terms of geographical areas, with each executive in charge of all administrative tasks and all commodities in his territory. A classification of expenses to reflect the territorial organization illustrated above would appear somewhat as follows:

2. *Operating expenses*
    21. Western-district expenses
    22. Central-district expenses
        221. Marketing expenses
            2211. Commodity A
            2212. Commodity B
            2213. Commodity C
        222. Production expenses
        223. Personnel expenses
        224. Financial expenses
        225. Controllership expenses
    23. Eastern-district expenses

A *commodity organization* is one in which the main administrative responsibility is apportioned to members of the firm on the basis of the commodities (rather than on the basis of territories or functions). Executives are selected to manage all affairs relating to given classes of commodities, without regard to territorial limitations. For example, a manager placed in charge of commodity A would be responsible for all the business operations connected with the manufacture and distribution of commodity A. He would establish his own sales branches, employ his own salesmen, and be responsible to the chief executive only for results connected with commodity A.

The operating expenses classified with commodities as the major grouping would be listed as follows:

2. *Operating expenses*
    21. Commodity A
        211. Marketing
            2111. Western
            2112. Central
            2113. Eastern
        212. Production
        213. Personnel
        214. Finance
        215. Controllership
    22. Commodity B
    23. Commodity C

The commodity type of organization is useful only when the physical differences between commodities are so great as to make it impracticable for one group of employees to deal with more than one class of commodities. For example, the administrative organization of a coal-and-ice company might be separated on a commodity basis. Likewise a meat-packing establishment might dispose of its by-products, such as soap, glue, hides, and perfume through distinct and separate channels of distribution.

Most enterprises make use of all the foregoing bases of organization in the establishment of administrative authority and responsibility. Consequently the classification of accounts to be selected will need to reflect various tendencies in the organization of the enterprise. There is no one form of organization which is best for all purposes; nor any one basis of accounting classification which may be adopted to the exclusion of all others, even within the limits of a single enterprise.

The classification of accounting data according to administrative responsibility is applicable most naturally to business operations, particularly expense. Units of organization make it possible to trace the responsibility for certain expenses, and to remedy undesirable conditions as well as to understand the causes of desirable conditions. The classification of expenses may well follow the lines along which an enterprise is organized. The various types of organization present in the administration of an enterprise may all be reflected in the classification of expenses, either as major or minor divisions. In some cases, the broad grouping will be made according to functions; in others, the main divisions will be in terms of territories or commodities, with functions as minor subdivisions under each general heading.

The balance-sheet data are not, in general, amenable to classification according to administrative responsibility. The merchandise inventories may, of course, be classified in terms of territories or commodities; but even in such cases, the subdivisions are usually limited to the subsidiary records. As far as fixed assets are concerned, the basis of administrative responsibility usually cannot be adopted to any great degree. Permanent assets in different territories vary in character, depending upon whether the territories contain factories, are selling organizations, or are mere warehouses for the supply of goods. Fixed assets cannot be classified according to the types of commodities with any degree of success; for most assets are used in the production or distribution of all or several commodities jointly. Likewise, fixed assets cannot usually be separated in terms of functions; for a building might be used to contain executive offices for the sales manager, production manager, chief accountant, and others.

Classification by funds cuts across the groups separating status and operations.[1]—Governments by legislative enactment appropriate private funds of individuals for the general uses of the public. Certain portions of the appropriated funds are selected as the bases for segregating and grouping accounting data. Assets received, liabilities incurred, and various income and expense transactions are all recorded as subsidiary to the broad divisions of the appropriated funds. The assets, liabilities, incomes, and expenses of a single "fund" are sometimes listed with all the detail

[1] Classification according to financial appropriations or ventures is in reality a special application of the division according to use or purpose. It is of such general significance that it was thought best to separate it for discussion in this text.

of the accounts of an independent enterprise; in fact, the governments can be said to regard as a separate business venture the collection and expenditure of the wealth classified under each fund. The government classification of data according to funds has a counterpart in private enterprise where certain amounts of wealth are accounted for as separate business ventures. For example, a shipment of consigned goods is sometimes treated as if it were a separate financial entity. Only the net results of the transactions find their way into the general accounts of the enterprise. Building contractors also use the "fund" concept in segregating their accounting records. Each construction project may be treated as a separate business entity, being charged with a certain amount of wealth to be used in carrying it on. This fund is increased and decreased, by contract receipts and expenditures, until a final summarization indicates the gain or loss from the project and the final status of the fund. Not infrequently, short-term trading ventures are handled as separate business entities, even though all parties to the venture might be engaged in other enterprises. The temporary venture is established as a business entity, and the status and transactions of the venture are classified under the main heading.

Detailed classification of accounts.—The detailed illustrative classification of accounts shown below is an elaboration of the general groups set forth earlier in the chapter. The account titles should not be taken to represent the author's recommendation of an ideal classification. They merely indicate typical groups and accounts which might be encountered in the ledger of a large enterprise. Many of the general ledger accounts indicated here may, in fact, be supported by elaborate subsidiary records of the detailed items. Moreover, some enterprises might regard as subsidiary accounts some of the items mentioned in this classification. The numbering system for distinguishing the accounts is not a special characteristic of this or any other scheme of accounting classification. However, an adequate numbering system is often a very important factor in the use of accounting data. Numerical symbols often can be substituted in the accounting records for a complete description of the accounts affected by certain transactions.

DETAILED CLASSIFICATION OF ACCOUNTS

1. **Assets**
    - 11. *Current assets*
        - 111. Cash
            - 1111. Petty cash
            - 1112. Branch funds
            - 1113. Bank No. 1
            - 1114. Bank No. 2
        - 112. Notes receivable
        - 113. Accounts receivable
            - 1131. Customers (subsidiary ledger)
            - 1132. Office employees (subsidiary ledger)
            - 1133. Subscriptions receivable (subsidiary ledger)
        - 113*a*. Allowance for bad debts (cr. bal.)
        - 114. Interest receivable
        - 115. Merchandise inventory (subsidiary ledger)
        - 116. Raw materials (subsidiary ledger)
        - 117. Goods-in-process (subsidiary ledger)
        - 118. Supplies
            - 1181. Factory supplies
            - 1182. Office supplies
        - 119. Temporary investments (subsidiary ledger)
    - 12. *Deferred charges*
        - 121. Prepaid insurance
        - 122. Prepaid interest
        - 123. Prepaid taxes
        - 124. Prepaid rentals
        - 125. Prepaid general expenses
        - 126. Small tools
        - 127. Office supplies
    - 13. *Fixed assets*
        - 131. Furniture and fixtures (subsidiary ledger)
        - 131*a*. Allowance for depreciation
        - 132. Delivery equipment (subsidiary ledger)
        - 132*a*. Allowance for depreciation
        - 133. Office equipment (subsidiary ledger)
        - 133*a*. Allowance for depreciation
        - 134. Machinery (subsidiary ledger)
        - 134*a*. Allowance for depreciation
        - 135. Buildings (subsidiary ledger)
        - 135*a*. Allowance for depreciation
        - 136. Land

- 14. *Permanent investments*
    - 141. Land, buildings, etc. (subsidiary ledger)
    - 142. Stock of other companies (subsidiary ledger)
    - 143. Bonds and notes (subsidiary ledger)
    - 144. Government securities (subsidiary ledger)
    - 145. Sinking-fund assets
- 15. *Intangibles*
    - 151. Organization expenses
    - 152. Patents, trade-marks
    - 153. Franchises
    - 154. Good-will

2. **Liabilities**
    - 21. *Current liabilities*
        - 211. Accounts payable (subsidiary ledger)
        - 212. Notes payable
        - 213. Accrued expenses payable
            - 2131. Taxes payable
            - 2132. Interest payable
            - 2133. Wages payable
        - 214. Dividends payable
    - 22. *Deferred credits*
        - 221. Advance rentals and royalties
        - 222. Advance customers' deposits
    - 23. *Fixed liabilities*
        - 231. Mortgages payable
        - 232. Debentures payable
        - 233. Bonds payable (subsidiary ledger)

3. **Proprietorship**
    - 31. *Capital stock*
        - 311. Preferred stock (subsidiary ledger)
        - 312. Common stock (subsidiary ledger)
        - 313. Common stock, no par value (subsidiary ledger)
    - 32. *Capital stock premium*
    - 33. *Capital stock subscribed*
    - 34. *Reserves*
        - 341. Reserve for plant extension
        - 342. Reserve for bond redemption
        - 343. Reserve for contingencies
    - 35. *Surplus*

4. **Clearing Accounts**
    - 41. *Manufacturing*
    - 42. *Trading*
    - 43. *Profit and loss*

5. **Income**
  - 51. *Gross income*
    - 511. Sales (subsidiary ledger)
    - 511*a*. Sales returns
    - 511*b*. Sales allowances
  - 52. *Non-operating income*
    - 512. Interest
    - 513. Rentals
    - 514. Royalties
  - 52*a*. *Non-operating expenses* (debits)

6. **Expenses**
  - 61. *Production expenses*
    - 611. Raw materials
      - 6111. Materials purchases
      - 6111*a*. Purchases returns (credits)
      - 6111*b*. Purchase allowances (credits)
      - 6112. Incoming freight charges
    - 612. Direct labor costs
    - 613. Manufacturing overhead
      - 6131. Factory-office salaries
      - 6132. Factory-office supplies
      - 6133. Stores department expense
      - 6134. Receiving-department expense
      - 6135. Power, heat, and light
        - 61351. Fuel
        - 61352. Wages
        - 61353. Oil waste
        - 61354. Purchased power
      - 6136. Plant and equipment expense
        - 61361. Depreciation
        - 61362. Repairs
        - 61363. Insurance
        - 61364. Interest on investment
        - 61365. Property taxes
        - 61366. Watchmen's salaries
      - 6137. Personnel supervision
        - 61371. Foremen's salaries
        - 61372. Infirmary
        - 61373. Pensions
  - 62. *Marketing expenses*
    - 621. Buying expenses
      - 6211. Purchasing agent's office
        - 62111. Salaries
        - 62112. Office supplies

6212. Research bureau
- 62121. Salaries
- 62122. Office supplies

622. Selling expenses

6221. General office
- 62211. Sales salaries
- 62212. Sales-office supplies
- 62213. Sales-office maintenance

6222. Traveling sales force
- 62221. Salesmen's salaries
- 62222. Salesmen's expenses
  - 622221. Car fare
  - 622222. Automobile expense
  - 622223. Meals, hotel, etc.

6223. Branch offices
- 62231. Branch-office salaries
- 62232. Branch-office supplies
- 62233. Branch-office maintenance
  - 622331. Rent
  - 622332. Heat, light, taxes, etc.
  - 622333. Insurance

6224. Advertising
- 62241. Direct by mail
  - 622411. Letters
  - 622412. Posters
- 62242. Outdoor
  - 622421. Bill boards
  - 622422. Road signs
- 62243. Periodical
  - 622431. Newspapers
  - 622432. Magazines

6225. Delivery expenses
- 62251. Depreciation on equipment
- 62252. Salaries
- 62253. Supplies and fuel
- 62254. Repair and maintenance

63. *Financial expenses*

631. General supervision
- 6311. Treasurer's salary
- 6312. Treasurer's office salaries
- 6313. Treasurer's office supplies

632. Cashier's department
- 6321. Cashier's salary
- 6322. Cashier's office salaries
- 6323. Cashier's office supplies

633. Pay-roll department
  6331. Paymaster's salary
  6332. Paymaster's office salaries
  6333. Paymaster's office supplies
634 Interest
  6341. Short-term notes
  6342. Long-term notes
  6343. Bonds
    63431. Series A
    63432. Series B
635. Credits and collections
  6351. Salaries
  6352. Supplies
  6353. Sales discount
  6354. Purchase discount (credit)

64. *Personnel department*
641. Personnel manager's office
  6411. Salaries
  6412. Supplies
642. Personnel activities
  6421. Entertainment
  6422. Hospital care
  6423. Public relations

65. *Controller's office*
651. Accounting and statistics
  6511. Salaries
  6512. Supplies
652. Budgetary control
  6521. Salaries
  6522. Supplies
653. Office management
  6531. Salaries
  6532. Supplies

66. *Executive supervision*
661. General manager's office
  6611. Salaries
  6612. Supplies
662. Director's salaries and fees
  6621. Salaries
  6622. Expenses
663. Legal counsel
  6631. Stock and bond issues
  6632. Trade relations

This chapter should not close without reference to two other bases for differentiating broad classes of accounting data, namely, *real* vs. *nominal*, and *personal* vs. *impersonal*. Where these terms are used, real accounts are the balance-sheet accounts—assets, liabilities, and proprietorship; nominal accounts represent business operations—income and expense. The terms "real" and "nominal" arose out of the original concept of double-entry, by which the balance sheet as the expression of financial status was supposed to represent the actual or real condition of a business; whereas income and expense data merely described temporary phases of the business affairs. "Personal," as opposed to "impersonal" accounts are those which have to do directly with persons—customers, creditors, proprietors. Impersonal accounts are all others. This distinction arose out of double-entry technique which began with keeping accounts with persons, rather than things or events. This practice continued for some time, and was ultimately revised by introducing "impersonal" accounts with tangible property and business operations.

QUESTIONS ON CHAPTER XXXIII

1. "*Classification* may be said to be the first step in *interpretation;* it is the beginning of accounting analysis." Explain.
2. The terms "current" and "fixed" are used continuously with reference to assets and liabilities? Would these terms be applicable also to proprietorship, income, and expense? Discuss fully. What are the merits of the classification according to *intended uses* for the main divisions of accounting data?
3. What is meant by classification of accounting data according to *inherent qualities* or properties of objects or phenomena? Is it possible to determine whether an article, such as an automobile, is a current or fixed asset by considering the capacity, shape, or dimensions?
4. Why is the *form of administrative organization* important in the classification of accounts? Which form of organization is best adapted to a classification of accounting data—territorial, commodity, or functional? Explain fully what these terms mean.
5. Why is the form of organization of an enterprise less applicable to the classification of balance-sheet data than of income and expense data?
6. What is meant by classification in terms of *financial appropriations*, or *funds?* What are its advantages? Its disadvantages?

CHAPTER XXXIV

BALANCE SHEETS AND OTHER SUMMARIES OF FINANCIAL STATUS

Accounting reports are summarizations of the accounting data in such form that they can be used for purposes of control. Reports may be very simple, covering only single aspects of status or operations, or they may be very complex, dealing with the enterprise as a whole or with several enterprises.

Accounting reports differ in their form and content.—Accounting reports may be classified in various ways. Two bases of classifying them will be indicated here: tabular as distinguished from graphic; summarized as distinguished from detailed.

Tabular, as distinguished from graphic, reports.—The accounting data of a business enterprise are usually set forth in tables which subdivide and group the important facts. The balance sheet and the statement of income and expense are, of course, tabular reports. Subsidiary schedules also may be presented in tabular form; for example, the total sales of an enterprise may be analyzed and summarized with columns and rows of data to group sales according to territories and commodities. A tabular report may contain much significant and detailed information and is particularly useful to those who are willing to study it with care.

Graphic reports attempt to portray economic status or operations by appeal to the eye rather than by numbers; they take the forms of charts, diagrams, or pictures, with differences in value or amount represented by straight lines, curves, areas, or volume. Graphic reports have the advantage of being easy to read and of presenting general impressions and relationships quickly. They bring important points to the attention of the reader and force out of the picture much irrelevant detail. Consequently graphic presentation is exceedingly useful as a device for administrative control; it tends to conserve the time and energy of busy executives. Graphic charts do not lend themselves to the expression of detailed data, even though such data may be very important for making special administrative decisions. An attempt to make a graphic report contain a large amount of detailed information may result in making it exceedingly complex and difficult of interpretation.[1]

Summary, as distinguished from detailed, reports.—Accounting reports may be classified as those presenting data in summary and as those which are detailed reports. The relation between summary and detailed reports is much the same as the relation between controlling and subsidiary accounts. For example, a balance sheet may be looked upon as a financial summary of economic status. A schedule of accounts receivable would be a detailed report subsidiary to the amount shown in the balance sheet as totaling the accounts receivable from customers. A schedule of the cost of goods manufactured would be a subsidiary schedule supporting the "Cost-of-goods-manufactured" item in a statement of income and expense.

Balance sheets vary in form and arrangement.—The balance sheet is the general financial summary of economic status. It combines in one report the central financial facts of an enterprise. Balance sheets are all alike to the extent that each one sets forth a statement of the property and property rights of a single enterprise; but balance sheets are all different to the extent that the enterprises differ in their organization and activities and to the extent that balance-sheet data vary as to grouping, terminology, and sequence.

The balance sheet of the North American Manufacturing Company (see pp. 432–33) illustrates how the classification of accounts set forth in chapter xxxiii could be applied to actual conditions. The exact grouping and account titles are departed from slightly in the balance sheet for two reasons: first, to avoid the impression that the suggested classification is an ideal one;

[1] The problem of graphic presentation is an important one, on which much has been written. A discussion of the subject, although pertinent in a treatise on accounting method, is beyond the scope of this text. The reader will find the subject fully treated in such well-known books as K. Karsten's *Charts and Graphs* and W. C. Brinton's *Graphic Methods for Presenting Facts.*

NORTH AMERICAN MANUFACTURING COMPANY

BALANCE SHEET—DECEMBER 31, 1928

ASSETS

Current assets:			
Cash:			
In bank and on call		$ 8,342.00	
Branch working funds		10,960.00	$ 19,302.00
Notes receivable			41,000.00
Accounts receivable:			
Customer's accounts		$203,000.00	
Officers and employees		6,100.00	
Interest receivable		1,900.00	
		$211,000.00	
Allowance for bad debts		12,030.00	198,970.00
Inventories (market prices 12/31/28):			
Raw materials	$ 86,030.00		
Goods-in-process	40,000.00		
Supplies	15,000.00		
Merchandise	110,000.00	$251,030.00	
Reserve for market fluctuations		30,000.00	221,030.00
Total current assets			$ 480,302.00
Deferred charges:			
Prepaid insurance		$ 1,200.00	
Prepaid interest		200.00	
Office supplies		800.00	
Small tools		3,917.00	6,117.00
Fixed assets:			
Furniture and fixtures (cost)	$ 24,000.00		
Allowance for depreciation	5,000.00	$ 19,000.00	
Machinery (original cost)	$179,883.00		
Allowance for depreciation	60,000.00	119,883.00	
Buildings (reproduction cost 1/1/28)	$400,000.00		
Allowance for depreciation	180,000.00	220,000.00	
Land (appraised value 1/1/28)		60,000.00	418,883.00
Investments:			
Land (building site at 60th and Kenwood. Present market value $18,000), cost-value		$ 10,000.00	
Stock in Mason Manufacturing Company (100 shares at cost, $104. Present market, $130)		10,400.00	
Sinking-fund assets (government bonds)		15,040.00	
6% Bonds of Lorton Dredge Co		4,560.00	40,000.00
Intangibles:			
Patents, formulas, trade-marks (at cost of development, less depreciation)		$ 16,000.00	
Good-will (purchase price at time of acquiring property of Sheldon Mfg. Co.)		40,000.00	56,000.00
Total			$1,001,302.00

NORTH AMERICAN MANUFACTURING COMPANY

Balance Sheet—December 31, 1928

LIABILITIES AND PROPRIETORSHIP

Current liabilities:			
Notes payable		$ 30,000.00	
Accounts payable:			
Merchandise creditors	$119,850.00		
Accrued interest	1,000.00		
Accrued wages	3,300.00	124,150.00	
Dividends payable (1/15/29)		6,900.00	$ 161,050.00
Deferred credits to income:			
Advance rentals		$ 600.00	
Customers' deposits		19,415.00	20,015.00
Fixed liabilities:			
5% First mortgage (60th St. property)		$ 6,000.00	
6% Bonds (factory building)	$120,000.00		
Less unamortized discount	1,526.00	118,474.00	
6% Ten-year serial gold notes		24,000.00	
Debentures of Sheldon Mfg. Co.		20,000.00	168,474.00
Total liabilities			$ 349,539.00
Capital stock:			
7% Preferred stock:			
Authorized	$400,000.00		
Unissued	300,000.00		
In hands of public		$100,000.00	
Common stock Class A:			
Authorized	$200,000.00		
Unissued	50,000.00		
In hands of public		150,000.00	
Common stock (16,240 shares no par value)		159,160.00	409,160.00
Reserves:			
Land and building revaluation		$ 20,000.00	
Workmen's compensation		16,000.00	
Bond redemption		14,000.00	50,000.00
Surplus:			
Balance 12/31/27		$115,894.00	
Net profit—1928		114,625.00	
Total		$230,519.00	
Dividends (during year 1928):			
Preferred stock	$ 7,000.00		
Common A	15,000.00		
Common (no par)	15,916.00	37,916.00	192,603.00
Total			$1,001,302.00

and second, to illustrate the fact that no group of account titles can be adopted completely for the ledger of more than one enterprise. The reader should observe that many of the groups and individual items are explained by parenthetical data as to the basis of valuation; also that heavy lettering, indention, or other devices have been resorted to in an effort to make the balance sheet clear.

The balance sheet of the Stewart-Warner Speedometer Corporation (see p. 435) illustrates a typical arrangement and grouping of accounting data. Observe that three main classes are recognized on the asset side of the report: "Current assets," "Deferred charges," and "Capital assets" (fixed assets). The intangible assets are listed at a nominal value of $1.00. The right side of the balance sheet is headed "Liabilities," under which appear not only the conventional classes of current and fixed liabilities but also "Capital stock" and "Surplus."[1] Under the "Fixed liabilities" are shown certain long-term notes of a subsidiary corporation, the Bassick Alemite Corporation. The "Capital stock" section includes certain shares of preferred stock in the Bassick Company. This item represents preferred shares which are owned by the general public rather than by the Stewart-Warner Speedometer corporation. The common stock of the Bassick Alemite Corporation is owned by the Stewart-Warner Company completely; consequently the common shares of the subsidiary company do not appear on the "consolidated" balance sheet here presented. The method of "consolidating" balance-sheet data of different corporations will be discussed in later paragraphs of this chapter.

The balance sheet of the Coca-Cola Company (see p. 436) presents a different picture in its portrayal of financial status. The company owns no expensive fixed assets and has only a small investment in merchandise inventory. Its earnings are derived in large part from the monopolistic character of the Coca-Cola

[1] The practice of listing proprietorship as a liability of a corporation emphasizes strongly the fundamental similarity of the proprietary rights of creditors and stockholders. The corporation is envisaged as a separate entity standing between the assets and the persons who have contributed them. The corporation is thus said to owe liabilities not only to creditors but also to stockholders.

STEWART-WARNER SPEEDOMETER CORPORATION[1]

CONSOLIDATED BALANCE SHEET—DECEMBER 31, 1926

ASSETS

Current assets:			
Cash in banks and on hand	$1,480,807.12		
U.S. govt. securities	1,369,856.25		
Investments in marketable securities at cost	510,213.74	$ 3,360,877.11	
Accounts receivable	$4,778,993.97		
Notes receivable	180,062.35		
	$4,959,056.32		
Less reserve	239,309.70	4,719,746.62	
Inventories of finished goods, material, etc. (at cost or market, whichever lower)		6,207,380.75	$14,288,004.48
Deferred charges:			
Prepaid insurance, advertising, royalties, etc.			309,367.38
Capital assets:			
Land, buildings, machinery, and equipment:			
Balance at December 31, 1925		$19,034,912.24	
Additions since (net)		1,540,671.91	
		$20,575,584.15	
Deduct—Reserve for depreciation:			
Balance at December 31, 1925	$5,513,548.07		
Additions since (net)	913,593.04	6,427,141.11	14,148,443.04
Patents, trade-marks, trade-names, and good-will			1.00
			$28,745,815.90

LIABILITIES

Current liabilities:		
Accounts and vouchers payable	$ 909,402.54	
Taxes, royalties, etc., accrued	440,289.45	
Provision for federal income taxes	661,271.39	$ 2,010,963.38
Fixed liabilities:		
Bassick Alemite Corporation: Collateral Trust 7% serial gold notes		1,000,000.00
Capital stock:		
Bassick Co. preferred: 7,830 shares of $100 each	$ 783,000.00	
Stewart-Warner Speedometer Corporation Common: 599,990 shares of no par value	19,155,458.77	19,938,458.77
Surplus		5,796,393.75
		$28,745,815.90

[1] Taken from the annual report of the Stewart-Warner Speedometer Corporation for the fiscal year ended December 31, 1926.

THE COCA-COLA COMPANY, ATLANTA, GEORGIA, AND ITS SUBSIDIARIES

Consolidated Condensed Balance Sheet[1]—December 31, 1926

ASSETS		
Current:		
Cash on deposit and placed on call	$ 4,600,793.82	
Government securities	4,013.75	
Notes receivable	139,964.77	
Accounts receivable	1,268,552.82	
Inventory—Merchandise on hand, priced at lower of cost or market	1,727,494.14	$ 7,740,819.30
Other assets:		
Sundry notes and accounts receivable		441,760.93
Permanent:		
Land	$ 1,042,512.29	
Buildings	3,853,339.90	
Machinery and equipment	2,520,659.72	
Bottles and cases	521,345.39	
	$ 7,937,857.30	
Less: Allowance for depreciation	1,848,158.09	6,089,699.21
Formulas, trade-mark, and good-will		20,745,676.91
Deferred charges:		
Unexpired insurance and prepaid expenses		31,902.62
		$35,049,858.97
LIABILITIES		
Current:		
Notes payable—For real estate, due 1927	$ 10,000.00	
Accounts payable	687,918.09	
Accrued accounts	1,437.42	$ 699,355.51
Reserves:		
Income taxes, contingent and miscellaneous operating reserves		3,557,583.10
CAPITAL		
Capital stock:		
Common	$15,010,000.00	
Profit and loss—Surplus	15,782,920.36	30,792,920.36
		$35,049,858.97

[1] Footnote by company: "During the year 1926, 60,000 shares, or $6,000,000.00 of the preferred stock were retired, of which 46,667 shares, or $4,669,700.00, were purchased out of current earnings, and 13,303 shares, or $1,330,300.00, were in the treasury."

formulas and trade-marks, which are carried on the balance sheet as 60 per cent of the total assets of the enterprise. The main groupings of balance-sheet data correspond to the conventional divisions encountered in other balance sheets. The term "Permanent" is used to designate the fixed assets of the company. There are no bonds or other fixed liabilities.

Principles underlying the consolidation of balance sheets.— Two of the balance sheets which have been illustrated in this chapter have been designated as "consolidated" balance sheets. A consolidated balance sheet is a report in which the accounting data of several related enterprises are combined; it is useful for expressing the aggregate financial condition of several companies when some of the corporations own shares of stock in the other corporations. A consolidated balance sheet is particularly applicable to a condition where one enterprise owns large portions of the capital stock of one or more corporations. The company owning shares in the other corporations is the "parent" company; the others are "subsidiaries." Corporations are sometimes organized for the primary purpose of owning ("holding") stock in subsidiary enterprises; such corporations are known as "holding" companies, to distinguish them from the "operating" companies the shares of which they own. A parent company may, of course, be organized both to carry on certain operations and to hold stock in subsidiary corporations, the activities of which it controls. The balance sheet of a holding company would normally list as assets the values of the shares in the subsidiary companies. Such shares would appear in the "Investment" section of the holding-company balance sheet.[1]

The following problem indicates in very simple form the relation of the balance-sheet data of the subsidiary enterprises to the balance sheet of the holding company which owns their stock. It indicates also the way in which the data may be consolidated to show the total assets and liabilities of the combined enterprises. Assume that three companies exist: the A Company, an operating enterprise which also owns all the capital stock of two subsidiary

[1] Compare chapter xxvi, where the valuation of stock investments was discussed.

A COMPANY

BALANCE SHEET

ASSETS		LIABILITIES AND PROPRIETORSHIP	
Sundry assets	$175,000.00	Sundry liabilities	$ 80,000.00
B capital stock	60,000.00	Capital stock	125,000.00
C capital stock	45,000.00	Surplus	75,000.00
	$280,000.00		$280,000.00

B COMPANY

BALANCE SHEET

ASSETS		LIABILITIES AND PROPRIETORSHIP	
Sundry assets	$100,000.00	Sundry liabilities	$ 40,000.00
		Capital stock	60,000.00
	$100,000.00		$100,000.00

C COMPANY

BALANCE SHEET

ASSETS		LIABILITIES AND PROPRIETORSHIP	
Sundry assets	$ 95,000.00	Sundry liabilities	$ 50,000.00
		Capital stock	45,000.00
	$ 95,000.00		$ 95,000.00

corporations; the B Company; and the C Company. The condensed balance sheets of the three companies appear on page 438. The capital stock of B Company and of C Company appear on the balance sheet of A company at $60,000 and $45,000, respectively. The capital stock of the two subsidiaries thus finds a place both in the balance sheets of the subsidiary companies as *proprietorship* and in the balance sheet of the holding company as *assets*. The data of the three related enterprises may be combined —incorrectly, it will be shown—as follows:

COMBINED DATA OF A, B, AND C COMPANIES

Sundry assets A..	$175,000.00	Sundry liabilities A.......		$ 80,000.00
Sundry assets B..	100,000.00	Sundry liabilities B.......		40,000.00
Sundry assets C..	95,000.00	Sundry liabilities C.......		50,000.00
Capital stock B...	60,000.00			
Capital stock C...	45,000.00			$170,000.00
		Capital stock A..$	125,000	
		Surplus A......	75,000	
		Capital stock B..	60,000	
		Capital stock C..	45,000	
				$305,000.00
	$475,000.00			$475,000.00

The items "B capital stock" and "C capital stock" appear on both sides of the foregoing statement; obviously there is a duplication in the summary as it now stands. These amounts must be removed from each side of the combined statement of condition. After such removal, the balance sheet may be correctly set forth as follows:

CONSOLIDATED BALANCE SHEET OF A COMPANY AND SUBSIDIARIES

ASSETS		LIABILITIES AND PROPRIETORSHIP		
Sundry assets A..	$175,000.00	Sundry liabilities A........		$ 80,000.00
Sundry assets B..	100,000.00	Sundry liabilities B........		40,000.00
Sundry assets C..	95,000.00	Sundry liabilities C........		50,000.00
				$170,000.00
		Capital stock A.	$125,000.00	
		Surplus A.....	75,000.00	200,000.00
	$370,000.00			$370,000.00

The "Capital stock" totals of the two subsidiaries originally appeared on the balance sheet of the holding company as assets. These "net worths" were replaced in the A Company consolidated balance sheet by the "gross" assets and liabilities of the subsidiaries. The substitution was accomplished by first adding all of the balance-sheet data of the B and C companies to those of the A Company, and then removing the items "B capital stock" and "C capital stock" from each side of the combined statement. Usually the consolidated balance sheet does not differentiate the assets and liabilities of the holding company from those of the subsidiaries. They may be combined in the fashion suggested below:

A COMPANY (AND SUBSIDIARIES)
CONSOLIDATED BALANCE SHEET

ASSETS		LIABILITIES AND PROPRIETORSHIP	
Sundry assets.......	$370,000.00	Sundry liabilities....	$170,000.00
		Capital stock.......	125,000.00
		Surplus............	75,000.00
	$370,000.00		$370,000.00

In the consolidation of more elaborate balance sheets the same principle as illustrated above is followed. Similar assets and liabilities of the subsidiaries are merged in the consolidated balance sheets, and investments in the subsidiaries are eliminated from the list of the assets of the parent or holding company. In cases where the parent company owns most, but not all, of the stock of the subsidiary, the interest of minority stockholders should be shown separately as a special proprietorship item on the consolidated balance sheet. If the holding company owns only a minority of the stock of the subsidiary corporation, such assets and liabilities of the subsidiary corporation should not be included in the consolidated balance sheet. The capital stock of the subsidiary should appear merely as an investment held by the parent company, and should be shown under the usual classification of investment assets.[1]

The statement of affairs represents status previous to liquidation.—Balance sheets are prepared with one general assumption in mind; namely, that enterprises will continue to function in the

[1] Complete discussion of the problems of consolidating accounting reports may be found in G. H. Newlove's *Consolidated Balance Sheets*.

future as they have in the past. This assumption is sometimes referred to as the assumption of the "going-concern";[1] for the accountant prepares his data in expectation of continued operations. There are times, however, when a financial summary must be prepared in anticipation of immediate liquidation. Such expectation may give an entirely different set of values to the assets which express economic status. For example, the fixed assets, such as land and buildings, might be worth more or less at the current market prices than the values given to them in the books. The same thing might also be true of merchandise or accounts receivable—in fact, of any assets except the cash. Deferred charges and prepaid expenses, such as office supplies, prepaid taxes, rentals, or insurance, are often of slight value at time of liquidation.

A financial summary of economic status in which the assets are presented at liquidation values is known as a "statement of affairs." It is sometimes prepared by receivers of insolvent enterprises preparatory to liquidation for the benefit of creditors. The statement of affairs may segregate the liabilities as those "preferred," "fully secured," "partially secured," and "unsecured." Thus the various interested creditors and proprietors can tell from the statement whether or not they will probably lose any invested funds at the time of liquidation. In some cases, liquidation may have the effect of merely "impairing the capital" of the proprietors; in other cases, it may result in actual losses to the outside creditors. The statement of affairs is not frequently encountered in business practice; however, it may serve as a useful device for appraising economic status, even though an enterprise has no intention of discontinuing business operations. The difference between a balance sheet and a statement of affairs is essentially one of point of view. This difference is reflected in two aspects of the report: the valuation of the assets, and the arrangement of the assets and the liabilities. In the balance sheet, assets and liabilities are evaluated on the going-concern assumption; in the statement of affairs, the assets and liabilities are evaluated in anticipation of immediate liquidation. The data in the balance sheet are typically arranged according to certain uses or purposes; the

[1] Compare chapter xxii, where the going-concern assumption was introduced as an underlying consideration in balance-sheet valuation.

assets and liabilities in the statement of affairs are arranged according to the conditions under which they will be realized or paid.[1]

QUESTIONS ON CHAPTER XXXIV

1. Observe the "Capital asset" section of the Stewart-Warner balance sheet. It shows the amount of assets on hand at the beginning of the period, the amount procured (additions), the amount disposed of (additions to depreciation reserve), and the balance at the end of the period. Is this statement analogous in any degree to the cost-of-goods-sold section on a statement of income and expense? Would it be possible or desirable to have all assets thus shown on the balance sheet?
2. The Stewart-Warner balance sheet lists the government securities and certain other "marketable securities" in the balance sheet among the "Current assets." What does this treatment imply as to the purpose for which the bonds are held; also as to the general financial status of the enterprise?
3. Notice the large amount of "cash" shown in the balance sheet of the Coca-Cola Company; also the portion of the total assets which consist of "Formulas, trade-marks, and good-will." Compare them with the proportions of similar assets on other balance sheets shown in this chapter.
4. The Federal Reserve balance sheet (see pp. 448–49) classifies cash, receivables, and inventories as *quick* assets, but excludes temporary investments from this group. In general, do you think this distinction is justified and well drawn? Can you think of any case where the investments might be more easily liquidated than the other current assets?
5. What advantages do you see in the division of current liabilities (that is, "Bills, notes, and accounts payable") into *secured* and *unsecured?* Is this division of more importance for a liquidating concern than for a going-concern?
6. The Federal Reserve balance sheet lists good-will as a deduction from capital stock and surplus rather than as an asset. Criticize this treatment, showing its advantages and disadvantages. Is it possible that such treatment might be helpful in comparison of the balance sheets of different companies? Might it at times also work an injustice to firms which have large amounts of good-will on their statements?
7. The Ohio Public Service Company balance sheet (see pp. 446–47) lists the following items as assets in its balance sheet: "Discount on capital stock," "Treasury stock," "Discount on bonds." Discuss other methods of treating these items.
8. How much of the "Surplus" on the Ohio Public Service Company balance sheet could be classed as "available"?

[1] Complete discussion of the form and preparation of a *statement of affairs* may be found in any of the following works: Hatfield, *Modern Accounting*, chap. xxi; Finney, *Principles of Accounting*, Vol. I, chaps. xxi, xxii; Kester, *Accounting Theory and Practice*, II, 644–59.

9. Why must the "investment" accounts of a holding company be eliminated from the balance sheet when the assets and liabilities of the subsidiaries are consolidated with those of the holding company?
10. What is a statement of affairs? What basic assumption of accounting valuation is ignored when the statement of affairs is prepared? How does the statement of affairs differ from the balance sheet?

APPENDIX TO CHAPTER XXXIV

The following balance sheets illustrate further some of the differences of form and content encountered in modern business practice. No attempt is made to give a complete list of all types of balance sheets, nor do the accompanying explanations discuss all of the important points which may be raised in connection with each statement. The reader should study these reports to observe the wide variety of terms which may appear in financial reports; he should also observe the difficulty encountered in trying to discover financial condition solely from the data of a balance sheet. The balance sheet, of itself, does not tell the reader what detailed items are included under each caption, nor does it usually give him any clue as to the bases of valuation adopted for establishing the amounts included in the reports.

The investment of the Yellow Cab Company (see p. 444) in cabs and equipment includes over 60 per cent of the total assets of the enterprise. Among the assets appears a heading entitled "Investments"; this includes the stock of the Hertz Drivurself Stations, Inc., a subsidiary company which rents automobiles to the general public at a fixed rate per mile or per hour. Intangible assets are shown at approximately one million dollars. The company has issued no bonds. The item "Reserve" appears in three places: to indicate the reserve for taxes (liability); to show the surplus appropriated to offset losses from injuries and damages (proprietorship); and to show the amount of accrued depreciation on cabs, equipment, etc. (asset deduction).

The balance sheet of the Woodlawn Trust and Savings Bank (see p. 445) is set forth under the heading "Statement of Condition." Its two columns are headed "Resources" and "Liabilities," respectively. Two items are worthy of special note. Among the assets the item "Loans and discounts" represents 60 per cent of the total resources. This resource is the amount receivable in

CHICAGO YELLOW CAB COMPANY, INC.[1]

Consolidated Balance Sheet—December 31, 1926

ASSETS		
Cash		$ 1,181,710.85
Accounts receivable		508,198.48
Notes receivable		4,300.00
Inventories of materials and supplies (at cost)		240,968.79
Insurance, etc., prepaid		113,319.37
Yellow Cab Company—Investment Department (representing accounts due by subscribers to stock of the Chicago Yellow Cab Company, Inc.)		658,729.94
Investments:		
Hertz Drivurself Stations, Inc., stock	$252,500.00	
Sundry	10,000.00	262,500.00
Special deposits		117,400.00
Deferred charges, including leasehold improvements being amortized over the terms of the leases		314,696.68
Cabs, equipment, etc		6,508,886.97
Good-will, privileges, and franchises		1,031,653.81
		$10,942,364.89

LIABILITIES AND CAPITAL		
Accounts payable		$ 437,856.70
Bonuses to officers and employees		496,510.10
Reserve for taxes:		
Federal income tax	$370,617.30	
Local taxes	75,176.07	
		445,793.37
Notes payable—banks:		
Yellow Cab Company—Investment Department (see contra)		968,991.81
Reserve for injuries and damages		400,352.83
Reserve for depreciation of cabs, equipment, etc		1,804,244.41
Capital stock:		
Authorized and issue—400,000 shares of no par value		2,200,000.00
Surplus		4,188,615.67
As at December 31, 1926		$10,942,364.89

[1] Taken from the annual report to the stockholders, 1926, Chicago Yellow Cab Company, Inc.

the form of notes (secured and unsecured) from customers of the bank. The largest liability is entitled "Deposits" and represents the liability to customers who have deposited funds in the custody of the bank.

The balance sheet of the Ohio Public Service Company (see pp. 446–47) presents an array of assets different from those of an industrial or financial firm. The current assets are a relatively small portion of the total resources of the company; in fact, almost 90 per cent of the total assets are *fixed* in character. The customers' accounts receivable are less than 2 per cent of the total

THE WOODLAWN TRUST AND SAVINGS BANK[1]
CHICAGO, ILLINOIS

STATEMENT OF CONDITION

RESOURCES		LIABILITIES	
Loans and discounts	$ 6,389,074.88	Capital stock	$ 500,000.00
Overdrafts	2,138.15	Surplus and profits.	460,094.82
Stocks and bonds	2,769,759.48	Reserve for interest and taxes	11,568.91
Customers' liability on letter of credit	4,300.00	Liability under letters of credit	4,300.00
Stock Federal Reserve Bank	21,000.00	Due Federal Reserve Bank	100,000.00
Furniture and fixtures	78,995.64	Deposits	9,415,786.87
Real estate	10,678.49		
Cash and due from banks	1,205,803.96		
Total	$10,491,750.60	*Total*	$10,491,750.60

assets; whereas the accounts receivable for other than electric service are approximately 3 per cent. The balance sheet includes no appreciable amount for merchandise salable to the public. The Stores and Supplies account includes unused materials for repairs and maintenance, as well as moderate stocks of electric appliances. The merchandise of the Ohio Public Service Company is electric power, an asset which is not stored. Electric power is a service rather than a commodity; it can be delivered to the customers only as they use it for lighting or industrial purposes, and does not accumulate during a period of business operations.

A uniform balance sheet has been prepared by the Federal Reserve Board (see pp. 448–49) for use by enterprises requesting

[1] As made to the auditor of public accounts, December 31, 1926.

credit from member banks. The subdivision of the data makes it possible for the statement to be used by different types of enterprises. The general groups, however, are clearly indicated in the suggested outline for the balance-sheet data.

THE OHIO PUBLIC SERVICE COMPANY

CONDENSED BALANCE SHEET—DECEMBER 31, 1926

ASSETS

Capital assets:			
Plant and investment		$45,652,358.56	
Discount on capital stock		461,853.41	
Treasury stock (preferred):			
Held in treasury	$832,800.00		
Less undelivered subscriptions	706,700.00	126,100.00	
Securities owned		25,607.92	
Sinking fund		259,155.01	
Total capital assets			$46,525,074.90
Current assets:			
Store and supplies		$ 905,068.57	
Notes receivable		139,191.34	
Customers' accounts receivable (current monthly)		875,946.64	
Merchandise sales and securities sales and other accounts receivable (less reserve for bad debts)		1,606,057.38	
Cash		497,109.22	
Total current assets			4,023,373.15
Other assets:			
Accounts receivable—Affiliated companies		$ 32,937.94	
Accounts receivable—Parent Company		305,488.90	
Special cash deposits (paving fund, etc.)		7,375.45	
Expenses paid in advance		227,505.62	
Discount on bonds		2,029,468.85	
Property amortization account		1,635,793.85	
Securities deposited with us (see contra)		1.00	
Endorsement recourse (contra)		300.00	
Total other assets			4,238,871.61
Total assets			$54,787,319.66

THE OHIO PUBLIC SERVICE COMPANY

CONDENSED BALANCE SHEET—DECEMBER 31, 1926

LIABILITIES

Capital stock:		
Preferred stock (see Schedule A)	$12,823,200.00	
Common stock	7,689,000.00	
Total capital stock		$20,512,200.00
Funded debt:		
Underlying bonds (see Schedule B)	$ 4,130,700.00	
First mortgage and refunding gold bonds (see Schedule C)	23,525,000.00	
Car trust certificates	8,333.54	
Total funded debt		27,664,033.54
Other capital liabilities:		
U.S. Government Loan	$ 250,000.00	
Municipal paving assessments	26,227.76	
Total other capital liabilities		276,227.76
Current liabilities:		
Notes payable	$ 150,000.00	
Notes receivable discounted	3,228.82	
Accounts payable	520,395.04	
Federal taxes accrued	267,248.56	
Interest, other taxes, etc., accrued	1,162,937.54	
Total current liabilities		2,103,809.96
Other liabilities:		
Customers and line extension deposits	$ 295,472.69	
Accounts payable—Affiliated companies	27,357.49	
Securities deposited with us (contra)	1.00	
Endorsement liability (see contra)	300.00	
Total other liabilities		323,131.18
Surplus and reserves:		
Replacement reserve	$ 2,880,600.31	
Contingent surplus	182,598.81	
Surplus	844,718.10	
Total surplus and reserves		3,907,917.22
Total liabilities		$54,787,319.66

UNIFORM BALANCE SHEET RECOMMENDED BY FEDERAL RESERVE BOARD

ASSETS

Current assets:		
Cash:		
1*a*. Cash on hand—currency and coin	......	......
1*b*. Cash in bank	......	......
Notes and accounts receivable:		
3. Notes receivable of customers on hand	......	
5. Notes receivable discounted or sold with indorsement or guaranty	......	
7. Accounts receivable, customers	......	
Less—		
13. Provisions for bad debts	......	......
14. Provisions for discounts, freights, allowances, etc.	......	......
Inventories:		
17. Raw material on hand	......	
19. Goods in process	......	
21. Uncompleted contracts	......	
Less payments on account thereof	......	
23. Finished goods on hand	......	
		......
Other quick assets (describe fully)	......	
....	......	
....	......	......
Total quick assets (excluding all investments)	......	......
25. Securities readily marketable and salable without impairing the business, stockholders, or employees	......	......
Total current assets		......
Fixed assets:		
31. Land used for plant	......	
33. Buildings used for plant	......	
35. Machinery	......	
37. Tools and plant equipment	......	
39. Patterns and drawings	......	
41. Office furniture and fixtures	......	
43. Other fixed assets, if any (describe fully)	......	
45. (Less) Reserves for depreciation	......	......
Total fixed assets	......	
Deferred charges:		
47. Prepaid expenses, interest, insurance, taxes, etc.	......	......
Other assets:		
49.	......	......
Total assets	......	......

LIABILITIES

Current liabilities:			
	Bills, notes, and accounts payable:		
	Unsecured bills and notes:		
2.	Acceptances made for merchandise or raw material purchased	......	
4.	Notes given for merchandise or raw material purchased	......	
6.	Notes given to banks for money borrowed	......	
8.	Notes sold through brokers	......	
10.	Notes given for machinery, additions to plant, etc.	......	
12.	Notes due to stockholders, officers, or employees	......	......
	Unsecured accounts:		
14.	Accounts payable for purchases (not yet due)	......	
16.	Accounts payable for purchases (past due)	......	
18.	Accounts payable to stockholders, officers, or employees	......	
	Secured liabilities:		......
20a.	Notes receivable discounted or sold with indorsement or guaranty (contra)	......	
20b.	Customers' accounts discounted or assigned (contra)	......	
20c.	Obligations secured by liens on inventories	......	
			......
22.	Accrued liabilities (interest, taxes, wages, etc.)	......	
	Other current liabilities (describe fully):		
	....	......	......
	....	......	......
	Total current liabilities		......
Fixed liabilities:			
24.	Mortgages on plant (due date ......)	......	
26.	Mortgages on other real estate (due date ......)	......	
28.	Chattel mortgage on machinery or equipment (due date ......)	......	
30.	Bonded debt (due date ......)	......	......
32.	Other fixed liabilities (describe fully)	......	......
	....	......	
	....	......	......
	Total liabilities		......

NET WORTH

34.	If a corporation—		
	a) Preferred stock	......	
	b) Common stock	......	
	c) Surplus and undivided profits	......	
	Less—		
	d) Book value of good-will	......	
	e) Deficit	......	......
36.	If an individual or partnership—		
	a) Capital	......	......
	b) Undistributed profits or deficit	......	......
	Total		......

CHAPTER XXXV

SUMMARIES OF BUSINESS OPERATIONS

This chapter continues the discussion of accounting reports, directing attention to the problems of preparing summaries of business operations, as well as to some general principles to be observed in the preparation of all types of accounting reports.

Summaries of business operations vary in form and content to serve the needs of each enterprise.—The published summaries of business operations are ordinarily of the "condensed" form, giving only the barest outlines of the nature of the income and expense transactions. This condition is characteristic, not only of the reports circulated for public inspection, but also of those distributed to stockholders of the corporation. Not infrequently the statement of income and expense consists merely of a statement that a certain net profit has been realized. For example, one well-known manufacturing concern, which set before its stockholders a complete and well-classified balance sheet, included in its annual report the following as a statement of operations:

Profit and *Income* for the nine months, after deducting all manufacturing, selling and administrative expenses, including adequate provisions for discounts and losses on doubtful accounts, depreciation on plant and equipment, but before providing for federal income tax:		
Three months ending March 31....	$1,200,000.00	
Three months ending June 30......	1,700,000.00	
Three months ending September 30..	1,850,000.00	$4,750,000.00
Less provision for federal income tax................		560,000.00
Net profit............................		$4,190,000.00

Types of summaries of business operations.—The statement of income and expense is the summary of business operations most commonly prepared; it is a very important summary and serves to inform the management of an enterprise as to the transactions

NORTH AMERICAN MANUFACTURING COMPANY

Statement of Income and Expense—For the Year Ended December 31, 1928

Sales			$1,660,000.00
Sales returns and allowances			13,000.00
Net sales			$1,647,000.00
Cost of goods sold:			
Cost of goods manufactured		$999,152.00	
Decrease in inventory		24,000.00	1,023,152.00
Gross profit on sales			$ 623,848.00
Operating expenses:			
Buying expenses:			
Purchasing agent's office	$12,000.00		
Research bureau	9,000.00	$ 21,000.00	
Selling expenses:			
Sales manager's office	$ 30,100.00		
Traveling sales force	138,010.00		
Branch offices	60,008.00		
Advertising	75,000.00		
Delivery expenses	18,000.00	321,118.00	
Financial administration:			
Treasurer's office	$ 15,004.00		
Cashier's department	10,020.00		
Pay-roll department	5,006.00		
Interest expense	25,006.00		
Credits and collections	12,098.00	67,134.00	
Personnel administration:			
Personnel manager's office	$ 7,115.00		
Welfare work	4,428.00		
Public relations	8,323.00	19,866.00	
Controller's office:			
Accounting and statistics	$ 30,004.00		
Budgetary control	12,048.00		
Office management	7,100.00	49,152.00	
Executive supervision:			
General manager's office	$ 22,048.00		
Directors fees and expenses	5,199.00		
Legal counsel	8,601.00	35,848.00	514,118.00
Operating profit			$ 109,730.00
Non-operating transactions:			
Income:			
Interest on investments	$ 1,000.00		
Royalties on patents	1,495.00		
Rent of warehouse space	2,600.00	$ 5,095.00	
Expenses:			
Repairs to accommodate tenant		200.00	4,895.00
Net profit			$ 114.625.00

which have resulted in increases or decreases of proprietorship during a period of time. The statement of income and expense has, however, two limitations as a complete summary of the business operations of an enterprise. First, it summarizes only the transactions which affect proprietorship, which is merely one of numerous balance-sheet items. The statement of income and expense gives no indication as to the various assets which have been increased or decreased or the liabilities which have been incurred or paid off. There are many other balance-sheet items which are of such importance that the transactions which affect their status might also be summarized as statements of business operations. Cash transactions, for example, are sometimes set forth in a "statement of cash receipts and expenditures."

Merchandise transactions illustrate another type which are of such importance that they might well be set forth in a special statement. Of course, the merchandise transactions are at times included in the portion of the statement of income and expense entitled "Cost of goods sold." This section might, however, be described more correctly as the "Statement of goods received and expended," or "Cost of goods purchased and sold." The cost-of-goods-sold section of a summary of business operations is essentially a transcript of the ledger data which affect the asset "Merchandise." Not infrequently the details of this section are removed entirely from the statement of income and expense, with only the resulting "Cost of goods sold" appearing as an expense item. Likewise a statement of the "Cost of goods manufactured" may also be prepared as a separate subsidiary schedule.

The second limitation of the statement of income and expense is that it does not necessarily account for all changes in proprietorship. Some transactions affect proprietorship directly, without passing through the income or expense classification. Illustrations of such transactions are the declarations of dividends, reservation of surplus, and sale or purchase of capital stock or bonds at prices other than par. To set forth all the various types of operations which affect proprietorship, a "statement of surplus" is sometimes also prepared. This statement reconciles the changes in surplus between the dates of successive balance sheets.

Statements of business operations vary in form and content.—The summaries of business operations vary greatly in their form and content. Any group of business operations may conceivably be summarized for use in administrative control. On the following pages the statements of business operations illustrate the differences in arrangement and classification which are encountered in practice.

NORTH AMERICAN MANUFACTURING COMPANY

SCHEDULE OF COST OF GOODS MANUFACTURED—DURING YEAR ENDED DECEMBER 31, 1928

Raw materials consumed:			
Inventory 12/31/27	$120,000.00		
Purchases	400,000.00		
	$520,000.00		
Inventory 12/31/28	85,000.00		$ 435,000.00
Direct labor			350,152.00
Manufacturing overhead:			
Factory office		$ 24,800.00	
Stores department		16,200.00	
Receiving department		12,300.00	
Power, heat, light		39,700.00	
Plant expenses:			
Indirect labor	$ 11,000.00		
Depreciation	34,000.00		
Repairs	23,200.00		
Supplies	4,800.00		
Maintenance	29,000.00		
Insurance	4,200.00		
Taxes	1,800.00	108,000.00	
Supervision		22,000.00	223,000.00
			$1,008,152.00
Goods in process 12/31/27		$ 31,000.00	
Goods in process 12/31/28		40,000.00	9,000.00
Cost of goods manufactured			$ 999,152.00

The first illustration is the statement of income and expense for the North American Manufacturing Company (see p. 451). This statement presents the income and expense data in accord with the typical classification set forth in chapter xxxiii. In many instances, however, both groupings and account titles have been changed. The "statement of income and expense" contains merely

THE COCA-COLA COMPANY, ATLANTA, GEORGIA, AND ITS SUBSIDIARIES[1]

CONSOLIDATED STATEMENT OF OPERATIONS—YEAR ENDED DECEMBER 31, 1926

PROFIT AND LOSS ACCOUNT

Sales			$30,107,272.29
Less: *Cost of goods sold*, including freight on sales and allowances			12,352,117.10
Gross operating profit			$17,755,155.19
Expenses—Selling, branch, administrative, and general			6,076,686.68
Net operating profit			$11,678,468.51
Other deductions, including income taxes, and contingent and miscellaneous operating reserves			3,274,814.88
Net profit			$ 8,403,653.63

SURPLUS ACCOUNT

Balance, December 31, 1925			$10,916,860.85
Net profits from operations for year ended December 31, 1926		$8,403,653.63	
Expense adjustments, prior years		118,441.87	8,522,095.50
			$19,438,956.35
Deduction for dividends:			
Preferred:			
July 1, 1926		156,035.99	
Common:			
March 28, 1926	$875,000.00		
June 29, 1926	875,000.00		
September 28, 1926	875,000.00		
December 28, 1926	875,000.00	3,500,000.00	3,656,035.99
Balance, December 31, 1926			$15,782,920.36

the net figure of "cost of goods manufactured." The details of this item are set forth in a schedule on page 453, entitled "North American Manufacturing Company, Schedule of Cost of Goods Manufactured."

[1] Taken from the annual report to stockholders, The Coca-Cola Company, Atlanta, Georgia.

The Coca-Cola Company's "statement of operations" (see p. 454) consists of two parts—the Profit and Loss account and the Surplus account.[1] The data of the Profit and Loss account set forth the total income and expense as summarized items; they are arranged in the conventional sequence usually adopted for a statement of income and expense. The Surplus account indicates the fact that the net profit is only one of the factors which have caused changes in the corporate surplus; other factors are the adjustments for previous years' expenses and the declaration of dividends on the outstanding stock of the corporation.

The "consolidated income account" of the Orpheum Circuit, Inc., and Subsidiaries displays data which are different from those of the ordinary commercial or industrial enterprise. The statement includes no cost-of-goods-sold item; for the product of the company is the entertainment which it provides patrons, and cannot be carried as an inventory of merchandise on hand. The Surplus account data are set forth in two columns—one, "Earned Surplus," the other "Capital Surplus."[2]

The business operations of a professional society consist essentially of the receipts and disbursements of cash. The "statement of income and expense" of the Illinois Society of Certified Public Accountants (see p. 458) illustrates this point. No merchandise is sold, nor is any inventory of salable goods held in stock. Copies of the annual publications are distributed gratuitously to all members. The assets consist entirely of cash and amounts receivable from members. The fixed assets are listed in the balance sheet for purposes of information only. The liabilities include "Accounts payable" and two deferred-income items entitled "Dues paid in advance" and "Membership fees, applications pending." The proprietorship is shown under the heading "Accumulated revenue."

The Federal Reserve Board has recommended an arrangement of income and expense data for use by firms when applying for

[1] The term "account" is often used in practice as synonymous with "statement," the implication being that each report is prepared directly from the data in the Profit and Loss account or in the Surplus account.

[2] See chapter xxx, "Valuation of Corporate Proprietorship," for a discussion of the meaning and use of the terms "earned surplus" and "capital surplus."

ORPHEUM CIRCUIT, INC., AND SUBSIDIARIES[1]

Consolidated Income and Surplus Accounts—For the Year Ending December 31, 1926

INCOME ACCOUNT

Gross income:		
Box-office receipts		$16,719,806.69
Rents, concessions, and other income		1,930,441.52
		$18,650,248.21
Expenses:		
Artists' salaries and film service	$6,726,149.98	
Other salaries	4,583,187.26	
Operating expenses and theatre overhead	3,718,576.15	
Interest and discount	444,415.06	
		15,472,328.45
Operating income, before deducting depreciation		$ 3,177,919.76
Deductions:		
Depreciation of buildings and fixtures	$ 621,910.53	
Amortization of leaseholds	169,830.16	
		791,740.69
Net income from operations		$ 2,386,179.07
Less: Reserved for contingencies		300,000.00
Net income, carried to "Earned surplus"		$ 2,086,179.07

SURPLUS ACCOUNT

	Earned Surplus	Capital Surplus
Surplus, December 31, 1925	$3,787,713.54	$30,653,641.53
Add: Net income for year 1926, as above	2,086,179.07	
	$5,873,892.61	$30,653,641.53
Deduct:		
Loss on disposition of leasehold property acquired in organization of company		$ 3,889,863.69
Prior year taxes paid in excess of accruals	$ 7,212.47	
Dividends paid on preferred stock	501,063.33	
Dividends paid on common stock	1,093,274.43	
	$1,601,550.23	$ 3,889,863.69
Surplus, December 31, 1926	$4,272,342.38	$26,763,777.84

[1] Taken from the annual report to stockholders of the Orpheum Circuit, Inc., and Subsidiaries.

loans to member banks. The sequence and grouping of data in this "statement of profit and loss" (see p. 460) provide for a functional classification of operating expenses; also for adjustments to reflect "other income." The blank forms for use by customers of the member banks are arranged in such manner that applicants may present a three-year comparative statement of profit and loss.

The term "gross income" on the Federal Reserve Board statement is equivalent to total "net profit" plus "non-operating income"; in a sense this amount is similar to the gross "income" as defined by the Federal Reserve Act. A difference arises, of course, out of the fact that the Federal Revenue Act excludes many items of income from taxation, and hence from the "inclusions," when prescribing items of "gross income." The term "gross income," as well as the term "deductions from income," is, of course, given an entirely different meaning in another portion of this text (chap. xii).

Accounting reports should possess certain features to insure their greatest usefulness.—Accounting reports are prepared for use. They should contain such information and be arranged in such form that they are of the greatest possible value to the interested persons. Certain characteristics of accounting reports fulfil the main purposes for which they are prepared. Among them are: simplicity, completeness, comparability, and clearness.

Simplicity.—Accounting reports should be simple. They should contain no irrelevant details and should, where practicable, be reduced to terms which are easily understood. Well-planned graphic reports usually meet this requirement admirably. However, there are cases where graphic reports are so poorly prepared that the accountant's attempts at simplicity are frustrated by his inexperience in graphic presentation. Condensed and brief tabular reports usually have the advantage of simplicity; they frequently are exceedingly useful in the presentation of central facts of financial status in a "condensed" balance sheet. The value of simplicity is limited, of course, by the inadequacy of the information for some purposes. Simplicity should not be confused with inadequacy; where simplification results in mere vagueness it cannot be regarded as a desirable procedure.

ILLINOIS SOCIETY OF CERTIFIED PUBLIC ACCOUNTANTS[1]

Balance Sheet—August 31, 1927

Assets:	
Cash	$2,391.06
Accounts receivable	51.67
Furniture and library, nominal value	1.00
	$2,443.73
Liabilities:	
Accounts payable	$ 324.00
Dues paid in advance	773.75
Membership fees, applications pending	160.00
	$1,257.75
Accumulated revenue	1,185.98
	$2,443.73

Statement of Income and Expenses—For the Year Ended August 31, 1927

Income:			
Annual dues		$5,266.26	
Entrance fees, 66 new members		330.00	
Interest		46.45	
			$5,642.71
Expenses:			
Quarterly and special meetings, less refunds		$ 413.90	
Annual golf tournament		207.36	
Printing and stationery		566.13	
Postage		312.00	
Year books		328.30	
Additions to library		8.00	
Medals		33.40	
Engrossing certificates		178.60	
Legislation and legal expenses, less specific contributions		951.00	
Secretary's allowance		75.00	
Services of secretary's assistant		175.00	
Miscellaneous		180.66	
Executive secretary's office (8 mos.)—			
Salaries	$3,028.44		
Rent	800.00		
Other expenses	506.05		
Furniture and equipment	490.50		
	$4,824.99		
Less: Contributions by members and firms	3,010.00		
		1,814.99	5,244.34
Excess of income over expenses			$ 398.37
Accumulated revenue, August 31, 1926			787.61
Accumulated revenue, August 31, 1927, as per balance sheet			$1,185.98

[1] Taken from annual report for the fiscal year ended August 31, 1927.

We have examined the accounts and records of the ILLINOIS SOCIETY OF CERTIFIED PUBLIC ACCOUNTANTS for the fiscal year ended August 31, 1927, and we certify that, in our opinion, the foregoing statements correctly reflect the financial condition of the Society as at August 31, 1927, and the income and expenses for the year ended on that date.

Chicago, September 10, 1927

WM. P. HAUWORTH
K. B. ELLIOTT } *Auditors*

Completeness.—Accounting reports should be complete; that is to say, they should contain all important material, with no omissions of data which are of value to the person examining the report. Completeness is not synonymous with complexity; for a report may be complete yet still be simple. Moreover, a report may be complete and still be short. Completeness may be defined as follows: "As long and complex as necessary, yet as short and simple as possible." Obviously this rule is much easier to state than to apply. Its meaning will become clearer with further discussion.

Comparability.—It is very important at times for business administrators to compare the results of different types of activity; consequently reports should, where possible, be prepared in such a manner that the data can be compared with those on other reports. It is impossible, for example, to compare $100 worth of merchandise with 24 pounds of merchandise. The reports to be comparable must be phrased in the *same* units of measure. Even the dollar itself is not always a constant unit of measure and is often unsatisfactory for a comparison of the fixed assets of an enterprise at moments of time. A building which was listed at a financial value of $10,000 at one time might be assigned a still higher financial value twenty years later. A comparison of the fixed assets of an enterprise, where such a condition prevailed, might well be accompanied by comments as to fluctuations in general price levels.

If reports covering similar facts are to be comparable over periods of time, or at the same time, the data should be similarly arranged. Consequently, uniformity in report construction plays a very important rôle in accounting control. Uniformity in bal-

COMPARATIVE STATEMENT OF PROFIT AND LOSS—FOR YEARS ENDING ______, 19__

(FEDERAL RESERVE BOARD FORM)

	Year Ending		
	19__	19__	19__
Gross sales	$......	$......	$......
Less outward freight, allowances, and returns	......	......	......
Net sales	......	......	......
Inventory beginning of year	......	......	......
Purchases, net	......	......	......
Less inventory end of year	......	......	......
Cost of sales	......	......	......
Gross profit on sales	......	......	......
Selling expenses (itemized to correspond with ledger accounts kept)	......	......	......
Total selling expense	......	......	......
General expenses (itemized to correspond with ledger accounts kept)	......	......	......
Total general expense	......	......	......
Administrative expenses (itemized to correspond with accounts kept)	......	......	......
Total administrative expenses	......	......	......
Total expenses	......	......	......
Net profit on sales	......	......	......
Other income:			
Income from investments	......	......	......
Interest on notes receivable, etc.	......	......	......
Gross income	......	......	......
Deductions from income			
Interest on bonded debt	......	......	......
Interest on notes payable	......	......	......
Total deductions	......	......	......
Net income—Profit and loss	......	......	......
Add special credits to profit and loss	......	......	......
Deduct special charges to profit and loss	......	......	......
Profit and loss for period	......	......	......
Surplus beginning of period	......	......	......
Dividends paid	......	......	......
Surplus ending of period	......	......	......
	......	......	......

ance-sheet construction makes it possible, for example, to compare the total current assets of one enterprise with the total current assets of another similar concern. Likewise, uniformity makes it possible to compare certain ratios appearing on different financial reports. Comparison of individual items, or groups of items, also may be facilitated by the form in which a report is prepared. Special indentations of similar details and the extension of similar totals into the same vertical column are ways in which comparability may be increased.

Clearness.—The quality of clearness may be said to overlap all of those which have been previously mentioned. However, there are certain detailed aspects of making a report clear that should be mentioned. It is very important that the items on a report be clearly set forth under descriptive account titles which indicate the nature of the items being considered. It may be advisable in the interest of clearness to call attention to the type of value which has been given to a particular asset. In the case of accounts receivable or accounts payable, some subdivision which would show the various maturity dates might prove to be of significance. The correct description of economic facts may sometimes be facilitated by free use of parenthetical explanations.

The basis of valuation is often indicated by putting two values on a financial report, or by indicating gross values with allowances for various deductions. This procedure is particularly common in the valuation of receivables and fixed assets, where allowances for bad debts and depreciation are subtracted on a balance sheet. The sequence in which items appear on a balance sheet or income sheet is at times of great significance. For example, a balance sheet which is being prepared as the basis for short-time credit should be organized in a way that will list current assets and liabilities in a conspicuous part of the report.

Offsetting of various items in an accounting report is often a useful method of pointing out significant characteristics. For example, the offsetting of gross sales against cost of goods sold may give a figure which is of great significance for some purposes. Clarity in accounting reports may also be achieved by free use of underlining, extension of totals, heavy lettering, and the segregation of similar data into special portions. Sometimes the segregation takes the form of actual removal of detail from the report and the placing of it in subsidiary schedules.

An accounting report should be organized in such a way that the data may be expanded or condensed to some degree without doing violence to its general structure. The framework of the classification should be such that details can be added from time to time without destroying the general outline. Very often the relevance or aptness of a report will contribute greatly to its clearness. Reports should be prepared in terms of the needs of the reader. Just what characteristics will make a given report significant to a reader cannot be answered in general terms. Data which would be significant for one purpose may be passed over entirely for another; similarly, data which would be very useful for the administrative problem of one executive might be of only passing interest to another.

QUESTIONS ON CHAPTER XXXV

1. Assume it to be true that the financial summaries of business operations of business enterprises are much more condensed than the balance sheets. What arguments can be advanced both to support and to discredit this practice, from the point of view of the management and of society at large?
2. How does a "statement of cash receipts and expenditures" differ from a "statement of income and expense?"
3. What is a "statement of surplus"? What types of transactions might affect the Surplus account directly without first appearing in the Income or Expense accounts?
4. What persons in a business enterprise might be interested in the following statements of financial operations?
   a) Cash receipts and expenditures
   b) Acquisition and disposal of fixed assets
   c) Incurrence and payment of accounts payable
   d) Increases and decreases in accounts receivable
   e) Issuance and redemption of long-term liabilities

   Suggest other reports of financial operations which might be prepared under special conditions.
5. The net profit of the Coca-Cola Company is something more than eight million dollars for the year 1926. Look at the balance sheet of this company in the foregoing chapter and estimate the rate of earnings on

the capital stock. In view of the circumstances, do you think the enterprise is justified in carrying a large amount for intangible assets on the balance sheet?

6. The Orpheum Circuit, Inc., classifies depreciation and the amortization of leaseholds as special deductions and does not list them under the heading of expenses. Comment on this treatment.
7. Note the term "Accumulated revenue" which designates the surplus of the Illinois Society of Certified Public Accountants. Might this term with propriety be adopted to represent the surplus of private enterprises organized for profit?
8. How complete should an accounting report be? Would the degree of completeness desirable vary with the purposes for which the report were prepared?
9. What do you consider to be the advantages and disadvantages of uniform financial reports?
10. Look over the financial reports in chapters xxxiv and xxxv to see to what extent the following devices have been availed of for purposes of clearness:
    a) Unusual account titles (for unusual data)
    b) Statement of basis of valuation
    c) Parenthetical explanations
    d) Sequence based on special characteristics (such as liquidity, security, tangibility, etc.)
    e) Underlining
    f) Heavy lettering
    g) Extension of totals into separate columns
    h) Offsetting of specific assets and liabilities

CHAPTER XXXVI

RATIOS IN ACCOUNTING REPORTS

Classification and summarization are really preliminary steps in the interpretation of accounting data. They separate data in terms of their differences and group them in terms of basis similarities. But the interpretation may be carried forward by comparisons between the various items and by the search for significant relationships in the data in the accounting reports, particularly those which can be expressed quantitatively.

Relationships between accounting data may be expressed as ratios, averages, and trends.—What are the important relationships between groups of data in an accounting report? What type of facts or estimates should the executives of an enterprise attempt to deduce from a report? These questions may be answered specifically only in terms of the needs and policies of each executive. There are, however, certain relationships which are of such general importance that they may be mentioned in a text which merely introduces the problem of interpreting accounting data for control. The following will be discussed.[1]

1. *Ratios.*—The quantitative relationship of one accounting fact to another is frequently of very great importance in planning operations or in determining status. The computation of the ratios between different data in the accounting reports will be discussed at length in this chapter.

2. *Averages.*—It is very often important to know what is the central tendency in a group or series of data. Such knowledge may be determined by computing the average of a set of measurements and discovering to what extent they vary from each other and from the accepted measure of central tendency.

3. *Trends.*—The analysis of a series of similar accounting data often enables a manager to discover significant trends which underlie the mass of facts displayed in the various reports. The trends may refer to series of single items, to ratios, or to averages.

[1] Readers acquainted with statistical method will recognize the terms "ratio," "average," and "trend" as familiar terms in that field. The fact is, of course, that all workers in quantitative methods have these devices available for their use. Statisticians have led the accountants in adapting them to their needs.

A ratio is a quantitative relationship between facts. Accounting ratios are, of course, the relationships between the financial measurements of certain objects or transactions, such as cash, merchandise, buildings, current assets, sales, purchases, and selling expenses. To illustrate, assume that the total sales of an enterprise were $13,000 and that total selling expenses were $2,000. Then the ratio between sales and selling expenses would be the ratio between $13,000 and $2,000. This may be expressed by the fraction $\frac{13,000}{2,000}$, which equals $\frac{13}{2}$, which equals $\frac{6.5}{1}$. The ratio may be expressed as the fraction $\frac{13}{2}$ or as the number 6.5. The ratio between sales and selling expenses, then, is the ratio between 13 and 2, or between 6.5 and 1, in which the former number represents sales and the second the selling expenses. When the larger item is expressed first in a ratio, the proportion is sometimes expressed as a number related to 1, such as 6.5:1, or merely as 6.5.

When the first item in a proportion is smaller than the second, there is frequently an advantage in reducing the fraction to percentage form. In the foregoing illustration, the ratio between selling expenses and sales is the ratio between 2,000 and 13,000, which may be expressed as $\frac{2,000}{13,000}$ which equals $\frac{100}{650}$, or 0.1539. This decimal may be expressed as a percentage, namely, 15.39 per cent. Selling expenses are thus said to be "15.39 per cent" of sales. In the following discussion, the ratios between accounting data will be expressed either as fractions, proportions, decimals, or percentages, depending upon the method which seems most convenient for the purpose.

Significance of ratios depends upon purposes of interpretation.—Comparisons may be drawn between any groups of accounting data; but the comparisons which will be most significant will vary with the circumstances under which, and with the persons for whom, they are made. The different persons interested in accounting reports—stockholders, directors, department managers, merchandise creditors, or banks—are not equally interested in the same relationships between the different accounting data. Consequently any discussion must recognize the fact that ratios derive their significance from the purposes for which they are computed. The general classes of accounting data, however, suggest a broad classification of the ratios which may be computed, namely: (1) ratios between balance-sheet data (general or subsidiary); (2) ratios between income and expense data (general or subsidiary); (3) ratios between balance-sheet data on the one hand, and income or expense data on the other (general or subsidiary). The number of ratios which might be computed from the data of a balance sheet, from a statement of income and expense, or from both combined, would be exceedingly large. Only a few will be illustrated. Those selected will be discussed as samples only, the discussion serving merely to emphasize the importance of a particular objective in the calculation of ratios. The following will be illustrated:

1. Balance-sheet ratios
   a) Between current assets and total assets
   b) Between net worth and liabilities
   c) Between current assets and current liabilities
   d) Between accounts receivable and merchandise
2. Income-and-expense ratios
   a) Between gross profit and sales
   b) Between operating expenses and sales
   c) Between net profit and sales
   d) Between classes of expense
   e) Between subdivisions of sales
3. Turnover ratios
   a) Between merchandise inventory and goods sold
   b) Other turnover ratios

The foregoing table of ratios is not all inclusive, for it does not include ratios between data on concurrent similar reports of different companies or on series of similar reports of the same company. The ratios between data on comparative statements are very important; in fact, they are so important they will be given separate treatment in chapter xxxviii, "Analysis of Comparative Balance Sheets." As a basis for the calculation of illustrative ratios, the balance sheet and statement of income and expense of the Modern Wholesale Company will be used (see pp. 467, 468).

Balance-sheet ratios reflect the various aspects of financial status.—Ratios between the various aspects of financial status of an enterprise may be differentiated from others by the term "balance-sheet ratios." Ratios which involve business operations may,

MODERN WHOLESALE COMPANY

BALANCE SHEET—DECEMBER 31, 1927

ASSETS		LIABILITIES AND PROPRIETORSHIP	
Current assets:		*Current liabilities:*	
Cash.............$	36,000.00	Accounts payable..$	188,000.00
Accounts receivable	150,000.00	Notes payable.....	62,000.00
Notes receivable...	78,000.00		$ 250,000.00
Merchandise inventory...........	320,000.00	*Fixed liabilities:*	
	$ 584,000.00	Mortgages payable.$	160,000.00
		Bond payable.....	264,000.00
			$ 424,000.00
Fixed assets:			
Office equipment...$	92,000.00	*Proprietorship:*	
Building..........	220,000.00	Capital stock.....$	250,000.00
Land.............	180,000.00	Surplus..........	168,000.00
Deferred charges...	16,000.00		
	$ 508,000.00		$ 418,000.00
Total assets.....$1,092,000.00		Total liabilities..$1,092,000.00	

in contrast, be delineated as "operating ratios"; this group includes the "income-and-expense ratios" and the "turnover ratios." The balance-sheet ratios will be discussed first.

Between current assets and total assets.—This ratio is a type of comparison which relates a "part" to the "whole."[1] The investment in an enterprise may comprise numerous assets, the com-

[1] J. H. Bliss in his well-known work entitled *Financial and Operating Ratios in Management* illustrates and discusses a large number of ratios. No clear line of distinction is drawn between "financial" and "operating" ratios; however, the classes appear to refer to the divisions suggested above, namely: "balance-sheet" and "operating" ratios.

MODERN WHOLESALE COMPANY

STATEMENT OF INCOME AND EXPENSE—FOR THE YEAR ENDING DECEMBER 31, 1927

Gross sales			$2,400,000.00
Cost of goods sold:			
Inventory, January 1, 1927	$ 190,000.00		
Purchases	1,644,000.00		
	$1,834.000.00		
Inventory, December 31, 1927	320,000.00		1,514,000.00
Gross Profit on sales			$ 886,000.00
Operating expenses:			
Buying expenses:			
Purchasing agent's office		$ 24,000.00	
Selling expenses:			
Salesmen's salaries	$ 232,000.00		
Travel expenses	150,000.00		
Advertising	26,000.00		
Freight out	10,000.00		
Delivery expenses	21,000.00		
Clerical expenses	26,000.00		
Miscellaneous	12,400.00	477,400.00	
Financial expenses:			
Salaries—Treasurer's office	$ 13,600.00		
Interest expenses	23,000.00		
Bad debts	5,000.00		
Sales discounts	18,000.00	$ 59,600.00	
Administration expenses:			
Executive salaries	$ 45,000.00		
Office salaries	35,000.00		
Heat and light	16,000.00		
Office supplies	28,000.00		
Telephone and telegraph	1,400.00		
Legal expenses	1,200.00		
Taxes	2,600.00		
Miscellaneous	13,400.00	142,600.00	703,600.00
Operating profit			$ 182,400.00
Non-operating income:			
Interest income	$ 2,200.00		
Warehouse rental	1,500.00		3,700.00
Net profit			$ 186,100.00

position of the whole being a very important element in financial success. The comparison of a part with the whole may, of course, be applied to various aspects of financial status; for example, one line of merchandise may be compared with the total inventory; accounts receivable with the total current assets; capital stock with total net worth.

The significance of the ratio between current assets and total assets is its presumed indication of the liquidity of the assets, in case an enterprise were to be dissolved or were to change the nature of its operations. Current assets are usually easier to dispose of than are fixed assets, for it is very often difficult to realize a satisfactory value for intricate machinery or specialized equipment; moreover, it is usually impossible to remodel elaborate equipment for use in the manufacture or distribution of a new line of merchandise. But it is not always desirable for current assets to bear a high ratio to the total assets of an enterprise. Extensive investment in labor-saving machinery is very often the factor in making possible a low unit cost of production, and hence a strong financial condition. This ratio, as all others, must be interpreted in each case in the light of particular circumstances. The ratio between the current assets and total assets on the balance sheet of the Modern Wholesale Company is approximately 0.54 to 1, or 54 per cent.

Between liabilities and net worth.—The ratio between liabilities and net worth illustrates the comparison of "one part" of the whole with "another part" of the same whole, the "whole" being the right side of the balance sheet. The liabilities and net worth together compose the entire right side of a balance sheet; the relation between them is very significant for purposes of the control of financial policy. It is impossible to say what are desirable proportions of liabilities and net worth, except in terms of a particular enterprise and a particular business policy. A high percentage of liabilities to net worth means that in a very prosperous concern the stockholders will reap a high rate of profit on their investment. In the case of the Modern Wholesale Company, the total liabilities are $674,000, whereas the total net worth amounts to only $418,000 ($250,000 of which represents capital stock). A high ratio between liabilities and net worth is not always desirable; it might result in net profit to stockholders being very small during dull times, because of heavy interest payments which must be paid to bondholders and other creditors.

Between accounts receivable and merchandise inventory.—This ratio compares one type of current asset with another; it is a ratio between one part and another part of the whole, the whole being the current assets. The comparison of different parts of the same whole may, of course, be applied to other balance-sheet data, to give such ratios as that between notes payable and accounts payable, between capital stock and surplus, between preferred stock and common stock. The importance of the ratio between accounts receivable and merchandise inventory arises from the fact that a great deal of merchandise is sold on credit terms, and the collection of accounts receivable is very often a prerequisite to the payment of debts or to obtaining additional goods.

The proper ratio between accounts receivable and merchandise inventory will vary with several considerations, among which are the length of the credit period for sales on account, the rate at which goods are sold, and the length of time it takes to procure additional goods by purchase or manufacture. If, for example, the terms of sale are 2/10/net/60,[1] it might be expected that at any one time there would be outstanding as accounts receivable an amount equal to more than ten, but less than sixty, days' sales of merchandise. In the case of the Modern Wholesale Company, the total sales were $2,400,000. Two months' sales would amount to $400,000; the accounts receivable at the end of the year are only $150,000. This may be due to several causes, such as a vigorous collection program which has induced a large number of customers to take advantage of the 2 per cent cash discount; or to a falling off in sales during the latter months of the year, which has resulted in a smaller total of accounts receivable to be collected. The explanation of this situation must be discovered by an analysis of the details in the Accounts Receivable and Sales accounts.

[1] For an explanation of the symbols expressing terms of sale, see chap. ix under the discussion of "Cash Discounts."

Whether or not a certain stock of merchandise is too large in proportion to accounts receivable will also depend upon the special facts of each situation. If the inventory appears unusually large, the condition may be due to a recent purchase under conditions which made possible the securing of a low price because of off-season purchases. On the other hand, a large inventory may indicate a falling off in sales, because of an ineffective sales program. In the case of a manufacturing concern, the presence of a large stock of finished goods may represent merely the accumulation of goods made in anticipation of a rush season which is to come soon, when orders will exceed production. The "Merchandise inventory" of the Modern Wholesale Company is shown as $320,000. This is approximately one-fifth of the total "Cost of goods sold" during the previous year. It represents, therefore, a normal stock of something more than sixty days' average sales. Whether or not this stock is too large will depend upon the time it takes to replenish stock, the price advantages to be derived from purchasing in large quantities, and the length of the credit period allowed by venders of merchandise.

Between current assets and current liabilities.—This ratio—commonly referred to as the "current ratio"—illustrates a comparison between data which do not form parts of the same whole; it is a comparison of a part of the assets with a part of the liabilities. The comparison of groups of assets with groups of liabilities may be carried on to any degree which suits the purposes of the interested persons; it may provide ratios between fixed assets and fixed liabilities, accounts receivable and accounts payable, intangible assets and common stock.

In the balance sheet of the Modern Wholesale Company shown above, the total of the current assets is $584,000; the total of the current liabilities is $250,000. The ratio between current assets and current liabilities is, therefore, 2.34:1. Current ratios indicate the availability of certain assets for the probable payment of short-term liabilities. Short-term creditors often regard the current ratio as a very important index of financial strength. Loans which are made for the purchase of merchandise are usually repaid by funds secured from the sale of these or other goods in the near future. Other things being equal, an enterprise is regarded as in good financial condition if its current assets are considerably larger than its current liabilities—if the "current ratio" is at least 2:1.

Just why a 2:1 ratio should be regarded as the ideal index of financial strength has never been demonstrated by business men or writers on the subject. No doubt there is a feeling that a 100 per cent margin of current assets over current liabilities is adequate, yet not so large as to compel a business man unnecessarily to tie up large amounts of capital in cash, receivables, and merchandise. Whether or not a 2:1 ratio is large enough or is too large in any given instance will depend on two things: (1) the forms which the current assets assume; (2) the nature of the business enterprise. It is conceivable, for example, that a retail furniture store which carries a large slow-moving stock and a large number of instalment accounts receivable might need to maintain a higher ratio than 2:1. On the other hand, an electric-light-and-power company might prosper with a much lower ratio. An electric-service company does not carry a stock of stored-up electricity. Its current assets consist primarily of accounts receivable from customers, which are due within ten or twenty days; in fact it is a common practice for public-utility enterprises to collect advance deposits to prevent losses on bad debts. Consequently all current assets of such an enterprise may be regarded as worth their value. In such a situation any current ratio greater than 1:1 might be perfectly safe; in fact, it is not uncommon for balance sheets of very prosperous public utilities to reveal current ratios of less than 1:1.

A ratio is sometimes computed between the total of cash and accounts receivable (sometimes cash and merchandise) on the one hand, and the short-term liabilities on the other. When these assets exceed the current liabilities, the financial condition of an enterprise is said to pass the "acid test." In the case of the Modern Wholesale Company, the total of cash and accounts receivable is $186,000; the total of current liabilities is $250,000; the proportion is approximately 0.74:1. It does not meet the requirements of the "acid test." Whether or not the acid test is important will depend upon the special conditions existing at the time.

Income and expense ratios compare various aspects of business operations.—Comparison of the data on the statement of income and expense may be made to provide ratios similar to those computed from items on the balance sheet. They also may be classified in terms of the relations between the various "parts" and the "wholes" on the statement, with the total income comprising one whole and the total expenses plus net profit comprising the other. Income-and-expense ratios have been referred to as a special type of "operating ratios," indicating that the comparison involves data which directly reflect business operations. Only a few of the possible income-and-expense ratios will be illustrated.

Between gross profit and sales.—Gross profit is the difference between total sales and the cost value of the goods sold. It is usually considered desirable for an enterprise to secure as high a percentage of gross profit on sales as possible, although in some cases a high gross-profit ratio may not lead to the greatest possible total profit or net profit. As an example of the importance of studying the gross-profit ratio, assume that goods are procured at a cost of $10 per unit of product and that 50,000 units are sold at a price of $20 each. In such a case the sales and cost of goods sold would appear on a statement of income and expense as follows:

Sales (50,000 units @ $20)	$1,000,000.00
Cost of goods sold (50,000 units @ $10)	500,000.00
Gross profit on sales	$ 500,000.00

The ratio of gross profit to gross sales is here 50 per cent, and the total gross profit is $500,000. But assume that 100,000 units could be sold if the price were lowered to $17.50 per unit. If such a policy were adopted, the sales would increase, and the income statement would be:

Sales (100,000 units @ $17.50)	$1,750,000.00
Cost of goods sold (100,000 units @ $10)	1,000,000.00
Gross profit on sales	$ 750,000.00

The "rate" of gross profit decreases when 10,000 units are sold; but the "amount" of gross profit increases. The lower rate of gross profit in the second instance gives the manager a higher total gross profit. On the statement of income and expense for the Modern Wholesale Company, the gross sales were $2,400,000; the gross profit on sales was $886,000. The percentage of gross profit to gross sales, therefore, is approximately 37 per cent. Whether or not this is a sufficiently high rate of gross profit for the enterprise will depend upon the total expenses of securing this amount of sales, upon the customary rates of gross profit in the industry, and upon the effect which a lowering or raising of the price would have upon the amount of goods sold.

Net profit to sales.—This ratio tells the manager how much of every dollar which is earned by the major operations of the enterprise represents a net profit to the stockholders.[1] The source of the major income of the Modern Wholesale Company is the sale of merchandise; the *net profit* is $186,100; the sales are $2,400,000. The ratio is therefore about 0.078:1, or 7.8 per cent. Whether or not this percentage of net profit to gross sales is a satisfactory rate depends upon many factors, such as the total investment of the proprietors, the risk encountered in the industry, and the total value of the assets employed in the enterprise.

Between operating expenses and sales.—The ratio between operating expenses and sales is a significant figure; it indicates in a measure the efficiency with which the major activities of an enterprise are being administered. By "operating expenses" in this paragraph are meant all expenses (except cost of goods sold) which are incurred to carry forward the major operations—the sale of merchandise. They include all of the "expenses" appearing in the typical statement of income and expense except those incurred merely to further incidental operations which are unrelated to the main purpose for which the enterprise is organized. In the case of the Modern Wholesale Company, the total "Oper-

[1] The term "gross income" could be substituted here for "sales"; the major income of some enterprises might come from sources other than the sale of merchandise. Illustrations of such enterprises are banks, professional firms, and hospitals.

ating expenses" are \$703,600. This figure, when compared to \$2,400,000, gives a ratio of 0.293:1, or 29.3 per cent. Wide fluctuations in the ratio between operating expenses and sales are significant facts in the planning of a sales program. It is conceivable, for example, that an expected increase in sales may be offset by a larger increase in operating expenses, which would result in an actual reduction of the net profit of an enterprise.

Between classes of expense.—It is often of interest to a manager to know specifically how certain expenses have been divided. He may wish to know, for example, the ratios between various operating expenses, as illustrated below:

Buying expenses	\$ 24,000.00—	3 per cent
Selling expenses	477,400.00—	68 per cent
Financial expenses	59,600.00—	9 per cent
Administrative expenses	142,600.00—	20 per cent
Total operating expenses	\$703,600.00—	100 per cent

Such general divisions enable a manager to see at a glance just what proportions of his total operating expenses are connected with the various activities of his enterprise. If any one type of expenses appears to be too large, the manager can examine the individual expense items to determine how the total of the group may be reduced.

Between subdivisions of total sales.—The foregoing discussion has been confined to facts which are apparent from the main summaries of status and operations—the balance sheet and the statement of income and expense. Any of the items on the summarized statements may be subjected to analysis by a business manager. He may, for example, ask for detailed data concerning the inventories on hand, the operating expenses, or the sales. An analysis of the sales transactions will be given below to illustrate some of the subsidiary data which may be utilized by a sales manager. Assume that the Modern Wholesale Company has three products—X, Y, and Z; also that it divides its sales territories into four districts—eastern, southern, central, and western. The sales manager desires to know in which territories each product is now being sold, with a view to expanding the sales of certain products in certain territories.[1] The total sales of the Modern Wholesale Company may be subdivided to show sales according to territories as follows:

Eastern district	$ 700,000.00	— 29 per cent
Southern district	200,000.00	— 8 per cent
Central district	1,000,000.00	— 42 per cent
Western district	500,000.00	— 21 per cent
Total sales	$2,400,000.00	—100 per cent

It may be determined further from the records that the total sales of lines of merchandise are divided as follows:

Line X	$1,600,000.00	— 67 per cent
Line Y	600,000.00	— 25 per cent
Line Z	200,000.00	— 8 per cent
	$2,400,000.00	—100 per cent

From this statement the sales manager can discover which line of merchandise is bringing in the major portion of the gross revenue. Obviously it is line X. But why are not lines Y and Z being sold in the same quantities? The answer may be, of course, that they are of such nature that the total sales will necessarily be less in proportion to the total than the sales of line X. But on the other hand, the explanation may be that the sales force is not pushing all lines with equal vigor; for example, the eastern and central districts (although they may be larger potential markets for the slighted commodities in lines Y and Z) may be concentrating on line X to the exclusion of the other lines. On the other hand, the southern district may be selling the major portion of the total amount of line Z. The data necessary to an intelligent approach to this problem are to be found in a further break-up of the total sales figures to show in what districts certain products are being sold in the greatest amounts. An analysis of the data may show the following facts:

[1] It is often impracticable to record such detailed information in the regular accounts of an enterprise, although such data might be so recorded if adequate subsidiary accounts were maintained to show the sales by products and by territories. More often the detail data of sales by products and territories are secured from special records prepared from the original invoices of sales.

	Line X	Line Y	Line Z	Total
Eastern district..	$ 500,000.00	$180,000.00	$ 20,000.00	$ 700,000.00
Southern district.	20,000.00	50,000.00	130,000.00	200,000.00
Central district..	800,000.00	160,000.00	40,000.00	1,000,000.00
Western district..	280,000.00	210,000.00	10,000.00	500,000.00
	$1,600,000.00	$600,000.00	$200,000.00	$2,400,000.00

The foregoing table permits the sales manager to determine at a glance in what territories the sales of certain lines of goods are most successful. He can see, for example, that the central district is selling 50 per cent of line X but is selling a much smaller percentage of the total of lines Y and Z. The southern district, on the other hand, shows quite a different condition. The southern district stands at the foot of the list in total sales; yet it is selling 65 per cent of the total of line Z. The reasons for such conditions may be apparent to the sales manager. His method of remedying the situation, if it appears to need remedying, will vary with the standards which have been set up in advance and which the various territories are supposed to meet.

Turnover ratios compare certain balance-sheet items with the business operations which effect them.—The essence of business activity is the exchange of economic values with a view to realizing a profit. One of the factors which makes for profit is the frequency with which the assets are utilized in business transactions. Obviously, more profit will be gained from two transactions than from one, if they are both profitable. The gain from an individual transaction, therefore, is only one factor in the gaining of net profit during a period of time. The other factor is the number of times the transaction is repeated. It is because of this obvious fact that business men set such a premium upon the rate at which their assets are exchanged—the "rate of turnover." The comparison of balance-sheet items with the transactions which affect them is, therefore, an important part of the discovery and presentation of significant relationships. Turnover ratios are a class of "operating ratios," as that term has been previously explained; they involve data which represent business operations. A turnover ratio must, of course, always be calculated in relation to a given period of time, such as a month, a year, or some other fiscal period adopted for the purposes of the computations.

Merchandise turnover.—Business men frequently speak of the advantage of a high rate of "merchandise turnover." By this term they mean the ratio between the goods sold during a period of time and the average inventory on hand during that period. The values of the merchandise may be computed in terms of cost price or sales price. Where the amount of the inventory fluctuates with seasonal requirements, the values on hand at the beginning and end of a period of business operations may be far from typical of the amount of merchandise inventory needed by the enterprise. In some cases, however, the inventories at the time of preparing financial statements are regarded as typical of the inventory during a period; the average inventory may be estimated by adding the book values of the beginning and ending inventories, and dividing the sum by two. The quotient thus obtained may then be divided into the cost of goods sold, to determine the rate of merchandise turnover for a period of operations. The merchandise turnover for the Modern Wholesale Company would be computed as follows:

Cost of goods sold		$1,514,000.00
Beginning inventory	$190,000.00	
Ending inventory	320,000.00	
Total	$510,000.00	
One-half of total (the average)		255,000.00

$$\frac{\text{Cost of goods sold, \$1,514,000.00}}{\text{Average inventory, \$255,000.00}} = 5.94$$

The turnover ratio is approximately 6:1; that is to say, the average cost-value of goods on hand at any one time is about one-sixth of the total cost value of goods sold during the period of business operations. A turnover ratio which will be considered satisfactory for the merchandise of an enterprise must be based upon knowledge concerning the ratio between gross profit and sales. Goods which are sold at a high rate of gross profit need not be sold as rapidly as those on which the percentage of gross profit is smaller. Most furniture stores and jewelry stores, for example, do not have a rate of merchandise turnover greater than twice per year. On the other hand, many grocery stores "turn over" their entire stock as often as twice a month, and some markets dispensing fresh meat carry only forty-eight hours' supply of provisions.

Other types of turnover ratios.—Many other types of turnover ratios may be computed for use in administrative control. Some of the turnover ratios most frequently used by accountants and business men are the following:

1. Between sales and total assets (capital turnover)
2. Between sales and current assets (working-capital turnover)
3. Between net profit and net worth
4. Between sales and net worth

Conclusion as to ratios.—This chapter has introduced some of the significant comparisons that can be drawn from the data appearing in financial reports. It has not attempted to illustrate or mention all the types of comparisons which may be of importance for a manager; nor has it attempted to extract from all the possible ratios those most significant for all purposes of administration. The ratios which are most significant in a particular situation will depend upon the existing conditions.

QUESTIONS ON CHAPTER XXXVI

1. Under what conditions might it be desirable for the current assets to be large compared to the total assets? And when to bear a low ratio? Compute the ratio between current assets and total assets for the balance sheets illustrated in chapter xxxiv. Note carefully any differences in the classifications of specific items which might tend to make the ratios not truly comparable.
2. Compare the ratios of net worth to liabilities in the balance sheets of the Coca-Cola Company (p. 436) and the Ohio Public Service Company (pp. 446–47). How do you explain the differences in the ratios?
3. What is meant by the term "current ratio"? Compute the current ratios of the balance sheets in chapter xxxiv. How many of these enterprises pass the "acid test"?
4. Compute the amounts of net working capital on all the balance sheets shown in chapter xxxiv.
5. The ratio of gross profit to sales for the Coca-Cola Company is very high. How is this fact to be explained? The Orpheum Circuit, Inc., shows no figure which would correspond to "gross profit.". Discuss.

6. Compute the ratio between net profit and sales or gross income for all the statements of income and expense shown in chapter xxxv. Explain, if possible, the differences in ratios which you discover.
7. What are the advantages of a high rate of turnover?
8. From the data of the Stewart-Warner Speedometer Corporation balance sheet (p. 435) compute the ratios between the following items: cash and accounts payable; accounts receivable and inventory; intangibles and total assets; current and fixed liabilities; fixed assets and capital stock.
9. Compute the ratios mentioned in question 8 for the Coca-Cola Company.
10. Compute the ratios mentioned in question 8 for the Ohio Public Service Company; also for the North American Manufacturing Company. Explain, if possible, the variations in the ratios in these balance sheets.

CHAPTER XXXVII

AVERAGES AND TRENDS IN ACCOUNTING DATA

The present chapter turns from the determination of ratios between classes of data to an attempt to discover averages in groups or series of similar data; also to the task of observing general changes in ratios and averages during a period of time.

Averages reveal central tendencies in groups of similar accounting data.—Groups or series of similar data—such as cash balances at different branches, or monthly sales of a certain article of merchandise—may be presented as accounting reports to interested executives; in fact, such data are often of more value to the treasurer or to the sales manager of an enterprise than the conventional balance sheets and statements of income and expense. Such reports may, of course, be analyzed by the calculation of ratios between the items, such as the ratio between the cash balance at one branch and the cash balance of the entire enterprise. But another technique is also available to the accountant: the calculation of *averages*. Averages are values which represent the central tendencies in groups or in series of similar data. To illustrate, assume that the total cash balance of an enterprise comprises the following amounts located at four different branch headquarters:

New York (eastern district)	$12,000.00
Atlanta (southern district)	8,800.00
Chicago (central district)	10,800.00
Denver (western district)	8,400.00
	$40,000.00

The total cash owned by the enterprise is $40,000. The average cash balance may be computed by dividing the total amount of the cash by the number of branches, which gives an average amount on hand of $10,000 per branch. This amount does not represent the amount on hand at any one branch; in fact, the actual amounts on hand vary from an amount as low as $8,400, at Denver, to an amount as high as $12,000, at New York. The average value of $10,000 cannot, therefore, be regarded in this case as the typical cash balance; it merely represents an amount which the cash balance at each branch would be if the balances were equal.[1]

Mention was made in the foregoing paragraph to "groups" and "series" of data. By a *group* of data is meant a number of similar data which are coexistent; they may actually exist at the same time (the average cash balances at different branches), or may be merely related to the same period of time, such as the sales by branches of different articles of merchandise. Groups of data are secured from phenomena measured concurrently. By a *series* of data is meant a set of measurements which express characteristics of the same phenomena at different points in time; illustrations would be the successive cash balances of an enterprise determined at monthly intervals, the monthly sales during an entire year, and the annual sales during a period of years. The various groups and series of data which will be subjected to the process of "averaging' will vary with the purposes of the executives using the data. Some of the uses to which averages may be placed are mentioned in the paragraph immediately following.[2]

Averages useful for administrative control.—An average possesses several advantages for use in the analysis of accounting data. In the first place, an average may be selected *to typify a group or series* of similar data. The average cash balance at a group of branch offices is not necessarily the amount which is on hand at any single branch office; yet the average balance may

[1] The reader should be warned at this point that there are several kinds of averages which may be used to indicate the central tendency of different groups or series. The arithmetic mean illustrated above, which is determined by dividing the total value by the number of items, is only one of various averages which may be selected to indicate a central tendency in a group or in a series of similar data.

[2] These illustrations of groups and series are all drawn from the internal accounting data of a specific enterprise. A firm might also be greatly interested in the comparison of its own status or operations with that of other firms. For example, a group of data might comprise the cash balances of a large number of similar enterprises. The manager of each firm could determine the average cash balance at the time for the different firms and compute the relationship of the condition of his own enterprise to that of the average. as well as to other firms.

very often indicate the central tendency as to cash balances and give an idea as to whether large or small amounts are kept in the branches. Likewise, the average inventory on hand on the first day of the various months during a fiscal year probably would not be identical with the actual amount on hand at the first of any particular month. Such an average would, however, give an idea of the tendency of the inventory to be large or small, and of the amount kept on hand.

A second advantage of the average is that it serves as *a basis for the comparison of the different groups or series.* The average inventory on hand is a useful figure in determining annual turnover of merchandise. Likewise, the average sales of a series of months might serve as a basis for comparing the average inventory each month with the average sales (or cost of goods sold) each month.

In the third place, averages serve as *a central point for measuring the variation* of individual items. For example, the average sales of a commodity during a month might be an amount midway between the sales of the months showing the highest and lowest figures. The variation from the average is very often as important a factor in the administrative control as the average figure itself.[1] The problem of variation is particularly important in enterprises which must maintain large stocks of merchandise inventory in order to supply unexpected demand at certain times during a fiscal period; for example, textbook-publishing concerns ship large numbers of school books during the month of August. The significance of variation is sharply emphasized in the activities of electric-light-and-power companies, which are forced to adjust their production of power to a fluctuating demand. The demand for electric current reaches very high peaks at certain hours of each day, while at other times the amount of current used is much less.

[1] Variation from the average is usually referred to by statisticians as "dispersion." Various measures of dispersion are offered by the technique of statistics for indicating the degree of variation from a given average. This fact of dispersion is another case in which the application of statistics as a quantitative tool often serves the manager in good stead. For a discussion of the problems of averages and dispersion, the reader is referred to Riegel, *Elements of Business Statistics*, chaps. x–xii.

Very often the average of a group or series of data serves as *the basis for establishing standards.* For example, the average inventory on hand in a group of branches doing about the same amount of business might be regarded as the desirable average amount for all branches to keep on hand. Similarly, the average sales of a group of salesmen during a period of time might be established as the minimum amount which must be sold by each one before he would be allowed a certain rate of commission on his sales.[1]

Various kinds of averages may be computed.—The simplest type of average is one which is computed by adding the various amounts to be averaged, and dividing the total by the number of different amounts. This average is known as the "simple arithmetic mean." It is very useful in some cases; but it has a tendency to emphasize the importance of extreme variations, especially where the variations are applicable to only a small number of items. If it were desirable to obtain the average cost of goods purchased during a given period of time, the simple average might be computed from the second column of the following table:

Items Purchased		Prices	Total Cost
400	@	$ 2.00	$ 800.00
500	@	2.25	1,125.00
25	@	4.00	100.00
350	@	2.30	805.00
50	@	3.40	170.00
1,325		$13.95	$3,000.00

The total of the various prices is $13.95. This amount, divided by 5, the number of different prices, gives an average price of $2.79. This price is obviously unsatisfactory for purposes of con-

[1] The establishment of standards, together with the method of keeping records and preparing administrative reports in terms of these standards, is sometimes referred to as "budgetary control." Obviously the accounting data play a very important rôle in the establishment and revision of administrative standards. The problem of budgetary control is an important one, which is closely related to the interpretation of accounting data. Many texts and special studies have been written on the subject during the last decade. The use of accounting records and reports in budgetary control is discussed fully by J. O. McKinsey in his *Managerial Accounting;* also in his *Budgetary Control.*

trol, for it does not represent the significant tendency in the inventory values. The manager can see, by casual observation of his report, that 1,250 of the total 1,325 units (nearly 90 per cent) were purchased at prices of $2.30 or lower; only 125 units were purchased at higher prices. The price of $2.79 per unit as an average price, therefore, is too high.

The remedy for the difficulty encountered in the simple arithmetic mean is to give proper weight to the prices applicable to large numbers of items purchased. This is accomplished by multiplying the number of items by the prices at which they were purchased. The total products are then added, and the sum divided by the number of items to be averaged. The quotient is the *weighted arithmetic mean*. The total cost of the goods purchased is $3,000. The number of items purchased is 1,325. The average price of each is approximately $2.26 per item. Such an average is more typical of the group of items to be averaged than the simple arithmetic mean. The weighted arithmetic mean is used extensively by business men; it is the figure always obtained where total cost is divided by a number of items. The average cost of units of output is the weighted arithmetic mean where it is computed by dividing cost of goods manufactured by the total number of units produced.

At times other averages are selected to represent the dominant characteristics of a group or series. For example, the most important value for some purposes may be the value which prevails for the largest number of purchases in some particular line. In the case of the article illustrated above, the price which prevailed for the largest number of purchases was $2.25; 500 items were purchased at this quotation. This value is reasonably close to the weighted arithmetic mean, which was $2.26; for purposes of administration, probably either figure would be satisfactory. This value which applies to the largest number of items in the group of prices is known as the *mode*, or modal value. The mode is a special type of average, applicable to some groups of data. In cases where the measurements tend to cluster about a certain value, it is very often satisfactory.

Another type of average sometimes encountered is the *median*.

This is the value attaching to the item midway between the highest and the lowest, when the items are arranged in the order of their values. In the case just illustrated, the median would be the value attaching to article number 663, which is midway between the first and last item in the group, reading either from the top or the bottom of the list of 1,325 items arranged according to prices.

Other averages are sometimes introduced to typify a group or series of data; they involve the use of somewhat elaborate mathematical formulas for their computation and will not be illustrated in this text. Similarly, certain measures of variation may be applied to the variation of the individual items from the average. The extent to which such averages and measures of variation will be applied to accounting data will depend upon the accuracy with which data are to be analyzed, the presumed advantages to be derived from such analysis, and the facility with which the accountant can use the tools of statistical analysis.

Averages and variations in series of accounting data.—The total sales of the Modern Wholesale Company were $2,400,000. The sales manager of the concern may be very much interested to know the way in which this total was distributed over lines of product and over sales territories; he may also wish to know in what months of the year the total sales were made. The average monthly sales for the year may, of course, be computed by dividing the total sales by the number of months. This would give average monthly sales of $200,000. Such a figure is important, but, alone, of slight use to a sales manager who is trying to equalize his sales throughout a fiscal period and to co-ordinate his activities with a uniform rate of factory production. Assume that the total sales were made during the various months as shown on page 487. A casual glance at this table indicates that the average monthly sales of $200,000 do not correspond with the typical monthly sales, at least not in the sense of being the amount which is usually sold during any given month. In fact, only two months of the whole year show sales of exactly $200,000; they are May and October. The average amount is doubled during the month of August; in January the monthly sales drop to $80,000. This is an

illustration of a case where tabulation of the accounting data appears to be inadequate. The accountant may improve the inter-

MODERN WHOLESALE COMPANY

MONTHLY SALES

January	$ 80,000.00
February	90,000.00
March	110,000.00
April	160,000.00
May	200,000.00
June	240,000.00
July	340,000.00
August	400,000.00
September	280,000.00
October	200,000.00
November	120,000.00
December	180,000.00
	$2,400,000.00

pretation of his data by using the graphic method of setting forth the wide variations in the data.

MODERN WHOLESALE COMPANY

MONTHLY SALES — 1927

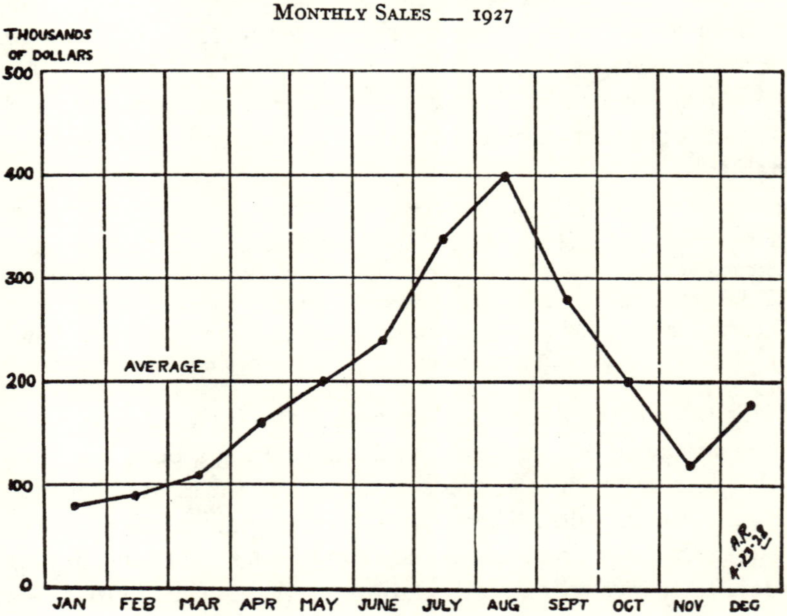

A chart for the monthly sales is shown on page 487. It shows that the sales for the year start at a low point, with January sales amounting to $80,000. They increase gradually during the first four months of the year; then increase rapidly until they reach a high point of $400,000 in August. They fall rapidly in amount during the remainder of the year, except for the increase in December. The horizontal line drawn at the level of $200,000 indicates the average monthly sales during the year. The line showing monthly sales is above the average at some points but lower at others. An executive interested in trying to improve sales during a certain part of the year can tell at a glance where the effort should be exerted.

Trends may be observed in series of ratios or averages.—The calculation of ratios has been limited to data on balance sheets and statements of income and expense which were interrelated. Similarly, the calculation of averages has been limited to data which constituted concurrent groups or which were series of similar data. Attention may now be turned to a treatment of the data in larger terms than individual ratios and averages; the ratios and averages themselves may be made parts of series of calculations with a view to discovering *trends* in series of ratios or series of averages.

Trends in a series of ratios.—Assume that the gross profit and the sales of a certain enterprise were represented by the following table:

	Gross Profit	Sales	Ratio of Gross Profit to Sales
First year.............	$20,000.00	$100,000.00	20.0 per cent
Second year...........	24,000.00	120,000.00	20.0 per cent
Third year............	30,000.00	155,000.00	19.4 per cent
Fourth year...........	35,000.00	170,000.00	20.6 per cent
Fifth year.............	42,000.00	210,000.00	20.0 per cent

This table illustrates a case where the ratio between gross profit and annual sales is practically constant during a period of time; the gross profit on sales tends to increase in the same proportion as the annual sales. There is a continuing interrelationship between the gross profit and the amount of sales. The tendency for data to change concurrently during a period of time illustrates a relationship of the type treated by statisticians under the general subject of "correlation." For a discussion of the methods of determining the degree of correlation between two or more variable phenomena, the reader is referred to standard works on statistical method, some of which are mentioned in the bibliography following the text material of this book.

A knowledge of the trend of any type of ratio during a period of time may prove very useful to an executive. In the first place, it may enable a manager to predict with reasonable accuracy what will happen under certain conditions. If, as in the foregoing example, he knows that gross profit has remained proportionate to sales for a period of five years (during which time sales have increased from $100,000 to $210,000), he may reasonably assume that the ratio will remain the same for another year. To be sure, other conditions—such as new inventions, a business depression, or cut-throat competition—might make such an assumption invalid; nevertheless, a business man must in practice actually attempt to predict his future activity. Any devices which will enable him to predict events more accurately should be used, if such use is practicable under the circumstances.

In the second place, knowledge of ratio trends makes it possible for a business man to know which types of business expenditures result in the greatest profit to him. For example, he may determine from a study of his reports that the sales in a given branch territory have borne a direct relationship to the amount spent for advertising in that territory during the years under examination. It is possible, of course, that the sales might have increased, whether the advertising expense had been incurred or not; but the interrelation is at least good evidence that the advertising was productive.

The determination of interrelationships between the various accounting data can be extended to any parts of the accounting reports. The knowledge of some interrelationships will be more useful than of others in the control of a business enterprise. It is the task of the business man or of his accountant to discover and measure those most significant for his purposes. Significant relationships may also be calculated among the non-financial data of a business enterprise; for example, between the number of employees in a department and the number of units of product they complete. The study of the continuing interrelationship of accounting data lies at the base of any development of a system of "budgetary control."

Trends in series of averages.—Trends may also be discovered in the *averages* applicable to the different members of a series of accounting data; that is to say, the accountant may compose series of the averages themselves. Such series reveal trends in business activity during a long period of time; they tend to minimize the effects of temporary variations during the shorter periods of time. The chart of the monthly sales of the Modern Wholesale Company revealed a wide variation between the sales in months during which the largest and smallest amounts were sold. The average sales, however, were shown to be $200,000 per month. A study of the trend of average monthly sales must include more than the transactions of a single year; otherwise a business man might make the mistake of assuming that his business was exceedingly prosperous during certain months and unprofitable during others. When an enterprise is committed to the carrying-on of its business year after year, it must recognize the seasonal variations in sales as a part of the circumstances under which it operates. The general trend of an enterprise is not to be measured by the seasonal fluctuations in sales but by the trend in average sales from year to year.

Assume the total sales of the Modern Wholesale Company for four years to be as follows:

First year..................	$1,800,000.00
Second year..................	1,500,000.00
Third year..................	2,400,000.00
Fourth year..................	2,700,000.00

It would be possible—in fact, desirable—to prepare a chart showing the trend of total sales during these four years. The chart might show the individual monthly sales for the period, or it may show only the average monthly sales for each of the four years. The average monthly sales would typify the general tendency in business during each of the years, and the information on such a chart would not be obscured by data showing monthly fluctuations resulting from seasonal variations in the demand. Reports showing the trend of business activities during a period of years may be very useful in the determination of profitable lines, especially where the total income or total costs are divided in terms of products or territories. A business might discover, for example, that although total annual sales were decreasing, the sales of certain products or in certain territories were increasing.

Conclusions on averages and trends.—Business men have, for the most part, limited their analysis of accounting reports to the computation of ratios; they have looked upon averages and trends as something mysterious, to be served up to them by statistical wizards. The calculation of some relationships may require the use of special mathematical devices; nevertheless, the principles underlying the discovery of averages and trends in accounting data may be grasped by anyone having a knowledge of simple arithmetic.

One more aspect of the recognition of tendencies remains to be discussed—the general changes in financial condition as revealed by a study of comparative balance sheets. The task is not different in principle from the calculation of the ratios between the data on the single balance sheets or statements of income and expense. There are, however, some aspects of the analysis of comparative balance sheets which deserve separate treatment. They will be discussed in the following chapter.

QUESTIONS ON CHAPTER XXXVII

1. Explain the difference between the following types of averages: simple arithmetic mean; weighted arithmetic mean; median; mode.
2. The Everready Fire Hose Company has purchased materials during the past accounting period in amounts and at prices as follows:

    20,000 pounds @ $0.30
    30,000 pounds @ 0.20
    50,000 pounds @ 0.35
    10,000 pounds @ 0.55
    5,000 pounds @ 0.40

    The manager decides that he will evaluate his remaining inventory (22,000 pounds) at the average price which has prevailed during the period. Compare the various averages which may be computed.

3. Assume that you wish to compare the sales in two territories during a period of two years and that you have data for the various months involved. How might the calculation of average monthly sales be advantageous in such a comparison?
4. Very often a business man is more interested in regularity of gross income than in the total amount of gross income. Why might this be true? Illustrate in the case of an electric light and power plant, a grocery store, a furniture factory, a publishing house.
5. Does the fact of variation from the average throw any light upon the efforts made by some enterprises to develop "off-season" business? Does it explain, for example, why some enterprises handle both coal and ice? why barber shops charge more for service on Saturday? why department stores hold sales on Mondays?
6. Assume that the gross profit of an enterprise is 20 per cent when sales are $24,000; 18 per cent when sales are $30,000; 15 per cent when sales are $35,000; and 12 per cent when sales are $40,000. On which amount mentioned above would the enterprise make the greatest net profit, assuming that operating expenses increase in direct proportion to sales? Operating expenses are $12,000 when sales are $24,000.
7. What is meant by "trend" in the interpretation of series of accounting data? Distinguish between series of individual items, of averages, of ratios.

CHAPTER XXXVIII

ANALYSIS OF COMPARATIVE BALANCE SHEETS

When a business man looks at the balance sheet of his enterprise and sees that his cash balance is a certain figure as of a certain date, he is informed only as to one phase of the cash—the amount on hand at a given moment. He cannot tell from such a figure whether this amount is too small, is too large, or is satisfactory. He may, of course, gain some useful information from a comparison of the cash balance with other items on the balance sheet or in the statement of income and expense. But still another important type of comparison may be made: a comparison of the present cash balance with the cash balances which have existed at certain other dates, or which now appear in the balance sheets of other companies.

Comparative balance sheets facilitate the analysis of statements.—A comparative balance sheet is one containing data of two or more balance sheets arranged in parallel columns. An illustration appears on the following page. In addition to the data of the two balance sheets, the report includes extra columns to indicate the increases or decreases in the various assets, liabilities, or proprietorship items.

The comparative balance sheet of the Modern Wholesale Company indicates that the "Cash" balance has been decreased by $6,000. The significance of such a decrease depends upon the collectibility of "Accounts receivable" and upon the due dates of "Accounts payable." The comparative balance sheet also indicates that "Merchandise inventory" has increased $80,000. The significance of this fact depends upon changes in other data expressing financial condition. The increase in the merchandise balance may mean any of the following: the enterprise has grown so rapidly that a large inventory is necessary to handle the demands of new customers; a decrease in annual sales has resulted in goods piling up on the shelves of the company; large amounts of goods have been bought at an unusually low price in anticipation of an increased market value. The comparison of items on successive balance sheets should be made with care. Relation-

MODERN WHOLESALE COMPANY

COMPARATIVE BALANCE SHEET—DECEMBER 31, 1927–28

(1)	(2) 1928	(3) 1927	(4) Increase	(5) Decrease
Current assets:				
Cash	$ 30,000	$ 36,000		$ 6,000
Accounts receivable	238,000	150,000	$ 88,000	
Notes receivable	42,000	78,000		36,000
Merchandise inven.	400,000	320,000	80,000	
	$ 710,000	$ 584,000	$168,000	$ 42,000
Fixed assets:				
Office equipment	$ 98,000	$ 92,000	$ 6,000	
Building	250,000	220,000	30,000	
Land	180,000	180,000		
Deferred charges	10,000	16,000		$ 6,000
	$ 538,000	$ 508,000	$ 36,000	$ 6,000
Totals	$1,248,000	$1,092,000	$204,000	$ 48,000
			Decrease	Increase
Current liabilities:				
Accounts payable	$ 130,000	$ 188,000	$ 58,000	
Notes payable	160,000	62,000		$ 98,000
	$ 290,000	$ 250,000	$ 58,000	$ 98,000
Fixed liabilities:				
Mortgages payable	$ 120,000	$ 160,000	$ 40,000	
Bonds payable	290,000	264,000		$ 26,000
	$ 410,000	$ 424,000	$ 40,000	$ 26,000
Net worth:				
Capital stock	$ 300,000	$ 250,000		$ 50,000
Surplus	248,000	168,000		80,000
	$ 548,000	$ 418,000		$130,000
Totals	$1,248,000	$1,092,000	$ 98,000	$254,000
Total changes	....	....	$302,000	$302,000

ships between the individual items can be fully understood only when thrown against the background of the complete business situation. For this reason, no sweeping conclusions may be drawn concerning the financial condition of an enterprise by the mere comparison of items appearing on successive balance sheets or statements of income and expense.

Analysis of comparative balance sheets reveals general financial changes.—It is possible and often desirable to attempt to draw some broad conclusions concerning business affairs by a general analysis of successive financial reports. Such comparisons must be made with care and with a realization of their limitations; however, they place before the business man a picture of the general changes in financial condition. The comparison and the grouping of the effects of similar items make it possible to discover important changes in the financial status of an enterprise. The comparison of large groups of items is most effectively carried on by setting them forth in a report in which the entire resources of the enterprise are considered as a unit. The changes in condition can be summarized in a statement which indicates both the sources of new funds which have become a part of the enterprise and the way in which the funds have been applied or expended. Such a statement is prepared from the facts of a comparative balance sheet and is known by various titles in practice. The title to be used in this text is "statement of sources and application of funds."[1] The net increases of the liabilities and proprietorship indicate the sources of the new funds from which assets have been procured. The net increases in the assets indicate the way in which these funds have been applied. The comparative balance sheet of the Modern Wholesale Company will serve as the basis for illustrating the analysis of the general changes in financial condition.

Statement of sources and application of funds illustrated.—In the comparative balance sheet shown on p. 494, two extra columns are provided in which are indicated the amounts of the increases or decreases in the various balance-sheet items. The changes will, of course, be equal in their amount and similar in

[1] The term "funds" as used in the following paragraphs refers to resources or wealth of any nature. It does not carry the technical limited meaning assigned to it in chap. xxvi, where it was discussed as a type of investment asset. Other titles for the "statement of sources and application of funds" are "general changes in financial position," "statement of application of funds," "changes in assets and liabilities," and "statement of sources and disposition of funds."

their tendency, for assets must always equal the liabilities plus the proprietorship. Column 4 lists the increases of assets ($204,000) and the decreases of liabilities and proprietorship ($98,000); column 5 lists the decreases of assets ($48,000) and the increases of liabilities and proprietorship ($254,000). The totals of these columns are the same. Some items increase; some decrease; but the net effect of the changes is to maintain the equilibrium of the balance sheet. The essential changes in financial condition during a period of time, as expressed by the data of a comparative balance sheet, may be classified as follows:

1. The *sources* of increased wealth (funds) of the enterprise (column 5).

2. The ways in which the funds have been *applied* by the enterprise (column 4).

The first group of changes comprises the items which are equivalent to the increases in liabilities and net worth. It also includes net decreases in specific assets, for the outgoing assets are the means of procuring the incoming assets. The second group includes the items which represent increases in assets and decreases in liabilities. From the standpoint of the enterprise as a whole, the increases of liabilities are "sources" of additional funds for the enterprise; the creditors by loaning money or selling goods on credit terms supply additional capital. Similarly the payments to creditors—the reductions of liabilities—represent ways in which the total funds are "applied." Not all funds received during a period are permitted to remain in an enterprise; new liabilities must be incurred to pay off old liabilities; certain assets must be surrendered to secure others.

A complete analysis of the changes in financial condition must subdivide the offsetting tendencies which make up the net change in the items. The changes in the items of a comparative balance sheet may be grouped as follows:

I. *Sources of funds* (column 5, comparative balance sheet)
   1. Increases of liabilities and proprietorship
   2. Decreases of assets

II. *Application of funds* (column 4, comparative balance sheet)
   1. Increases of assets
   2. Decreases of liabilities and proprietorship

The changes in the balance sheet of the Modern Wholesale Company may be set forth as follows;

STATEMENT OF SOURCES AND APPLICATION OF FUNDS

Sources of funds:		
Increased liabilities:		
Notes payable	$98,000.00	
Bonds payable	26,000.00	$124,000.00
Increased proprietorship:		
Capital stock	$50,000.00	
Surplus	80,000.00	130,000.00
Decreased assets:		
Cash	$ 6,000.00	
Notes receivable	36,000.00	
Deferred charges	6,000.00	48,000.00
		$302,000.00
Application of funds:		
Increased assets:		
Accounts receivable	$88,000.00	
Merchandise inventory	80,000.00	
Office equipment	6,000.00	
Building	30,000.00	$204,000.00
Decreased liabilities:		
Accounts payable	$58,000.00	
Mortgages payable	40,000.00	98,000.00
		$302,000.00

In the foregoing statement, the balance-sheet items are listed individually; but a condensed statement of the changes is sometimes more desirable. In the first place, fluctuations in the forms of certain assets or liabilities are not always significant; consequently only net changes in the total assets and liabilities need be shown. In the second place, if the changes in the certain assets are significant in nature or amount, they can often best be set forth in a subsidiary supporting schedule. A condensed statement might appear as follows:

Sources of funds:		
Increased liabilities	$124,000.00	
Increased proprietorship ...	130,000.00	
Decreased assets	48,000.00	
		$302,000.00
Application of funds:		
Increased assets	$204,000.00	
Decreased liabilities	98,000.00	
		$302,000.00

This latter statement may be altered by offsetting the current assets against current liabilities, to determine their net effect on working capital and by reinstating the fixed assets and liabilities and the proprietorship in the body of the report. Giving effect to the procedure just mentioned, the statement becomes:

Sources of funds:		
Increased fixed liabilities:		
Bonds payable		$ 26,000.00
Increased proprietorship:		
Capital stock (additional issue)	$50,000.00	
Surplus (profit)	80,000.00	130,000.00
Decreased fixed assets:		
Deferred charges		6,000.00
		$162,000.00
Application of funds:		
Increased net working capital		$ 86,000 00
Increased fixed assets:		
Office equipment	$ 6,000.00	
Building	30,000.00	36,000.00
Increased fixed liabilities:		
Mortgages payable		40,000.00
		$162,000.00

In the statement of sources and application of funds shown above, the fixed assets and liabilities are shown separately in the statement. The details of changes in current assets and liabilities are set forth in a subsidiary statement which explains the change in net working capital. An illustration of such statement is shown below:

STATEMENT OF WORKING CAPITAL

Changes in current assets:		
Increases:		
Accounts receivable.....	$ 88,000.00	
Merchandise...........	80,000.00	
	$168,000.00	
Decreases:		
Cash..................	$ 6,000.00	
Notes receivable........	30,000.00	
	$ 42,000.00	
Net increase..................		$126,000.00
Changes in current liabilities:		
Increase: Notes payable...	$ 98,000.00	
Decrease: Accounts payable	58,000.00	
Net increase..................		40,000.00
Increase in net working capital....		$ 86,000.00

When net working capital is reduced as the result of the operations of a fiscal period, the decrease must be listed in the first section of the statement of sources and application of funds. The statement thus presents net working capital as a source from which the new funds are procured; for it means that current assets have been liquidated or current liabilities incurred to purchase fixed assets or to pay fixed liabilities.

The statement of sources and application of funds interpreted.—What significant facts may be deduced from the data of the statement of sources and application of funds? May it be substituted for a statement of income and expense? Obviously not, for it gives the reader knowledge concerning only the general changes in financial status. It may be determined from the statement illustrated above that the financial status of the Modern Wholesale Company has been strengthened by funds received from two main sources—the issue of capital stock, and the net profit of the period.

Some additional bonds have been issued, and a portion of the deferred charges have been applied to the foregoing period. The benefits of these funds are reflected in two main divisions of the balance sheet—the current capital section and the fixed-capital section. Both the net working capital and net fixed capital have been increased as result of the operations of the period; the former was increased by $86,000; the latter by $44,000. As far as the working capital is concerned, it is apparent that the current ratio has been materially improved; the large increase in the current assets has been accompanied by a relatively small increase in the current liabilities. Whether this change is a good thing will depend upon the collectibility of the accounts receivable; also upon the salability of the merchandise, in which forms most of the increase of current assets is represented. As far as the fixed assets are concerned, it may be seen that the increase of fixed assets is not accompanied by an increase of fixed liabilities; in fact, there has been a decrease in total fixed liabilities, for the decrease in mortgages payable more than offsets the slight increase in bonds payable. The main source of funds, therefore, is shown to be the increase of proprietorship resulting from the issuance of additional Capital stock and the retention of current profits by the enterprise.

Conclusions on the interpretation of accounting reports.—The interpretation of accounting data is an integral part of the accounting process. It is the way in which the important facts of business status and operations are placed before interested parties, especially the managers responsible for the administration of the enterprise. The method of interpretation comprises the classification and summarization of accounting data, as well as the discovery of important relationships among the groups of data. The relationships may be expressed as ratios between different items on similar reports, or between similar items on different reports. In addition to the computation of ratios, the accountant may concern himself with the computation of averages to typify groups or series of data, and also with the discovery of trends in the accounting data. Ratios and averages may themselves be used as the basis for measuring variations from a central tendency in status and operations. The only limits to the refinements of accounting interpretation are the limits of usefulness to the interested parties, the ability of the accountant to apply special technique, and the cost of applying the more elaborate methods to the data at hand.

QUESTIONS ON CHAPTER XXXVIII

1. What is a comparative balance sheet? Might such a report be prepared to show financial status at more than two points in time?
2. What is a statement of sources and application of funds? Would such a statement be of any advantage to a business man who was unfamiliar with the principles of double-entry bookkeeping? Explain.
3. A person once characterized the statement of sources and application of funds by the following: "It tells you where they [meaning funds] came from, and where they went." Is this statement essentially true, if assets themselves are a designation of where funds "went"?
4. Another person called it the "whence-whither" statement. What might such an expression mean?
5. In what sense are reductions in specific assets to be considered as sources of funds? Are they not rather transactions which reduce funds? Discuss fully.
6. If the comparative balance sheet shows that the net values of fixed assets have been reduced by allowances for depreciation, would you classify the allowances for depreciation as sources of funds? Explain fully why or why not.
7. What advantages can you see in the separation of the changes in working capital from the other changes set forth by the statement of sources and application of funds?
8. What is the justification for grouping increased assets and decreased liabilities in the same class as types of "applications" of funds? Discuss fully in what way these changes are similar from the point of view of financial status.

CHAPTER XXXIX

ADMINISTRATIVE USES OF COST DATA[1]

What has it cost? What will it cost? Such questions are asked daily by business men; and the answers to them, whether right or wrong, are used as the bases for important administrative decisions. The present chapter will explain and illustrate some of the uses of cost data in the management of an enterprise, and the methods by which costs are classified and summarized.

The concept of "cost-units."—Chapter xxxii introduced the problem of identifying expenses with periods of time; it emphasized the importance of stating clearly just when various expense transactions occur. This chapter directs attention to a different aspect of expenses—their identification with particular services, departments, transactions, or products, rather than with particular accounting periods. These units of business, in terms of which expenses are grouped or clustered, may be spoken of as "cost-units"; the identification of the expenses of a period with these cost-units is the essential problem of cost accounting.[2] The difficulties of cost accounting are of two types: (1) selecting

[1] This chapter illustrates the fact that accounting method is affected by the uses to which the accounting data are to be placed, with particular reference to administrative, rather than social, control. The "application" of accounting data is not a part of accounting method; however, the whole advantage of the "measurement" and "interpretation" of business transactions is lost unless the accounting data are to be used in some way. Accordingly it has been thought best to close this text with two chapters selected to illustrate the point of the opening chapter, namely, that accounting is a "tool for economic control," administrative and social. Many administrative uses of accounting data could be selected for discussion. The importance of "cost" in administrative action justifies, it is felt, selecting the determination and use of cost data as a typical administrative problem which accounting helps to solve.

[2] Strictly speaking, "expenses" and "costs" are identical terms, although there persists a feeling in the minds of many accountants and business men that costs are expenses identified with particular cost-units. Thus one speaks of "cost of goods sold," but of "selling expenses" or "administrative expenses." It would be more descriptive of the actual situation to refer to each of these groups as a *cost:* cost of goods (which were) sold; cost of selling (them); cost of administration (of the enterprise).

and defining cost-units which are significant for given purposes; (2) identifying expenses with the proper cost-units. Cost-units may vary greatly in their scope and in their nature, the unit in each case being a definite quantum of some type of business activity. The cost-unit may be an activity which continues throughout an entire fiscal period, such as soliciting business in a certain territory, advertising a given commodity, or maintaining a continuous service. The cost-unit may be an activity during a shorter period of time, such as the delivery of ten tons of coal, the assembly of an automobile, or the mixture of a group of chemical substances. The cost-unit may be stated, of course, in terms of actual commodities, such as hats, boxes, or machines; in such cases the term "cost" usually refers to the cost of manufacturing the articles to a point of completion where they may be sold or delivered to another enterprise, and does not include costs of distribution.

The chief purposes of cost determination.—The task of identifying the expenses of a period with specific cost-units may, and often does, require extensive reclassification of the data set forth in the conventional ledger accounts. The selection of significant cost-units is affected greatly by the purposes for which the costs are determined. Some of the most important purposes for which costs are computed will be discussed in the following paragraphs.[1]

Establishment of a selling price.—In the long run, business men will not continue to sell a product or render a service below cost; for, although it may be necessary to dispose of purchased or manufactured products below cost, it is not necessary to replace such products unless the expected selling price will exceed the expected outlay. A manufacturer of certain products at a cost of $6.00 may be able to sell them for only $4.00 each. But he will not prepare other similar products for the trade if he thinks that costs will exceed selling prices. A knowledge of past costs is an important element in administrative policy formation, for such information provides a clue to probable future costs. Future costs will not be incurred by business men unless there is some promise of their being exceeded by the resultant income.

[1] Many of the ideas in the present chapter have been suggested by J. M. Clark's *Economics of Overhead Costs*, particularly chaps. iii, ix–xii.

Costs do not determine selling prices; they merely form the basis for estimating normal or satisfactory selling prices over periods of time. This fact is not clearly understood by all business men; for in many instances they seem to feel that the public is under a moral obligation to pay prices which will cover past costs. A merchant not infrequently makes a statement such as the following: "I cannot sell this article for less than $10.00, for it cost me $9.00, not including the cost of transportation or of handling it in my store." Such explanation of a relatively high price falls upon deaf ears when addressed to an audience of buyers in a competitive society. A merchant will, of course, ordinarily refuse to secure an article or to render a service for a customer unless he can realize a price which will cover his expected total costs; but he cannot force a customer to pay a certain price just because certain past costs have been incurred. It is the costs "not yet incurred"—not the costs "already incurred"—which have an effect on selling price.[1] The estimates of future costs will vary when made by different persons; it is just this fact, however, which is the basis for distinguishing good management from bad. Enterprises which continually underestimate future costs to the degree that selling prices do not cover actual costs of business activities are traveling the road to financial insolvency, however much their operations may benefit society at large.

Determination of profitable lines.—The comparison of total income and expense reveals the net effect of business operations of a given period upon financial status. But such comparison gives no clue to the products or services which are most profitable. When certain services are being rendered for prices which do not cover their costs, the question immediately arises as to whether the services should be discontinued or the price raised. For example, a bank might discover that the cost of handling small

[1] There are some cases where goods are sold (in advance of procurement or production) at prices which are a certain percentage or amount above actual cost. Such contracts are usually referred to as "cost-plus" contracts; they are common in various transactions which continue over periods of time, such as the construction of buildings or the total yearly supply of raw materials to another plant. For example a large manufacturer of automobiles may procure his tires for original equipment at a price equal to a constant percentage above actual costs, computed monthly.

checking accounts is greater than the financial income from the funds on deposit. To meet this situation, it establishes a minimum average limit below which checking-account balances may not fall, without being made subject to a "service charge."

The fact that the total cost of a service or product is greater than the income which can be directly ascribed to it does not, of course, necessarily mean that such service or product should be discontinued. There may be other reasons for continuing them, such as the sales advantages of producing a "full line," or the advertising value of a particular service. Banks, for example, often perform minor clerical and legal duties for their customers gratis, such as the preparation of mortgages and leases and the giving of advice on income-tax returns. Regardless of the resulting decisions, accounting makes possible the comparison of the income and expense attributable to separate products or services of an enterprise, and the determination of profitable lines.

Comparison of the efficiency of departments or processes.—The cost-unit may be a department of an enterprise. Assume that the cost records of the paint department of a furniture factory show that 5,000 tables were stained and varnished at a total cost of $30,000; this is an average cost of $6.00 per table. This cost of $6.00 may be compared with the costs in the paint department for previous years, or with the costs of paint departments in other factories. Where there are several similar departments in an enterprise, the comparative costs of performing certain tasks may be very useful as a gauge of the efficiency of the departments. Such data often aid in revealing unsatisfactory conditions which may be improved by study and special treatment. The cost-unit may be also a process in the manufacturing operations; such a unit is very useful for comparing the efficiency of different methods of accomplishing the same objective.

The control and evaluation of inventory.—Where the cost-unit is a manufactured product, or where merchandise inventory is kept on hand in relatively large amounts, the problem of adequate cost determination is very important. Cost accounting makes possible the valuation of the goods on hand at any one time; at least, it provides the cost data which may serve as the basis for arriving at satisfactory inventory values. Correct inventory valuation in turn enables an enterprise to calculate the actual costs of carrying a stock of goods of a certain size, and thus it makes possible intelligent consideration of the problem of how large an inventory of goods should be maintained.[1]

Types and classes of cost dependent upon purposes.—We now turn from a consideration of the different purposes for which cost may be determined to the problem of what types of costs may best serve the various purposes. This consideration involves a twofold application of cost analysis: the concept of cost which is to be adopted in forming administrative decisions, and the classes of costs which comprise the total expenses connected with the cost-unit.

Average vs. differential cost.—One of the most important concepts in the calculation of costs is the distinction between a distribution of total cost, on the one hand, equally among a total number of cost-units and, on the other hand, according to the causal responsibility for, or benefits resulting from, the costs incurred. The one method of identifying total costs with cost-units assumes that all expenses are to be shared equally by similar cost-units; it provides an "average" cost of producing certain articles or rendering certain services. The other method attempts to allocate total expenses by a differential analysis of the data; by apportioning to different cost-units those portions of total cost which they "cause" or from which they benefit. "Average cost" is the figure determined by dividing total cost by the number of

[1] One of the bookkeeping devices generally made part of a cost-accounting system is a complete perpetual-inventory record of the inventories of raw materials, goods-in-process, and finished goods. These records consist of subsidiary-ledger cards or sheets supporting the respective controlling accounts with the various inventories. The perpetual inventory cards for raw materials are commonly designated as "balance-of-stores" cards, and each card carries a record of the materials of a certain kind that have been received and issued. The individual entries are authorized by invoices and requisitions, which are periodically summarized for an adjustment of the controlling account. The subsidiary records for finished goods are less frequently kept and are known variously as "balance-of-finished-goods" cards or "balance-of-stock" cards. The subsidiary records for goods-in-process are not generally considered as illustrations of the perpetual-inventory principle, although they may be so regarded. They are usually referred to as "cost-sheets," or "job-order sheets."

units produced. "Differential cost" is the additional cost (above that already incurred) of producing additional units, as illustrated by the following table:

COMPARISON OF AVERAGE AND DIFFERENTIAL COSTS OF PRODUCTION

No. of Articles Produced	Total Cost	Average Cost per Article	Differential Cost of 10 Additional Units	Differential Cost of Each of 10 Additional Articles
10	$240.00	$24.00	...	...
20	400.00	20.00	$160.00	$16.00
30	540.00	18.00	140.00	14.00
40	600.00	15.00	60.00	6.00

In the foregoing illustration the average cost per article of output decreases with increased production. The average costs of producing forty units is $15.00 per article. Yet the additional cost of producing the last ten articles is only $6.00 per article. What is the real cost of each of the last ten articles—$15.00 or $6.00 per article? The accountant typically would answer the question by using the average cost. In the first place, the double-entry accounts do not separate the costs of additional units of output; the only figure available in the double-entry records when forty articles have been produced during a period of time is the total expense of producing the forty articles—$600. In the second place, the accountant frequently uses accounts to establish a normal or long-run desirable selling price, which must be high enough to cover total cost. Assuming that all units of output are to be sold at the same price and in the same market, the figure to be used for this purpose is "average cost."

Yet if it were possible to sell the first thirty units of the article at a price which would cover the average cost of producing them, it might be desirable to sell the next ten articles at any price exceeding the "differential cost" per unit, which is $6.00. It is exactly this principle which is applied by some factories when they attempt to sell additional output at a lower price in some distant market, or under some special brand in the same market. The process of unloading increased output at any price which exceeds differential cost is known as "dumping." It has been followed frequently in the past in foreign trade, much to the discomfiture of manufacturers in the market receiving goods which were produced and sold at prices based on differential costs. The principle of differential costs will be mentioned again in the discussion of the different classes of partial costs, where the problem is one of deciding whether to incur costs in addition to those which cannot be avoided or which have already been incurred and are irrecoverable.

Classes of partial costs.—The concept of the total costs of given cost-units may be supplemented by a study of the different types of cost which comprise the total. Many different aspects may be mentioned, varying with the point of view from which they are observed. Two bases of classification only will be explained in the following paragraphs: current expenses vs. fixed charges; direct vs. indirect expenses.[1]

Current expenses vs. fixed charges.—The terms "current expenses" and "fixed charges" are used in a variety of ways by accountants and business men. "Current expenses," as here used, refer to those expenses incurred solely to carry on the operations of a given fiscal period; they are expenses which would not be incurred at all if the enterprise were to discontinue operations. "Fixed charges," on the other hand, are the expenses which continue regardless of business operations. The expenses which will be classed as current expenses[2] and fixed charges will vary with the particular enterprise under consideration. It is possible, however, to give some typical illustrations which are of practical value. In the case of a factory, for example, one may say that the current expenses consist of such items as salaries and expenses of the sales and clerical forces, advertising, materials consumed in factory

[1] J. M. Clark, in his *Economics of Overhead Costs*, pp. 46–55, discusses other bases for classifying partial costs. Among them are the following: variable vs. constant; sunk vs. recoverable; urgent vs. postponable; manufacturing vs. selling.

[2] The current expenses here contrasted with *fixed charges* are not the same group as the *operating* expenses which were contrasted with *non-operating* expenses in chapter xiii. In chapter xiii the term *operating* was synonymous with *major*, as contrasted with minor or incidental expenses; it included interest, taxes, and depreciation, and all other expenses connected with business operations.

operations, factory labor employed in manufacturing, and fuel for power generation; typical fixed charges would be depreciation on building and equipment (the portion due to the passage of time or action of the elements), interest on bonded indebtedness, property and other general taxes, salaries of permanent executive staff, and wages of watchmen to protect the property.

In the long run, prices should be high enough to cover the total current expenses and fixed charges of an enterprise. But it is conceivable that an enterprise might choose to accept any price which was high enough to cover more than the current expenses of manufacturing a product. Accepting such a price would be better than permitting the plant to lie idle, with fixed charges continuing unabated. The following table will illustrate the point:

INCOME AND COST DATA OF A PLANT WHEN IDLE AND WHEN PRODUCING 3,000 UNITS AT A LOSS OF $3.00 PER ARTICLE

	Units of Production	
	None	3,000
Selling price per unit	....	$ 14.00
Total income	....	42,000.00
Fixed charges	$25,000.00	25,000.00
Current expenses	....	26,000.00
Total cost	25,000.00	51,000.00
Cost per unit	....	17.00
Total net loss	25,000.00	9,000.00

The data shown above illustrate the paradoxical situation of its being profitable to operate an enterprise at a loss. It is more profitable to continue operations at a slight loss than to discontinue operations at a great loss. The total net loss to the enterprise is $9,000 when it is operated; $25,000 when it is closed down. With an output of 3,000 items during a fiscal period, it would be necessary to receive a price of at least $17.00 per unit to cover the total current expenses and fixed charges. At a price of $14.00, a $3.00 loss is borne on each article produced, giving an average loss which totals $9,000 during the fiscal period. Unfortunate as this situation may appear from the standpoint of the manufacturer, it may be preferable to the discontinuance of operations.

The current expenses of an enterprise may be regarded as a special type of differential cost. They are the costs of operating a manufacturing plant, which would not be incurred if the plant were to remain idle. If any amount of product can be disposed of at a figure higher than the additional cost incurred to produce it, profits will be larger than if production were discontinued. In the case of additional output of a factory which is already operating, it may be necessary to sell the additional product in a distant market or under conditions which would not spoil the market for other goods. The possibility of spoiling the market for a later period when higher prices might be secured may, of course, act as a deterrent to unlimited price-cutting. Nevertheless, there are many cases where it will never become possible to secure prices for articles which will be high enough to cover both current and fixed charges incurred in making them. For example, a large amount of expensive specialized machinery may have been purchased to manufacture a product for which public demand has fallen off, or which can be manufactured by competitors according to improved and more economical processes. In such cases, the manager must choose between operating his plant at partial capacity, on the one hand, and cutting prices, on the other; neither policy, presumably, will make it possible for him to recover total expenses. He will follow the policy which permits him to reduce his loss to the smallest amount.

Direct expenses vs. indirect expenses.[1]—Total cost may also be classified as "direct" and "indirect." By "direct expenses" is meant that group of costs directly traceable to specific cost-units; such expenses may be illustrated by the lumber used in the manufacture of a table, or the wood-carver's labor applied to the decoration of a molding. Direct expenses (direct costs) are usually presumed to vary with the amount of business transacted; to the extent that they do so, they are similar to current expenses.

[1] The concept of direct vs. indirect expenses was introduced in chapter xx of this text, in the discussion of the accounts subsidiary to the Goods in Process account. The indirect expenses were there summarized under the general caption "Burden"; they are also referred to in practice as "overhead" costs. Other terms similar to the terms "direct" and "indirect" expenses are "prime" and "supplementary," and "special" and "general."

Direct costs per unit do not always vary directly with the amount of business transacted. For example, an employee may perform labor on twenty-five articles in one day at a daily wage of $5.00, which is 20 cents per article. On the other hand, if he were to be paid at a rate of 18 cents per article, he might increase his speed of work and thus complete forty articles in one day. The total direct-labor cost would increase from $5.00 to $7.20, or 44 per cent over the original cost. However, the total output would be increased 60 per cent over the original production.

"Indirect expenses" are those costs which are not directly traceable to specific products or services. To some degree they are similar to the fixed charges of an enterprise; for in many instances they are of such nature that they continue even when no product is being manufactured or no service rendered. No single definition will serve to explain all the different aspects of indirect expenses. Indirect expenses are to be differentiated from direct expenses by the methods of identifying them with cost-units rather than by any intrinsic qualities which characterize them.

Indirect expenses present special problems to the accountant. —The characteristics of indirect expenses make it difficult to identify them with specific cost-units. Some of the special characteristics of indirect expenses and the peculiar problems of their allocation will be discussed at this point.

Criteria of indirect expenses.—Certain expenses are incurred which *render simultaneous service* to various portions of output or to the business as a whole. A foreman may supervise the operations involving five or six different products which come from a factory. Taxes assessed upon the value of a factory building must be charged against all the different types of output. The salary of a factory manager and the cost of generating current for power likewise represent services rendered simultaneously to different units of output or to an entire business.

Some expenses are incurred primarily to serve one unit of the business, but may *indirectly benefit others*, either at the same time or in future periods. For example, the advertising of hams may increase the sale of bacon, or the advertising of tooth paste may increase the sale of shaving cream. A lawsuit incurred to settle an important question of business policy and legal privilege may be of indirect advantage to numerous other transactions in the future. The expense of maintaining a research bureau may be incurred to increase sales during a given period of time; it may indirectly reveal facts about customer preferences which lead to far-reaching changes and economies in the manufacturing processes.

Expenses may be regarded as indirect costs because of the *mere difficulty of apportioning* them directly to any particular units of service of a product. For example, a foreman may supervise a wide variety of different activities throughout a day; a watchman may protect numerous products during the night; a general workman may be employed in several departments in the course of a week.

The allocation of indirect expenses to cost-units.—The total expenses of an enterprise, it has been shown, may be charged against particular cost-units. A cost-unit may be a specific transaction (such as the shipment of a hundred crates of fruit), a subdivision of the administrative organization (such as the finishing or assembling department of a factory), a commodity (such as a motor car, a ton of soap, or a dozen hats), or a business process (such as enameling or packing). Some of the expenses are charged directly to specific costs-units because the materials or services they represent may be physically identified with these units in a visible and unmistakable fashion. The expenses which cannot be identified with cost units in this direct fashion—the indirect expenses—are allocated on some predetermined basis to the particular transactions, departments, commodities, or processes. The allocation of indirect expenses involves a judgment as to what causes govern the amount of the indirect expenses; in some cases the governing factor may be discovered by an analysis of interrelationships among the accounting data; in other cases the basis of allocation must be determined by expert opinion advanced by technicians.

The theory underlying the allocation of expenses is that cost-units should be charged with the costs which are incurred for their benefit and which would not be incurred if the product were not made or the service were not rendered. Each item, therefore, should be charged with the "differential cost" of producing it. The concept of differential cost was discussed in connection with successive increments of identical cost-units. It is also applicable to the apportionment of a given total cost to a group of cost-units which have been completed. The question is: What indexes may be used to identify certain parts of the indirect expenses with particular cost-units? This question is one of the most difficult which accountants face in the calculation of costs. It can be answered only by the most careful statistical analysis of the ways costs behave under different conditions and rates of manufacture; data should also be available concerning cost behavior when the proportions between the different products are changed. In practice, cost accountants have adopted various rules of thumb which appeared to be useful for the purposes at hand. Where such rules of thumb are applied with full knowledge of their arbitrary character, they provide a satisfactory guide to administrative control. Where, however, such methods of allocating expenses are looked upon as indisputably correct and logical, they may lead to error in dealing with cost problems. Some of them will be illustrated in the following paragraphs.

Bases for allocation.—It is not necessary that all expenses be allocated to a cost-unit on the same basis, or that a given type of expense be allocated to all cost-units on the same basis. The following table indicates typical bases which might be adopted where certain indirect expenses are to be allocated to departments, the departments being the cost-units.

Basis for Allocation to Departments	*Types of Indirect Expenses to Which Applicable*
Value of departmental machines	Depreciation and taxes (on machines and equipment)
Floor space of department	Depreciation and taxes (on building)
Cubic air space in department	Light, heat
Number of employees in department	General office expenses, foremen's salaries

Groups of indirect expenses may be allocated as a whole to a cost-unit. This procedure is often followed where the cost-unit is a physical commodity rather than a department or process. An attempt is made to discover some characteristic of the product itself, or of its components, which will serve as the proper index for apportioning indirect expenses. Some of the aspects of commodities which have been used as the basis for apportioning indirect expenses to them are: (1) cost of direct labor involved in manufacture (the labor-cost method); (2) number of hours of direct labor involved in manufacture (the labor-hour method); (3) length of time during which the commodity remains at, or receives the services of, a special department, machine, or process (the production-center method). The advantages and limitations of each of these methods arise out of the particular conditions under which they are applied. No one process can be said to be superior to the others for every purpose and in all circumstances. The establishment of satisfactory rules for allocating indirect expenses and the application of the rules in practice are the special tasks of the "cost accountant."[1]

Joint-costs of raw materials present special problems of allocation.—"Joint-cost" is a term which describes a certain type of expense incurred to further the output of several products or the rendering of several services.[2] When a meat-packing establishment purchases a live hog for its packing operations, it may pay a price of 10 cents per pound for the entire animal. If the animal weighs 400 pounds the total cost is $40. But after the pork operations and other factory processes have been completed, the various parts of the animal are offered for sale in such different items as hams, bacon, shoulders, pickled feet, and hide. These articles are "joint products," and the cost of the live hog is the "joint-cost" of bringing them all to market. But how much shall each one of these products bear of the total price paid for the original animal? Shall each product be charged 10 cents per pound for the material entering into it? If so, some of the articles

[1] For extensive treatments of the technique of cost allocation, the reader is referred to such texts as J. L. Dohr, *Cost Accounting;* W. B. Lawrence, *Cost Accounting;* P. M. Atkins, *Industrial Cost Accounting;* and J. M. Clark, *Economics of Overhead Costs*, chaps. xi, xii.

[2] Many indirect expenses are "joint-costs" in the sense that they must be allocated to different cost-units. The use given to the term in the present discussion is a limited, technical sense encountered in business practice and in accounting literature.

may sell at net losses, while others will show enormous profits; for the different portions of an animal are sold at widely different prices.

The phenomenon of joint-costs is frequently encountered in practice. The cost of raising sheep is the joint-cost of raising wool and mutton. The cost of handling eastbound and westbound railroad traffic is a joint-cost; for if cargo is not hauled each direction, certain costs must nevertheless be incurred to return empty cars to a point of reloading. The cost of mining coal is the joint-cost of producing coke, coal-gas, and kerosene. The salary and expenses of a salesman who solicits business for several lines of goods represents a cost incurred in the distribution of several products. Wheat ground in a flour mill is the common source of first-grade flour, second-grade flour, and bran. A final illustration is the cost, at a saw-mill, of logs which are made into boards of different widths and grades. In order to saw wide boards from the central section of a lot, it is necessary to manufacture narrower boards from the outer edges. Such boards are sometimes regarded as second grade because of the knots which appear at the points branches join the central trunk or limb.

Joint-costs include only those which are incurred up to the point where the joint products begin to emerge as separate items. Costs incurred after separation may, of course, be assigned directly to each of the final products. In some cases, the joint-costs comprise all or nearly all of the costs of the final products, as in the case of the mutton and wool produced by the growing of sheep. In other cases, the additional costs added to the separate products comprise a relatively large portion of the total costs, as in the cases where hides are subjected to elaborate tanning and finishing processes in the production of fine leather.

The problem of apportioning joint-costs to different joint products is one that very often defies logical solution. Where one of the joint products is of relatively small total value, it is often referred to as a "by-product." The income from the sale of a by-product can be regarded as an offset to the cost of the main product; in cases where joint products are produced in relatively equal quantities, some other method of treatment must be devised.

Very often the joint-cost is imputed to the various final products in proportion to the selling prices less the costs of selling them. Whether or not this method suffices is a question dependent for its answer upon the uses for which costs are determined. The method is used frequently by packing houses, where costs are used to compare the relative profitableness of different lines.[1]

Interest on invested capital as a part of cost.—The question arises continuously in cost computation as to whether a charge which represents interest on the invested capital should be included in the cost of specific commodities or services. An examination of the problem shows that it may properly be excluded for some purposes but must be included for others. For purposes of measuring the net financial income of an enterprise during a given period, only actual interest paid on borrowed capital need be considered; in such cases, the interest on net worth is included in the return to the proprietors as part of their annual profits. But when attention is turned to the establishment of a normal or satisfactory selling price, interest on total capital must be considered; for capital must earn a normal rate of interest or it will, if such procedure be feasible, be transferred to other lines of industry.

For the purpose of determining profitable and unprofitable lines, comparison of data must recognize the total investment required to carry on the production of each line. Similarly, in the comparison of the efficiency of departments or processes, the amount of investment is an important factor. A process which requires a large investment may, of course, reduce the cost of a commodity, or it may not. In either case, the recognition of interest on investment makes it possible to compare processes cor-

[1] The solution of the joint-cost difficulties lies in turning out the joint products in such proportions that the greatest total net profit can be secured from the sale of them all. In some cases the proportions cannot be changed; for the production of one article necessitates production of the same relative amount of the other; for example, the number of hides produced in the slaughtering of a given number of steers will necessarily equal the number of beef carcasses. In other cases, it may be possible to change proportions of the output by variations in the processes. For example, it may be possible to secure more gasoline from crude petroleum by processes which affect the portion which would otherwise be used to produce lubricating oil, and vice versa. Cf. J. M. Clark, *Economics of Overhead Costs*, pp. 98–104.

rectly. In deciding whether to accept an order for additional product which can be produced without an increase in equipment, interest computations need not be included. On the other hand, if the additional amount of business will require the investment of additional capital, interest becomes a factor for consideration.

The question of whether interest on total capital is a cost or not has been discussed heatedly by accountants; however, much of the argument has arisen from misunderstandings as to the points of view of the disputants.[1] In some cases the argument has been merely one of how interest expense was to be classified, whether as an expense of production, or as some other type of expense, such as "selling" or "administrative." The solution of the problem in this form depends, of course, on the particular classification of accounts which an enterprise has adopted; it assumes that interest is to be accounted for in the double-entry records.

A sharper line of difference of opinion arises over the question of whether interest on invested capital (if a cost of operation) should find explicit recognition in the books of account. Practical accountants assert that such treatment gives rise to accounting difficulties which confuse the records and serve no useful purpose; for debits to an Interest Expense account require offsetting credits to an Interest Income account representing the earnings on owned assets. The interest comes out of one pocket and goes into the other. Such a paradoxical situation is one which many practical men refuse to recognize in accounts which purport to contain data of bona fide financial transactions.

Among enlightened accountants the question of whether interest is a cost seems to have been reduced to a question of whether it should be entered in the general financial accounts as affecting net income. Interest on investment is obviously an important element in cost determination, though its recognition is not necessary to the computation of net financial income. If it does not appear in the double-entry records, it must be added for certain purposes; if it does appear in the accounts, it must be subtracted for certain purposes.

[1] A lengthy discussion of the economic and accounting aspects of "interest as a cost" appears in the *Year Book of the National Association of Cost Accountants, 1921*, pp. 45–96; also in C. H. Scovell's *Interest as a Cost*.

QUESTIONS ON CHAPTER XXXIX

1. What is meant by a "cost-unit"? Illustrate.
2. State briefly and illustrate the chief purposes of cost determination.
3. For what purposes is "average cost" of greatest use in management? Is average always practicable as a guide in the establishment and carrying out of business policies?
4. Distinguish "current expenses" and "fixed charges"? Differentiate "current" expenses as explained in chapter xxxix from "operating expense" as described in chapter xiii.
5. What are some of the various criteria by which expenses are said to be "indirect" rather than direct?
6. There may be said to be two theories of allocating indirect costs to cost units: the "responsibility theory" and the "benefit theory." Do you think that in the long run the cost units which are responsible for certain expenses are also the ones which receive the benefits from them?
7. A third theory, or rule, for allocating indirect costs is that of charging a cost unit with all of the indirect expenses it can stand, under the circumstances. It is a sort of "ability-to-pay" theory. Do you think that this theory at times influences the costs imputed to certain joint products of an enterprise?
8. Explain the various bases sometimes used for apportioning different costs or groups of costs to special departments or products: labor-hour, labor-cost, machine-rate.
9. What are "joint-costs?" How do they differ from indirect costs?
10. Is "interest on invested capital" a part of the cost of carrying on certain activities or manufacturing certain products by an enterprise? Should it be recorded in the books of account?

CHAPTER XL

SOCIAL CONTROL THROUGH ACCOUNTS

The present chapter deals with some special applications of accounting as a tool for "social control" of economic activity. These are (1) accounting as a tool for controlling governmental activities—the administration by a government of duties which are primarily economic in nature; (2) accounting for non-profit institutions; (3) government uses of accounting to control private enterprises—both public utilities and those enterprises which are not so commonly recognized as being of a public or quasi-public nature; (4) the uses of accounting by groups of private enterprises in an attempt to co-ordinate their activities and to increase their individual efficiency. The chapter closes with brief mention of the profession of accountancy which has developed in the modern economic order.

The rôle of accounting in government administration.—The place of accounting in government administration corresponds in most respects to the field it covers in the administration of private enterprise. There is scarcely a function or activity of a private corporation but can be or has been performed by a government. But the conditions of government administration are peculiar in their nature—so much so, that the problem of governmental accounting may well be regarded as a special problem, in many respects different from that of accounting for a private enterprise. The proprietorship of a government is vested in the entire group of citizens. General governmental activity is not carried on for the benefit of a few persons; in fact, it is not even carried on for the benefit alone of those persons who contribute to the cost of governmental operations. Any wealth appropriated by a government is, therefore, to be regarded as belonging to the citizenry; the government, considered by itself, is a peculiar entity dependent upon the consent of the citizens for the continued appropriation of wealth and the application of funds to the citizens' own benefits.

The government must be considered as the "agent" of the citizens, the financial representative of the people in the collection and expenditures of the common funds. Consequently a government must be limited in the scope of its activities. The citizens may be said to appoint the government merely as their fiscal agent. The rôle of the government as a mere collecting and disbursing agent of the citizens explains in a measure the "red tape" so often encountered in governmental financial operations. The restrictions on government finance are established as matters of public policy (good or bad) which must be recognized and allowed for by the government accountant. A government may also play the rôle of a mere "custodian" of public funds. As such it is required to hold for periods of time funds which are placed under its control; such funds are not to be expended immediately upon receipt but to be kept either for gradual use over a long period of time or for ultimate payment of obligations. Illustrations of such wealth placed in the custody of a government are the funds used as working capital for a publicly owned utility, and the sinking-funds for the retirement of public debts.

The objective of governmental activity is not primarily to increase the wealth of the government. As was indicated in a foregoing paragraph, the objective is rather to carry out the wishes of the citizens, regardless of what these wishes may be. Private enterprises attempt to earn the greatest possible income with the least possible expense; the amount by which income exceeds expense is the measure of the success of a private enterprise. A government, on the other hand, attempts merely to collect sufficient income to cover an agreed expense program over a given period of time. In fact, the income program cannot properly be established until probable expenses have been estimated in detail. An expense program is, of course, often limited by the possibilities of raising certain funds from the public; nevertheless, the expense program comes first in planning the financial operations of a government.

Fund accounting differentiates government procedures from those of private enterprise.—The first official step in the procurement of government funds is a declaration by the legislative body that a certain amount of wealth may be appropriated from the citizens and used for a governmental purpose. The act of the legislature may, and usually does, indicate specifically the procedure to be followed in collecting funds, as well as the government activities to which they must be devoted. Each parcel of wealth thus specially appropriated is classified under the heading of a certain "fund." Each fund is accounted for as a separate financial entity.[1] The custodian of the fund is expected to collect the wealth according to the process authorized by law, and to disburse it according to instructions. His responsibility is to make sure that all moneys are collected and spent in terms of the appropriation acts affecting the various funds. "Fund accounting" has been the core of governmental accounting records. It is fund accounting which has distinguished governmental accounting most sharply from the accounting practices of private enterprises.

The scope of fund accounting.—Immediately upon the passage of an appropriation act, the governmental units which are to act as the agents and custodians for certain funds make the first financial records for each fund. An appropriate title is given to the fund itself, and accounts are opened under captions which make possible a determination of the financial status of each fund at any time. The accounts are grouped in terms of the assets on hand, the encumbrances (liabilities), and the available balance (proprietorship) of each fund. Assume that a legislative enactment authorizes the appropriation of a certain sum for the maintenance of public highways (e.g., the sum to be collected by a special tax upon automobiles). A "fund" might be established under some general title such as "Highway Maintenance." Highway Maintenance would then be regarded as an enterprise with a distinct financial entity similar to that of any private enterprise. Highway Maintenance would be as much a separate economic unit for purposes of governmental accounting as would the business of a grocery store or of a small factory.[2]

[1] Compare chap. xxxiii where the "financial appropriation" was introduced as a classification basis for the accounting data of a private enterprise. The basis which is used only occasionally by private business is the foundation of adequate government accounting.

[2] The technique of accounting for governmental funds is explained fully in L. Morey's *Introduction to Governmental Accounting*. A discussion of the administrative uses of governmental accounting data may be found in W. F. Willoughby's *Public Administration*, chaps. xxxv–xliii.

Limitations of fund accounting.—It should be obvious from the foregoing discussion that the segregation of the resources of a government into funds requires a high degree of decentralization in the accounting records, a condition which makes very difficult the classification of data in such form as to set forth completely governmental status or operations. A statement of governmental financial condition might, therefore, be nothing more than a list of the available appropriations in the various funds existing at a given time. Fund accounting requires that the custodian of a fund submit a report of all receipts and expenditures. It does not provide data, however, which will tell whether resources have been spent wisely, as well as within the limits of the intended purpose. It has been remarked by students of governmental accounting that fund accounting accomplishes its greatest purpose by making sure that all money is spent, that none remains for the operations of ensuing fiscal periods. At the present time, citizens have come to be interested in *how* money has been expended, as well as in the fact that *it has been* spent. This has led to a demand for further classification of governmental expenditures beyond the classification of funds which would provide some measure of the efficiency of government representatives.

Administrative uses of accounting data.—Governments use accounting data in much the same manner as do private enterprises: as the basis for comparing the efficiency of departments or processes; as the basis for establishing a normal or satisfactory tax rate; as the basis for evaluating the assets on hand and unexpended at any given time; as the basis for placing responsibility upon the executives in charge of important governmental functions. Central governments have found accounting control very important in their fiscal relations with subsidiary governments. This is particularly true of state governments which have financial relations with the counties as collecting agents for the general taxes of the commonwealth. Many of the state governments have established uniform accounting systems which must be adopted and maintained by the counties, cities, and other governmental units within their jurisdictions. The chief accounting officer of the state in many cases maintains a complete staff of assistants whose duty it is to instal such systems and to audit the accounts of cities and other political subdivisions from time to time.

The Census Bureau of the United States Department of Commerce has been collecting for some time financial statistics of the various states and of the cities with populations of more than 30,000. The reports are prepared according to a uniform classification of accounting data, although the states and municipalities are not required to maintain their current accounting records according to the classification. The Bureau maintains a large office force and a field staff whose function it is to assist the state and municipal accountants in summarizing the data for the report.

> The purpose of the reports is to provide information in regard to the financial administration of the states [and cities] in such form as to be comparable, with the hope that it may be of assistance to the officials who are charged with the responsibilities incident to the administration and betterment of the individual states [and cities]; directly, through personal study of the reports, and indirectly, through the interpretations and recommendations of the practical students of state [and municipal] affairs.[1]

Accounting for non-profit institutions similar to that for governments.—The problems of non-profit institutions are different from, yet similar to, those of governments. The primary difference lies in the fact that only a limited group of persons are directly interested in the financial operations of a club, church, educational institution, or technical society. The similarities arise out of the fact that non-profit institutions plan operations in such manner that income will be equal to the necessary expenses. The need for accurate accounting for non-profit institutions is no less important than in the management of private gain-seeking enterprises. Not infrequently the resources commanded by a social club or an educational institution exceed those of some of the large commercial or industrial corporations. Cost data in

[1] *Financial Statistics of States, 1925*, p. 11: "The report presents statistics of: (1) the total and per-capita receipts of states from revenues and from the principal classes thereof; (2) the total and per-capita payments of states for expenses, for interest, and for each of the principal classes of expenses, and the total for outlays [capital expenditures]; (3) the total value of state properties; (4) the total and per-capita indebtedness of states; (5) the total and per-capita assessed valuation of property subject to taxation, and the total and per-capita levy of taxes."

such institutions may be exceedingly important in the proper administration of the funds intrusted to the organization. Some typical sources of revenue to non-profit institutions are contributions, endowment earnings, fees, tuition, sales of merchandise, ward or dormitory rentals, and café or restaurant charges. The number of sources of income to a non-profit institution would ordinarily be greater than to a private enterprise with the same gross revenue. The problem of expense classification for a non-profit institution is essentially the same as for a private enterprise.

Governments regulate various public-service corporations by the use of accounting data.—Governments have found accounting to be a very useful device in the control of the financial policies of corporations affected with a public interest. The United States government through the Interstate Commerce Commission and other agencies has established a system of accounting for railroads and telephone companies which prescribes in detail a complete classification of a balance-sheet and income and expense accounts. With the establishment of the Interstate Commerce Commission in 1887, Congress made its first attempt to regulate interstate commerce by preventing the railroads from charging rates under such conditions as to abuse the privileges granted them by the government. Effective control of railroad operations was impossible until the passage of the Hepburn Act, February 25, 1906, which gave the commission sweeping control in matters of accounting. The commission was given authority to require monthly reports of revenues and expenses, and to obtain special reports when needed. It was also empowered to prescribe a uniform classification of accounts and to compel its adoption. The Transportation Act of 1920 has carried farther the problem of accounting control by empowering the Commission to determine a "fair value" on which the railroads should be allowed to earn a "fair return," which has been set by the Commission at 6 per cent.

State governments, likewise, in their regulation of public service corporations have depended to a great extent upon the accounting records and reports which they were authorized to demand from the companies under their supervision. The public-utility commissions of the various states usually prescribe the classification of accounts which the companies must use in their annual reports. They do not, however, demand that no other accounts be kept, if other accounts would be useful for administrative purposes. The public-utility commissions of the various states are vested with full authority over the operations of utilities, such as electric, gas, and water companies. They do not control the activities of the railroads and telephone companies, inasmuch as these enterprises come under the jurisdiction of the Interstate Commerce Commission, except in the rare cases where the operation of such enterprises is entirely confined within the limits of the state.

Governments regulate the activities of private enterprise with the aid of accounting data.—The many ways in which the various governmental agencies use accounting to control private enterprise will be commented on briefly in this present discussion. Three national agencies will be mentioned: the Federal Trade Commission; the United States Tariff Commission; the Bureau of Internal Revenue.

Federal Trade Commission.—The Federal Trade Commission was created by an Act of Congress, September 26, 1914, to prevent persons, partnerships, or corporations, except banks and common carriers,[1] from using unfair methods of competition in commerce. Section 6 of the act gives the commission power to "investigate from time to time the organization, business, conduct, practices, and management" of the enterprises under its jurisdiction. This power includes the right to investigate the accounting records and reports, including the methods of computing costs and of calculating income and expense. The Commission has been instrumental in the promotion of uniform classifications of accounts in various industries and has published numerous pamphlets on the benefits of improved accounting systems (two of those most widely circulated are entitled *Fundamentals of a Cost System for Manufacturers* and *System of Accounts for Retail Merchants*, both published in July, 1916).

United States Tariff Commission.—The present Tariff Com-

[1] Banking operations are under the jurisdiction of the Federal Reserve Board; common carriers, under the Interstate Commerce Commission.

mission was created by the revenue act of September 8, 1916, to serve as an advisory body which should gather and prepare for the use of the president and Congress "industrial and economic information concerning the foreign and domestic trade of the United states as related to and affected by customs, duties, laws, regulations"[1] of the United States and other nations. Special provisions of the act were enacted in 1922: section 315, sometimes called the "flexible" provision, authorizes the president to adjust tariff rates, within the limits of 50 per cent, in order to "equalize ascertained differences in costs of production of like or similar articles in the United States and in the principal foreign countries." The work of carrying on the investigation of costs of production in the United States and various competing countries is under the supervision of the Tariff Commission. With the aid of a staff of full-time economists and accountants, the Commission continuously carries on investigations of production costs of different articles. These inquiries may be carried on under the terms of section 315, at the request of interested parties, or under section 318, which permits investigations whenever in the opinion of the Commission it is practicable.

Bureau of Internal Revenue.—The income-tax legislation of the past two decades, beginning with the act of 1909, has had a profound influence upon the accounting procedures of American individuals, partnerships, and corporations. It has not only influenced accounting procedure; it has actually been the cause of instituting accounting procedure in many cases where no accounts of any kind had been previously maintained. The federal revenue acts of recent years require the filing of several million returns by the individuals and enterprises of the United States. The data recorded thereon must all be classified in terms of the subdivisions of income and expense specified on the income tax returns. The Commissioner of Internal Revenue, or his representatives, may require that adequate records and evidence be produced to explain how the data were compiled.

Other methods of accounting control.—Many more illustrations of the uses which governments make of accounting data in the

[1] *Tenth Annual Report of the United States Tariff Commission* (1926), pp. 2–3.

control of private enterprise could be mentioned, such as the control of banks by the state bank-examining departments and the Federal Reserve Board, and the creation of commissions in the various states to regulate the issue of corporate securities. Those which have been mentioned serve to illustrate the fact that accounts play an important rôle in governmental regulation of business.

Associations and groups of similar private enterprise use accounts for control of the industry and its members.—The scope of accounting activities which have been undertaken by various associations of private enterprises has been very broad. Most of the attention has been directed to the development of uniform classifications of accounts, uniform systems of records and forms, and methods of budgeting administrative activities. The benefits which are alleged to arise from attention by the associations to matters of accounting are improved methods of internal administration, an improved attitude on the part of the public, the elimination of cut-throat competition arising from ignorance of costs.[1] The United States Chamber of Commerce has actively promoted the adoption of uniform systems of computing manufacturing costs and has issued bulletins from time to time pointing out the advantages to be gained from uniformity. A series of three bulletins was released in 1923 by the Department of Manufacture which dealt fully with the topic "Uniform Cost Accounting in Trade Associations." The number of associations which have made some attempts to adopt uniform systems of accounts or to benefit by the interchange of accounting information cannot be determined. There are several thousand commercial and industrial organizations in the United States;[2] the records of the United States Department of Commerce indicate that probably two

[1] Some of the generalizations in this section are based upon the studies of F. H. Sumrall, reported in an unpublished manuscript entitled "Accounting Activities of Trade Associations."

[2] A pamphlet containing a list of such organizations was published by the United States Department of Commerce in 1926. It contained the names of approximately one thousand national and international organizations, and about four thousand local associations. The pamphlet is entitled *Commercial and Industrial Organizations of the United States*.

hundred of the associations have made some attempt to interest members in uniform accounting systems.

Accountancy as a profession.—Two main types of professional accountants may be distinguished in modern economic organization: (1) the heads of the accounting departments in single enterprises—the private accountants; (2) the specialists who render certain types of accounting service to various firms—the public accountants. The scope of the activities of the private accountants will be discussed first.

Private accountants.—In every enterprise there is some individual who devotes part or all of his time to the supervision of the accounting records. Some of the titles most frequently used to designate this person are "auditor," "chief accountant," "chief clerk," "controller," "head bookkeeper." There is no title which may be said to be preferable for designating the chief accounting officer of an enterprise. There seems to be some tendency at the present time to adopt the title "controller" more extensively than in former years.

The place which the private accountant takes in the administration of a particular enterprise varies greatly. His duties in some instances are limited to the routine recording of transactions which are evaluated and interpreted by other persons or departments. In other cases, the chief accountant is regarded as an important member of the executive personnel of his company. The organization of an accounting department is, of course, affected by the organization and administration of the enterprise it serves. Typical subdivisions of the accounting activities are grouped around the maintenance of special types of records, such as cost accounts, the pay-roll, accounts receivable, cash receipts and disbursements, and inventories. In some cases one executive will be responsible for such varied duties as double-entry accounting procedure, statistical analysis (including that of non-value data), office management, and budgetary procedure.

The accountant occupies a unique position from which to view the general status and operations of an enterprise. Records of all other departmental activities—production, sales, purchasing, finance—come under his supervision. These records enable him to maintain a correct perspective of the enterprise and to measure its progress in terms of general success rather than of the activity of a single department. Consequently accountants are by training equipped to diagnose business ills and recommend remedies for administrative difficulties. An understanding of the broader aspects of accounting is often the basis on which success in business administration is founded.

Public accountants —Some accountants devote their talents to the service of several enterprises concurrently, consulting with business men or examining financial data on a strictly professional basis.[1] The original reason for the growth of public accountancy was the need for independent verification of the financial records of businesses and governments. At the present time, however, the duties of public accountants extend beyond the verification of the financial correctness of accounting records. The following activities may be recognized in modern practice:

1. Auditing: "A systematic examination of the books and records of a business or other organization, in order to ascertain or verify, and to report upon, the facts regarding its operations and and the results thereof."[2]

2. Constructive accounting: The recommendation and installation of bookkeeping systems adapted to the particular needs of a given enterprise.

3. Income-tax counsel: The determination of taxable income, to avoid the burden of taxes improperly assessed.

4. The appraisal of property values: The accountants have, of course, been assisted by engineers and economists in the valuation of fixed assets.

5. General business counsel: The analysis of accounting rec-

[1] A "certified public accountant" (C.P.A.) is an accountant who has satisfied the legal requirements of some state as to his general proficiency, either by passing an examination or by submitting evidence of successful practice, or both. The educational and experience requirements for permission to take the C.P.A. examinations vary with the individual states. Governmental approval of financial policies is sometimes dependent upon the records having been "certified to" by a certified public accountant; likewise certain business contracts are dependent upon the professional opinions of certified public accountants. In most states the holding of a C.P.A. certificate is not a prerequisite to independent professional practice.

[2] R. H. Montgomery, *Auditing Theory and Practice* (4th rev. ed., 1927), p. 3.

ords to indicate trends in business activity and to suggest courses of action.

The universality of accounting method.—This chapter brings the reader back to the point at which the discussion of accounting method was opened: "accounting as a tool for economic control" —a tool which may be used in the administration of a specific enterprise or in the co-ordination and direction of social economic energy. Accounting is a method of evaluating and interpreting the business transactions which may be measured in terms of financial value.

The present trend toward a livelier interest in accounting in educational institutions is not merely a reflection of the modern flare for practical subjects. It is a recognition of the fact that an understanding of our modern economic order can be derived only from learning the language in which economic affairs are expressed. Accounting is the process by which the transactions of an economic enterprise are described, discussed, and interpreted. A knowledge of accounting thus opens the way to a wide range of experience and understanding, much like that made available through the mastery of a foreign language. Accounting is not a technique separate from the facts of everyday existence; it pervades every branch of practical affairs. Accounting may be regarded as part of a complete education for the purpose of living as well as for making a living; it is possible that some day it will be looked upon as necessary equipment for a citizen who wishes to play his proper rôle in a democratic society.

QUESTIONS ON CHAPTER XL

1. In what ways does governmental accounting differ from private accounting? Are the differences to be explained by the differences between governmental enterprise and private enterprise?
2. What is meant by "fund accounting" when applied to governmental accounting procedure?
3. What are some of the limitations of fund accounting for purposes of administration?
4. It is suggested that governmental balance sheets cannot be prepared by merely listing all the resources and liabilities at their cost price, and the liabilities at their face values. Could the same thing be said about the financial reports of private enterprises? Discuss.

5. What advantages arise from the uniform methods of classifying governmental accounting data? Would the work of the Census Bureau in securing financial statistics of cities and states be possible unless the data were uniformly classified in the reports?
6. Think over the names of some large non-profit institutions. Estimate the total amount spent during a year by any one of them and suggest records and reports which would be useful in its control.
7. What are some of the governmental agencies which regulate the public service corporations of the United States and the various states?
8. Explain briefly the work of some of the national commissions which base their decisions upon the accounting data of private enterprises.
9. How do associations of private enterprises use accounting data in the formation and carrying out of business policies?
10. Assume that a citizen had no thought of engaging in business or becoming a public administrator. Would there be any advantage gained from his becoming familiar with the problems of accounting method?

BIBLIOGRAPHY

BIBLIOGRAPHY

The following classification of references does not imply that each work mentioned can be adequately distinguished as belonging only to one group. Some of the books cover a wide variety of topics and could be classified under several of the general headings. The reading-list is intended to suggest, however, that the books mentioned are particularly useful in study of the special topics under which they are grouped.

The bibliography does not include all, or all kinds of, accounting books. No elementary textbooks are included, the list being intended for supplementary, rather than complementary, reading. No books are included which treat the problems of particular industries. American texts are listed in classified groups. Following these are certain texts written by European authors.

DOUBLE-ENTRY THEORY AND TECHNIQUE (SPECIAL APPLICATIONS)

BENNETT, G. E., *Advanced Accounting* (New York, 1922).

FINNEY, H. A., *Principles of Accounting*, Vols. I and II (New York, 1923).

KREBS, W. S., *Outlines of Accounting*, Vol. II (New York, 1927).

PATON, W. A., *Accounting Theory*, Part I (New York, 1922).

SPRAGUE, C. E., *Philosophy of Accounts* (New York, 1907).

ACCOUNTING VALUATION

GENERAL TREATMENTS

HATFIELD, H. R., *Accounting* (New York, 1927).

KESTER, R. B., *Accounting Theory and Practice*, Vol. II (New York, 1925).

PATON, W. A., *Accounting Theory*, Part II (New York, 1922).

SPECIAL TREATMENTS

CLARK, J. M., *Economics of Overhead Costs* (Chicago, 1923).

DEWING, A. S., *Financial Policy of Corporations*, Book III (New York, 1926).

FINNEY, H. A., *Actuarial Science* (New York, 1920).

KOHLER, E. L., *Federal Income Taxes* (Chicago, 1927).

ROBBINS, CARL M., *No Par Value Stock* (New York, 1926).

PINKERTON, P. W., *Accounting for Surplus* (New York, 1923).

REITER, PROSPER, *Profits, Dividends and the Law* (New York, 1926).

YANG, J. M., *Goodwill and Other Intangibles* (New York, 1926).

INTERPRETATION OF ACCOUNTING DATA

BLISS, J. H., *Financial and Operating Ratios on Management* (New York, 1923).

COUCHMAN, C. B., *The Balance Sheet* (New York, 1924).

Day, E. E., *Statistical Analysis* (New York, 1925).
McKinsey, J. O., *Managerial Accounting* (Chicago, 1924).
Mills, F. C., *Statistical Methods* (New York, 1924).
Newlove, G. H., *Consolidated Balance Sheets* (New York, 1926).
Riegel, R., *Elements of Business Statistics* (New York, 1924).
Young, B. F., *Statistics as Applied in Business* (New York, 1925).

USES AND APPLICATION OF ACCOUNTING DATA

Bennett, G. E., *Accounting Systems* (Chicago, 1926).
Bliss, J. H., *Management through Accounts* (New York, 1924).
Bruere and Lazarus, *Applied Budgeting* (New York, 1926).
Church, A. H., *Manufacturing Costs and Accounts* (New York, 1917).
Dohr, J. L., *Cost Accounting* (New York, 1924).
Hilgert, J. H., *Cost Accounting for Sales* (New York, 1926).
Hodge, A. C., *Retail Accounting and Control* (Chicago, 1926).
Jackson, J. Hugh., *Audit Working Papers* (New York, 1923).
Jordan, J. P., and Harris, G. L., *Cost Accounting* (New York, 1925).
Kohler, E. L., and Pettingill, P. W., *Auditing Procedure* (Chicago, 1924).
Lawrence, W. B., *Cost Accounting* (New York, 1926).
McKinsey, J. O., *Budgetary Control* (New York, 1922).
Montgomery, R. H., *Auditing Theory and Practice* (New York, 1927).
Morey, L., *Introduction to Governmental Accounting* (New York, 1927).
Schlatter, C. F., *Cost Accounting* (New York, 1927.)

EUROPEAN REFERENCES

Carter, R. N., *Advanced Accounts* (London).
Dicksee, L. R., *Advanced Accounting* (London).
Fischer, R., *Die Bilanzwerte* (I. Bd., 1925; II. Bd., 1908; Leipzig).
Garnsey, G., *Holding Companies* (London, 1922).
Gerstner, P., *Revisions-Technik* (Berlin, 1926).
Herzog, S., *Industrielle und Kaufmännische Statistik* (Stuttgart, 1926).
Masi, V., *La ragioneria come scienza del patrimonio* (Bologna, 1927).
Müller-Bernhardt, *Industrielle Selbstkosten bei schwankendem Beschäftigungsgrad* (Berlin, 1925).
Pixley, F. W., *The Accountant's Dictionary*, Vol. I–II (London, 1922).
Ryall, R. J. H., *Dictionary of Costing* (London, 1926).
Schmalenbach, E., *Grundlagen dynamischer Bilanzlehre* (Leipzig, 1925).
———, *Grundlagen der Selbstkostenrechnung und Preispolitik* (Leipzig, 1925).
Schmidt, F., *Bilanzwert, Bilanzgewinn, und Bilanzumwertung* (Berlin, 1924).
Walb, W., "Die kaufmännische Betriebswirtschaftslehre," in Rothschilds *Taschenbuch für Kaufleute* (Leipzig, 1922).

LABORATORY EXERCISES

LABORATORY EXERCISES

The exercises recommended in the following pages are composed with a view to testing the students' grasp of the principles developed in the text. The symbols by which the exercises are designated refer to the chapters in *Accounting Method.* In so far as practicable, specific instructions accompany the data of each exercise; where no instructions are given (beyond the mere requirements of the problem), the student is expected to use his judgment in arriving at solutions. Consequently, in some cases alternative solutions may be regarded as corrrect. Where a student makes specific assumptions in his attack upon an accounting problem, a clear statement of the assumptions should accompany the solution.

No exercises are assigned which relate to Part I "The Rôle of Accounting on Modern Economic Life." The first exercise, therefore, is based upon the material in chapter iii.

EXERCISES ON DOUBLE-ENTRY ACCOUNTING—PART II

III—1

The following data are secured from the accounting records of the Lindbergh-Wright Airplane Company on January 1, 1928. Arrange them in the form of a balance sheet, indicating which are assets, liabilities, and proprietorship, respectively: land, $16,000; delivery equipment, $13,000; airplanes for sale, $34,000; notes payable to C. N. Coolidge, $29,000; note receivable from H. L. Nungesser, $3,600; account payable to Aircraft Corporation of America, $27,000; machine shops and hangars, $39,000; cash, $4,100; C. C. Lindbergh, capital, $30,000; mortgage on land, held by H. Rickenbacker, $10,000; Orville Wright, capital, $28,000; account receivable from L. Pinedo, $15,200.

III—2

The following transactions are to be analyzed in terms of assets, liabilities, and proprietorship. Indicate in each case the title for, and nature of, the items increased or decreased as a result of the transaction. Prepare a single balance sheet giving effect to all the transactions.

1. Mr. Brown invested $10,000 in the wholesale hardware business.
2. Borrowed $5,000 by giving a note to a bank.
3. Purchased furniture and fixtures on credit terms, $7,000.
4. Purchased a delivery truck for cash, $3,600.
5. Gave a note for $4,500 in partial payment for the furniture and fixtures.
6. Mr. Brown withdrew $6,000 cash from the business for his own personal use.

7. Paid the bank $5,000 cash in payment of note due them.
8. Admitted Mr. Smith as a partner on his investment of $8,000 cash in the business.
9. Mr. Smith paid out of his own personal funds the note for $4,500 due for the furniture and fixtures, counting it additional investment.
10. Mr. Smith retired from the business, selling his interest to Mr. Jones for $12,500.
11. Mr. Brown withdrew as a proprietor, accepting the firm's note for $4,000 in exchange for his proprietorship.

Example (1): Cash (asset) increased........... $10,000
Brown, capital (proprietorship) increased.. $10,000

IV

Indicate the debits and credits resulting from the transactions listed in Exercise III—2. Place the debits and credits in the proper columns of appropriate accounts. Test the accuracy of your work by adding the totals of the debits and credits. The totals should, of course, be equal.

V

a) Indicate the debits and credits arising from the following transactions, showing in each case whether the account affected refers to an asset, a liability, an expense, an income, or proprietorship.

b) Prepare accounts for each of the following items, entering debits on the left and credits on the right sides, respectively: Cash; Merchandise; Accounts Receivable; Notes Receivable; Sales Salaries; Office Salaries; Advertising; Delivery-truck Income; Insurance; X, Capital; Rent; Furniture and Fixtures; Office Expense; Accounts Payable; Notes Payable; Sales; Delivery Equipment.

c) Test the accuracy of your analysis and record by totaling debits and credits to insure their being equal.

1. Mr. X invested $10,000 cash in a mercantile enterprise.
2. Paid $200 for one month's rent of a store building.
3. Transferred from previous business fixtures valued at $2,000, and set them up for use in the new business.
4. Bought, for $500 cash, additional fixtures for new building.
5. Paid in advance the monthly telephone charge of $12.50.
6. Bought for cash merchandise, $2,500.
7. Purchased on account from Byron & Company, merchandise, $5,000.
8. Sold on account to R. W. Watson merchandise, $450.
9. Sold for cash to Mr. Watson merchandise, $350.
10. Received from Mr. Watson a note for $300 on account.
11. Paid miscellaneous office expenses of $45.
12. Paid sales clerk $50. Paid office help $35.
13. Received from Mr. Watson, $125 on account.

14. Gave Byron & Company a note on account, $2,500.
15. Paid Byron & Company cash on account, $2,000.
16. Bought on account a delivery truck for $1,500.
17. Mr. X withdraws $500 for his own personal use.
18. Sales to M. W. White on account, $350. Cash sales, $550.
19. Received cash for use of delivery truck, $45.
20. Purchased from Jones & Company merchandise, $3,000. Gave a note for $1,000, cash for $1,250, remainder on account.
21. An advertising bill for $35 received but not paid.
22. Paid insurance on stock of merchandise and fixtures, $50.
23. Sold merchandise to M. W. Johnson, $1,250. Received from him a note for $500, cash for $400, and remainder on account.
24. Paid sales clerk 50. Paid office help $35.

VI—1

Journalize and post the transactions of Exercise V, using the standard journal and standard ledger pages. Use the same account titles as were selected for the analysis in Exercise IV. Give particular attention to the proper uses of the date columns, account-title-and-explanation columns, and the money columns; also to the technique of cross-indexing the journal data and ledger data.

VI—2

1. R. M. Whitney bought the business of G. D. Ramsey. The fixtures were valued at $1,500; the merchandise at $5,000; the delivery truck at $500. Mr. Whitney paid one-half in cash and one-half with a note payable. He placed in the business an additional $5,000 cash.
2. Paid the rent for the month, $75. Paid for heat and light, $25.
3. Insured his stock, fixtures, and delivery truck, at a cost of $160. Cash sales for the day were $350; sales on account, $450.
4. Bought merchandise on account, $5,500; bought merchandise for cash, $1,500; paid repair expense on truck, $65.
5. Gave a note on account to a trade creditor, $3,000. Paid cash on account to a trade creditor, $1,000.
6. Cash sales were $350; sales on account were $600. Received a note on account from a customer for $400. Received cash on account from a customer, $350. Paid clerk $25; paid delivery boy $20. Mr. Whitney drew out $500 for his own personal use.
7. Purchased for cash, office supplies, $35. Received a bill for fuel, $65 (to be paid at the end of the month). Paid $35 for advertising. Paid $15 for a license for a street sign. Donated $5.00 to the local ball club. Cash sales were $350. Sales on account were $200. Paid freight on purchases of merchandise, $35.
8. Fixtures repaired and a bill rendered for $50. A customer paid a note due Whitney, $400. Whitney paid the note due a creditor, $3,000.

a) Journalize the foregoing transactions, using account titles listed below.

b) Post all items to the ledger accounts.

c) Balance the Cash account and prepare pencil totals of all accounts which contain more than one debit or credit.

Use the following accounts in the ledger, giving each account a separate page number (not necessarily a separate page): Cash; Accounts Receivable; Accounts Payable; Merchandise; Sales; Notes Payable; Notes Receivable; Furniture and Fixtures; Delivery Equipment; R. M. Whitney, Capital; Freight-In; Selling Expense; General Administrative Expense.

VII

a) Prepare trial balances from the accounts of R. M. Whitney in Exercise VI—2, consisting of: (1) debit and credit totals; (2) account balances.

b) Close the accounts with financial operations, assuming that merchandise has been sold which has a cost value of $1,500.

c) Prepare a balance sheet.

d) Prepare a statement of income and expense.

VIII

Journalize the following transactions, using appropriate account titles. The transactions are to be considered independently of each other and are *not* to be posted to accounts.

1. A lot and building are valued at $125,000. A vacant lot adjoining and similar to this one is valued at $25,000. There is a mortgage of $50,000 against the first lot and building. We purchase the two lots and the building on the following terms: we assume the existing mortgage of $50,000; we give a second mortgage on the one lot and building for $20,000; we pay the balance of $80,000 in cash.
2. Cash paid for fixtures, $5,000. Note given for truck, $3,000. Cash received from customers on account, $4,000. Note given to creditor, $500.
3. Bonds sold for cash, $50,000.
4. A, proprietor, increased his investment by $5,000 by paying that amount from his own funds to a creditor.
5. B, proprietor, has recently borrowed $1,000 from the firm on his personal note. He now decides to consider this as a permanent withdrawal of capital.
6. New machinery is purchased on account, $1,500.
7. $10,000 is borrowed from the bank on our sixty-day note and used to pay creditors.
8. An employee draws a week's salary in advance, $45.
9. Office supplies are purchased for cash, $350. Factory supplies are purchased on account, $500.
10. Surplus cash of $25,000 is invested in Liberty bonds.
11. Bonds payable of $20,000 are redeemed at maturity.

12. Capital stock of X Company is purchased as an investment, for $10,000.
13. A small fire destroys $1,000 worth of fixtures, and the insurance company pays us, in cash, the amount of the loss.
14. An addition to a building is constructed at a total cost of $25,000, which we pay in cash.
15. A new building is constructed at a cost of $150,000. We finance this by selling $75,000 of bonds; by borrowing $25,000 at the bank on our note; by selling Liberty bonds which we hold, $20,000; and by drawing down our cash balance by $30,000.

IX

a) Journalize the following transactions, using the standard form of journal and the account titles as given below. Do not write out explanations.

b) Post the data to ledger accounts.

c) Prepare a trial balance.

d) Save the ledger and trial balance for future reference. (It will be used in connection with Exercise XI—1).

Account Titles

Cash; Accounts Receivable; Buildings; Accounts Payable; Notes Payable; Mortgages Payable; L. W. Burrows, Capital; L. W. Burrows, Personal; Purchases; Purchases Returns and Allowances; Rent Expense; Interest Expense; Bad Debts; Sales Discounts; Taxes; Salaries; Advertising; Building Repairs; Office Supplies; Sales; Sales Returns and Allowances; Purchases Discount; Rent Income; Interest Income.

Transactions

The numerals identifying the transactions may be used as dates of the month of January for purposes of making complete journal and ledger entries of this group of transactions. It will be apparent to the student that all of these transactions could not possibly have occurred during any one month.

1. Lowell W. Burrows starts business with a cash capital of $5,000.
2. He purchases merchandise on account from sundry creditors amounting to $3,000.
3. Cash payments for the day consist of: rent $175; office supplies, $100.
4. Sales on account are $525.
5. Goods values at $275 are returned to creditors.
6. Cash purchases are $850.
7. Sales on account are $920.
8. Goods are returned from customers, amounting to $65.
9. Accounts payable, amounting to $1,200, are paid on which the creditors allow a discount for prompt payment amounting to 2 per cent of invoice price. Cash sales, $1,200.
10. Received on account from customers, $180, less 1 per cent discount.
11. Mr. Burrows withdrew $100 in cash for temporary use.

12. A note for $400 is given to a merchandise creditor.
13. A note is received from a trade debtor amounting to $500.
14. Interest on the notes receivable is received amounting to $25.
15. Interest on notes payable is paid, amount $20.
16. An allowance of $16 is made to a customer for goods damaged in transit.
17. A merchandise creditor permits a reduction in his bill to cover articles which were not correctly designed but which have been received and placed in stock, $75.
18. Salaries are paid, $200.
19. Taxes are paid, $350.
20. A bill of $140 for advertising is received and approved.
21. An account receivable of $126 is determined to be uncollectible.
22. A building is purchased for $10,000 and paid for as follows: cash, $1,000; mortgage, $5,000; four notes of $1,000 payable at six-month intervals during the next two years.
23. A building is repaired, and the bill for $185 received from the carpenters is paid by applying the amount against the carpenters' debt as customers of the business. Sales on account, $1,400.
24. The note receivable for $500 is paid in full, and the final interest payment of $25 is received at the same time.
25. Mr. Burrows advanced $200 cash from his personal funds to pay an account. He intends to withdraw this amount as soon as it is convenient.
26. The note payable for $400 is paid with interest amounting to $15.
27. Sixty dollars cash is received for rent on a portion of the building.

X

Analyze the following business situations, and make the necessary journal and ledger entries to adjust the accounts affected. Indicate in regard to each debit and credit whether it is a balance-sheet account or an income or expense account.

1. At the time of adjustment, the Merchandise Inventory account showed a balance of $2,500. The actual inventory on hand was $4,600.
2. The accounts showed $1,600 of fuel purchased. One-half of this amount had been consumed.
3. An inspection of the office supplies on hand indicate their value to be $300. The Office Supplies account carried a debit balance of $700.
4. A note receivable for $5,000 had been discounted at the bank two months prior to this date. This discount was $100 and had been debited to Prepaid Interest. The note is due in two more months.
5. An insurance policy for one year with a face value of $10,000 had been taken out one month prior to the date of closing. The first annual premium of $240 was paid at that time, and the amount was debited to Prepaid Insurance.
6. Liability insurance payable to the amount of $200 is unpaid and not yet recorded in the books.

7. Wages payable to the amount of $1,000 had been incurred at the time of closing. They were due and payable three days later.
8. Rent to the amount of $600 was due to the landlord.
9. A sixty-day 6 per cent note for $3,000 was received from a customer on the day the books were adjusted. The interest was paid in advance by the customer in cash. Journalize the receipt of the note and the cash.
10. Accrued interest on notes receivable amounted to $75.
11. Space in warehouse had been rented to another company. Two months prior to this date $150 was received from them in advance payment for three months' rent. The amount had been credited to Advance Rentals.
12. Interest accrued on notes payable amounted to $125.
13. The $3,000 note receivable mentioned in situation nine (9) above is paid. Journalize the receipt of the cash and the recognition of the interest income on the note on the date of maturity, bearing in mind the records made when the note was received.

XI—1

a) Adjust the accounts of L. W. Burrows, assuming the following facts as of January 31, 19__:

1. Merchandise on hand, $1,600. (Use a special account for Merchandise Inventory.)
2. Salaries due but not yet payable, $120.
3. Office supplies on hand, $35.
4. Interest receivable, not yet due, $85.
5. One-fourth of rent income must be deferred.

b) Close the income and expense accounts, after adjustment of the ledger.

c) Prepare a balance sheet.

d) Prepare an eight-column work sheet to show the effects of the adjusting and closing entries, and to verify the correctness of the closing procedure.

XI—2

Certain of the accounts of a firm contain the following balances on December 31:

Merchandise Inventory, December 1.......	$ 7,000.00
Purchases..............................	19,000.00
Freight-in..............................	200.00
Sales returns and allowances..............	400.00
Sales..................................	30,000.00
Interest on notes receivable...............	100.00
Salaries................................	3,000.00
Insurance..............................	1,200.00
Advertising.............................	600.00

An inspection of merchandise on hand, December 31 reveals that it should be valued at $15,000.

a) Set up the information in accounts.

b) Make the journal entries to adjust and close the accounts.

c) Post the journal entries, using a Profit and Loss account and transferring the net profit to an account entitled "Proprietor, Personal."

XII—1

From the following trial balance and supplementary data taken from the books of H. V. Tugg, on December 31, 19—, make (*a*) a work sheet; (*b*) a balance sheet; and (*c*) a statement of income and expense.

Cash	$ 2,000.00	
Accounts receivable	8,000.00	
Notes receivable	500.00	
Merchandise inventory, January 1	10,000.00	
Furniture and fixtures	5,000.00	
Allowance for depreciation on furniture and fixtures		$ 500.00
Delivery equipment	21,000.00	
Allowance for depreciation on delivery equipment		6,000.00
Buildings	16,000.00	
Allowance for depreciation on buildings		3,000.00
Bonds	18,000.00	
Land	16,000.00	
Accounts payable		23,000.00
Notes payable		600.00
Mortgage payable		10,000.00
Sales		63,000.00
Purchases	44,000.00	
Advertising	1,500.00	
Sales salaries	2,000.00	
Office supplies	1,000.00	
Office salaries	5,000.00	
H. V. Tugg, capital		44,500.00
Delivery expense	600.00	
	$150,600.00	$150,600.00

Final inventory of merchandise	$15,000.00
Inventory of office supplies	300.00
Accrued office salaries	150.00
Accrued sales salaries	250.00
Advertising to be deferred to next period	450.00
Accrued interest on bonds held	900.00
Accrued interest on mortgage payable	500.00

Allowance for doubtful accounts, 2 per cent of accounts receivable.

Depreciation: Buildings, 5 per cent.
Furniture and Fixtures, 10 per cent.
Delivery Equipment, 20 per cent.

XII—2

JOHN JONES

Trial Balance, December 31, 1922

Account	Debit	Credit
Cash	$ 41,000.00	
Accounts receivable	80,000.00	
Notes receivable	20,000.00	
Merchandise inventory (initial)	75,000.00	
Furniture and fixtures	5,000.00	
Delivery truck	4,000.00	
Purchases	200,000.00	
General expenses	10,000.00	
Salaries	15,000.00	
Buildings	50,000.00	
Insurance	6,000.00	
Sales		$300,000.00
Interest income		1,000.00
Allowance for depreciation of furniture and fixtures		1,000.00
Notes payable		15,000.00
Bonds payable		50,000.00
Bonds interest	2,000.00	
In-freight	10,000.00	
John Jones, capital		150,000.00
Prepaid rent income		1,000.00
	$518,000.00	$518,000.00

Adjustment Data, December 31, 1929

Final inventory of merchandise	$50,000.00
Accrued salaries	1,000.00
Accrued interest income	100.00
Unexpired insurance	1,000.00
Allowance for bad debts, ½ per cent of sales.	
Depreciation:	
Ten per cent on furniture and fixtures.	
Twenty per cent on delivery equipment.	
Two per cent on buildings.	
Prepaid rent income (included in $1,000)	100.00

a) Set up ledger accounts showing as "balances" the data of the trial balance.

b) Make adjustment entries on journal paper (general journal).

c) Prepare a work sheet.

d) Make a balance sheet.

e) Make a statement of income and expense.

f) Post adjusting entries in ledger.

g) Journalize and post appropriate closing entries.

XIII

The following is trial balance of the Stevens Mercantile Company on December 31, 1928, *after* all adjustments have been entered in the accounts, but *before* closing.

Account	Debit	Credit
Cash	$ 5,000.00	
Sales		$100,000.00
Cost of goods sold	75,000.00	
Buildings	35,000.00	
Accounts payable		9,000.00
Accounts receivable	11,000.00	
Allowance for depreciation of fixtures		2,000.00
Inventory merchandise, December 31 (1928)	10,000.00	
Sales returns	1,000.00	
Purchases allowances		200.00
Sales discount	500.00	
Sales allowances	400.00	
Purchases returns		1,200.00
Bad debts	600.00	
Fixtures	5,000.00	
Land	15,000.00	
Allowance for depreciation of trucks		3,000.00
Sales salaries	5,195.00	
Advertising	600.00	
Allowance for depreciation of buildings		15,000.00
Trucks	5,000.00	
Purchases discount		750.00
Notes payable		4,000.00
Office salaries	800.00	
Office-supplies expense	275.00	
Insurance expense	150.00	
Rent income		105.00
Interest cost	125.00	
Notes receivable	3,500.00	
Donations and memberships	50.00	
Interest income		70.00
Income from use of trucks		200.00
Taxes	185.00	
Building repairs	500.00	
Bonds	2,000.00	
Mortgage payable		10,000.00

Mortgage interest expense	$ 300.00	
Freight-in	1,350.00	
Freight-out	150.00	
Telephone and telegraph	50.00	
Surplus		$ 5,475.00
Light, heat, and water	1,500.00	
Miscellaneous general expense	400.00	
Loss by fire	1,300.00	
Capital stock		30,000.00
Accrued interest payable		25.00
Accrued interest receivable	20.00	
Accrued salaries payable		195.00
Insurance	50.00	
Advertising expense	400.00	
Advance rentals		45.00
Allowance for bad debts		1,200.00
Office supplies	125.00	
Accrued taxes payable		60.00
	$182,525.00	$182,525.00

Required: Prepare a balance sheet and a statement of income and expense, having regard for the proper forms of the financial reports.

XIV

Using the following transactions of John L. Handley, journalize and post them from a special-column general journal with the following columns: Accounts Receivable, Dr.; Accounts Receivable, Cr.; Accounts Payable, Dr.; Accounts Payable, Cr.; Purchases, Dr.; Sales, Cr.; Cash, Dr.; Cash, Cr.; Sundry, Dr.; Sundry, Cr. Set up the accounts as they would appear after being posted from the special-column journal, using any other accounts which are necessary, in addition to those at the heads of the special columns. Record transactions as of the month of May.

1. John L. Handley invested $6,000 cash in a business.
   He paid $350 for two months' rent of a storeroom.
   He bought for cash, furniture and fixtures, $1,750.
   He bought a delivery truck for $1,500, giving a note for $1,000 and cash for the balance.
2. He bought merchandise on account, $3,000.
   Sold merchandise for cash, $500.
   Sold merchandise on account, $1,250.
   Bought office supplies for cash, $75.

3. Handley took merchandise for his own use, $100.
   Advertising bill for $85 was received from a newspaper but was not paid.
   Sales for cash, $250.
   Sales on account, $50.
4. Bought merchandise on account, $1,500.
   Sold a small amount of the office supplies for $1.00.
   Bought an office safe for $250 cash.
   Sold merchandise to a customer for $800, who paid $400 in cash and gave a note for $250, leaving the rest on account.
5. Sales for cash, $460.
6. Cash sales were $750.
   Paid weekly salaries: office clerk, $20; saels clerks, $50; delivery boy, $25.
   Drew for personal use, $75 cash.
8. Paid garage bill for delivery truck, $35.
   Bought for cash a typewriter for the office, $105.
   Gave a 6 per cent, ten-day note for $2,000 due a creditor.
   Paid $1,000 on account, less 2 per cent discount.
   Paid $50 for coal; paid $10 for sign in front of store; paid $10 for repair of delivery truck.

XV

The following are the transactions for George Carpenter for December:

1. Carpenter put $7,000 into a retail coal business.
2. He paid $100 for rent.
3. Bought coal on account from the Gibson-Spence Coal Company for $600.
4. Bought furniture and fixtures for cash, $600.
5. Sold coal on account to Gene Tunney, $75.
   Bought on account from City Coal Company, $350.
6. Bought on account from Burns Coal Company, $500.
   Paid for telephone service, $10.
7. Made a cash purchase of coal, $1,000.
   Paid Gibson-Spence Coal Company, $150.
9. Cash sales, $300.
   Sold merchandise on account to J. Dempsey, $100.
   Sold merchandise on account to Forty Acres Hotel, $200.
11. Paid remainder owed Gibson-Spence Coal Company.
    Sold Gene Tunney, $50 on account.
13. Received from Dempsey, $75 on account.
    Cash sales, $375.
15. Paid clerk's salary, $50.
18. Paid Burns Coal Company, $200 on account.
    Cash purchases, $500.
21. Received a note of $100 from Tunney, to apply on account.

23. Dempsey paid the remainder of his bill.
Sold Forty Acres Hotel, $125 on account.
26. Cash sales, $350.
Bought from Burns Coal Company, $350 on account.
28. Gave a note to Burns Coal Company for $200 to apply on account.
Sale to H. C. Story, $75 on account.
30. Received $300 from Forty Acres Hotel to apply on account.
Sales on account to Tunney, $100.
31. Clerk hire, $50, paid.
Cash sales, $300.

a) Make all entries in a special-column journal, using the same special columns as were used in exercise XIV—1. Use more special columns if they seem to be appropriate.

b) Post the entries, using controlling and subsidiary accounts for customers and creditors.

c) Prepare schedules of accounts payable and accounts receivable to verify the net balances in the controlling accounts.

XVI—1

The following transactions are made by the business of E. L. Devitt during the month of March, 1926:

1. Devitt invested $3,500.
Paid for office rent, $100.
3. Received on account from the Lenglen Company, $500.
5. Paid Tilden Company on account, $150.
7. Cash sales, $175.
Purchased merchandise for cash, $50.
9. Received on account from V. C. Richards, $80.
11. Paid for delivery, $15.
13. Purchased merchandise for cash, $40.
15. Advertising expense paid, $10.
Clerk's salary paid, $30.
17. Cash sales, $130.
19. Received from V. C. Richards on account, $100.
21. Paid Tilden Company on account, $25.
23. Paid freight and drayage, $15.
Received from W. T. Johnston, $50.
26. Paid delivery boy, $1.00.
Paid for stamps, $2.00.
Advertising expense, $5.00, paid.
30. Received from F. H. Terrill, on account, $30.
31. Paid administrative expense, $45.
Paid heat and light, $10.

Paid clerk's salary, $30.

a) Prepare a cash book, and record the above entries, using the special columns illustrated in appendix to chapter xvi.

b) Set up the necessary accounts, and post them, maintaining controlling accounts with Accounts Receivable and Accounts Payable.

XVI—2

The following transactions represent three days' sales of the Norton Company. (*a*) Record them in a two-column sales journal, making proper provision for entries to the subsidiary accounts with customers. (*b*) Post the transactions individually to subsidiary accounts, and in total to the appropriate general-ledger accounts; (*c*) verify the accuracy of the posting by comparing the sales-ledger balances with the controlling account total and preparing a schedule of accounts receivable.

Sales on Account

March 1.	Invoice No. 51.	T. A. Jorgensen	$80.00
	Invoice No. 52.	L. D. White	70.00
	Invoice No. 53.	H. C. Boucher	64.00
	Invoice No. 54.	T. A. Jorgensen	52.00
	Invoice No. 55.	T. A. Jorgensen	88.00
	Invoice No. 56.	H. C. Boucher	30.00
March 2.	Invoice No. 57.	L. D. White	90.00
	Invoice No. 58.	L. D. White	42.00
	Invoice No. 59.	H. C. Boucher	81.00
	Invoice No. 60.	J. O. McKinney	47.00
March 3.	Invoice No. 61.	T. A. Jorgensen	51.00
	Invoice No. 62.	J. O. McKinney	73.00
	Invoice No. 63.	L. D. White	61.00
	Invoice No. 64.	T. A. Jorgensen	58.00
	Invoice No. 65.	J. O. McKinney	94.00

Sales for Cash

March 1.	Sales slips 650–96	$375.00
2.	Sales slips 697–741	519.00
3.	Sales slips 742–57	428.00

Sales for Notes

March 1.	Alexander Graver	$49.50
	J. H. Cissell	47.25

XVI—3

The following purchases of merchandise are made by R. W. Stone during the first four days of April. (*a*) Journalize and post the transactions to the general ledger and to subsidiary creditors' accounts, using a two-column purchases journal with columns for "Sundry" entries and for "Accounts Payable." (*b*) Prepare a schedule of accounts payable.

PURCHASES ON ACCOUNT

	Vendors	Amount	Our Invoice No.
April 1.	J. C. White	$120.00	43
	J. W. Charlton	30.00	44
2.	W. E. Dickerson	41.00	45
	J. B. Heckert	36.00	46
	W. E. Dickerson	52.00	47
	J. W. Charlton	67.00	48
	J. C. White	59.00	49
	J. W. Charlton	72.00	50
3.	J. B. Heckert	83.00	51
	W. E. Dickerson	55.00	52
4.	J. W. Charlton	61.00	53
	J. B. Heckert	87.00	54

CASH PURCHASES

April 1.	B. L. Dowers, Check No. 87	$117.00
3.	R. M. Manly, Check No. 94	89.00

XVI—4

1. John Jones invested $100,000 in business (cash).
2. He rented a building, paying six months' rent, $6,000.
3. He purchased for cash, $10,000 worth of fixtures.
4. He purchased on account from Smith Bros., $60,000 worth of merchandise.
5. He sold for cash, $1,000 worth of merchandise.
6. He bought for cash, $20,000 worth of merchandise.
7. He sold on account to Will White, $5,000 worth of merchandise.
8. Cash sales for month, $40,000.
9. Salaries for month, $2,000, paid in cash.
10. General expenses for the month, $5,000, paid in cash.
11. He gave Smith Bros. a note on account for $20,000.
12. Will White paid on account, $1,000.
13. Will White gives a note on account for $2,000.
14. He pays on account to Smith Bros., $30,000.
15. He buys on account from Johnson & Son, one delivery truck for use in the business, $5,000.

16. He receives one month's rent for small store room in building, $50.
17. He pays the note to Smith Bros., $20,000, with $40 interest.
18. Will White pays his note for $2,000 with $10.00 interest.
19. Will White buys on account, merchandise, $5,000.
20. He buys on account from Smith Bros. merchandise, $1,000.

a) Enter the transactions in cash book, purchase book, sales book, and general journal, using special columns in the specialized journals. Establish subsidiary sales ledger and purchases ledger.

b) Post to ledger, opening all accounts necessary.

c) Take a trial balance.

XVII—1

Vouchers were issued by the Hill Furniture Company during the month of February for the following:

Feb. 1. Administrative salaries for—

January	A. E. Hill	$600
	William H. Stanton	400

2. *Chicago Tribune*, for advertising, $1,500.
3. Adler Printing Company's invoice for (1) office stationery, $30, (2) advertising material, $75.

Pay-roll for the week:

Sales salaries	$320
Sales commissions	240
Shop laborers	255
Shop foreman	50
Receiving and shipping	115
Garage labor	90
Drivers	140

5. Davis and Company's invoice for merchandise, terms 3/10/n/30, $1,250, dated February 1.
7. Purchase from Marshall Field & Company, on monthly account, materials for window decoration, $75.
8. Bill from E. L. Burke for garage supplies, $85. This is to be paid immediately.
9. Purchase posting machine from Burroughs Company, net cash, $600.
10. Pay-roll, same as February 3.
12. Invoice from Anson and Burgess for merchandise, terms 2/10/n/30, $1,500, dated February 8.
13. Receive recapitulation of petty cash expenditures as follows:

Telegrams	$ 6.75
Express	15.25
Repairs office equipment	6.00
Selling expense	9.60
Advertising	4.40
Other office expense	8.20

A check is to be drawn to renew this fund.

14. Invoice from the Phoenix Company, dated February 12, for shop supplies, $145. Terms, n/30.
16. Bill from Illinois Central R. R. Company for freight on incoming shipments, $75.
17. Pay-roll, as on February 3.
20. The firm's sixty-day note to the Northern Trust Company, for $2,000, without interest is due on the 21st, and should be vouchered and paid.
21. Thomas Connor, a customer, is allowed a $50 refund on merchandise returned, and check is to be sent him immediately.
23. Invoice from the Pullman Couch Company, dated February 20, for merchandise, terms 3/10/n/60, $950.
24. Pay-roll, as on February 3.
26. Prepare a voucher for the first instalment of the firm's income tax, $2,875.50, to be paid immediately. (Check to collector of internal revenue.)
28. Mr. J. L. Shean, buyer, submits a statement of his expenses on a buying trip east, amounting to $225. The amount is O.K'd, payment to be made today.

a) Rule a voucher register containing columns headed "Vouchers Payable—Credit," and various debit columns as follows: "Merchandise," "Freight In," "Shop Supplies," "Shop Labor," "Receiving and Shipping," "Selling Expense," "Advertising," "Delivery Expense," "Sundry." Record in this register the vouchers indicated above.

b) Rule a check register, and enter in it all payments indicated as falling within the month of February, assuming that no discounts are neglected. The bank upon which checks are to be drawn is the Northern Trust Company.

c) Post all entries affecting general ledger accounts, allowing four lines to an account.

d) Take a trial balance of the accounts affected by the foregoing transactions. This is, of course, only a partial trial balance of the accounts which would appear in a complete ledger.

XVII—2

The A. F. Rood Corporation operates a clothes shop for men. A summary of the transactions for March 1, 19__, were as follows:

Merchandise Purchases

Abrams and Company, 2/10/n/30	$575.50
Wilson Brothers, 1/10/n/30	325.00
The Crofut-Knapp Company, 2/10/n/30	400.00
Cluett, Peabody, and Company, 2/10/n/30	275.00
Abrams and Company, n/30	55.00

Merchandise Charge Sales

Inv. 111.	J. O. Murdock	$65.00
Inv. 112.	R. L. Coles	70.00
Inv. 113.	W. J. Torr	17.75
Inv. 114.	J. L. Hardy	45.00
Inv. 115.	H. H. Core	60.00
Inv. 116.	Robt. Ames	12.00
Inv. 117.	J. O. Murdoch	80.00
Inv. 118.	J. C. Crane	87.50
Inv. 119.	Robt. Ames	75.00
Inv. 120.	R. L. Coles	18.75
Inv. 121.	W. J. Torr	65.00
Inv. 122.	H. H. Core	8.00

Cash Sales

No. 409	$ 67.85	No. 119	$ 97.00
No. 410	42.25	No. 420	110.00
No. 411	37.45	No. 421	175.50
No. 412	58.20	No. 422	77.80
No. 413	661.75	No. 423	91.30
No. 414	48.50	No. 424	105.50
No. 415	115.15	No. 425	86.70
No. 416	69.70	No. 426	118.45
No. 417	83.40	No. 427	221.25
No. 418	74.50	No. 428	108.00

Cash Disbursements

Check No. 561. Paid Cluett, Peabody & Co., $50 less 2 per cent discount.

Check No. 562. Paid Abrams and Company, $350 less 2 per cent discount.

Check No. 563. Paid office expense, $40.

Check No. 564. Paid salaries, $150.

Check No. 565. Paid rent, $200.

Check No. 566. Paid Crofut-Knapp Co., $200 less 2 per cent discount.

Check No. 567. Paid office expenses, $30.

Check No. 568. Paid Wilson Brothers, $125 less 1 per cent discount.

Cash Receipts from Customers

J. O. Murdock	$30.00
R. L. Coles	15.00
W. J. Torr	12.00
H. H. Core	60.00
J. C. Crane	50.00
Robert Ames	55.00

Miscellaneous Transactions

Goods returned from customers:

W. J. Torr	$ 8.00
J. C. Crane	17.50

Good returned to creditors:

Abrams & Company	$80.00
Wilson Brothers	85.00

a) Prepare journal entries to represent the effects of journal vouchers which summarize the transactions of March 1, 19—. Post the entries to the general-ledger accounts.

b) Prepare, also, subsidiary sales and purchases ledgers in which the customers and creditors accounts may be posted. Post to the subsidiary accounts.

c) Prepare a trial balance of the general ledger.

XVIII—1

a) X, Y, and Z are equal partners, each possessing a capital of $5,000 in the partnership. W buys all of X's interest for $5,000 and one-half of Y's interest for $2,500, and is admitted as a partner. Journalize the transactions upon the books of the partnership.

b) Assume the same conditions as stated in the foregoing problem except that W pays X $6,000 for his interest and pays Y $2,000 for one-half of his interest. How will this affect the entries to be made on the books of the partnership?

XVIII—2

A, B, and C are equal partners, each owning a capital of $10,000 in the partnership. The debit balance in the personal accounts at the end of the year are as follows: A, $1,000; B, $1,500; C, $2,000. After the distribution of the net profits for the year, $9,000, the partners dispose of their undrawn profits as follows: A leaves one-half of his as permanent capital and one-half as a loan to the firm; B withdraws one-half of his and leaves one-half as permanent capital; C leaves all of his as permanent capital.

Required: Construct the necessary Capital, Personal, and Loan accounts for each partner, giving effect to all of the transactions described above.

XVIII—3

A & B, partners, contract to transfer their assets and liabilities to the Western Manufacturing Company for a consideration of 500 shares of the corporation's stock, par value $100 per share. The balance sheet of the partnership at the date of transfer, March 15, 19—, showed the following condition: assets, $90,000; liabilities, $40,000; A capital, $25,000; B capital, $25,000. After the consummation of the transaction, the stock was divided between A and B and the partnership dissolved.

Required: The journal entries to record these transactions on the books of the partnership.

XIX—1

Assume the same conditions as stated in Exercise XVIII—3.

Required: The journal entries to record these transactions on the books of the Western Manufacturing Company.

XIX—2

The Timpton Company was incorporated in the state of Illinois December 23, 1924, to engage in the manufacture and sale of glass. Capital stock authorized, 1,000 shares, each of $100 par value. Eight hundred shares were subscribed at par at the date of organization. These subscriptions were paid up in two equal instalments on January 1, 1925, and February 15, 1925, respectively. Certificates were issued upon receipt of the second instalment. Journalize the necessary entries.

XIX—3

a) The Ibex Manufacturing Corporation is organized with an authorized capital stock of 1,000 shares of common stock with a par value of $100 per share and 1,000 shares of 6 per cent preferred stock with a par value of $50. One-fourth of the common is subscribed for at $90 per share, and one-fourth of the preferred is subscribed for at $45 per share. These subscriptions are paid in two instalments and the stock issued. Later an additional 100 shares of common stock is subscribed for at 110, and one-half of the subscription is paid in cash. An additional 100 shares of preferred stock is subscribed for at $55. A bond issue of $100,000 7 per cent twenty-year bonds is sold at par.

Required: (1) Journal entries to record all transactions in connection with the authorization, subscription, payment, and issuing of capital stock; (2) journal entries for the sale of the bonds, the first annual payment of interest, and the redemption of the bonds at maturity.

b) The profits of the Ibex Corporation for the first year of operations amounted to $10,000 after payment of the bond interest. Dividends were declared and paid on the preferred stock; a 6 per cent dividend on the common stock was declared and paid. (Only the *issued* stock shares in the dividends.)

Required: Journal entries to record the declaration and payment of the dividends.

XX—1

Assume that the following account balances appear in a ledger at the close of a fiscal period on June 30:

Merchandise inventory (January 1), $1,840; Merchandise purchases (January 1–June 30), $17,620; Purchases returns, $316; Purchases allowances, $150; Sales, $28,160; Sales returns, $219; Purchases discounts, $314; Freight-and-cartage (on incoming merchandise), $1,112; Sales allowances, $420. The Merchandise inventory, as determined by actual appraisal on June 30, is $2,200.

Prepare a trading account.

XX—2

The following balances appear on the books of the Chicago Manufacturing Company on December 31, 19__:

Account	Debit	Credit
Accounts payable		$ 40,000.00
Accounts receivable	$ 50,000.00	
Accrued bond interest		3,000.00
Accrued federal income tax		14,000.00
Accrued wages		2,000.00
Advertising	10,000.00	
Allowance for bad debts		1,000.00
Allowance for depreciation on factory building		50,000.00
Allowance for depreciation on machinery and equipment		100,000.00
Allowance for depreciation on office furniture and fixtures		2,000.00
Allowance for depreciation on patents		10,000.00
Bad debts	4,500.00	
Bond interest expense	6,000.00	
Bonds payable		100,000.00
Capital stock		500,000.00
Cash	40,000.00	
Depreciation on factory building	10,000.00	
Depreciation on machinery and equipment	30,000.00	
Depreciation on office furniture and fixtures	500.00	
Depreciation on patents	4,000.00	
Factory building	500,000.00	
Factory pay-roll, direct	70,000.00	
Factory pay-roll, indirect	80,000.00	
Factory supplies	35,000.00	
Federal income taxes	14,000.00	
Freight and cartage in	20,000.00	
Freight and cartage out	2,000.00	
Insurance on factory and equipment	10,000.00	
Insurance on finished goods	1,500.00	
Interest on notes payable	3,000.00	
Interest on notes receivable		2,000.00
Land	100,000.00	
Legal expense	2,000.00	
Light, heat, and power (factory)	15,000.00	
Machinery and equipment	300,000.00	
Maintenance of building and equipment	15,000.00	
Notes payable		50,000.00
Notes receivable	30,000.00	
Office expenses	10,000.00	

Office furniture and fixtures	$ 5,000.00	
Office salaries	25,000.00	
Officers' salaries	40,000.00	
Patents	60,000.00	
Postage	2,000.00	
Printing and stationery	7,000.00	
Raw materials	460,000.00	
Purchases discount		$ 8,000.00
Purchases returns and allowances		10,000.00
Rent (office)	3,000.00	
Sales		1,050,000.00
Sales discount	20,000.00	
Sales returns and allowances	20,000.00	
Salesmen's salaries and commissions	50,000.00	
Superintendence (factory)	15,000.00	
Surplus		261,000.00
Taxes (factory)	5,000.00	
Tools	10,000.00	
Tools expense	5,000.00	
Traveling expenses (salesmen)	15,000.00	
Unexpired insurance	7,000.00	
Watchmen (factory)	4,000.00	
Workmen's compensation insurance	7,500.00	
Goods-in-process inventory, January 1, 19—.	50,000.00	
Finished-goods inventory, January 1, 19—.	30,000.00	
Total	$2,203,000.00	$2,203,000.00

The following are the inventories at December 31, 19__:

Inventory—raw materials	$50,000.00
Inventory—work in process	55,000.00
Inventory—finished goods	35,000.00
Inventory—factory supplies	6,000.00

Required:

1. Journalize the necessary entries: (*a*) to summarize the direct and indirect manufacturing costs in the Goods in Process account; (*b*) to summarize the sales and cost-of-goods-sold data in the Trading account; (*c*) to summarize the gross profit on sales and the other income and expense data in the Profit and Loss account; (*d*) to close the Profit and Loss account to the Undivided Profits account.

2. Prepare Goods in Process, Trading, and Profit and Loss accounts, as they would appear after the foregoing entries had been posted.

3. Prepare a balance sheet.

4. Prepare a statement of income and expense.

5. Prepare a schedule of the cost of goods manufactured.

PRACTICE SET

JOHN EVANS, PROPRIETOR

NOTE: This practice set involves the use of the specialized journals, and carries the transactions of a small business through a complete set of operations. It may be given as a special review of chapters vii–xx, at the time the first half of the text is completed. Or it may be assigned for the purpose of review in smaller portions, to be worked while the exercises in valuation and interpretation are being solved.

Instructions

a) *Enter the transactions in books of original entry*, using for this purpose sales journal, purchases journal, cash journals, and general journal. The journals should be ruled as follows: (1) five-column sales journal with columns headed "Sundry Dr.," "Accounts Receivable Dr.," "Cash Dr.," "Notes Receivable Dr.," and "Sales Cr."; (2) five-column purchases journal with columns headed "Sundry Cr.," "Accounts Payable Cr.," "Cash Cr.," "Notes Payable Cr.," and "Purchases Dr."; (3) five-column cash receipts journal with columns headed "Sundry Cr.," "Notes Receivable Cr.," "Accounts Receivable Cr.," "Sales Discount Dr.," and "Cash Dr."; (4) five-column cash disbursements journal with columns headed "Sundry Dr.," "Delivery Expense Dr.," "Accounts Payable Dr.," "Purchases Discount Cr.," and "Cash Cr."; (5) ten-column general journal with account titles and explanations between the debit columns and the credit columns, the money columns being headed "Sales Returns and Allowances Dr.," "Accounts Payable Dr.," "Notes Receivable Dr.," "Accounts Receivable Dr.," "Sundry Dr.," "Sundry Cr.," "Accounts Receivable Cr.," "Notes Payable Cr.," "Accounts Payable Cr.," and "Purchases Returns and Allowances Cr."

b) *Post the journal entries to accounts in the ledgers.* Use subsidiary ledgers for accounts receivable and accounts payable. The accounts in the general ledger will be as follows (allow ten lines for each account): (1) Cash; (2) Notes Receivable; (3) Accounts Receivable; (4) Allowance for Bad Debts; (5) Merchandise Inventory; (6) Furniture and Fixtures; (7) Allowance for Depreciation of Furniture and Fixtures; (8) Delivery Equipment; (9) Allowance for Depreciation of Delivery Equipment; (10) Notes Payable; (11) Accounts Payable; (12) John Evans, Capital; (13) John Evans, Personal; (14) Sales; (15) Sales Returns and Allowances; (16) Purchases; (17) Purchases Returns and Allowances; (18) Freight-In; (19) Office Salaries; (20)

Prepaid Insurance; (21) Cash Short and Over; (22) General Expenses; (23) Delivery Expense; (24) Sales Salaries; (25) Advertising; (26) Freight-Out; (27) Bad Debts; (28) Interest Cost; (29) Sales Discount; (30) Purchases Discount; (31) Interest Income; (32) Depreciation on Furniture and Fixtures; (33) Depreciation on Delivery Equipment; (34) Office Supplies Inventory; (35) Prepaid Rent; (36) Insurance Expense; (37) Prepaid Advertising; (38) Accrued Interest Receivable; (39) Accrued Interest Payable; (40) Office Supplies Expense; and (41) Cost of Goods Sold; (42) Profit and Loss (twenty lines).

c) Take a trial balance on eight-column or ten-column analysis paper, to be used for work-sheet.

d) Prepare a work-sheet, giving effect to needed adjustments.

e) Make adjusting entries in the general journal.

f) Post the adjusting entries.

g) Prepare a balance sheet and a statement of income and expense. Check this with work-sheet.

h) Make the entries in the general journal to close the expense and income accounts.

i) Post the closing entries.

j) Take a post-closing trial balance.

Transactions for February, 19__

1. John Evans invests in a business: $10,000 in cash and $15,000 in merchandise. (NOTE TO STUDENT: All transactions are to be recorded from the point of view of the accounts of John Evans. Where descriptions of transactions do not mention specifically the name of any person, it is to be assumed that the transactions are those of John Evans and are to be recorded from the point of view of his business enterprise.)
   He paid $350 for two months' rent of a storeroom.
   He bought for cash, furniture and fixtures, $1,750.
   He bought a delivery truck for $1,500, giving a note for $1,000 and cash for the balance.
2. He bought merchandise on account from Butler Brothers, $3,000.
   Sold merchandise for cash, $500.
   Sold merchandise on account to R. B. Black, $1,250.
   Bought office supplies for cash, $75.
3. Evans took merchandise for his own use, $100.
   Advertising bill for $85 was received from *Daily News* but not paid.
   Sales for cash, $250.
   Sales on account to E. R. Brown, $50.
4. Bought merchandise on account from Welton & Company, $1,500.
   Sold a small amount of the office supplies for $1.00.
   Bought an office safe for $250, cash.
   Sold merchandise to G. R. White, $800, for which White paid $400 cash and gave a note for $250, leaving the rest on account.

5. Evans pays one-half of the amount due Butler Brothers, less 2 per cent discount for cash.
Sales for cash, $460.
Sales on account to R. S. Green, $375; to T. B. Gray, $350; to R. B. Black, $250; to E. R. Brown, $100.
Purchased on account from Gorham and Rogers, merchandise for $1,500.

6. Cash sales were $750.
Paid office clerk his weekly salary, $20; also salaries of sales clerks, $50; delivery boy, $25. Drew for personal use, $75 cash.

8. Paid garage bill for delivery truck, $35.
Bought, for cash, a typewriter for the office, $105.
Paid Butler Brothers $1,000 on account, less 2 per cent discount.
Gave Butler Brothers a 6 per cent, ten-day note for the $500 balance due them.
Paid $50 for coal; paid $10 for sign in front of store; paid $10 for repair of delivery truck.

9. Bought merchandise on account from Butler Brothers, $2,000.
Sold merchandise to E. R. Brown and took his check in payment, $50.
Paid $50 for Commerce Club dues.
Paid $50 for office supplies.
Sold merchandise on account to R. S. Green, $500.

10. R. B. Black paid his bill of the 2d, less 2 per cent discount.
E. R. Brown paid his bill of the 3d in full.
Evans took merchandise for his own use, $50.
Paid the advertising bill received on the 3d.
Paid Welton & Company the amount due them, less 2 per cent discount.

11. Returned as unsatisfactory $300 worth of the merchandise purchased from Gorham and Rogers on the 5th.
Cash sales were $750.
Purchased for cash from Butler Brothers, merchandise for $500.

12. Paid freight bill of $75.
Received from G. R. White the balance due on bill of the 4th.
Received payment from G. R. White of his note for $250, plus $1.00 interest.
Cash sales were $500.

13. Paid office clerk's salary, $20; sales clerks, $50; delivery boy, $25; drew for personal use, $65 cash.
Cash sales, $750.

15. Received payment in full, less 2 per cent discount, from R. S. Green, T. B. Gray, R. B. Black, and E. R. Brown, for merchandise sold to them on the 5th.
Paid Gorham and Rogers balance of bill of the 5th, less 2 per cent discount.
Paid garage bill for delivery truck, $30.

16. Received returned merchandise from R. S. Green, $75.
Sales on account: to R. B. Black, $500; to T. B. Gray, $450.
Purchased merchandise on account from Gorham and Rogers, $750.
Cash sales, $1,500.
17. Purchased from R. M. House a desk for use in the office, $75.
Mr. House took merchandise in part payment, $50, and the balance left on open account.
Allowed R. B. Black's claim for $50 for spoiled merchandise.
Returned merchandise to Gorham and Rogers as unsatisfactory, $75.
Received $50 cash from Butler Brothers in payment of claim on account of unsatisfactory merchandise in bill of 11th.
18. Sales on account: to E. R. Brown, $750; to R. S. Green, $375.
Sales for cash, $600.
Sales to G. R. White, $450. Received cash for $200, a note for $150, and the balance left on open account.
Received a note on account from R. B. Black, $350.
Paid to Butler Brothers the ten-day note due them, plus interest.
Bought office supplies, for cash, $65.
Paid freight on merchandise in, $85; paid freight on merchandise out, $35.
19. Sold to T. B. Gray, merchandise, $385. Received cash, $85, Gray's note for $100, R. M. House's note for $125, the balance being left on open account.
Bought merchandise from Welton & Company, $6,750; paid $1,000 in cash, transferred White's note for $150, Black's note for $350, gave personal note for $2,500, and left the remainder on open account.
20. Paid office clerk's salary, $22.50; sales clerks, $55; delivery boy, $25.
Drew for personal use, $100.
Cash sales were $500. Cash purchases were $1,500.
22. Evans drew for his own personal use, merchandise, $350.
Purchased from Butler Brothers on account, merchandise, $1,500.
Return defective merchandise to Welton & Company, $450.
Collections were: E. R. Brown, $85; G. R. White, $75.
23. White's note for $150, which was transferred to Welton & Company, is not paid when due. They charge it back to Evans, who charges it back to White's account. It was a non-interest-bearing note.
We find a counterfeit bill in the cash drawer, $50.
24. Paid insurance for three months beginning February 15, $100.
We send a check for $250 to Welton & Company on account. This payment is within the 2 per cent discount period.
Sales on account to T. B. Gray, $270.
25. White pays the $150 note he had failed to pay Welton & Company on the 22d.
Welton & Company return Black's note unpaid. It is charged to Black's account.

Mr. Black goes bankrupt and pays only 25 cents on the dollar. Evans receives a check for one-fourth of the debt, this being the final payment from Black.

Drew a thirty-day non-interest bearing draft on T. B. Gray against bill of the 24th and sent the draft to Welton & Company to apply on account, $100.

26. Purchased merchandise on account from Butler Brothers, $1,250.

Sales on account to R. S. Green, $460.

Cash Sales were $350.

Received defective merchandise returned by T. B. Gray, $75.

Accepted Butler Brothers' thirty-day non-interest bearing draft for $1,000 against bill of the 26th.

27. Paid the week's salaries: office clerk, $22.50; delivery boy, $25; sales clerks, $55. Drew for personal use, $125. Paid telephone bill, $20; advertising bill, $35; freight on merchandise in, $50; freight on merchandise out, $10.

Paid electric light bill, $14.

Sales on account to E. R. Brown, $450.

Cash sales were $1,000.

Additional information at end of month:

Inventory of merchandise, $21,000.

Office supplies inventory, $70.

Prepaid rent, $175.

Interest accrued on notes receivable, $0.35.

Interest accrued on notes payable, $9.00.

Advertising expense to be deferred to next period, $50.

Depreciation of furniture and fixtures, 1 per cent for the month.

Depreciation of delivery equipment, 2 per cent for the month.

Reserve for bad debts, ½ per cent of net sales.

Prepaid Insurance, ⅙ expired.

EXERCISES ON ACCOUNTING VALUATION—PART III

XXI—1

A manufacturer of cement blocks owns equipment which was purchased ten years previously at a cost price of $12,000. The equipment is in good physical condition, but new inventions make it appear probable that an ultimate saving could be effected by purchasing a new machine at a cost of $30,000. A junk dealer has offered $600 for the old equipment. Similar new equipment could be purchased for $18,000. If it had not been for the new inventions, the machine would have been used for ten additional years. A small competitor has offered $3,500 for the machine, but the sales manager says that if the competitor buys the machine he will also cut prices in the local territory and take away business which would otherwise yield a net profit of $2,500. Depreciation allowances to the total of $5,500 have been made in the accounts.

Required: Indicate the possible accounting values of this machine to the company owning it, and state the conditions under which each would be applicable.

XXI—2

Suggest the proper balance sheet value for forty filing cabinets to the following enterprises and under the following conditions:

a) The enterprise which has produced them at an average cost of $24 each, not including any costs of distributing them to agents or dealers.

b) A wholesale concern which has purchased them from the manufacturer at an average price of $30 and holds them for sale to retail agencies at $36 each.

c) A retail concern which has purchased them for $36 and offers them for sale to the public at $45.

d) A user of the filing cabinets, who is a manufacturer of an entirely different product and who instals them as office equipment.

e) An enterprise which has discovered that the filing cabinets are of the wrong size and style for use in its office.

XXII

No exercises are suggested to accompany chapter xxii. The assumptions and common rules of accounting valuation are illustrated in the problems of all the chapters from xxiii–xxxii, inclusive.

XXIII—1

The net debit balance in the Accounts Receivable account in the general ledger is $80,000. The following additional data are secured by an accountant who is examining the records: 5 per cent of the accounts are entirely uncollectible; 20 per cent are thirty days past due, with approximate loss estimated at 10 per cent; 10 per cent are sixty days past due, with loss on them estimated to be 40 per cent; of the remainder, $40,000 are subject to 2 per cent cash discount, if paid within ten days (according to experience, 80 per cent of the accounts will probably be "discounted"); the costs of collecting the accounts will probably be $3,000; the average time between the date of sale and date of payment is sixty days (the prevailing rate of interest is 6 per cent).

Required: Calculate the probable "present value" of the Accounts Receivable, considering all factors.

XXIII—2

On May 15, the Z Company discounted two notes with the Lansdowne State Bank at a rate of 6 per cent—J. R. Philip's sixty-day non-interest-bearing note for $5,000, due in 30 days; and P. A. Aldworth's ninety-day non-interest-bearing note for $2,000, due in $60 days.

The bank notified the company on June 15 that J. R. Philip's note had been paid at maturity.

The company received notice July 15 that the note had been presented to J. R. Aldworth, payment had been refused, and the amount of the note together with $2 protest fees was being charged back to the company's account at the bank. The company took up the note and secured a settlement with Aldworth on August 23 for $1,800. The balance was charged off as uncollectible.

Frame the journal entries to take up these transactions on the books of the Z Company.

XXIII—3

The following entries appear in the debit column of the account for a particular item of merchandise:

January 1	Balance— 100 units @ 1.00.......	$100.00
February 15	Purchases—600 units @ 0.92.......	552.00
April 7	Purchases—300 units @ 0.95.......	285.00
May 12	Purchases—100 units @ 1.05.......	105.00
June 4	Purchases— 50 units @ 1.10.......	55.00
June 22	Purchases— 40 units @ 1.15.......	46.00

The accountant is making up the balance sheet of the enterprise and finds that 240 units of this article are on hand. The market price at the time (June 30) is $1.10. The accountant wishes to evaluate the merchandise on a conservative basis, applying the rule "cost or market whichever is the lower." What is the "cost"? Indicate the various meanings that the term cost may assume for merchandise. Compute the various types of cost which may be applied, and indicate which are higher and which are lower than the prevailing market on June 30.

XXIV—1

A machine is purchased at an invoice cost of $27,000. Other expenses incurred which relate to the machine are: incoming freight, $250; installation, labor, $180; fees to expert engineer who supervised testing, $300; costs of adjustment and re-installation on recommendation of engineer, $125; interest on ninety-day note payable for $25,000, the loan being negotiated at 6 per cent to purchase the machine and maturing at the time the machine was put into actual use. It is expected that the machine will be used in the manufacture of goods for a period of five years, at the end of which time it will be in good physical condition but inadequate for the needs of the plant. Its sale value will probably be about $7,000 at the end of the five years.

Required: (*a*) Compute the total original cost of the machine; (*b*) calculate the depreciable value; (*c*) estimate the total cost of operating the machine for a year, assuming that it is used at uniform rate of speed and the maintenance and repairs average $300 per year.

XXIV—2

A brick factory building, referred to by the owners as "Building No. 2," which originally cost $100,000, has been depreciated at the rate of 2½ per cent annually for twenty-four years. The net book-value is $40,000 at the beginning of a fiscal period. During the ensuing year the following transactions occur:

a) Doors and windows are repaired at a cost of $300. The walls, ceilings, and floors are painted at a cost of $800, this being required every three years because of the climate in which the building is located.

b) The building is remodeled for light manufacture, a process which involved moving certain heavy machinery to another plant at a cost of $2,000. The remodeling consists of tearing out partitions and instaling elevators and carrying devices in order that the upper floors can be used for other than storage purposes; the cost of the remodeling is $8,000, and it is estimated that the change in production plans will prolong the life of the building fourteen years.

c) A small wing is constructed as part of the building for a research laboratory at a cost of $4,000.

d) During the year the costs for fuel and supplies to operate both the old and new equipment were $3,600.

e) Shortly before the decision to remodel the building, the firm refused an opportunity to sell the building for $50,000 cash.

Required: Make such journal entries as seem to you appropriate to reflect the foregoing transactions. Show the condition of the account for Building No. 2. Ignore any consideration of changes in the value of the land site on which the building is located, assuming that the opportunity to sell involved the building only and that the land would have been leased under a separate contract.

XXV—1

A machine which was purchased January 1, 1924, for $1,000 was replaced January 1, 1928, by a larger machine costing $1,600. Depreciation has been recorded at the rate of 10 per cent each year on the diminishing-balance basis and credited to an allowance account. On the sale of the old unit $800 was realized. The removal of the old machine cost $100, and the installation of the new equipment cost $200.

Required: Assuming the proper balance in the accounts as of January 1, 1927, journalize all subsequent transactions and set up the ledger accounts.

XXV—2

A machine is purchased at a cost price of $14,000, with an estimated service life of six years and a scrap value of $2,000. It is expected to be serviceable for the manufacture of 24,000 units of product. At the end of three years the asset is disposed of at a cash price of $6,500. Make the journal entries to close the account with the fixed asset, estimating accrued depreciation on the following bases: (*a*) straight-line; (*b*) 30 per cent of diminishing balance; (*c*) sinking-fund method, $1,800 first year, increased on 6 per cent basis; (*d*) service method—outputs for three years were 7,000, 5,000, 4,000 units, respectively.

XXVI—1

A company purchases 100 bonds, with a face value of $1,000 each, for $90,000. They have twenty years to run before maturity, and they bear interest at 4½ per cent. It is decided to amortize the discount on a straight-line basis. Journalize the following transactions: (*a*) purchase of the securities; (*b*) receipt of a semiannual interest payment. Show the condition of the discount account as it would appear at the end of three years after the date of purchase.

XXVI—2

Journalize the following transactions: (*a*) purchase of 40 bonds, each of $500 face value, with fifteen years to run before maturity, bearing 5½ per cent interest, at 103; (*b*) receipt of an annual interest payment, assuming that the premium is to be amortized on a straight-line basis. Show the condition of the account at the end of two years.

XXVI—3

The proprietorship section of the balance sheet of the Anderson Snow Shoe Company on January 1, 19—, is as follows:

Common stock (1,000 shares)....	$100,000.00
Surplus........................	20,000.00
Total.....................	$120,000.00

On January 15, 19—, the Jensen Ski Manufacturing Company purchases 800 shares of the Anderson Company at $120 per share. On July 1, 19—, the Anderson company computes the earnings for the first half-year at $35,000. On August 1, 19—, the Anderson Company declares a 30 per cent cash dividend. On December 31, 19—, the second half-year's profits are estimated at $15,000.

How would you show the investment in Anderson stock on the books of the Jensen company, December 31, 19—? How would the proprietorship section of the balance sheet of the Anderson company appear on December 31, 19—? Would you have treated these transactions in the same way if the Jensen company had bought only 200 shares of Anderson stock? Journalize on the books of the Jensen company the first record of the purchase of the investment, also all subsequent transactions affecting the Jensen books.

XXVII—1

On the balance sheet of the Holten Trading Company as of December 31, 1928, the "Good-will" appears stated at $160,000. An analysis of the account reveals that it is made up of these items:

1. Patent (appraised value)	$25,000.00
2. Discount on stock	20,000.00
3. Organization expense (incurred in 1913)	6,000.00
4. Excess of purchase price over net worth of subsidiary	14,000.00
5. Deferred good-will advertising expense	30,000.00
6. Good-will spread on books upon resolution passed by the board of directors	65,000.00

The patent was secured five years ago at a cost of $8,500. The sum of $1,000 has just been expended in a successful defense of the patent.

a) State how each of these items should be treated in the accounts.

b) Construct the intangible-assets section of the balance sheet.

XXVII—2

A manufacturer obtains two patents at the same time, as follows: (*a*) He purchases outright for the sum of $5,000 a patent which has only ten more years to run, which he terms his "patent No. 1"; (*b*) he invents a contrivance and obtains a patent on it, the cost of which he estimates at $13,000, and which he styles his "patent No. 2." At the end of three years he expends the sum of $5,000 in defending his patent No. 2, the decision being given in his favor. One year later he spends $2,000 in a suit he brings against a competitor for the infringement of his patent No. 1, which suit he also wins.

By using the actual figures, state how you would treat all the foregoing transactions and arrive at a valuation of these two patents six years after he had obtained them, giving reasons therefor.

XXVII—3

Two concerns, A and B, are consolidating; and their balance sheets show net worths of $2,000,000 and $3,000,000, respectively. The average net earnings of A during the past five years has been $400,000; the earnings of B have been $300,000 annually. Both firms have paid dividends equal approximately to their earnings; so the net assets referred to above may be regarded as the average net capital of the two companies during the five years. The question arises as to whether the excess earnings of A should be given consideration in the distribution of stock of the consolidated company among the "A" and "B" stockholders.

Required: (*a*) Indicate whether the A stockholders should receive more than two-fifths of the stock of the new company. (*b*) State what, in your opinion, should be the total capital stock of the new corporation, assuming that both A and B would have continued to earn the same rates of return for ten years. (*c*) If good-will is to be introduced into the accounts, how much should appear therein?

XXVIII—1

On January 1, 1914, the Ames Corporation finished the erection of a factory building at a cost of $102,400, which covered all expenditures for materials, labor, supervision, etc., exclusive of bond interest during construction. Six months prior to the completion of the building, in order to finance the project, the company floated a ten-year $80,000 bond issue, bearing interest at the rate of 6 per cent per annum, payable semiannually. The bonds were sold at 95. The service life of the building was estimated to be twenty years; and the scrap value, $5,000. The building and the land on which the building was erected were sold January 1, 1924, for $60,000 (original cost of the land $15,000). The bonds were redeemed at maturity by cash payment.

Journalize entries for: (*a*) floating the bond issue, (*b*) the payment for the construction of the building, (*c*) the first interest payment, (*d*) the second interest payment, (*e*) the liquidation of the bond liability at maturity, and (*f*) the sale of the factory and factory site.

XXVIII—2

Journalize the following transactions: (*a*) issuance of $3,000 bonds at 5 per cent premium, face value $500, interest rate 6 per cent, maturing in twenty-five years; (*b*) payment of a semiannual interest instalment, assuming bond premium to be amortized on a straight-line basis.

Show the condition of the Bond Premium account as it would appear at the end of two years.

XXIX—1

a) A and B are partners, A owning capital of $10,000 and B capital of $5,000 in the partnership. C makes an investment to secure a one-fourth interest in the business, paying for it in cash on the basis of book values as stated on the books of the existing partnership. Journalize the transaction on the books of the partnership.

b) Assume the same conditions as stated above, except that C invests $6,000 to secure a one-fourth interest in the business; the necessary adjustments are made in the capital accounts of the partners so that C's interest becomes exactly one-fourth of the total net worth of the business. (A and B have been sharing profits on the basis of their capital investments.) Journalize the transaction.

c) Assume the same conditions as stated in (*b*), except that the credit to C's capital account will be the amount of his contribution and adjustment must be made on the books of the partnership to give him exactly a one-fourth interest in the partnership.

d) Assume the same conditions as stated in (*b*) above, except that C pays $4,000 for a one-fourth interest.

e) Assume the same conditions as stated in (*d*), except that the credit to C's capital account will be the amount of his contribution and adjustment must be made on the books of the partnership to give him exactly a one-fourth interest in the partnership.

XXIX—2

The profit of the X, Y, and Z partnership for the year ending December 31, 19—, before providing for salaries or interest to the partners, is $11,000. The agreement provides that salaries shall be allowed as follows: A, $3,000, B, $2,500, and C, $4,000, that interest at the rate of 6 per cent shall be allowed on the capital of each partner; and that the final balance of profit or loss shall be distributed equally. The Capital accounts of the partners showed: A, $40,000; B, $20,000; and C, $15,000. Their Personal accounts reflected debit balances for drawing against their salary allowances; A, $2,500; B, $2,500; and C, $3,750. The resulting "Personal" balance of each partner is to be closed into his Capital account.

Journalize the entries to dispose of the balances in the P. & L and Personal accounts as of December 31, and set up the necessary ledger accounts.

XXIX—3

a) A has $10,000 invested in his business. He sells to B, a one-half interest in the assets and liabilities and in the future profits for $6,000. The money is *not* placed in the business.

b) X has $10,000 invested in his business. He admits Y as a partner with one-half interest in the assets and liabilities and future profits upon Y's investment in the business of $9,000.

c) Assume the same circumstances as in (*b*), except that Y contributes $12,000.

Required: Journalize the entries to record the admission of the new partner in each of the foregoing cases. Give two possible solutions for each case.

XXIX—4

A, B, C, and D are partners in an enterprise sharing profits and losses equally. Investments of partners are as follows: A, $20,000; B, $15,000; C, $10,000; D, $5,000. The first year of operations is unsuccessful and the partnership is dissolved. After payment of all liabilities, $10,000 cash is available for distribution among the partners. D has no assets outside of the partnership enterprise, while all the other partners have their major business interests outside of the partnership.

Required: (*a*) Journal entries to record the apportionment of the losses and the distribution of the cash among the partners; (*b*) the Capital accounts of the partners showing the effects of the foregoing transactions, and these accounts finally closed. Omit Personal accounts and make entries direct to Capital accounts.

XXIX—5

S, M, and C are partners with Capital accounts as follows: S, $1,000; M, $4,000; C, $7,000. The following personal accounts also appear on the books: (*a*) debit balances: C—Borrowings, $300; M—Salaries, $400; S—Interest, $100; (*b*) credit balances: M—Loan, $375; C—Interest, $125.

The assets of the enterprise (after payment of all outside liabilities) amount to $9,000. Journalize the entries (*a*) to account for the gain or loss at liquidation, (*b*) to make the proper allowances for the personal relationships of the partners, (*c*) to distribute the cash among the partners.

XXIX—6

Handle problem xxix–5 on the assumption that the net assets of the partnership proved to be $15,000 at liquidation.

XXX—1

The Ottawa Furniture Company secured a charter from the state of Illinois March 13, 1924, granting it the right to engage in the manufacture and sale of furniture. The authorized capitalization consisted of 20,000 shares of stock, no par value. Of these, 10,000 shares were subscribed at $10 per share as of the date of incorporation. (The minimum value of no par stock in Illinois is $5.00 per share.)

The subscriptions were paid up April 1, 1924. On September 15, 1924, $5,000 additional shares were sold for cash at $11 per share. Journalize these transactions.

XXX—2

Prior to the transactions recorded below, the Lambert Company had an authorized capitalization of 5,000 shares preferred stock, par value $100; and 10,000 shares common stock, par value $50. Four thousand shares of preferred and 9,000 shares of common stock were outstanding.

The common stockholders donated 1,000 shares of their stock to the company March 21, 1923, to be sold to obtain additional working capital. On April 6, 1923, 700 shares were sold at 48; and on April 14, 1923, 200 shares were sold at 53. The remaining shares were kept in the treasury.

Two years later (February 1, 1925) the company bought up 20 shares of preferred stock at 100. It disposed of 15 shares for 100 on March 10, 1925.

Required:

a) Journalize the foregoing transactions and set up the corporate proprietorship accounts.

b) Construct the net-worth section of the balance sheet as of March 31, 1925. Assume that the surplus (exclusive of any changes arising out of the foregoing transactions) is $300,000.

XXX—3

Dividends are declared as follows: (*a*) 30 per cent dividend on 500 shares, common stock, par value, 100; (*b*) $1.75 per share on 300 shares no-par-value common stock; (*c*) semiannual dividend on 300 shares, 7 per cent, $100 par value, preferred stock. The methods of paying the aforementioned dividends were: (*a*) in shares of common stock; (*b*) in cash; (*c*) in scrip, payable in sixty days from date of the dividend declaration.

Required: Journalize the declaration and payment of the dividends mentioned above.

XXX—4

The Surplus account of the Pseudo Corporation contains a credit balance of $32,000, prior to entry of the following transactions:

1. Declaration of 6 per cent dividend on 400 shares preferred stock, $100 par value.
2. Declaration of 8 per cent dividend on 300 shares common stock, par value $50.
3. Net profit from operations of $6,000.
4. Issuance of $10,000 worth of twenty-year bonds at 3 per cent discount.
5. Purchase of 50 shares of outstanding preferred stock at $90, to be held in the treasury for reissue.
6. Payment of $2,000 for damages caused by a company-owned truck, a reserve for such contingencies having been previously established.
7. Receipt of a gift of land from a municipality, contingent upon continued operation in the city for four years. The land has a market value of $7,500.
8. Shares of stock held as an investment were disposed of at $6,500. They had originally cost, and were carried in the accounts at, $8,000.

Required: Journalize the foregoing transactions, using such account titles as seem to you appropriate under the circumstances. Show the Surplus account as it would appear after the entries were posted.

XXXI—1

Journalize and post the following transactions, making all entries in terms of controlling accounts only, without reference to subsidiary data. Show the status of each of the accounts affected.

1. C.O.D. sale, $200.
2. Sale on approval, $85.
3. C.O.D. sale, $100.
4. Receipt of cash from C.O.D. customer, $200.
5. Sale on instalment plan, one-fifth of sale price received in cash, $120.
6. Return of goods sold on approval, $85.
7. Receipt of cash from instalment customer, $24.
8. Sale on approval, $125.
9. C.O.D. sale, $135.
10. Receipt of cash for goods sold on approval, $50, and return of the other goods on approval.

XXXI—2

Journalize the following transactions on the books of the consignor and consignee:

1. Shipment of goods, cost price of which is $1,400.
2. Payment of freight by consignor, $74.
3. Payment of storage by consignee, $81; this is ultimately to be borne by the consignor.
4. Sale of half the goods for $1,000.
5. Payment of cash for amount owed by consignee to consignor, 5 per cent commission being deducted.

Set up the consignment accounts as they would appear on the books of the consignor and consignee at the end of these transactions. Journalize and post the entries necessary on the books of the consignor for the purpose of closing the consignment account and preparing a balance sheet. Indicate how the transactions would be reflected on the balance sheet and the statement of income and expense of both companies.

XXXI—3

March 8, 1925, the Trumbell Company ships to Summers and James a consignment of goods costing $6,000, which it is expected will be sold for $7,500.

Mar. 9. The Trumbell Company pays drayage out $20 and insurance $10.

12. Summers and James receive the goods and pay freight, $65.

15. Summers and James advance $3,000 on account to Trumbell Company.

26. Summers and James have disposed of the consignment. Credit sales have been $4,000; and cash sales, $3,800. Collections on credit sales have totaled $2,500 to date. Summers and James render a tentative account sales to the Trumbell Company and remit the net proceeds to date less 3 per cent on sales.

28. The Trumbell Company receives the account sales and remittance.

Apr. 12. $1,400 of the balance of the accounts receivable outstanding April 26 has been collected. A $25 allowance was made one customer, and $75 was written off as a bad debt—these expenses to be borne by the consignor. The proceeds less the 3 per cent commission on sales are forwarded to the consignor.

16. The Trumbell Company receives the final remittance.

Journalize these transactions and set up the ledger accounts (*a*) on the books of the consignee and (*b*) on the books of the consignor.

XXXII—1

Consider the following transactions as separate operations affecting the financial status of an enterprise.

1. Receipt of a gift of land from a municipality, contingent upon continuous operations in the city, $300,000.

2. Receipt of land from municipality, free of all incumbrances of any kind, $100,000.
3. Declaration of the existence of good-will in an enterprise, $16,000.
4. Operating profit of $140,000 before allowing for depreciation or interest on bonds of $30,000.
5. Receipt of cash dividends from subsidiary corporation, $12,000.
6. Revaluation by an appraisal company, resulting in write-up of fixed assets, $75,000.
7. Refund of income taxes erroneously assessed by the federal government, $17,000.
8. Issue of $30,000 bonds at 106.
9. Issue of 100 shares capital stock, par value $100, at 110.
10. Purchase of 50 shares of company's own stock at 80.
11. Resale of treasury stock at $90 per share.
12. Redemption of $10,000 bonds at face value, having been issued at 106.

Required:

a) Journalize the foregoing transactions, using such account titles as seem to you appropriate.

b) Discuss each one in terms of whether the net gain arising from it can be classified as: (1) an increase of net worth; (2) a net profit from operations; (3) available for dividends (assuming no other surplus exists from which dividends may be declared).

XXXII—2

You are requested to examine the books of account of the Jasper Manufacturing Company and to prepare a balance sheet which will correctly reflect the condition of the business. A balance sheet taken from the general ledger accounts is submitted to you.

Balance Sheet—December 31, 1923

ASSETS

Land	$ 80,000.00	
Building	127,500.00	
Machinery	224,000.00	
Furniture	5,000.00	
Good-will	100,000.00	
Cash	33,800.00	
Receivables	120,000.00	
Investments	50,000.00	
Inventory	155,000.00	
Prepaid expense	2,575.00	
Total		$897,875.00

LIABILITIES

Notes payable	$120,000.00	
Creditors	62,000.00	
Bonds	100,000.00	
Total		$282,000.00
Net worth:		
Capital stock	$500,000.00	
Undivided profits	115,875.00	
		$615,875.00

Your examination discloses the following:

a) The land was valued by an appraisal company as at July 10, 1923; and the appraisal increase of $39,500 was credited to undivided profits.

b) The building, machinery, and furniture were recorded at cost. Depreciation had been written off regularly and at an adequate rate, viz.: buildings, $22,500; machinery, $96,000; furniture, $3,000.

c) The good-will has been estimated by the officers of the corporation, and the amount credited to undivided profits, July 1, 1923.

d) The cash balance is composed as follows:

On Hand	$ 2,000.00
Defunct state bank	1,800.00
X national bank	33,000.00
Y state bank (overdraft)	12,000.00
Sinking-fund trustees	9,000.00
	$33,800.00

The cash on hand includes I.O.U.'s of a former salesman, $175.00; the defunct state bank has been closed for some time; the receiver expects, eventually, to pay 50 cents on the dollar; the overdraft in Y state bank is caused, partly, by holding open the cash book and entering, as of December 31, 1923, checks issued to creditors in January, 1924, amounting to $9,000.

e) The receivables include: $15,000 initial payment for new machinery ordered by us under contract, in amount, $45,000; $20,000 consignment sales on which a profit of $6,000 is expected; claim $16,000 for refund, treasury department. This claim, with an amended return for 1921, was filed with the local collector December 27, 1923.

f) Investments consist of U.S. Liberty bonds at par which are pledged on notes payable.

g) The inventories, priced, at cost, are as follows:

Raw materials	$ 52,000.00
Goods in process	16,000.00
Finished goods	87,000.00
	$155,000.00

h) Prepaid expense consists of prepaid insurance, $1,650. and office supplies, $925.

i) Notes payable include a demand note due the president in amount $30,000; and $50,000 due X national bank and secured by the U.S. Liberty bonds; the balance to other banks.

j) Creditors' account includes pay-roll, $18,000, and accrued interest, $320.

k) Bonds, issued January 1, 1921, at 103, thirty years; 7 per cent, sinking-fund payment required, $3,000 yearly.

l) Capital stock:

Six per cent preferred, authorized and issued	$300,000.00
Common, authorized, and issued	200,000.00

Dividends were declared and paid in July, 1923, 3 per cent on preferred and 2 per cent on common. On January 15, 1924, 3 per cent was declared on preferred and 4 per cent on common, payable February 15, 1924.

m) The Undivided Profits account showed:

Debit balance, January 1, 1923	$ 27,825.00
Credits for the year 1923	156,700.00
	$128,875.00
Dividends, July, 1923	13,000.00
Credit balance, December 31, 1923	$115,875.00

Required: Prepare your own balance sheet from the foregoing data, and accompany it with a report containing comments explaining the nature of and reasons for the adjustments you have made.

NOTE: This problem is a review of many of the points discussed in the twelve chapters on accounting valuation. It should be solved in accordance with the problems treated in the entire section dealing with valuation.

EXERCISES ON INTERPRETATION—PART IV

XXXIII

Using the data of the Chicago Manufacturing Company trial balance of Exercise XX—1, rearrange the account titles to agree with the sample classification of accounts shown in chapter xxxiii. Many of the account titles of the Chicago Manufacturing Company ledger will not agree with the illustrative classification of this chapter. In such cases the student should group the accounts under such general classes as seem most appropriate. No new groups of accounts need be created, although new detailed accounts will be required.

XXXIV—1

Prepare the balance sheet of the Yellow Cab Company, giving effect to such groupings as the following: current assets, deferred charges, fixed assets, investments, intangibles, current liabilities, capital stock, surplus, reserves. Use the account titles of the balance sheet of the Yellow Cab Company appearing in the appendix to chapter xxxiv.

XXXIV—2

The following balance sheets of X Company and its subsidiaries, Y and Z, show their financial status as of December 31, 1928:

	X Company	Y Company	Z Company
Assets:			
Cash	$ 3,000.00	$ 2,000.00	$ 8,000.00
Merchandise	24,000.00	15,000.00	30,000.00
Receivables	15,000.00	35,000.00	14,000.00
Investment—Y Co	36,000.00	....	....
Investment—Z Co	20,000.00	....	....
Buildings	40,000.00	28,000.00	....
	$138,000.00	$80,000.00	$52,000.00
Liabilities:			
Accounts payable	$ 10,000.00	$16,000.00	$21,000.00
Notes payable	5,000.00	15,000.00	....
Bonds payable	30,000.00	13,000.00	....
	$ 45,000.00	$44,000.00	$21,000.00
Proprietorship:			
Capital stock	$ 60,000.00	$20,000.00	$20,000.00
Surplus	33,000.00	16,000.00	11,000.00
	$ 93,000.00	$36,000.00	$31,000.00
	$138,000.00	$80,000.00	$52,000.00

Required: Prepare a consolidated balance sheet of X Company and its subsidiaries. Assume that the X Company owns all of the stock of companies Y and Z.

NOTE: The capital stock of Z Company is carried as an investment of $20,000 on the books of the X Company, whereas the balance sheet of Z

Company reveals a total net worth of $31,000. This discrepancy may have resulted because profitable operations of the subsidiary have not been given recognition on the books of the parent company. The consolidation of the three balance sheets must reconcile the difference. The "Capital stock" of Z Company "cancels out" with the "Investment" on the books of X Company. The "Surplus" of Z Company does not cancel out in the consolidation; it has the effect of increasing the surplus of the consolidated balance sheet above that on the balance sheet of the holding company.

XXXV—1

Prepare a statement of income and expense for the Chicago Manufacturing Company (see Exercise XX—1), arranging the data according to the classification worked out in Exercise XXXIII.

XXXV—2

The Anson Mercantile Company balance sheet of December 31 shows a credit balance of $122,000 in a "Capital Surplus" account, and $50,000 in an account entitled "Surplus." Calculate the balances in these accounts after giving effect to the following transactions, setting forth a statement of surplus similar to that of the Orpheum Circuit Company.

1. Net profit, not including any of the items mentioned later, $89,000.
2. Sale of a machine at $18,000 above book value.
3. Declaration by board of directors of $18,000 preferred stock dividends and $24,000 common stock dividends.
4. Appraisal of factory building which results in changing book value from $240,000 to $360,000.
5. Amortization of good-will, $75,000.
6. Loss on sale of leasehold $20,000.
7. Unanticipated obsolescence of delivery equipment, $32,000.

XXXVI-XXXVIII—1

The data of the Progressive Furniture Company, shown below, will serve to illustrate the interpretation of accounting reports by the various techniques illustrated in chapters xxxvi, xxxvii, and xxxviii. The application of interpretive technique cannot be separated in practice into the independent classes implied by the divisions of the chapters; nevertheless, certain aspects of the data may be analyzed in accord with the suggestions of the various chapters. For example, requirement (*a*) may be based on chapter xxxvi; (*b*) and (*c*) on chapter xxxvii; (*d*) and (*e*) on chapter xxxviii.

The Progressive Furniture Company, Jamestown, Michigan, is a close corporation, engaged in the manufacture and sale of good-quality mahogany and walnut bedroom furniture. Raw materials are obtained from 200 different vendors. The finished product is sold to some 325 retail furniture and department stores, which purchase two-fifths of their requirements at the

PROGRESSIVE FURNITURE COMPANY

COMPARATIVE BALANCE SHEET FOR THREE YEARS, ENDED DECEMBER 31, 19__

(All Figures with 000 Omitted)

	Third Year		Second Year		First Year	
Assets:						
Cash		$ 10		$ 20		$ 16
Notes receivable		45		20		10
Accounts receivable		70		40		24
Inventories:						
Raw materials		60		35		20
Goods in process		140		70		40
Finished goods		155		70		40
Deferred charges to expense		15		10		5
Land		50		50		50
Buildings	$140		$110		$110	
Reserve for depreciation	20	120	15	95	12	98
Equipment	$320		$245		$240	
Reserve for depreciation	80	240	60	185	48	192
Total assets		$905		$595		$495
Liabilities:						
Notes payable		$155		$110		$ 45
Accounts payable		90		35		20
Bonds payable		300		100		100
		$545		$245		$165
Net worth:						
Capital stock		$300		$300		$200
Surplus		60		50		130
		$360		$350		$330
Total liabilities and proprietorship		$905		$595		$495

semiannual furniture exhibitions and the balance from the company's salesmen on the road. Perpetual inventory records are maintained for finished goods but not for raw materials or supplies.

PROGRESSIVE FURNITURE COMPANY

Comparative Consolidated Statement of Income and Expense for Three Years, Ended December 31, 19—

(All Figures with 000 Omitted)

	Third Year	Second Year	First Year
Sales (net)	$1,200	$750	$500
Cost of goods sold	870	500	300
Gross profit	$ 330	$250	$200
Selling expenses	$ 155	$100	$ 70
Administrative expenses	120	105	100
Operating profit	$ 55	$ 45	$ 30
Non-operating income	$ 12	$ 3	$ 6
Non-operating expense	17	10	7
Net profit	$ 50	$ 38	$ 29
Dividends	40	18	8
Carried to surplus	$ 10	$ 20	$ 21

Comparative Schedule of Cost of Goods Sold for Three Years Ended, December 31, 19—

(All Figures with 000 Omitted)

	Third Year	Second Year	First Year
Materials, beginning inventory	$ 35	$ 20	$ 15
Purchases	380	225	115
	$ 415	$245	$130
Materials, ending inventory	60	35	20
Cost of materials	$ 355	$210	$110
Direct labor, cost	320	170	105
Manufacturing expense	350	180	115
Total cost of manufacturing	$1,025	$560	$330
Goods in process, beginning inventory	70	40	25
	$1,095	$600	$355
Goods in process, ending inventory	140	70	40
Cost of goods manufactured	$ 955	$530	$315
Finished goods, beginning inventory	70	40	25
	$1,025	$570	$340
Finished goods, ending inventory	155	70	40
Cost of goods sold	$ 870	$500	$300

Required:

a) Calculate and arrange in tabular form for the three years such ratios as you think would be useful in determining and controlling the business policies of the company. Include the following ratios.

1. The current ratio
2. The acid test
3. Current to total assets
4. Net worth to liabilities
5. Net working capital to net worth
6. Selling expenses to sales
7. Administrative expenses to sales
8. Operating profit to sales
9. Net profit to sales
10. Merchandise turnover
11. Working capital turnover
12. Total capital turnover.

b) Compare the trends in the ratios computed as part of requirement (*a*) above. Observe any outstanding features among the interrelationships between the data, particularly continued increases in or decreases in ratios, as well as constant relative quantities.

c) Prepare a *statement of sources and application of funds* for the third year, using the data of the balance sheets as of December 31 of the second and third years.

d) Draft a written report for a prospective investor on the condition and operations of the company as reflected in the financial statements. Make such comments and recommendations as seem to you appropriate. Make any assumptions you wish, but state them explicitly either as part of your text or in the form of footnotes.

XXXVI–XXXVIII—2

THE JENNINGS WHOLESALE COMPANY

COMPARATIVE BALANCE SHEET, DECEMBER 31, 1919–20

Assets:	1920	1919
Cash	$ 30,000.00	$ 36,000.00
Notes receivable	142,000.00	78,000.00
Accounts receivable	138,000.00	109,000.00
Merchandise inventory	810,000.00	420,000.00
Office equipment	32,000.00	30,000.00
Building	126,000.00	120,000.00
Land	210,000.00	180,000.00
Deferred charges	20,000.00	16,000.00
Good-will	60,000.00	62,000.00
	$1,568,000.00	$1,051,000.00

Liabilities and net worth:		
Notes payable	$ 390,000.00	$ 52,000.00
Accounts payable	150,000.00	88,000.00
Mortgages payable	90,000.00	60,000.00
Bonds payable	80,000.00	64,000.00
Capital stock	750,000.00	750,000.00
Surplus	108,000.00	27,000.00
	$1,568,000.00	$1,051,000.00

COMPARATIVE STATEMENT OF PROFIT AND LOSS FOR THE YEARS ENDING DECEMBER 31, 1919–20

Gross sales	$1,800,000.00	$1,200,000.00
Less: Sales returns and allowances	3,600.00	12,000.00
Net sales	$1,796,400.00	$1,188,000.00
Cost of goods sold:		
Inventory beginning of year	$ 420,000.00	$ 190,000.00
Purchases	1,902,000.00	1,244,000.00
	$2,322,000.00	$1,434,000.00
Less: Ending inventory	810,000.00	420,000.00
Total cost of goods sold	$1,512,000.00	$1,014,000.00
Gross profit on sales	$ 284,400.00	$ 174,000.00
Operating expenses:		
Buying expenses	$ 15,000.00	$ 15,000.00
Selling expenses:		
Salesmen's salaries	$ 40,000.00	$ 22,000.00
Salesmen's expenses	60,000.00	30,000.00
Advertising	36,000.00	16,000.00
Clerk hire	8,000.00	6,000.00
Miscellaneous	2,400.00	2,400.00
Total selling expenses	$ 146,400.00	$ 76,400.00
Administrative expenses:		
Office salaries	$ 26,000.00	$ 15,000.00
Heat and light	6,000.00	6,000.00
Clerk hire	8,000.00	8,000.00
Telephone and telegraph	600.00	500.00
Legal expense	2,000.00	500.00
Total administrative expenses	$ 42,600.00	$ 30,000.00
Total operating expenses	$ 204,000.00	$ 121,400.00
Operating profit	$ 80,400.00	$ 42,600.00

Other income:		
Interest on notes receivable............	$ 1,000.00	$ 1,000.00
Discount on purchases................	11,600.00	19,000.00
Total other income...............	$ 12,600.00	$ 20,000.00
Gross income.....................	$ 93,000.00	$ 72,600.00
Deduction from income:		
Interest on notes payable..............	$ 4,000.00	$ 3,000.00
Interest on mortgages payable.........	3,800.00	3,600.00
Interest on bonds payable..............	4,000.00	2,000.00
Sales discounts......................	200.00	8,000.00
Total deductions from income......	$ 12,000.00	$ 16,600.00
Net income.....................	$ 81,000.00	$ 56,000.00

Required:

a) A statement of application of funds.

b) The financial statements so arranged as to facilitate their analysis and interpretation, accompanied by percentages and other ratios which indicate significant relationships.

c) A written report on the condition and operations of The Jenning Wholesale Company based on the analysis and interpretation of its accounting statements.

NOTE: Observe that the income and expense groups of these reports do not correspond with the typical classification illustrated in chapter xxxiii; they correspond rather with the arrangement of items in the Federal Reserve uniform statement of profit and loss, which was shown in chapter xxxv. No attempt need be made to change the classifications of items as shown above.

XXXIX—1

The M Company manufactures and sells within the United States an average monthly output of 10,000 units of product. The components of the average factory cost of the product are: materials, $2.50; direct labor, $1.75; overhead expenses, $2.75. Selling and general administrative expenses average $3.00 per unit. By expanding the volume of operations from 10,000 units to 11,000 units per month, it is estimated that the *average* factory cost per unit can be reduced $0.15, due entirely to the spreading of overhead over a larger volume of output. The additional 1,000 units are to be sold in European markets. Considering that the cost of shipping and selling attributable to the extra output will be $3,300, or $3.30 per unit, and allowing 5 per cent of the extra cost as the minimum margin of profit which will compensate for the risk involved, what is the lowest price at which the company can afford to sell the goods abroad?

XXXIX—2

An enterprise owns a plant which has been constructed at a cost of $100,000 and which is adapted to the manufacture of a special type of product which may be designated as "product A." Product A has normally sold for $60 per article. When the company was manufacturing 1,000 articles per year, it made a net profit of $15,000 annually, total expenses being calculated as follows:

Materials and labor (direct and indirect)....	$22,000.00
Depreciation..............................	5,000.00
Interest on investment....................	6,000.00
Selling expenses..........................	7,000.00
Administrative expense....................	5,000.00
	$45,000.00

Special conditions of competition make it impossible to sell product A at a price higher than $38 per article; but it is estimated that 800 articles can be sold at this price, and that materials and labor would be $15,000, selling expenses, $7,000, and administrative expenses $3,000.

Required:

a) Compare the financial effects of manufacturing and selling 800 items, with the alternative of letting the plant lie idle. Assume that the administrative expenses would be $3,000 in case the plant were closed down.

b) Would it be advantageous to accept a proposition to rent the plant for $9,000 per year, in which case the administrative expenses, such as taxes, insurance, and repairs, would be $2,500?

c) Would your answer to the rental proposition be different if you could sell articles direct to a jobber at $35 and thereby cut your total selling expenses to $1,000 and administrative expenses to $3,000?

XXXIX—3

Certain products—A, B, and C—are being manufactured. The total costs of manufacturing 3,000 (1,000 each) of these products during a given period of time is computed as follows: direct materials, $25,000; direct labor, $40,000; factory burden, $30,000. The costs of the direct materials are allocated to the products in the following amounts: A, $10,000; B, $6,000; C, $9,000. The total number of direct labor-hours worked during the period is 60,000, a labor-hour being one hour of the labor of one man. The total direct labor is traceable to the different products as follows:

A.	6,000 labor-hours	@ $1.66............	$10,000.00
B.	24,000 labor-hours	@ .50............	12,000.00
C.	30,000 labor-hours	@ .60............	18,000.00
	60,000		$40,000.00

Required: Compute the total and average cost of manufacturing each of the products, allocating the correct amount of the factory burden, $30,000, to each line of product (*a*) in proportion to the direct-labor-costs expended on each; (*b*) in proportion to the direct-labor-hours expended on each.

XL

No exercises are practicable for this chapter.

INDEX

[PRINTED IN U·S·A]